Ethics and Values in
Industrial–Organizational Psychology

SERIES IN APPLIED PSYCHOLOGY
Edwin A. Fleishman, George Mason University
Jeanette N. Cleveland, Pennsylvania State University
Series Editors

Gregory Bedny and David Meister
The Russian Theory of Activity: Current Applications to Design and Learning

Michael T. Barannick, Eduardo Salas, and Carolyn Prince
Team Performance Assessment and Measurement: Theory, Research, and Applications

Jeanette N. Cleveland, Margaret Stockdale, and Kevin R. Murphy
Women and Men in Organizations: Sex and Gender Issues at Work

Aaron Cohen
Multiple Commitments in the Workplace: An Integrative Approach

Russell Cropanzano
Justice in the Workplace: Approaching Fairness in Human Resource Management, Volume 1

Russell Cropanzano
Justice in the Workplace: From Theory to Practice, Volume 2

James E. Driskell and Eduardo Salas
Stress and Human Performance

Sidney A. Fine and Steven F. Cronshaw
Functional Job Analysis: A Foundation for Human Resources Management

Sidney A. Fine and Maury Getkate
Benchmark Tasks for Job Analysis: A Guide for Functional Job Analysis (FJA) Scales

J. Kevin Ford, Steve W. J. Kozlowski, Kurt Kraiger, Eduardo Salas, and Mark S. Teachout
Improving Training Effectiveness in Work Organizations

Jerald Greenberg
Organizational Behavior: The State of the Science, Second Edition

Uwe E. Kleinbeck, Hans-Henning Quast, Henk Thierry, and Hartmut Häcker
Work Motivation

Martin I. Kurke and Ellen M. Scrivner
Police Psychology Into the 21st Century

Ethics and Values in
Industrial–Organizational Psychology

Joel Lefkowitz
Baruch College, City University of New York

LEA
2003

LAWRENCE ERLBAUM ASSOCIATES, PUBLISHERS
Mahwah, New Jersey   London

Lawrence Erlbaum Associates, Inc., Publishers
10 Industrial Avenue
Mahwah, NJ 07430

Cover design by Kathryn Houghtaling Lacey

Cover art © Fotosearch.com, LLC, Waukesha, WI.
Reprinted with permission.

Library of Congress Cataloging-in-Publication Data

Lefkowitz, Joel.
Ethics and values in industrial-organizational psychology / Joel Lefkowitz.
    p. cm.
Includes bibliographical references and index.
ISBN 0-8058-3353-6 (c: alk. paper)
ISBN 0-8058-3354-4 (pbk. : alk. paper)
1. Psychology, Industrial. 2. Business ethics.   I. Title.

HF5548.8 L3644 2003
174'.915—dc21   2002035390
                                            CIP

Books published by Lawrence Erlbaum Associates are printed on acid-free paper, and their bindings are chosen for strength and durability.

Printed in the United States of America
10 9 8 7 6 5 4 3 2 1

This book is dedicated to back-office clerks doing data entry in the financial districts of New York, goldminers in the dark and the wet and the heat more than a mile beneath the Black Hills of South Dakota, a Dayton police officer alone in his cruiser at 3:00 a.m. after several days of street violence, young women high school graduates learning power sewing machine operation for piece rates in Pennsylvania and New England, partially literate washers and pressers in a steamy industrial laundry in rural Louisiana, aircraft parts production employees in Cleveland … and many more. Because they graciously allowed themselves to be observed, interviewed, surveyed, tested, evaluated, or trained, I came to appreciate what it is like to work in America.

Moral thought just is difficult: humans cannot do it at all well.
—R. M. Hare

All science, and all philosophy, are enlightened common sense.
—Karl R. Popper

Contents

III. The Ethical Context of Research

IV. Conclusion

List of Figures/Tables

Series Foreword

Series Editors
Edwin A. Fleishman
George Mason University

Jeanette N. Cleveland
Pennsylvania State University

There is a compelling need for innovative approaches to the solution of many pressing problems involving human relationships in today's society. Such approaches are more likely to be successful when they are based on sound research and applications. This Series in Applied Psychology offers publications that emphasize state-of-the-art research and its application to important issues of human behavior in a variety of societal settings. The objective is to bridge both academic and applied interests.

Recent years have seen an increasing interest in ethics and morality in various segments of our society. Current events have underscored the relevance of many of these issues for organizations and their management. This book, *Ethics and Values in Industrial–Organizational Psychology* by Joel Lefkowitz, is a major contribution to our discussion of beliefs and assumptions about ethics in the profession of psychology, especially industrial–organizational psychology, in the world of business, and in the nature of our society.

As one reviewer of the manuscript for this book pointed out "the timing for this book could hardly be better. Our culture is facing massive ethical crises in many sectors of society. Psychologists who work with organizations cannot escape being touched by these forces." This book deals with issues involved in our roles as applied psychologists working in complex social settings. These issues also include potential ethical dilemmas which may confront academic colleagues engaged in basic research. The author challenges us to examine our beliefs in "value-free" science and research in the context of our service in the highly competitive world of professional practice and amid the values and goals of the corporate world.

The breadth of the domain addressed by Professor Lefkowitz is truly remarkable. The innovative manner in which the broad array of relevant topics is organized and clustered together will motivate scholars in the fields of I/O psychology and related disciplines to think about ethics in ways they haven't up to now.

This scholarly, comprehensive, and superbly organized treatment of ethics and values in industrial and organizational psychology is a significant contribution to the professional literature. It should find its way for use in many graduate courses, including research methodology. The book is essential reading for those academics who do research in this field as well as for psychologists who consult or work in organizations.

The book provides an entry into the realm of ethical decision making for behavioral scientists and other human resource specialists who work in organizations and shows the important role of values that underlie both science and practice. On a broader level, the book provides a philosophical foundation for morality and applies the principles derived to a wide range of contemporary problems. The book is provocative and will certainly engage the reader.

1

Introduction

A prolific academic author once told me that an effective book is generally based on just one idea—irrespective of how broad the topic or complex the material. I took the comment to mean that in order to make a point one should at least have a point to make. The overarching thesis of this book is that, contrary to an attitude often expressed or implied, professional ethics is not an unreasonable set of rules or expectations designed by intrusive idealists to make our lives more difficult. As psychologists we study human behavior. To do so, we depend on the goodwill and trust of the persons who cooperate with us voluntarily, sometimes revealing their private selves to us, enabling us to do our work and research. As industrial and organizational (I/O) psychologists we further depend on the goodwill of organizational decision makers who trust us when we say that we can improve the effectiveness of their enterprises. As professionals, we cannot do that work very well, at least not for very long, if we do not treat all of those persons ethically—that is, honestly, fairly, and with respect and dignity.

But our motives ought not be solely instrumental. Indeed, as reviewed in chapter 3, the hallmark of some moral theories is the rejection of such utilities, or "cost–benefit analyses," as a means of judging ethical behavior. As is characteristic of all professionals, we assume the responsibility of "the service ideal." As psychologists, we carry with us a humanistic tradition that includes a concern for promoting people's welfare, some of which is formalized in our ethical codes. Thus, ethical issues of fairness and justice and of duty and beneficence are central to our core values as professional psychologists. Some of the more controversial portions of this book, however, include the criticism that much of I/O psychology has drifted rather far from those core values and has to a considerable degree replaced them with a narrow version of business values that are not commensurate with psychology's humanistic heritage.

Portions of this book are concerned with matters that probably go beyond what many of my colleagues may view as the appropriate domain of professional ethics. In my opinion—which is explained clearly in later chapters—we cannot avoid the economic, sociopolitical, and human developmental antecedents of individual and organizational ethical behavior any more than we could hope to understand the functioning of an organization as if it were a closed system, ignoring its cultural history and the social, political, and economic environments that influence and set constraints on its internal policies and external actions (D. Katz & Kahn, 1978). A similar conclusion seems justified with respect to the consequences of organizational actions. For example, I/O psychology studies as legitimate and important facets of employees's job performance their organizational citizenship behaviors (OCBs) because such prosocial behaviors contribute to organizational effectiveness, even though they may not be part of the prescribed work role (Podsakoff & MacKenzie, 2000). By extension, we cannot ethically ignore the moral qualities and actions of the organizations to which we devote our efforts—in effect, the organization's citizenship behavior— with respect to the society that legitimizes and supports it and in which it functions. Just as we study employee perceptions of organizational justice (Cropanzano, 1993; Gilliland, Steiner, & Skarlicki, 2001) vis-à-vis an organization's internal human resources activities, we should also be concerned with the social justice implications of the organization's external actions, which characterize the probity of its role in society. This perspective is in keeping with that of other psychologists who have begun to express concern for the way in which professionals carry out *good work*—"work that is both excellent in quality and socially responsible" (Gardner, Csikszentmihalyi, & Damon, 2001).

As far as I have been able to discern, there are essentially four kinds of publications concerned with ethics. Each type is rather different from the others and makes a relatively unique contribution, notwithstanding that there is some inevitable overlap among them. The first category of publications consist of ethical codes that have been promulgated by governments, professional and trade associations, individual organizations (including business corporations), and others. Such codes are offered as helpful guides to ethical behavior, generally within particular domains such as business management or the professions. A primary limitation of ethical codes is that they are often written either in overly general terms focusing on aspirational ideals or they are highly specific and idiosyncratic, leading one to exclaim in frustration, "I can't find my problem in the code!" In the first instance one may be at a loss as to how to apply the ethical principles, so that an explanatory casebook is necessary (e.g., Lowman, 1998; Nagy, 2000); in the second instance the code may need further elaboration to be useful, such as that provided by Canter, Bennett, Jones, and Nagy (1994) for the American Psychological Association's (APA) code. Similar to codes are legal and professional standards that set forth specific obligations of professional practice or scientific research (e.g., American Educational Research Association [AERA], APA, & National Council on Measurement in Education [NCME], 1999; APA, 1987; Equal Employment Opportunity Commission, Civil Service Commission, Department of Labor, & Department of Justice, 1978; Office for Protection From Research Risks, National Institues of Health, Department of Health and Human Services [referred to hereafter as OPRR],1991; Society for Industrial and Organizational Psychology [SIOP], 1987).

In contrast, the second category of publications consists of highly theoretical and philosophical treatises. Primary among these are original expositions by moral philosophers, as well as reviews of moral theories by other philosophers—frequently in the form of critiques in which one theory "wins" and the others "lose" because they are deemed logically less consistent and/or less comprehensive. Chapters 2, 3, and 4 of this book present a distillation of moral philosophies in which, although I have not shied away from offering criticisms, no attempt is made to assess "winners" and "losers." Rather, my intention is to familiarize the reader with the varieties of ethical reasoning and to offer alternative conceptual approaches that may be useful in anticipating, evaluating, and resolving ethical dilemmas—even when you cannot find your problem described in the code. Different ethical problems, even within a single domain such as business practices, may induce different types of ethical reasoning corresponding to different moral theories (Fritzsche & Becker, 1984).

A third category of publications consists of illustrative casebooks that contribute to our understanding by providing specific applications of ethical principles and guidelines that may otherwise be ambiguous or poorly comprehended. But they tend to be limited by the same factors that limit the codes themselves, and no one person or even small number of persons is likely to have direct experience with enough real cases to represent anywhere near an entire code. Good casebooks, therefore, almost always need to be collaborative enterprises—perhaps developed by members of an ethics committee with considerable experience evaluating complaints.

The last major category of ethics publications are books that aim to impact people's lives and, by extension, society by showing how ethical considerations are relevant to everyday affairs. These books deal with applied ethics, practical ethics, or social criticism (from an ethical or moral perspective). Perhaps the best known contemporary example of this genre is P. Singer's (1993) wide-ranging *Practical Ethics*, which tackles issues like euthanasia, animal killing, environmental degradation, the distribution of wealth, and much more from a consistent theoretical position (that of

consequentialism, see chap. 4). Other examples are targeted for a specific audience, such as books on business ethics (e.g., Schminke, 1998).

With perhaps more than a little hubris, this book touches all four of those
bases and emphasizes primarily the ubiquitous, but often unacknowledged,
role played by personal and institutional values in shaping moral action. Although the book develops a framework for ethical decision-making, culminating in a model of ethical reasoning for taking moral action, I emphasize
throughout the important role played by the values that underlie our reasoning. That orientation is responsive to the concerns expressed by T. R.
Mitchell and Scott (1990):

> Currently it is popular to treat ethical and moral issues as problems to be
> solved. The tendency in business schools is to consider them, in Edmond
> Pincoff's words, as quandaries. Quandary ethics concern tangible and con-
> crete moral dilemmas, case studies, engaging in role playing, or solving critical
> incidents....
>
> The step beyond quandary ethics in schools of business curricula is moral dis-
> course.... Moral discourse is a process of rhetorical engagement by students
> and professors in free and open forums of conversation and debate. One tries
> to persuade others of the truth of his or her point of view on moral issues. In
> the process, widely divergent opinions are expressed and each individual is
> exposed to alternative propositions about values. The whole point is to pro-
> vide knowledge of moral options and the opportunity to choose among differ-
> ent values systems. In the academic atmosphere of modern business schools,
> in which bottom-line thinking is supreme, the chance that such forms affords
> for students to hear something different is essential to their moral develop-
> ment. Students need to know that people make decisions using guidelines
> other than those suggested by expected value and maximization. (pp. 28–29)

The situation described by Mitchell and Scott (1990) is no less true regarding the ethical education of I/O psychologists, and I hope that this book
contributes to fostering the sort of "moral discourse" they advocate. Psychologists seem to have shown less interest in studying how ethics is taught
in their profession than have business scholars concerning the teaching of
business ethics. Perhaps that is because business ethics may be taught at the
college level by business professors, philosophy professors, or social scientists (D. Morris, 2001), whereas ethics for psychologists are more likely to be
taught by other psychologists.

An explosion of interest in ethics and morality has taken place over the
past 20 years. It is erupting all around us, in many spheres of life. Social scientists (e.g., Etzioni, 1996) and revered religious leaders (e.g., Dalai Lama,
1999) have felt the need to offer prescriptions for improving the moral dimension of society, and in the United States displays of public religiosity and
calls for moral rectitude are at a level and scale probably not seen since the

17th and 18th centuries. The number of books published on business ethics has soared and professional journals, such as *Ethics & Behavior*, *The Journal of Business Ethics*, *Business Ethics Quarterly*, and *Business and Society*, have flourished. The surefire indicator that a scholarly field has achieved a critical mass of attention—an edited handbook—now exists as well (T. L. Cooper, 2001). Consultants teaching business ethics or "values clarification" in corporations and "character training" in the schools constitute a new growth industry, and instructional books holding out the promise of being able to raise moral children become best-sellers (Coles, 1997). Within my profession the APA (1992) revised its ethical code relatively recently yet has just revised it again (APA, 2001a, 2002). And in conjunction with the APA, SIOP revised and expanded its casebook on ethics (Lowman, 1998). Morality and character issues have become preeminent screening criteria for those who wish to serve in public office. If further demonstration were needed to make the point, the Sunday magazine section of my hometown paper, *The New York Times*, now publishes an advice column titled "The Ethicist" for those who find themselves ethically challenged.

Why all this attention? In part, I believe it is because ethics is intimately reflected in the essence of what it means to be a sentient person. Human beings seem to have evolved several potential answers to the fundamental existential questions of "Why?" and "What?" (As in "Why are we here?" and "What is the purpose of life?"). They invoke five domains:

1. The intellect—understanding the natural world.
2. The family and extended social relations—finding meaning in intimate and just relationships.
3. & 4. Work and play (both of which are contained in the arts as well) through which we experience forms of meaningful expression, accomplishment, and recognition.
5. Faith—a religious or secular sense of transcendence.

They all reflect basic human needs for achieving psychological fulfillment through our ways of being in the world.

The fifth domain is rather distinct from the first four insofar as faith is the only one that ostensibly entails a direct and explicit engagement with the existential questions. What I mean by *faith* follows the notions of the comparative religionist W. C. Smith (1963), who distinguished it from both religion and belief. Although Smith did not define the term precisely, it is clear that faith is an attribute of people—of personality—whereas religion refers to a social, cultural, and historical tradition, encompassing symbols, stories, theologies, ethical teachings, architectural styles, and so on. Among those elements of any religion are its beliefs, which represent ideas about its tradition. Faith, however, is the aspect of human personality to which religion and its associated beliefs appeal for adherents; but faith itself refers to a more fundamental and transcendent way of being in the world. It accounts for the similarities in religious experience among believers of many different religions. The relevance of all this for our purposes is found in the writings of Fowler (1981) who advanced a clearly psychological and humanistic conception of faith as reflecting people's attempt to shape and provide meaning to their lives, noting that the process is informed by one's values and reflected in the nature of one's relationships with others—which is, of course, what ethics is all about.

From Smith (1963) and Fowler's (1981) perspective, religion is one of the possible manifestations of faith. As P. Singer (1995) pointed out, religion provides a ready answer to the question of the meaning of life in general and by extension, to the meaning of each believer's life. Belief in a god as creator generally presupposes a divine purpose for that creation, so that meaningfulness for the religious entails divining and fulfilling that purpose—achieving that goal. Secular faith-based views tend to sound rather metaphysical, such as that of Kohlberg and Ryncarz (1990), psychologists for whom the answer to questions like "Why be moral?" or "Why live?" is provided by "identify[ing] ourselves with the cosmic or infinite perspective and valu[ing] life from its standpoint" (p. 192), that is, to "sense the unity of the whole and ourselves as part of that unity" (p. 195).

Those who possess neither strong religious belief nor a sense of cosmic unity are limited to the remaining sources for answers, and the experience of fulfillment and meaning via these four domains is as much a matter of process as goal achievement. It is in the acts of attaining understanding, experiencing loving and respectful relationships, expressing ourselves, accomplishing meaningful tasks, and realizing worthwhile objectives that we potentially answer questions like "Why?" Although the capacity to experience these varieties of meaning is probably universal, there appear to be culturally rooted values differences in the relative salience of each, and the vagaries of upbringing and other circumstances produce considerable individual variation in people's capacity and inclination to do so. All five facets of human existence concern the ways in which we conduct ourselves in this world in order to find fulfillment and meaning in it; to a considerable degree, they all entail interpersonal, including intergroup, relations. For most of us even the intellective aspects of our lives are not conducted entirely in solitude. In fact, the new multidisciplinary field of *relationship science* is based on the premise that, "because interpersonal relationships are the foundation and theme of human life, most human behavior takes place in the context of the individual's relations with others" (Reis, Collins, & Berscheid, 2000, p. 844). As Emler and Hogan (1991) cogently expressed it, "there is very little of any consequence, including mischief, that any individual can do entirely alone" (p. 81). Therefore, *ethics*, the study of how one should properly live one's life, especially with respect to behavior toward others, is tied to the very essence of meaningful existence.

But that still does not address why attention to ethics and morality has recently increased. I do not know that anyone has provided a fully satisfactory nonmetaphysical explanation for the current eruption, but there are a number of factors that may have contributed:

1. The world has been astounded by biomedical advances such as mapping the human genome, genetic engineering of food crops and livestock, the cloning of a living mammal, and the creation of human embryos in order to extract undifferentiated stem cells that can be "directed" into becoming a variety of specialized tissues—and many have become more than a little frightened by the ethical implications of those achievements.[1]
2. The globalization of American corporations has led to a growing awareness of differences in what are considered ethically acceptable business practices in other cultures and to the passage and amendment of the Foreign Corrupt Practices Act (U.S. Congress, 1977/1998), as well as to a concern for the extent to which U.S. corporations maintain working conditions and terms of employment in third-world production facilities that would not be tolerated in the United States.
3. The proliferation of the Internet and people's access to the World Wide Web have led to concerns regarding privacy and confidentiality in business transactions, as well as paradoxically to a growing sense of anonymity.
4. There had been a growing fearfulness associated with rising crime rates from the 1960s through the 1980s, especially with respect to apparently random street crime and a few highly publicized murderous rampages—all of which were viewed by many Americans as evidence of moral failing rather than emotional disturbance.
5. There has been an extraordinary increase in the power exercised by business corporations over people's lives—virtually tearing up the old implied social contract—as well as the shift from a manufacturing to a service economy with the attendant job losses through the 1980s and 1990s, loss of a sense of economic security, and destruction of the sense of commitment and loyalty to a long-term employer.

---

[1]Four years after the sheep named Dolly was successfully cloned, scientists have had a success rate of only 3% with subsequently cloned animals—mice, cows, pigs, and goats. More disturbing has been the high incidence of serious anomalies, such as developmental delays, heart defects, lung problems, and malfunctioning immune systems. "Some scientists say they shudder to think what might happen if human beings are cloned with today's techniques. . . . It would be morally indefensible" (Kolata, 2001, p. 14). But human embryonic stem cell research and extrauterine cloning for medical purposes holds enormous potential for the treatment of many serious diseases.

6. There have been so many high profile instances of unethical behavior on the part of corporate leaders that it is characterized in the popular press as a "scourge" (Zipkin, 2000).

7. A series of disturbing and highly publicized ethical and moral lapses at the highest level of government, starting with President Nixon's Watergate, to President Reagan's "Irangate," to President Clinton's "Monicagate," with many other (bipartisan) lapses in between, have taken place.

The behavioral scientist who is not well read in philosophy and ethics may be surprised by the extent to which much of the content of ethical thought deals with familiar psychological issues. Assumptions about human nature and motivation abound in ethical treatises, and the personal behavioral observations and interpersonal experiences of the moral philosophers are frequently generalized by them as characteristic of all humankind. In addition, the nature of the processes by which intellectual progress is achieved in philosophy seems highly similar to the nature of psychology as it existed roughly 100 years ago. Psychology used to focus on grand theories that attempted to explain the entire domain of human behavior, each criticizing and supplanting one that preceded, as with the so-called "schools of psychology"—structuralism, functionalism, and behaviorism. Even more so in moral philosophy, philosophical *thought* has taken the form of philosophical *argument*—a dialectic in which theories are developed largely in response to perceived weaknesses and criticisms of the one(s) before. However, the criteria for acceptance have become very different in the two fields. In moral philosophy it is a matter of which theory is more robust in withstanding the rational attacks of its competitors—such as meeting the criticisms of logical inconsistency, lack of inclusiveness, and practical implausibility. In the social and behavioral sciences it is a matter of which theory is more effective in generating testable hypotheses that are confirmed by systematic observation—i.e., empirical evidence. As explored further in chapter 5, psychology moves beyond simply considering the logical sufficiency of moral theories by attending to the non-rational emotional, cognitive, and social antecedents of moral behavior, as well as to the issue of moral development in childhood. But we should recognize some overlap: even to philosophers the plausibility of an ethical theory is a psychological criterion that is implicitly empirical (even if that sounds like an oxymoron). Philosophers generally recognize that it makes little sense to advocate an ethical model that is based on unrealistic assumptions and expectations about human behavior.

Indeed, Steininger, Newell, and Garcia (1984) argued that the several putative differences that have frequently been advanced as distinguishing between ethics and psychology fail to establish a clear demarcation. For example, one of the primary distinctions has to do with the presumed differences between description and explanation—which is what psychologists do—and the ethical justification of behavior. But, on analysis the differentiation between the causes of behavior and the reasons for engaging in it turns out to be not so clear-cut. Why some accountants at Arthur Anderson shredded documents from Enron would seem to be an entirely different question from whether they should have done so. But scientific explanations of behavior often involve the actor's justifications; and moral justifications generally depend on assumptions about the causes of behavior. "In the domain of human action, it is difficult, perhaps impossible, to explain without assuming or implying values, and the 'why?' often refers to both" (Steininger et al., 1984, p. 262). When someone asks why those accountants shredded the documents, they are probably seeking both the explanation and the justification for the actions. "Both the psychologist who tries to explain behavior in morally [i.e., values-] neutral terms and the ethicist who tries to justify judgments about the moral rightness or wrongness of an action independent of any psychological considerations are denying the inevitable overlap of their two disciplines" (p. 266). A related point is made by Alderfer (1998), who emphasized that scientific theory, data, methods, and values all interact, and that there is an "interdependence between what is known scientifically and what is judged ethical at any point in history" (p. 67).

The reader may find one of the moral theories discussed in chapters 2, 3, and 4 more useful or otherwise more compatible than others, so that it might be adopted as a consistent perspective within which to approach ethical deliberations. Alternatively, I have found different models with their associated ethical principles to be more or less helpful and appropriate with respect to different types of problems. Either perspective necessitates becoming familiar with the general issues and alternative approaches offered by the various moral philosophies. Consequently, my primary aim in this regard was to produce a usable synthesis that would be helpful in decision making, not just for the rare ethical crisis one might face but for the "quiet, steady, day-to-day choices that add up to a career characterized by integrity or moral malaise and/or conflict. It is for the quotidian choices that moral guideposts are most needed and most wanting" (Lowman, 1991, p. 196). Aiding ethical decision making is just one of the main purposes served by moral theory for professionals such as applied psychologists (Knapp, 1999). The other purposes are to help explain the fundamental moral underpinnings of society and its institutions, to identify and justify the general principles on which our ethical standards and codes are based, to encourage moral behavior, and to assist in the education and self-regulation of the profession by providing a basis for compliance with those standards.

This book is premised on a number of personal beliefs and concerns about ethics, the profession of psychology, I/O psychology in particular, the contemporary world of business, and the nature of society. Many of them become apparent in later chapters, but it is constructive and fair to the reader to make some of them explicit at this point.

The first concern can be introduced conveniently with an anecdote. On the first day of SIOP's 2002 annual conference in Toronto I met an old friend and colleague whom I had not seen for quite a while. The ensuing conversation began like many in that circumstance, catching up on each other's life. In response to a question about what I'd been doing professionally, I told him that I was writing a book on ethics and values in I/O psychology and was almost finished. His quick and sardonic reply was "Well, that must be a slim volume!" Because we got distracted by the arrival of others; I never got to inquire whether his wit reflected the sarcastic view that we did not need any, or that we did not have any! In any event, concern about a high level of unethical behavior by I/O psychologists, or even a high incidence of ethical dilemmas in the field, was not among the motives for writing this book.

Although based on limited data, self-reported ethical problems in I/O psychology do not seem to be a prevalent problem (Pope & Vetter, 1992). In the domain of professional psychological practice, the bulk of ethical complaints brought to the attention of the APA concern clinical practice—especially sexual misconduct by therapists with clients (APA, Ethics Committee, 2000, 2001). In the research domain, the controversial practice of deceiving research participants about some features of the study seems to be a less significant issue for I/O psychology than for experimental social psychology (cf. Baumrind, 1985). However, despite the critical determinative role played by values in one's experience of and reactions to ethical dilemmas, discussions concerning the foundational values of the field are not well represented in the professional literature of I/O psychology. And so this book is as much or more about values as it is about ethics per se.

Young I/O psychologists and business managers have come of age professionally at a time when the U.S. business world has been marked by momentous displays of greed, self-aggrandizement, and disregard on the part of its leaders for the well-being of workers and sometimes even shareholders. One of the issues to be considered later is whether this merely represents the actions of a relatively few "bad apples" or whether there may also be systemic influences at work. Especially germane to the aims of this book, I have observed a variety of unfortunate adaptations to the prevailing zeitgeist exhibited by many of these nascent professionals. Some seem resigned to accepting it as a natural reflection of the essentially egocentric nature of human beings in a competitive environment. Similarly, some seem to view it as representing unfortunate excesses of the free-enterprise system—minor costs to pay as the price for harnessing the enormous productive potential of individual ambition and incentive. Some I/O psychologists appear to be exercising some form of "technocratic denial"—retreating behind our armamentarium of assessment and selection devices, training modules, quasi-experimental interventions, competency models, and performance appraisal systems—as if the moral actions of the enterprises in which these are implemented were none of our concern. This adaptation is reminiscent of much of the history of I/O psychology as a compliant handmaiden to corporate-defined objectives and values. But others hold an alternative view of the possibilities and justification for moral and ethical corporate behavior and the salience of more altruistic concerns. In fact, there is a substantial, albeit loosely organized coalition of business scholars, social critics, and progressive business leaders who have been pressing the moral dimension of capitalism and promoting *corporate social responsibility* as well as models of *corporate social performance*. I/O psychologists, however, have been conspicuously absent in this alliance; thus, one of the aims of this book is to promote this perspective in our field.

An adequate consideration of professional or applied ethics entails incorporating the domain it shares on one side with models of personal ethical decision making—what the father of *utilitarianism* Jeremy Bentham referred to as *private ethics*—and on the other side with the moral aspects of institutional decision-making, social policy, and political economy at the macro-level. Both levels of activities reflect underlying values positions concerning interpersonal and group relations and pertain to deliberations about what is appropriate in that regard. This accounts for the existence of professional journals like *Philosophy and Public Affairs, Business and Society,* and *Psychology, Public Policy and Law.* For example, Cohen (2002), noted that ethical virtues are expressed not only in the individual's behavior toward others but in the quality of the societies we create; they should be identified with civic virtue. Therefore, it is to be expected that a book on ethics and values in I/O psychology would range beyond the specific ethical issues we face in our research and practice to include discussions of such topics as business ethics and the morality of corporations—focusing on the domains in which we conduct our research and practice.

As I/O psychologists we share with our colleagues in the other subspecializations of psychology a common heritage regarding what it means to be a psychologist. We have acknowledged and prided ourselves on adhering to some aspects of those traditions (e.g., the epistemic values of empirical science) but have given short shrift to other aspects, such as its humanistic ideals. Chapter 12 explores some of the consequences of having largely abandoned those ideals and offers some suggestions for their redevelopment.

In our role as applied psychologists working in complex social settings we encounter a host of additional potential ethical dilemmas that for the most part, do not confront our academic colleagues engaged exclusively in laboratory or basic research. Some of those potential dilemmas are the result of conflicts between the humanistic value system of psychology alluded to previously, and the value system of the organizations within which we work—the values of a competitive free-enterprise, profit-driven economic system.

Complicating the situation, but also rendering it more interesting, is the fact that a dominant ideology in I/O psychology is the belief in value-free science and research (e.g., the distinction between the putatively neutral and scientific issue of *test bias* and the value-laden social issue of *test fairness*). This view is advanced by those who believe improbably that the field is entirely objective and scientific despite our service to the highly competitive world of business in which our professional practice and much of even our research agendas are shaped by the values and goals of the corporation and the ideology of the economic system. When one's personal value system is largely consonant with that of the social systems within which one acts, the absence of "moral friction" can make it seem as if the systems are value free.

As noted sagely in the *Canadian Code of Ethics for Psychologists* (Canadian Psychological Association, 2000), "Although it can be argued that science is value-free and impartial, scientists are not" (p. 1). One of the advantages of a single-author book is the opportunity to express a particular point of view—especially so in the realm of applied ethics because real world moral decisions are value driven. I cannot claim that my own values and views regarding a variety of issues have not influenced the content of this book—in choice of topics, opinions expressed, what I have criticized, what I have lauded, and how they impact my ethical analyses. But I tried to make those values explicit and thereby subject to scrutiny. My hope is that this prompts the reader to consider the ways in which his or her own values disagree or are in accord with mine, and—more importantly—how they affect the reader's ethical deliberations. In that way we may together raise the level of discourse, if not necessarily of agreement, in moral reasoning among I/O psychologists.

I

Moral Philosophy
and Psychology

2

Meta-Ethics

Despite the efforts of Descartes and his successors to elaborate a method—based, in different versions, on clear and distinct ideas, dialectics, mathematical logic, phenomenological intuition or conceptual analysis—philosophers have never agreed on a way to resolve their disputes. At the same time, the area of competence in which they roam has steadily diminished, as the natural and then the social sciences developed bodies of theory and methods of investigation calling for specific apprenticeships, not general wisdom. Philosophers have been left with commentary on the sciences and arts, along with musings on morality whose superiority to anyone else's, when there is any, is due to a higher degree of self-conscious organization of thought rather than to some special knowledge or method.

—Paul Mattick

Professor Mattick is unnecessarily apologetic on behalf of his profession and colleagues. There is much to be said for a high degree of self-conscious organization of thought—especially when it illuminates a domain not well explored by others. As behavioral scientists we are quite used to refining ambiguous constructs operationally and resolving theoretical contradictions empirically. It is precisely when we enter the realm of values and ethics that we are largely left in the lurch by the scientific method and must call on the "general wisdom" and the "musings on morality" by philosophers to help us light the way. For example, the more optimistic philosopher A. Rosenberg (1995) pointed out, philosophy has always addressed the questions that the sciences cannot answer, such as what ought to be the case as opposed to what is, as well as the epistemological questions concerning why science cannot answer them. These musings concern questions like "What is the right thing to do in this situation?," "How should I live my life, in general?,"

"What ought she have done then?" Attempts to provide systematic answers to these questions by defining *right* and *wrong* or *good* and *evil* and justifying rationally what one should or ought to do constitute the substantive matter of ethics or moral philosophy. This is referred to as normative ethics.[2]

Before embarking on a survey of normative ethics, however, it is helpful to begin by discussing some of the fundamental issues that provide its underpinnings. What, for example, is the nature of morality or ethics and of ethical theories? How does one go about arriving at the definitions of *right*, *wrong*, or *good*? These concerns are commonly referred to as *meta-ethical issues* and they are embedded at least implicitly in all normative ethical theories. Figure 2.1 presents a list of eight meta-ethical questions that constitute the subject matter of this chapter. At the end of the chapter I present a set of conclusions that may be drawn from the consideration of these questions and, therefore, provide us with the beginnings of a framework for ethical decision making.

META-ETHICAL ISSUES

The ancient Greeks dealt with meta-ethics explicitly or indirectly along with their deliberations about the content issues of normative ethics. In contrast, the great 17th, 18th, and 19th century "modern" philosophers (e.g., Thomas Hobbes, John Locke, David Hume, Immanuel Kant, John Stuart Mill, G. W. F. Hegel) were primarily concerned with developing normative theories. However, in the 20th century meta-ethical concerns have seen something of a revival. The most important meta-ethical issue is whether answers to the fundamental ethical questions (e.g., what does it mean when we say something is morally right?) are in some way potentially verifiable objectively. In other words, do morals represent "truths" to be uncovered, or are they entirely subjective? All of the classical ethical theories may be categorized as explicitly or implicitly *objectivist* or *subjectivist* in nature. The second major meta-ethical issue concerns the perspective from which the conclusions of right or wrong are made. Here, the issue is a dichotomy between a consideration only of the person who is doing the deciding (e.g., one's own happiness) and a more encompassing perspective (e.g., the well-being of all involved). This is the issue of whether normative ethical theories are *egoistic* or *universalistic* in nature. It is rather remarkable that the roots of both the *subjectivist–objectivist* and the *egoist–universalist* controversies in ethical thinking originate in western thought from the same source—the *Sophists*.

---

[2]There is frequently a nuanced distinction between the terms ethics, which is of Greek origin, and morality, which is Latin: The latter term is often used with a religious implication, whereas ethics is invariably used when referring to professional issues, as with ethical codes of conduct. I follow customary practice by using the terms roughly synonymously.

META-ETHICAL QUESTIONS

1. Are ethical principles entirely subjective expressions of personal values and attitudes or do they represent objective truths to be discovered?

2. If they are only subjective does that mean that each person's ethical standards (and by extension, each society's) must be considered "right" for them, even if they seem patently immoral?

3. If they are "objective" what is the nature of those truths, and how might we ascertain them?

4. What about religion? Is secular morality compatible with religious precepts, or perhaps even dependent on them? Isn't religious belief the source of all morality?

5. What about conclusions drawn from the biological, behavioral and social sciences that study human behavior? Shouldn't the nature of humankind tell us something about ethical behavior?

6. What is meant by the ethical constructs "right" and "wrong," "good" and "bad," "justice" and "injustice"? How are they to be defined?

7. In deciding whether an action is right or wrong whose interests should be considered: only those of the "actor", the subgroup(s) in which the actor is a member, or all those directly affected by the action? Aren't we all governed primarily by self-interest?

8. What about the distinction between knowing the right thing to do and doing it? Why should one do the correct thing?

FIG. 2.1. Some important meta-ethical questions to be considered.

Origins of Subjectivism

Approximately 2,500 years ago in Greece a very bright group of itinerant teachers earned their living by helping their fellow citizens be successful politically and commercially. These Sophists were generalists, teaching much of what we would call the liberal arts curriculum. But they specialized in teaching public speaking, debate, or rhetoric because rhetoric was a critical skill for success in public life. However, they were not well liked in many quarters because of their emphasis on the arts of persuasion, convincing others, or winning an argument rather than on illuminating truth. That reaction has extended until today; the characterization of one's views as sophistry is a serious put-down. But some of the Sophists were not only rhetoricians but philosophers who dabbled in the ethical dialogues of 5th century BCE Athens. Their reaction to the criticism they received was not simply to defend their activities on pragmatic grounds—much like their contemporary counterparts in the fields of public relations, advertising, and political consulting may be expected to do. Instead, they took the philosophical offensive by questioning the very existence of objective truth.

They advanced a point of view that thousands of years later psychologists refer to as a *phenomenological perspective*. Because we each experience the world through our separate senses, process those experiences, and interpret them through our separate nervous systems and cognitive processes, there is no objectively verifiable truth to be known. How one person experiences the world cannot be exactly the same as another person experiences it. This leads to a position of *ethical relativism* at the individual level—what is right for me is not necessarily right for you—and of *cultural relativism* at the societal level. The Sophists' growing awareness of diverse social practices and customs among the many societies to which sophisticated Athenians were exposed undoubtedly influenced the development of their notion of cultural relativism. Because all societies have a set of moral conventions—albeit different in each case—morality must simply be a matter of social convention. The moderates among the Sophists accepted the necessity for each society to have its own conventional morality, but there was a more radical group that rejected it. If morality and laws are mere conventions, and if those rules are enacted by the powerful in society, then there is no moral reason to obey them. (This is the origin of the view that "might makes right.") But this leads to a problem for these radicals: What is correct? What should replace conventions?

Objectivist Rejoinders

Their answer was the introduction of the concept of *natural law*—a notion that plays a key ingredient in the philosophies of the "big three" who follow: Socrates, Plato, and Aristotle. Obedience to conventional law is supplanted by obedience to natural law by which they meant *human nature*. And what is the nature of human behavior, according to these radical sophists? It is simply the pursuit of one's own self-interest, undeterred by conventions. Now, the radical Sophists were not so naive as to fail to recognize that a society in which everyone pursues only their own self-interests is likely to run into some difficulties concerning a lack of integration and cooperation, frustration of objectives, conflict, and aggression. Consequently, they acknowledged the necessity for laws to provide protection against exploitation of the weak. But, having no inherent value, these laws were to be obeyed only if and when one had to in order to avoid punishment.

The radical Sophists provided Plato and Aristotle with a conceptual point of view called *ethical naturalism*, which they elaborated in order to refute the subjectivist view that all morality is relative. They reasoned that the best way to live can be inferred from human nature, which is an objective, potentially knowable aspect of the real world. But before Plato there was Socrates, who was no less iconoclastic and as annoying to much of Athenian society as were the Sophists; in fact, his incessant (he lived well into his 70s) challenges and refutations of accepted conceptions of virtue got him killed.[3] He, like the Sophists, challenged the conventional morality but did so by poking holes in the customary views of what is meant by moral principles like justice or personal virtues such as honesty. Unlike the Sophists he believed that these virtues were potentially knowable by the good person—indeed, it is such knowledge that renders the person good, because that is all that is necessary in order to *be* good. Although that seems psychologically naive to us today, giving short-shrift to motivational determinants of behavior, the important point is that he laid the groundwork for the importance of logical reasoning in deciding what is justifiably good or right. It is worth noting that attempts to integrate the cognitive dimension of ethics ("what is the right thing to do, and how can I know it?") with the pragmatic motivational dimension ("why should I do what's right?") have plagued moral philosophers for centuries—ever since Socrates simply finessed the question.

Plato, Socrates' pupil, developed a very modern sounding answer to the questions, what does it mean to be just or good, and how will we know? His answer is psychological in nature and draws on sociology and physiology by analogy. A *just* society is one in which the three major social classes—guardian, military, and economic—perform their functions well so that the society as a whole functions harmoniously. Similarly, individual physical health is a reflection of the various parts of the body functioning properly, and we experience that as pleasurable. By extension the just (moral) person is one for whom the three aspects of human nature are in harmonious balance under the control of reason which, with the help of spirit, keeps desire in check. "Goodness, then, is the health and harmony of the personality" (Norman, 1983, p. 20). Thus, Plato did provide an answer to the problem that Socrates simply defined out of existence. The reason we act in accord with reason and justice is that it is pleasurable to do so.

As a student of Plato's, Aristotle's meta-ethics also represents a version of ethical naturalism and also gives a prominent position to the role of reason. But he changed the criterion. According to Aristotle the ultimate aim of human behavior is happiness.[4] His thinking here is akin to

---

[3]There is no direct written record of Socrates' views. Virtually all of what we know of his thought is from how he is represented in the writings of Plato, and scholars are uncertain about how much of those representations are actually Plato's views, not those of Socrates.

[4]That is the usual closest translation of the Greek *eudaimonia*, but the word is generally conceded to include the state of being fulfilled or actualized, as well as simply feeling happy.

what I/O psychologists recognize as second-, third-, or higher-order instrumentalities in valence–instrumentality–expectancy theory. I may
work in part to earn money. Why? To purchase material goods. Why do I
want to do that? It satisfies the needs and wants I have. Why is that important? Because it is a source of gratification and happiness. Happiness
is taken as the ultimate human objective needing no further explanation
or justification. It is the ultimate good that results from acting in accord
with all of the customary human virtues (honesty, bravery, prudence,
etc.). In fact, the reason the virtues *are* virtues is that behaving in that
manner produces happiness.

Although Aristotle assumed that happiness needs no additional
justification, he was very concerned with defining what it is. His answer
is consistent with Plato's views in that it consists of reason, although his
argument is rather tortuous and, in terms of modern biology and
psychology, simply invalid. Aristotle believed that all things, both
inanimate objects and living beings, have a function and what is proper is
to fulfill that function. Knives are to cut well; cows provide good milk;
trees provide fruit and shade; slaves are to serve. The proper function for
a human being is indicated by that which is unique to humans—the
capacity to reason. Thus, the most rewarding existence will be had by
developing and utilizing one's powers of reasoning. The flaws in the
model are obvious. First, modern science has revealed that living
creatures develop according to the principles of evolutionary biology and
environmental adaptation, not in teleological fashion to fulfill some a
priori purpose. Second, even if we accepted the teleological view, it
simply does not follow that what is putatively unique about us necessarily
defines our proper function as human beings; that is an invalid
essentialist argument. After all, we use our unique powers of reason for
such immoral or harmful activities as planning bank robberies, swindling
investors, and discriminating against people who are different from us.
(It took the *Stoics*, modifying Aristotle's natural law, to specify that
because reason could be corrupted, the use of reason should be *right
reason*.) And the last criticism, as we know now, is that the capacity to
reason is not in fact unique to our species.

Egoism Versus Universalism

All of the ancient Greek philosophers I have noted, including the Sophists,
Socrates, Plato, and Aristotle, shared the same meta-ethical position concerning whose interests should be considered in attempting to understand
what is good or right: one's self. This is reflected in the Sophist's pursuit of
self-interest generally and in Aristotle's focus on happiness (limited exclusively to one's own). This position is referred to as *ethical egoism* and charac-

terizes relatively few normative ethical theories, although it is well represented in modern economic theory and business values (cf. Chap. 10 and chap. 11). Perhaps the best known example among the classical moral theories is that of Thomas Hobbes, and among more contemporaneous social thinkers the views of Ayn Rand.[5]

Aristotle did not feel that this position needed any particular justification because he simply did not acknowledge any distinction or potential conflict between self-interest and morality or altruism. In fact, as we have seen, the Aristotelian view is that the human virtues, even the altruistic ones like honesty, sympathy, charity, and so on, represent the reasoned and correct moral choice because they are inherently bound up with the experience of happiness. Perhaps that is why there is a considerable amount of evidence to suggest that people are less motivated by self-interest than even they would describe themselves to be (D. T. Miller, 1999). In our highly individualistic society we are taught that rational self-interest is not only natural but also appropriate and good. Therefore, Miller suggested, we may be more influenced by not violating a social norm of rational self-interest and thereby appearing to be a "do-gooder" or "bleeding heart" than by genuine motives of self-interest. In fact, it may be entirely natural to be altruistic (Simon, 1990). The sociobiological theories of kin selection, reciprocal altruism, and multilevel selection explain why altruistic behavior is evolutionarily adaptive at both the individual and family level, as well as for larger unrelated groups that are in competition with other groups (McAndrew, 2002). Recent evidence indicates that cooperative behavior in humans is hard-wired (Rilling et al., 2002). The other side of this coin concerns the extent to which the justifications provided by ethical egoism and the promotion of self-interest are partly responsible for the paroxysms of greed and corruption that have marred the past 2 decades of American business.

Rand's (1964) version of ethical egoism rests on the belief that altruism (the opposite of egoism) is so all-consuming that it entails the virtual inability to lead a meaningful, productive, and independent life. That is, it is quite literally and intensely self-sacrificing. Consequently, ethical egoism—a concern solely for one's own interests—is the only morality that respects the integrity of the individual. And so, the welfare of society must always be subordinate to individual self-interest. One of the reasons that Rand's work re-

---

[5]Ethical egoism is a meta-ethical view that it is right and proper for each of us to pursue our own selfish interests. This is invariably based on an assumption of *psychological egoism*, which has to do with a particular view of human nature. It is the view that we are predominantly if not exclusively motivated by selfish concerns—a view that does not withstand psychological scrutiny. However, one could be a psychological egoist without necessarily being an ethical egoist. Whereas Rand was for the most part what I would call an unqualified or unrestrained ethical egoist, Hobbes was a qualified or enlightened ethical egoist (see chap. 3). *Rational egoism* is a separate construct in moral philosophy, referring to the relatively tenable assertion that it is reasonable or rational to act in accord with one's self-interests, although that may not be the moral thing or necessarily even the best thing to do. Simon (1985) described "rational" as being "behavior that is appropriate to specified goals in the context of a given situation" (p. 294).

mains controversial is the vehemence and, to many critics, gratuitous hostility she directs toward the politically weak and powerless among us. In any event, there is little reason to accept her assumption about the extremity of the consequences of behaving altruistically; concern for others need only be one of the several considerations that govern our actions in any instance, along with self-interest; and there seem to be many examples of accomplished autonomous people who nevertheless engage in substantial altruistic, even charitable, activities. In fact, many distinguished scholars view altruistic behavior as having evolved by natural selection because of the advantages it conveys to the population (Simon, 1990, 1993). Moreover, as D. T. Miller (1999) suggested, the extent and preeminence of self-interest motivation may be highly exaggerated in our society, and this is confirmed by the prevalence of altruistic endeavors.[6] Of special interest to I/O psychologists is Simon's (1993) observation that economic analyses should pay more attention to the motivational effects of forms of altruism derived from group and organizational loyalties.

As Barry and Stephens (1998) summarized, philosophical views such as Rand's (1964) single-minded focus on self-interest have not generally been well-received among modern moral philosophers or as an avowed foundation for applied business ethics. In fact, one recently proposed model of fairness in the context of organizational justice emphasizes the limitation of the traditional definitions of justice that are restricted implicitly to the domain of self-interest, rather than including a more pluralistic set of motives, including altruistic concerns (Folger, 2001). However, views like Rand's are not totally without adherents (Becker, 1998; Locke, 1988; Locke & Becker, 1998; Locke & Woiceshyn, 1995). In general, ethical egoism seems to be most well-received by those who see themselves as holding sufficient social advantage to successfully promote their self-interests even though everyone else is trying to do the same. Rachels (1993a) described succinctly two arguments that many philosophers believe sink unconditional egoism as a viable meta-ethical position.[7] The first argument is contingent on accepting a particular conceptualization of what ethics is all about, which I do. That is,

---

[6]The more cynical among us may accept the appearance of altruism within one's family as being natural, but when such behavior is directed toward others it is frequently rationalized as mere reciprocal altruism—undertaken with an expectation of reciprocation, hence not really altruistic at all. Similarly, many take a Hobbesian position that altruistic feelings are merely a version of self-satisfaction. The economist Samuelson (1993) replied: "When the governess of infants caught in a burning building reenters it unobserved in a hopeless mission of rescue, casuists may argue: 'She did it only to get the good feeling of doing it. Because otherwise she wouldn't have done it.' Such argumentation (in Wofgang Pauli's scathing phrase) *is not even wrong*. It is just boring, irrelevant, and in the technical sense of old-fashioned logical positivism 'meaningless' " (p.143, italics in the original).

[7]They do not threaten seriously Hobbes' version of qualified or enlightened egoism (cf. Arrington, 1998; Copleston, 1994; Kymlicka, 1993). And they do not necessarily contradict a benign interpretation of Rand's (1964) views as reflecting mere rational egoism rather than ethical egoism (Locke & Woiceshyn, 1995). Refer to Baier (1993) for a critique of the several versions of egoism.

one of its primary objectives is the resolution of interpersonal conflict (as well as intrapersonal conflict). In other words, moral guidance comes into being as a means of reducing conflict and enhancing cooperation among members of society. If one accepts this as a legitimate conceptualization of ethics, it is clear that unqualified ethical egoism provides no basis for contributing to this enterprise; if universally adhered to it would, in fact, exacerbate tensions and conflict. This outcome has been well documented at the macrolevel in economics by the *fallacy of composition*—what is best for each person need not be best or even good for all (Samuelson, 1993). In fact, the overwhelming prevalence in the United States of what is referred to as the ethic of personal advantage, is viewed by the management scholars T. R. Mitchell and Scott (1990) as the fundamental cause of "American decay." They describe decay as environmental degradation (also see Karp, 1996), the growth and exclusion of a permanent social underclass and managerial corruption: "What began as the decade of the entrepreneur is becoming the age of the pinstriped outlaw" (p. 25). However, we can see in Hobbes' work (summarized in chap. 3) how a cooperative ethical model—the social contract—can be developed within a framework of egoistic assumptions about human behavior.

The second argument places unrestricted egoism in a class of usually implicit moral views that makes a priori distinctions among people and views as morally correct the practice of treating them differently based on those distinctions (e.g., racism, sexism, and anti-semitism). In this case, the distinctions consist of there being just two classes of people—one's self and everyone else. In both cases, of course, there is no a priori morally acceptable justification for treating groups of people (or one's self) as differentially worthy of respect or consideration: *"We can justify treating people differently only if we can show that there is some factual difference between them that is relevant to justifying the difference in treatment"* (Rachels, 1993a, p. 88). In this context we can understand the process of stereotyping a group as an attempt to provide such factual differences to justify discriminatory treatment. So this refutation of ethical egoism leads us to acknowledging that there can be no a priori moral basis for considering anyone's interests as having precedence over anyone else's. P. Singer (1995, chap. 2) elaborated these views considerably into a riveting discussion of "equality and its implications." His major point has to do not with factual equality because individual differences among people are clearly evident, but with *equality of interests*—one's rights and freedoms—that are independent of those individual differences in ability, talent, intelligence, and so on.

Ethical egoism is in opposition to the more numerous normative ethical theories characterized as universalist in nature because they take into account the concerns of a wider array of folks—typically all who are affected by the actions under consideration. Examples include the theories of Hume,

Kant, Mill, and Hegel, as well as Christian ethics. For example, one variety of *consequentialist* theory (that of Mill) holds that the most morally defensible action is that which results in the greatest happiness for all those affected. Some of these normative theories are discussed in the following chapters. But now, after having discussed two of the fundamental meta-ethical issues in moral philosophy, we will consider, albeit briefly, some illustrative meta-ethical theories.

EXAMPLES OF META-ETHICAL THEORIES

Objectivist Theories

The following two meta-ethical theories are objectivist in nature. This attribute is sometimes referred to as *moral realism* (cf. M. Smith, 1993). As M. Smith outlined, there are two basic tenets of moral realism. First, as with all of normative ethics, the focus is the very practical goal of providing the basis for doing what is morally right or making the ethically correct choice. Second, and this is the essence of the issue, objectivist or moral realist theories are based on the assumption that those right actions and correct choices exist as a body of "moral facts" that are potentially knowable and verifiable, just as are empirical scientific facts, although the means of doing so differ among different objectivist theories.

Ethical Naturalism

The earliest version of a naturalist theory in ethics was, as discussed, the model of natural law developed by the ancient Greeks. Aristotle defined the essence of human functioning as our reasoning capacities that, if adopted as the guiding principle of our lives, will result in achieving fulfillment and happiness. The Stoics stipulated that this should mean "right reason" so as to preclude mere selfishness, and the model is later taken up and systematized further by the Roman Cicero. The theme survives to the Middle Ages at which time it is given perhaps its most well known expression by Thomas Aquinas:

> Whatever is contrary to the order of reason is contrary to the nature of human beings as such; and what is reasonable is in accordance with human nature as such. The good of the human being is being in accord with reason, and human evil is being outside the order of reasonableness…. So human virtue, which makes good both the human person and his works, is in accordance with human nature just in so far as it is in accordance with reason; and vice is contrary to human nature just in so far as it is contrary to the order of reasonableness. (Cited in Buckle, 1993, p. 165)

One of the major difficulties with natural law theory is its ambiguity: Natural law theorists rarely specify just what actions are natural and which unnatural; when some behaviors are specified as unnatural, the justifications tend to be vague condemnations that they are self-destructive (without specifying how or in what way). That is, the stipulation concerning "right reason" often seems to be given short shrift. In the terms of modern psychology the construct is inadequately operationalized. This is true even of the most popular contemporary versions of ethical naturalism—theories of human rights—as developed by J. Locke (1988) and culminating in such grand statements as the United Nation's *Universal Declaration of Human Rights* (1948).

An exception to the ambiguity is the version of natural law employed by orthodox religious groups, especially Roman Catholics, in condemning some sexual behaviors like homosexuality, masturbation, and contraception. The natural law objection (and there are other bases of objection as well) is that these practices are unnatural because they violate the basic biological function of sex, which is procreation for species propagation. As Buckle (1993) pointed out, this argument makes little sense as a justification for condemning these activities. Biological function is a rather restricted conceptualization of the nature of human beings. Moreover, no individual instance of masturbation or contraception or homosexual encounter has had any deleterious effect on the overall fecundity of the breeding population of *Homo sapiens*, yet it is the discrete acts that are condemned. Moreover, this point of view would require us to condemn as immoral a man who has sex even though he knows he is sterile or a woman who is menopausal.

Evolutionary Psychology.   More potentially justifiable is the contemporary naturalist position represented by the newly developed field of *sociobiology* or *evolutionary psychology* (E. Wilson, 1975/2000): the systematic study of the biological basis of all social behavior. One of the more interesting features of sociobiology is that it posits an evolutionary origin for intraspecies cooperation, including the altruistic actions that characterize what we call ethical or moral behavior. It views altruistic behavior as well as the accompanying thoughts about altruism (i.e., our ethical beliefs) as a human adaptation: our ancestors who thought and acted in that fashion survived and reproduced better than those who did not (Ruse, 1993). Contemporary economists have also indicated that altruistic behavior is an underrecognized human motive in social and economic behavior (Samuelson, 1993; Simon, 1993). Sociobiology or evolutionary psychology as a meta-ethical theory is rightly considered an example of ethical naturalism, positing a biological basis for the very existence of morality itself. However, at this point in time not much can be said about it from the standpoint of normative ethics—that is, what the *content* of an ethical theory based on evolutionary psychology might be.

The overarching criticism from which most versions of ethical naturalism cannot recover is that the essential nature of the thesis is a non sequitur. It represents a case of the *naturalistic fallacy*, which consists of defining something (a concept such as goodness) by means of the object(s) that possess that thing or ability. It is a conflation of two separate realms of meaning. For example, because reasoning is good, it does not follow that we can define good exclusively as reasoning. In particular, Hume (1978) pointed out in what has become known as *Hume's Law*, it is a logical fallacy to believe that empirical facts, even if correct, tell us anything about moral judgments. Arrington (1998) summarized the point well: "From the fact that human beings are constituted in a certain way and behave in certain ways, nothing follows about how they *ought* to behave and about the character they *ought* to have. Being what they are, human beings may in fact never do or be what they ought" (p. 242). One can not justifiably infer what ought to be merely from what is.[8] A dramatic illustration of this point was occasioned recently by an extremely controversial article that made an informed case for rape being an evolutionary adaptation—a way for less "attractive" men (from an evolutionary perspective) to perpetuate their genes (Thornhill & Palmer, 2000). The thesis can be refuted at the empirical level (the pregnancy rate from rape is very low; attractive, physically fit, wealthy, and even married men commit rape; men rape other men), but the more relevant point concerns Hume's Law. Suppose Thornhill and Palmer's thesis is correct. Are we willing to thereby accept rape as a morally justifiable activity because it is natural?

All of this should not be taken as an attack on the legitimacy of sociobiology. Investigating the possible hereditary foundations of moral behavior is a perfectly appropriate enterprise; what is at issue is whether the heritability of any particular behavior pattern that is relevant to a consideration of ethics justifies it as a definition of morality. De Waal (1996) overstated the case when he asserted that "we seem to be reaching a point at which [biological] science can wrest morality from the hands of philosophers" (p. 218). The position argued here is that the nature of morality—as a matter of human values—is defined in the humanities, social sciences, and religious teachings. It is in those realms that we forge the essence of morality as dependent on the socially constructed meanings of responsibility, duty, fairness, and justice, as well as the human qualities of empathy, caring, altruism, honesty, reasoning ability, susceptibility to social influences, and so on. It is fascinating and extremely important to our conception of human nature to learn that protobehaviors reflecting those qualities are observed in infrahuman species, especially the other hominids and species of monkeys.

---

[8]Arrington also noted, however, that Hume's famous "is/ought" distinction has not gone unchallenged by other philosophers and that there is a considerable controversy over its validity.

Religion

In recent years in the United States, morality, virtue, and ethics have become very much a matter of public, even political discourse—although the terms of discussion have been co-opted largely by those who share a particular narrow view of morality. A position taken by some of the more vocal proponents of this new morality (e.g., fundamentalist Christians who profess to having been "born again," as well as other "dogmatic religionists"; Ellis, 1992, p. 428) is that there can be no true morality divorced from religious faith.

This issue has also become very popular in recent years in the context of the resurgence of *virtue theory*.[9] Recall that for the ancient Greeks the study of ethics had only secondarily to do with questions concerning "what is the right thing to do?" and more to do with "what is the right kind of person to be?" or "what does it mean to be 'good' or 'just'?" Thus, they focused on human nature with particular reference to the so-called virtues (and vices)—what some personality theorists would refer to as *character*. They enumerated many virtues, the essence of which could presumably be subsumed by the four cardinal virtues of prudence, temperance, justice, and courage (or fortitude). Christian moral theology has added to these natural virtues the theological virtues of faith, hope, charity (or love), and obedience. Virtue theory responds to a perceived overemphasis in modern western ethical theories on right actions and on the efficacy of ethical reasoning, to the exclusion of the moral character of the actor. It has been faulted, however, for going overboard in the opposite direction by eliminating the ethical principles or rules that are needed to properly define and justify what is meant by a *virtue*, and by overlooking the guidance that may be necessary sometimes to know what to *do* in order to be virtuous. The interested reader can find readable critiques in Pence (1993) and Rachels (1993a).

But the larger meta-ethical issue concerns the relation between ethics and religion. There are several different things that theologians and other religious peoples might have in mind when they say that ethics and religion are inseparable. To begin with, it should be acknowledged that moral philosophy and religion have long been intertwined. In the *Vedas*, from about 1500 BCE India, enlightenment and righteousness are inextricably connected. Similarly, much of the old testament, including more than half of the Ten Commandments, are concerned with how we are to treat one another. For Jews, treating others with loving-kindness is one of the ways to worship God

---

[9]There is nothing intrinsic to virtue theory that renders it necessarily religious. For example, its recent resurgence is generally attributed to a secular treatise (Anscombe, 1958). It happens, however, that religious moralists in the contemporary United States frequently express their moral theology in such terms. And it seems to me, based on unsystematic observations, that the virtues extolled are generally those having to do with control, such as obedience, politeness, sexual abstinence or fidelity, loyalty, and honesty, as opposed to those having to do with altruism, such as compassion, kindness, generosity, helpfulness, considerateness, and sympathy (cf. Blum, 1987).

because we were all made in His image. With the addition of a greater emphasis on forgiveness, Jesus follows in that tradition (think of the Sermon on the Mount). Obviously, the Judeo–Christian ethic is eminently compatible with the basic idea of secular ethics—the right treatment of others. The same is true of the teachings of Islam, which emphasize redressing injustices. But that is not the issue here. It is whether, as many of the contemporary American moralists avow, ethics *depends* on religion.

According to Berg (1993) there are three ways in which ethics may be dependent on religion: (a) God as the source of that which is good, which is known as the *divine command theory* of ethics; (b) God as the source of moral knowledge; and (c) God as the source of moral motivation, that is, as the provider of the reason(s) for behaving morally. None of these ideas is very successful at making a case for the indispensable reliance of morality on religion.

Divine Command Theory.   This is the point of view that holds that what is "good" (i.e., moral, just, or right) is equivalent to "God's will." In other words, there can be no conception of the good without God. The difficulties encountered by this view were elucidated even before the spread of monotheism by Plato: "Do the gods love holiness because it is holy, or is it holy because they love it?" (cited in Berg, 1993, p. 527). If one chooses the first option, that God wills us to be good because it is good, it must mean that there is an independent standard or criterion of "goodness" that is separate from God's will. This would appear to be, from a religious standpoint, an unacceptable infringement on the omnipotence of God. Conversely, one may believe that it is only by virtue of God's will that what we think of as good is good. But that renders the notion of good extremely arbitrary. If God had willed torture, slavery, and genocide to be good and helping others in need to be bad would we believe so? A religionist rejoinder to this argument is that God is good and, therefore, could not possibly will those things. But that, in effect, puts one back on the other horn of the dilemma.

God as the Source of Moral knowledge.   Perhaps it can more reasonably be concluded that our knowledge of good and evil and of right and wrong depends on God.[10] One of the problems with this view is that it flies in the face of our common experience. We know that there are plenty of atheistic and agnostic people who know right from wrong, and some of them even demonstrate extremely moral behavior; thus, morality cannot depend on knowing or believing in God. In addition, to accept this point of view would necessarily mean denying all of the alternative nondeistic means of justify-

---

[10]As Berg (1993) pointed out, this does not refer to the unhelpful belief that God is the source of everything in the universe including whatever it is that we know. The directly relevant issue is whether God is the source of moral knowledge in some special way that is not true for, say, scientific knowledge.

ing moral and ethical beliefs (e.g., all of the moral philosophies), which seems unreasonable. Perhaps what is meant by this view is simply that, for each of us, our moral sense is God-given whether we realize it or not. That may be a comforting source of faith for some, but it is simply an inadequate justification.

God as the Source of Moral Motivation. This point of view pertains to the issue I referred to earlier regarding the distinction between the cognitive aspects of normative ethical theory (knowledge of what one ought to do) and the motivational aspects (why one should do it). The answer traditionally provided by religion to the question "why be moral?" is so that one can hope for the reward of heaven and avoid divine punishment. This is probably the least justifiable of the three bases considered. Again, it seems apparent that there are many reasonably moral people who do not believe in heaven and hell. Clearly, their motivation must have other sources.

All of this should not be misconstrued as antireligious. In fact, a major concern of this book is the ethical issues of justice and care, and religious principles are among the prominent sources supporting concern for economic and social justice (cf. chap. 7). For example, the National Conference of Catholic Bishops (1986) asked Americans to consider "How do my economic choices contribute ... to a sensitivity to those in need?" and "With what care, human kindness and justice do I conduct myself at work?" (para. 23).

Subjectivist Theories

Suppose I were to ask you, somewhat rhetorically, "Aren't affirmative action programs just wonderful?" and you reply "Are you kidding? They are awful and destructive." What do these verbalizations mean? Surely, at the very least, I am expressing a positive attitude about affirmative action, and you are expressing the opposite. But which of us is correct? *Simple subjectivism* is the ethical meta-theory that views this question unanswerable. That is, we are each simply expressing our attitude and values and there is no basis to choose between them. You have your opinion; I have mine, and truth does not enter into it. This is very different from the objectivist belief in the existence of moral facts, however they are defined. There is no valid position for a pure subjectivist.

To clarify, that is not generally what the participants in a dispute believe. Each of us may personally be convinced that we are correct—that we are on the side of truth. But that is not how a simple subjectivist would see it. The simple subjectivist would assert that at the level of whatever is factual in this situation—as paradoxical as it seems—you and I are probably in agreement. That is because all that our respective statements mean to the subjectivist is I approve of affirmative action and you disapprove. Both of those clauses are true, and each of us would probably have no difficulty agreeing to their accuracy (i.e., I agree with the fact that you disapprove of affirmative action, and you probably agree with the fact that I approve of it). This points out the most serious flaw associated with simple subjectivism: It trivializes moral expression and does not account for the substantive differences among obviously oppositional views. This is true because it implicitly treats our moral judgments merely as factual statements about our attitudes: In this instance, I feel affirmative action is good; you feel that it is bad. Surely this is a rather frustrating and inadequate state of affairs. But there have been subsequent modifications designed to improve the simple version of the theory.

Emotivism and Prescriptivism

Stevenson (1944) developed a partially successful advance over simple subjectivism based on linguistic analysis. He pointed out that language is used for more than merely stating facts—whether they are descriptive facts (e.g., "Since the advent of affirmative action the employment rate of ethnic minorities and women has increased") or facts about attitudes ("I think affirmative action is good"). Moral language, according to Stevenson, is *emotive*; that is, it is used to express attitudes ("Thank goodness for affirmative action") and to influence other people's behavior ("You should consider implementing an affirmative action program in your organization"). The positive contribution over simple subjectivism is that this expressiveness and influence more clearly separates the factual realm from the attitudinal. You and I may agree or disagree about the relevant facts regarding affirmative action and its effects. But even if we agree on most of those facts, emotivism shows that we may still disagree in our attitudes. Our disagreement is, according to Stevenson, a moral one—meaning that it is a difference in attitude, rather than a disagreement about attitudes.

The problem with emotivism is that even after this elaboration we still are left with the expression of potentially conflicting ethical attitudes with no basis to choose among them. That is because the theory does not concern itself with the processes by which those competing points of view may be evaluated. That's where reason comes in. Contemporary philosophers have refined emotivism by emphasizing that any value judgment, especially moral points of view, must be supported by reasons. (Attitudes about more trivial issues, e.g., mere matters of taste, can get by with no greater justification than an expression of the preferences of the speaker: No particular reason is required for the assertion that you enjoy Chevy Chase movies.) Moreover, it is generally accepted that the explanations should be relevant and not merely expressions of self-interest or bias. Recall that this harks back to the Stoics and their emphasis on right reason. Rachels (1993b) pointed out that it is consonant with several contemporary ethical theories, such as ideal observer theory, which holds that the ethical choice is the one a perfectly rational, impartial, and benevolent observer would make.

By far the best known of the contemporary elaborations of subjectivism is Hare's (1981, 1993) universal prescriptivism. By *prescriptivism*, Hare emphasized the emotive nature of moral language as expounded earlier by Stevenson: Moral statements always contain an implicit action recommendation of what one ought or ought not to do. And it is that implicit (or explicit) prescription or proscription that needs justification. If I cannot produce good answers to the question "Why should my company implement an affirmative action program?," then my prescriptive statement that you ought to do so cannot claim to be an ethical position.

According to Hare (1993), the fundamental justification of moral prescriptives is their *universalizability*: If, in a particular situation, I believe that you ought to do such-and-such, my viewpoint can be accepted as an ethical one only if I accept that anyone (including myself) in the same situation ought to do the same thing. If the principle of universalizability sounds familiar, there is good reason it should. It is reminiscent of the various versions of the Golden Rule ("Do unto others only that which you would have them do unto you") that are found in Confucianism (ca. 500 BCE), in both the Old and the New Testaments, and as reflected in Kant's famous categorical imperative ("Act only on that maxim which you can at the same time will that it should become a universal law"; see chap. 3). Erikson (1964) viewed the rule, in all its many cultural versions, as a foundation of morality. It is the universalizable characteristic that makes a particular "ought statement" moral and differentiates it from an ordinary imperative like "Close the door." (Not every open door warrants being closed.)

The last aspect of universal prescriptivism I note is one that relates to the issue of moral knowledge as being distinct from moral behavior: knowing what one ought to do versus doing it. Remember that for Socrates it was not an issue. He assumed that merely knowing what was good will result in one's being good. Plato recognized the distinction but believed it presented no problem because acting properly (with reason and justice) is the most pleasing alternative. In moral theology, conversely, the issue is quite a big deal. Acting morally and for the right reasons is influenced by anticipation of what one may refer to as the ultimate in extrinsic reinforcement contingencies—nothing less than eternal bliss or eternal damnation. Hare (1981, 1993) appears to be rather Socratic on the question. Prescriptivism holds that a moral statement inherently implies a commitment to action in accord with the statement. It would be intolerably inconsistent, according to Hare, to accept the view that "I ought to do such-and-such, but I don't want to" or "I ought not do such-and-such, but I am going to do it anyway." I think that, as psychologists, we may be more receptive than Hare to accepting the inconsistencies involved in those examples of behavior not in accord with one's ethical conclusions. After all, behavior—even morally relevant be-havior—is multiply determined (cf. the model of moral action in chap. 5), and moral behavior may be influenced by intuitive emotional reactions as much as by moral reasoning (Haidt, 2001).

Relativism

At the beginning of this chapter the origination of the idea of cultural rel-ativism by the Greek Sophists was noted. It has remained a seductively at-tractive notion all this time—probably because it seems to fit so well our common experience of the enormous variation in customs, practices, and institutions of the world's diverse cultures (to say nothing of the variability even within pluralistic societies like our own). The 16th century essayist de Montaigne appears to be the first to have publicized the often-repeated ac-count by Herodotus of the Persian King Darius's famous little practicum demonstration in social science. He summoned to his court some Greeks who were in town and asked them how much money they would require in order to eat the bodies of their dead fathers. Well, the Greeks—whose cus-tom it was to cremate their corpses—were horrified and indicated indig-nantly that no amount would be sufficient. He then summoned a group of Callatians from India (who customarily did, in fact, maintain the aforemen-tioned dietary practice); in the presence of the Greeks he asked them what he would have to pay for them to burn their dead fathers's bodies. Needless to say, they were very upset and asked him not to even speak such a thing. Each of us can probably think of many such examples of contrasting prac-tices from our own knowledge of the world's cultures.

It has become common for many business people in this age of "globaliza-tion" and international corporate mergers to encounter foreign business people, government officials, and customers whose business practices are not merely different but seem exceedingly strange and perhaps even unethi-cal by our standards (e.g., distortions of the facts or bluffing, and bribes or side payments in contract negotiations). The effects of cultural differences on organizational functioning have been studied extensively (Hofstede, 2001), and a theoretical case has been made for the impact of cultural differ-ences not only on the content of ethical principles but as influencing ethi-cal-reasoning processes as well (Thorne & Saunders, 2002)

Even though at this descriptive level of analysis we are dealing with a question in social science, particularly cultural anthropology and sociology, the relevance for an understanding of ethics is, as the Sophists first indi-cated, direct. Isn't it self-evident that what is morally correct varies as a function of what each society deems it to be? However, when the question is approached from within one's own cultural perspectives and biases, most of us find it extremely difficult to accept as normal—much less, moral—cus-toms that are shocking to our encultured sensibilities: "One's own morality

lies deeply internalized, and it is not easy to overcome ethnocentric prejudice when confronted by behavior which prima facie offends against it"
(Silberbauer, 1993, p. 15). Consequently, we tend to view those other folks
as primitive, uncivilized, and downright immoral, or simply weird.

Looking beneath the apparent descriptive accuracy of cultural relativism,
the analytic justification for it among modern social scientists is a variant of
themes that we have seen in the writings of Aristotle and in the tradition of
ethical naturalism. Its modern representation can be traced back to the theory of *functionalism* in sociology developed by Durkheim (1898/1953,
1893/1956), and advanced by his successors in sociology (Parsons and Merton) and anthropology (Malinowski). This point of view starts from the assumption that societies must fulfill certain functions in order to survive effectively as an organic whole. It proceeds with the inference that each society
then develops customs and folkways that reflect those functional accomplishments. As there is no independent standard of right or wrong, each society's
functional adaptations may be unique; each culture's traditions are correct by
virtue of their satisfying the society's needs. Again, although this appears to be
an acceptable explanation in the abstract, there is something disquieting
about a point of view that seems to preclude any moral condemnation of a set
of cultural practices that effectively fulfills the designated functions of Ger-
man society during the 1930s and 1940s or of the Soviet Union during Stalin's
regime or of South Africa during apartheid. Rachels (1993a) pointed out that
an uncritical acceptance of the cultural relativist position also would preclude
our condemning customary aspects of our own society as immoral (e.g., eth-
nic- or sex-based employment discrimination) during a period of time when
they are considered acceptable and legal.

These criticisms of its consequences have tended to give cultural relativism a bad name. In addition, as Hatch (1983) and many others pointed out,
there appears to be an inherent contradiction in the cultural relativist position in so far as it involves the nonrelativist values of tolerance and rational
understanding of all cultures. (On what basis could we condemn a society
for being intolerant?) If these conclusions make little sense to us, how can
the meta-theoretical position have any credibility? Conversely, as covered
in our earlier discussion of objectivism, the opposite point of view—that
there exists some independent universal standard of morality that pertains
to all cultures—also does not fare well upon analysis.

A Rapprochement.   The philosopher Wong (1993) observed the
following:

> Almost all polemics against moral relativism are directed at its most extreme
> versions: those holding that all moralities are equally true (or equally false, or
> equally lacking in cognitive content).... One reason, in fact, that not much
> progress has been made in the debate between relativists and universalists is

that each side has tended to define the opponent as holding the most extreme position possible. (pp. 446–447)

Wong took as his starting point the view that all human beings have developed some form of moral system. This is so because it serves two universal human needs: regulating interpersonal conflict and regulating intrapersonal conflict due to competing motives. Therefore, some commonality among those systems is likely to exist. Rachels (1993a) would have agreed with him because he asserted that there is actually less disagreement among cultures than it appears. He reasoned that the relevant commonalities exist at the level of societies' values, not their overt customs and practices. In particular, Wong stated, "We cannot conclude, then, merely because customs differ, that there is a disagreement about *values*. The difference in customs may be attributable to some other aspect of social life. Thus there may be less disagreement about values than there appears to be" (p. 23). Using a variant of the societal functions argument presented previously, he went on to suggest that there are certain values that must be more or less universal because they seem important for the maintenance of virtually any functioning society. These would include objectives such as the care and protection of infants, telling the truth, and prohibiting willful murder—notwithstanding that there may be some exceptions under certain conditions and that the relative importance of each of them may vary. Other scholars believe that there is an even longer list of principles and practices that may be universally represented in virtually all moral codes: keeping promises, protecting the vulnerable, avoiding incest, justice, unprejudiced judgment, reciprocity, and respect for personal property (Shweder, Mahapatra, & Miller, 1987). According to this view these shared values represent the core of a more-or-less universal set of moral principles: That is, many (but not all) of these values are shared by many (but not all) societies because they are adaptive. But even so, they may be expressed in rather divergent practices at the behavioral level because overt social practices and customs reflect not only a society's moral values and principles but are also influenced by environmental and contextual factors, such as the form and level of economic development, historical and religious beliefs, traditions and folkways, as well as by its cultural conventions and institutions, such as its political system. In the field of international business, in which these academic considerations take on a very pragmatic cast, such broad-based normative or ethical principles have been conceived as hypernorms that provide the basis for macrolevel social contracts (Donaldson & Dunfee, 1994). The conception still allows room for the existence of more idiosyncratic microlevel social contracts, as long as they don't contradict the hypernorms. Similarly, Donaldson (1989) presented a common ethical core of 10 fundamental rights to be respected by all corporations wherever they conduct business.

The view represented by both Rachels (1993a) and Wong (1993) is a modified or attenuated version of cultural relativism. (Alternatively, it could just as readily be referred to as an attenuated version of universalism.) They held that all societies develop moral systems because of a need to regulate conflict among their members so that the societies can function. Similarly, they argued that there is a certain degree of similarity in human nature as well (without pushing the point too hard). Based on those two sets of constraints, ethical systems are developed that are comprised of a certain number of core values that generalize across cultures but may be expressed in a variety of social practices due to the influence of other antecedent influences, such as historical tradition, environmental context, nature of the political system, and level of economic development of the society. This view leaves open the question of how much commonality or uniqueness one may find across cultures. A prominent example of this approach at the empirical (i.e., non-normative) level with which I/O psychologists may be familiar is Hofstede's (1980, 2001) description of complex national cultures by means of just five core values orientations: power distance, uncertainty avoidance, individualism/collectivism, masculinity/femininity, and time orientation.

A Final Challenge.   Geertz, an anthropologist, wrote extensively in this area, and no discussion of this topic should conclude without a consideration of his views. In particular, it would be misleading to leave the reader with the impression that the existing proponents of cultural relativism are all necessarily naive or uncritical in their approach. Geertz (1973) was rather disparaging of what he referred to as "a hunt for universals in culture," although he acknowledged that it is a scientifically and emotionally appealing position:

> In essence, this is not altogether a new idea. The notion ... that there are some things that all men [sic] will be found to agree upon as right, real, just, or attractive and that these things are, therefore, in fact right, real, just or attractive—was present in the Enlightenment and probably has been present in some form or another in all ages and climes. It is one of those ideas that occur to almost anyone sooner or later. (pp. 38–39)

In the late 19th and early 20th centuries, he observed, this "hunt" took the form of a search "for empirical uniformities that, in the face of the diversity of customs around the world and over time, could be found everywhere *in about the same form*" (p. 38, italics added). This approach was largely a failure: The forms (behavioral patterns) are simply different. In modern anthropology beginning in the 1920s, according to Geertz, this hunt adds something new: "It added the notion that ... some aspects of culture take their specific forms solely as a result of historical accidents; others are tailored by forces which can properly be designated as a universal" (p. 39). This, of course, is the conceptual approach on which Rachels (1993a) and

Wong (1993) have constructed the modified cultural relativist (or modified universalist) position previously described. The universals are based on core values embedded in the requirements for developing and maintaining any human society, whereas some cultural practices do not imply any such core values but merely reflect historical tradition, particular political systems, or environmental factors and the like.

Among the several telling criticisms that Geertz (1973) offered of that view, the most relevant for us is the challenge that even if such substantial universals can be demonstrated (and he by no means concedes the point) the question still remains:

> should [those universals] be taken as the central elements in the definition of man [sic], whether a lowest-common-denominator view of humanity is what we want anyway. This is, of course, now a philosophical question, not as such a scientific one; but the notion that the essence of what it means to be human is most clearly revealed in those features of human culture that are universal rather than in those that are distinctive to this people or that is a prejudice we are not necessarily obliged to share. (p. 43)

And thus we can detect what is for our purposes a meaningful distinction: Geertz is an anthropologist debating meta-theoretical issues in the social science of anthropology. His concern for the grand question of what may be justifiably accepted as the central elements in the definition of humanity need not be ours with respect to (merely) whether there are some common moral values that underlie social custom. We can be more accepting of the middle-ground position emphasizing the search for core values that may underlie some of the great diversity among cultures.

TOWARD A FRAMEWORK FOR ETHICAL DECISION MAKING

So, where does all this leave us? This brief overview of meta-ethics has yielded six points that provide the beginning of a useful framework for ethical decision making to which we can add in later chapters.

1. **The use of ethical reasoning is critically important.** The major meta-ethical issue that we have dealt with is the tension between subjectivist and objectivist views. Rachels (1993a) warned that we should not fall into the trap of structuring the issue as a dichotomous choice between two extremes: Either (a) there are objective moral facts just like empirical facts in science, or (b) our moral principles and values are merely reflections of our idiosyncratic subjective feelings and beliefs. As we have seen there are substantial problems with both stances. He pointed out the following:

> This is a mistake because it overlooks a crucial third possibility. People have not only feelings but reason, and that makes a big difference. It may be that ... moral truths are truths of reason; that is, *a moral judgment is true if it is backed by better reasons than the alternatives.* (p. 40, italics added)

Similarly, P. Singer (1995) concluded that "The non-existence of a mysterious realm of objective ethical facts does not imply the non-existence of ethical reasoning.... So what has to be shown to put practical ethics on a sound basis is that ethical reasoning is possible" (p. 8). And that is what has preoccupied many analytic philosophers in the 20th century: "By focusing on the 'logic' of moral argumentation, they shifted the focus of attention from the question of whether moral judgments are true or false to the question of what constitutes a 'good reason' for a moral conviction" (Arrington, 1998, p. 384).

But that conclusion can seem inadequate to psychologists who are trained in the traditions of empirical science:

> Human cognitive ability is so flexible and creative that every conceivable moral principle generates opposition and counterprinciples.... However, whereas oppositional thought in science is checked by empirical constraints, it goes unimpeded in ethics. Ethics, unlike science, as repeatedly noted, has no extrinsic criterion, shared by all, that can be used to judge the validity of moral principles.... A moral pluralism appears to be a psychological end product of a democratic society whose members are free to express their ethical views.... (Kendler, 1999, p. 832)

But then Kendler went on to discuss the necessity for moral pluralism to be conceived as an ongoing set of guidelines that "require constant evaluation to determine their consequences so that the functional value of moral pluralism will not be endangered either by disruptive moral conflicts or by intolerant restrictions" (p. 832).[11] I assume that what Kendler envisioned as the evaluation of alternative moral principles is a process akin to the ethical reasoning advocated by the moral philosophers, so there is little distinction between his position and the one advocated here.

Even though Rachels (1993a) acknowledged that if our reasoning is flawed we may be led to incorrect conclusions about what is good and bad or right and wrong, in my opinion, he still underestimated both the psychological complexity of logical reasoning and the potentially distorting influences of which humans are capable. For example, he believed that "reason

---

[11]Kendler's (1999) remarks were written in the context of the ongoing debate regarding the relation between values and science and in defense of the position that psychology must adhere to the model of value-free science. There are many proponents of the alternative view that values are always inherent in the scientific enterprise and that the value-free model of the natural sciences is an ideal that has never characterized science as it is actually practiced. These matters will be discussed in chap. 8.

says what it says, regardless of our opinions or desires" (p. 40). But even emotionally neutral rules of logic may yield ambiguous determinations of whether deductions are correct or inductive inferences are warranted (Rips, 2001). And we know all too well that personality factors and strongly held political, social, and religious beliefs and values influence the premises on which our reasoning processes are based and our evaluation of alternatives. As a consequence of different strongly held attitudes, what seems reasonable (i.e., appropriately reasoned) to me may not appear so to you and vice versa. The best we can do is to be aware of those potentially distorting influences, try to be honest with ourselves by unmasking those hidden blinders, and expose our views to others who are likely to not share the same biases—that is, to attempt always to engage in what I have emphasized as right reason.

2.   **An indispensable aspect of moral reasoning is the universalizability of an ethical decision.** Most people probably accept this principle implicitly, but it bears being made explicit. I cannot give you advice regarding what to do in a difficult situation and expect it to be considered an ethical recommendation if I would not advise myself similarly in the same situation. Universalizability is responsive to the principle that there should be consistency in what is considered ethical behavior, irrespective of individual personalities.

3.   **I reject egoism in favor of the universalist tradition.** Despite how well thought out the basis for one's behavior, it will not in these pages be considered ethical if the justification is entirely self-interest. The position I have adopted is reflected in the moral philosophies reviewed in the next two chapters and is consonant with that of P. Singer (1995): "Self-interested acts must be shown to be compatible with more broadly based ethical principles if they are to be ethically defensible, for the notion of ethics carries with it the idea of something bigger than the individual" (p. 10). That is, no one's interests and concerns, especially one's own, can be held to have a greater a priori moral claim than anyone else's. We may take this principle to refer equally to the self-interest of one group (e.g., senior executives) over all other groups as well (e.g., shareholders, employees, or consumers). It should be acknowledged, however, that there is a tradition in moral philosophy perhaps best expressed by Hume (see Arrington, 1998) to the effect that the two motives are not mutually exclusive. The mere fact that we have sentiments of benevolence and concern for the public good means that acting on them is personally gratifying and pleasurable. This was Aristotle's view as well: Acting in accord with the social virtues is inherently pleasing. It is this connection that I believe Singer alluded to in the previous quote regarding the potential compatibility of self-interest and broader ethical principles. Some philosophers believe that there is no antagonism between

selfishness and altruism. For social beings, as we are, self-interest and social-mindedness are entirely compatible, if not indistinguishable.

4. **There is a potential distinction to be acknowledged between moral knowledge and moral action.** On one hand, we can agree with *universal prescriptivism* (Hare, 1981, 1993) that knowing the correct thing to do in the face of an ethical dilemma always carries with it the implicit commitment to act accordingly. And we can further agree, therefore, that the failure to do so renders our behavior unethical. Nevertheless, as psychologists we know that most behavior is multiply determined, and we should bear in mind that moral dilemmas can be complicated and stressful, with several competing motives. Consequently, if the situation warrants, and if significant harm has not been done, we should be prepared to cut others (as well as ourselves) some slack in terms of the severity of condemnation that an ethical violation deserves. Chapter 5, which introduces the psychological perspective as distinct from the philosophical, explores further the issue of moral choice and action as discrete steps following moral reasoning.

5. **The problem represented by cultural relativism in ethical thinking remains incompletely resolved.** The middle-ground position discussed in this chapter may be useful. That is, judgments regarding the degree of similarity or difference among cultures in their ethical standards ought to consider not merely the surface manifestations or social practices of the societies but the meaning of those practices in terms of their implicit ethical values. It is to be expected that at the level of values there will be greater cross-cultural similarity than at the level of social customs because the latter are determined by a variety of nonmoral antecedents as well as by those values.

6. **We should remember Hume's Law.** As social scientists we may be especially vulnerable to slipping into the "ought" from "is" trap. We may be so accustomed to looking to our empirical data as the means of resolving ambiguities, discrepancies, and disagreements in our work that we uncritically generalize that procedure to our deliberations regarding ethical matters. Natural phenomena, including even those aspects of human behavior that may have a high genetic component (assuming there were unanimous agreement on which those were), carry no particular moral capital by virtue of their naturalness. Ethical reasoning cannot be co-opted legitimately by recourse to putative scientific facts.

3

Normative Ethical Theories:
I. Deontology

The word *philosophy* means the love of wisdom, but what philosophers really love is reasoning. They formulate theories and marshal reasons to support them, they consider objections and try to meet these, they construct arguments against other views. Even philosophers who proclaim the limitations of reason—the Greek skeptics, David Hume, doubters of the objectivity of science—all adduce reasons for their views and present difficulties for opposing ones. Proclamations or aphorisms are not considered philosophy unless they also enshrine and delineate reasoning.

—Robert Nozick

Most contemporary philosophers agree that there are two broad categories of normative ethical theories, albeit with many examples and variations within each: *deontological theories* and *teleological theories*. *Deontology* derives from the Greek word *deon*, meaning duty, and refers to points of view in which actions are viewed as inherently ethical or not. *Teleology* derives from the Greek *telos*, or goal, and is used to label theories in which what is ethical or moral is determined by the effects or consequences of the actions. Rawls (1971) explained the conceptual distinction between the two as determined by the way in which a theory defines and relates the two notions of (a) right and wrong and (b) good and evil (or bad).

Teleological ethical theories—more frequently referred to nowadays as *consequentialist theories*—give primacy to the good: That is, they focus on the good and bad that will result from an act, or from two or more alternatives, and they define the rightness or wrongness of the action(s) in terms of the net amount of goodness that results from each. Deontologists essentially do not deal with the notions of good and bad; the rightness or wrongness of an act is intrinsic to the nature of the act, based on whether or not it violates a moral principle, and is independent of its consequences. Whether or not I may ethically mislead the student–participants in a psychological experiment will depend, for the consequentialist, on the balance of benefits likely to result from the research, in comparison with the likely harm that may ensue from the deception. For the deontologist, deceiving the participants—that is, not providing fully informed consent—is wrong irrespective of how much good might result from the research. The deontologist will view me as having *wronged* those students even if I have not *harmed* them.

A dramatic contrast between these two ethical perspectives was brought to the public's attention in the summer of 2001 by President Bush's highly publicized decision concerning public funding for embryonic stem cell research.[12] The *consequentialist* view emphasizes the enormous potential *good* that may result from such research—possible cures for Alzheimer's disease, Parkinsonism, diabetes, and others—with virtually no downside risk beyond the financial commitments. Some deontological positions focus on the fact that an embryo must be destroyed in the process of obtaining the stem cells and that the destruction of human life, at any stage, is unequivocally *wrong*. Of even greater importance for our purposes, the controversy also illustrates that (a) ethical issues exist within a context of underlying definitional and conceptual concerns (e.g., When does life begin? and Is an embryo a person?); (b) the resolution of moral dilemmas is invariably linked to, and in many cases dependent on, factual or empirical matters (e.g., the scientific breakthroughs that occasioned the ethical dilemma; estimates of the likelihood of developing the anticipated medical treatments, and at what costs); (c) ethics and morality are inherently political in nature because they involve interpersonal norms, social values, and, in many instances like this one, social policy decisions; and (d) because many of the available "lines" of stem cells available for medical research were developed and are controlled by private firms, issues of commercialization, business values, and the relations among government, business, and the common good are also invoked.

DEONTOLOGICAL THEORIES

Most of the moral rules or principles that constitute a deontological position are phrased in the negative as a proscription. In other words, deontological morality generally has to do with defining what is permissible or impermissi-

---

[12]Stem cells have the potential to develop into any kind of specialized cells, thus holding out the promise of renewing diseased or damaged organ systems that, up to now, have been irreparable. Embryonic stem cells are derived from a human embryo and are thought to be much more flexible, hence useful, than adult stem cells that can be derived from more mature organisms.

ble—not what is required.[13] For example, in a treatise on ethical concerns in conducting organizational surveys, 23 ethical principles are promulgated all of which begin "You shall not ..." (Sashkin & Prien, 1996). As N. A. Davis (1993) pointed out, although the rules might be rephrased in the positive (e.g, "always tell the truth") the negative formulation focusing on the impermissible is not accidental in the deontological perspective. There is both a pragmatic and a theoretical reason for it. The practical reason is that it would be extremely difficult to stipulate everything that a person should do: The possibilities are virtually infinite; specifying what is wrong is a more limited enterprise. The theoretical reason has to do with the distinction that must be maintained by deontologists between intended and unintended effects. Within this view one would violate the proscription against harming others only if one did so intentionally; if our behavior harms others unintentionally, we have not transgressed—even if we anticipated the harmful results of our actions! It is apparent why this is a theoretically necessary aspect of a deontological position: If it were not, one would have to come perilously close to adopting a consequentialist position (foreseeing negative consequences is a teleological reason to refrain from carrying out such a bad act).[14]

However, some versions of deontology, therefore, encompass an arguably untenable position. Suppose one evening, on leaving my office and arriving at the corner of Park Avenue South and 25th Street, while waiting for the traffic light to change to green so that I can cross the street, I notice that the blind woman standing next to me has started to cross before the light has changed and is about to be hit by an automobile. I do not violate the proscription against doing harm to people if I simply stand there and do and say nothing, allowing her to be hit. Deontological rules are narrowly phrased: If I refrain from doing what is impermissible, I am behaving morally. You might respond by asking whether there is an offsetting rule that says, in effect, "Try to help others in need whenever you can." There may be; in this instance, the two rules are complementary. But that is not always the case; sometimes they are contradictory. Let us change the scenario a bit. Suppose a father is standing just in front of the blind woman and, because he is distracted by his two rambunctious children he fails to see the car bearing down on us. It's too noisy for him to hear a warning shout, but I can get to him and pull him and the kids to safety—if I push the blind lady out of the way, perhaps into the path of the car. If I intentionally harm her, I have violated the deontological rule and behaved immorally, notwithstanding the fact that I may have saved

---

[13]There are exceptions, such as theories that focus on one's duties.

[14]This is referred to as the *doctrine of double effect* and is common in Roman Catholic moral theology. It explains why causing the death of the mother is not viewed as immoral if the intended effect was to save a viable fetus—even if the mother's death was foreseen. Similarly, it would not be viewed as immoral for a doctor to cause the death of a terminally ill patient by administering morphine—even at potentially lethal dosages—if the ostensible purpose was only the alleviation of pain.

three other lives. Conversely, if I do nothing and the father and children are seriously injured, I incur no moral accountability. But reason tells us that failing to act can sometimes be equivalent to acting wrongly.[15]

The sorts of deontological theories I have been alluding to are examples of *rule deontology*. They entail the establishment of general moral rules to be followed. A rule-deontological theory does not assume that following the rule is necessarily the best thing to do in each and every instance, just that it's the best *general* rule, so that the specifics of any situation are simply not considered. Obviously, basic questions for deontology are "What are those moral rules," and "How are they determined?" The different answers to those questions constitute different normative ethical theories. One of the essential problems for rule deontologies has to do with situations in which the rules are in conflict. What if I feel professionally obligated to advance psychological knowledge and understanding, and also to refrain from deceiving or manipulating research participants, but I am contemplating a project in which accomplishing the former objective entails violating the latter principle? Rule deontology has no fully satisfactory answer to this dilemma because all the rules are conceived as absolutes.

However, compromises are possible. For example, one could rank order the rules to establish some prioritization. But that certainly is a lot more complicated to deal with than a simple list of universals (e.g., whose preferences will hold sway in determining the rankings?). This approach is illustrated prominently by a rank ordering of the four principles that comprise the organizing structure of the *Canadian Code of Ethics for Psychologists* (Canadian Psychological Association, 2000). Barring exceptions having to do with imminent danger to someone's physical safety, respect for the dignity of persons is expected to take precedence over responsible caring, which in turn is viewed as more important than integrity in relationships, which outweighs responsibility to society. Another possibility is that the rules could be formulated as less general and more specific so that the incidence of conflict among them is diminished. This is exactly what has been done for millenia even with respect to the biblical commandment not to kill: It has been interpreted in western civilization as a prohibition only against taking innocent life. Other exceptions are routinely made even by religious people, such as wartime killing. In our field, one might operate under the qualified rule that "it is wrong to deceive research participants unless the study is breaking important new ground." Of

---

[15]The fact that my ultimate goal is to save the father and his children, not to harm the woman, does not get me off the hook with a deontologist as long as I have intentionally put her in harms way. The deontological conception of intentionality refers to *means* as well as to *ends*. Conversely, as will be discussed later, one may be just as uncomfortable with a strict utilitarian argument that justifies intentionally harming one lady in order to save three others. How one reacts to dilemmas of this sort may have much to do with how personally involving the situation is (refer to the discussion of the trolley problem and the footbridge problem in chap. 5).

course, the difficulties are apparent. "Important" according to whom? By what standards, and to what degree? How new is "new"?

Religious precepts tend to be deontological in nature: They set forth specific rules to follow in a legalistic fashion (Fletcher, 1966). Over the years, however, circumstances change and empathic motives of sympathy, fairness, and justice lead to modifications, exceptions, and qualifications to the rules that, in Chandler's (2001) ironic characterization, take the form of "rules for breaking the rules" (p. 187). The most extreme compromise is called *act deontology* in which each specific alternative in a particular situation (or act) is evaluated as an independent entity in light of the relevant deontological principles, which are treated more as guidelines than absolute rules. The question to be answered is whether following the rule(s) is the best action in this particular instance. But note that the evaluation is still within the boundaries of deontological considerations—presumably ignoring the teleological issue concerning consequences. However, many consequentialist philosophers are of the opinion that these individual situational act-deontological evaluations inevitably involve a consideration of the relative good or harm associated with the available options, thus constituting a utilitarian justification.

Probably the quintessential deontological theory is that of Immanuel Kant, who ultimately offered a single moral principle that may be said to underlie all others: Do not violate anyone's dignity, respect, and autonomy, which are everyone's rights.

Immanuel Kant

Immanuel Kant (1724–1804) probably has been the most influential philosopher in western culture since Aristotle despite the fact that his work has been criticized extensively (cf. Arrington, 1998; O'Neill, 1993). The importance of his work stems from three sources. First, his elaborate theoretical formulations come close to representing an appealing common sense view of ethics. Kant conceived of moral behavior as answering the call of duty, of doing what one ought to do, despite having motives—what he termed *inclinations*—to the contrary.

Second, he has been so influential because many of the principles he introduced or systematically elaborated have become generally accepted foundations for moral positions that many ethicists and laypeople take for granted. Those include most of the points noted at the conclusion of the previous chapter constituting the beginnings of a general framework for ethical decision making: (a) the essential role of reasoning or the rational self as the source of morality; (b) the criterion of consistency or universalizability in the application of ethical principles (i.e., that the same moral rules should apply to everyone); (c) the requirement of universalism (i.e., everyone's interests and autonomy must be respected) because of the inherent worth and dignity of all human beings; and (d) an elaboration of the relation between moral knowledge and moral action by virtue of Kant's emphasis on the criticality of the motives for an action in judging its ethicality, not merely the behavior itself or its consequences. His work also provides a philosophical underpinning for political democracy insofar as he emphasized that each of us, as autonomous rational people, should view ourselves as not only obedient to moral law but as the creator of it. And last, his work influenced greatly the theoretical formulations of 20th century moral psychologists, such as Jean Piaget and Lawrence Kohlberg. We will explore how these great ideas play out in his philosophy.

The Centrality of Motivation and the Function of Reason

According to Kant there is only one thing in the world which can be taken as good (i.e., moral or right) without qualification. That thing is what he called *good will*, or what we might think of as right motives. Even Aristotle's criterion of happiness cannot be taken as an unqualified good: A person might be pleased, for example, at someone else's misfortune. Because right motives are unqualifiedly good, their moral value does not depend on the person's good actions in implementing them because the person might not be very capable. If I see a child drowning in the ocean at a nearly deserted beach and I plunge into the surf to rescue her but am too poor a swimmer to reach her before she disappears, my behavior is no less moral for its ineffectiveness. Similarly, suppose I do rescue her but unfortunately she is too far gone and cannot be revived. My behavior is no less moral because of the negative outcome. This definition of moral behavior independent of its consequences is one of the attributes that clearly renders Kant's philosophy deontological in nature and is one of its features that resonates with people's general notions of morality as having to do with good intentions. These intentions or motives—more particularly, the underlying principle(s) that they reflect (e.g., one should try to save an innocent person's life if there is the possibility of doing so)—Kant called a *maxim*.

None of this emphasis on intentions or maxims would make much sense if Kant didn't assume that we are all autonomous beings free to choose (or not) the correct thing and that we have the reasoning capacity to do so. It is reason that guides the operation of free will. Each of us, as rational agents, prescribes for ourselves what is moral.[16] How that comes about takes us to the next elements in his philosophy.

---

[16]One might question, "Why should reason be given this preeminence? Why be rational?" However, as Norman (1983) pointed out, one who poses such a question has already accepted the truth of the assertion.

Duty. Kant was the first one to put the notion of *duty* at the core of an ethical theory. Norman (1983) pointed out that Kant's parents were devout Lutherans, and he undoubtedly was influenced by the ideas of the Protestant ethic, which viewed the fulfillment of one's duties in everyday life (e.g., duties as a parent, good citizen, and loyal employee) as the highest calling in life. Kant contrasted duties with those aspects of our behavior influenced by our desires, temptations, preferences, or what he referred to as our *inclinations.* What makes an act moral is its being motivated by a sense of duty rather than by our inclinations. The prototypical moral act is one we initiate out of a sense of duty despite feeling compelled by inclination to do otherwise. And it is not enough for Kant that the action merely is *in accord with* a sense of duty; for it to have moral worth it must actually *be motivated by* a sense of duty rather than inclination.

Therefore, referring to my previous hypothetical encounter with a drowning child, if my motives for attempting her rescue were entirely egoistic (e.g., fantasies about being hailed as a hero) or instrumental (anticipation of a monetary reward) or even a reflection of my basically kind-hearted, generous, and altruistic nature, then for Kant my actions are without moral worth. If I had been quaking with fear and wishing I had not come along at just that time, but managed to overcome that trepidation to dive into the surf after the child, then my behavior would be morally worthy. One of the interesting implications of Kant's position is the indeterminacy of judgment in those mixed-motive situations in which our inclinations and our duty coincide. Kant did not have a good answer for that. Conversely, he should not be misinterpreted as proposing that any involvement of our inclinations precludes moral value. He was saying only that acting from duty is the necessary condition.

Kant went a step further and radicalized the notion of duty. He divorced it from its specific mundane referents, transformed it to an abstract generalized duty, and suggested that morality consists in adherence to this sense of duty for its own sake, without reference to any specific purposes or outcomes. And we are able to do our duty (i.e., do what we ought to do or what is right) by following the dictates of reason. To summarize, ethical behavior is that which is motivated by good intentions, or the aim of doing one's duty, which is most clearly evidenced when one has to overcome contrary inclinations in order to do so. A contemporary application of the importance placed on duty is the perceived prevalence of promise keeping as a core ethical value in the business world (R. D. Haas, 1997). Unfortunately, however, the empirical evidence is that keeping one's promise does not fare well when it conflicts with competing work-related values—unless there is the force of legal sanctions backing up the promise (Oakley & Lynch, 2000).

But what does Kant mean by generalized duty? If duties are not to be defined by their particular purposes or consequences, then what is this "duty"? It has no content. We will see how he answered this question.

Universal Law and the Categorical Imperative

Kant said that "duty is the necessity to act out of reverence for the [moral] law" (cited in Arrington, 1998, p. 267). This is important because only rational beings can have laws and intentions to follow them, so that the highest purpose of reason is to provide the motivation to follow moral law. But, wait a second. Kant seems to have merely shifted the focus without answering the question. If duty consists of obeying moral law, but the content or substance of the duty is undefined, what is this "law"? His answer is brilliant. Because the law, like duty, cannot be defined by its content (which can at best refer only to a qualified good) or by its unreliable consequences, it can only be defined by the formal quality of law itself, which boils down ultimately to its universal nature, or what I have previously referred to as universalizability. For a principle or maxim such as "never tell a lie" or "help others whenever you can" to qualify as a moral law, it must be one that we can be assured all people would be obliged to obey.

For Kant (as with Hare's universal prescriptivism 2 centuries later; see chap. 2) a moral principle or maxim has the nature of a command: "Do this" or, more frequently, "don't do that." The reason that we experience it as an imperative is because we have inclinations that may be in opposition to our duties and need to be overcome. According to Kant, an imperative that is conditional on an inclination is a *hypothetical imperative*. "If you want to graduate and receive your PhD degree you must complete your doctoral dissertation." "The honest thing to do is to return that money." Completing your dissertation and returning the money are imperatives only if you accept the conditional purposes of wanting to graduate and being honest, respectively. In contrast, universal moral laws are expressed as *categorical imperatives*, meaning that they have no conditional purpose(s). Obedience to them is absolute, that is, unconditional: "Do not lie [ever, under any circumstances]."

"Do not lie" is a categorical imperative because it is universalizable. "It's okay to lie under some circumstances" is not universalizable. That is, if society operated according to that qualified principle presumably no one could know whether or when they were being lied to so no one's word could be accepted, and society could not survive. I qualified the previous sentence with the word *presumably* because the determination of whether a maxim is universalizable is generally not based on any empirical data but on a thought experiment, imagining what society would be like if everyone always behaved in accord with it. For example, could there be a viable society in which no one was ever sure whether he or she were being lied to?[17]

---

[17]It is just this sort of reasoning, however, that leads consequentialists to charge that Kantian deontology, in the process of analyzing the universalizabilty of an imperative, actually resorts to a utilitarian assessment of consequences, illustrating that deontology cannot stand on its own independent of a consideration of outcomes.

Although there are many maxims that could be formulated as potential categorical imperatives, there is one overall categorical imperative—The categorical imperative: "Act only on that maxim whereby you can at the same time will that it should become a universal law." Thus, universalizability is the hallmark of morality; because we are all rational beings, we all will agree on what is universalizable. Kant developed a few other formulations of the categorical imperative that are meant to be expressed in more practical terms. The most important of these is referred to as the *formula of the end in itself* or the *formula of humanity*.

Respect for People as Ends in Themselves

Just as Kant reasoned earlier that there is only one unqualified good (good will), he also reasoned that there is only one thing that has absolute, objectively verifiable value: human beings. The value of all other things such as physical objects or even individual qualities of people (e.g., their wit or intelligence) varies; in fact, human beings, through their inclinations, impart value to all other things. Because the values of things vary some things may be perceived and used as *means* of obtaining other valued things. This cannot be true of human beings because their value is absolute; they are *ends* in and of themselves. Moreover, it is self-evident to Kant that each of us, as rational agents, conceives of ourselves as having unconditional value, that is, as being ends. Arrington (1998) pointed out that this is entirely consistent with the universalizability promoted by the categorical imperative; in fact, it provides it with additional justification:

> If all rational beings are ends-in-themselves, we treat them as such only if we refuse to make any arbitrary distinctions among them, distinctions that would demote some of them to the status of mere things to be used by others. We must, that is to say, act consistently toward all rational beings. Hence whatever we conceive to be right for ourselves, we must also conceive to be right for other rational creatures—all of them. And whatever commands to action we give to others, we must also give to ourselves as well; whatever duties we assign to them, we must also impose on ourselves. (p. 277)

Therefore, Kant was led to this revision or corollary of the categorical imperative: "So act as to treat humanity, whether in your own person or in that of any other, never solely as a means but always also as an end." The qualifiers *solely* and *also* are important. Kant recognized that we may, with no adverse moral implications, use people as appropriate to the circumstances—to cook a meal for us, drive us to the airport, or mentor the development of our careers. Kant's formula of humanity is generally viewed as one of the most fundamental moral principles ever developed. It dictates that we never lose sight of the view of all human beings as having absolute worth in and of themselves and thus should be treated with dignity and respect. Far from being a trite platitude, the implications of this view, as Norman (1983) articulated, are profound. It suggests that we be concerned for other people's objectives as well as our own. It means recognizing that the pursuit of our own goals is limited by their potential infringement on the rights of others; we should not manipulate or use others merely for our own purposes, regardless how worthwhile those purposes may be. It implies respect for the liberty and autonomy of others to pursue their own ends freely. Thus, Kant's views have also found expression in later rights-based theories of ethics (cf. Tuck, 1979; Waldron, 1984) and in the ideas articulated by the intellectual and political leaders of the American and French revolutions and the Declaration of Human Rights of the United Nations in 1948.

Thomas Hobbes

Suppose you lived in a world in which each person was motivated exclusively by her own selfish interests; there was no political, legal, or social machinery to enable or enforce cooperative relations; the predominant attitude with which you and everyone else engaged the world was a mixture of distrust, fear, competition, and aggression; and most of your existence was focused on the struggle to survive. (Think of the movie Mad Max.) That is what Thomas Hobbes (1588–1679) envisioned as the natural *state of nature* of humankind without the mechanisms of civilization—what he characterized as a perpetual state of war. His description of the likely devastating consequences of these conditions is one of the most widely quoted passages in all of philosophy:

> In such condition there is no place for industry; because the fruit thereof is uncertain: and consequently no culture of the earth; no navigation, not use of the commodities that may be imported by sea; no commodious building; no instruments of moving and removing such things as require much force; no knowledge of the face of the earth; no account of time; no arts; no letters; no society; and, which is worst of all, continual fear and danger of violent death; and the life of man, solitary, poor, nasty, brutish and short. (From *Leviathan*, cited in Arrington, 1998, p. 161)

What Hobbes meant by "no society," among other things, is an absence of morality or of any sense of good and evil, right and wrong, or justice and injustice. Under these conditions, each person has what Hobbes called the *right of nature*, which is nothing less than the freedom to do anything he or she wants in order to protect and enhance his or her life. Because living under such conditions of continual fear and insecurity is untenable, it is clearly in humankind's self-interest to escape this brutish existence. And this we do, according to Hobbes, by means of the *laws of nature*.

The Laws of Nature and the Idea of the Social Contract

Fortunately, according to Hobbes, we possess the powers of reason that enable us to find a way out of this horrible life. Reason leads us to a number of principles (19 in all) that he referred to as the laws of nature. The first two of these emphasize that it is in our own self-interests to abandon the state of war and to seek peace, and to give up our unlimited freedoms under the right of nature, providing others do so as well. The condition is important: Hobbes was a "psychological egoist" as well as an "ethical egoist." People cannot be expected to relinquish their freedom to pursue their exclusive self-interests if others are not abiding by the same ground rules.[18]

When people mutually renounce some of their rights they enter into an agreement that Hobbes referred to as a *contract*; to the extent that the contract entails commitment to future actions, it is a *covenant*. The third law of nature is that we are required to live up to the obligations incurred by our contracts and covenants with others; otherwise, peace cannot actually be attained. Thus, it is the existence of the explicit and implicit laws and agreements that you are expected to live up to and your being able to count on others doing the same that comprises the substance of morality. *Justice* entails abiding by these *social contracts* that structure civilized social life; *injustice* is failing to do so.

But, one might reasonably question at this point, given Hobbes' decidedly pessimistic view of human nature, how can he expect people to abide voluntarily by their social contracts? This is a good question. The answer is he does not. Included in the liberties that we relinquish is the establishment of a superordinate agent that we all empower to enforce the laws and covenants. This agent Hobbes called the *Sovereign*, and it is only as a consequence of our fear of punishment by the sovereign for committing an injustice that we achieve a workable social system that he referred to as a *commonwealth*. (The commonwealth may exist in any political form, democracy or totalitarianism; Hobbes himself was a staunch monarchist.) The alert reader may note that this sounds reminiscent of the stance taken by the radical Sophists who saw the need for the existence of laws to temper our unbridled pursuit of self-interest. But there is an enormous difference between them and Hobbes. For the Sophists morality consisted in *expressing* our self-serving human nature; they advocated a grudging acceptance of law only as necessary to avoid punishment. Conversely, for Hobbes, it is the social contracts and laws that comprise morality, enabling social and commercial discourse of all kinds by *limiting* human nature. Moreover, the security afforded by the commonwealth allows us to temper our potentially unlimited pursuit of self-interest by enabling some expression of altruistic motives.

---

[18]It is this emphasis on the renunciation of some personal liberty to achieve peaceful conditions allowing all to pursue their limited self-interest that makes Hobbes an *enlightened* ethical egoist.

That is a theme developed more fully by Jean Jacques Rousseau in *The Social Contract*, published more than a century after *Leviathan*.

The Relation Between the Individual and Institutional Power

Hobbes' discussion of the powers of the sovereign betrays a rather authoritarian if not totalitarian point of view. The powers of the sovereign are virtually unlimited. Hobbes undoubtedly was led to this position by virtue of his rather disquieting view of the nature of human behavior in an unregulated state, as well as by his personal observations of social disorder during the English civil wars (1642–1651). But the purpose of the sovereign is to maintain overall peace and security and the survival and gratification of all members of the commonwealth (i.e., the state), so the powers are not completely unlimited. Hobbes specified that we are absolved from obeying the sovereign (i.e., the laws of the land) if the sovereign is not able to provide the protections that are its reason for being. Moreover, the individual's basic right to pursue his or her self-interests (within the limits of the law), the right to self-defense, and protection against self-incrimination (i.e., thwarting one's own self-interests) are never surrendered.

One of the values of Hobbes' theory is the integration of what is essentially a political philosophy concerning the acquisition and exercise of institutional power, along with morality. Ethical issues surrounding the use and abuse of institutional power are certainly relevant topics for organizational psychologists, notwithstanding our focus on corporations or other social organizations as the institution rather than the state. It is not much of a stretch to cast the modern corporation in the role of sovereign, and its relationship with its employees, as well as the relationships among employees, as governed by social contracts and covenants more familiarly referred to as organizational policies and regulations, employment contracts, collective-bargaining agreements, and other artifacts of organizational culture, as well as implicit psychological contracts (Rousseau, 1995; Rousseau & Schalk, 2000).

Rachels (1993a) elaborated the application of social contract theory to the issue concerning when it might be appropriate to break the rules of the commonwealth or, on a larger scale, to engage in civil disobedience. As already noted, Hobbes provided the rationale: When the sovereign is unable to provide the protections or other benefits that are due under the terms of the social contract, it may morally be disobeyed. The rules of the social contract are based on an implied or explicit reciprocity: I give up my freedom to act unilaterally in my own interest in order to obtain the longer term benefits that will accrue to me by everyone else doing the same. Therefore, if someone violates that reciprocity we are morally released from our obligations (within the limits allowed by law). Similarly, Rachels pointed out that social contract theory provides a meaningful rationale for the explicit defiance of the law—civil disobedience—under certain circumstances:

Why do we have an obligation to obey the law in the first place? According to The Social Contract Theory, it is because each of us participates in a complicated arrangement whereby we gain certain benefits in return for accepting certain burdens.... In order to gain these benefits, we agree that we will do our part to uphold the institutions that make them possible....

But what if things are arranged so that one group of people within the society is *not* accorded the rights enjoyed by others?... If the denial of these rights is sufficiently widespread and sufficiently systematic, we are forced to conclude that *the terms of the social contract are not being honored.* Thus if we continue to demand that the disadvantaged group obey the law and otherwise respect society's institutions, *we are demanding that they accept the burdens imposed by the social arrangement even though they are denied its benefits.* (p. 154)

Critique.   It is easy to criticize Hobbes on a factual basis. We know his view of human nature to be at best a pessimistic unidimensional view that emphasizes a narrow range of human motivation. Factually, there is no historical or anthropological record of humans living in a "state of nature," as he visualized it, or of them ever having entered into an actual contract of some sort that marked a transition from the state of nature to civilized society. In fairness to Hobbes, he did not actually advance the latter point as an historical event, but he accepted the social contract as implied by the relatively uniform conventions that characterize society. Some philosophers (e.g., Arrington, 1998) are severe in their criticism of the social contract theory even when conceived as merely implied agreements and obligations: "I must *actually* promise something in order to be obligated to do what I promise" (p. 183).

On the one hand, I accept these criticisms as accurate; on the other hand, they may be moot. The contemporary study of social psychology, sociology, anthropology, political science, and economics all take for granted the existence of socialization processes and unarticulated cultural values, assumptions and normative expectations that serve to regulate our interpersonal, commercial, and legal interactions without benefit of formal contractual arrangements or explicit recognition.[19] I am willing to acknowledge the usefulness of the contractarian approach as a helpful model by which to understand a range of interpersonal phenomena, especially in organizational settings, without assuming the existence of myriad formal contracts. On the other hand, the social contract is not mere metaphor: There are in fact sets of social rules by which we live our lives, and this arrangement benefits all of us. As Rachels (1993a) recognized, "the story of the 'social contract' need not be intended as a description of historical events. Rather, it is a useful an-

---

[19]See Danley (1994) for a discussion of the distinctions among actual, tacit, and hypothetical contracts.

alytical tool, based on the idea that we may understand our moral obligations *as if* they had arisen this way" (p. 156). Perhaps most important, Hobbes' approach provides the essence of one of the major general conceptions of what is meant by justice: that is, justice as mutual advantage (e.g., see Barry, 1989). Within the meta-ethical context of ethical egoism, in which each party to the eventual contract is concerned exclusively with maximizing his or her position, negotiators bargain as best they can to advance their self-interests based on their likely positions of differential power. The outcome of such bargaining will probably reflect the differential bargaining power of the participants. That seems to be a potentially flawed conception of justice (see section on John Rawls that follows).

John Locke and Natural Rights

The 17th century philosopher Hugo Grotius (1583–1645) is generally credited with being the first modern exponent of the tradition of ethical naturalism stretching from Aristotle to the Stoics, Cicero, and Thomas Aquinas. The natural law tradition emphasizes the role of rationality (right reason) in revealing the best (i.e., the moral) way to live. It does so in this view because the capacity for reason was implanted in us by God (see the God as the Source of Moral Knowledge section in chap. 2). The key to understanding the significance of any ethical naturalist theory is that it is a reaction against the skeptical or relativist view that morality is essentially a matter of cultural (i.e., local) conventions.[20] Grotius' contribution was to interpret the nature of morality as consisting of universal individual rights (Buckle, 1993) that we expect to be respected by society even though significant compromises may be needed to gain the security that society provides (Schneewind, 1993). (Note the similarity with social contract theory, which Hobbes developed 26 years after Grotius' major work.) Although most rights theorists view human rights as self-justifying—either by revelation or reasoning—they are not absolute rights because some potentially conflict with others, and no one is free to exercise his or her rights by infringing on those of others.

Although John Locke (1632–1704), extended Grotius' work concerning human rights and Hobbes' work regarding the social contract, he also challenged their conceptualizations. He opposed Grotius by emphasizing that some of our rights are inalienable and thus may not be abridged by society (i.e., government). This is the origin of the *classical liberal* tradition in political philosophy which influenced the American and French revolutions. And he opposed Hobbes by positing a very different state of nature than the devastating warfare Hobbes envisioned. Recall that for Hobbes the state of

---

[20]In this sense, natural rights theory, as with all ethical naturalist theories, has much in common with those that espouse a belief in universal (i.e., pan-cultural) moral values.

nature consists in an absence of society, which meant to him an absence of morality. Morality is achieved only by people agreeing reluctantly to creation of the commonwealth. For Locke, morality is based on our natural rights and precedes society. In the state of nature, all are free and equal: "Men living together according to reason, without a common superior on earth with authority to judge between them, is properly the state of nature" (cited in Copleston, 1994, p. 128). And if all people are fundamentally equal, independent, and rational, reason clearly indicates that no one should deprive another of life, health, liberty, or their possessions; the state should not deprive people as well, except in defense of these liberties on someone's behalf. That is what he meant by natural moral law. Hence, there are moral limits to what governments may legitimately do.

The fact that Locke very much emphasized the right to private property is frequently attributed to the fact that he moved among the landed gentry of England, who were his patrons (Copleston, 1994). His views form the kernel of what is characterized as the classical liberal tradition in western political philosophy, especially as applied to economic theory (Danley, 1994). In current political parlance, it is a libertarian or conservative theory (see chap. 7) in comparison with contemporary liberalism, which from this perspective is a revisionist liberal point of view. What is frequently ignored by libertarians and other contemporary proponents of a minimalist government is that Locke's defense of private property was clearly a limited one. What justifies entitlement to private property is one's labor in producing and enjoying it. Amassing more than one can reasonably use and enjoy personally, especially if it is to the detriment of others, is "more than one's share" and is not justifiable. Also, emphasizing rights is not incompatible with notions of overall utility and social responsibility insofar as "the assertion of rights necessarily involves recognition of the rights of others as well as one's own" (Almond, 1993, p. 267), and Locke viewed the primary role of the state as promoting the common good. It is here and in his consistent antiauthoritarian themes that we see the seeds of political liberalism in the contemporary, rather than classical, meaning.

Most rights-based theories share the common flaw of the natural law meta-theories on which they are based (see chap. 2). What is the justification for these rights? How were they determined? On what basis do we accept them as the basis for morality? Normative theories of human rights have great difficulty answering such questions other than by recourse to religious beliefs of their having been God given, which most scholars do not accept as a sufficient philosophical or rational justification. Moreover, even if one did accept that explanation, on what basis do we honor Locke's list of rights (or anyone else's) as the correct ones? Locke himself provided no particular justification. The most frequent justifications have probably been utilitarian (liberty and justice contrib-

ute to human happiness; Almond, 1993), but that breaches the deontological aims of the theory.

John Rawls: A Contemporary Contractarian View

Perhaps the most salient criticism of Hobbes' moral philosophy and its version of the social contract theory is that it is not really a moral theory
(Kymlicka, 1993). Although Hobbesian theory contains the notion of justice—living up to one's social obligations—those obligations reflect contracts negotiated by people who may differ substantially in bargaining power,
and they are incurred by people merely as necessary constraints on one another's otherwise self-serving actions. A barely hidden flaw in this conception of justice is that it matters not a whit what the basis is for one's superior
bargaining power: high social status or positional status in a corporate hierarchy, racial identity, sex, inherited wealth, lack of scruples, willingness to
lie, lack of regard for others, and so on. There is an implicit acceptance of the
sociopolitical status quo regardless of how it came about. Moreover, within
this conceptualization of morality or justice people cannot necessarily be relied on to honor their social contracts; it requires the authorization of a sovereign with the power to punish to establish a workable society or
commonwealth. In other words, a conception of justice posited entirely on
the expression of regulated self-interest, which ignores social inequities, and
is enforced in great measure by external authority and the threat of punishment is viewed by some critics as not being about morality at all.

It is worth noting, however, that there is a contemporary version of social
contract theory in the tradition of universal human rights and Kantian morality, which "uses the device of a social contract in order to develop, rather
than replace, traditional notions of moral obligation; it uses the idea of the
contract to express the inherent moral standing of persons, rather than to
generate an artificial moral standing" (Kymlicka, 1993, p. 191). This point
of view is represented by John Rawls' (1971) work, in which the "inherent
moral standing of persons" is reflected in the Kantian and Lockian ideas of
universalizability or the moral equality of persons, and respect for people as
autonomous "ends in themselves." Therefore, for Rawls, the social contract
reflects the natural duty of justice we *owe* to one another by virtue of our existence, not the artifice of a mechanism of mutual restraint:

> It is to avoid the appeal to force and cunning that the principles of right and
> justice are accepted. Thus I assume that to each according to his threat
> advantage is not a conception of justice. It fails to establish an ordering in the
> required sense, an ordering based on certain relevant aspects of persons and
> their situation which are independent from their social position, or their
> capacity to intimidate and coerce. (p. 134)

Rawls used the contractarian approach as a mechanism to articulate the somewhat vague natural duty of justice. Starting from Hobbes' rather pessimistic and totally egoistic state of nature, he asserted that morality (i.e., justice) can be achieved only if we can obviate the natural inequalities among people because contracts negotiated among parties of unequal power are not likely to be fair. For example, a growing number of companies—estimated at 19% in 1997 by the federal General Accounting Office and 23% by a later survey (L. Greenhouse, 2001)—require employees to surrender their right to sue their employer (e.g., for employment discrimination, wrongful dismissal, or sexual harassment) as a condition of employment—substituting due process procedures, such as arbitration by an internal tribunal of employees and managers or by external arbitrators. Although some management scholars view such *alternative dispute resolution* (ADR) *programs* as effective and safe forums for employees to express grievances (McCabe, 1997), the coercive aspect seems contradictory. Employers have unilaterally applied these due-process rights (which may require many levels of expensive hearings before the employee even reaches the arbitration stage) to existing employees who have had no voice in the implementation of this retroactive condition of employment (Walsh, 2000).[21] Conversely, the more important issue may be the vast majority of employees who enjoy little due-process job protection at all and work under the dominant model of at-will employment in which, with a few exceptions, an employer can hire or fire at will with no explanation required (Werhane, 1999). Dunford and Devine (1998) provided an overview of the common law history of employment at will in the United States, as well as recent legal developments. The topic is discussed further in chapter 12 in the context of employee rights.

The issue of power differentials has been a long-recognized weakness of the contractarian model of corporations as voluntary associations of people united by a network of contracts (e.g., Hessen, 1979). Kelley (1983) pointed out the following:

> All kinds of organizational agreements are actually 'contracts of adhesion,' that is, agreements containing standardized terms set by dominant parties and only marginally negotiable, if understandable, by weaker parties to a transaction.... In these contracts, terms often have been skillfully designed to minimize the legal liabilities of their authors; and, although the 'adhering' party theoretically is free to shop around for a better deal, one finds similar terms offered by competing organizations. (p. 382)

---

[21]The power imbalance in this agreement is reflected in the facts that the employers determine the dispute resolution rules—which may not be questioned as part of the arbitration—and frequently choose the arbitrators as well. They also may have many experiences with the process, whereas a complainant or employee is likely to be going through the process for the first time–an inequality that is exacerbated by the closed-door feature of the arbitrations, in which even the decisions remain unpublished and therefore unavailable to potential future complainants. Thus, it has been reported that the arbitration forum "tends to favor repeat users—management—over individuals who use it only once" (L. Greenhouse, 2001).

The metaphorical device Rawls created to achieve fairness is the *veil of ignorance*. If we designed our social relationships without knowing beforehand our own particular talents and weaknesses, our personal preferences, or our position in society, Rawls assumed that we would simply have to decide what is best for society impartially. And that, he asserted, would lead to a self-protective attitude in which everyone would favor benefitting those who are the worst off (which might turn out to be oneself).[22] Thus, justice is conceptualized within the Kantian tradition of fairness, impartiality, and universalism based on the assumption of respect for the autonomy of all rational people.

Georg Wilhelm Friedrich Hegel

It seems fitting to end this sampling of deontological ethical theories primarily with the views of G. W. F. Hegel (1770–1831) and secondarily with some elaborations of Hegelian notions by Karl Marx (1818–1883). That is because (a) Hegel's ethical theory emphasizes greatly the social nature of our existence, including our participation in the institutions of our society, which is very much in keeping with the points of view expressed elsewhere in this book; and (b) he utilized in his ethical ideology—200 years ago(!)— quite a number of modern psychological constructs with which professionals in developmental, social, as well as I/O psychology would feel quite comfortable. One finds in Hegel consideration of the following topics (albeit not always expressed in our current jargon): development of the self concept and self-identity as a process of psychological individuation; processes of primary and secondary socialization; the notion of alienation, and of social relations and the development of a social identity as the means of overcoming it; human behavior as seen in the context of social role theory, including the importance of work roles; the central importance of self-realization in a social context, as well as effectance motivation and job enrichment at work.

The overriding principle that is reflected in Hegel's philosophy is that humans start life in an alienated state; through a series of developmental stages, we ultimately achieve self-realization through our intimate involvement in social life—through our families, our civil life (e.g., involvement in local community and our work), and the larger society or state. A necessary component of that approach is acceptance of the social character of the individual. We are born into a family and nurtured by its members and others in the local community. Our cognitive and emotional development occurs in a highly social context, and we continue to expand our relationship to the external world largely through involvement in larger and more varied social organizations and institutions. The implications are that (a) the crux of

---

[22]This is the so-called *maximin utility* solution, which is the common interpretation of Rawls's (1971) position, although Barry (1989, p. 83) asserted that it is a misinterpretation.

what we mean by ethics, according to Hegel, has to do with the very special character of interpersonal relationships, which are based on trust, loyalty, cooperation, emotional commitment, and the like, initially just to one's family and then to the wider circle of interdependent social and economic institutions he referred to as *civil society*, including those at work, and ultimately to the state; and (b) these social relations are not merely things we do and peripheral aspects of our personality, but they are intrinsic aspects of our self-identity. Thus, when I extend my trust to a close friend, family member, or good colleague, it is not because it will increase the overall level of happiness or good in the world (Utilitarianism; see chap. 4) or because it is a dutiful thing for me and everyone else to do (Kant), but because my relationships with these folks are part of my psychological identity and it gives my life meaning to do so. However, extending this principle to an ever-widening social world—for example, loyalty to fellow employees and one's employer, relations with community members, and identification with one's country—depends on the quality of one's relationships with those people and entities. We do not, according to Hegel, owe blind loyalty irrespective of the worthiness of those people, organizations, and institutions.

The Development of Self-Identity[23]

Hegel took a developmental perspective concerning the process whereby we achieve an ethical existence, which he referred to as *self-realization*. Because, as already noted, the essence of the ethical sphere is social, self-realization is the realization of the social self. That is the ultimate goal of human development. The developmental process starts with us as mere physical beings until, through interacting with the environment, we begin to be aware of ourselves as conscious and willful beings. The basis for all personality development is this initial undifferentiated self-consciousness and what Hegel called the *imperative of right* associated with it (i.e., the right of all humans to be). Personality—and especially one's sense of personal freedom—begins to become differentiated through engaging with objects, possessing, using, and ultimately exchanging them with others (e.g., a young child in a sandbox tightly in possession of his or her pail and shovel, not yet able to share). Hegel placed great store on the notion of private property as the means whereby we learn to express our individual rights and freedom, as well as how to interact socially.

These exchanges of private property ("My Michael Jordan trading card for your Mark McGwire?"), which Hegel referred to as *contracts*, are the means whereby we acquire normative notions of right and wrong, which are formalized in the laws and customs of society. From these particularized notions of right and wrong develop a more elaborated sense of morality, which

---

[23]This discussion is based largely on analyses by Arrington (1998).

consists of a generalized notion of how one ought to be. And it is a critical point for Hegel that this generalized notion includes recognition that we share this morality with others; in that way, our identity is transformed from an individual, isolated selfhood to that of a social being. It is at this point in his ethical theory that Hegel's notions of universal subjectivity become rather metaphysical. But we need not be too put off. The essence of the concept is that "The self which I am to realize is a social self—not the self which I am as an isolated particular, but the self which I am through my relations to other selves, the self which I share with others, as a social being" (Norman, 1983, p. 149). On this basis, therefore, the substance of morality becomes welfare, not only my own but universalized as that of others as well.

But what does everyone's welfare consist of? How does one know what is the good thing to do? What are one's right duties? Hegel specifically rejected Kant's answer to these questions. Recall that Kant believed that moral law and its attendant duties could not be specified by their substance (which represent only qualified goods at best) or by their consequences (which are unreliable), but only by the formal quality of the law itself—its universalizability, or the categorical imperative. Hegel's answer is very different and is highly susceptible to misinterpretation and distortion (as was, in fact, done by European Fascists in the 1920s and 1930s), but it is consistent with his focus on our social character. He asserted that the only possible objective ethical content, free of individual subjective distortions, are the "absolutely valid laws and institutions" of our social existence that are embodied in the family, civil society, and the state. "In an *ethical* community, it is easy to say what a man must do, what are the duties he has to fulfill in order to be virtuous: he has simply to follow the well known and explicit rules of his own situation. Rectitude is the general character which may be demanded of him by law or custom" (cited in Arrington, 1998, p. 309). In this regard F. H. Bradley (1935), a foremost interpreter of Hegel, is responsible for publicizing the phrase "my station and its duties." In this way, Hegel defined our ethical obligations in a concrete and specific manner, between the ambiguous and unhelpful abstractions of moral law on one hand and the potentially biased and self-serving subjectivity of personal conscience on the other hand.

A casual reading of these notions might create the impression that, far from leading to the freedom of self-realization that was Hegel's objective, this is a very conservative and constraining conception of the ethical life: mere reverence to the status quo traditions, obligations, and laws of one's society. But that overlooks two matters. First, for Hegel, the institutions, work organizations, and the state in which we perform our duties are assumed to be ethical ones, by which he meant that these organizations can justify the rationality or validity of their laws and regulations and demonstrate that their functioning is compatible with the personal objectives of their constituents or citizens. Second, contingent on our acceptance of the institutions as ethical, Hegel assumed we do not experience them as coercive or antagonistic. In fact, it is presumed we identify psychologically with them and with our duties; they in part identify who we are—as a family member, a member of the larger society in which our well-being is interwoven with that of others, and a citizen of the state.

Self-Realization

An additional brief word seems in order concerning what Hegel meant by "self-realization." In this regard, he accepted Kant's emphases on respect for the individual and on each of us as an end in our own right, but he rejected Jeremy Bentham's utilitarian ideal of maximizing pleasure as the hallmark of individual actions (see chap. 4).[24] That is because he viewed the utilitarian approach as atomistic, whereas self-realization involves a more inclusive and coherent affirmation of one's whole social being. As Norman (1983) put it, "the accumulation of superficial satisfactions may leave one's life incomplete" (p. 169). That coherence is frequently attained by virtue of having a dominant focus in one's life around which all else revolves—it is frequently one's work or career, commitment to a political or religious movement, or family relationships. In all cases, it generally provides a sense of social recognition for the individual and a sense of identity.

Especially apropos is Hegel's focus on the importance of work as a means of self-expression that provides one with a sense of identity. It is in this rich context that we should understand the meaning of "my station and its duties." Bradley (1935) elaborated this Hegelian theme by enunciating the principles of what, many years later, psychologists would refer to under the rubrics of *effectance motivation, activation theory,* and *job enrichment* (e.g., see Deci & Ryan, 1991). That is, the process of self-realization is not one of mere passive enjoyment; it requires action and accomplishment—in particular accomplishing meaningful and challenging tasks. Boring, repetitive, and unchallenging activity does not provide the means for realization. That is a point of view espoused by another renowned 18th century figure not ordinarily associated with a sympathetic view toward the worker:

> The man whose life is spent in performing a few simple operations, of which the effects too are, perhaps, always the same, or very nearly the same, has not occasion to exert his understanding, or to exercise his invention in finding out expedients for removing difficulties which never occur. He naturally loses, therefore, the habit of such exertion, and generally becomes as stupid and ignorant as it is possible for a human creature to become. (Adam Smith, 1776/1976, p. 303)

[24]Hegel's familiarity with utilitarianism was limited to his knowledge of Betham's work. Hegel died when Mill was only 25 years old.

Karl Marx

There is an irony about Marx being considered in a work focused on ethics or moral philosophy that would probably annoy the heck out of him, given his rejection of moral theorizing and the very notion of morality as we conceive it. However, quite a few interpreters of Marx have suggested that Marxist theory itself is rather ironic in this regard because of the highly moralistic nature of its denunciation of capitalism for stifling human freedom.[25] In any event, there are several reasons for his inclusion. Early in his intellectual life Marx was a Hegelian, and several aspects of Hegelian ethics are represented in Marxist theory, including the notions of alienation and the expression of self-identity through work, the interdependence of the individual and society, the objectives of freedom and self-realization, and a rejection of Kant's abstract formalism. (Ultimately, of course, Marx rejects Hegel's view of the psychological importance of private property ownership and the rectitude of accepting one's station in life and fulfilling its duties.) In addition, as indicated by such earlier works as Plato's *Republic*, as well as those of Hobbes, Hegel, and others, Marx was not the first to illustrate that reflections on ethics inevitably lead to a consideration of the social, economic, and political institutions by which society regulates the behavior of its members toward one another.

Historical Materialism and the Rejection of Morality

To put it succinctly, Marx was a sophisticated Sophist. He believed, as did they, that society's laws, customs, and morality simply reflect the self-interests of the dominant members of the society. This is elaborated within the larger context of his theory of *historical materialism*. Historical materialism views history as divided into eras characterized by a particular mode of economic production that is controlled by a particular segment of society, which also is the primary beneficiary of that production. Other segments of society are relegated to other roles. To the extent that each segment of society is represented by relatively organized political and social representation it becomes a *class*, and it almost goes without saying that the particular class that is in control of the means and rewards of production is highly motivated to maintain that position, and those not in control are motivated to acquire it.

According to Marx, virtually all aspects of culture—religion, art, literature, science, and morality—are *ideological*, meaning that they represent and reinforce the class interests of those who are in power at any particular time. "Morality is a system of ideas which both interprets and regulates people's behavior in ways which are vital for the working of any social order"

---

[25]Of course, the greatest irony, as pointed out by A. Wood (1993), is the number of horrific atrocities of the past century as a consequence of the moral failings of political forces using his name.

(Wood, 1993, p. 516). Most people remain unaware of this, even with respect to their own motives and behavior—they lack *self-transparency*—and so remain in a state of "unfreedom." For example, we may kid ourselves, a Marxist might assert, that our ethical notions of universalizability and universalism (i.e., impartiality and equivalence of interests) represent key elements of a just moral system. But given the nature of the class structure—one class that rules at the expense of all others—any apparent impartiality is illusory: It merely furthers the interests of those in power. Similarly, the free trade, free competition, and freedom of the worker to contract his or her services in the capitalist system are all illusory insofar as they are actually structured and constricted by the economic system that serves the interests of the ruling class. Therefore, Marx's views in this regard are diametrically opposed to Hegel's and Bradley's focus on "my station and its duties." Note that Marx believed that the self-serving advancement of one's own class interests would be no less characteristic of the motives of the working class if it was in power. That is why the proletarian revolution was conceived as merely a step toward the ultimate goal of a classless society, which would actually accomplish what illusory morality pretends to do, so that ideology would be unnecessary.

Alienation, Realization, and Work

Marx believed, as did Hegel and many industrial and organizational psychologists today, that work provides a critical source of self-identity, social recognition, and self-realization—when it is meaningful work that allows the expression of some autonomy. This focus on the ideal of a fully realized life through meaningful productivity makes Marx no more radical than Plato, Aristotle, Hegel, Kant, or Mill, or the psychologists Maslow (1998), Herzberg, Mausner, and Snyderman (1959), or Hackman and Oldham (1980), for that matter. However, he further believed, as most I/O psychologists do not, that those objectives are precluded by work as it exists within the capitalist system, namely, *wage labor*: working for others who own the capital and means of production.

Marx borrowed Hegel's notion of alienation to describe the consequences of wage labor. As Norman (1983) summarized, Marx identified four dimensions of *alienated labor*:

1. Alienation from the product of one's labor: That is, the worker has little or no concern for the qualities of the product and does not own it. It is merely a means of earning a wage.
2. Alienation from one's own productive activity: By this he meant working under conditions of external structure and substantial controls with no expression of individual autonomy.

3. Alienation from our distinctly human capacities: such as intelligent, creative functioning.

4. Alienation from others: When work is motivated solely by extrinsic financial reward, especially when based on individual performance, it precludes the social rewards of a cooperative, shared experience.

How is this to be overcome? How is the worker to move from a state of alienation to self-realization? Marx's answer may be viewed as an exaggeration (quite an extreme exaggeration) of a theoretical position with which most contemporary social scientists and psychologists are comfortable in one form or another—situational determinism. There may be quite some distance between job restructuring or reinforcement contingencies near one end of a continuum and the revolutionary restructuring of the entire society at the other end, but they are nevertheless all on the same continuum formed by a belief in the efficacy of social–structural or contextual determinants of behavior. For Marx, the only solution is bringing the means of production under the ownership and control of the workers themselves. "Only then can work be experienced by the workers as the putting into effect of their own communally formulated projects and aspirations. Only then can it be experienced as an activity in which each individual finds his own identity confirmed by others in a shared enterprise" (Norman, 1983, p. 179).

Critique. Given the general historical failure of communism as an effective economic and political system for enhancing individual freedom, it seems most useful for our purposes to focus on the positive features that we can glean from Marxist theory. From our vantage point 1½ centuries later it seems clear that Marx's empirical observations were mostly correct. The importance of people's social and psychological growth needs and the salience of work as a sphere uniquely suited for expressing and gratifying them is widely accepted now. Similarly, his characterization of the stultifying conditions under which most workers labored in the early stages of the industrial age remained widely true for over a century (cf. C. R. Walker, 1952) and, for many workers, remains true today. Moreover, contemporary criticism of the economic and social power and political influence wielded by corporations, especially the precipitate exodus of capital and production facilities from communities that have both supported and come to depend on them to cheap labor markets around the globe, is at least compatible with Marx's views of historical materialism and class divisions, if not necessarily supportive of the entire theory. Last, as Norman (1983) pointed out, "Marx's recognition that the human good requires not just individual action but political change remains of very great importance" (p. 200). This is in keeping with the view of many philosophers that ethics consists of both "personal morality" and "a social institution analogous to law ... [that] is part of the apparatus of power" (Seckel, 1987, p. 69).

....

Additions to the framework for ethical decision-making are deferred until after the following chapter so as to integrate suggestions drawn from both deontological and consequentialist views.

4

Normative Ethical Theories:
II. Consequentialism

An ethical judgment that is no good in practice must suffer from a theoretical defect as well, for the whole point of ethical judgments is to guide practice.
—Peter Singer

CONSEQUENTIALIST THEORIES

As noted at the outset of the previous chapter the teleological or consequentialist point of view asserts that the morality of our actions is to be judged by the relative goodness of their effects rather than by their inherent rightness or wrongness. Pragmatists, such as business managers, economists, and applied psychologists, who are accustomed to making their professional choices based on the anticipated consequences of their actions, have generally felt more comfortable with consequentialism than with deontological theories (Fritzsche & Becker, 1984). For example, a proposed model of ethical decision making in organizations defines a moral issue entirely in terms of harm or benefit to others (T. M. Jones, 1991). The first systematic formulation of this approach, *utilitarianism*, was presented by Jeremy Bentham (although it was suggested earlier by Hume) and it was expanded and refined by his student, John Stuart Mill. The resulting composite of their work is usually referred to as *classical utility theory*, and it has undergone further refinements in response to the criticisms raised by Bentham and Mill themselves, as well as by other vociferous critics. Contemporary consequentialist theories retain much of the essence of classical utility theory but with several substantial modifications, as I will show.

Jeremy Bentham

Jeremy Bentham (1748–1832) was a philosophical radical who aimed to rid moral philosophy of reliance on what he considered to be irrational notions, mystical and religious justifications, and abstract moral rules, such as natural law or natural rights. Moreover, he was also a social and political radical who simultaneously hoped to transform English institutions by ridding them of their ill-conceived conventions and traditions which he held responsible for much social injustice and unhappiness. In fact, his major work is entitled *The Principles of Morals and Legislation*. Both of these aims were to be accomplished by adherence to the one ultimate moral principle, the principle of utility, which refers to:

> ... that principle which approves or disapproves of every action whatsoever, according to the tendency which it appears to have to augment or diminish the happiness of the party whose interest is in question: or, what is the same thing in other words, to promote or to oppose that happiness (cited in Arrington, 1998, p. 320).

Bentham, therefore, was a hedonist—a position he arrived at by adherence to his belief in empirical science. That is, human beings encounter the world through our senses, and our actions are determined entirely by the experience and/or anticipation of pleasure and pain. Realistically, therefore, maximizing pleasure and avoiding pain (i.e., increasing happiness) is the only justifiable moral principle. And the principle is applicable at the individual level with respect to one's private morality as well as at the public level so that legislators ought to design laws in light of people's propensity to promote their own happiness, and all government officials should base their policy decisions on the criterion of maximizing public welfare. Therefore, although Bentham was a psychological egoist (he believed that people tend to act in their own self-interest), he was not an ethical egoist. He believed that moral actions are those that produce the greatest happiness for oneself and others. For Bentham, the great appeal of the principle of utility is that it puts moral philosophy on an objective base. The justification of its ultimate principle does not rely on deontological abstractions or appeals to the revealed word of God but on the objective consideration of real-world consequences. But how is this objective consideration to be accomplished?

The Hedonic Calculus.   Bentham meant nothing less than that Utility was a measurable (i.e., quantifiable) construct. Although this was a somewhat radical notion, it was not new: His ideas were based on Bernoulli's (1738/1954) mathematical expression of psychological utilities in decision making. Bentham conceptualized the construct as multidimensional, and contemporary psychologists would recognize the conceptual antecedents of modern attitude measurement, economic utility theory, and cognitive decision theory. Each action we take may have a variety of consequences, each of them being relatively pleasurable or painful. And pleasure and pain can be assessed quantitatively by measuring the seven dimensions of which, according to Bentham, they are comprised. Pleasure and pain vary in duration, intensity, certainty or uncertainty (the likelihood that the action will result in the sensation), propinquity or remoteness (the immediacy or distal nature of the occurrence of the effect; e.g., contrast the immediacy of the discomfort of a visit to the dentist vs. the delayed effects of failing to study for a midterm exam), fecundity (the probability that the pain or pleasure will be followed by more of the same kind; e.g., the additional ramifications of failing that midterm exam), and purity (the probability that the pain or pleasure will not be followed by the opposite sensation). To determine the goodness of an act or the relative goodness of several alternative options, (a) each of the six attributes are to be assessed by the individual for each of the consequences of every option: (b) a net effect for each option calculated as a multiplicative function of the six dimensions, and (c) a seventh dimension should be considered, extent, by adding algebraically for each option the net pleasure and pain experienced by all other people affected, as calculated in the same manner. The best—that is, most morally defensible—action is the option whose consequences have the highest overall net pleasure score or the lowest overall net pain score.

Bentham did not presume that this complicated and time-consuming set of psychometric calculations—what Knapp (1999) referred to as *felicific calculus* and we might neologize as *ethimetrics*— is carried out prior to every individual action or governmental decision.[26] And it is beyond our purposes here to consider all of the difficult scaling and other measurement issues to overcome in operationalizing this ethimetric system (see Arrington, 1998, and Goodin, 1993, for succinct summaries). Nevertheless, Bentham said that this is just the sort of reasoning that people intuitively approximate when confronted with difficult choices. And he held it up as a model to be achieved if possible because it represents the ideal of a rational underpinning for ethical decision making. Similarly, Pettit (1993) made the point that consequentialist approaches in general are more validly thought of as a theoretical way of justifying ethical decision making than as a blueprint for actual deliberation. However, we know that contemporary behavioral theories of decision making and gaming in psychology and economics do make use of subjective expected utility as a basis for understanding and predicting choice behavior (Barry, 1989; Mellers, 2000;

---

[26]Although something very much like it in principle, cost–benefit analyses are indeed frequently carried out in the process of planning or evaluating social programs.

Savage, 1954), despite evidence suggesting that people's preferences or values are unstable and biased by the particular measurement operations used to estimate them (Kahneman, Slovik, & Tversky, 1982; Slovik, Fischoff, & Lichtenstein, 1985). Recent psychological research on decision processes has focused on subjective expected pleasure as a key evaluative process. That is, evidence indicates that people make decisions by anticipating the relative pleasure or displeasure associated with outcomes, weigh those by their perceived likelihoods of occurrence, and choose options with the highest anticipated average pleasure (Mellers, 2000; Mellers & McGraw, 2001; Mellers, Schwartz, Ho, & Ritov, 1997). Unfortunately, however, people may not be very accurate in anticipating their affective reactions (Mellers & McGraw, 2001). To my knowledge, this decision affect theory has not yet been applied to the realm of ethical decision making.

John Stuart Mill

John Stuart Mill (1806–1873) was the son of James Mill who was a close colleague and collaborator of Bentham. So John's philosophical education was dominated by utilitarianism, and he maintained an adherence to its basic tenets, such as what he referred to as "the greatest happiness principle." But he also was dissatisfied with several aspects of the theory and so is responsible for having modified and refined it in a number of ways. For example, although Bentham included consideration of others' welfare as well as one's own, Mill emphasized even more the criterion of the greatest overall happiness for everyone, with no person's well-being counting more than anyone else's. Mill's views are a clear example of what I referred to as the universalist tradition in moral theorizing. Most important, he expanded the hedonistic conceptualization of pleasure to include a more complete picture of human nature and thus enlarged the notion of what is meant by the ultimate principle of happiness.

The Pleasures of Swine

Because of his strong preference for empiricism, Bentham's notions of pleasure and pain were limited essentially to the sensual level of experience and so, to Mill, could be considered "a doctrine worthy only of swine." Mill corrected this limitation of the theory by introducing a consideration of higher pleasures—so characterized because he viewed them as superior to the baser pleasures to which Bentham attended. They are superior insofar as they depend on the functioning of the higher human faculties: intellect, abstract thought, aesthetic appreciation, a sense of freedom and autonomy, personal security, social gratification, and so on. Mill would feel quite comfortable with a consideration of Maslow's hierarchy of human needs stacked on the base of physiological drives or with Hegel's notion of self-realization. In fact, Mill redefined Bentham's limited conception of happiness into one that is more compatible with Aristotle's *eudaimonia* or fulfillment (see chap. 2).

However, because these pleasures are different in kind from each other and—especially from the lower pleasures—they can be considered only qualitatively, not quantitatively. He did not reject the quantitative hedonic calculus of Bentham (e.g., he continued to consider the *greatest* happiness) but, as Norman (1983) pointed out, Mill tended to exclude a consideration of the lower pleasures and so it is unclear how he intended to integrate both the quantitative and qualitative dimensions of the varieties of pleasure. Perhaps this is not such a serious criticism in light of the general recognition that utilitarian calculations are more often than not implicit and intuitive in any event and thus should be able to accommodate the qualitative considerations. For example, Mill wrote at length about *secondary principles* that represent generalizations and extrapolations regarding the relative benefit to society of various kinds of actions. Over the span of civilization we have learned that, for example, truthfulness and respecting others are generally beneficial in the long run and that deceitfulness is generally harmful. In most instances these sorts of guidelines make it unnecessary for us to engage in detailed ethimetric calculations for each specific decision. Those analyses can be reserved for instances in which two or more secondary principles may conflict.

Contemporary Consequentialism

A variety of consequentialist theories remain popular in ethical thought today. They generally represent modifications of classical utilitarianism developed in response to significant criticisms of the narrowly hedonistic view of the classical Bentham—Mill model, so it makes sense for us to understand them in that context.

Responses to the Limits of Hedonism. Many philosophers have argued that the pursuit of happiness—even Mill's expanded version of the construct—is at least a myopic, if not completely flawed vision of morality. It ignores much of what we view as noble in human behavior, expressions of virtue as well as the many other values that guide people's attempts to do what they perceive as right. In chapter 2 I made the point that contemporary virtue theory is a response to a perceived overemphasis on right actions and ethical reasoning to the exclusion of considering one's moral character, as reflected in attributes such as courage, beneficence, or integrity. Some of these criticisms were made even in Mill's time, and his response is viewed by some philosophers as inadequate. Simply put, Mill acknowledged that, although virtue is not an intrinsic aspect of hedonistic utilitarianism, it is readily incorporated into the theory to the extent that people who are virtuous behave that way because it pleases them to do so. At least for those folks, then, virtue is simply a component of happiness. The reader may recall from chapter 2 that this is essentially Aristotle's position as well. Nevertheless, many view this as an inadequate tautological explanation: From an initial premise that the pursuit of happiness is the ultimate objective of all behavior, one simply infers inappropriately that anything we do must therefore have been done because it contributes to our happiness.

Early in the 20th century G. E. Moore (1903/1993) gave a more satisfactory answer to this challenge by acknowledging that human beings intuitively recognize the intrinsic value or good of other things like aesthetic beauty, knowledge, and feelings of friendship and love—independent of whatever role they may have in contributing to happiness. His version of *ideal utilitarianism* maintains a utilitarian focus on maximizing the overall good of outcomes, but it permits a wider variety of goods to be included in the calculus. It does little, however, to address another sticky issue for utilitarianism: that is, the need to accurately predict the future to compare the consequences associated with each decision option.

The theory of *preference utilitarianism* is similar to the ideal version in that it maintains the basic structure of utilitarianism (i.e., the maximization of utility) but sidesteps entirely the definition of what is good. Happiness, virtuous action, loving relationships, the appreciation of beauty—whatever!—can be considered as legitimate preferences for each individual, the relative satisfaction of which is what gets considered in the evaluation of utility. This approach from philosophy corresponds to psychological *decision affect theory* (Mellers & McGraw, 2001), which focuses on anticipated pleasure as the key ingredient.[27] Perhaps more important, preference utilitarianism also obviates the other difficulty for utilitarianism as a system of ethical decision making: the difficulty in predicting with any certainty or known probability all of the consequences of one's potential actions. Therefore, the calculations of the hedonic calculus, whether explicit or implicit, are invariably incomplete and inaccurate when applied to anticipated consequences. In contrast, one's a priori preferences are more readily specified and evaluated; thus, preference utilitarianism is the version most often used by economists in theorizing about political economy (Danley, 1994; cf. chap. 10).

The theory of *welfare utilitarianism* is another variant that considers people's welfare or interests as the basis on which utility should be assessed. Whenever our best interests and conscious preferences coincide there is no

---

[27]As with Moore's ideal utilitarianism, the subjective expected pleasure that provides the focus of decision making in decision affect theory is not limited to a narrow hedonistic definition of pleasure. It may be derived from actual or anticipated selfless acts of virtue (Mellers & McGraw, 2001).

difference in those two models. When they do not coincide, the two sets of utility analyses will diverge. Unfortunately, there are many reasons to presume that preferences and interests will frequently not be the same, such as having incomplete information about the available options or conflicting motives concerning them. For example, smoking cigarettes might be relatively high on your list of preferences to be satisfied frequently; it is hardly in your long-term best interests.

This example brings to mind Mill's classic liberal (in current political parlance it would be called *libertarian*, cf. chap. 7) statement on the relation between the state and the individual. Recall that this issue seems to arise almost inevitably in the deliberations of many moral philosophers and social thinkers, from Plato to Hobbes, Hegel, Marx, and B. Russell. In his essay "On Liberty," Mill expressed his views on personal freedom, independence, and autonomy in a utilitarian context: Freedom should be virtually limitless up to the point at which one harms the interests of others. Therefore, at the individual level, self-protection or preventing harm to others is the only justification for interfering with the actions of others. Not even the person's own welfare is a legitimate justification for restricting his or her autonomy. Extrapolating to the state, the only justification for government interference is the prevention of harm to others. This is the classical liberal position regarding civil liberties and also provides the basis for the minimal government conceptualization of laissez-faire capitalism. Mill would likely have concluded that we have no ethical right to prevent people from acting against their own interests by smoking cigarettes or failing to use seat belts in their automobile or a helmet when on their motorcycle. (Note, however, the enormous public medical costs associated with the long-term effects of smoking should be weighed in this evaluation as harming others.)

The Exclusion of Justice, Duties, Rights, and Obligations.   Other modern criticisms of classical utilitarianism are that it ignores and cannot account for such obvious bases of morality as the commonly felt imperative of living up to one's obligations, promises, and duties. It betrays this weakness, the criticism holds, because of its teleological nature (i.e., a forward-looking perspective focused on consequences), whereas obligations and promises (e.g., keeping one's word) are what Rachels (1993a) referred to as "backward-looking" (p. 108). Norman (1983) presented the following example:

> Suppose that I have arranged to visit a friend on my bicycle, and have promised my daughter that I will take her with me on the child-seat of the bicycle. As I am about to leave, my son says that he wants to go with me. I cannot take them both. Now suppose that my son and my daughter would equally enjoy going with me, and would be equally disappointed if they cannot go (and suppose that this is the case, even when we take into account

the added disappointment which my daughter will feel as a result of having had her expectation roused). Or suppose that my son will even enjoy it very slightly more than my daughter would. The utilitarian will have to say that if my son would enjoy it even more, I ought to take him; and that if they would both enjoy it equally, it would be equally right for me to take either my son or my daughter. To say this, however, is to deny all significance to what is, in fact, the crucial difference between the two alternatives, the fact that I have made a promise to my daughter, but not to my son. In virtue of that fact it is clear that, even though the consequences might be just as good in either case, I ought to take my daughter. This shows that there is a duty to keep one's promises, quite apart from utilitarian considerations. (p. 134)

Although this criticism may be apropos of classical utilitarianism, it can be rebutted successfully if we think in terms of some combination of ideal and preference utilitarianism, in which one's intentions to live up to one's obligations, responsibilities, and commitments are represented in the utilitarian equation. The satisfaction or fulfillment of those intentions may be included among the benefits, or goods that contribute to one's sense of well-being. All else being equal, Norman will feel better and more righteous if he takes his daughter.

Similar arguments against utilitarianism have been made with respect to the concepts of justice and individual rights. Assume that I am a utilitarian. Suppose I am an organizational consultant conducting individual and group on-site interviews with employees of a large department store in connection with the development of an overall competency model for the store. Suppose that during the few days that I spent meeting with people in a particular department, a large amount of merchandise was stolen from that area in a manner that could only have been accomplished by an employee. Assume further that the store is owned by a parent corporation located in another city, whose managers care little for employee relations. The corporation just announced that if the culprit is not identified within 2 days it will take retributive action against all eight employees who had access to the merchandise. As a respected and impartial observer whose word will be accepted, why shouldn't I, as a utilitarian, accuse one person of the crime in order to prevent the adverse consequences to several innocent employees? The lie seems defensible in utilitarian terms. Although it is true that the one falsely accused person will be harmed, he or she will probably just lose the job; there won't be enough proof for a criminal charge. But there will be a great deal of benefit done: saving the jobs of the other innocent employees.[28] Clearly, my behaving as suggested would be wrong. Most people have no difficulty recognizing that I will have violated a moral right of the accused, which would

---

[28]Do not get hung up on the extremely unlikely nature of the scenario and the relevant aspects of the situation that I am not considering, such as the effect of this action on my continuing relationship with this client and its employees. It is not meant to be a realistic case, just an illustration.

be unjust (in deontological terms, I will have intentionally wronged this person), so that the utilitarian analysis therefore cannot be correct. This is the sort of argument that is used to illustrate the presumed weakness of utilitarianism in failing to account for such values as rights and justice.

There are in actuality two related but distinct criticisms being subsumed in this illustration, and they lead to two more modifications of classical utilitarianism. The first criticism is that because utilitarianism emphasizes the greatest good for all concerned it ignores potentially relevant distinctions among people. In other words, it doesn't matter who benefits or who is harmed. The classical theory does not deal with the notion that people may differ in the extent to which they deserve the outcomes in question. The person I was to falsely accuse is no more deserving of punishment than any of the other innocent employees. A research psychologist may decide that the likely aggregate scientific and educational benefits of a research study outweigh the possible harm resulting from deceiving participants about a noxious or emotionally stressful experimental manipulation to be employed. But the benefits accrue to the researcher (and perhaps to society), whereas the harms are visited on only the research participants.

Focusing on the overall level of happiness or well-being also ignores instances in which the injustice has more to do with some people benefitting unjustifiably more than others. This becomes an extremely important consideration when the analysis is elevated to the institutional or societal level. For example, some people have characterized the mid-1980s to mid-1990s as a decade of unparalleled economic success for the United States because of the steady growth in *overall* wealth and earnings. For example, median family income continued to rise. But others point to increasing and (to them) unjustifiable *discrepancies* in wealth between the very few fabulously wealthy families on one extreme and the persistently large proportion of very poor, including working poor families, at the other extreme, whose earning power in constant dollars has actually declined over the past generation or so (Gottschalk, 1993). As will be discussed in chapters 7 and 10, a focus on maximizing the production of aggregate wealth or on issues of its equitable distribution mark two divergent models of political economy with significant social and moral implications for business and its relation to the rest of society and government.

This criticism has led to a transformation in our understanding of the nature of the universalist tradition from its original characterization in classical utilitarianism. In chapter 2's discussion of egoism versus universalism, I made the point, following the utilitarian P. Singer (1995), that a moral perspective does not require treating everyone equally, but that everyone's interests—their rights and freedoms—should be given equal consideration. The quotation from Rachels (1993a) bears repeating: "We can justify treating people differently *only* if we can show that there is some factual difference between them that is relevant to justifying differences in treatment" (p. 88). So it is simply not true that modern utilitarianism overlooks deserved distinctions among people; it emphasizes the need for a moral justification of those distinctions.

The second criticism implicit in the store theft illustration is that utilitarianism condones or even requires on occasion that we lie, cheat, steal, or engage in other obviously immoral acts if the balance of good over bad consequences is notable. The aspect of Bentham's classical utility theory that renders it susceptible to this criticism is that it is an *act utilitarianism*. That is, it presupposes that the hedonic calculus is applied, even if implicitly, to each contemplated action with moral implications. Mill's response to this criticism involves his conceptualization of secondary principles noted earlier. I mentioned this notion previously in the context of Mill's acknowledgment that much of utilitarian ethical reasoning is likely to take place only intuitively and implicitly, using general guidelines, rather than by means of a detailed ethimetric analysis of each specific situation. According to Mill, these guidelines are developed inductively by a society and learned by its members as part of their culture based on the primary principle of utility. In other words, we have learned collectively, for example, that lying is generally likely to have more harmful than beneficial consequences and respecting other people's property is generally likely to yield more positive than negative repercussions. In the language of modern computer software, these secondary principles become ethical "default options," to which exceptions may be applied if and when they are clearly warranted.

Mill's invocation of secondary principles brings his version of the classical theory close to a *rule utilitarianism* in which the general utilitarian rules are employed as guidelines by which to judge the ethicality of actions. A rule utilitarian will apply an implicit utilitarian analysis to generalized moral principles rather than to the actions possible in a particular situation.[29] It is viewed frequently as a more relevant approach than the original act-based theory (Knapp, 1999), and the two approaches may lead to different ethical conclusions about the same situation (Fritzsche & Becker, 1984). If two or more secondary principles that produce equal aggregate benefit (or are equally preferred) are in conflict (e.g., being truthful to participants in our psychological research and conducting the research in a fashion that will

---

[29]There is considerable disagreement among philosophers over whether Mill is truly a rule utilitarian. (The term was coined long after his death.) The secondary principles appear to indicate that he is, but his acknowledgment of possible exceptions to the rules seems to place him back in the act-utilitarian camp. There has also been a sizable debate concerning whether strict rule utilitarianism—adherence to general principles—is even utilitarianism at all, as it does not involve an assessment of utility for the specific situation.

yield unambiguously interpretable findings), then recourse to the primary principle of act utility and its calculations is called for in this particular situation.[30]

ADDING TO THE FRAMEWORK
FOR ETHICAL DECISION MAKING

The brief survey of prominent normative ethical theories presented in this chapter and the previous one suggests that we add the following considerations to the framework begun at the end of chapter 2.

7. **Neither deontological nor utilitarian approaches emerge unscathed and intact from analyses by their critics, so we should accept both the principled expressions of rights, duties, virtues, and justice, as well as analyses of consequences, as legitimate bases for ethical decision making.** In fact, as discussed, there are many instances in which the two modes of thought appear to merge, such as when a Kantian assessment of whether a maxim is universalizable seems to rest on implicit utilitarian analyses of its consequences or when a utilitarian incorporates adherence to duty in the hedonic calculus as a source of preference satisfaction or happiness. It has been my experience that some ethical dilemmas seem to be more amenable to analysis by one or the other of these paradigms, so we are best served by keeping both doors open. In other words, in some situations right or wrong seems to be a more appropriate and/or salient criterion than the extent of benefit or harm to those involved; for some other situations, the opposite seems to hold. In chapter 5 I will introduce the notion, based in part on the work of Carol Gilligan, that these two philosophical paradigms may correspond to two independent psychological aspects of human moral development and action.

I am indebted to R. Cohen (2000) for calling attention to a relatively mundane dilemma that provides a good example of a situation that may be viewed deontologically or as a consequentialist, with a different conclusion resulting from each. How many times have you attended a sporting event or the theater and during intermission or a break in the action moved from your inexpensive seat to a more expensive seat with a better view? (Or perhaps you've been embarrassed by a companion who insists on doing that, to your chagrin.) Viewed deontologically, it is clearly wrong (i.e., against the rules). You did not pay for the seat. Some might even consider it theft of service. But, from a consequentialist perspective, no one has been harmed. In some venues this practice may even have the status of a normative tradition. (I'm assuming that you have accomplished this migration discretely and politely, without disturbing other patrons or performers, and

---

[30]It is certainly debatable, however, whether the two principles are actually of equal value—that is, are likely to produce the same overall benefits—or are of equal preferential interest to all researchers.

are prepared to graciously surrender your seats to their rightful occupants should they show up late.) If the same action can be viewed as unethical within one of the two normative moral traditions and acceptable by the other, it stands to reason that we ought to be familiar with and able to reason with both of them. People who have adopted different personal moral philosophies are likely to differ in their moral judgments of things like questionable business practices (Forsyth, 1992).

With regard to further comparing the two it is interesting to note that whereas act-deontological theory is a position that was developed in response to major criticisms of the traditional rule-deontological theories, just the opposite is true with regard to consequentialist positions. The rule-utilitarian model evolved to meet significant criticisms of the classical act-utilitarian model. Theoretically, the dialectic modifications should have worked better for the deontologists than for the consequentialists. That is because an absolute adherence to rules is not an easily defended ethical position, irrespective of whether the rules have an abstract deontological justification or a generalized consequentialist justification. However, act deontology is not a very popular position—perhaps for psychological reasons. People who are most comfortable with the absolutist rule-deontological view may be less disposed to accept the uncertainties in moral reasoning that are part of the modified act-based theory. And given many of the pragmatic difficulties in implementing thorough act-utilitarian analyses for every moral dilemma, the world of practical ethics tends to be represented most frequently by both rule-based models (and approximations to act-utilitarian analyses). But there is a difference between the two. Rule-deontological positions are invariably unconditional and admit of no qualifications (although the possibility of rank ordering principles as a feasible, albeit imperfect, way of dealing with conflicts is available), whereas rule utilitarians are more likely to conceptualize and use the rules as general guides open to challenge in a particular instance (cf. Baumrind, 1985, regarding the ethics of deception in psychological research).

Present day moralists who are uncomfortable with the indefiniteness of act-based ethical analyses (of either stripe), often refer to them derisively as *situational ethics*. Presumably, the epithet is meant to indicate unprincipled or amoral acts, which of course is incorrect (Fletcher, 1966). These moralists, however, rarely acknowledge in their frequent public admonishments the theoretical inconsistencies and pragmatic difficulties sometimes associated with attempts to adhere to absolutist deontological principles. Numerous instances can be found of ethical disagreements between those adopting consequentialist positions and those advocating essentially deontological positions; some of them even played out in the political arena. For example, some critics of current environmental policy in the United States are skeptical of many existing environmental rules on the basis of their cost effectiveness. According to these folks cost–benefit analyses indicate that some regulations are astronomically expensive.[31] Conversely, adopting a more deontological point of view, "the Supreme Court this year upheld a prohibition in the Clean Air Act and other environmental legislation that expressly forbids federal agencies from considering costs as a factor in their decision making, directing that the agencies seek to do everything feasible to protect human health" (Jehl, 2001, p. 28).

8.   **Our initial predilections or gut reactions may be unreliable indicators of what is the correct ethical choice.** It is sometimes assumed, extrapolating from Kant, that doing the right thing will invariably be experienced as painful, necessitating a struggle against our more selfish interests. That is not always the case. The assumption underestimates the extent to which most of us have incorporated society's values—at least as ideals for which to strive. Therefore, sometimes there is no marked conflict between our inclinations and doing the right thing. And the converse is also true. Our conscience is not an infallible indicator of unethical choices to be avoided. In the first place, there is great interindividual variability in the voice of conscience. Moreover, it is unfortunately true that human beings have an almost unlimited capacity for guilt and anxiety. Some of us, due to the nature of our primary socialization experiences, have grown up with overly restrictive superegos that are not to be entirely trusted as objective moral barometers. As B. Russell (1987) pointed out, the study of the unconscious has revealed the often mundane causes of our pangs of conscience. So what should we do? Which of our reactions are to be trusted? The answer is to return to the advice offered in chapter 2: ethical reasoning. One will always be on surer footing if one can articulate the rationale for one's choices and actions and subject them to the impartial scrutiny of others.

9.   **A few core values appear to underlie many different normative ethical theories and, therefore, seem worthy of our allegiance.** The first two were introduced in chapter 2.

a.   Universalizability or consistency of judgment. One of the hallmarks of an appropriate ethical decision is that it remains appropriate in the same situation, irrespective of who the actor is, or for the same person in a recurrence of the same situation.

b.   Universalism: Each person's interests are morally equivalent to everyone else's. As noted in chapter 2, I have rejected the perspective of unqualified ethical egoism in which one's own interests count as more important than the interests of others in one's ethical

---

[31]Frequently glossed over, however, are the difficulties inherent in trying to quantify some costs and effects—problems in what I have called the ethimetrics of the analyses. For example, in evaluating certain Environmental Protection Agency regulations there is a dispute regarding whether one should determine the cost for each life saved or the total years of life saved. The different units of analysis yield very different estimates of program cost.

deliberations. This is reflected in both the universalist utilitarian position that everyone's interests are equal (unless there is some morally relevant factual basis for treating people differently) as well as in the deontological concern for fairness, impartiality, and justice.

However, there is an unresolved difficulty with this value that needs to be illuminated. Such impartial treatment assumes an impersonality that most of us do not possess or, in many instances, even desire. For example, people will generally not find it at all mystifying or necessarily inappropriate if one cares more about one's own interests than for the interests of others (rational egoism) or that you care more for your family than you do for almost anyone else. As a pragmatic matter we can expect a declining degree of concern as one considers the well-being of one's own family and friends to that of neighbors, colleagues and acquaintances, to that of strangers merely of the same nationality, to strangers in some distant land, and so forth. Prior to our era of rapid travel around the world, instantaneous global communications, and international connectedness of political and economic institutions, this gradient of unconcern could be attributed entirely to a combination of ignorance and ineffectualness:

> All men [sic], even those at the greatest distance, are no doubt entitled to our good wishes, and our good wishes we naturally give them. But if, notwithstanding , they should be unfortunate, to give ourselves any anxiety upon that account seems to be no part of our duty. That we should be but little interested, therefore, in the fortune of those whom we can neither serve nor hurt, and who are in every respect so very remote from us, seems wisely ordered by Nature.... (A. Smith, cited in Barry, 1989. p. 5)

But we now recognize that social relations and social identity are emotionally salient considerations that lead to a declining sense of responsibility and obligation to those further removed from our core identities, irrespective of physical distance. We grow up caring more for those close to us emotionally. Nevertheless, one must acknowledge a potential slippery slope in this regard. It is not a very far slide from the modestly distasteful practice of nepotism to a host of even more repugnant "isms"—chauvinism, sexism, ethnocentrism, and racism. In addition, as Barry (1989) pointed out, it has only been since the time of Adam Smith 200 years ago that unequal economic development has opened up such enormous disparities among nations that they cannot be ignored in any general treatment of social justice. I would add, moreover, that the current international economic and political forces that we call *globalization* now render it more relevant as well as feasible to include such concerns.

I do not believe that there is any fully satisfactory resolution to the incompatible values of impersonal universalism (fairness as impartiality) and personal commitment, duty, or obligation based on individual social relations. Situations in which they actually conflict are likely to be uncomfortable. As I stated earlier in chapter 2, "as psychologists we know that most behavior is multiply determined, and we should bear in mind that moral dilemmas can be complicated and stressful, with several competing motives." Moreover, an important point made by the psychologist Carol Gilligan, and expanded in the next chapter, is that the motive of interpersonal caring is not outside the domain of morality but should be viewed as another dimension of it, along with the principle of justice. Writing in his newspaper column "The Ethicist," in the aftermath of the destruction of the World Trade Center in New York, Cohen (2001) reflected:

> We are not solitary. We live among others, and we rely on them—on strangers—for society to function, for any kind of life to be possible. Honesty demands that we acknowledge this; ethics demands that we act upon it. As we mature, both physically and morally, we are able to see beyond ourselves and embrace the concerns of a widening circle—family, friends, community and further. No one may be forced to live for others—to donate an organ, for example, let alone a life. But each of us must see the reciprocal ties we rely on every day. Passivity in the face of the current calamity not only weakens these essential communal bonds; it also diminishes our own humanity. (p. 30)

c.   The essence of ethics and morality is the right treatment of others, and the overarching principle is that people are to be treated with maximum respect, meaning that our own motives and intentions cannot ethically be realized at the cost of violating the dignity, autonomy, or legitimate objectives of others. Whatever moral or political rights or liberties we envision ourselves as possessing are enjoyed equally by others.

d.   The attainment of a worthwhile personal identity, social recognition, and rewarding personal relationships, as well as the opportunity to engage in meaningful and rewarding work, appear to be extremely widespread if not universal meta-objectives of people that should be facilitated and promoted. I will argue later (in chap. 7) that, as psychologists, we are especially obligated to take a proactive stance promoting this value and the previous one, not merely be alert for possible derelictions. Moreover, the observation that people differ systematically in their inclinations to fulfill these objectives is of no moral significance with respect to our obligation to promote the widespread availability of conditions enabling their attainment.

10.   Ethics is inevitably political. "Ethical beliefs, throughout recorded history, have had two very different sources, one political, the other concerned with personal religious and moral convictions" (B. Russell, 1987, p. 89). The focus of ethics is on the processes whereby interpersonal relations are most appropriately regulated and controlled for the benefit of all concerned,

from the microlevel of individual face-to-face interactions to institutional, governmental, and international actions. These activities are conditioned by explicit rules, regulations, policies, laws, and agreements, and by implicit values, customs, norms, and social contracts—all of which serve to specify the appropriate distribution of expected power relations among individuals and between individuals and organizations. It is in that sense that ethics is political.

11.   To the extent that loyally fulfilling one's duties and responsibilities to one's employer is a justifiable ethical requirement it is contingent on the corresponding ethical behavior of the employer in furthering and not thwarting the legitimate interests of all those who are affected by its actions. Of particular concern to I/O psychologists is the considerable power wielded by business organizations to impact people's economic, social, and emotional well-being, along with people's rightful expectations that employers behave responsibly in the exercise of that power.

5

Moral Psychology

Philosophers tell us that there is an element of rational choice in human morality, psychologists say that there is a learning component, and anthropologists argue that there are few if any universal rules. The distinction between right and wrong is made by people on the basis of how they would like their society to function. It arises from interpersonal negotiation in a particular environment, and derives its sense of obligation and guilt from the internalization of these processes.

—Frans de Waal

The preceding three chapters have focused on some of the metatheoretical issues and normative theories constituting moral philosophy. The primary concerns of philosophers have been the specification of prescriptive models of moral reasoning, the metatheoretical assumptions on which they rest and the logical adequacy of the criteria that define each model. Philosophers have not been unmindful of such important related topics as the association between moral judgments and the motivation of moral behavior (cf. Adams, 1976; Stocker, 1976) or the practicality of their normative theories. However, those are empirical issues that have remained largely secondary in terms of their expertise and interest.

In contrast, a growing domain of *moral psychology* that consists of "attempts to analyze moral phenomena in terms of psychological concepts and processes" (Emler & Hogan, 1991, p. 72), has developed during the past century, especially the last half. Although moral psychology has not reached the degree of institutional structure to be designated as a formal specialty area in psychology akin to experimental, clinical, social, or I/O psychology, it has a rather clearly articulated domain of theory, research, and, more recently, application (cf. Rest & Narvaez, 1994). Contrasted with moral philosophy moral psychology is a broader field of inquiry that might even be more accurately described as the "behavioral and social science of morality." It has the following interrelated attributes:

1. **Multidisciplinary:** The field counts among its participants developmental, social, and clinical psychologists, as well as psychoanalysts, evolutionary biologists and psychologists, sociologists, and anthropologists.

2. **Process oriented:** Beyond studying the content of moral reasoning, there is a focus on the developmental, social, and contextual antecedents that influence such judgment processes as well as the determinants of whether and how such judgments lead to moral behavior.

3. **Empirical:** As with any facet of the behavioral and social sciences, the ultimate criteria for the evaluation of theoretical explanations (e.g., hypothesized stages of moral development) are empirical research findings, not mere logical consistency.

4. **Comprehensive and multidimensional:** As a consequence of its process and multidisciplinary orientations it includes study of a wide array of relevant factors: the inborn capacities for moral behavior like empathy and other individual-difference variables; the maturational bases for the appearance of moral reasoning and altruistic feelings in children as well as the developmental sequences by which they unfold; the social influence processes by which cultural norms, values, and standards are imparted; the interplay between motives to behave ethically and motives driven by competing values; and other situational and contextual influences affecting moral actions, including those pertaining to employment in organizations.

5. **Theoretically driven:** The empirical study of moral behavior has been organized around a relatively few fundamental theoretical issues: (a) the specification of what is meant by moral behavior; (b) the extent to which moral behavior is unique to humans or is also reflected in the social lives of the other hominids, all primates and/or even lower species; (c) the relation between general cognitive and emotional development in humans and their moral development; (d) the extent to which moral development progresses innately as a reflection primarily of maturational processes, as opposed to being socially constructed as a consequence of the transmission of cultural norms and values; (e) whether moral development proceeds in an orderly sequential fashion and, if so, whether the sequence is hierarchical (i.e., cumulative), and if so whether it is characterized by discretely separable stages; (f) whether the fundamental features of moral development are invariant across cultures; and (g) specifying the multiplicity of antecedents of moral behavior, often in theoretical causal models.

I have organized a synthesis of the field into a developmental model of moral action (DMMA) that is presented as Fig. 5.1. *Moral action* refers to all of the psychological and social processes involved from the time at which one is confronted by and apprehends an ethical problem, with its attendant emotional arousal, to the process of moral reasoning that culminates in a moral choice and some eventual behavioral response (which may or may not correspond to the moral choice), as well as the factors that moderate those hypothesized causal sequences. In Fig. 5.1 moral action is represented by the sequences that comprise all of the causal relations following Category III and the relations among variables within each of those categories.

Note that several theoretical models of ethical reasoning and behavior have been presented previously in the literature. Although I have drawn from them, the model presented in Fig. 5.1 is more general and conceptual, hence, less directly testable than those (e.g., it is comprised of classes of constructs rather than individual variables), and it purports to be a more comprehensive and developmental model, encompassing a life-span perspective.[32]

A DEVELOPMENTAL MODEL OF MORAL ACTION

Based on the preceding chapters we can conclude—as have many moral psychologists—that human social interactions can be segmented into three broad domains: (a) *egoistic behavior* that is dominated by self-interest, with little or no consideration of other people except as they impact the gratification or frustration of our needs and are the source of consequent emotional reactions; (b) *conventional behavior* that constitutes much of our social interaction and heteronomously reflects society's consensual rules and customs, whether construed pessimistically as a necessary restraint on our unbridled egoism (as per Hobbes' account) or optimistically as reflecting the worth of each individual (cf. Rawls); and (c) moral behavior that reflects principled and autonomous adherence to a higher level of rules and regulations governing our interpersonal lives than those based on mere social consensus and sanctions. Much individual behavior is, of course, motivated by a combination of influences from more than one of these realms, and as discussed later there is some disagreement regarding whether they deserve to be thought of as separate domains.

Following a common theme in moral philosophy (Frankena, 1973) psychologists have generally viewed moral behavior as two-dimensional,

---

[32]Those models are presented, elaborated, and investigated in the following sources: Bommer, Gratto, Gravander, and Tuttle (1987); D. Cole, Sirgy, and Bird (2000); Dubinsky and Loken (1989); R. C. Ford and Richardson (1994); Hunt and Vitell (1986); Jansen and Von Glinow (1985); T. M. Jones (1991); G. E. Jones and Kavanagh (1996); Loe, Ferrell, and Mansfield (2000); Near and Miceli (1995); Rest (1986b, 1994); Schminke (1998); and Trevino (1986).

84

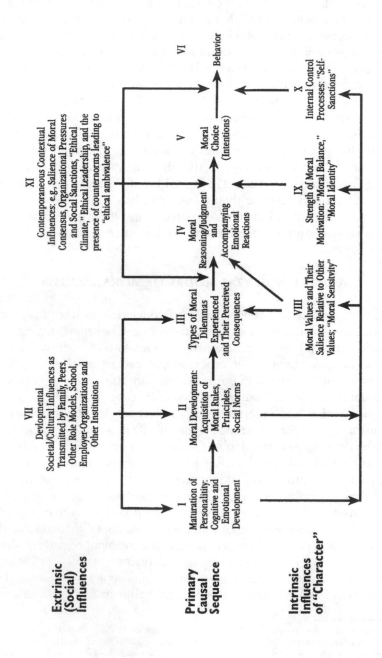

FIG. 5.1.   A developmental model of moral action (DMMA).

corresponding roughly (but not entirely, as discussed shortly) to the deontological and consequentialist traditions in moral philosophy. The two dimensions of morality, or sets of criteria by which to evaluate the morality of social behavior, are (a) *justice*, with its attendant criteria of fairness, impartiality, and universalizability, in the Kantian tradition of treating people with respect and dignity; and (b) *welfare*, with its criteria of beneficence, harm, caring, and altruism, that has been proposed as an important yet underappreciated qualification for effective management (Kracher & Wells, 1998). As noted later in this chapter and discussed further in chapter 6, I will nominate another relevant dimension: (c) *honesty* or *virtue*, with its criteria of character, fidelity, trustworthiness, and responsibility in one's dealings with others. Although justice is most frequently construed as an abstract deontological principle, it can be defined in consequentialist terms, such as the equitable allocation of society's (or the organization's) rewards. Conversely, although welfare clearly implies a utilitarian focus on the consequences of social acts, it may entail generalized rule-based proscriptions against certain actions.

This compact three-component traditional view of the moral domain is reflected in many somewhat more detailed contemporary statements of ethical standards such as the APA's (2002) *Ethical Principles of Psychologists and Code of Conduct*, M. B. Smith's (2000) outline of the moral foundations of psychological research with human participants, and the *Canadian Code of Ethics for Psychologists* (Canadian Psychological Association, 2000).

The model described in Fig. 5.1 begins with a discussion of the maturational bases for the eventual expressions of moral behavior— behavior reflecting considerations of justice, welfare, respect, and honesty. The Roman numeral following each of the sections in the following discussion refers to the labeling of latent constructs in Fig. 5.1.

Maturational Underpinnings: General Cognitive and Emotional Development (I)

It seems clear to most developmental psychologists that minimum requisite levels of maturation must be reached to develop the protobehaviors that will eventually be recognized as expressions of morality. However, "recent research on infancy provides compelling demonstrations that the foundations of morality are present early in child development—in the infant's responsiveness to the feelings of others and the young child's appreciation of standards" (Gilligan & Wiggins, 1987, p. 280). There is less agreement on identifying those behaviors, the timing of their appearance, their degree of heritability, and what, if any, are the necessary social circumstances for their emergence. Much of the disagreements about those matters need not concern us here. It is sufficient for our purposes to start out with the knowledge that largely during the second through fifth years of life the capacities to engage in moral reasoning, to appreciate the benevolent and harmful consequences of events (including one's own actions) on others, and to feel concern for others develop. These changes can be thought of as analogous to the cognitive and social growth that is prerequisite for speech and the neural and psychomotor development necessary for locomotion (Kagan, 1987).

In general, some of the biopsychosocial changes (Bandura, 1991) that constitute the developmental trends associated with moral development are a shift from concrete to more abstract forms of reasoning so that more sophisticated moral judgment becomes feasible; a broadening social reality that expands the relevant domain of moral concerns, moral choices, and the potential influence of social sanctions; a shift from external (heteronomous) regulation of behavior to increasing autonomy and self-regulation; and the adoption of standards reflecting the child's more sophisticated cognitive functioning and more complex social world in which he or she functions. These trends are all influenced greatly by—and, reciprocally, influence the potential effectiveness of—familial and societal factors such as the nature of social sanctions used (e.g., threats, discipline, and reasoning); the modeling of interpersonal behavior by parents, siblings, peers, and teachers; cultural and subgroup values; and various indirect forms of cultural communication, such as television.

In particular, some of the most important emerging capacities that have been highlighted by empirical findings as providing the soil in which moral development ripens are as follows:

1. The development of fundamental ego processes (abstractions of the psychological operations that mediate intrapsychic events and external behavior) necessary for all complex behavior (Bredemeier & Shields, 1994): For example, the ability to concentrate on a moral dilemma so as to engage in the moral reasoning necessary to resolve it is dependent on the attention-focusing ego function of selective awareness.

2. The perceptual, cognitive, and affective process of *decentration* (Gibbs, 1991): To cope with more and more complex and difficult intellective problems and social situations, the young child must gradually move away from the limitation of being able to concentrate or center on only one or a few salient components of a situation (centration) to achieve a more comprehensive and balanced view of all of the relevant issues (thus, decentration). Without a maturing of these abilities we could not hope to deal with a moral dilemma characterized by competing interests, potentially conflicting values of our own such as professional integrity and career advancement, and complex moral standards and ethical guidelines of ambiguous applicability.

3.   A cognitive grasp of one's self as distinct from the rest of the world, including other people, which when combined with a sense of empathy—the ability to respond affectively to someone else's situation—enables a growing ability to demonstrate care for others (Hoffman, 1988).

4.   An altruistic responsiveness to the distress of others: De Waal (1996) pointed out the irony that the biological principle of natural selection, which functions through the process of competition, has given rise to enormous capacities for caring and sympathy (not restricted to *homo sapiens*) because they are so adaptive for the species. In this context it should come as no surprise that organizations and I/O psychologists have come to value the advantages of cooperative team performance (Ilgen, 1999; Levine & Moreland, 1990) and prosocial and organizational citizenship behaviors (OCBs; Podsakoff & MacKenzie, 2000).

5.   An ethical sensitivity based on awareness of the nature of our own actions, especially its effects on others (Rest, 1994): To develop this disposition even more basic capacities need to have been realized, such as a grasp of means–ends relationships or cause-and-effect in interpersonal affairs, and role-taking skills—that is, the ability to appreciate another person's perspective.

Moral Development (II)

The topic of moral development has been for the past century one of the most frequently researched and debated topics in psychology, escalating in volume during the last 50 years. Virtually every major discipline and subdiscipline in the social and behavioral sciences (not to mention evolutionary biology, as noted earlier) has weighed in heavily on this topic: sociology, cultural and physical anthropology, psychoanalytic theory, and behavioral psychology—both traditional operant views as well as more contemporaneous social learning theory, cognitive psychology, and humanistic faith-based views (both religious and secular varieties). Notwithstanding that enormous diversity of input, it is generally acknowledged that there have essentially been just two dominant paradigms in the social-scientific study of morality: the cultural transmission model and one or another form of cognitive stage theory.

Morality as Based on the Transmission of Cultural Standards

For most of its history, the developmental aspects of moral psychology have reflected the sociologist Emil Durkheim's (1858–1917) theory of functionalism (cf. the consideration of cultural relativism in chap. 2). As applied to social behavior functionalism emphasizes the socialization processes by which we internalize society's norms, values, traditions and conventions, and it is represented most prominently in the work of psychologist Martin Hoffman (1977, 1988; discussed shortly). Ironically, however, Durkheim (1898/1953, 1893/1956) was very concerned with establishing the legitimacy of sociological analyses and argued against the reductionist view that social phenomena were explicable at the level of individual psychology or biology. For him social phenomena are social facts that exist outside of and independent of the individual. The duties we feel in connection with our roles as spouse, parent, or employee; the legal obligations we accept as a result of our citizenship or as a consequence of being an employer; the good manners we exhibit to behave properly all derive from external laws, norms, customs, and so on that existed prior to our birth and are independent of our individual consciousness. Among these social facts are the moral standards and principles characteristic of our society in general as well as those that pertain to someone who occupies our particular role(s) in it. For Durkheim, society's rules, norms and values provide the social integration that is indispensable for the effective functioning of society and the individual.

In Durkheim's view, because the maintenance of social integration is so important for the perpetuation of society and for individual adjustment, it is not based solely on external controls like laws, customs, parental sanctions, teacher discipline, company regulations, and so forth. Through the psychological process of internalization those standards, including morality, become part of each one of us in the form of common sets of values, assumptions, and expectations. As a consequence of these socialization mechanisms society is both an external social fact and present within all of us.

Virtually all psychological theories of moral development since Durkheim have shared the notion that we internalize the conventions, values, and standards of our society as they are taught to us directly by an ever-widening array of educators, from parents and siblings to peers, teachers, and colleagues, and indirectly via other mechanisms of socialization, such as television and film. Among the first such theories was Freud's *psychoanalytic theory* that emphasizes the oedipal situation and the child's introjection of parental prohibitions as the foundation of superego development. *Social learning theory* focuses on the generalization of aversive or positive emotional reactions to social reinforcers or the observation and imitation of models being reinforced for their actions.

Hoffman's Empathy-Based Model of Internalization.

Hoffman's (1977, 1983, 1988, 1991) model of moral development is a very sophisticated version of socialization theory in that it emphasizes the individual's active participation in the internalization process (i.e., the child is not simply a passive recipient of society's mores in the process of making them his or her own) and it employs an integration of both cognitive and affective processes to understand the child's readiness for socialization, especially the capacity for empathy. Hoffman (1991) described his theory as essentially an information-processing approach, and it is comprised of three major components: (a) three ideal types of moral dilemma from which one may, subject to appropriate child-rearing practices, develop an internalized sense of morality, guilt, and prosocial concern for others; (b) consideration of the nature and development of our capacity for empathy; and (c) the nature of the discipline procedures by which one acquires an appreciation for the effects of our behavior on others. It is worthwhile to consider, albeit briefly, each of Hoffman's three ideal types of moral problems because they can serve as a means of further structuring our understanding of the ethical challenges we are likely to encounter as adults.

Hoffman's first ideal type of moral problem, being an innocent bystander to someone else's pain or distress, engenders the motivation to help because of our capacity for empathy. Hoffman defined empathy as "a vicarious affective response that is more appropriate to someone else's situation than to one's own (1988, p. 509) and believed that this capacity is inborn as a product of natural selection. That belief is supported by the knowledge that highly similar caring behavior occurs in infrahuman species (de Waal, 1996; Strum, 1987) and that cooperative behavior in humans is mediated by that part of the brain associated with experiencing pleasure (Rilling et al., 2002).

A great many experimental and observational findings indicate that the expression of empathic behavior becomes more complex and sophisticated concomitant with the individual's social–cognitive maturation. Hoffman (1988) described the process as beginning with the generalized emotional contagion of a *global empathy* in which the very young child lacks sufficient sense of self to apprehend that the source of distress is someone else. As he or she develops a sense of self as distinct from others, that child is able to distinguish the distress as emanating from another. Nevertheless, it is an immature *egocentric empathy* in which he or she cannot yet appreciate that the other's affect may be different from his or her own emotional reactions. At this stage of development the child may begin to experience feelings of compassion or *sympathetic distress* for the victim, generating motives to help because of feeling sorry for the other person rather than just to ease his or her own empathic discomfort. That shift is enabled when the child acquires the cognitive capacity to make causal attributions for behavior—for example, that the other person's distress is not their own fault.

Empathy for another's feelings and empathy for another's life condition are the highest levels of empathy in Hoffman's scheme. These affective reactions depend on the child's becoming able to understand that other people's feelings, based on their needs, may be different from one's own and may be related to more generalized conditions than the immediate situation. But not only does one's perception of the world become more complex, so too does one's affective empathic reactions. For example, if a third party is to blame for someone's pain, sympathetic distress may also lead to *empathic anger* at the perpetrator. And if the victim is seen as undeserving of this treatment, what Hoffman referred to as a sense of *empathic injustice* may be engendered.

Hoffman's second ideal type of moral problem, being the cause (or potential cause) of harm to another, is the type of situation in which moral behavior is acquired as a function of the discipline procedures used frequently by our caregivers when we are children. For example, Minton, Kagan, and Levine (1971) found that mothers of 2-year-olds attempt to change the behavior of their children against their will an average of every 6 to 7 minutes!

Hoffman (1988, 1991) outlined three basic kinds of disciplinary techniques, and he concluded that they have different consequences with regard to the internalization of moral mechanisms (e.g., anxiety, guilt, altruistic feelings, and justice principles). They include power-assertive discipline, consisting of physical or psychological punishment, commands, threats, or deprivations; and love-withdrawal techniques, which may be needed to get the child to stop what he or she is doing and pay attention to what the adult is communicating, but which by themselves are actually inimical to the internalization of moral standards. According to Hoffman (1988) the acquisition of a moral orientation consisting of internal motives to act morally irrespective of external sanctions is achieved via the use of *inductions*—"disciplinary techniques that point up the effects of the child's behavior on others, either directly ('if you keep pushing him, he'll fall down and cry') or indirectly ('don't yell at him, he was only trying to help')" (p. 524). These inductions serve to generate guilt feelings that, when repeated many times, may produce a moral motive, and they also provide the content within which those motives are embedded: for example, why certain things are right or wrong, what the values are that are being expressed, and so forth.

The essence of why Hoffman (1991) referred to his model as an information-processing theory is that in his view the child "semantically integrates the information contained in many inductions over time ... this results in an increasingly complex structure of knowledge about the harmful effects that one's actions may have on others" (p. 107). Further, this knowledge structure is charged with the empathic and guilty feelings that were generated by the inductions and thus has motivational force. For that reason, and because the source of the induction (the parent or other caregiver) lacks salience and a connection to the knowledge structure and so is forgotten, the product of the information processing—a moral standard—is experienced as one's own (i.e., it is internalized).

Hoffman's third ideal type of moral problem, having to reconcile competing obligations to two or more persons, is a common adult dilemma encountered, for example, by parents who have more than one child or by managers who must make personnel decisions affecting several subordinates. In such instances Hoffman (1991) noted that empathy-based moral considerations alone may be insufficient. For example, the decision maker may have equal or equivalent empathic concerns and attachments to all those involved. Hoffman emphasized that "mature moral judgments in these situations may therefore require the application of moral principles that transcend empathy and contribute a note of impartiality" (p. 108). The moral psychologists who have most concerned themselves with such "impartial principles" have been the cognitive stage theorists to whom we now turn our attention.

Morality as Reflecting Cognitive Stages of Development

Piaget's Stages of Moral Development.[33]   Jean Piaget's (1896–1980) work on moral development was an outgrowth of his work on cognitive development, which was his primary concern. He began his research in the 1920s when learning theory, in particular behaviorism, was the dominant view in American psychology, that is, when intellectual growth and development was viewed largely as a quantitative phenomenon—an increase in associations and reinforcement connections. But Piaget was a European who had studied both philosophy and zoology as well as clinically oriented psychology with C. G. Jung and E. Bleuler; based on his experiences administering reading tests to Paris schoolchildren, he came to appreciate the cognitive development of children as representing qualitative changes.

In particular, he viewed such development as progressing through four qualitatively distinct stages, increasing in intellectual sophistication and culminating in a stage of thinking that is akin to adult reasoning: the *sensorimotor* stage during the first 2 years of life; the *preoperational* stage, from age 2 to 6 or 7, during which we learn to manipulate the world psychologically through words, images, and thoughts; the *concrete operational* stage, from approximately age 7 to 11 or 12, marking the beginning of logic, classifying objects according to their differences and similarities, and developing abstract notions like number and time; and the *formal operations* stage, extending through adolescence into adulthood, during which an adult-like mastery of logical thought and the capacity to manipulate abstract notions and foresee the implications of ideas develops.

Piaget (1932/1965) carried over fundamental aspects of this model of cognitive development into his views on moral development as well: (a)

---

[33]Much of the discussion of Piaget's work on moral development is informed by Lickona's (1994) helpful and succinct review.

development moves through sequential stages that are cumulative, each one necessary for passage to the next; (b) passage from one stage to the next, although conceived as universal and innately based, is nevertheless constructed uniquely by each individual based on stimulating interactions with environmental objects; and (c) each stage is constituted of successively more mature cognitive operations, allowing for increased success with handling more complex situations and a more sophisticated and abstract conceptualization of the world. But most important of all is his assumption that moral development depends on, first and foremost, general intellectual growth—an assumption that has been largely supported by the empirical literature of the past 60 years (see Lickona, 1994).

As shown in Table 5.1, Piaget's theoretical formulation of the stages of moral development consists of only two stages in contrast to his more refined four-stage model of cognitive development. The shift from the less mature to the more mature level of morality is accomplished for most healthy children during the preoperational or, at the latest, the concrete operational stage of cognitive development. The shift is conceived to be a gradual one, and there may be a considerable period of time in which both modes of thinking coexist until the more mature one comes to dominate due to its greater utility as a basis for shaping the child's social interactions. In fact, reviews of the available research suggest that the dimension changes outlined in Table 5.1 do not represent qualitative shifts in thought processes (Gelman & Baillargeon, 1983) but may best be viewed as "steady age increases under most circumstances, rather than as closely knit *stages* of moral thought" (Lickona, 1994, p. 331, italics added).

The early stage *morality of constraint* (also referred to as *heteronomous morality* or *moral realism*) is largely shaped, according to Piaget, by the child's limited intellectual capacities and his or her unconditional subservience to adults. The gradual shift to a *morality of cooperation* entails a growing capacity to appreciate the separateness and worth of others as social equals to oneself. Piaget hypothesized that shifts, especially in the first four dimensions of the moral stages (see Table 5.1), were the aspects of the child's moral system most dependent on cognitive development, and this has largely been supported by empirical research (Lickona, 1994). Cognitive development enables the child to acquire a set of moral beliefs based on the variety of social interactions with peers and adults that typifies middle childhood, and an absence or a distortion of reciprocal childhood social interactions can result in a retardation of moral development.

Overall, Piaget's theories of cognitive and moral development reveal a growth from externally controlled or heteronomous behavior to more autonomous functioning. In his morality of cooperation we see the influence of Kantian notions of respect for all individuals as our moral equals (cf. Dimensions 1, 5, 6, 7, 8, and 9), the conception of the moral person as one

TABLE 5.1

A Comparison of Piaget's Stages of Moral Development and Their Constituent Dimensions

Early Stage of Moral Development: The Morality of Constraint		Later Stage of Moral Development: The Morality of Cooperation
1. Absolutist or egocentric moral perspective. There is only one viewpoint on right and wrong, and it is held by everyone.	vs.	1. Awareness that there may be alternative views of right and wrong and that people may differ in that regard.
2. Rules are permanent and unchangeable largely because they emanate from powerful adults.	vs.	2. Rules are flexible and can be changed, and that is not the same as breaking the rule.
3. Belief in immanent justice that punishment for wrongdoing is automatic and inevitable.	vs.	3. Punishment, like the misdeed itself, is a social phenomenon and so not necessarily inevitable.
4. Responsibility for behavior is judged objectively in terms of its consequences or effects on others.	vs.	4. Responsibility for actions is judged subjectively based on the actor's motives or intentions (i.e., intentionality).
5. What is morally wrong is defined in terms of external sanctions of what is prohibited and/or punished.	vs.	5. Moral wrongness is defined in terms of that which violates notions of fairness, trust, or cooperation.
6. Acceptance of arbitrary or expiatory punishment (e.g., spanking) that bears no intrinsic relation to the offense.	vs.	6. Belief in restitution or reciprocity-based punishment, allowing the offender to suffer the adverse consequences of his or her actions.
7. Approval of punishment for peer-initiated aggression administered by an authority.	vs.	7. Approval of direct retaliation to the culprit.
8. Acceptance of the arbitrary and unequal distribution of goods or rewards by an authority.	vs.	8. Insistence on the equal distribution of goods or rewards.
9. Duty is conceived as obedience to authority.	vs.	9. Allegiance to the notion of equality, equal relations with peers, and concern for the welfare of peers.

Note. Based on Lickona (1994).

with good intentions (cf. Dimension 4), and the reasoning capacity and freedom to acquire an independent sense of morality beyond mere obedience to external constraints and sanctions (cf. Dimensions 1, 2, 4, 5, 6, and 9). In addition, we can see in Piaget's focus on cooperative social relations as the ultimate criterion of morality the influence of social contractarian ideas, especially Rawls' view (cf. Dimensions 3, 5, 6, 7, 8, and 9).

Kohlberg's Cognitive Stage Model.[34]   For the past generation or so the dominant view of moral development among psychologists and other social and behavioral scientists has been Lawrence Kohlberg's (1981, 1984) individualistic *cognitive stage theory*. To fully understand the development of Kohlberg's theory it should be appreciated as a reaction to the then-prevailing socialization models of moral development. Although Piaget's study of moral development was secondary to his involvement in exploring cognitive development in general, the outlines of his theoretical approach and the assumptions on which they rest accrued great significance because of their influence on Kohlberg's thinking. Kohlberg expanded on Piaget's work philosophically, psychologically, and methodologically. The substance of his theory is informed even more than Piaget's was by philosophical thought (especially Kant, Hare's universal prescriptivism, Rawls, and Habermas). In fact, he even attempted a sort of reconciliation of the long-standing philosophical dispute between consequentialism and deontology, viewing them both as providing the basis for the highest level of moral judgment (although, as discusssed later, he did not see them as equivalent). His psychological theory is much more elaborate than Piaget's; it is more complex—three broad levels of moral development are recognized, with at least two stages each (depending on which version of the theory is used). And from a methodological perspective much greater attention is paid to the development of a reliable measuring instrument by which to operationalize the constructs.

There are six basic aspects or assumptions underlying Kohlberg's theory and research, all of them with roots in Piaget's model: (a) in contrast with the dominant socialization view of moral development in the 1950s and 1960s when Kohlberg started his work and the influence of behaviorism in American psychology prior to the so-called "cognitive revolution," Kohlberg's focus was on the cognitive processes by which individuals construct a system of moral reasoning for themselves; (b) moral development proceeds invariantly through successive stages (six of them in the most widely cited version), without regression to an earlier stage or skipping a stage; (c) the stages are defined by the nature of the moral reasoning

---

[34]This review of Kohlberg's theory was aided by comprehensive yet succinct summaries by Kagan (1987), Kegan (1993), and Rest (1994).

engaged in, that is, as prevailing cognitive operations for the person, with each successive stage representing more complex judgment processes; (d) because of the focus on reasoning processes, as well as the inclusion of children as research participants, the empirical method of choice was the oral presentation of social dilemmas or conflicts with free, open-ended responses that could reveal those processes; and (e) as the child gets older, movement from one stage to the next is dependent on both the increasing capacity to engage in the more complicated cognitive reasoning required and on being confronted with more complex social situations for which the old reasoning is inadequate. As a consequence, Kohlberg extended the domain of empirical research beyond Piaget's focus on early and middle childhood into adulthood; (f) the stages are conceived as universal across cultures and historical eras back as far as classical Greek civilization. This assumption is not based on a strong biological determinism but—as with Piaget—on the presumed logical sequence by which simpler reasoning processes must precede and form the foundation for more complex solutions to interpersonal problems.

An outline of Kohlberg's stage model is presented in Table 5.2. There have been several versions of the stages, with attendant theoretical revisions advanced over the years most notably by Kohlberg, Levine, and Hewer (1983; but also see Sonnert & Commons, 1994). The most frequently seen formulation is comprised of three levels of moral development, each in turn comprised of two stages, for a total of six. At various times, Kohlberg and his collaborators also utilized transitional stages between each of the six, as well as two substages within each one; toward the end of his life, Kohlberg was concerned with elaborating a somewhat metaphysical seventh stage (see Kohlberg & Ryncarz, 1990, published after Kohlberg's death). Table 5.2 omits the substages, Stage 7, and all but one of the transitional stages (Stage 4½ has been the most frequently considered one).

A good way to approach Kohlberg's work is operationally, by understanding the methodology by which a person's current level of moral reasoning is assessed. Kohlberg presented his participants, frequently children who were reexamined and assessed every few years, with a series of moral problems (one at a time) and asked them to explain what they would do in the situation (this is the Moral Dilemmas Interview or Moral Judgment Interview) (MJI) (Colby & Kohlberg, 1987). The most widely known of these is the Heinz dilemma, a slightly abbreviated version of which is as follows:

> Mr. Heinz's wife is dying from cancer and the only thing that can save her is a new drug that has recently been developed by a druggist, who is its only source. The druggist, however, is charging a great deal for the drug—more than Heinz has or could hope to raise. [A contemporary updating of the story should

TABLE 5.2
Kohlberg's Stages of Moral Development

Level and Stage	Normative Definition of What is Right	Motivation: The Reasons for Doing Right	Meta-Ethical Issue: Who Counts? (Social Perspective)	Example of Moral Reasoning
A. Preconventional				
Stage 1. Punishment and Obedience	Obedience to rules and authority for its own sake and avoiding doing physical harm to others and property.	Avoiding punishment and deference to the superior power of authorities.	Egocentrism. A person at this stage does not consider the interests of others or recognize they differ from one's own. Does not relate two points of view. Actions judged in terms of physical consequences, not psychological interests of others. Confusion of authority's perspective with one's own.	"I don't pad my expense account because they watch that like hawks."
Stage 2. Individual instrumental purpose and exchange	Following rules when it is in someone's interest. Acting to meet one's own interests and if necessary allowing others to do the same. Right is also what's a fair exchange, a deal, or an agreement.	Serving one's own needs or interests in a world where one must recognize that others have interests too. "You scratch my back, and I'll scratch yours."	Individualism (qualified egoism). A person at this stage separates own interests from others' and is aware that different persons' interests may conflict, so that right is a fair exchange, deal, and instrumental agreement.	"If you cover my shift this Friday, I'll work two shifts for you early next week."

B. Conventional

	What is right	Reasons for doing right	Social perspective	Example
Stage 3. Mutual interpersonal expectations, relationships, and conformity	Living up to what is expected of someone. Occupying one's social role(s) as child, sibling, friend, and so on. Being good is an important aim and means showing concern for others and maintaining their trust, loyalty, and respect.	Needing to be a good person in one's own eyes and others', caring for others, and respecting the Golden Rule. Being good by being nice.	Group perspective. A person at this stage is aware of shared feelings, agreements, and expectations, which take precedence over individual interests. Relationships based on a concrete use of the Golden Rule; generalized social systems not recognized.	"I'll stay late to help you with that problem because we're on the same team here, and I know you'd do the same for me."
Stage 4. Social system and conscience maintenance	Fulfilling the duties to which one has agreed and contributing to the group, an institution, or society. Laws to be upheld except in extreme cases when they conflict with other fixed social duties or rights.	Maintaining one's self-respect or conscience by meeting one's obligations or facing the consequences ("what if everyone did it?"). Also, wanting to keep the institution going as a whole.	Societal perspective. A person at this stage takes the viewpoint of the relevant social system, which defines law and order, roles, and rules. Interpersonal relationships are considered in terms of people's places in the system.	"I will work this weekend to finish the proposal—afterall, satisfying the client is what our business is all about."

B/C. Transition

	What is right	Reasons for doing right	Social perspective	Example
Stage 4.5. Postconventional but not yet principled	One's personal and subjective choices, because duty and right are arbitrary and relative.	Emotional reactions concerning maintaining one's sense of integrity as an individual irrespective of society's particular mores or norms.	An asocial perspective (subjectivist). A person at this stage stands outside his or her own society and makes decisions without any generalized commitment or contract with society. One can pick and choose obligations, but one has no principles on which to base it.	"I don't care if the company regulations say we should do that. I just don't feel like doing it."

(continued on next page)

TABLE 5.2 (continued)

Level and Stage	Normative Definition of What is Right	Motivation: The Reasons for Doing Right	Meta-Ethical Issue: Who Counts? (Social Perspective)	Example of Moral Reasoning
C. Postconventional & Principled				
Stage 5. Prior rights and social contract or utility	Awareness that people hold a variety of values and opinions, that most values and rules are relative to one's group but should be upheld in the interests of fairness, impartiality, and because they are part of the social contract. Some nonrelative rights and values must be upheld regardless (e.g., life and liberty).	Feeling obligated to obey the law as an expression of one's participation in the social contract, which is for the benefit of all. Family, friends, and work obligations are also voluntary social contracts to be respected. Laws should be based on rational assessment of overall utility: the greatest good for the greatest number.	Prior-to-society perspective (universalism). A person at this stage has a rational awareness of values and rights prior to social attachments and contracts. The person integrates perspectives by formal agreements, objective impartiality, and due process. He or she recognizes that the moral and legal points of view may conflict and finds it difficult to integrate them.	"I'm really sorry that I can't go with you to the Knicks game this evening, but I promised that I'd finish the ABC company report today; they really need it."
Stage 6. Universal ethical principles	Abiding by those laws or social agreements that rest on universal ethical principles and refusing to obey those which violate them. Principles are universal principles of justice: equality of human rights and respect for the dignity of human beings as individuals.	Belief in the validity of universal moral principles and a sense of personal commitment to them, based on rational evaluation (i.e., exercising one's individual conscience).	A principled moral point of view on which social arrangements are grounded. It is self-chosen based on reason. A person at this stage recognizes the nature of morality—that persons are to be respected as ends in themselves, not means.	"I know my boss doesn't like her and I won't win any points for doing it, but she deserves an increase and I'm going to fight for it."

probably include that Heinz's HMO won't approve payment for the drug.]
Should Heinz steal the drug in order to save his wife's life? Why, or why not?

The essence of Kohlberg's theory is reflected in the fact that it does not matter what choice the respondent makes; it's the nature of the judgment processes by which the decision is reached that gets assessed, that is, how the moral choice is justified. This is so because "the reasoning by which different people arrive at a moral conclusion can be structurally the same even though the specific issues attended to, the circumstances modifying the problem, and the concrete details may be different" (Snarey, 1985, p. 221). Over years of research the scoring system by which the open-ended responses are scored was revised and refined several times until it now consists of a quite elaborate set of guidelines and scoring examples that yield reliable results (Colby & Kohlberg, 1987).[35] In addition, Rest (1986a) developed a widely used self-administered, paper-and-pencil, multiple-choice inventory, the Defining Issues Test (DIT), which employs some of the same content as Kohlberg's dilemmas. Rest (1994) was noncommital on the issue of whether the DIT measures the same constructs as the MJI procedure, but Eckensberger and Zimba (1997) indicated that it does not.

Children who are at the first (preconventional) level of moral reasoning can think only in subjective terms. They are incapable of taking another perspective, of putting themselves in someone else's shoes, so their reasoning entails consideration only of their own needs and feelings. At Stage 1 the young child's reply might be something like "Well, if the druggist is the only one in the store and he can't see you do it, I'd take the drug," or perhaps "You're bound to get caught stealing, so I wouldn't do it." A child in Stage 2 might reflect that "It depends on how nice his wife is; if she is really good to him then he should steal it." Older children who are at the second, or conventional, level of morality have grasped Piaget's cognitive principle of reversibility so they are able to engage in reciprocal role taking socially and understand the ongoing nature of social relationships. Consequently, at Stage 3—during which social morality is exclusively dyadic, involving only one's personal relationships—they may respond "If they are married then he must love her, so he should get the drug; it's not like stealing for himself." If they are in Stage 4—at which time their sociomoral meaning making has led to a conception of social relations extending beyond merely one's personal contacts, and so requires a formal system of institutions and controls—the response might entail "Stealing is against the law, so he shouldn't do it. It's too bad for his wife, but we can't just let everyone go around stealing whatever they want." The transitional Stage 4½ represents an ambiguous

---

[35]That's the good news—increased reliability. The bad news is that, as Snarey described (1985), it is extremely difficult to compare and integrate studies that were conducted over a period of years with different scoring criteria and algorithms.

period of cultural and ethical relativism in which the societal, conformist views of Stage 4 are seen as unjustifiably arbitrary, but a principled morality has not yet emerged to take its place. A person at this stage somewhat ambivalently reverts to a less social, more individualistic sensibility.

Young adults and older persons who have reached the principled morality of Level 3 have resolved the ambiguities of the transitional stage by the cognitive construction of objective universalizable principles that can be justified rationally. As Kagan (1987) interpreted:

> "Rightness" and "wrongness" are defined by reference to objective principles detached from the subjective feelings and perspective of either the self or the group. What is correct and virtuous is defined in terms of universalizable standards, reflectively constructed by the individual, of justice, natural rights, and humanistic respect for all persons.... For the post-conventional thinker, there are objective obligations that any rational person can come to discover and is bound to respect, that stand above the feelings of the self or the demands of others. (p. 5)

In the first segment of Level 3, Stage 5, those standards and obligations reflect notions of the social contract and utilitarian fairness that are owed deference by virtue of their value in promulgating a just society in which rules and norms are based on the greatest good for the greatest number. An adult in Stage 5 might respond to the Heinz dilemma: "That's really tough; I'm not sure what I'd do. The druggist has a right to his profit, and I don't condone stealing, but ... I guess I'd try to arrange for installment payments ... It might depend on whether he was gouging people: that's unfair. If that was the case, maybe I'd steal it." Kohlberg's highest stage of moral reasoning, Stage 6, consists of having an inclusive moral system that, in the Kantian tradition, rests on a belief in the worth and dignity of all people and their equal entitlement to fair consideration. An adult at this stage might reply "I certainly respect the druggist's right to earn a living, but isn't someone's life more important? If I couldn't convince him of that or make some sort of deal, I'd have to steal the drug and just take the consequences."[36]

A fuller understanding of Kohlberg's theory can be facilitated by noting some of the criticisms that have been leveled at it.

Critique of Kohlberg. One indicator of how widely researched and influential Kohlberg's views have been is the depth and variety of criticisms to which it has been subjected. Poignantly, because his theory represents an attempt to integrate both psychological and philosophical thought, it has

---

[36]Note that researchers, including Kohlberg, have always had difficulty in scoring Stage 6 and differentiating it from Stage 5. The incidence of people scored as at Stage 6 has been minuscule (Kagan, 1987); in the revised scoring manual for the MJI, Stage 6 is not scored (Colby & Kohlberg, 1987). Similarly, the DIT collapses Stages 5 and 6 to form a single composite *principled stage* (Rest, 1986a).

enticed criticism from both disciplines. The major charges are as follows: (a) the model is an incomplete representation of moral behavior; (b) there is insufficient justification to characterize the transitions in reasoning processes as progressive invariant stages with no regression, rather than as continuous changes; (c) the theory contains an ideological philosophical bias; (d) the theory is culturally biased; and (e) it is also biased against women.

Incompleteness.   The elements of Kohlberg's theory are comprised exclusively of modes of reasoning concerning social relations that are based on fundamental cognitive operations. Kohlberg's focus on reasoning or judgment processes was probably overdetermined by his reliance not only on Piaget, but on his attempt to embed his psychological model of morality in the historical philosophical tradition that, as shown in chapters 2 and 3, focuses on moral reasoning. Consequently, if one is interested in understanding the processes by which people act morally (or fail to do so), it is clear that a great deal more is involved than the conscious rationales by which moral choices are reached. As noted earlier, it is one of the substantial differences between moral philosophy and moral psychology. Figure 5.1 suggests that there are many other social, emotional, motivational, and institutional factors that come into play in the relation between moral choice and moral action. Consequently, the correlations between moral judgment and real-life moral behaviors are generally reported as no more than .30 to .40 (Rest, 1994). This criticism of incompleteness has been raised frequently (cf. Snell, 1996; E. V. Sullivan, 1994), and it was acknowledged early by Kohlberg (1973) himself who referred modestly to his theory as one of moral reasoning not of morality in general. One of the major areas of deficiency has been a failure to consider the critical directive role played by relatively stable personality attributes, such as the moral dimensions of one's character and values—thus the significance of a book title that includes both *Being Good* and *Doing Right* (Dobrin, 1993).

Not "Stages."   The reader may recall that it is generally conceded that Piaget's characterization of the changes that occur in the nature of moral reasoning are more justifiably thought of as "steady age increases" rather than discrete "stages" (Lickona, 1994). The same may be true for Kohlberg's stages as well. The available empirical research does not establish the levels of moral development as discrete stages characterized as structured wholes, that is, by consistent intrastage uniformities and between-stage differences. Eckensberger and Zimba (1997) observed that "most cross-cultural Kohlbergian research provides very little information about the homogeneity of stages.... Quite generally, it seems that inconsistencies are more frequently reported by researchers outside Kohlberg's group" (p. 312). That opinion was reached independently by other reviewers as well (Bandura, 1991; Krebs, Vermeulen, Carpendale, & Denton, 1991).

Complicating matters is the fact that the vast body of empirical research is based on several different operational measures that employ as few as 5 to as many as 13 stages, with varying degrees of psychometric reliability (Snarey, 1985). Where are the stage demarcations? Moreover, although the moral development score that characterizes each person's stage admittedly tends to show an upward progression with few regressions in both cross-sectional and longitudinal research, it is always an average score with considerable variation in the individual's many responses to the dilemmas. In fact, it is not unusual for participants to be categorized as at two or more stages simultaneously, and it is not known the extent to which this may reflect mere measurement (rater) error as opposed to a disconfirmation of the stage model.

In addition, the work of Turiel (1983) and his colleagues (Nucci & Turiel, 1978; Nucci & Weber, 1991; Turiel, Killen, & Helwig, 1987; Turiel, Smetana, & Killen, 1991) also challenges the sequencing of Kohlberg's stages from another perspective. They produced and reviewed a considerable amount of evidence in support of the theoretical view that conventional understanding, having to do with social customs and practices (equivalent to Kohlberg Stages 3 and 4), represents a "conceptually and developmentally distinct form of social knowledge" (Turiel et al., 1991, p. 319) that is independent of moral understandings having to do with issues of harm, welfare, fairness, and justice. They are coexisting but separate social orientations. The moral orientation having to do with justice, fairness, rights, obligations, and others' welfare is based on intrinsic (i.e., context-independent) notions of rightness, wrongness, and harmfulness. The conventional orientation is based on elements of social organization, authority, and custom, which tend to be context-dependent. And their view is that the rationales underlying morality are cognitively more accessible to young children (the harmful consequences of transgressions, e.g., hitting a playmate) than those of social conventions (learning the rules of social behavior) so that "children's commitment to upholding moral rules consequently develops *earlier* than their commitment to conventional rules" (R. Edwards, 1993, p. 95, italics added). Therefore, conventional values and moral values are viewed as distinct domains; the former is not a stage on the way to the latter. In fact, according to these scholars, principled morality precedes conventionality.

Shweder et al.'s (1987) work tends to confirm the potential independence of the two domains but suggests that the distinction may exist only in certain cultures, including our own. Orthodox Hindus in India made no distinction between morality and convention. I believe that most Americans probably experience and conceive the two domains as independent: For example, most of us have probably observed that the appropriateness of people's behavior may be very different in each. A business acquaintance's adherence to respectable business attire, proper etiquette, and norms of sociability is not likely to tell us much about whether he or she may be cheating customers, exploiting subordinates, or cooking the books. By all accounts, several executives at Enron who deceived and swindled their employees and shareholders were well-liked and charitable pillars of their communities (Eichenwald, 2002b).

Philosophical Bias. Is it justifiable for Kohlberg to have singled out a particular moral philosophy as the culmination of his entire stage sequence—that is, as the epitome of human moral development?[37] Is it defensible to assume as a result that consequentialism (utility theory) entails a less complex, less mature stage of moral reasoning (Stage 5) than does deontology (Kant & Rawls, Stage 6)? Philosophers (and others) who have attended to the issue generally think not (Puka, 1991; Thomas, 1993). As E. V. Sullivan (1994) put it, Kohlberg's "stage 6 becomes 'the model of moral man' rather than 'a model of moral man' " (p. 51, italics added). Puka (1991) was, nevertheless, sympathetic to Kohlberg's likely intent:

> When Kohlberg entered the field of research on "morals," he encountered a relatively simple-minded relativism. A credible source of nonrelativistic thinking was needed simply to distinguish moral norms among the diversity of norm systems. Kohlberg turned to moral philosophy to find sophisticated distinctions between the moral and nonmoral, along with well-justified criteria of adequacy in moral reasoning. (p. 374)

But, Puka speculated, Kohlberg could have simply extracted and synthesized the best and most relevant of what the diverse moral philosophies might contribute to psychology. Instead, he "became a philosophical convert and partisan, to some extent.... He decided that a particular philosophical tradition had defined the scope and adequacy of morality best. Then he set its view up as a somewhat a priori standard for moral psychology and development" (p. 375). Thomas (1993) added, with respect to the implicit view that utilitarian thinking is less cognitively mature than deontological thinking, that "The very idea seems ludicrous when one

---

[37]It is both interesting and ironic that Kohlberg seemed to have committed the obverse of the naturalistic fallacy (Moore, 1903). Recall, from chapter 2, that Hume's Law refers to the inappropriateness of justifying what ought to be (e.g., normative moral standards) merely on the basis of what is (empirically prevalent patterns of behavior). Here, Kohlberg seemed to have defined what is—the empirical nature of moral behavior—largely as a reflection of his preferred normative standard, Rawls' and Kant's moral philosophies. As E. L. Simpson (1994) noted, "The distinction between normative philosophy and empirical psychology remains blurred, and normative thinking especially governs the description of what [Kohlberg] calls empirically derived categories of 'post-conventional' or principled reasoning" (p. 21).

considers the long line of distinguished thinkers who have embraced some form of utilitarianism: Jeremy Bentham, John Stuart Mill, and Henry Sidgwick" (p. 468).

Compounding this criticism are the empirical findings that, as noted previously, the incidence of research participants scoring at Stage 6 was so low, and the reliability of such scores so poor, that Stage 6 was eventually dropped from Kohlberg's scoring scheme, and Stage 5 and Stage 6 were condensed into a single category by Rest (1986a) in the DIT. Therefore, as measured operationally by the two primary measuring instruments in the field, Kohlberg's stage model consists of only a single stage of principled morality that is comprised of an amalgam of ethical relativism, Hobbesian social contractarianism, as well as the Rawlsian variety, utilitarianism (variant unspecified), Kantian notions of respect for people, and universalizability of moral principles, as well as elements of natural law theory in the form of universal rights!

Such a conglomeration of principles derived from multiple ethical theories is unlikely to be able to satisfy reasonable criteria for an internally consistent structural stage because several of these theories are philosophically incompatible. Nevertheless, that is not necessarily a grave problem for Kohlberg's theory—especially if one simply drops the strict stage assumptions that are not supported empirically in any event. One of the criticisms that has been leveled by philosophers doing what they do best—analyzing the logical consistency of a theory—is that, whereas the first four stages adhere more or less to Kohlberg's intent that they be defined by the nature of the reasoning processes by which moral judgements are achieved, Stages 5 and 6 do not. Content issues were smuggled into the definition of those stages. That is, they encompass particular moral values (e.g., the right to life and liberty) and personal attributes (e.g., the moral courage to stick to one's principles despite social disapproval; Thomas, 1993). Truncating the third level, principled morality, to a single stage corresponding to principled moral reasoning of whatever stripe (i.e., content neutral) may actually enhance the logical consistency of the theory. The composite Stage 5/6 would not be limited to any particular version of moral reasoning, as long as some rendering of morally right reasoning is the basis for moral choice.

Cultural Bias. Kohlberg's theory has been charged with being culturally biased from both a conceptual as well as empirical point of view, thus challenging his claim that the stage progression model is universal. Clearly, the normative philosophical theories that inform and define the substance of principled morality are western philosophies (Kant, Rawls, Mill, Dewey, and Habermas). They are part of a tradition emanating from the classical Greeks that embodies substantive notions of social relations and morality (beliefs, attitudes, and values) not necessarily shared by the non-western world, that is, most of humanity (E. L. Simpson, 1994). For example, the ideals of life, liberty, and adherence to principle are defined within the western model of individualism and having the courage to "buck the crowd" (Sampson, 1977). But political philosophers point out that individual autonomy and liberty are not universal values (Gray, 2000). In contrast, eastern and Asian cultures emphasize communal contribution and fitting in. These two sets of values correspond to Stages 5 and 6 and to Stages 3 and 4, respectively.

Perhaps even more important in this regard are the findings of systematic differences in perceptual and cognitive style and reasoning processes between easterners and westerners. That is because the primary meta-concept on which Piaget's and Kohlberg's theories of moral development are based is that modes of cognition, including moral reasoning, are universal and thus provide a culture-free (i.e., content-free) means of evaluation.[38] Nisbett, Peng, Choi, and Norenzayan (2001) produced and reviewed a great deal of evidence from a variety of psychological domains indicating that westerners tend to be analytic, "paying attention primarily to the object, categorizing it on the basis of its attributes, and attributing causality to the object based on rules about its category memberships," whereas "East Asians are held to perceive and reason holistically, attending to the field in which objects are embedded and attributing causality to interactions between the object and the field" (Choi, Nisbett, & Norenzayan, 1999, p. 48). As a consequence, westerners are more likely to attribute the causes of people's behavior to their dispositional attributes, whereas easterners are more likely to attribute the causes to features of the situation or context within which the person acts. Therefore, in that sense, the reasoning processes by which, according to Kohlberg, moral development is defined may not be content- or culture-free.[39] Because these tendencies extend to self-descriptions as well as to descriptions and attributions about others, they may be reflected in the judgment narratives offered in response to Kohlberg's moral dilemmas.

To what extent does the empirical research reflect the biases suggested by these cultural differences? One way of examining the question is an assessment of the extent to which Kohlberg's claim of universality holds up—that all stages will be found, at least to some degree, in all societies. To begin with, the reader should recall that Stage 6 was dropped from the Colby and Kohlberg (1987) scoring scheme, so is not even assessed. Snarey (1985) reviewed 45 studies of Kohlberg's theory in 27 different cultural areas and

---

[38]Although, as was just described, Kohlberg failed to adhere to that assumption with respect to Stages 5 and 6, which are defined by their normative philosophical content.

[39]Of further relevance is the position advanced by Nisbett et al. (2001) that it is simply not possible to clearly separate cognitive processes and cognitive content.

observed that, among the 25 studies conducted with participants who were at least 18 years old, nine studies reported having no one scoring as high as 4/5 or 5.[40] However, those nine studies were not all of nonwestern societies; they were classified as tribal or village folk societies—western European, nonwestern and non-European. Snarey (1985) concluded that "the available data thus suggest that the significant difference lies between folk versus urban societies rather than between Western versus non-western societies" (p. 218). However, that conclusion may be premature as even the nonwestern European samples were categorized by Snarey (1985) as "Westernized, urban complex societies" (p. 217) (including Hong Kong, Israel, Japan, Puerto Rico, and Taiwan).

Another question one could ask of the empirical research is whether Kohlberg's six (operationally, only five) stages are exhaustive. Are there other cultural variants of principled morality that do not seem to be recognized by the theory? After examining this question Snarey (1985) concluded:

> In sum, the evidence from the Israeli kibbutz, India, Taiwan, New Guinea, and Kenya suggests that some culturally unique moral judgments do not appear in the theory or scoring manual. Collective or communalistic principled reasoning, in particular, is missing or misunderstood. (p. 226)

For example, in response to the Heinz dilemma, a village leader from New Guinea responded by placing blame on the community: "If nobody helped him [to save his dying wife] and so he [stole to save her], I would say we had caused that problem" (Snarey, p. 225).

Thus, the bias toward moral individualism as just discussed seems to infect the Kohlberg system, but it is not, as anticipated, reflected in a clear east–west dichotomy. Similarly, the cross-cultural studies reveal significant class differences in moral development scores within cultures: In virtually all cases, upper middle- and middle-class respondents scored higher than lower and working-class participants. This is also associated with significant differences in educational level, and Snarey (1985) concluded that these differences suggest the "possibility of a bias in the scoring system" (p. 221). Similarly, Eckensberger and Zimba (1997) reviewed evidence indicating that moral stage development correlates with socioeconomic status, urbanization, religiosity, modernization, and educational level and/or intelligence, "but the psychological meaning of these sources of variance are usually difficult to interpret" (p. 317).

---

[40]Similarly, Rest (1994) presented a summary of DIT P-scores (a continuous-scale measure of principled morality) from six countries, including western and nonwestern societies, in which the oldest participants, all college students at least 20 years old, averaged approximately only 46 on a scale with a theoretical range up to 95.

Sex Bias.   We have seen that restricting the definition of morality to western notions of justice principles and individual rights does not appear to be justified epistemologically (elevating a philosophical theory to an empirical psychological ideal), and its operationalizations may contain cultural and class biases. Gilligan (1982) and Noddings (1986) argued that Kohlberg's theory is also biased against women, even urban western women. The central argument they advanced is that an objective and rational approach to moral dilemmas, consisting of a dispassionate search for the operative principles of equity or justice or deliberations on the relative credence to be given to conflicting justice principles, is (a) a typically male orientation and (b) overlooks the orientation more typical of women, characterized as one of caring. That orientation involves attending to the contextual elements of a social dilemma, especially the needs, feelings, and interests of the people involved. Not only are such social concerns not likely to be scored any higher than Stage 3 on the MJI, but, the brief bare bones presentations of the moral dilemmas do not include the rich contextual material in which real-life ethical problems are encountered—and which comprise the most salient aspects of the situation for women.

Gilligan and Wiggins (1987) agreed with Piaget and with developmental psychologists in general that the origins of morality depend on differentiation of the self in relation to others. One element of that differentiation involves the young child's initial sense of helplessness, powerlessness, and dependence on others—one of inequality. Another simultaneous facet of differentiation is the child's growing attachment to caregivers. These two dynamics are seen as laying the groundwork for two social orientations or moral visions—justice and caring. "Since everyone is vulnerable both to oppression and to abandonment, two stories about morality recur in human experience.... Two moral injunctions—not to treat others unfairly and not to turn away from someone in need—define two lines of moral development, providing different standards for assessing moral judgments and moral behavior ... " (Gilligan & Wiggins, 1987, p. 281).

The hypothesis of sex bias in the measures of morality has generally not been demonstrated empirically. When proper controls are used for age, class and educational level neither Kohlberg's MJI nor Rest's DIT reveal statistically significant sex differences (Kohlberg, 1984; Snarey, 1985; L. Walker, 1984).[41] And the latest meta-analysis of sex differences in moral orientation reveal relatively small differences, albeit in the predicted directions: Males were higher in justice orientation and females higher in

---

[41]The lack of significant differences may, in part, be artifactual. Recall that both the MJI and the DIT are restricted at the upper level of principled morality at which the putative sex differences are expected to be manifested. Stage 6 scoring has been abandoned in the measuring instruments, and the incidence of respondents at Stage 5 is very low. Thus, the measures do not appear capable of providing an adequate test of the sex-bias hypothesis.

care orientation (Jaffee & Hyde, 2000). Although it might reasonably be concluded therefore that this critical feminist position has lost the battle over whether our measures of morality are biased, they have clearly won the war in that caring has been firmly established as a dimension of morality.

It is clear that over the past 20 years moral psychologists have routinely accepted the duality of morality as including both justice concerns and caring (frequently labeled *welfare*). The latter is prominent, for example, in Hoffman's (1977, 1983, 1988) influential empathy-based socialization model. Moreover, the caring orientation may be an indication of healthy psychological adjustment. For example, it has been shown that degree of prosocial behavior, including instances of caring, among 8- and 9-year old boys and girls is significantly predictive of their academic achievement and positive relations with peers 5 years later (Caprara, Barbaranelli, Pastorelli, Bandura, & Zimbardo, 2000). The investigation and interpretation of sex differences in morality ought to explore potential differences in the patterning of these two equally relevant perspectives, perhaps in response to varying situational or cultural demands, rather than focusing on comparisons in which one sex is, in effect, deemed morally deficient by virtue of a lower mean score on a single criterion.

The Nature and Experience of a Moral Dilemma (III)

The immediate results of moral development, regardless of which theory is used to conceptualize the process, are internalized sets of cognitive schemas with associated motivational and emotional components. These consist of generalized social orientations, personal values, behavioral norms, social expectations, conceptions of fairness and justice, and prosocial motives, as well as motives to avoid causing harm. These schemas provide the bases by which one perceives, defines, and evaluates the sorts of social problems that we label *moral* or ethical. Most research in moral psychology is focused on determining what processes can be generalized across social classes and even cultures. Consequently, not a great deal of evidence has been gathered with respect to the delineation of individual differences in those processes. Nevertheless, it seems evident that there exists considerable interindividual variation—for example, in what ethical situations different people will experience as particularly upsetting. Much of that variation is undoubtedly attributable to differences in the socialization experiences among people— even among those in the same national, cultural, religious, and social class groupings.

But another group of potentially relevant variables has to do with the nature of the ethical dilemma itself with which one is confronted. Several factors are important. For example, a pertinent aspect of any such dilemma is its complexity. *Moral complexity* reflects the number of values and concerns elicited by the stimulus array and the relations among them. Of particular relevance, of course, are situations in which conflicting or incompatible values are evoked. An example encountered frequently in the moral philosophy literature illustrates the common conflict between interpersonal commitments (e.g., duty and responsibility) and personal ambition, needs, or objectives. It is called the *Gauguin dilemma*, representing the conflict between a self-actualizing motive—in this case, to go off to the South Seas to paint—and the responsibilities one has to one's spouse and family. Similarly, many philosophers have introduced the issue by means of a question reputedly first posed by Jean Paul Sartre concerning the young Frenchman during World War Two who was torn between the desire to leave home and join the resistance to fight the Nazis and the duty to stay home to care for his elderly mother. What should he do?

Those are particularly vexatious dilemmas insofar as there may be little possibility for compromise. When we can compromise between competing ethical and social imperatives, we often do so; when we cannot, we may vacillate painfully. An example is provided in Stanley Milgram's (in)famous experiments in which research participants were instructed by the experimenter, under the guise of a learning experiment, to administer higher and higher levels of (fake) electric shock to experimental confederates when they made errors. Most of the participants did so, even reaching levels of shock at which the confederates were apparently in considerable discomfort and pain. Turiel et al. (1991) noted that the research participants were actually confronted by "two separable contextual elements in conflict with each other. Embedded within the experimental situation is what [has been] referred to as a moral context and a social organizational context (p. 315)."[42] The moral dimension had to do with the issue of inflicting harm on others; the social organizational dimension had to do with the implicit rules and authority relations of the social system established by the experiment, including its scientific aims and legitimacy. To comply with the social influence meant violating the morality of care; to avoid inflicting harm meant denying the social dictates of the study. Most subjects, whichever choice they made, betrayed considerable ambivalence and reluctance in doing so, as a reflection of the conflict and the attempt to arrive at a psychological compromise of sorts.

T. M. Jones (1991) was among the first to point out that theories of moral reasoning such as Kohlberg's and models of ethical decision making in organizations have uniformly omitted consideration of characteristics of the situation itself. In his theoretical exposition of an issue-contingent model, he introduced the multidimensional construct *moral intensity* that "captures

---

[42]Turiel et al. (1991) did not use the term *context* as it is customarily used and as I used it in Fig. 5.1 (see Category XI). What they referred to as the moral context and social organizational context of the situation refer to dimensions or facets of the ethical problem itself, not its surround.

the extent of issue-related moral imperative in a situation" (p. 372). It is comprised of six characteristics of a moral issue:

1. **Magnitude of the consequences** of the decision, defined in accord with general utility theory as the sum of the harms (or benefits) done to potential victims (or beneficiaries).
2. The **social consensus** surrounding the ethical issue, defined as "the degree of social agreement that a proposed act is evil (or good)" (p. 375).[43]
3. The **probability of effect** (or likelihood of the consequences) is an expectancy-like notion corresponding to the joint probability that the contemplated act will occur and will result in the consequences anticipated.
4. **Temporal immediacy** refers to the interval between taking moral action and the onset of its consequences.
5. By **proximity** is meant the degree of social, cultural, psychological, or physical "nearness" that the actor feels for the potential victims or beneficiaries of the action. This seems to reflect the empathy-based considerations discussed earlier (Hoffman, 1988).
6. The **concentration of effect** of the ethical behavior is an inverse function of the number of people affected by the act (assuming overall magnitude is constant). In other words, it is the average consequence per person affected. Thus, cheating an individual out of a given sum of money has a greater concentration of effect than cheating a corporation out of the same sum.

T. M. Jones (1991) proposed that dilemmas of high moral intensity are more likely to be recognized as moral issues, will elicit more sophisticated moral reasoning as well as a greater intent to act on a moral decision, and will thus more likely result in ethical behavior. The empirical results appear to generally support the importance of moral intensity, but they are limited primarily to the first three of the six components (Chia & Mee, 2000; Frey, 2000; Harrington, 1997; S. A. Morris & McDonald, 1995; Paolillo & Vitell, 2002; M. Singer, Mitchell, & Turner, 1998; Weber, 1996).

In a similar fashion, D. Collins (1989) proposed that value judgments regarding potential ethical transgressions (defined in terms of harms) will be influenced by three factors. The first is the *nature of the harm*, in which Collins suggested—following distinctions made in jurisprudence—that physical harms are viewed as most severe, followed by economic harms and psychological or emotional harms—in that order. The second component is the *nature of the harmed*, in which it is postulated that harm to persons is

---

[43]Note that, whereas most of T. M. Jones' (1991) six issues are consequentialist in nature, social consensus has a decidedly deontological cast.

viewed as more serious than harm to nonhuman entities, as is harm to many people than to few and to those with higher social status people than to those of lower social status. The third factor is the *stage of the resource transformation process* at which the harm occurs. Whereas the first two factors pertain to any consequentialist analysis, regardless of venue, the third refers specifically to transgressions within organizations in which, for example, ethical issues concerning hiring practices, promotion policies, and dismissal procedures correspond to the resource input, throughput stage, and output stage of human resource management, respectively. Collins suggested that, all else being equal, organizations are likely to be held more blameworthy for harms in the input and output stages because they are more visible to a greater number of observers. Certainly, the enormous focus on the fairness of employee selection testing and on the justification for repeated organizational downsizing of workers is consonant with that inference, although there does not seem to be many direct empirical tests of the hypotheses. However, as expected, Weber (1996) found that managers use successively higher stages of moral reasoning in dealing with dilemmas involving psychological, economic, and physical harm.

Complicating still further our attempts to understand the nature of an ethical situation are some results obtained by applying the methods of cognitive neuroscience to the field of moral psychology. J. D. Greene, Sommerville, Nystrom, Darley, and Cohen (2001) investigated a long-recognized puzzle among moral philosophers. The moral dilemma posed by the trolley problem and the footbridge problem are alike, but people typically endorse different actions in each. In the former, a runaway trolley is headed for five people who will be killed if it continues on that track. You can save them by switching the trolley to another track where it will kill one person. Should you turn the trolley and save five people at the expense of one? In the latter problem, as before, there is a trolley bearing down on five people. You are standing next to a large stranger on a footbridge spanning the tracks between the trolley and the people. The only way to save the five people is to push the stranger off the bridge onto the tracks; he will die, but the trolley will be stopped. Should you do so? Most people respond yes to the first scenario and no to the second. Why? The difference between the two dilemmas is that the first appears to be indirect or relatively impersonal whereas the second involves more direct and personal action.

Greene et al. (2001) found that dilemmas characterized as personal in nature, like the footbridge problem, activated areas of the brain associated with emotion, whereas structurally similar impersonal moral dilemmas, like the trolley problem, activated areas associated with working memory during cognitive processing. The results suggest, therefore, that there are systematic differences in moral judgment associated with the degree of emotional arousal inherent in the dilemma, having little if anything to do with a rational assessment of the situation. More important, as the experimenters pointed out, the personal–impersonal distinction is merely "a useful 'first cut,' an important but preliminary step toward identifying the psychologically essential features of circumstances that engage, or fail to engage, our emotions and that ultimately shape our moral judgments" (p. 2107). This may also be a good example of the contribution of psychology (and brain science) to moral philosophy. The apparently illogical (i.e., inconsistent) typical responses to the two situations may correspond to and explain what the deontologists characterize as intended as opposed to unintended effects (see chap. 3); the determinative factor may actually be the active–personal–emotional versus the passive–impersonal nature of the behavior.

Societal and Cultural Influences on Moral Development (VII)

The astute reader of this chapter so far will not have missed the fact that it was impossible to discuss the developmental aspects of moral behavior without considerable reference to interpersonal transactions. Even the cognitive self-construction model of moral development does not require the view that children simply construct their moral standards endogenously:

> Rather they "reconstruct" or "re-create" culturally appropriate moral meaning systems. That is, with increasing age and experience, children apply progressively more complex and mobile logical schemas to cultural distinctions and categories; they transform what they are told and what they experience into their own self-organized realities. These realities are idiosyncratic to each individual child and yet bear witness to extensive cross-cultural commonalities in early moral reasoning. (C. P. Edwards, 1987, p. 149)

As Aronfreed (1994) summarized, moral judgment and conduct are best characterized "by the view that they evolve from continuities in the interaction between the child's cognitive capacity and his social experience" (p. 185). At the microlevel the earliest and most fundamental of these social experiences are parental inductions and modeling, as well as peer encounters reinforced by praise, rewards, punishment, witholding affection, scolding, reasoning, teasing, shaming, and so on. For adults who work in or for large organizations, later socialization processes continue somewhat more indirectly and subtly in the form of organizational roles, rules and regulations, performance objectives, norms, values, and other mechanisms of assuring behavioral consistency and predictability (D. Katz & Kahn, 1978). In the next chapters I discuss the values-shaping aspects of one's professional training and experiences.

One aspect of the socialization process is the production of a certain degree of fundamental commonality among members of the moral community, which enables society to function in a relatively frictionless manner. For example, it is generally taken for granted in the United States that concepts of fairness and justice are defined according to merit and the equity principle, rather than by equality. However, it is important to avoid an erroneous conception of the social environment as homogeneous and producing homogeneous social orientations (Turiel et al., 1991). These authors reviewed experimental and field research from several areas indicating that the contextual influences of any given social situation may be complex and that they vary as a function of the particular domain of social interaction—particularly with respect to the distinction between conventional and moral behavior.

Moral Reasoning (IV) and Choices (V)

Little commentary seems necessary concerning these two components of the DMMA: They comprise the entire substance of chapters 2, 3, and 4. As noted several times, what seems to have been relatively underappreciated by the moral philosophers whose work is reviewed there is the relation of moral reasoning and choice to real-life behavioral outcomes.[44] As reflected in the content of this chapter, that is a major contribution from moral psychology. A portion of that contribution also consists of attempts to delineate the influences had by other individual difference variables that have behavioral implications, such as moral sensitivity, moral motivation, moral identity, and self-control, as well as additional contextual influences on moral reasoning, choice, and behavior, as discussed later. The general relation of attitude and cognition to behavior has also, of course, been the focus of a great deal of work in social psychology. In Ajzen's (1988; Ajzen & Fishbein, 1980) model, a person's intention to perform a volitional action is the proximal determinant of behavior, just as moral choice influences moral action in Fig. 5.1. That is why intentions correlate more highly with behavior than do attitudes toward the behavior. For example, I/O psychologists typically find that the intention to quit one's job is more highly related to subsequently leaving than is one's level of job satisfaction or dissatisfaction (Mobley, Griffeth, Hand, & Meglino, 1979). However, the developmental model depicted in Fig. 5.1 differs from Ajzen and Fishbein's insofar as it assumes that external control processes such as organizational norms and ethical climate and internal control processes

---

[44]There are exceptions, however. Some philosophers, like P. Singer (1995), have expressed concern for the psychological realism of moral theorizing. For example, it has been observed a number of times (e.g., Krebs et al., 1991) that the moral dilemmas utilized in Kohlberg's MJI are not sufficiently realistic and that the responses people make to other dilemmas are frequently not the same as those they make to the MJI dilemmas.

like self-judgments moderate the relation between choice (or intention) and action. In Ajzen's model, they impact intention directly, so that intention is defined as the subjective probability of performing the action.

Potentially very important is work that emphasizes the primacy of affective reactions as antecedent to cognitive processes (Zajonc, 1980), including moral judgment processes (Haidt, 2001). Haidt pointed out that, since the cognitive revolution in psychology in the 1960s, the dominant conception guiding work done in the study of moral psychology has been the rationalist model "in which moral judgement is thought to be caused by moral reasoning" (p. 814). In contrast, he made a well-supported case for an intuitionist approach in which morally relevant situations unconsciously elicit immediate intuitions (Reber, 1993) that are experienced as intrinsic, automatic, or self-evident moral judgments, such as the immediacy of most people's reaction to a story of incest in our culture. Those automatic reactions then, according to this model, may elicit moral-reasoning processes that are "engaged in after a moral judgment is made, in which a person searches for arguments that will support an already-made judgment" (p. 818). Note that, in Fig. 5.1, I indicated that moral reasoning and judgment processes are accompanied by emotional reactions, admittedly begging the issue at this stage of our knowledge whether those reactions might be antecedents leading to moral judgment.

Interestingly, Haidt (2001) acknowledged two instances in which the traditional rationalist model may be an accurate depiction. The first is that we use moral reasoning as an ex post facto process (after the emergence of our immediate moral judgments) to influence the intuitions and judgments of others. The second, relevant to our concern with ethical dilemmas, is when a situation elicits multiple competing intuitions. Under those circumstances, the expectation is that the several intuitions trigger contradictory judgments which then elicit the sort of reasoning processes being considered here, resulting in a comparative analysis of the alternative justifications. Thus, it may be that both the intuitionist and the more rationalist models predict similar psychological processes in response to the multifaceted situations likely to comprise professional ethical dilemmas.

Character: Moral Values and Sensitivity (VIII), Motivation (IX), and Internal Controls (X)

The primary preoccupation of moral psychology has been the adequate explanation of the biopsychosocial processes responsible for moral development. This is a point of view that, according to some critics, has paid inadequate attention to matters of *virtue* or *character*. That is a legitimate issue to be acknowledged, especially with respect to the Kohlbergian cognitive stage model perspective. As noted earlier the substance of Kohlberg's theory, the moral stages, consist of structured reasoning processes; they are not to be misconstrued as characterizations of types of people. The emphasis on cognitive processes has contributed to a sense that "there's no 'there' there" in the study of moral psychology. Where is the locus of morality, the person, in this psychological theory? As indicated in chapter 2, this is an Aristotelian criticism in that he construed morality not in terms of "what is the right thing to do?," but "what is the right sort of person to be?" Although the criticism is much less applicable to the socialization models of moral development (e.g., Freudian theory, cognitive–social learning theory, or Hoffman's empathy-based model) it has proven to be a salient appraisal because of the preeminence of Kohlberg's theory and because of the prominence of virtue theory in contemporary religious culture. The concern has been seen as critical in the selection of public sector administrators (Hart, 2001), and taken up in the business world with calls for greater attention to the "identification of those already predisposed to live according to high moral standards" (H. B. Jones, 1995, p. 867).

Character is one of those elusive terms that is more frequently used than defined and understood. Following Boyd's (1994) approach in a general way, I refer to relatively stable dispositional aspects of personality that account for relatively consistent attitudes and behavioral tendencies across a variety of circumstances. I would have no great quarrel with a reader who views character traits as having much in common with values and one's character as reflected in one's value system (see chap. 6). Among the differences, however, is one of vantage point. One's character is invariably judged or inferred by others, whereas one's values are more frequently a matter of self-reflection and revelation. These dispositional tendencies are what allow us to "characterize" people in terms of particular trait descriptions; they are what we mean most frequently when we say that we know what someone is like.

Nevertheless, it has been recognized for quite some time that there is considerable intraindividual variation in the expression of personality traits, including indications of moral behavior or values such as honesty (Hartshorne & May, 1928; Murphy, 1993). This variability is an outcome of competing motives and/or varying contextual influences, and it requires us to recognize these characterological influences primarily as nascent tendencies, not as rigid determinants. Most psychologists accept an interactionist perspective of behavior as due to the interplay of dispositional attributes of personality, including character, and situational influences (Kenrick & Funder, 1988). In fact, some scholars have reconceptualized the notion of the consistency of personality to include not only stable individual differences, but also "distinctive and stable patterns of situation–behavior relations (e.g., she does X when A but Y when B)" (W. Mischel, Shoda, & Mendoza-Denton, 2002, p. 50).

Not all aspects of character are moral in nature. *Moral character* refers to those dispositional tendencies that relate to some normative moral stance, most frequently reflecting aspects of one or both of the two widely recognized dimensions of moral behavior emphasized in the study of moral psychology: justice–fairness and welfare–beneficence. To describe your friend as very friendly, sociable, and outgoing does not ordinarily have the same moral implication as describing him or her as very caring. But in some circumstances it might. If your friend were going out of his or her way at a social event to be especially welcoming to someone who is a shy outsider that would be, according to this definition, a positive reflection of his or her moral character because of its beneficent aim. Positive traits of moral character may sometimes be the same as those attributes commonly labeled as virtues—loyalty, courage, patience, and so on. I agree with Boyd (1994), however, that these attributes are best thought of as subordinate character traits that may be expressions of or derived from the primary traits of moral character: "That is, they can be considered *moral* character traits only insofar as they are put into context by the moral point of view framed by benevolence and justice" (p. 119). For example, loyalty to a dishonest employer or having the fortitude to follow company directives to fire someone unjustly or being gratuitously hurtful to a colleague under the guise of being honest are neither virtuous acts nor indications of good moral character.

The bottom portion of Fig. 5.1 presents three sets of latent variables that have been studied to some degree by moral psychologists, which I construe to be aspects of moral character.

Moral Values, Moral Sensitivity, and Moral Imagination

Moral values and *moral sensitivity* reflect those aspects of moral character that play a directing and defining role in determining whether one experiences a situation as morally challenging. "People's values and beliefs affect what information they seek and how they interpret what they see and hear" (Bandura, 1991, p. 94), and individual differences in values have generally been acknowledged as an important element in managerial ethics and organizational conflict (Gortner, 2001). The personal values of managers have been shown to be related to their stage of moral reasoning (Weber, 1993) and to their ethical judgments (Douglas, Davidson, & Schwartz, 2001), although the influence of personal values on their ethical decision making may be suppressed if the managers are accountable to a higher authority whose preferences are known (Brief, Dukerich, & Doran, 1991)—an important contextual/organizational effect to keep in mind (discussed later). Not only may managers be expected to differ in values, and those differences result in different ethical outcomes, but the pattern of value differences that accounts for the different outcomes may vary as a function of the nature of the ethical dilemma (Fritzsche, 1995).

In other words, just as important as one's individual values is the relation among a person's values—his or her *value system*. Not only do interindividual differences in values contribute to what often seem to be irreconcilable differences among people, the multiplicity of values we each possess is a potential source of intrapersonal conflict. Fortunately, their relative ordering in importance is a mechanism by which such conflicts can be obviated or resolved. "Intraindividual conflict can be traced in part to the clarity with which values are crystallized and prioritized. A critical first step in the decision-making process is to reduce this source of uncertainty" (D. Brown & Crace, 1996, p. 212). But it is probably to be expected that the complexity and ambiguity of professional and business decisions will engage multiple motives within a person, reflecting diverse values and goals (DiNorcia & Tigner, 2000).

Suppose the organization for which you work decided to "restructure" its operations and in so doing terminated the most experienced older (i.e., middle-aged) employees and after a short period of time replaced many of them with younger, part-time, and supposedly more vital workers who "coincidentally" were able to be hired at much lower salaries with virtually no benefits.[45] Whether you perceive this as a possible moral transgression by the company, how suspicious you may be of management's motives, and your readiness to concede them some benefit of the doubt will depend on, among other things, your values and opinions regarding management prerogatives, obligations and motives, employee rights, principles of justice and fairness, and the relation among them.

Perhaps your values are such that viewing the company as a transgressor is not untenable, but you simply failed to put two and two together regarding the dismissals and subsequent acquisitions of younger replacements. That lack of perceptiveness might reflect your low level of moral sensitivity, an attribute that has been viewed as a salient component of professional ethics. *Moral sensitivity* is probably better understood from a phenomenological perspective as "the awareness of how our actions affect other people. It involves being aware of different possible lines of action and how each line of action could affect the parties concerned. It involves ... knowing cause–consequence chains of events in the real world; it involves empathy and role-taking skills" (Rest, 1994, p. 23). Given the haphazard nature of moral development and ethical training, it is likely that people's degree of moral sensitivity is not uniform across domains of potential transgression. For example, an I/O psychology professor might be more sensitive with

---

[45]"Restructuring" is frequently a euphemism for the less-palatable "downsizing," which may be aimed at "enhancing our profit margin," by "selecting out" people—which are of course additional euphemisms for the act of dismissing people from their jobs (Bandura, 1991). Euphemisms are used frequently by organizations to provide a "language of nonresponsibility" (Gambino, 1973, p. 7) in which ethically questionable behavior is described in the passive form, with no agent, so as to seem that no people are responsible (Bolinger, 1982).

respect to the ethical implications of his or her behavior toward employees in an organization for which he or she consults than toward students in his or her classes.

Figure 5.1 construes moral intensity as influencing the nature and extent of our perception and experience of moral dilemmas as well as our reactions to them. Recent empirical research has confirmed that moral sensitivity influences the recognition of moral issues; both of them, in turn, influence moral evaluation processes (D. R. May & Pauli, 2002). The conception of moral sensitivity as a dispositional variable is supported indirectly by the finding that it was unrelated to industry and organizational environment among a sample of accountants (Patterson, 2001). However, it apparently can be successfully taught, as it has been to dentists and nurses (Bebeau, 1994; Duckett & Ryden, 1994).

Moral sensitivity is probably reflected in one's *moral imagination* (Carroll, 1987; Werhane, 1999), although I am not aware of any empirical investigations of the matter. Moral imagination refers to one's ablility to think beyond the situational particulars and moral guidelines that may define a dilemma and it probably depends in part on one's powers of empathy (Hoffman, 1991). Werhane (1999) views it as an inherent aspect of business and economic relations and has applied the notion to organizations as follows:

> In managerial decision-making, moral imagination entails perceiving norms, social roles, and relationships entwined in any situation. Developing moral imagination involves heightened awareness of contextual moral dilemmas and their mental models, the ability to envision and evaluate new mental models that create new possibilities, and the capability to reframe the dilemma and create new solutions in ways that are novel, economically viable, and morally justifiable. (p. 93)

Moral Motivation, Balance, and Identity

Once a situation is encountered in which our values and moral sensitivity lead us to recognize as morally relevant our moral cognitive schema are engaged, consisting of those problem-solving processes that I described as moral reasoning. Hopefully, this results in some solution or choice (or set of alternative choices needing further resolution), which then leads to action. Relatively little research has been performed regarding the processes whereby values are translated into ethical action. Weber (1993) presented an example, utilizing stage of moral reasoning as a mediating variable. In the model presented in Fig. 5.1 motivational issues are implicated in moderating the relation between moral judgment processes and the choice: The option chosen is not necessarily what one has reasoned to be the most ethically defensible action. For example, in response to a scenario in which they imagined taking an important qualifying exam unsupervised, 80% of a sample of third-year university students maintained that it would be wrong to cheat, but 50% indicated that they would nevertheless decide to do so (Nisan, 1991). Motivational (control) processes are also implicated with regard to the relation between the choice and behavior. What impels implementation of the choice or failure to act in accord with it? These control processes are discussed in the following section.

Some philosophers have acknowledged that most moral theories deal only with reasons, values, and justifications, and that "they fail to examine motives and the motivational structures and constraints of ethical life. They not only fail to do this, they fail as ethical theories by not doing this" (Stocker, 1976, p. 453). Similarly, another philosopher observed:

> Many philosophical views of morality show little or no concern for any psychological substratum that explains how a human being does, or can come to, live in accordance with morality.... If rational argument can demonstrate a certain view of morality to be compelling, that is all the philosophical grounding it needs. Some conceptions, for example Kant's, make the further assumption that such rational acceptance is sufficient to motivate conformity to the morality. But it must be admitted that many philosophical views take no stance either way on this point, assuming tacitly that philosophical acceptability has no connection to psychological reality. (Blum, 1987, p. 307)

Not to be outdone, psychologists have also been as critical of psychological theories on similar grounds: "A theory of morality must explain both the motivators for cognitive change in moral principles and the motivators for acting morally. Stage theorists address the motivation for cognitive change but largely ignore the motivation for pursuing moral courses of action ... " (Bandura, 1991, p. 61).

Reviews of a fairly substantial amount of empirical research indicate that there is a measurably significant relation between people's scores on measures of moral judgment (the MJI and DIT) and relevant behavioral outcomes concerning delinquency, honesty, altruism, and so on. (Blasi, 1980; Thoma & Rest, 1986). In the nomenclature of Fig. 5.1 those are correlations between variable Categories IV and VI. As Thoma (1994) pointed out, the relations are modest—at best 10% to 15% variance in common—and "the nature of the typical study rarely suggests the conditions under which the judgment and action links vary, nor does it help us understand the processes that actually describe how judgments inform actions" (p. 202). He suggested that such understanding will be advanced, and statistical effect sizes increased, by a consideration of other relevant individual difference variables of the sort Rest (1984) incorporated into a Four Component Model and which I subsumed under the rubric of moral character in Fig. 5.1 (Categories VIII, IX, and X). The model presented here, moreover, explicitly includes consideration of social, situational, and contextual influences (Categories VII and XI), which are at best only implied in the Four Component Model.

One of the most interesting motivational constructs relevant to the connection between moral judgment and choice is Nisan's (1990, 1991) concept of *moral balance*. He presented evidence in support of his model which specifies that one of the important determinants of moral choice making is the maintenance of a sort of implicit moral balance sheet for oneself, based on a review of all of one's comparatively recent morally relevant actions. Thus, he was quite explicit in indicating that for many of us moral choices are not merely a reflection of moral judgments focused on each individual situation in isolation, but they reflect a limited morality in which we allow ourselves some deviations from the ethically ideal choice— as long as the transgressions do not fall below some personal standard of minimal acceptability.

Whereas moral philosophies and even psychological theories like Kohlberg's focus exclusively on moral judgments, Nisan's (1990, 1991) model includes consideration of the actor's personal characteristics, current circumstances; and—most important—past behaviors. Moreover, deviations from the ethical ideal should not be interpreted as stemming from insufficient willpower, disaffection with moral standards, or other inferred moral failings. They are generally motivated by an attempt to reconcile conflicts between various components of one's personal identity, of which *moral identity* is just one. Similarly, from a psychodynamic perspective, moral identity has also been defined as the "use of moral principles to define the self" or the "level of integration between self-identity and moral concerns" and viewed as "the key source of moral commitment throughout life" (Damon, 1999, pp. 76, 78). From a content perspective, moral identity has been defined as a "commitment consistent with one's sense of self to lines of action that promote or protect the welfare of others" (D. Hart, Atkins, & Ford, 1998, p. 515).

The moral balance model is in opposition to two other motivational models, the ideal or maximization model of moral action and the slippery slope model. The maximization model is generally implied by the moral philosophies reviewed in this book: That is, we always strive to ascertain and do the morally best thing, as determined by the finest moral reasoning of which we are capable. The slippery slope model posits that individuals avoid even minor transgressions because of the fear that they will lead inevitably to greater and greater breaches. That is, it suggests that one violation of moral standards will lead to self-deprecation and lower self-expectations, predisposing to further violations. In contrast, the maintenance of moral balance renders it more likely for us to indulge ourselves in a limited moral transgression following a period in which we have been relatively good, whereas a recent history of ethically wrongful behavior is more likely to be followed by righteousness. Although Nisan found more empirical support for the moral balance model than for the other two, he acknowledged that there may be individual differences among people in their characteristic modes of acting. Circumstances are also expected to play a role: When the potential transgression is so severe that it represents an intolerable deviation/threat to one's moral balance, we are more likely to see the inhibitions of the slippery slope in action. Or when individuals in an organization are held publicly accountable for their actions to those who have the power to reward or sanction, their behavior is more likely to conform to the expectations of the audience (Beu & Buckley, 2001; Tetlock, 1992). Indirect evidence for the operation of moral balance dynamics comes from a study indicating the existence of contrast effects in ethical judgments. Boyle, Dahlstrom, and Kellaris (1998) found that students rating the ethically ambiguous behavior of a salesperson tended to rate the target as more ethical if they had previously been exposed to an unethical scenario and as less ethical if they had been primed with an ethical scenario. This suggests that organizations should provide behavioral examples of ethical and unethical behavior to serve as anchors for their policy statements to avoid this unacceptable type of moral relativism.

Internal Control Processes

Moral balance and moral identity may be viewed in the larger context of the self-regulation of behavior. However, whereas those conative aspects of the moral action sequences seem most relevant as moderators of the link between moral reasoning and moral choice, the influences of self-regulation pertain more to the processes by which moral choices are or are not reflected in behavior. Virtually every theory of moral behavior, both secular and models embedded in religious teachings, incorporates notions of inhibition, self-regulation, or self-control. These notions are indicated by terms such as conscience, superego, duty, denial, sin and willpower, and they reflect what some people mistakenly think of as the entirety of character. Implicit in several of those views is the assumption that human beings are in some fundamental or essentialist way driven primarily by egoistic motives unless otherwise deflected from that path. My theoretical preferences in this regard are the explanations of cognitive social learning theory (Bandura, 1986, 1991) which do not entail that assumption.

In social cognitive theory the expression of ethical behavior is controlled by two anticipatory regulatory mechanisms—social sanctions and internalized self-sanctions. In this section I discuss only the self-regulatory mechanisms. And they consist of three components: self-monitoring, self-judgments, and self-reactions. Once a tentative choice or a number of alternative potential choices have been arrived at, they are subject to a process of self-scrutiny and evaluation in light of one's moral identity and the current level of one's moral balance in relation to the specific contextual situation. According to Bandura (1991), however, the most important elements in the process are the resultant "affective self-reactions [that] provide the mechanism by which standards regulate conduct. The anticipatory self-respect and self-censure for actions that correspond with, or violate personal standards serve as the regulatory influences" (p. 69). In other words, the primary internal regulators are the anticipated experiences of self-satisfaction and self-respect associated with the confirmation of our moral ideals and the contemplated sense of self-condemnation or self-contempt ensuing from ethical and moral transgressions. These feelings are the result of repeated and eventually internalized inductions during one's childhood, which form the basis for Hoffman's (1991) empathy-based model of moral development. Bandura (1991) also made an important point concerning the influence of more fundamental personality attributes on these moral self-sanctions: "Effective self-regulation of conduct requires not only self-regulatory skills but also strong belief in one's capabilities to achieve personal control.... The stronger the perceived self-regulatory efficacy, the more perseverant people are in their self-controlling efforts and the greater is their success in resisting social pressures to behave in ways that violate their standards" (p. 69). He went on to highlight that, unlike internalization theories that emphasize constantly vigilant control mechanisms like conscience, self-reactive influences do not operate unless we engage them. Selectively activating and disengaging internal controls allows for our engaging in different behaviors even under the same moral standards—a situation akin to what Nisan (1990, 1991) described as the limited morality enabled by maintaining one's moral balance.

A somewhat different perspective is suggested by moral psychologists who have resurrected interest in the moral emotions, such as empathy and sympathy (M. Davis, 1994; Eisenberg & Miller, 1987), guilt and shame (Baumeister, Stillwell, & Heatherton, 1994), feelings of moral obligation (Gorusch & Ortberg, 1983), forgiveness (Kurzynski, 1998), and gratitude (McCullough, Kilpatrick, Emmons, & Larson, 2001). Such moral affects or the anticipation of such are important both as reactions to moral behavior or as potential motivators of it, respectively. In addition, the appropriate expressions of these affects serve to reinforce the people who are the objects of the emotional responses, thus encouraging further moral behavior (i.e., beneficent actions). A student's expressions of gratitude at being allowed to hand in a paper late with no penalty make it more likely that I will repeat that action in the future with other students.

The Situational Context of Moral Action (XI)

Even within behaviorist learning theory it is understood that the same stimulus conditions do not always lead to the same responses, resulting from the social context in which the stimuli appear (Gewirtz, 1972). And of course in social psychology the effects of situational variations on perceptual judgment processes, bystander intervention, conformity with instructions from an authority, and so on, have long been the very focus of investigations. Consequently, it should come as no surprise to learn that contextual influences on ethical behavior have been of some interest to moral psychologists. For example, ethical judgments have been shown to be biased as a function of contrast effects dependent on whether one has just previously observed an instance of ethical or unethical behavior (Boyle et al., 1998) and whether one is primed to identify with the perpetrator or the victim of a moral transgression (Kronzon & Darley, 1999). One of the more dramatic illustrations of situational effects comes from Milgram's (1963, 1974) "shocking" experiment mentioned earlier. Under experimental conditions in which some contextual elements were manipulated, such as the distance of the participant from the experimenter or from the "victim," participants showed greater resistance to compliance with the authority figure.

I conceive of the variety of contextual influences on moral action as having moderating effects—rather than affecting the dependent variables directly (cf. Barnett & Vaicys, 2000)—on three causal relationships: (a) the nature of the moral judgment processes that are invoked in response to a perceived ethical dilemma (Categories III→IV in Fig. 5.1), (b) the ethical choices and behavioral intentions that are arrived at as a consequence of the moral reasoning processes (Categories IV→V), and (c) the connection between moral choice–intention and behavior (Categories V→VI).

Organizational Influences

The ethicality of employees's behavior in organizations is subject to the same situational influences that impact other role-related and extrarole behaviors, including one's position and status in the organization, its ethical climate—as communicated by top management and reinforced by the normative expectations, social sanctions, and reward structure of the company—and how one is treated. For example, in writing about honesty in the workplace, Murphy (1993) noted that "to understand honesty in the workplace, we must examine the norms, customs, and assumptions of members of the organization, as well as the messages conveyed by the organization about the range and limits of acceptable behavior" (p. 6), and interest in the social determinants of ethical behavior seems to be growing among organizational psychologists (Darley, Messick, & Tyler, 2001). Moreover, underlying even those proximal situational influences are the morally relevant social, political, and economic macrolevel assumptions and values that provide the context within which the organization, especially corporations, function. Those meta-issues are taken up in chapter

7 regarding matters of social justice, in chapters 8, 9, and 12 concerning the rights and responsibilities of those in the professions in general and in psychology and I/O psychology in particular, as well as in chapters 10 and 11 pertaining to alternative models of political economy such as *laissez-faire* profit maximization versus corporate social responsibility.

Positional Status.   Organizational scholars have long recognized that the nature of the scientific, economic, and market environments within which a firm operates serve to shape its structure and function—at least for successful adaptive organizations (Lawrence & Lorsch, 1969). These in turn influence the concerns, beliefs, and attitudes of managers in different segments of the organizational structure, so that structure influences individual values (Hinings, Thibault, Slack, & Kikulis, 1996). Thus, one's position in the organization may be expected to influence the problems and dilemmas one is most likely to encounter, both technical and ethical. In fact, Victor and Cullen (1988) found that the several dimensions of ethical climates in organizations varied within organizations as a function of position, tenure, and work group membership.

Among a sample of almost 1,500 American supervisory, middle, and executive managers, it was found that judgments that their organizations were administered ethically were related positively to job level; whether the managers sometimes had to compromise their personal principles to conform to organizational expectations was related inversely to job level (Posner & Schmidt, 1987). That is, high-level managers, who are more involved in policy-setting activities and in determining and implementing strategic decisions are more likely to see their organizations as ethical and less likely to experience pressure to conform or compromise personal principles than lower level managers and supervisors.

Organizational Ethical Culture and the Climate for Ethical Behavior.[46]   A major social contextual component of the way in which we experience an ethical dilemma and how that experience structures our moral reasoning and intentions has to do with the relative salience of moral standards in the pertinent domain. This is the advantage of having a clearly

---

[46]The constructs of ethical culture and ethical climate have not been well differentiated in the literature. Sometimes they have been used interchangeably (R. C. Ford & Richardson, 1994; Loe, Ferrell, & Mansfield, 2000). I follow traditional social science custom by using the term *ethical culture* to refer to a shared commonality of values, goals, and norms regarding the ethical behavior to be expected from the members of a social system, such as a work group or an entire organization; whereas *ethical climate* refers to the individual perceptions of members of the system with respect to their personal experience of the ethicality of organizational practices, which may include their perceptions of the system's ethical culture. The distinction between the two is often blurred operationally because aspects of culture (e.g., normative expectations) are frequently measured via individual perceptions. Moreover, those individual-level perceptions are often taken inappropriately to be measures of culture without demonstrating that they represent a shared commonality of views.

explicated ethical code, conducting ethical instruction, and otherwise engaging in activities that promote the awareness of a moral perspective and encourage ethical behavior (Fudge & Schlacter, 1999). Personality and social psychologists characterize social situations as relatively strong or weak as a reflection of the extent to which they include salient cues as to how one should behave, and this has been applied to an understanding of the expression of honesty and dishonesty in the workplace (Murphy, 1993). In settings as disparate as sports and international accounting firms, such influences have been referred to as *moral atmosphere* (Bredemeier & Shields, 1994) or *organizational ethical culture* (Douglas, Davidson, & Schwartz, 2001). For example, one well-documented finding with implications for us as I/O psychologists is that a competitive environment tends to lower one's sensitivity to the concerns of others and focuses attention on one's own needs and goals (or that of one's team, work unit or company, as a whole), resulting in less prosocial and more aggressive behavior (Bredemeier & Shields, 1994). This seems to be a contemporaneous extension of the well-known earlier social psychological research findings indicating that intergroup cooperation or conflict is fostered by the cooperative or competitive nature of the situation (Sherif, Harvey, White, Hood, & Sherif, 1961).

Victor and Cullen (1988) developed a multidimensional conception and measure of nine types of ethical work climate, and subsequent research has demonstrated that at least some of those categories are associated with different forms of organizational governance (Wimbush, Shepard, & Markham, 1997a), although there may be some question regarding the nine-factor structure of the scale (Wyld & Jones, 1997). Several dimensions have been found to be related significantly to ethical intentions or organizational misbehavior (Wimbush, Shepard, & Markham, 1997b; Vardi, 2001) or to moderate the relation between ethical judgment and behavioral intentions (the IV→V causal path in Fig. 5.1; Barnett & Vaicys, 2000). Others have similarly documented the relation between the organization's ethical climate and responses to ethical problems (Bartels, Harrick, Martell, & Strickland, 1998; Falkenberg & Herremans, 1995; R. L. Sims & Keon, 1999).[47]

Leadership and Other Interpersonal Influences. In an extremely interesting discussion Peterson (2001) illustrated that the broad sweep of classic social psychological research of the last half of the 20th century concerning the effects of group membership, intergroup conflict and other group processes, social power, attitude change, leadership style, group decision making, compliance with authority, and procedural justice are all intrinsically concerned with what are essentially moral issues of behavioral

---

[47]The interested reader can refer to integrative summaries of the empirical research literature concerning ethical decision making in organizations (R. C. Ford & Richardson, 1994; Loe et al., 2000).

influence. He concluded that our caution regarding direct influence attempts by powerful leaders and other authority figures (e.g., directing the outcome of a decision problem) overlooks the importance of more subtle and indirect authoritarian strategies, and that these generally constitute matters of procedure, not outcomes, denying subordinates the respect and autonomy inherent in a fair decision process. This seems to be commensurate with appeals to institutionalize organizational ethics through the use of transformational leadership which appeals to the moral values of employees and emphasizes benefit to the organization over narrow self-interest (D. S. Carlson & Perrewe, 1995; also see B. M. Bass & Steidlmeier, 1999, regarding the moral foundations of transformational leadership). Top management's commitment to ethics influences the nature of the organization's control systems with respect to ethical behavior (Weaver, Trevino, & Cochran, 1999). However, acting on behalf of the organization is no guarantee against unethical or illegal behavior (see the discussion of groupthink that follows and chaps. 10 and 11 regarding the excesses of profit-maximizing values). In fact, those with a traditional business orientation (the only legitimate managerial objective is maximizing shareholder value) are more likely than nontraditionalists to view ethically questionable actions as justifiable—as long as the conduct is aimed at benefitting the organization rather than being self-serving (Mason & Mudrack, 1997).

Dealing more directly with the issue of ethical decision making, Wimbush (1999) suggested that level of cognitive moral development (as per Kohlberg's scheme) interacts with supervisory influence such that "highly cognitive morally developed subordinates are not influenced by supervisors when resolving ethical dilemmas. While, on the other hand, subordinates at levels one and two of cognitive moral development look to supervisors for guidance concerning what is considered to be appropriate ethical behavior" (p. 392). Unfortunately, no data are presented. D'Aquilla and Bean (2000), using an experimental procedure with college accounting students, found that three levels of organizational ethical "tone at the top" were related to degree of ethical financial reporting. And confirming the influence of modeling behavior, Fritz, Arnett, and Conkel (1999) found that, for organizational associates (those with no supervisory responsibilities), awareness of the organization's ethical standards and organizational commitment were predictable from their perception of the extent to which managers adhere to the organization's ethical standards.

Schminke and Wells (1999) demonstrated that the ethical predispositions of college students were enhanced by their participation in a 4-month interacting group strategic-management simulation, although they offered no explanation of why that should be so or how it might have occurred. Of particular interest, however, are the findings that degree of group cohesiveness was predictive of the increase in utilitarian perspective but not of the increase in formalism (i.e., a rule-based or deontological approach); a structuring leadership style by group leaders was predictive of changes in formalism but not in utilitarianism. In other words, interpersonal processes may affect ethical behavior differently as a function of the ethical orientation of the actor, as well as the nature of the ethical problem.

We know that group processes can have maladaptive consequences as well as positive effects. Perhaps the best known example(s) of the influence of group dynamics on decision making concern the deleterious effect of what Janis (1982) termed *groupthink*—a collective pattern in cohesive decision-making groups of defensively avoiding contradictory information, suppressing alternative arguments, reinforcing the dominant group perspective, and otherwise pressing for uniformity of opinion, thus leading to ineffective outcomes. R. S. Peterson (2001) listed 21 high-profile documented cases of groupthink-induced disasters, and R. R. Sims (1992) extended the application of the phenomenon as a precursor to unethical as well as merely inept actions. He observed that the prospect of groupthink occurring is enhanced by three factors: (a) when decisions are made under stressful circumstances (e.g., financial or time pressures), (b) when the group is characterized by a degree of arrogance, and (c) group members are loyal to one another. These are circumstances not infrequently found in large business enterprises. To avoid the disastrous consequences of groupthink Sims recommended that groups intentionally program conflict into the decision-making process by having someone (on a rotating basis) play the role of devil's advocate or by instituting dialectic methods. "The dialectic method calls for structuring a debate between conflicting views regardless of members' personal feelings. The benefits of the dialectic method are in the presentation and debate of the assumptions underlying proposed courses of action. False or misleading assumptions become apparent and can head off unethical decisions that are based on these poor assumptions" (pp. 268–269). The idea is to promote legitimate dissent.

Bandura (1991) sounded a similarly cautionary note. Recall, from the preceding section that presented the social cognition theory view of internal controls that social sanctions exist as a regulatory mechanism parallel to the internalized self-sanctions. Just as a positive climate for ethical behavior can encourage it, Bandura (1991) noted that there are innumerable contextual factors that may serve to facilitate our engaging in the sorts of questionable behaviors that we would ordinarily repudiate in the absence of those factors. For example, institutions or organizations may provide a moral justification for reprehensible behavior, allowing the person to cognitively reconstrue its moral qualities. Thus, killing is admirable in wartime and manufacturing cigarettes is respectable because it is legal and provides employment to lots of people. Other institutional mechanisms include (a) the use of euphemisms as part of the "language of nonresponsibility" to mask ethically questionable activities (see footnote 45), (b) displacing responsibility for one's actions on to an authority figure, (c) diffusing responsibility entirely to others as a function of the division of labor (e.g., contributing to the success of a cigarette manufacturer is fine—"I'm only in Human Resources, I don't manufacture or sell the product"), and (d) diffusing responsibility to a collective group decision in which no one is individually accountable. For example, on January 19, 2001, then-Secretary of Defense William S. Cohen endorsed the conclusions of a long Navy report to the effect that "responsibility for not preventing the suicide attack on the destroyer Cole in Yemen [which killed 17 American sailors] extended throughout the Pentagon's leadership—from those aboard the ship to himself—and he recommended that no individuals be disciplined" (Myers, 2001, p. A1).

A final mention is warranted of an important and underappreciated point raised by Jansen and Von Glinow (1985) regarding ethical ambivalence. As already reviewed, we know that social sanctions play a critical role in shaping ethical climate and behavior, as do the nature of organizational reward structures (Loe et al., 2000). Based on earlier theoretical writings by the sociologist Robert Merton, Jansen and Von Glinow illustrated how organizational reward systems may shape behaviors in directions opposed to the prevailing norms such as those promoting ethical conduct, thus establishing *counternorms*. Dominant norms generally express positively valued standards of conduct ("abide by the rules"), whereas counternorms may express implicit, largely unacknowledged expectations that conflict with the norms ("do whatever it takes to get the job done on time"), thus leading to ethical ambivalence. Counternorms may be related to the financial reward system of an organization, as with individual incentive pay when the organization otherwise promotes team effort and responsibility. The resulting ethical ambivalence can be personally upsetting and induce actions that are dysfunctional for the organization. Remedying the situation may be extremely difficult if key policy makers are not prepared to acknowledge the problem and redesign those portions of the organizational reward systems that are at variance with the ostensibly desired culture of the organization. For example, Wal-Mart was recently indicted for requiring employees to work overtime for no pay (Greenhouse, 2002). Despite official policies to abide by wage and hour regulations, the company also pressured store managers to keep payroll costs down and provided substantial bonuses for them based on the profit of their stores. According to some managers, payroll and staffing levels were set so low that it was nearly impossible to run the stores adequately unless they forced off-the-clock overtime work.

ADDING FURTHER TO THE FRAMEWORK
FOR ETHICAL DECISION MAKING

12. The psychological capacities that develop into a mature moral perspective (e.g., empathic sensitivity, an appreciation for standards of conduct, and the consequences of one's actions) appear very early in life in virtually all cultures, suggesting that ethical behavior is a critically important and indispensable feature of human existence. This implies that ethical considerations should be afforded considerable deference and not conceived of as a discretionary afterthought.

13. The three general types of moral problems studied by Hoffman (1988) seem sufficiently inclusive to provide the basis for expansion into a useful taxonomy of ethical challenges (including situations that may entail combinations of two or more of them).

(a) Awareness or anticipation of someone else's being harmed or wronged by a third party. Having a personal relationship with either the transgressor(s) or the victim(s) makes this type of situation more salient emotionally. Having a formal relationship with the transgressor(s), (e.g., being employed in the same organization) may implicate one's own ethical sensibilities ("Is this the kind of company for which I should be working?"). And if the nature of the transgression involves one's personal domain of organizational responsibility (e.g., human resource practices), the situation may rise (or sink?) to a genuine ethical dilemma.

(b) Contemplating an action in accord with some self-serving motive, goal, or ambition that would be unjust, deceitful, or cause harm to another. The classic example of this dilemma in modern moral philosophy is the Gauguin problem noted earlier. Of particular relevance for organization members are situations in which the contemplated action is self-serving by proxy (i.e. your behavior serves the objectives of the organization) and is communicated by the external pressures of organizational policies or managerial directives—for example, being instructed to do something that one considers ethically wrong.

(c) Facing competing obligations or responsibilities to two or more persons such that fulfilling one means failing to meet the other(s). This type of dilemma is complicated in accordance with the nature of the personal relationships between the actor and the others. It may be especially painful for the actor when he or she is involved personally with all of the competing beneficiaries of his or her obligations. A personal relationship or identification with only some of the potential beneficiaries invites unfair bias.

Another paradigmatic situation, not enumerated explicitly by Hoffman, is as follows:

(d)   Facing conflicting and relatively equally important personal values so that expressing one entails denying the other(s) expression (cf. chaps. 6 and 8).

14.   An as yet small body of empirical evidence suggests that many cultures are characterized by moral principles and standards other than the individualistic rights-based notions of fairness and justice that characterize western morality. In portions of Africa, the Middle East, Southeast Asia, and the Far East communitarian group-based concerns are more salient. Westerners need to be mindful of this when interacting with and/or judging the behavior of nonwesterners.

15.   The study of moral psychology reveals that ethical behavior is like other complex, intentional, interpersonal, and patterned action sequences. That is, (a) it has perceptual, cognitive, and motivational dispositional components on which people may be expected to vary; (b) it involves schema-based reasoning processes informed by the acquisition of prior knowledge and principles; and (c) despite the existence of some tendency toward consistency of character or maintenance of one's moral identity, it is subject to considerable intra-individual variability due to competing values and intentions, past reactions to ethical dilemmas, unrecognized differences in the nature of the dilemmas such as their personal or impersonal nature, and a variety of contemporaneous contextual influences including organizational determinants that may include countervailing pressures for both ethical behavior and misbehavior. Consequently, there is no good reason to anticipate that consistently behaving ethically is necessarily very easy to do.

II

Values

6

The Central Role of Values
in Ethical Decision Making

The concepts of value and value system are among the very few social psychological concepts that have been successfully employed across all social science disciplines. Anthropologists, sociologists, political scientists, and organizational and individual psychologists are all accustomed to speak meaningfully about values and values systems at different levels—cultural values, societal and institutional values, organizational and corporate values, and individual values....

—Milton Rokeach and Sandra Ball-Rokeach

Suppose that, as an organizational consultant, you receive a request from a manufacturing company to conduct an attitude survey for the company. Knowing something about the dynamics and pitfalls of organizational consultation, you spend considerable time up front talking with key managers and other potential stakeholders so that you can consider their expectations and objectives for the survey in designing its implementation. The senior managers reveal nothing particularly surprising: They seem to have a genuine concern for employee relations and would like help in identifying the company's strengths and weaknesses so they can build on the strengths and, to the extent possible, correct or improve the weaknesses. No problem.

Further suppose, however, that the management of this company has privately learned—without revealing it to you or acknowledging it publicly—that in the coming year the company is to be the target of an organizing drive by a national labor union and that the purpose of the survey is to identify the company's points of vulnerability to lessen the likely success of the potential union certification election. What's your reaction?

When I have posed this scenario to classes of I/O psychology doctoral students, most of them immediately take umbrage at being deceived by these managers. Surprisingly, there are often a few students who do not take offense at being treated in this fashion. Those students seem to have no problem (at least at this point in the discussion) being used for an ulterior purpose and view it as a reasonable management prerogative for the company executives to maintain the secrecy of their "war plans," even to the extent of such deceit. More unsettling, in recent years I have noted the appearance of a few students who are somewhat incredulous as to why I or anyone else should be surprised at having been lied to by the managers. As one student put it, "That's what managements do, they lie!" She went on to add, "If you're uncomfortable with that, then you shouldn't be going into this field." To these students, the incidence of shameful executive behavior has resulted in normative expectations that they take for granted. Such views do not bode well for the likelihood that these students will serve as ethical role models (Wiley, 1998) for their organizations. The class discussion eventually gets around to uneasy reflections on what else might have been withheld by these managers, what other deceits might be going on, and what kind of company this might be to have as a client or employer.

At that point, one or more of the students who don't mind very much being lied to sometimes change their minds about the situation and become more skeptical about this consulting assignment. Alternatively, sometimes an offended student, upon reflection, voices an opinion like "Oh, what the heck ... I don't like being lied to, but a job's a job." At this point, there is frequently a cloud of considerable uncertainty in the seminar room—a stage in group processes that the venerable Kurt Lewin referred to as "unfreezing." As a consequence, the students sometime begin to consider such issues as (a) the relative importance of money in our lives and what we are willing and not willing to do for it; (b) the distinction between being a full-time consultant dependent on this client and being a salaried professor with a part-time consultancy; or (c) whether our views would be any different if we were an employee of this company serving as an internal, rather than external, consultant; and (d) the possibility of accomplishing positive change in this organization despite the circumstances. These are all relevant and interesting points, and consideration of them is invariably instructive. But those matters, including even the issue of being deceived, are not the reason I introduce the case.

"Now, what if," I say at this point, "the managers had been completely honest with you and told you that you are being enlisted in a confidential corporate effort to keep out the union," what then? After a brief pause, and with an almost palpable feeling of relief at not having to compromise one's self-respect to work with clients who have treated them dishonestly, many of the I/O psychology students whom I have taught affirm their unambivalent willingness to proceed with the project. They see nothing wrong with management's perfectly legal objective or with their contributing to its accomplishment. In contrast, I would be very opposed. What is the nature of that difference, and what accounts for it?

In part—but probably only in small part —the answer lies in my foreseeing some difficulties with this client and some problems with the way in which this company relates to its employees, which the students, being exposed to the case for the first time, have not had the opportunity to think through. The students are generally of the opinion that, irrespective of the actual objectives of management, there is positive value in implementing a project that is ostensibly aimed at benefitting employees ("Hey, if management is going to respond positively to employee complaints and end up improving things, what does it matter if there's an ulterior motive?"). At first blush that may seem reasonable, but the more one thinks about it the more one might be disturbed by some nagging questions. Why has this management apparently not shown such concern for employee well-being until threatened by unionization? Why do they require an external survey to find out this information? Even if they implement positive changes as a consequence of our survey, what is the likelihood that the changes will be maintained—especially if the union subsequently fails to win certification? And should we not be concerned about management's deceitfulness to its employees who, afterall, will be *our* survey respondents? If we are questioned by employees concerning the purpose of the survey, are we expected to lie too?

Much more important, I have come to recognize, is the difference between many (but by no means all) of my students and myself in our assumptions, attitudes, and expectations regarding labor unions and labor–management relations. During my formative years in the 1950s, when my father was a union member, I learned about the history of the labor movement in the preceding decades as one of workers struggling against terrible exploitation and violence on the part of politically influential employers. The formative years of the students in my classes were a generation or more later, by which time those early struggles had become ancient history, union membership had declined drastically in the United States, and many unions had made themselves irrelevant or otherwise become superfluous or, in a few instances, corrupted by gangsters. It is not surprising to learn that the free associations of some of these students to the stimulus *labor unions* tend to include responses such as "irrelevant," "wasteful," "inefficient," "uncooperative," "corrupt," and "pain in the butt." It certainly makes sense that those students would have little resistance to participating actively in management's objective in this scenario. They view themselves as simply contributing to the overall effectiveness and productivity of the organization.

Unfortunately, however, the students' attitudes are more reflective of social biases than of economic reality. Quantitative studies indicate that the presence of unions is generally associated with *higher* productivity, although organized firms tend to have lower rates of profit than nonunion firms because they are frequently unable to pass on the entire cost of the higher wages to customers or consumers; when unionization is associated with lower productivity, it is usually in the context of a poor labor-relations climate (Belman, 1992). And, in his review of the data, Pfeffer (1994) concluded that the commonplace suppositions that unions have (a) raised wages to noncompetitive levels and thus compromised the position of U.S. firms in the world economy and (b), in an effort to protect the jobs of their members, retarded the introduction of technology that would enhance U.S. organizations' competitiveness are both incorrect.

In contrast to those of many of the students, my free associations tend toward responses like "worker protection," "industrial democracy," "autonomy," "bargaining power," and "dignity." I am also sensitive to the ways in which I/O psychologists have contributed in the past to unethical employment practices by management under the guise of union busting (cf. Chap. 12 for a brief review of the historical relationship between I/O psychology and organized labor). I tend to be skeptical, if not downright suspicious, of organizations for which preventing unionization is a primary objective, per se, absent specific justifications. That is because "By focusing on productivity, costs, prices, and profits, we have neglected the fundamental reasons for the existence of unions: protection of the economic interests of employees, provision of due process, and the betterment of the physical and moral work environment" (Belman, 1992, p. 72). Consequently, I would be unlikely to accept this consulting assignment without some written safeguards and reassurances from the management. For example, employees surveyed should be informed of the context in which the survey is being conducted; no attempts should be made to use the survey for purposes of identifying individual employees and their views regarding unionization. Of course, my conditions are likely to be moot as I suspect that at this point my chances of being retained by this company are not great. The broader point, however, is that family background attributes as well as personal experiences are related to the formation of personal values and work values (Hofstede, 2001; Kinnane & Bannon, 1964; Paine, Deutsch, & Smith, 1967).

The critical issue to be appreciated is that whether one even experiences a situation as an ethical dilemma—as well as how one defines, analyzes, and responds to it—depends greatly on one's values concerning issues relevant to the situation.[48] Our value systems define the parameters of potential ethical dilemmas we will experience in life: their extent, the particular domains of life activities in which they occur, and the specific instances. If we have different values we will likely not experience the same ethical challenges.

In the DMMA presented in chapter 5 moral values were presented briefly as one of the characterological determinants that play a primary role in defining and shaping the ethical conflicts with which we are confronted. It's time to pay more attention to what is meant by values in general. Notwithstanding the positive epigram from Rokeach and Ball-Rokeach (1989) that starts this chapter, the construct has not been an easy one to define in psychology, and at least one respected personality theorist has acknowledged that "I still cannot make sense of most talk about values" (Batson, 1989, p. 214).

THE DEFINITION OF VALUES

The reader may recall the discussion in chapter 2 of subjectivist meta-ethical theories, such as Stevenson's (1944) emotivism and Hare's (1981, 1993) universal prescriptivism, in which I explored the various meanings of a hypothetical difference between the reader and myself regarding our views of affirmative action programs. The hypothetical difference is one of values: That is, as part of a constellation of associated personal and social values I hold such programs to be morally right and I see them, despite some drawbacks, as effective and beneficial for society and thus to be promoted; you perhaps maintain opposing views. As suggested by the example, virtually every philosophical and psychological definition of values is rooted in the notion of *evaluative preferences* (e.g., Rokeach, 1973), although philosophers have sometimes used the term *interests* instead (Perry, 1963).[49] In fact, the major criticism I offered in chapter 2 of subjectivist ethical theories is that, as moral theories, they are deficient because they are *merely* expressions of preference. Consequently, as reflected in the model of moral action presented in chapter 5, although values define and shape the process of moral reasoning, they are just one among many determinants of moral choice and behavior. Also common to virtually all definitions of values is the assumption that they are rank

---

[48]My choice of this particular illustration was not accidental. As Pfeffer (1994) indicated, "the subject of unions and collective bargaining is, in my experience, one that causes otherwise sensible people to lose their objectivity" (p. 160).

[49]This definition is limited to *values* used as a noun in the substantive sense, that is, a value or someone's system of values. That is not the same referent as when value refers to the attribute of how valuable something is, which implies some sort of empirical confirmability. Thus, the statement that social justice is valuable for society is not the same as the statement that I value social justice or that it is an important component of my value system. This usage is consistent with the way values are generally conceptualized in the study of organizational behavior (cf. Meglino & Ravlin, 1998).

ordered according to their importance in the psychological economy of the person so that we may speak of the person's value profile, pattern, or value system (Roe & Ester, 1999).[50]

But even when considered as just a component in the process of moral behavior, preference by itself is an unsatisfactory defining construct because of its ambiguity. It is both too inclusive a term by which to define values and too narrow. It is too inclusive because it fails to distinguish values from interests and attitudes, which also entail preferences. In a concise and informative review of the area Dawis (1991) differentiated values from attitudes in that the former are "more ingrained, permanent, and stable, more general and less tied to any specific referent, and provide a perceptual framework that shapes and influences behavior" (p. 838). Values differ from interests in that their affective quality pertains to the quality of relative importance rather than degree of liking. The distinction harkens back to the earliest scholarly treatments of the concept of values, in which Dewey (1939) and Kluckhohn (1951) contrasted what is merely desired or preferred with what is desirable or preferable, the latter including beliefs about what *ought* to be. For example, one ordinarily thinks in terms of how *important* truth, justice, or caring are to the individual, not how much they are *liked*. In addition, we need to restrict the term's referents to things that are truly important to the person—even if we remain somewhat flexible in how we define what is important. Thus, Rokeach (1973) viewed values as central aspects of one's self concept—relatively stable but not permanent—and in the model of moral action presented earlier I have similarly placed them among the characterological components of personality. Some psychologists have restricted the term to preferences regarding the well-being of others and society (cf. Eisenberg, Reykowski, & Staub, 1989). However, I follow more customary usage and refer to those as moral values that fall within the domain of social values (as distinct from personal values).

There are several reasons why preferences is also too narrow a definition. Although values generally refer to preferences regarding desired objectives or end-states, we think of them as having a broader referent than is frequently connoted by the term *goal* which also refers to a desired end-state. Values refer to generalized end-states or classes of objectives that serve to invest specific circumstances and goals with positive or negative valence. Your general reactions to the scenario presented at the outset of this chapter were determined in great measure by your values concerning

---

[50]The conception of the relative ordering of a person's values does not necessarily imply a particular set of measurement operations. In fact, there is evidence that rating procedures may yield more valuable assessments than direct rankings of values (Maio, Roese, Seligman, & Katz, 1996), although Ravlin and Meglino (1987) as well as T. J. Reynolds and Jolly (1980) reported opposite findings. Meglino and Ravlin (1998) presented a thorough discussion of the issue.

worker representation, labor unions, management prerogatives, and so on. But values do not only pertain to end-states; they may also refer to generalized behavioral tendencies or modes of conduct (e.g., respect for research participants)—what Rokeach (1973) referred to as *instrumental values*, in contrast with *terminal values* that pertain to end-states. The generality of values is another way in which they can be distinguished from *attitudes* as well: Attitudes refer to evaluative beliefs about specific goals, situations, or behaviors, whereas values refer to evaluative beliefs about generalized end states or modes of conduct.

What psychologists have added to the understanding of values, which has more frequently been the focus of attention of philosophers, sociologists, and anthropologists, is the recognition of its cognitive, affective, and behavioral components. For example, Feather's (1992) definition of values is typical in that he "treats values not only as generalized beliefs about what is or is not desirable, but also as motives ... that influence people's actions" (p. 111). All in all, values may be defined as relatively stable cognitive representations of what the person believes are desirable standards of conduct or generalized end states. They have affective and evaluative components in that they are experienced in terms of their relative importance in the person's ideal self-concept; they have a motivational component in that they serve to initiate and guide people's evaluations, choices, and actions.

Normative and Normal Values: Dual Systems?

S. Epstein (1989) suggested that we actually have two relatively independent value systems. The first is a *rational conceptual system* in which our values are expressed as conscious beliefs about the relative desirability of outcomes, along with associated attitudes. The beliefs tend to be relatively rational, analytic, and motivated by a need for empirical and logical confirmation. Thus, we tend to experience them as under volitional control. Reese and Fremouw (1984) referred to these as *normative* or *prescriptive values*—what ought to be—and Argyris and Schon (1978) referred to them similarly as *espoused values*. The second is an *experiential conceptual system* which is tied more closely to preconscious, emotional, and affective processes. Consequently, these are experienced as more automatic and are more action oriented. These have been characterized as *normal values* (Reese & Fremouw, 1984) or as *values in use* (Argyris & Schon, 1978). All of these scholars viewed the two value sets as overlapping, not discrete. That is, some rational, espoused, and normative values may also be expressed in normal or customary behavior. Nevertheless, the distinction between the two components is important both theoretically and because of its measurement implications. The typical survey inquiry or standardized inventory assessing people's values depends on verbal report; hence, it reflects mostly the first system. The second system is more likely to be reflected in people's behavior and may not be accessible for self-report. The fact that the two systems are relatively independent (having different determinants and reflecting different psychological processes) means that discrepancies between the two—for example, behaving in ways inconsistent with the values one professes—does not necessarily imply that one is being hypocritical. It also does not necessarily mean that the measurement operations lack construct (i.e., convergent) validity.

Apropos of the existence of these two value systems is D. T. Miller's (1999) explanation, mentioned in chapter 2 in connection with the meta-ethical position of egoism, that people tend to verbally express greater adherence to a social norm (or value) of self-interest than is actually reflected in their motives and behavior. In other words, many of us are more good-hearted and less self-serving than we are willing to let on—even to ourselves. This is the precise opposite of the more frequently voiced view that "because values are socially desirable, there are strong pressures to publicly express and validate [altruistic or prosocial] values whether or not they are held internally" (Meglino & Ravlin, 1998, p. 356). D. T. Miller's more optimistic interpretation is commensurate with other indications of widespread altruistic behavior, such as the increased philanthropic activities of members of the approximately 600,000 U.S. households with wealth exceeding $5 million (Abelson, 2000) and the national collegiate program Campus Compact, that promotes community service opportunities for students. Approximately 700 colleges and universities and hundreds of thousands of students have participated since its inception in 1985, demonstrating the salience of beneficent moral values among recent generations of college students.[51] In 5 years, the number of college students paying for the privilege of doing volunteer work during spring break has doubled (Wilgoren, 2001a). Similarly, many colleges and universities are participating in the Graduation Pledge Alliance, in which graduating seniors "pledge to explore and take into account the social and environmental consequences of any job I consider or any organization for which I work" (Murray, 1999, p. 34). Of course many other examples of widespread beneficence could be listed.

A Definitional Taxonomy of Values

There are two (nonorthogonal) dimensions on which a taxonomy of specific values can be based. The first has to do with the issue of generality or domain

---

[51]Campus Compact was initially part of the Education Commission of the States and now operates under the auspices of the Taubman Center for Public Policy and American Institutions of Brown University.

specificity in which we can distinguish between *general values* or *life values* of broad relevance and more narrow domain-relevant attributes such as *family values* or *work values*. The second dimension has to do with the level of analysis at which a value or value system is considered—that is, who is it that holds the values? This book so far has implicitly considered only the individual level of analysis—that is, values from an individual-differences perspective. But it is also common to speak of values at the group or institutional level (e.g., the values of a political party and Judeo-Christian values or business values) in which the value holders share group membership or other social identity. And it is not uncommon for social scientists to study the values of larger social units such as the *cultural values* of an entire country or ethnic group (Hofstede, 1980, 2001), or of even larger historical–cultural units as when we speak of *western values* of individualism in comparison with *eastern values*, which are more collectivist (Triandis, 1995). Macrolevel values are considered in the next chapter.

THE VARYING GENERALITY OF VALUES

General or Life Values

General values or life values are usually segmented into the two categories of *personal values* and *social values*, referring to self-centered or interpersonal concerns, respectively. Personal values refer to important attributes of the person's own self (evaluatively preferred modes of action and classes of objectives). As such, they correspond closely to what has long been studied in personality theory as the ideal self (Wojciszke, 1989). Social values refer to one's preferred broad objectives and modes of accomplishing them that are interpersonal and society centered. Among the more frequently noted and studied social values are those involving power (e.g., social status and prestige, and dominance over others), universalism (e.g., social justice, equality, and protecting the environment), benevolence, tradition, conformity (e.g., polite and obedient) and security (e.g, safety and stability of society and social order; cf. Ros, Schwartz, & Surkiss, 1999).

Because general values have frequently not been differentiated clearly from beliefs, attitudes, interests, preferences, and other personality attributes, the number of values that have been itemized in the literature is vast. A review of the topic is not possible here, but concise summaries that focus on definitional problems are available (Dawis, 1991; Elizur & Sagie, 1999; Musser & Orke, 1992; Roe & Ester, 1999). One approach to developing a more manageable number of values is the rational construction of a conceptual typology such as Rokeach's (1973) dichotomy of 18 *instrumental values* such as ambitious, broadminded, helpful, and honest, and 18 *terminal values* like a comfortable life, a world at peace, and inner harmony. Rokeach also categorized the 36 values as either personal or social. A similar typology is Elizur and Sagie's (1999) three-modality classification of *material values* (having to do with physical and economic conditions), *affective values* (concerning interpersonal relationships), and *cognitive values* (e.g., achievement, independence, freedom, and curiosity). Another example is S. H. Schwartz's (1999) seven values categories: harmony, egalitarianism, intellectual autonomy, affective autonomy, mastery, hierarchy, and conservatism. A more prevalent procedure is the use of mathematical techniques such as factor analysis or smallest space analysis to derive an empirically based taxonomy. These procedures have been performed frequently on data from samples obtained from several nations in the hopes of identifying a modest set of basic values with great cross-cultural generality. Overall, the results have been disappointing, resulting in the "theoretically unsatisfactory situation of having a multitude of 'basic dimensions' that are difficult to compare and to combine" (Roe & Ester, 1999, p. 7). Going in the opposite direction, England (1967) itemized no fewer than 66 personal values concepts by which to assess the values of American managers. In keeping with those findings, McDonald and Pak (1996) found that managers from Hong Kong, Malaysia, New Zealand, and Canada did not differ significantly in the ethical frameworks they used when considering ethical business dilemmas. Their examples of ethical frameworks consisted of values such as self-interest, duty, and justice.

This theoretically messy situation is reflected in the conclusion reached by I/O psychologists concerning "the generally disappointing performance of these measures [of values, preferences, and interests] in personnel selection.... By the late 1950s and early 1960s, industrial and organizational psychologists were looking at other ways of viewing work motivation" (Dawis, 1991, p. 836). By the 1970s and 1980s values had staged a substantial comeback among I/O psychologists—but restricted to the more focused study of work values. The study of general values has remained largely the domain of personality, developmental, and social psychologists until the recent outpouring of concern for morality in society and for business ethics in particular, which are seen as partly reflective of general life values. These social forces have more recently also been reflected in I/O psychology by a focus on employee honesty (Murphy, 1993), the concomitant emergence of integrity testing as a significant component of personnel selection (Bolin & Heatherly, 2001; Sackett & Wanek, 1996), and the study of *organizational citizenship behavior*, defined in terms of values like altruism, civic virtue, and conscientiousness, as a major aspect of employee performance (Organ & Ryan, 1995; Podsakoff & MacKenzie, 2000).

One of the perennial concerns in the study of values has been the frequently observed discrepancy between a person's espoused values and his or her actions. We have, of course, considered a similar issue previously with respect to the connection, or lack thereof, between moral reasoning and moral behavior. In fact, if we understand moral values to be the internalization of moral principles, it is essentially the same issue. A modification of Wojciszke's (1989) views, when combined with those of S. Epstein (1989), may contribute to an acceptable answer. Recall that S. Epstein's understanding of values is that:

> Values exist at two levels, a conscious, verbal level and a preconscious, experiential level. The values at the two levels can differ in content and degree, as they are embedded within different conceptual systems that not only differ in content but also operate by different rules. This does not mean that the two systems never correspond; they often do, but it is important to note that they need not correspond, and, when they do not, self-reported values are often poor predictors of emotions and behavior. (p. 13)

Although Epstein went on to explore the way in which values from each system may be assessed (verbal report vs. actions); he did not offer us much help regarding the issue of which system will be activated at any particular time, other than indicating that the experiential system is more closely linked to emotional arousal. This is an important question with respect to the relation between ethical deliberations or moral reasoning and eventual ethical behavior. Because our moral values serve a directing and shaping function in our perception and definition of ethical dilemmas (cf. Fig. 5.1), it is obviously critical to know when the experiential system, which is the one presumably more apt to affect behavior, is likely to be activated.

Wojciszke's (1989) theoretical views do not include the existence of a second, experiential value system, but he nevertheless attempted to account for the situation in which assessments of people's ideals do not correspond with their actions. He attributed it to the idea that such verbal expressions may be forthcoming even from people who do not have a conscious cognitive system of such ideals, but who declare some ideals in response to the demand characteristics of the assessment situation. Only for people who do, in fact, have such a set of ideal-self cognitive schemata and who use it as a source of information directing their behavior will there be a correspondence between the verbal and behavioral expressions of values. He referred to such persons as *idealists*, whereas *nonidealists* are those "whose ideal selves are less established and/or not used in the regulation of behavior" (p. 233). But, if Epstein's theory is correct (and I do find it persuasive), Wojciszke's idealists may actually be those who are sufficiently curious and insightful to ascertain their preconscious experientially based values; these values then provide the motivation for modifying one's rational system accordingly. The rational verbal system for such people would be more concordant with the experiential system and would correlate more highly with behavior.

This theoretical analysis has not been subjected to systematic empirical investigation but it seems consistent with descriptions offered by an experienced business ethicist who has written about defining moments for managers, by which Badaracco (1998) meant choosing among two or more deeply held ideals. He noted that the business leaders who are most satisfied with their resolution of such ethical dilemmas:

> are able to take time out from the chain of managerial tasks that consumes their time and undertake a process of probing self-inquiry ... They are able to dig below the busy surface of their daily lives and refocus on their core values and principles. Once uncovered, those values and principles renew their sense of purpose at work and act as a springboard for shrewd, pragmatic, politically astute action. (p. 116)

Two Definitions of Social Values

D. J. Mueller and Wornhoff (1990) called attention to a frequently unnoticed ambiguity in the definition, measurement, and interpretation of social values. Social values have traditionally been defined in terms of whether the value inherently involves interpersonal behavior, as with honesty, friendship, or justice (in comparison with self-centered personal values like achievement or independence). The ambiguities derive from a second possible meaning that pertains to the valuation of goals and activities for others or for society at large. In other words, values may also be defined according to who is the referent—that is, according to whom the value is being applied—to oneself, or to others, even if the value is not inherently interpersonal in nature (i.e., even if it is not a social value according to the first definition). As an example, consider the value independence. How important independence is to you, personally, is not the same question as how important you think it should be for young people growing up or for all people in general. And contrary to what one might expect, Mueller and Wornhoff observed only a modest correlation between scales measuring each of those conceptualizations ($r = .39$).

The two definitions are conceptually independent. For example, an inherently social (i.e., interpersonal) value such as tolerance could be defined entirely in terms of a self-referent ("Is tolerance of opposing points of view an important value by which you live your life?"). Conversely, although the extent to which one personally espouses the Protestant work ethic is not a social value according to the first definition, it is frequently given a social referent as reflected in one's views regarding government policies, such as unemployment insurance or workfare requirements. The social issues that have roiled our country for the past generation or more (racial prejudice and affirmative action, sex-based discrimination, abortion rights, capital punishment, privatization of public education, etc.) all involve social values as per the second definition. What makes the issues contentious is the attempt by adherents of a particular view to apply these very important self-affirming beliefs—values—to everyone, that is, to the institutions whose rules determine the nature of our society. They become matters of social policy for the country as a whole. We would be wise, when considering the topic of social values, to be clear which definition is being used.

Social values (generally defined as per the first, traditional conceptualization) are frequently an object of study by social scientists interested in the relation between individual attributes such as personal and social values and meaningful outcomes that have real-world moral significance. Whereas "attitude theory ... suggests that global attitudes are poor predictors of specific behaviors ... values are important because of their measurable impact on behavior, despite the generality" (Karp, 1996, p. 115). A prominent recent example is the work of Felicia Pratto and her colleagues (Pratto & Shih, 2000; Pratto, Sidanius, Stallworth, & Malle, 1994; Pratto, Stallworth, Sidanius, & Siers, 1997; Sidanius, Pratto, & Bobo, 1996) on *social dominance orientation*, defined as one's desire to have one's own in-group dominate and be superior to other groups. It has been found related to sex (men are higher), a belief in ideologies that enhance hierarchical group differences (anti-African-American racism and nationalism), political conservatism, and career aspirations for occupations that preserve existing social hierarchies (e.g., business), rather than for hierarchy-attenuating roles (e.g., counseling). Other related examples include a significant relation between commitment to democratic values and tolerance for the unpopular political views of others (J. L. Sullivan & Transue, 1999) and the finding that readiness for social contact with an out-group member is related positively to having universalist values (concern for the welfare of all people) and negatively to strong tradition, security, and conformity values (Sagiv & Schwartz, 1995). Similarly, possessing prosocial or universalist values has been found to be related positively to proenvironmental behavior, whereas proself and self-enhancement values were related negatively to such environmental concerns (Cameron, Brown, & Chapman, 1998; Karp, 1996).

Domain-Relevant Values

I refer to domain-*relevant* rather than domain-*specific* values because many work values, family values, or scientific values are not limited to one domain, although their specific content and expression may vary among each. Not surprising, the domain of values that has most interested I/O psychologists is that of work values.

Work Values

A detailed treatment of this topic is not germane to the purposes of this text, but it should be noted that work in this area is characterized by considerable concern for defining the domain. The questions addressed most frequently are "What are work values?" and "What is their relation to general values?" (Bolton, 1980; Carter, Gushue, & Weitzman, 1994; Dawis, 1991; Elizur, 1984; Elizur & Sagie, 1999; R. Pryor, 1979, 1982; Roe & Ester, 1999; Ros et al., 1999; Sagie, Elizur, & Koslowsky, 1996). Most scholars working in this area have adopted a position similar to that of Ros et al's. (1999) to the effect that general values are seen as "desirable, trans-situational goals that vary in importance as guiding principles in people's lives" (p. 51) and that work values "are specific expressions of general values in the work setting" (p. 54).

However, the conceptualization of work values as expressions of general life values fails to specify whether work values are *merely* the expressions of personal values in the work setting. Take the value honesty, for example. Are my professed values regarding honesty the same with respect to the domain of work as in my social life? Is my behavior, when this value is challenged, similar at work and on the tennis court? With regard to my entire system of values, is the relative importance of honesty at work equivalent to its relative importance when I am out shopping? Is my conception of what I even mean by honesty the same for all these circumstances? In fact, Elizur and Sagie (1999) found that "the comparability between life and work values was observed mainly in their structure rather than in the relative importance of individual values. The differences that were found between the rank orders of certain life and work values indicate that the importance of a personal value is not context-free. Rather, it depends on the environment in which the value is considered" (p. 85). These findings support the domain-specificity effects first reported systematically by Hartshorne and May (1928) as well as more recent findings that people's rank-ordering of values in the context of their personal lives is different than when focusing on their societal life (Braithewaite & Law, 1985) and that managers rank values differently in the context of their work lives and personal lives (Chusmir & Parker, 1991). Considerable attention has been paid to comparing the work values of men and women (e.g., J. E. Walker et al., 1982).

Moral or Ethical Values

In chapter 5 I concluded that human social interactions can be segmented conveniently into three domains: (a) egoistic behavior dominated by self-interest; (b) conventional behavior reflected in society's consensual rules and customs; and (c) moral behavior reflecting higher level rules, principles, or values. I further observed in chapter 5 that moral psychologists, following a long tradition in moral philosophy, have generally conceived the last category, moral behavior, as consisting of two dimensions: (a) *justice issues*, which are intimately bound up with the notions of fairness, as well as rights and duties, and which we owe much to the work of Piaget (1932/1965) and Kohlberg (1981, 1984); and (b) *welfare* or *caring*, involving issues of beneficence and harm or wrongdoing, which owes much to Hoffman's (1977, 1983, 1988) work on empathy and to Gilligan (1982; Gilligan & Wiggings, 1987). Those two dimensions are sometimes construed as reflecting the two main categories of normative ethical theories, deontology and consequentialism, respectively. However, modifications and elaborations of both normative positions have rendered them more similar than their idealized versions (e.g., the development of act-deontological and rule-utilitarian views). Moreover, as I will discuss, the principles of justice are frequently defined in consequentialist terms of reward allocation, and welfare may entail rule-based proscriptions against certain wrong actions. Consequently, it is an oversimplification to entirely equate the dimensions of justice and caring with deontology and consequentialism, respectively.

The Case for Virtue. As noted in chapter 5, I believe a reasonable argument can be advanced for adding a third moral dimension of *honesty* or *integrity*. That is, to acknowledge the contribution to be made by including some notion of *moral virtue*. This dimension is not independent of the first two: Issues of honesty and integrity are clearly reflected in justice principles and may be implicated in the dimension of caring or beneficence as well. It does not demarcate a separate content domain of morality, but I propose its consideration because it emphasizes the nidus of morality in the character of the person. The contribution consists of articulating clearly that the domain of ethics and morality extends beyond that of mere decisional considerations (i.e., ethical decision making) to include consistent attributes of the decision maker. By its inclusion the ethical question shifts from a focus entirely on "What shall I do?" to include "Who shall I be?" (Jordan & Meara, 1990). This point of view has been advocated by the virtue theorists and has been applied enthusiastically to the role of management:

> When the defenders of the paradigm ... of the modern management orthodoxy consider administrative ethics, they most often do so within the framework of a morality of rules, which are attached to organizational positions, and ignore the issue of the moral character of the incumbents. This is intentional, because it corresponds to the cardinal rule of the management orthodoxy that an organization must never allow itself to be dependent upon individuals. (Hart, 2001, p. 135)

Indeed, the importance of virtue and personal integrity has provided the framework for comprehensive treatments of business ethics (Petrick & Quinn, 1997; Solomon, 1992). Dyck and Kleysen (2001) operationalized Aristotle's cardinal virtues in a fashion similar to Fayol's familiar functions of management and Mintzberg's managerial roles in an effort to show that the virtues may "provide a useable framework for integrating moral concerns into a holistic view of management" (p. 570).

I have previously defined character as referring "to relatively stable dispositional aspects of personality that account for relatively consistent attitudes and behavioral tendencies across a variety of circumstances." Because of the essentially interpersonal and societal quality of morality, it is not enough for one to simply espouse a moral principle on occasion. People with whom we are engaged need to be assured that we truly hold those principles: that is, that we believe them to be correct and right and can be counted on to behave accordingly (Nozick, 1993). Character is the aspect of personality that provides that reassurance, but not all aspects of character are moral in nature. For example, among the four cardinal virtues in western culture (prudence or discretion, justice, fortitude or bravery, and temperance) only one is unambiguously moral in nature. Similarly, only one of the three Christian virtues, charity or love, is clearly moral (the other two, of course, are faith and hope).[52] The attributes of character that are moral relate to values and behavior concerning justice and welfare, the two irreducible dimensions of morality (Boyd, 1994; Frankena, 1973). Just as values may be thought of as personal or social in nature, so too are the virtues that relate to them. According to this conception, personal virtues like industriousness, thrift, perseverance, sobriety, and so on have few moral implications. They are what Hume (1978) referred to as *selfish virtues*. They are virtues insofar as they are useful or valuable attributes to their possessor. But "it is only when we are motivated by sentiments favoring our fellow human beings that we enter the realm of morality" (Arrington, 1998, p. 252). The moral virtues, therefore, are comprised of attributes such as generosity, honesty, and integrity—by which I mean adhering consistently to principles of justice and caring despite countervailing pressures. Hume, who wrote a great deal about virtue, was (unlike Rand, 1964) adamant that these are not at all antagonistic to self-interest. He held that acting on these sentiments is in fact more gratifying than the sort of satisfaction derived from accomplishing purely selfish aims.

Therefore, the addition of virtue contributes to a more complete understanding of the nature of ethics or morality. Let us not, however, make three mistakes that I believe characterize the views of many contemporary

---

[52]There is nothing necessarily restricting the list of virtues to the traditional seven. Contemporary philosophers have made a case for as many as 18 discriminable virtues (Comte-Sponville, 2001).

virtue theorists, especially those with a religious perspective: (a) the tendency to overestimate the consistency of behavior (i.e., one's general character) irrespective of the situation, with the corresponding tendency to underestimate the social and contextual influences on behavior, as illustrated in the top portion of the model of moral action (Fig. 5.1). Evidence regarding the substantial stability of values, for example, is generally assessed at the group not the individual level of analysis (illustrating merely the stability of group means), such as for samples of managers (B. L. Oliver, 1999); (b) the inclusion of the selfish virtues in the conception of morality; and (c) the promotion of a particular societal agenda that emphasizes the virtues of self-denial and obedience to authority (e.g., abstinence as the only solution to the problem of teenage sexuality or strict rules accompanying rote learning of the basics as the only appropriate classroom strategy). These inclinations result in a highly moralistic (and here I use the term pejoratively) outlook in which people are characterized as uniformly good or bad, strong or weak.

DEALING WITH VALUES CONFLICT: RESOLUTION OR RATIONALIZATION?

Both social psychologists (D. Katz, 1960; M. B. Smith, Bruner, & White, 1956) and clinicians (Horney, 1950) have for quite some time viewed attitudes and values from a functional perspective. There are two broad facets to this point of view. The first is one that has been implicit throughout this chapter and is inherent, for example, in the work of I/O psychologists who study work values. That is, that the formation of generalized values preferences and priorities determine people's attitudes toward more specific objectives and instrumentalities, which in turn influence overt behavior (Ball-Rokeach, Rokeach, & Grube, 1984). In other words, one's most salient attitudes frequently reflect one's important values.

The more intriguing aspect of the functional perspective, however, is the ego defensive role that values may play in maintaining self-esteem. Rokeach (1973) indicated that values:

> ... tell us how to rationalize in the psychoanalytic sense, beliefs, attitudes, and actions that would otherwise be personally and socially unacceptable so that we will end up with personal feelings of morality and competence, both indispensable ingredients for the maintenance and enhancement of self-esteem. An unkind remark made to a friend, for example, may be rationalized as an honest communication ... The process of rationalization, so crucial a component in virtually all of the defense mechanisms, would be impossible if man did not possess values to rationalize with. (p. 13)

Counselors have recognized the self-limiting and self-deceiving potential of this process and have focused on how to recognize such defensiveness and help their clients overcome it (Hultman, 1976). For example, socially insecure people might throw themselves into their work as a defensive means of avoiding social situations and interpersonal relationships and rationalize it as an expression of their work ethic and career aspirations.

Social psychologists have extended Rokeach's (1973) suggestion to a formal value justification hypothesis concerning attitudes toward social issues and interpersonal relations (Eiser, 1987). The notion is that people who hold different attitudes about a social issue such as economic globalization or toward a targeted group such as Latinos or labor unions employ different values to justify or account for their attitudes (Kristiansen & Zanna, 1988). Elsewhere, those authors explain:

> Although attitudes may originally stem from the relative importance that people ascribe to various values, once formed, attitudes may well produce self-serving biases that affect both the values that people deem relevant to an issue and the complexity or open-mindedness of their reasoning about an issue. In addition, just as people may appeal to values to justify their attitudes toward social issues such as nuclear weaponry or abortion, data suggest that people may exaggerate perceptions of intergroup value differences in an effort to rationalize prejudicial intergroup attitudes and justify discrimination. (Kristiansen & Zanna, 1994, p. 47)

Kristiansen and Zanna reviewed several studies that demonstrated that these value justification effects occurred over and above differences in value priorities (i.e., value importance was controlled), indicating that "*values play a stronger role as defensive justifications of already established attitudes rather than as guides to the development of people's attitudes and related behaviors*" (Kristiansen & Zanna, 1994, p. 61, italics added). This is one of the reasons that conflicts regarding social issues are so difficult to resolve: People on different sides resort to different, frequently incompatible values to support their attitudes and beliefs. Similarly, when faced with some personal preferences or values that are more salient than their ethical aspirations, people may deceive themselves by means of rationalizations or evasions that attempt to "deny the [ethical] shortfall" (Litz, 1998, p. 132).

Thus, although personal, professional, and social values play an undisputable role in directing the way in which we experience social events, including potential ethical dilemmas, as well as provide an indispensable source of moral motivation, they also constitute a potential difficulty. Tetlock and Mitchell (1993) emphasized the extent to which researchers' normative assumptions, especially their sociopolitical views, affect the conduct of supposedly neutral psychological research, especially research concerning public policy. Without subjecting our ethical judgments to the standards of right reason and the scrutiny of others who are relatively neutral on the issue at hand, even the most apparently principled ethical stance can be a mere post-hoc rationalization of self-serving goals and objectives. Habermas (1990) emphasized that the resolution of interpersonal values conflicts depends on people understanding the cultural influences that underlie the differences and engaging in the necessary moral discussion to resolve them. This is commensurate with the first point raised in the Framework for Ethical Decision Making in chapter 1, emphasizing the critical importance of ethical reasoning. In the absence of such open examination of our positions as well as the other person's, we run the risk of operating more like ideologues or partisan politicians in service to their political party or ideology than like ethically responsible citizens, scientists, or administrators.

I suggest that we extend to the realm of contentious social issues and interpersonal or intergroup conflict a stratagem that has been advocated regarding the effective clarification of individual, that is, intrapsychic, values. Kinnier (1995) suggested that the rapid dissipation of the once-popular educational programs of values clarification in the 1970s was due in part to an inappropriate and inadequate focus on individual values: "Individuals do not consider one abstract value at a time until all of their values are finally clarified. More realistically, they attempt to resolve specific conflicts [between values] as they become salient in their daily lives" (p. 21). I suggest a similar resolution process with respect to conflicting social values—that we substitute a reasoned comparative analysis of the opposing viewpoints, rather than the repetitive restatement of one's favored position, which usually characterizes such exchanges. The process is similar to the dialectic method R. R. Sims (1992) suggested as a means of avoiding the deleterious effects of groupthink on group decision processes (cf. Chap. 5). But these considerations have already led to the topic of the next chapter—values at the group level.

ADDING FURTHER TO THE FRAMEWORK
FOR ETHICAL DECISION MAKING

16.   Values are relatively stable cognitions concerning the importance of generalized end-states or standards of conduct. They have salient affective, evaluative, and motivational components and guide the
formation of a variety of more specific beliefs and attitudes and consequent behaviors. Therefore, it is at the level of one's values that one must
look to understand principled conflicts, including ethical dilemmas.

17.   One's values may not be self-evident or readily amenable to assessment. Espoused (normative or prescriptive) values may coexist with an experiential set of normal values in use that are preconscious yet more closely
linked to action. Because the two value systems are not identical people
may sometimes behave in ways that reflect values that are inconsistent with
their espoused principles. This is not necessarily an indication of hypocrisy.

18.   Ethical or moral values are those that have to do with issues of fairness and justice, duties and responsibilities, beneficence and caring, or honesty and integrity.

19.   In addition to the proactive guiding role that values serve in attitude formation, they may also serve—especially moral values—a somewhat insidious role of providing post-hoc rationalizations or justifications for attitudes whose perhaps less savory origins are elsewhere. For example, one variant of this dynamic is that prejudicial attitudes toward some disliked social group are frequently justified by exaggerating perceptions of values differences between them and ourselves as a means of rationalizing those attitudes and justifying discriminatory policies and actions. A critical factor with respect to understanding one's own attitudes and personal conflicts as well as contentious social issues is being able to differentiate the proactive role of values as guiding principles from their ego-defensive function as rhetorical devices for rationalization.

7

Values at the Group Level

Civil society is beginning to play a central role in the growing awareness
that respect for human rights is a private sector as well as a public sector responsibility.

—Wesley Cragg

When the unit of analysis for a consideration of values is larger than the single
individual, the concept of culture is inevitably engaged. Whether speaking of
groups identified by a common social identity (e.g., their ethnicity or
nationality), common social role (e.g., work groups), or both (e.g., members of
the same occupation), values are incorporated within a multilevel conceptualization of culture in which they represent the more deeply embedded core,
which influences the overt patterns of behavior and their artifacts at the
periphery (Cooke & Rousseau, 1988; Rousseau, 1990; Schein, 1990).
Rousseau and Schein distinguished between values, by which they meant the
espoused or normative values that are readily articulated and the deeply held
assumptions of the social group or organization, which correspond to what
Epstein (1989) referred to as *experiential values* or values in use (Argyris &
Schon, 1978). In their extremely informative review of research on business
values, Agle and Caldwell (1999) emphasized the importance of the multiple
levels of analysis at which values may be studied. They articulated five levels
as appropriate for this domain, as well as research concerning the relations
among levels. In addition to individual values that represent the bulk of
empirical research, there are four levels of macrovalues or group values:
organizational, institutional, societal (i.e., national), and global (i.e.,
universal). In addition, sub organizational units of analysis are important to

consider (e.g., work-group or team-level goals and values), as well as units of analysis based on biosocial and social identity.

A STRUCTURAL–FUNCTIONAL PERSPECTIVE

A particularly nettlesome issue is the relation between values (or culture in general) and social structure. For example, with respect to organizational structures, Hinings et al. (1996) discussed several theoretical alternatives concerning the relation between the two, including (a) the primacy of the values of senior managers who shape structural arrangements to reflect their personal values; (b) the role played by social position and status in influencing the attitudes and values of individuals by virtue of their different perspectives, experiences, and concerns (cf. Lawrence & Lorsch, 1969); (c) the influence of external societal values in producing organizational forms that must adapt accordingly (cf. D. Katz & Kahn, 1978); and (d) that "organizational arrangements develop from the ideas, values, and beliefs that underpin them" (Hinings et al., 1996, p. 890). It is intriguing to contemplate, moreover, that the same general approach may be applied with respect to collectivities of individuals who share a social, but not necessarily organizational, identity. That is, those who occupy a similar location in the larger social structure by virtue of their age, ethnicity, sex, occupation, or other personal attributes tend to develop common values as a consequence of their shared experiences and cultural identity.

These perspectives are essentially functionalist in nature, reminiscent of the sociologist Emil Durkheim's view of social norms, rules, and values serving to provide the integrative glue by which society holds together and functions effectively. (A more apt metaphor, in this instance, may be rubber bands.) This functionalist approach has been elaborated in social science into the view that all human societies must provide answers to a number of metaproblems such as the following: What is the character of innate human nature? What is the basis for human relationships? The answers comprise value orientations; because there are presumably only a limited number of potential answers to each question, there are likely to be substantial values commonalities across cultures. This has given rise to a universalist perspective in which it is believed that all cultures and societies can be described adequately on the same set of universal values. Among organizational scholars probably the best known work conducted in this tradition is that of Hofstede (1980, 2001; also see Oyserman, Coon, & Kemmelmeier, 2002), and the contemporary conceptualization that aims at achieving the most widespread generality is that of S. H. Schwartz (1992, 1994, 1999; S. H. Schwartz & Bilsky, 1987, 1990; also see Karp 1996; Stern, Dietz, & Guagnano, 1998).

This functionalist perspective can be extended to the level of social institutions within our society, as depicted in Table 7.1. Because it is based on an analysis of the societal functions performed by the fundamental categories of social structure, or institutions, of society I refer to it as a structural–functional analysis. The values—those that are espoused and/or values in use—are inferred from the functions. In other words, I make the assumption that each institution generates values supportive of its objectives. "A social institution embodies individual values when, in the normal course of its

TABLE 7.1

A Structural–Functional Analysis of the Values of Major American Institutions

Societal Institution	Functions Served	Espoused Values or Values In Use
Family	Assure physical survival. Foster emotional well-being. Accomplish primary socialization, including the capacity for moral development.	Interpersonal trust. Empathy and love. Loyalty and responsibility.
Schools	Create an educated citizenry. Accomplish secondary socialization, including the capacity to adhere to social norms and conventions.	Excellence (knowledge, competence, achievement, and creativity). Conformity to legitimate authority.
Government (political)	Maintain domestic order and peace. Represent those governed. Advance the commonweal by raising and spending monies. Advance the nation's international goals and relations.	Fairness and justice. Egalitarianism. National pride.
Government (military)	Provide national security and defense. Advance and enforce international goals and relations.	Patriotism. Honor, valor, and self-sacrifice. Obedience to legitimate authority.
Economic (business)	Foster physical survival. Advance material, psychological, and social well-being. Provide profit for owners.	Profitability (productivity and efficiency). Accumulation of wealth. Competition.
Religion	Provide transcendent meaning to life. Advance moral and ethical standards of conduct.	Subordination to an unknowable higher authority. Belief in a unifying metaphysical explanation of all. Moral treatment of others.
Science and its applications	Produce knowledge and expertise. Enhance physical survival, health, and well-being. Provide transcendent meaning to the natural world.	Belief in the utility and heuristic value of scientific methods and explanatory systems.
Aesthetic–Cultural	Provide expressive and transcendent meaning to life.	Self-expression and artistic creativity.

operation, the institution offers people roles that encourage behavior expressing those values and fosters conditions for their further expression" (B. Schwartz, 1990, p. 7). The analysis represents something of an oversimplification in that, although the different institutions can be reasonably clearly demarcated, there is overlap in some functions and values among them. This helps facilitate the integrity of society as a whole. For example, much of the primary socialization of children that occurs within the nuclear family enables the secondary socialization that begins with early school experiences which, in turn, facilitates the still later accommodation to the role requirements of employment.

A couple of observations should be made regarding the analysis of the American economic institution comprised of free-enterprise capitalist businesses. First, although it is clear that business contributes a great deal to the material and social well-being of society in many ways beyond the mere production of resources, goods, and services, I have implied (by their absence) that those social factors find relatively little representation in the value system of business. Thus, we see the overwhelming dominance of the profit motive in the value systems of business to the detraction of potential social contributions. In other words, for the time being I am assuming the dominance of the classical laissez-faire free-market model of business activity in which the sole responsibility of business is to make a profit. But this is an important ethical and social issue that will be considered explicitly in chapters 10 and 11. Second, note that in the classical model there is just one overriding terminal business value—profitability. Productivity and efficiency are instrumental values that support it. Frederick (1995) referred to this value cluster as *economizing*. In addition, whereas I think it is legitimate to infer the espoused value of competition for the economic institution at that macrolevel, it should be clear that it is not generally a value of the specific business organizations that comprise the institution or of the individual leaders of those organizations. Even Adam Smith (1976) noted that if left to their own devices businesses would always form anticompetitive monopolies.

Empirical Research

A great deal of the empirical research on values consists of group comparisons among those who differ in social identity and/or roles. Without purporting to summarize this vast literature in anything near a representative manner, it appears that the comparisons are generally of three sorts. In the first type of study the entire human population is segmented into just two groups that are sampled and compared—men and women. For example, a meta-analysis of 20,000 respondents indicated that within student samples women are more likely than men to perceive specific business practices as unethical (Franke, Crown, & Spake, 1997)—what I would take to be an indication of their greater moral sensitivity (Rest, 1994; see chap. 5). However, the effect size is rather small and, in a tribute to the secondary socialization effects of adult experience, the difference virtually disappears with samples of men and women who have greater work experience.

The second large body of empirical research, following Hofstede's (1980, 2001) seminal work, limits the domain of values to a comparison between individualist and collectivist work values. The comparisons are generally cross-national (cf. Earley & Gibson, 1998; Hofstede, Neuijen, Ohayv & Sanders, 1990; Singelis, Triandis, Bhawuk, & Gelfand, 1995; Triandis, 1995). However, individualism–collectivism has also been investigated within cultures: for example, among work groups in the same occupation within the same company (Workman, 2001) or at different organizational levels (Hofstede & Spangenberg, 1987); as an individual-difference variable related to organizational citizenship behavior (Moorman & Blakely, 1995), and as a basis for assessing person–organization fit (Robert & Wasti, 2000). The reader interested in this cultural issue should refer to the major analysis by Oyserman et al. (2002) and the accompanying commentaries. In addition, note that individualism–collectivism is just one among five core values on which Hofstede (2001) compared cultures, including power distance, uncertainty avoidance, masculinity–femininity, and time orientation.

The third area of research pertains to the relation between occupations and values. Although some of these studies treat values as an independent variable influencing occupational choice (Duff & Cotgrove, 1982; Feather, 1982; Rosenberg, 1957; Wooler, 1985), most focus on post-hoc characterizations of particular occupational groups or on comparisons of two or more groups. Consideration of the substance of that research would take us too far afield from the focus of this book on ethical issues and moral values in particular.[53] What is of special concern for this section, however, is the representation of ethical and moral issues at the societal level. That is the issue of social justice.

---

[53]Among the occupational groups whose values have been assessed are psychological counselors (Carter, 1991; Chapman, 1981; E. W. Kelly, 1995); military personnel (Clymer, 1999; Guimond, 1995) and police officers (Hazer & Alvares, 1981); physicians (Blackburn & Fox, 1983); organization development practitioners (Church, Burke, & Van Eynde, 1994); and, of course, managers, both as an individual description (England, 1967; Sikula, 1973) as well as in comparison with other groups such as labor union leaders (J. Giacobbe-Miller, 1995), public administrators (DeLeon, 1994; Posner & Schmidt, 1996), entrepreneurs (Kecharananta & Baker, 1999), and organization development practitioners (Goodstein, 1983), or as within-group comparisons across functional areas (Posner, Randolph, & Schmidt, 1987), and as cross-national comparisons (England & Lee, 1974; Hofstede, 2001; Ralston, Gustafson, Elsass, Cheung, & Terpstra, 1992).

SOCIAL JUSTICE

M. S. Singer (2000) pointed out that the notion of justice has always been accorded a pivotal status in normative theories of ethics. For example, it was considered "the sum of all virtues" by Aristotle; in Kantian terms it involves a rational balance between people's rights and duties. Its relevance to the study of ethics may be illustrated by the distinction between injustice and mere misfortune. Misfortune refers to external, frequently unavoidable natural events, whereas injustice generally refers to socially mediated, often intentional human acts (Shklar, 1990).[54] The concept has generally been studied within the context of the second of Mueller and Wornhoff's (1990) two definitions of social values. That is, social justice pertains to the fairness or morality of a social system such as an organization, an entire society, or even as reflected in international relations, including the principles by which the system determines the distribution of rewards and resources (power, status, or money) as well as its avowed standards of right and wrong. At the societal level the most prominent venues of social justice concerns in recent generations have included such contentious issues as abortion rights, physician-assisted suicide, sexual morality, pornography and censorship, sexism, racism and affirmative action, world hunger, environmentalism, animal rights, and economic justice—particularly the role of business in society (Mappes & Zembaty, 1997). Of most relevance for us as contributors to the effective functioning of economically and politically dominant business enterprises is the issue of economic justice and the distribution of society's benefits. Those allocations are determined by the operating principles of the various relevant institutions of the social system that comprise its structure. At the broadest societal level those principles are determined by the nature of the political and economic systems of a nation; at the organizational level it is a matter of specific human resource practices and actions and of administrative programs such as those for determining compensation. In other words, the values of the economic system determine the form that the value of justice takes throughout society and, by extension, within most organizations.

Three scholarly traditions can be discerned in the study of justice: two empirical ones from psychology and the other constituting normative theory from political and moral philosophy. One of the lines of study in psychology is in the tradition of decision theory, for example, studying the decision heuristics people use to satisfy a particular criterion of justice, such as equality

---

[54]There is some conceptual confusion regarding the distinction, if any, between justice and fairness. Most often they are used synonymously, as I do. Finkel, Watanabe, and Crystal (2001), however, presented evidence that to some extent unfairness and injustice are given more similar meanings by people with respect to outcomes and equity, whereas they are more likely seen as separate notions with respect to process and equality issues.

(Messick, 1993). The other psychological line of research includes I/O psychology as represented by studies of organizational justice and equity theory (see Colquitt, Conlon, Wesson, Porter, & Ng, 2001; Cropanzano, 1993; Gilliland et al., 2001; R. J. Harris, 1993). After briefly comparing the psychological and the normative social theory approaches, I focus on the normative, relying heavily on Barry's (1989) illuminating work because it is more relevant to our understanding of the nature of ethical issues.

Not surprising, justice is invariably defined in psychology as a psychological variable—that is, as *perceived* justice. For example, "By organizational justice we mean individuals' and groups' perceptions of the fairness of treatment (including, but not limited to, allocations) received from organizations and their behavioral reactions to such perceptions" (K. James, 1993, p. 21). Such perceptions and reactions are also invariably understood to include evaluative and emotional components so that we speak of feelings of injustice in terms of relative deprivation (Cropanzano & Randall, 1993). And even when focusing on groups, the implied or explicit level of measurement is at the microlevel of the individual's attitudes, even if aggregated across people to provide a social index. Whether institutional procedures are fair or just is inferred ex post facto from people's reactions to their experiences with it—frequently just a single experience such as an unexpected corporate layoff or an anticipated promotion not received. The advantage of this approach is that it does not require an a priori definition of justice. Just as preference utilitarianism finesses the issue of defining aggregate utility by allowing each person's preferences into the definition of what is utile, perceived justice is given a similarly phenomenological definition. However, that this approach does not require an a priori definition of justice is also its major weakness. It means that we avoid proposing a standard of justice and defending it as the morally correct choice. Hence, we are precluded from taking a normative or prescriptive stance.

All of that is in contrast with the structural orientation in political and moral philosophy in which the definition of social justice frequently reflects a priori judgments regarding the actual terms of the allocation system at the macrolevel. The focus is on the conditions necessary to arrive at a just system in accord with the assumptions of a particular model (cf. Barry, 1989; Mappes & Zembaty, 1997). Those conditions include the motives of the parties determining the system and the contextual circumstances under which an agreement is reached; any arrangement that is developed under the appropriate conditions is presumed to be just, and there may be many different ones that qualify.[55]

---

[55]Obviously, it is not so cut and dry. The requisite conditions may be only partially met, resulting in *relatively* fair or unjust decision rules and/or procedures.

An important difference between the work in psychology and social theory that I just alluded to pertains to the fact that applied psychologists, in studying people's reactions to events, generally adopt a purely scientific approach. We define our task as describing and explaining the basic rules or principles of the allocation system, which we generally accept as givens. Normative or prescriptive views of the conditions or outcomes that *ought* to pertain are usually considered to be outside the domain of scientific study.[56] For example, in studying organizational justice in the employment setting I/O psychologists ignore the moral implications of the fact that the terms of social exchange are established under conditions in which one party (a corporation) has infinitely greater power than the other (an individual job applicant or employee). In a similar fashion, social psychologists study the experiences of litigants or defendants in the courts—taking the essential features of the legal system as given.

The prevalence of the descriptive approach has not entirely deterred applied psychologists from investigating the determinants of perceived justice with an eye toward improving the system. But, since the 1980s, the study of distributive justice has largely been abandoned in favor of a focus on *procedural* or *interactional justice* (Schminke, Ambrose, & Noel, 1997), which is the perceived fairness of the manner in which allocations have been administered (cf. Cropanzano, Byrne, Bobocel, & Rupp, 2001). The fact that procedural justice is frequently found to be a more salient issue in organizations than distributive justice (Folger & Lewis, 1993; Landy, Barnes, & Murphy, 1978; Viswesvaran & Ones, 2002) probably reflects the extent to which most people take for granted the culturally dominant values definition of distributive justice which is, in our society, the principle of equity or merit. As a consequence, the resulting procedural recommendations for improvement are generally restricted to attempts at enhancing the fairness by which the distribution rules are implemented, as opposed to establishing or challenging their fundamental distributive assumptions.

In contrast, moral and political philosophers and their intellectually related colleagues in economics, political science, and social theory are more likely to be using a combination of moral philosophy and mathematical decision theory and game theory to model what a just system would look like. Moreover, in the tradition of *social contract theory* (see chap. 3) their focus is on modeling the process whereby the parties affected by the distribution of power, status, or money (or their representatives) engage in an agreement-reaching process of stipulating the terms of the contract. Their approach may be criticized as paying insufficient attention to the messy empirical realities that have to be contended with in order to

---

[56]It is likely, however, that normative expectations of psychologists—even one's sociopolitical views—nevertheless impact the study of social phenomena like justice (Tetlock & Mitchell, 1993). The role of personal and social values in scientific research is considered in chapter 9.

implement a justice model, especially insofar as the prerequisite conditions for justice may not exist in a particular situation. Conversely, the idealized models of justice enable us to focus more clearly on the underlying moral assumptions of practices that we take for granted and on ways in which our real-world social systems may be deficient in that regard.

Distributive Decision Principles

How should the wealth, rewards, and benefits of society be distributed to achieve an economically just society (or organization)? In general, cultural norms are highly related to a country's economic system, and both determine the prevailing criterion of distributive justice (cf. K. James, 1993, for a brief review). For example, individualistic cultures with free-enterprise economic systems value people for their perceived contribution to the productivity of the society (most frequently by means of contributing to the effectiveness of a single organization) and so reward people in accord with their economic utility (i.e., "equitably"). The psychological hegemony of cultural values is reflected in the fact that the question I posed will be viewed by many as moot or as unworthy of consideration. In our own culture, the answer taken for granted is that income and wealth should be based on what one has achieved or contributed—that is, what one has "earned." This is viewed as morally right and proper. It also tends to be taken for granted on pragmatic grounds in that it is demonstrably the allocation system that has produced the greatest aggregate amount of wealth for a society. But social scientists have listed as many as 5 (Mappes & Zembaty, 1997), 7 (Bar-Hillel & Yaari, 1993), or even 11 (Deutsch, 1975) possible distributive principles. They are usually condensed into the following three. The economic benefits and burdens of society could accrue to individuals (a) equally, (b) according to need, or (c) according to merit or equity. Following the publication A *Theory of Justice* (Rawls, 1971), another has been considered frequently, emphasizing that (d) benefits should accrue to those who are the least well off.[57]

Those principles will be considered later in the context of a discussion of some contractarian models of justice. But first, as Mappes and Zembaty (1997) pointed out, note that judgments about these four alternatives involve values concerning the ideals of liberty and equality and the proper role of government as a reflection of the society's economic and political values. We will unavoidably return to these issues in chapters 10 and 11 when considering the moral values and role of business organizations in a

---

[57]This is the principle of maximin utility, and it is frequently misunderstood or misrepresented. Maximizing the benefits received by the least well-off will invariably require increasing benefits to those better off as well. It does not entail elevating the least advantaged to a position superordinate to others, as those others would then become the least advantaged.

democratic society and, by extension, those of I/O psychology which serves those organizations. Mappes and Zembaty suggested that three primary sociopolitical conceptions of justice can be articulated, as follows.

The Libertarian View.   Libertarianism can be viewed, in part, as a political representation of the egoist tradition in moral philosophy. It holds that people have the moral right to life, liberty, and property, and the only legitimate function of government is to protect these (cf. section on John Locke and Natural Rights in chap. 3). All else is a matter of individual responsibility and achievement. Thus, libertarianism is most compatible with the merit or equity principle of distributive justice. It is the contemporary label for the 18th century liberal tradition in western thought, referred to as classical liberalism, which is today more associated with conservative political positions. People (or their representation in the form of the state) do not have the right to interfere in the affairs of the individual—unless of course the person is threatening someone else's life, liberty, or property.

It is this minimalist conception of the state, restricted to preventing harm, that gives rise to a serious limitation to the morality of classical liberalism. Avoiding harm and wrongdoing is only one portion of what is ordinarily construed as the substance of moral action. It disregards the positive side of the coin, so to speak, having to do with empathic caring and beneficence. It also disregards the moral dimension of justice or fairness as related to human need. For example, the minimalist view is advocated because it presumably provides the liberty that enables the greatest aggregate welfare for society. Thus, its adherents reject as immoral even modest government interventions such as a progressive income tax that in effect distributes some wealth to the poor at minimal cost to the wealthy. It is important to recognize that liberty is not synonymous with freedom; liberty pertains only to the absence of coercion or intentional restraint, especially as might emanate from government. But libertarians tend to be not much concerned with other manifestations of freedom or the constraints thereon. For example, a libertarian would be quite sanguine about your "freedom" to obtain any job you desire, notwithstanding your poor judgment at having been born and raised in a situation with numerous social, economic, and educational constraints such that many of the most rewarding and prestigious jobs are now beyond your reach. As Anatole France is reputed to have said (more or less), both the rich and the poor are free to sleep under the bridges of Paris. Classical liberalism is the philosophical underpinning for much of laissez-faire economic theory and its assumptions regarding the social and moral responsibilities of business (cf. chap. 10).

The Socialist View.   Socialism may be interpreted to some degree as the political equivalent of the universalist Kantian tradition in moral philosophy in that there is a commitment to the ideal of equality, both pragmatically and morally. The moral dimension refers to what is called "equality of interests" (see chap. 2). The pragmatic aspect envisions a genuine equality of opportunity for everyone, to the extent that it can be enabled by social conditions. If that requires some restrictions on individual liberty, so be it. The socialist tends to view the liberty advocated by liber-tarians as meaningless or cynical under conditions in which some people have inadequate food, shelter, health care, and inferior educational and job opportunities. Such disparities are considered ethically unjustifiable as we are all moral equals. Some forms of socialism hold that equality can be achieved only under an economic system in which there is public ownership of the means of production, but there are other varieties in which that is not so, most notably the Social Democrat parties of western Europe.

The View of Contemporary Liberalism.   The liberal tradition has been important in Western moral and political thought since its classical manifestation during the Enlightenment. That libertarian point of view, and the revisionist liberal perspective that we now call *liberal* in the United States (Danley, 1994), join in viewing some freedoms as important—free speech, assembly, privacy, and so on (Mappes & Zembaty, 1997). But the contemporary liberal outlook also tends to agree with the socialist view that the social and economic constraints that de facto confine certain freedoms to the privileged are not morally justifiable, so that society does have an obligation to aid those less well off. To the extent that freedom, especially in the economic sphere, is likely to lead to disparities in income and wealth, it will conflict with egalitarian principles and so require compromises. In an extension of Rawls' (1971) views Barry (1989) pointed out that we cannot fail to acknowledge, as an empirical psychological reality, the importance of economic incentives in achieving optimum individual performance and maximum overall financial utility for society as a whole. However, most liberals want also to attend to the *distribution* of benefits in society, not just aggregate utility, and will be concerned that a free market also increases income disparities. They hold that a system of justice in which the gains accrue virtually entirely to those already best-off is not morally justifiable—especially when the entire social system favors those people to begin with. Thus, in comparison with an ideal of equality, even though economic incentives may be necessary to promote overall utility, the resulting large disparities in income and wealth are viewed as not morally justified and should be attenuated.

The conviction is held widely that the proper role of societal institutions is the attempt to increase aggregate utility or well-being by promoting both individual freedoms and assuring at least a minimal level of need gratification for all. This has been seen in contemporary western society as a prescription for the simultaneous functioning of a relatively free-market system for the generation of wealth along with a governmental system for the partial redistribution of wealth so as to provide a safety net or to more closely approximate the moral ideal of equality.

The economic manifestation of the universalist moral tradition and egalitarian political tradition rests on a rather radical position to which I have alluded a number of times but have not stated explicitly. It is radical in the sense that it is seemingly at odds with the dominant American values of meritocracy, although various declarations of the position can be found in moral philosophy (e.g., Barry, 1989; Rawls, 1971; P. Singer, 1995). It is that income and wealth disparities based on principles of merit or equity reflecting differences between people in occupational achievement are not morally justifiable.

That the assertion seems shocking and indefensible is an indication of the extent to which we in the United States take for granted, based on our economic system and supporting cultural norms, the exclusive rightness of the equity principle (Deutsch, 1985). For example, in the recent development of a four-dimension scale of organizational justice (procedural, distributive, interpersonal, and informational), the distributive justice items reflect only the equity criterion (Colquitt, 2001). Moreover, it has recently been reported that Russian managers, no less than managers in the United States, prefer the equity standard when the focus is on productivity (Giacobbe-Miller, Miller, & Victorov, 1998). However, the Russians were more likely to also make allocation decisions based partially on the basis of equality in the interests of preserving group harmony. The empirical data indicate that individual financial incentives are indeed related to productivity, although they seem to have no impact on the quality of performance (Jenkins, Mitra, Gupta, & Shaw, 1998). However, as Jenkins et al. pointed out, not explored in their meta-analysis was the possible influence of work groups or other interdependencies among employees. In a team context both individual and organizational performance have been found to be related inversely to the degree of dispersion of pay level among team members. Thus, under those conditions, the operation of the equity principle in the form of merit-based incentive pay "may create motivational problems that work against both an organization's goals and, perhaps, the compensation plan itself" (Bloom, 1999, p. 38).

As startling as the moral contention regarding occupational achievement may sound, it is merely a representation in the field of moral values and social justice of a commonly accepted notion in I/O psychology and human resources administration. Two examples can illustrate the principle. The first concerns the perennial issue in I/O psychology of the so-called *criterion problem* (Austin & Villanova, 1992), that is, the attempt to develop fair and valid measures of individual employee performance. A measure is biased (*criterion contamination*) if the assessments it generates are influenced to an appreciable degree by determinants that do not reflect performance elements under the employee's control. That is, these extraneous sources of variance do not really indicate how well or poorly the employee is performing, so the measure is biased. The classic example is the case of two factory workers each producing widgets, one on an old piece of widget-manufacturing machinery with a maximum capacity of 200 widgets per hour and the other on a more efficient state-of-the-art widget machine with a capacity of 235 widgets per hour. Other things being equal, we would hold a simple output criterion to be a biased representation of the relative performance of these two workers and their productive contribution to the organization. The second example stems from the use of personal history information (biodata) as predictors in personnel selection. The issue pertains to the *controllability* of the item content, "the extent to which the item addresses events that were under the direct control of the respondent (e.g., prior behaviors), as opposed to events over which the respondent had little or no control (e.g., demographics, parental behavior)" (Stokes, Mumford, & Owens, 1994, p. 4). It is generally conceded that it would be improper (unfair, biased or unethical, and in some instances illegal) to premise employment decisions on such factors (Lefkowitz, Gebbia, Balsam, & Dunn, 1999; Mael, 1991).

In both instances, the operative principle is that it is inappropriate (i.e., unethical or unjust) to base the allocation of organizational resources such as performance-based rewards or societal benefits like obtaining a job on attributes of the individual over which he or she has had no control. Now, we normally ascribe occupational achievement to people's intelligence and talents as these have been nourished in stimulating and supportive home environments and reinforced with effective educational and social experiences, as well as to their affective and motivational traits such as perseverance, interpersonal skills, and the like, similarly conditioned by the nature of the social environment in which they were nurtured. None of the determinants of the individual's capacities or performance in these realms are under his or her control. Certainly not the social and economic circumstances into which the person is born, nor the quality of the educational system in which he or she gets enrolled or the person's hereditary endowment, which is the primary determinant of individual differences in intelligence. Some moral philosophers who espouse this position by denying the moral legitimacy of ability-based allocation systems are more sympathetic to an allocation system reflective of people's differential effort (e.g., P. Singer, 1993). But effort (i.e., one's strength of motivation, conscientiousness, or perseverance) also reflects those innate and socially determined disparities that we are dealt and over which we have had little or no control.

Many people might agree with Prilleltensky's (1997) assertion that "Under conditions of equality of opportunity, the principle of merit may apply, but an argument can be made that in conditions of inequality, need is the more appropriate criterion" (p. 522). But the more telling moral issues are how we define equality of opportunity and whether it ever really exists. Economists concerned with social ethics have noted that, whereas people may indeed be held responsible for their own choices, it is not reasonable to hold the least skilled responsible for the impoverished set of opportunities from which they have to choose (Schokkaert & Sweeney, 1999).

In this vein of social justice theory it has been asserted that "material incentives should not be necessary in a society whose members are committed to justice" (Barry, 1989, p. 393). However, as psychologists we know that self-interest is a salient (if not necessarily always the most important) motive and that people do expend effort for the attainment of productive goals and personal rewards. That is, the incentive-based free-enterprise system (when supported by a democratic political and legal system) does, in fact, appear to be the most effective economic arrangement for maximizing aggregate material benefit for society as a whole, partly because it does provide for many people the freedom to maximize their accomplishments in the expectation of personal gain. In the words of the business ethicist Patricia Werhane (1999): "I believe that free enterprise is the least worst economic system, given the alternatives" (p. 237).[58] One conclusion that might be reached is that, as a compromise between the conflicting objectives of material success and social justice, the best society potentially available to us is one in which material incentives exist as a means of maximizing the production of overall income and wealth, but that the means of attenuating potentially egregious economic and social disparities are institutionalized and supported. Two related ways of doing this is by implementing compensation policies that limit the dispersion of pay distributions within organizations—preferably as part of a program of reducing hierarchical status differences in general and by basing performance incentives on work group, team, or even organization accomplishment rather than on individual productivity (Pfeffer, 1994, 1998). Pfeffer (1998) pointed out that it is the contingent nature of the reward that has a motivating effect, not the level at which it is applied (individual, group, or organizational). He reviewed evidence that group- or organiza-

---

[58]There are critics, however, who believe that this too readily concedes to free-market capitalism results that may be due to a mix of factors (Donaldson, 1982). For example, the most successful capitalist countries (the United States, Western Europe, and Japan) had relatively high levels of education and technology even before the emergence of capitalism, and they are all political democracies. Others point to the likely effectiveness of cultural factors having to do with work habits, religion, and primary socialization experiences. And governmental policies that encourage capital investment may also play a part (e.g., capital gains are taxed at a lower rate than normal income).

tional-level rewards are at least as effective as individual incentives and present fewer associated problems.

The aim of attenuating extreme income disparities is certainly not a particularly radical notion as it represents a reasonable description of the dominant sociopolitical philosophy of the United States since the presidency of Franklin D. Roosevelt. The macrolevel social contract that has characterized the western industrial democracies since the end of World War II has entailed a de facto division of responsibilities between the private sector, which is involved solely in generating wealth and maximizing profits, and the public or governmental sector, which is concerned with issues of social justice, human rights, and the equitable sharing of wealth (Cragg, 2000). What is new, and perhaps more socially challenging, are three recent aspects of the situation: (a) the explosive growth in the magnitude of the income disparities between the extremes of the distribution in the United States and between the have and have-not nations of the world, (b) the need to consider matters of economic social justice in international terms, and (c) questions regarding the allocation of responsibility for attenuating these disparities in the name of decency and social justice. Should it be left entirely to government in the form of redistributions, or should the institutions that generate the wealth themselves have a hand? This last point refers not only to alternative compensation systems, as Pfeffer suggested, but also to the growing concern for socially responsible business (to be discussed in chap. 11). At this point, we observe: "The ethical challenge for business is to think about creative ways of reintegrating the lower skilled in the production process ... Even in a period of rapid technological change, there is room for the creation of low productivity jobs" (Schokkaert & Sweeney, 1999, p. 265).

Income and Wealth Disparities

The economic disparities among nations have been widening for almost 200 years (United Nations Development Programme, 1999). Guillen (2001) similarly concluded "The evidence unambiguously indicates that there is today *more* inequality across countries than ten, twenty, fifty or even one hundred years ago. Stunningly, the gap in per capita income between rich and developing countries has grown five-fold between 1870 and 1990" (p. 247). Similarly, wage inequalities within countries have also grown in most advanced countries during the last 3 decades. In fact, the last quarter of the 20th century saw an explosion in family income disparities in the United States between the top of the income distribution and everybody else, but especially in comparison with those at the bottom including the so-called working poor (see Fig. 7.1). Recent U.S. census bureau data confirm that the gap in income between the top and bottom 20% of families has widened over the past 20 years in 45 of the 50 states (Bernstein, Boushey, McNichol, & Zahradnik, 2002) and the within-nation disparities are more extreme than elsewhere in the industrialized world (Gottschalk, 1993). "The United States has the most unequal income distribution and one of the highest poverty rates among all the advanced economies in the world. The U.S. tax and benefit system is also one of the least effective in reducing poverty.... Contrary to widely held perceptions, the United States offers less economic mobility than other rich countries" (Mishell, Bernstein, & Schmitt, 2001, pp. 11–12). This has been viewed as extremely alarming not merely by those ideologically devoted to narrowing such gaps (e.g., C. Collins, Hartman, &

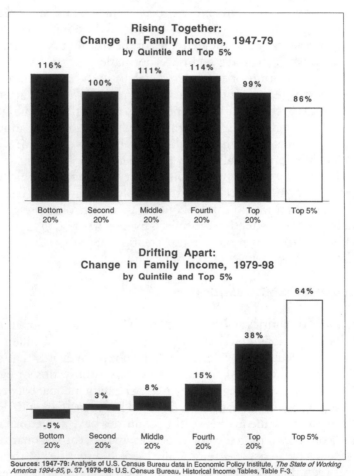

FIG. 7.1.   Changes in family income, by level of income, over 50 years. From *Divided Decade: Economic Disparity at the Century's Turn*, by C. Collins et al., 1999, Boston: United for a Fair Economy. Copyright © 1999 by United for a Fair Economy. Reprinted with permission.

Sklar, 1999) but by mainstream economists (e.g., R. B. Freeman, 1996) and the popular press (Johnston, 1999). Alarms have been raised even by business scholars such as the founder of the World Economic Forum: "Despite all the gains of globalization, there's a widening gap between the haves and have-nots. This simply is not sustainable. So it's in the self-interest of the privileged to make sure that the gap is closed. All this may sound idealistic, but it's not idealistic, it's pragmatic. In our interdependent world, you can't afford to let people lose out in pursuit of a decent life. Everyone must be a winner" (Schwab, 2000, p. 82).

One side of the coin of income disparity is wage stagnation. Although productivity in the United States grew 46.5% in the quarter-century beginning 1973, workers were not allowed to share in those gains (C. Collins et al., 1999; R. B. Freeman, 1996). At least part of the reason was due to a wage squeeze by the increased rates of profit taken, which generated a stock market boom that overwhelmingly benefitted the richest families (Mishell, Bernstein, & Schmitt, 1999).[59] If workers had shared proportionally, the median hourly wage in 1998 would have been $17.27, rather than $11.29. Approximately one third of American workers are paid less, in terms of purchasing power, than their Western European counterparts; adjusted for inflation, earnings of the median U.S. worker in 1997 were approximately 3.1% lower than in 1989 (Mishell et al., 1999). Several factors appear to account for most of the income disparity: (a) decline in the number and bargaining power of unionized workers, (b) decline in the real value of the federal minimum wage, (c) decline in higher wage manufacturing jobs and corresponding growth in lower paying service sector jobs, (d) effects of globalization (U.S. manufacturing moved abroad, and increased immigration of unskilled workers), and (e) growth in temporary and part-time jobs whose incumbents typically earn less and receive few if any benefits. On the positive side, fueled by a tight labor market and some earlier increases in the federal minimum wage, real wages started to grow appreciably from 1995 to 1999 (Mishell et al., 2001). However, that was due primarily to a substantial increase in the number of hours worked by families during the year.

The other side of the coin of disparity depicts the income growth of those at the top, most notably the managerial elite. Perhaps nothing else epitomizes for the working and middle classes the issue of economic injustice within the United States over the past several years as much as does executive compensation, which even a former chief executive officer (CEO) referred to as "obscene" (Lear, 2000). The growing enormous disparity in compensation

---

[59]In the 10 years from 1989 to 1999 the share of income paid out by corporations to owners of capital rose from 18.2% to 20.5% (Mishell, et al., 2001). One hears frequently that the stock market boom of the 1980s and 1990s benefitted almost everyone, not just the wealthy. Although the share of households owning stock did increase appreciably in the 1990s, by 1995 almost 60% of households owned no stock in any form, and fewer than one third of all households owned stock valued at more than $5,000 (Mishell et al., 1999).

between the top and bottom of the corporate hierarchy has been found worrisome, even by those who embrace the principles of equity, merit, and individual recognition. As reviewed in *Barron's*, while corporate profits grew 116% from 1990 to 1999, and average worker pay failed to keep pace at 32%, CEO pay rose 535% (all unadjusted for inflation; Blumenthal, 2000; also see Anderson, Cavanagh, Collins, Hartman, & Yeskel, 2000). Those sources reported that in 1980 the CEO-to-worker pay ratio was 42:1 and by 2000 it had risen to 475:1. Mishell et al. (2001) reported a more modest increase in the difference between average CEO and average worker pay: an increase from 56:1 to just 107:1. According to the *Forbes* compensation survey the average total compensation of the top five CEOs in America during 2000 was $275,409,000.[60] Since 1960 the ratio between the average CEO's pay and the pay of the President of the United States has jumped from 2:1 to 62:1.

A decade ago it was believed, and some people still believe, that a significant factor accounting for this trend is the composition of Boards of Directors' compensation committees—specifically, that most committees were dominated by company insiders (e.g., present and former employees). But many committees are now independent and still approving deals just as generous as those authorized by insider committees (Lavelle, 2000). Of course, many of those committee and board members are themselves chief executives of other firms, and most board members are in effect appointed by the CEO who approves their perks and whose compensation they will ultimately be asked to approve (Nichols & Subramaniam, 2001). Studies have often concluded that these managers have "considerable power to shape their own pay arrangements" (Bebchuk, Fried, & Walker, 2002, p. 1). Calls have been made for increasing the leverage of compensation committees and of shareholders in general over CEO compensation packages (Walters, Hardin, & Schick, 1995).

The typical justification for the very high levels of compensation is the principle of merit or equity. That is, that a CEO, because of his or her impact on corporate performance, deserves to be compensated grandly. Moreover, a sharply increasing proportion of executive compensation has taken the form of stock options so as to align managers' interests with those of shareholders (Ozanian, 2000). A leading executive compensation consulting firm reported that at 100 large U.S. firms surveyed 59% of CEO pay was in the form of such options and an additional 32% was based on performance incentives (Pearl Meyer & Partners, 2000). It would seem reasonable that when the company (or, more specifically, the company's stock) does well, the CEO deserves to be rewarded accordingly (Weinberg, 2000). However, although there is some evidence that in high-technology industries,

---

[60]Charles B. Wang of Computer Associates, $650,048,000; Bobby R. Johnson, Jr., of Foundry Networks, $230,544,000; Mel Karmazin of CBS, $201,939,000; Millard Drexler of The Gap, $172,816,000; and John T. Chambers of Cisco Systems, $121,700,000.

executive compensation is associated with objective indicators of company innovation (Balkin, Markman, & Gomez-Mejia, 2000), the relation between innovation and financial performance of the companies was not investigated, and other evidence indicates that the overall relation between stock performance (i.e., shareholder reward) and CEO compensation is not particularly apparent (Gomez-Mejia & Balkin, 1992). More important, as we have seen recently linking executive pay to stock price, which generally reflects profitability, created for some executives—with the apparent collusion of their outside auditors and bankers—an irresistible incentive to hide portions of their companies' debt, exaggerate earnings, and disseminate intentionally misleading information to their shareholders and the public. As the economist Paul Krugman (2002) put it, "Let me be clear: I'm not talking about morality, I'm talking about management theory. As people, corporate leaders are no worse (and no better) than they've always been. What changed were the incentives" (p. A19).

Based on the *Business Week* 2000 executive compensation survey (Executive Compenstaion Scoreboard, 2000) of the top two executives (generally the CEO and the Chief Operating Officer) of 364 companies, I noted which companies had actually produced a negative return on equity for the preceding period from 1997 to 1999. There were 146 of them—not an easy task to have accomplished in the stock market of the late 1990s. Of the 279 chief executives of those companies for which compensation data could be obtained, 210 (75.3%) of them received *increases* in their salary plus bonus packages in 1999. It should be borne in mind, moreover, that salaries and bonuses amount to only about 23% of chief executives's realized compensation (Ozanian, 2000). But maybe CEOs are being rewarded for increased corporate revenues and profitability that are not being reflected in stock prices. Uh-huh. Ozanian also reported that, whereas in 1995 chief executives earned on average a dollar for every $2,533 of sales, in 1999 it was a dollar for every $1,085. Not even *The Wall Street Journal* believes that executive compensation is based on merit: "Pay for performance? Forget it. These days, CEOs are assured of getting rich—however the company does" (Lublin, 1999, p. R1). Following a year of sharply declining profits and share values in 2001, median compensation for chief executives increased by 7%, to $9.1 million, at 200 large companies that showed an average 35% drop in profits (Leonhardt, 2002b).

Continuing surveys of chief executive compensation and analyses of successful executive negotiations with sympathetic compensation boards reveal extraordinary examples of selfishness, greed, and injustice (Leonhardt, 2001a, 2001b). As the stock market was plummeting during most of 2000, many CEOs convinced their boards to give them additional stock options, actual shares of stock (that have immediate value), and even increases in their base salaries, bonuses, and perks (i.e., cash). Thus, the CEOs continued to increase their compensation substantially (approximately 22%) even while average investors lost 12% of the value of their portfolios. Particularly noteworthy were the executives of technology companies who, like a former executive vice president of Priceline.com, anticipated the downturn in technology stocks and sold his shares for a profit of $74 million before the company's shares dropped 97%. (So much for aligning executive interests with those of shareholders, much less what it implies regarding the executives's own appraisals of their ability to run their companies successfully!) The new chairman of The Coca-Cola Company was given a $3 million bonus despite the fact that Coke missed its financial goals, because—in the opinion of the Coke board's compensation committee—the chair had inherited a difficult situation and had quickly developed plans to deal with it, which involved cutting thousands of jobs. Similarly, it has been observed that newly appointed CEOs tend to cut allocations to research and development and to capital equipment and pension funds to drive up short-term profits and secure their positions (J. S. Harrison, & Fiet, 1999).

Probably the most egregious example of greed and immorality is that provided by the 29 executives and directors of the Enron corporation who gradually sold 17.3 million of their shares in the corporation (most, if not all, probably purchased at discount prices via options) as the price dropped from over $80 per share to approximately $30 over the course of less than 1 year, from late 2000 to mid-2001, for a total of $1.1 billion (Eichenwald, 2002a, b; Wayne, 2002). One executive alone sold shares worth $353.7 million. They had created hundreds of dubious financial partnerships designed to hide the true financial condition of the company by overstating its profits by almost $1 billion; when the house of cards began to crumble, they put out deceptive favorable commentary about the company's health (Van Natta & Berenson, 2002). When the share price was around $20 in October 2001 they froze the assets of the company's 401(k) employee retirement plan, more than half of which consisted of Enron stock, "to allow for administrative changes" to the plan. By the time employees and retirees could sell their shares they were virtually worthless. (In mid-January 2002, the shares were valued at less than 60¢.) Not only have many thousands of Enron employees lost their jobs, they have also lost nearly all of their retirement savings.[61, 62]

---

[61] As of January 2002 at least one civil suit has been filed on behalf of employees and other investors, and the U.S. Department of Justice is opening a criminal investigation of the company's collapse. Attorney General John Ashcroft recused himself from the investigation because the chairman and CEO of the company, Kenneth L. Lay, had contributed $50,000 to Mr. Ashcroft's 2000 senatorial campaign. In July of 2002 an investigative panel of the U.S. Senate found that Enron's Board of Directors knew about and could have halted many of the deceptive accounting practices and disguising of debts that led to the company's demise (Oppel, 2002).

[62] The more important issue, from a justice perspective, are the systemic advantages enjoyed by executives investing in the same 401(k) plans as their employees (Uchitelle, 2002). The executives are relatively insulated from the losses to which ordinary workers   (continued on next page)

It should be especially interesting and gratifying for I/O psychologists to learn that one of the significant determinants of a company's general reputation and of its CEO's compensation was found to be its use of popular human resource techniques such as quality assurance programs, self-managed work teams, and employee empowerment (Staw & Epstein, 2000). Ironically, however, use of such techniques had no effect on company financial performance. And in keeping with prior observations (Barkema & Gomez-Mejia, 1998; Crystal, 1991), firm performance did not have any significant effects on CEO pay. However, there is evidence that some high-performance human resource practices do impact favorably on productivity (Pfeffer, 1994, 1998). Of special interest is the finding that high-performance practices for workers such as investing in their education and having incentive pay policies are associated with higher pay not only for the workers, but for managers as well (Colvin, Batt, & Katz, 2001).

Why should we care about the greed manifested by chief executives and the growing inequalities such as those depicted in Fig. 7.1? There are both moral reasons having to do with justice and fairness and pragmatic reasons (I do not suggest that the two are necessarily independent). Focusing on employees's experiences of fairness in organizations Cropanzano et al. (2001) recently pointed out, "sometimes what we *do not* say about human behavior is as important as what we *do* say. If organizational justice theorists include only economic and social considerations, and exclude morality and ethics, then it is a short step to inferring that the former are important and the latter are not…. It is important to recognize that human beings are sometimes motivated by moral principle and beliefs, as well as by economic and social concerns" (p. 199). However, I am not aware of the justifiability of executive compensation or its impact on employee perceptions of fairness, ever having been the focus of organizational justice research. This may, in part, reflect the primary emphases on procedural and interactional justice and the paucity of research concerning distributional justice that characterize this field of study. In addition, as Meara (2001) pointed out, "an important prior question to discussing organizational justice is what kind of person or organization we want to make the fairness decisions that affect us or those close to us" (p. 230).

I/O psychologists ought to be disquieted by the scandal of executive compensation because of the roles we play in developing and implementing performance appraisal systems by which most of those below the level of chief executive are held to the espoused organizational values of equity and merit for purposes of compensation, advancement, and even job retention.

(*continued*) are exposed because they generally know early on when their company is in trouble, and can act accordingly; in addition to their stock options, chief executives generally receive several million dollars annual compensation in cash, thus permitting greater diversification in holdings outside the company, frequently with the aid of financial advisors paid for by the company; and employer contributions to the 401(k) for senior executives are often in cash, rather than inflexible securities.

And from a pragmatic organizational perspective, a degree of wage compression can lead to overall efficiency gains (Pfeffer, 1994). In contrast, extreme "vertical pay dispersion sends a signal that the lower-paid, lower-level people matter comparatively less. This may be fine in some technologies and under some strategies, but it is quite inconsistent with attempting to achieve high levels of commitment and output from *all* employees" (Pfeffer, 1994, p. 52). It is destructive of the sense of community, empowerment, common fate, and personal reinforcement that most I/O psychologists would agree contribute to organizational success.

   Wealth.   Income inequality in the United States is exceeded by the degree of inequality in the distribution of wealth. Although wealth has been distributed unequally in the United States throughout the 20th century (up through the mid-1950s, the top 1% owned approximately 30% of total net worth), the disparities grew during the 1980s and 1990s so that by 1995 it was 38.5% (Keister, 2000; Mishell et al., 2001; Wolff, 1995). "In the past, Americans smugly assumed that European societies were more stratified than their own, but it now appears that the United States has surpassed all industrial societies in the extent of its family wealth inequality" (Keister, 2000, p. 4). Keister went on to explain that the reason this is important is because, despite the general focus on income and income disparities (largely because income is relatively easy to measure), "wealth comes closer both theoretically and empirically to our general understanding of well-being.... Wealth implies a more permanent notion of security and an ability to secure advantages in both the short and long terms. It is this latter concept that likely fits our shared conception of well-being" (p. 11).

   Because, surprisingly, wealth and income are not very highly correlated, looking at wealth yields a different picture of economic advantage and disadvantage.[63] For example, pronouncements about the emergence of an African-American middle class, with an attendant narrowing of the racial disparity with White Americans, are based on average income figures, not wealth (S. A. Holmes, 1996), and generally ignore the expansion of a chronic African-American underclass (W. J. Wilson, 1996). Considering family wealth rather than income suggests no such narrowing (M. L. Oliver & Shapiro, 1995). Survey data and simulation studies indicate that the racial disparity in wealth is largely attributable to differences in the extent of stock ownership, level of incomes, and education levels, among other things (Keister, 2000).

   From a societal perspective extreme disparities in income and wealth do not just happen inevitably as a consequence of exogenous economic processes; they do not merely reflect individual and group differences in

---

[63]In 1 year, the correlation between wealth and income was found to be .49. When asset income (i.e., income that is produced from wealth) was removed from total income, the correlation was .26 (Lerman & Mikesell, 1988).

effort and accomplishment. To a considerable degree they reflect the unequal distribution of political power and intentional governmental policies. For example, a chart similar to Fig. 7.1 depicting *after-tax* family income would show even more, not less, disparity. Net changes in tax regulations since 1977 (including even some progressive changes in 1986 and 1993) have resulted in a decline in the tax bill of the wealthiest 1% of families by $36,710 (Mishell et al., 1999). And not content with this state of affairs, some actual and potential presidential candidates have in recent years advocated strongly for a low 17% flat tax on income that would do away entirely with even the vestiges of progressive taxation and would eliminate taxes on investment income entirely (Wayne, 1999).

Although the United States has experienced three previous gilded ages, in the 1790s, 1880s, and 1920s, in each instance just like the 1980s and 1990s they were promoted by power elites (including the Founding Fathers) advancing their own "familiar conservative economic and demographic patterns of preferment" (K. P. Phillips, 1990, p. xx). Phillips further pointed out, "Since the American Revolution the distribution of American wealth has depended significantly on *who controlled the federal government, for what policies, and in behalf of which constituencies*" (p. xix). He went on to describe how this played out in the 1980s, with President Reagan's policies rewarding those who voted in support of them. (People in the top two quintiles of the income distribution accounted for more than 50% of the voter turnout in Reagan's 1984 landslide victory. The voter turnout was only about 25% in the South Bronx.) A good example of the role of government policy in this regard is the stagnation of the real value of the minimum wage. It has *declined* 27% since 1968. It now does not bring a full-time worker with one child above the poverty line ($13,003 for a family of three).[64] The economic metaphor of a rising tide lifting all boats becomes a cynical caricature when a very few are luxuriating in comfortable yachts (as likely to have been inherited as earned) whereas many others are working longer and longer each week to acquire vessels that are barely seaworthy.

From a pragmatic perspective the dramatic decline in real earnings has numerous adverse consequences on those directly affected such as poor health and the absence of adequate medical care (American Psychological Society [APS], 1996a, 1996b; E. Goode, 1999; New York Academy of Sciences, 1999), inadequate access to quality education, job insecurity and dissatisfaction, a decline in the growth of home ownership for those under 55 years of age, and so forth. A reported 34% of the homeless people in Santa Clara County, Silicon Valley, in 1999 had full-time jobs but could not find affordable housing (Nieves, 2000). Similarly, 41% of the homeless in

---

[64]The poverty line for a family of four is $16,600, and except for inflation adjustments the criteria have not changed since they were created by President Lyndon Johnson as part of his war on poverty.

Minneapolis and St. Paul in 2000 were employed, with an average monthly income of $622 (Fountain, 2002). The average rent in the Twin Cities area for a one-bedroom apartment was $664. Perhaps the most serious effects, though, are the ones on the fabric of society as a whole: "Rising inequality and falling real earnings reduce the living standards of individuals and families on the lower rungs of the income distribution. Many of those affected will feel alienated from society and behave accordingly" (R. B. Freeman, 1996, p. 119). The perpetuation of such an underclass, with a consideration of all its determinants and ramifications, is arguably the most important social issue facing the United States (Krugman, 1994).

Among the many possible means of addressing these social and economic conditions a consensus seems to be building around the following objectives: (a) focus on the educational system and on corporate training programs so that more people qualify for better paying jobs and to reduce the competition for marginal jobs; (b) rethink whether the decline in organized labor is such a good thing for the country; (c) avoid the quick-fix of protectionist trade policies; and, recalling Phillips' (1990) observation regarding the role of governmental policies in all of this, (d) focus on progressive programs and policies such as increasing the minimum wage and the earned income tax credit, reducing the regressive payroll tax for low paid workers, and reforming medicare and medicaid (R. B. Freeman, 1996; McDonough, 1996; J. Mueller, 1996; Reich, 1996; Sweeney, 1996; Weston, 1996).[65]

An International Perspective on Economic Justice

What is the appropriate moral response to the information that many American manufacturing companies, drawn by cheap labor, lucrative tax breaks, remission of tariffs, and minimal labor and environmental regulations, have abandoned the communities that supported them, in some cases for generations, to set up shop along the U.S.–Mexican border (as well as in Southeast Asia and the Far East)?[66] By 2001 there were approximately 3,400 foreign-owned assembly plants or *maquiladoras* throughout Mexico—almost 300 in just one of the several border cities, Ciudad Juarez, with an average of two new plants opening each month

---

[65]Regarding the issue of labor unions, it is instructive to learn that workforce unionization has been found to be positively related to *management* compensation—via the union's uplifting effect on workers' base pay and the company's attempt to maintain pay equity (Colvin et al., 2001). Even more interesting is the observation that the union organizations nevertheless also had more egalitarian, that is, lower, manager:worker pay ratios.

[66]Merely posing this admittedly tendentious question implies adherence to a moral and economic model regarding the responsibilities of corporations extending beyond the solitary duty to maximize profits. This is a model that is not accepted by everyone (cf. Chaps. 10 and 11).

(Thompson, 2001a).[67] On the plus side, the more than 1 million Mexicans drawn to the border by the lure of jobs earn an average daily wage of approximately $4—almost triple the Mexican minimum wage—yet less than 1 hr's wage of an American worker.[68]

Extrapolating from Rawls' (1971) distributive justice principle of benefitting the least well off, it may seem entirely reasonable to view as moral an economic alternative that improves the well-being of these poor Mexican workers. But to what extent has it actually done so? And to what extent ought we consider, from a utilitarian perspective, the offsetting loss of jobs north of the border? In many instances the utility gain for Mexican workers does not appear to have exceeded the loss for American workers so as to have increased total well-being. But, of course, one has to acknowledge the usual difficulties in operationally measuring aggregate utility so as to demonstrate that conclusion (see chap. 4). Moreover, there is certainly a legitimate pragmatic defense to be made of these southern job migrations to the extent they maintain the viability of companies that might otherwise go out of business—when that is in fact the case. But that rationale is undercut by the exploitative actions of many of the companies against their new employees at a level that does not appear requisite for the mere survival of the organization.

In the spring of 2000 a group of unhappy workers who were earning about $12 a day including benefits in a *maquiladora* owned by a large American–Japanese corporation actually induced the chairman and chief executive of the corporation to visit and listen to their complaints. The complaints included the workers's profit-sharing payments of around $40 the previous year—the same year in which the chief executive exercised $33 million in stock options in addition to his $3 million salary (Dillon, 2001). Poignancy is added to these workers' complaints in light of the research which ordinarily finds Mexican workers agreeing unconditionally with their bosses, and very disinclined to challenge a management decision because of the value placed on workplace harmony (DeForest, 1994; Martinez & Dorfman, 1998; Stephens & Greer, 1995). Conversely, some researchers have described the young unskilled employees of *maquiladoras* as relatively satisfied with their jobs—at least as "a temporary stop on the way to something better" (Sargent & Matthews, 1999, p. 225). Their findings, however, were based on a small

---

[67]As with Hosmer and Masten's (1995) analyses, Mexico is used in this discussion as a symbol of the much wider potential transfer of manufacturing facilities from the U.S. to low wage areas throughout the western hemisphere. Those authors also enumerated the benefits and harms of the *maquiladoras* and presented an illuminating debate between a business ethicist and an economist over the issue of free trade. Also see Post, Frederick, Lawrence, and Weber (1996, pp. 641–650) for a summary of conditions in the *maquilas* and the northern border towns of Mexico.

[68]Over the past decade the wages in the *maquiladoras* have increased. In 1990, average wages there were appreciably less than even the Mexican average (Hosmer & Masten, 1995). They are still sufficiently economically unattractive that the workforce is overwhelmingly young and female.

sample that was 2/3 men—not representative of the population of *Maquila* workers, who are mostly women.

In the past it had not been unusual in the United States for a corporation building or expanding facilities in a community, in exchange for certain tax incentives or zoning variances, to help finance directly or indirectly through taxes needed improvements to the infrastructure to sustain the community, ensure a stable labor supply, and/or improve the quality of life: access roads, public transportation, affordable housing, schools, recreational facilities, and so on. Relatively little of this has been done in the industrial zone of the Mexican border communities. Most of these workers and their families are living in the squalor of makeshift shelters with no running water, sanitation facilities, or school buildings.[69] The mayor of Juarez stated:

> The reality of Juarez is the reality of the whole border.... You have a city that produces great wealth, but that sits in the eye of a storm. In one way it is a place of opportunity for the international community. But we have no way to provide water, sewage and sanitation for all the people who come to work.
>
> Every year we get poorer and poorer even though we create more and more wealth....
>
> [The annual contributions made by maquiladoras to their local governments are] better than nothing, but really what they give is a minuscule part of all the money they are able to make by having their factories in Mexico... What the maquilas provide to Mexico are jobs. And that is good. It is very good. But it is not enough. (Thompson, 2001a, p. A6)

Perhaps of even greater long-term significance, a combination of the U.S. recession of 2001 on one hand and increased rates of pay (to an average of approximately $8 an hr) on the other hand has had very deleterious effects on the limited positive contributions of the *maquilas*. It was reported that by the end of that year 200,000 workers along the border had lost their jobs—in many cases as a result of factories having moved to even lower priced labor markets in countries such as El Salvador, the Dominican Republic, Indonesia, and China in which low-skilled factory workers earn around $1.59, $1.53, $1.19, and 43¢ per hr, respectively (Thompson, 2001b).

Meanwhile, moreover, just to the north, due in great measure to the flight of manufacturing facilities south, 6 of the 15 poorest metropolitan areas in

---

[69]This is not a fully developed discussion of the globalization of manufacturing, markets, and money, so no elaboration is offered of other relevant justice issues like forced labor, child labor, inadequate wages and substandard working conditions, physical mistreatment of workers, environmental degradation, and so on. It is obviously a very complicated issue involving third-world governments who, in competing for foreign investment, are complicit in the exploitation of their own nationals. The ethics of employment and the social responsibility of business loom as inescapable issues because the fact of the matter is that there are no substantial solutions to the problem of world poverty other than business investment and trade.

the United States are on the border with Mexico. In the first 7 years after the North American Free Trade Agreement took effect on January 1, 1994, El Paso lost more than 10,000 manufacturing jobs. The 9% unemployment rate was approximately double the national average, and the $17,000 per capita income was just 60% of the U.S. average (these data are prior to the recession of 2001). However, the shameful level of poverty in the United States is not a regional issue. Among the 17 industrialized nations surveyed recently the United States has the highest rate of poverty (United Nations Development Programme, 1999).

Even assuming there were a national moral consensus on these matters, the problems may not be amenable to solution at the national level, that is, by individual countries alone. As Carruth (1999) noted, " ... the transnational nature of information-based capitalism with its overriding emphasis on international capital formation, workforce mobility and foreign direct investment; technological innovation; and cross-border competition strategies at the expense of the public interest and collective good has eroded national sovereignty" (p. 403). Complex global cooperation is necessary among national governments and international nongovernmental organizations, and it may be that the transnational corporations themselves must be persuaded to play a key role beyond that of exploiting third-world workers as a fungible resource; governments do not seem to be able to do it. That is precisely the role attempting to be played by organizations such as the Coalition for Justice in the Maquiladoras, comprised of several dozen labor, religious, women's, environmental, and Latino organizations. They have promoted standards of conduct for companies doing business along the border and have initiated shareholder resolutions concerning socially responsible conduct in the region. Similar organizations in the United States, such as the Workers Rights Consortium, comprised of students and administrators from 85 American colleges and universities, have successfully pressured manufacturers such as Nike to substantially revise their relationships with their third-world contractors and suppliers.[70] According to Nike, Inc. the company employs 50 people whose job it is to assure compliance with fair labor practices in these companies.

Not all contemporary scholars of globalization believe that it has rendered the traditional nation–state irrelevant (cf. Guillen, 2001, for a review of the issues). The highly respected United Nations Development Programme (2000) emphasized the inadequate role played by many governments in alleviating poverty within their borders: "Effective governance is often the 'missing link' between national anti-poverty efforts and poverty reduction. For many countries it is in improving governance that external assistance is

---

[70]More can be learned about these organizations from their web sites: http://www.coalitionforjustice.net/ and http://www.workersrights.org/

needed" (p. 9). This view is reinforced by news reports describing the failure of some third-world governments to enforce even those worker protections that exist, such as minimum wage requirements (L. Kaufman & Gonzalez, 2001). Similarly, T. L. Friedman (2000) asserted:

> Creating a stable political, legal and economic environment friendly to entrepreneurship in which people can start businesses and raise their productivity, is the precursor for effectively fighting poverty anywhere.... Poor countries such as Kenya and Zambia have fallen behind in the globalization age not because globalization failed them, but because they failed to put in place even the minimum political, economic and legal infrastructure to take advantage of globalization. (p. 356)

So, what is the correct moral position regarding all of this? There are probably several that are defensible, but here is one with which I am comfortable. In the instance in which a company is in danger of failing largely because of its labor costs (as opposed to, e.g., egregious levels of debt-service as a consequence of ill-advised acquisitions) and no other reasonable solutions are available, the traumatic transfer of manufacturing facilities to the cheap labor markets of the less-developed nations of the world seems justifiable. However, even in that instance the organization should be expected to act in ways so as to improve the quality of life of its employees there, not to merely exploit their availability. From a moral perspective note that the intended objectives of such moves are not to provide employment for and better the lives of the Central American, Malaysian, Cambodian, or Chinese peasants who become the company's employees—even if, hopefully, that is precisely what happens. In fact, one could argue that the willingness to tolerate wages and working and environmental conditions for third-world workers that would not be tolerated in the United States is a chauvinistic violation of the ethical principle of universalizability. If the company's position can be defended morally it will be from a consequentialist perspective, with a special focus on the populations most directly affected— the lowest socioeconomic (SES) groups. The company should create more aggregate good for its new employees and contribute to the economic and social development (and, in some instances, political freedom) of workers in the host nation than the aggregate harm it does to its former employees. The former employees are themselves frequently unskilled or semiskilled production workers whose most optimistic prospects are to obtain a much lower paying job in the service sector, at a distant commute from home, after a considerable period of unemployment.[71]

---

[71]Following the massive layoffs of the 1980s and restructuring of the labor force, many people managed to get training and eventual employment in the new economy high-technology industries. That is, at least for the time being, no longer a viable option. During 2000, over 50,000 jobs were eliminated from internet companies in the United States, and the rate is increasing (J. Lee, 2001). Approximately 51,500 more such jobs were eliminated in the first 4 months of the following year (Richtel, 2001).

Modeling Justice

Brian Barry's (1989) illuminating A Treatise on Social Justice: Vol. 1. Theories of Justice points out that the issue of justice arises when it is recognized that social, political, and economic inequalities are largely the consequence of human conventions so that we feel the need for some justification of them. If we largely reject metaphysical justifications such as "God intends it to be that way" and so-called natural justifications like social Darwinism, virtually the only type of justifications left are rational agreements that are acceptable to those involved. Looking proactively, the question of justice occurs when two or more parties (individuals, work groups, organizations, or nations) have a conflict of interest over resources; and Barry proposed that:

> Whether we are dealing with individual acts or whole social institutions, justice is concerned with the way in which benefits and burdens are distributed. The subject of justice is the distribution of rights and privileges, powers and opportunities, and the command over material resources ... And if we ask what we are saying about an action or an institution when we say it is unjust, the general answer is, I suggest, this. We are claiming that it cannot be defended publicly—that the principles of distribution it instantiates could reasonably be rejected by those who do badly under it. (p. 292)

In other words, even though some people may be unhappy with an agreement and experience a felt sense of relative deprivation and so want more, the situation is not unfair if they cannot rationally and reasonably justify a claim for more.

Most institutions in society are not directly involved in issues of justice, so that social justice is not the only, or necessarily even the primary, criterion by which they should be judged. Primary criteria relate to the essential objectives of the institution. Corporations are in business primarily to provide goods and services to society at a profit for the owners. Schools exist to educate our children to become knowledgeable, happy, and effective citizens. Thus, productivity and profitability in the first instance and quality of education delivered in the second are primary criteria. But institutions and individual organizations may also be evaluated from the standpoint of their contribution to or detraction from the overall quality of society. With regard to the two examples, principles for the allocation of employment opportunities and the extent of income differentials in corporations and the determinants of disparate educational preparation for desirable occupational positions in our school systems are relevant justice issues. This is in contrast to the point of view that business corporations, as long as they obey the law and adhere to minimal standards of ethical conduct, should not be held to any evaluative criteria other than making profits for their owners. Barry (1989) developed a taxonomy of eight models (actually, eight families of models) of justice based primarily on two alternative assumptions regarding the motivation of people to reach an agreement and two different structural assumptions.[72] The assumed motivational alternatives are (a) people are motivated primarily, if not exclusively, by the pursuit of self-interest so that the primary motivation to be just is that it is to one's own long-term advantage; or (b) people are motivated to a considerable degree by the attempt to be fair and impartial without consideration of morally irrelevant bargaining strengths and weaknesses. These stem from the egoist and universalist meta-ethical traditions, respectively, in moral philosophy, and both are within the tradition of social contract normative theory. The structural distinction is between (a) two-stage models in which there is an explicit or implied baseline from which to compare the advantageousness of the agreement and (b) baseline-free "original position" models. Figure 7.2 outlines and compares the bare-bones features of three of the eight models. Actually, there are four models represented because Model III summarizes two versions.

Model I: Bargaining or Gaming.   This is the embodiment of classical social contract theory as developed by Hobbes and Hume. It is the quintessential representation of a family of two-stage models in which it is assumed that the parties to a potential agreement start out in a preagreement stage of independent self-striving or direct competition (the nonagreement baseline). The parties achieve an agreement (a metaphorical contract) because they each anticipate some advantage to themselves from the bargain. "Justice consists in playing one's part in mutually advantageous cooperative arrangements, where the standard of comparison is some state of affairs defined by absence of cooperation" (Barry, 1989, p. 361). Taking his lead from Hume, Barry pointed out that it is the circumstances of justice (see Fig. 7.2, col. 3) that enable the operation of this state of affairs. Some level of "scarcity" of benefits must pertain; if there were complete abundance notions of justice would be moot. The second critical component is that the nature of the self-interest that motivates the participants needs to be more in line with what I referred to in this book as *enlightened self-interest*, and what Barry called *intelligent self-interest*. This means that people simply give a higher priority to personal security (which entails constraints on one's selfishness and aggressiveness) than to the ability to aggress freely (which would involve the cost of susceptibility to the same from others). And the third critical component of predicate conditions is the relative equality of power among the participants. Because one party is not so much more powerful than any other, reaching an agreement is the only way (under this model) to achieve a mutually advantageous outcome. Given the salience of self-interest motivation, if

---

[72]Several other attributes are used as well to develop the classifications. These two are the most important for understanding his work.

Model	Structure of the Model	Predicate Conditions	Motives of the Participants	Nature of "Justice"
I Bargaining or Gaming (Thomas Hobbes, David Hume)	"Two-Stage Model"	"The Circumstances of Justice": • Moderate Scarcity • Moderate Selfishness • Relative Equality of Power	Egoism: Maximizing Self-Interest, in the Context of Others Attempting to do the Same	Justice as Mutual Advantage: Compliance With Cooperative Agreements Based on Long-Term Mutual Advantage
II Decision-Making Under Uncertainty (John Rawls)	"Original Position" (baseline independent)	The Three "Circumstances of Justice": • Moderate Scarcity • Moderate Selfishness • Relative Equality of Power ⊥ Quasi-Impartiality (see below)	Egoism: Maximizing Self-Interest, Constrained by Ignorance of Personal Circumstances ("Veil of Ignorance")	Justice as Mutual Advantage: Compliance with Cooperative Agreements Based on Long-Term Mutual Advantage
III Persuasive Debate (David Hume, John Rawls)	"Original Position" (baseline independent)	"The Circumstances of Impartiality": • Comparable Organization and Resources • Comparable Political Representation • Common "Fellow-feeling" • Politics as Genuine Debate	Universalism: Achieving Terms that None Can Reasonably Reject (The "Justice Motive"). Either With Full Knowledge or Under a "Veil of Ignorance"	Justice as Impartiality: Compliance With Cooperative Agreements Based on Their Impartiality (fairness & reasonableness) to All With no Consideration of Personal Advantage

FIG. 7.2. Three models of social justice. Based on *A Treatise on Social Justice: Vol. 1. Theories of Justice* (Barry, 1989). The dotted lines indicate aspects of different models that are the same or similar.

one party were so powerful as to be able to impose his or her will on the other(s), justice would not be possible. An agreement might be coerced, but the disadvantaged party would not accept it as just. Hume, in fact, used the behavior of Europeans toward native Americans in the 18th century as an illustration of that state of affairs. But any agreement reached *under the circumstances of justice* is to be abided. And, following the Hobbesian tradition, abiding by such covenants is taken as the definition of justice. It is a content-free definition because there is no a priori definition of what constitutes a fair agreement.

The reader may recall that in critiquing Hobbes's social contract theory in chapter 3 I raised the issue of whether such a scheme, based merely on constrained self-interest could reasonably be considered a moral theory of justice at all. Barry (1989) made a similar point by noting what seems to be a fatal flaw in this model: the boundary condition that excludes from consideration situations in which there is a great imbalance of power among the parties. When there is such a power imbalance that one party can arbitrarily impose its will, the circumstances of justice are not met and the resulting agreement will not be accepted as just by all affected. But it is precisely under those circumstances that one needs a serviceable concept of justice!

Model II: *Making Decisions Under a Veil of Ignorance.* This is one of Rawls' celebrated challenges to the classical contractarian model. He objected to the assumption of a strategic self-serving baseline condition that operates as the starting point for the establishment of fairness. He substitutes the concept of the *original position* in which the parties are free to bargain under the circumstances of justice of the two-stage model, but the circumstances are modified so that no party garners an advantage by virtue of superior power or bargaining strength. The implicit moral view is that the fairness of an outcome has nothing to do with people's relative strategic positions to begin with, so those factors are metaphorically removed from the situation by a *veil of ignorance* under which all bargaining is to occur. The so-called veil of ignorance conceals from the parties all information regarding who they are, their social position, and the time and place in which they live—in short, all of the morally irrelevant potential determinants of an agreement. Thus, no real bargaining is necessary. In this manner Rawls overcomes the fatal weakness of the classic bargaining model.

It is unlikely that we (or Rawls) believe that the veil of ignorance is a realistic or even feasible device. But it is also not so unrealistic or metaphorical as might first appear. Rawls pointed out that we may accept as fair agreements reached under circumstances in which it is *as if* all parties were in the same position. We intuitively recognize the validity of this view whenever, in the midst of a disagreement, we challenge our opponent with the statement "You wouldn't be taking that position if you didn't [have some particular advantage]." And, of course, to convince us of the fairness of his or her views, your adversary responds "Oh, yes, I would. My [advantage] has nothing to do with it."

Under the constraints of the veil of ignorance, which forces a degree of impartiality, virtually any criterion of distributive justice may be arrived at: maximizing overall utility, equity, equality, or need-based allocations. Under these conditions, according to Rawls, the parties would agree on two fundamental principles of justice. First, equal civil and political rights for all. Second, that the economic inequalities resulting from open competition among people with unequal qualifications should be organized so that the least advantaged group in society (e.g., the bottom quintile in annual income) could not do any better under an alternative arrangement. Rawls referred to that as the *difference principle*.[73] A recent and heart-warming example of the moral motive underlying the operation of this principle was the organized fight to *retain* the federal estate tax by a large group of multi-millionaires and billionaires in response to President George W. Bush's proposed repeal of it. The organizer of the protest, William H. Gates, was quoted as saying "Ever since I heard that somebody was trying to repeal the estate tax I have been angry.... [The money to be devoted to repeal could be put to better use] to reduce other taxes, which affect the other end of the economic spectrum" (Johnston, 2001, p. A16).

Model III: Persuasion.   This differs from the first two models by virtue of introducing a different assumption about human motivation. As originated by Hume and developed further by Rawls, in this model self-interest is replaced by the justice motive as the operative force. This is akin to a progression from Stage 4 or 5 of Kohlberg's moral reasoning to Stage 6 and is consonant with the universalist tradition in moral philosophy. The essence of moral justice becomes *impartiality*, the ability to defend a single decision or distributional system from the standpoint of its fairness and reasonableness to all those with different vested interests. That is, an agreement is reached that no one can reasonably reject. This is enabled not only by the justice motive but also by the circumstances of impartiality, which include the assumption that the parties enjoy comparable resources and political representation so that all sides may be represented adequately in the persuasive debate, and the existence of a common fellow-feeling among all parties (cf. Hoffman's work on empathy in chap. 5). In other words, people must be willing to be convinced by the positions of others even if it runs against one's self-interest. This model can operate either under the veil of ignorance or with full knowledge of one's position. Given

---

[73]The difference principle is a dynamic not a static criterion. It is not met if we improve the lot of the least fortunate by having them rise above another group—that would then become the least advantaged.

the salience of the justice motive in this model (desire for fairness, reasonableness, and impartiality), the veil becomes moot.

ADDING FURTHER TO THE FRAMEWORK
FOR ETHICAL DECISION MAKING

20. A structural–functional perspective on values formation suggests that the particulars of our upbringing, social status and identity, occupation, organizational position, and so on result in individual differences in values, attitudes, and beliefs, including notions of what is just. Hence, people are likely to differ in their perceptions of potential ethical dilemmas. That is why devices such as ethical codes and casebooks are helpful despite their limitations; they promote uniform standards of evaluation.

21. From a moral perspective a convincing argument can be made for the superiority of the distributive justice criteria of equality or need over merit or equity. Conversely, from a historic and empirical perspective one cannot fail to recognize the aggregate economic utility of the merit principle. The latter is consonant with our cultural norms, the character of our economic system, and with the nature of human motivation. However, it also seems clear that merit is frequently used as a justification for the maintenance and promotion of morally questionable social inequities and extreme disparities in income and wealth. A reasonable compromise between the often conflicting objectives of individual economic success and social justice is the acceptance of material incentives as a means of maximizing efficiency and the production of income and wealth, while also promoting social programs, government policies, corporate actions, and international arrangements that will attenuate the resulting extreme disparities—primarily by enhancing the capabilities of the have-nots to contribute to and share in the rewards.

22. The functioning of most institutions of society as well as individual organizations can be evaluated from an ethical standpoint, for example, with respect to their promotion of or detraction from social justice, irrespective of their primary functions. This is especially true of business—most especially large corporations—if for no other reason than because of their extraordinary power and dominance in our society. As professionals who contribute to the maintenance and effectiveness of those organizations, these ethical considerations are legitimate matters of concern regarding our personal decision to participate in a particular organization.

8

Values and Value Conflicts in the Professions

Why is it that experts primarily teach *techniques* to young professionals, while ignoring the values that have sustained the quests of so many creative geniuses?

—Gardner, Csikszentmihalyi, & Damon

This chapter and the remainder of Part II deal with professional values, values conflicts, and role conflicts that are attributable to the complex nature of any profession and the settings in which it is performed. Some reflect strains within the field of psychology and the sciences in general; some characterize the interface between the values of psychology and those of business, which is, of course, the meeting ground on which I/O psychology is practiced. First, I discuss the professions in general.

It is quite obvious that the particular ethical issues and dilemmas that arise in the practice of medicine, law, psychology, anthropology, policing, accountancy, and so on are very different. The knowledge bases of the fields, as well as the nature of the services provided and their setting, the degree of autonomy enjoyed by the practitioners as sanctioned by society, and the norms and values characterizing each are all rather different. Consequently, the ethical guidelines adopted by members of these occupations are distinctly different. Accordingly, there are some scholars who believe that a consideration of professional ethics must be particular to each profession— or occupation aspiring to the status of a profession. Supporting that view is research indicating that the values of those in different professions, even at the time of their graduate training, are different (J. T. Edwards, Nalbandian, & Wedel, 1981) and that different professional groups within the same employing organization may experience values conflicts (Davidson, 1985; DeLeon, 1994). But there are some scholars who emphasize that there is a common underlying set of norms and values by which all professional practice may be linked. This view holds that professional ethics are built on a core of common or personal morality that transcends occupational distinctions. For example, Brien (1998) focused on trust as the essential ingredient in all professional relationships. And "While formal codes of conduct can sometimes be a useful guide, developing those traits of character that are particularly suited to the lawyer's role is at the core of what we ought to mean by professional ethics" (Wilkins, 1996, p. 250). Consistent with this cross-disciplinary view, Wilkins went on to describe the development of a single ethics course for both law students and medical students at Harvard that is being expanded to include students of business and government as well.

Although it is not necessary for us to take a stand on this issue, it does implicitly raise a point that is of some value to consider. If there is anything at all to be said for the conceptualization of a generic approach to professional ethics—or more likely, in my opinion, professional values—one should at least be able to specify more or less unambiguously what are the professions that rest on this common moral bedrock. Although there are some social theorists (e.g., Wilkins) who are of the opinion that it is impossible to generate a set of ahistorical criteria for designating some occupations as professions and not others, a great deal of work of that sort has been conducted by sociologists who study the occupational structure and professions. I assume that the reader will agree with me that psychology, including I/O psychology, is in fact a profession, so it is important to explore what that means—including what values inure to the field by virtue of that status.

WHAT IS A PROFESSION?

It is not coincidental that the origin of the word *profession* is theological. In the Middle Ages it denoted a "declaration, promise or vow made by one entering a religious order" (Kimball, 1992, p. 19). Gradually, it came to stand for the group of people who made the vow, that is , a particular order of monks, nuns, or other professed people. By the 15th and 16th centuries the term had expanded to include the learned professions—not only theology but also law, medicine, and education. By far the most esteemed among the four was theology; education sort of snuck in the back door by virtue of the medieval universities being a site of scholarship regarding the first three. That is pretty much how things stood until the colonization of the new world. In the 17th century and early 18th century in the colonies, ministers were most esteemed, and it is they who imparted special dignity to the notion of a profession as referring to a "particular calling" with an "ethic of selfless service" (Kimball, 1992, p. 302). By the late 18th century in America politics and the law became the preeminent professions. However, it was an idealized politics having to do with the noble enterprise of developing a legal and political system by which to order society (think of the greatly esteemed founding fathers: Washington, Jefferson, Madison, Adams, Franklin, etc.).

From the late 19th century and into the early years of the 20th century law and politics declined in status (perhaps as a consequence of the civil war), education greatly increased in status (being a professor was a very highly esteemed occupation), and science entered the picture—the natural sciences, not social science. The university as the nidus of scientific scholarship and activity served to reinforce the status of education and to merge the identification of science and learning. Medicine also increased greatly in status, as an integral aspect of biological science. In fact, the continued supremacy of medicine resulted in its being held as a model of "the true professional ideal" in America during the 20th century (Kimball, 1992, p. 308). Throughout the 20th century scholars flirted with the idea of whether business had become a profession. Louis Brandeis (1914/1971) thought that it already had, and others such as R. H. Tawney (1920) and Talcott Parsons (1937) thought that it had not yet but ought to become so—to attenuate its acquisitiveness and self-interest with the altruistic service character of the professions. But whether an occupation is a profession is not simply a matter of its being anointed as such; if it were, attention would certainly shift to whoever had acquired the authority to perform the ritual. After considering the attributes that exemplify professions we will be in a better position to consider the extent to which business satisfies those criteria and the role that the professionalization of management plays concerning the putative social responsibilities of business.

The last half of the 20th century witnessed a rapid increase both in the professionalization of occupations, with more and more of them claiming that mantle, as well as an explosion in scholarship devoted to the topic. The study of the professions is now a full-fledged sub-specialization in sociology. It was during this time that the notion of a "true professional ideal" developed denoting "a dignified vocation practiced by 'professionals' who professed selfless and contractual service, membership in a strong association, and functional expertise modeled on the natural sciences" (Kimball, 1992, p. 303). The fruits of that scholarship will help us understand better what is meant by a profession.

Attributes of Professions[74]

The historical evolution of what Kimball (1992, p. 303) referred to as "the true professional ideal" is more frequently characterized less grandilo-

---

[74]This discussion draws substantially on the work of R. T. Hall (1975), Lynn (1965), Etzioni (1969), Elliott (1972), and W. J. Goode (1960, 1969).

quently by sociologists as "the professional model" (e.g., R. T. Hall, 1975, p. 72).[75] The ideal is a distillation of characteristics by which occupations that are professions may presumably be distinguished from those that are not (Freidson, 1986; Haber, 1991). It is important to recognize, however, that it is indeed a model—that is, it is a prototypic representation that may not be fulfilled by every profession. And the attributes are not "all-or-none": Professions will vary in the extent to which they meet each of the components. "There is no absolute difference between professional and other kinds of occupational behavior, but only relative differences with respect to certain attributes common to all occupational behavior" (Barber, 1965, p. 17). Some of the components are structural in nature, referring to the social organization of a profession and/or its position in society; some are functional, referring to the nature of professional activities; and some refer to the characteristics or attitudes of the members of a profession themselves. Almost all can be viewed from a values perspective, reflecting the profession's generalized preferences concerning goals and objectives as well as the means of achieving them.

Point 1: Professions Are Organized Around a Systematic Theoretical Body of Knowledge

The nature of the theories may be either pure, as with scientific inquiry, or pragmatic, as with the application of knowledge. Some professional occupations are primarily pure and research oriented, such as cosmology; some are largely practice oriented, such as dentistry or the clergy; and some are comprised of significant components of both, like medicine and I/O psychology. The relative balance doesn't matter with respect to the designation as a profession. "If some occupations become professions by developing an intellectual interest, others do it by becoming more practical" (Hughes, 1965, p. 6). Within those professions that have significant pure and applied components, some members may be involved in both sets of activities, but most adherents tend to be involved primarily in one or the other. For example, practitioners tend not to do research; only about 10% of the published scientific research in I/O psychology is authored by organizationally based practitioners (Sackett, Callahan, DeMeuse, Ford, & Kozlowski, 1986).

---

[75]The positive—some would say idealized—view of professions characterized by the professional ideal, the professional model, or the service model is offset by a negative and rather cynical—some would say realistic—view. In this power-oriented conception, professions are simply economically successful monopolies that have managed to persuade society to honor their claims for special privileges (Brien, 1998). That is, whatever altruistic public service may exist is simply a byproduct of the primary motivation which is self-interest. It seems to me that one can accept the ubiquitous existence of a certain amount of self-interest (a modified *psychological* or *rational egoism*) without adopting such a one-sided unflattering portrait. We can take mixed motives as the expected basis for most complex human behavior.

Point 2: Society Confers Legitimate Authority to the Profession Over the Interpretation and Application of Knowledge in Its Domain in Providing Services to Clients

A major implication of a profession's being organized around a specialized body of knowledge is the presumption that clients are at best incompletely and inadequately informed about the best course of action in the profession's domain, and so they depend on the professional's judgment. Another important aspect of this attribute is that the profession is accepted as the arbiter of any disputes over theoretical or technical matters within its domain.

Thus, for example, the AERA, APA, and NCME (1991) *Standards for Educational and Psychological Testing* and SIOP's (1987) *Principles for the Validation and Use of Personnel Selection Procedures* are afforded great deference in legal deliberations concerning alleged discrimination involving employment testing. An important aspect of this attribute is that the professional implicitly asks to be trusted by those whom he or she serves (Hughes, 1965). In contrast to the marketplace in which the prevailing ethos might be caveat emptor, within the sphere of professional practice it is *credat emptor.*

Point 3: Society Also Confers Considerable Formal and Informal Sanction Power to the Profession

This is reflected in the substantial role that professions play in determining the educational and training requirements necessary to enter the profession, including providing input into the standards for licensing and accreditation. R. T. Hall (1975) also pointed out that, to the extent professional–client communications are privileged, it not only protects the right of the client but also asserts the authority of the professional. The extent to which some form of accreditation characterizes professions and fields aspiring to that status is indicated by the finding that more than 1,000 fields have professional certifications (McKillip & Owens, 2000).

Point 4: Professions Generally Have Some Form of Ethical Code as a Guide to Appropriate Action Regarding Clients, Colleagues, and the Public at Large

Concomitant with a code is a set of administrative regulations by which the code is putatively enforced—for example, through the agency of a professional association, such as the APA. However, there is considerable disagreement among scholars and social critics, practitioners of the professions, and public advocates concerning the extent to which professions may be relied on to sanction the behavior of their members. R. T. Hall (1975) suggested that the norm of professional self-regulation does not

work all that well because of the absence of observability of much professional work, by which he meant observation by those who are capable of
judging its appropriateness. In any event, the development of an ethical
code is one of the clearest specific indications of an occupation or subfield of
specialization aspiring to the status of profession.

Point 5: Professions Have Their Own Culture of Values, Norms, and Professional Opinion

These serve to present a relatively "uniform face" to the public regarding
such matters as standards for training and admission to the profession, as
well as structuring the nature of client–professional relationships. The
culture is generally represented by a formal association. In fact, the presence
of such a professional association may be taken as an indicator that an
occupation has reached the status of a profession (Lounsbury, 2002). One
interesting aspect of professional culture has to do with the relative degree
of specialized knowledge and terminology that characterizes the field. Such
specialization serves to mark the distinctiveness of a profession from the rest
of society, thus enhancing its status, while accentuating its separation.
Professionals sometimes exacerbate the social consequences of that
separation by adopting an attitude of superiority. Elliott (1972) pointed out
that professionals tend to justify their activities as not merely useful but
"right." The authority conferred on a profession combined with that sense
of separation and superiority may set up a professional group as a potential
object of public hostility—especially if its members are particularly well
paid. Think, for example, of the anger frequently directed toward medical
doctors and of the many hostile lawyer jokes.

Point 6: Professionals Have a Professional Attitude Toward Their Work

We ordinarily think of a professional as one who is intrinsically motivated
by the inherent nature of the work, with a high degree of personal involvement in his or her activities and a sense of commitment and obligation to
those served. A professional attitude also involves a sense of identification
with one's colleagues through membership in professional organizations and
personal interaction. This serves to solidify a degree of cohesion to the field,
as reflected in a common culture, as already noted.

Point 7: The Service Provided by the Profession Is Deemed Important by Society

This attribute is implied by several of those preceding. It underlies the
authority and power conferred on the profession by virtue of its unique

capabilities. The essentially monopolistic control over a particular domain of knowledge and its application would not mean much if they were not considered to be important.

Point 8: Professionals Typically Undergo a Longer Period of Socialization Than Is Associated With Other Occupations

The specialized education and training that is required to master the knowledge domain and its applications means a longer period of time in professional or graduate school, as well as in some form of internship. Moreover, professional knowledge acquisition does not end with graduate education: It is a lifelong process. An often overlooked aspect of these educational experiences is the process of occupational socialization that occurs frequently. The common socialization experiences contribute to a substantial degree of commonality of attitude and outlook among professionals in the same field, perpetuating the profession's culture. Elliott (1972) emphasized that "through socialization, students acquire built-in regulatory mechanisms. These can be measured as the norms, values and attitudes they hold" (p. 89). These homogenizing forces can be overstated however: Of course, individuals' outlooks may differ in many ways. Moreover, the degree of subspecialization that marks many ostensibly uniform professions (the APA, e.g., has 55 divisions) as well as the differing role requirements and values associated with the "theoretical" versus the "practice" dimensions of a field assure a certain heterogeneity of outlook.[76]

Point 9: The Power and Responsibility of a Profession Extend Beyond Its Direct Clients to Society at Large

This is a consequence of the public's relative ignorance regarding the technical expertise nearly monopolized by the profession (cf. Point 2), the profession's power to control its own standards and discipline its own members (Points 3 and 4), the attitude of professional responsibility assumed to be characteristic of its members (Point 6), and the importance of the service provided in the eyes of society (Point 7). This extension of power is reflected, for example, in the influence wielded by a profession over the shaping of legislation concerning the profession itself. Hughes (1965) described the attribute well:

---

[76]The ever-finer gradations by which professions have become subspecialized raises the interesting question as to what are the boundaries of a particular profession. For example, the salient knowledge domain as well as the norms, values, attitudes, and ethical concerns of an emergency room doctor in a public hospital and a dermatologist on Park Avenue (New York City) who does not accept medical insurance reimbursements vary considerably. The same may be said regarding a comparison of experimental cognitive psychologists, as opposed to colleagues in clinical or I/O psychology. Whether there is (or should be) a common core curriculum in psychology has long been a matter of some dispute (Benjamin, 2001, 2002).

Physicians consider it their prerogative to define the nature of disease and of health, and to determine how medical services ought to be distributed and paid for. Social workers are not content to develop a technique of case work; they concern themselves with social legislation. Every profession considers itself the proper body to set the terms in which some aspect of society, life or nature is to be thought of, and to define the general lines, or even the details, of public policy concerning it. The mandate to do so is granted more fully to some professions than to others; in time of crisis it may be questioned even with regard to the respected and powerful professions. (p. 3)

The recent role of accountants in the Enron, WorldCom, and Global Crossing scandals (and others) has precipitated a "time of crisis" for that profession, resulting in a questioning of their mandate to report and audit corporate finances. As a consequence, additional external regulation has been introduced by the government, in response to the public outcry, despite the 30-year trend of business deregulation (Uchitelle, 2002c).

Point 10: A Profession Is Typically a Lifelong Commitment for Its Members

In contrast to many occupations in which changing jobs is common, the length of training and preparation as well as the socialization and identification with the field that takes place usually makes a profession the terminal occupation for members. The fact that professionals are generally well paid probably also contributes to occupational longevity. R. T. Hall (1975) made the point that these factors tend to render the professional incapable of changing occupations because of relatively fixed skills and attitudes. A major partial exception to this observation—especially germane to I/O psychology—pertains to professionals who are employed in large organizations and who advance hierarchically by becoming administrators or managers and largely abandoning their professional functions. That suggests the next important topic.

PROFESSIONAL WORK SETTINGS

Professionals work in four primary settings: (a) as individual practitioners, (b) as members of autonomous professional organizations, (c) in heteronomous professional organizations, or (d) in professional departments in larger organizations (R. T. Hall, 1975). The individual practitioner, as exemplified by a one-person law practice, an independent psychotherapist, your neighborhood dentist, or an I/O psychology consultant, is the prototypic ideal type of professional. However, not much is known empirically about the nature of this work arrangement across the professions in comparison with the other three. That is probably because most professionals are employed in organizational settings (Freidson, 1986). For our purposes, probably the most striking fact about being an independent private practitioner is its potential isolation when faced with values conflicts and potential ethical dilemmas. On those occasions the wise solo practitioner will attempt to make full use of informal personal consultation with colleague–friends and other resources available through the appropriate professional associations. For example, the Ethics Committee of the APA welcomes proactive letters of inquiry seeking advice.

Autonomous professional organizations, such as an I/O psychology consulting firm, are settings in which professionals establish the organization's structure, norms, policies, and so on—presumably in accord with the culture of the profession and the particular expectations of the members. Thus, the goals of the organization are essentially those of the professionals employed. It may be impossible to generalize much about these work settings, which may range from a pair of consulting I/O psychologists to a private medical clinic comprised of 10 doctors to a firm of 50 consulting engineers with almost as many draftspersons to a Wall Street law firm of several hundred attorneys, paralegals, and other support staff. Hypothetically, at least, in comparison with the single practitioner these arrangements permit professional collaboration and consultation, the advantage of performance standards being set by fellow professionals, and greater observability of potential ethical transgressions. However, R. T. Hall (1975) reported conflicting findings from studies of law firms and medical clinics regarding the effectiveness of the self-regulation systems. Another matter that is frequently a salient issue for the principals of such consulting firms is the pressure for revenue flow due to having established a considerable level of overhead. Although it is not an infrequent topic at social gatherings, I am not aware of any extensive or systematic published material in I/O psychology regarding the potential impact of these pressures on professional concerns, such as choice of clients or projects, methodologies employed, substance of findings, or integrity of evaluations reported to clients. Anecdotal evidence suggests that the pressure for billable hours frequently conflicts with professional ideals and is especially discomforting to young practitioner–consultants.

Heteronomous organizations, in which professional employees are subordinated to an overall administrative structure and granted little autonomy, represent a structure typified by teachers in secondary schools, social workers in welfare agencies, or librarians in libraries. It is a form of organizational work setting that is not (to my knowledge) represented in the field of I/O psychology.

In contrast, many I/O psychologists are employed in professional (human resources) departments in large private-sector organizations or governmental agencies, as are chemists in pharmaceutical companies, librarians in law firms, engineers in manufacturing companies, and economists in brokerage houses—to name just a few other examples. This is an arrangement that has considerable potential for conflict related to the disjunction between professional and organizational norms and values—even to the point of potentially precipitating organizationally deviant (i.e., maladaptive) behavior by the professional (Raelin, 1984, 1989, 1994).[77] Consequently, it has been the object of study by organizational scholars and social theorists for at least 50 years (Parsons, 1954).

Professional–Organizational Conflict

The predominant view of the nature of the relation between professionals and the large business organizations in which they are employed has been one of inevitable conflict, as illustrated by W. Kornhauser's (1962) well-known research documenting the adverse effects on scientists of working in an industrial setting. Typical of this line of thought, Etzioni (1969) and Hughes (1965) emphasized the contrast between a professional's need for autonomy and freedom to innovate or take risks without undue fear of failure and the hierarchical administrative authority structure of most organizations. A contrary, and what appears to be a minority, opinion is offered by Lipartito and Miranti (1998) to the effect, that rather than serving to corrupt professional values, corporations have actually enhanced the development and status of many occupations. I return to this view shortly.

W. Kornhauser (1962) found that there are four areas of values conflict that may be expected between industrial scientists and engineers and the large organizations that employ them, and I believe they are potentially relevant for I/O psychologists as well. First is the conflict between the scientists' adherence to professional and scientific objectives and standards and the organization's continuous demands for productivity and profitable developments. For example, the organization's standards for evaluating the effectiveness of a popular pilot project (e.g., initiation of a "flex-time" work schedule) might be very different from those of a conscientious I/O psychologist. W. Kornhauser outlined the quandary for the professional:

> Opposition to professional expertise is illustrated by the client's impatience with the niceties of professional procedure. The consequence is pressure to evade that procedure in order to get immediate results or operational ease rather than technical perfection. Professional autonomy clashes with the client's desire to exercise control over actions that vitally affect his [sic] interests. *When the client is also the employer, the conflict often is severe....*

---

[77] A related issue that has interested some scholars is the potential conflict among different professional subgroups within the same organization (Davidson, 1985; DeLeon, 1994). That topic is not reviewed.

If professions seek to accommodate internal strivings and external pressures by lowering standards, they dilute their values. If, on the other hand, professions respond merely by conforming to their standards without finding ways of taking client and member interests into account, they run the risk of losing their effectiveness. (p. 2, italics added)

This potential strain between corporate and professional standards was brought to my attention by a former student of mine shortly after he began work for a very large multinational corporation. He was asked to continue the development of a competency model that had been initiated prior to his arrival on the job. Following some discussion with him of the situation, I was prompted to write the hypothetical discussion case presented in Fig. 8.1, which in fact describes the situation accurately. I offer it here without further comment.

The second area of potential conflict concerns the nature of control over the scientists' work. "Control over work performance is of course the basic prize over which occupation and administration contend in particular work settings" (Freidson, 1973, p. 33). In many organizations the work is arranged based on rational principles of hierarchical administration that may not be the most effective for facilitating scientific creativity. Supervision in particular may be a significant problem. The reliance on formal organizational authority, as opposed to technical expertise and professional autonomy, represents a major clash of normative expectations (Bledstein, 1976). In general, "professionals feel that only members of one's profession are capable of judging one's work" (J. T. Edwards et al., 1981, p. 126). For example, many I/O psychologists in corporations, who are engaged in sophisticated technical applications (e.g., test validation, the evaluation of training programs, theory-based work reorganization, and other organization development interventions) report to managers of human resources who are not psychologists. These administrators usually have no training in research methodology, and all too frequently have even had careers outside the sphere of human resources administration. Achieving an appropriate understanding and evaluation of the professional I/O psychologist's performance may be a daunting task under those circumstances. However, the opinion expressed by Edwards et al. may be only partially correct—more true with respect to process than outcome. A patient may not be able to judge the skillfulness of a surgeon's technique, but frequently he or she will have some postoperative indications whether the surgery has been successful. Similarly, neither the human resources nor the line managers of a manufacturing company may be able to judge the quality of the selection test validation study or team-building intervention implemented by an I/O psychologist, but they will probably be able to evaluate in the first instance whether there has been an improvement in the

You have been retained, at a hefty salary, by a large multinational corporation with headquarters in the U.S. to develop and implement a world-wide management development program, based on a model of corporate leadership that was developed before you were hired. You shortly learn that this "model" consists merely of: (a) rather abstract, undefined or poorly defined platitudes— e.g., "does what it takes," "dynamic people-manager;" (b) socially-desirable stereotypes—e.g. "smarts," "trustworthy," "passion to win," "fires up people;" and (c) undefined outcome indicators, with no hint of how those outcomes are, or ought to be achieved—e.g., "does what it takes," "world-class business manager."

You learn that this model was developed entirely from interviews with approximately 20 very senior managers and essentially violates much of what you have learned about doing good applied organizational research—e.g., no behavioral representation of what is meant by these attributes was developed, nor how they may be achieved; no representative sampling was conducted nor any investigation of possible differences in requisite attributes as a function of hierarchical level or functional area in the organization; no exploration was undertaken of possible national or cultural differences in effective leadership style across countries, or other possible context effects; there has been no confirmation that these attributes in fact are related empirically to effective leadership; and there is an emphasis on dispositional attributes unlikely to be amenable to the ostensible goal of the program, which is management *development.*

Upon reflection it appears that the only positive contribution that might be made by this project is the relatively minor one of providing a common vocabulary for managers to use in describing or evaluating other managers irrespective of whether that vocabulary stands for anything useful. Yet, an enormous investment in resources is planned for this development program. You realize the fallaciousness of the enterprise, based as it is on unsophisticated and unprofessional HR research, and you feel that you ought to say something to your superiors—after-all, what did they hire you for if not for your expertise? But you're new to the job, the salary and perks are all you dreamed of, senior management seems committed to this program, and who are you to rock the boat? On the other hand, you have considerable misgivings about participating in the implementation of a very expensive program based on such shoddy personnel research. You have said to yourself, wouldn't the company save a lot of wasted money and effort and derive much positive benefit if you could get them to do it correctly? .... What do you do?

FIG. 8.1. Organizational versus professional standards.

quality, productivity, or longevity of new hires and whether there has been a decline in intergroup conflict in the second instance (assuming those were the objectives).

This view of the large, nonprofessional employing organization as constraining the professional's expected autonomy, leading to interpersonal and organizational conflict, has been the dominant model guiding research in the area. The research has tended to confirm that professionals working in highly formal or bureaucratic organizations are indeed less likely to perceive themselves as autonomous and more likely to experience role conflict (e.g., Engel, 1970; Organ & Greene, 1981). However, research has also indicated that the organizational structure variables are not the only significant antecedents; the outcomes also depend on the nature of the professionals' psychological identifications. Those who, in fact, have a high bureaucratic (i.e., organizational) orientation, irrespective of whether they may also have a high professional orientation, are likely to be high in job satisfaction (Sorenson & Sorenson, 1974) and experience less role conflict and alienation than those who identify strongly with their profession (C. N. Greene, 1978).[78] Greene also found that the two factors interact: The most dysfunctional reactions were experienced by those who identified with their profession (senior scientists and engineers) and were in more formalized organizational settings.

The third area of likely conflict identified by W. Kornhauser (1962) relates to differences in the incentive systems between the scientific community and the organization. Professional recognition for scientific accomplishment is achieved in the world or national community of one's disciplinary colleagues, whereas organizational recognition is achieved locally by advancement within it. "The organization expects its members to be local in orientation, with loyalty to the organization and its purposes, but the scientist is cosmopolitan in that his [sic] rewards and references are in the wider scientific community. For the cosmopolitan, advancement in the local organization may not be an attractive incentive" (R. T. Hall, 1975, p. 104). Confirming this aspect of the scientist versus practitioner split, I/O psychology practitioners tend to feel that the research published in our journals has little impact on what they do in their organizations, and they are not rewarded for publishing research and so don't do it much (Campion et al., 1986; Sackett, 1986; Sackett et al., 1986). The issue of knowledge transfer between academe and professional practice has been a perennial problem (Rynes, Bartunek, & Daft, 2001).

The fourth source of potential tension stems from the decision-making authority residing in the organizational hierarchy, including dominion over the scientists' activities. Organizational criteria (e.g., rapidity, marketability, and productivity) are the controlling factors, not scientific standards (e.g., statistical effect sizes and internal validity of a program's effects or their generalizability).

---

[78]Professional and organizational identification have been found to be orthogonal (i.e., independent) orientations. Respondents are typically categorized as having a professional identification (high on professional but low on organizational identification), an organizational identification (high on organizational and low on professional identification), a mixed orientation (high on both), or as being indifferent (low on both).

In a very real sense, higher level managers determine the meaningfulness of the professional's work to the organization; the professional may have very little influence in that regard. It is true that in many instances the scientist can acquire such influence by advancement up the managerial hierarchy, but that may be at the cost of relinquishing the role of scientist and technical competence as the basis for authority. And not all professionals have the motivations to express power and influence and the needs for dominance and upward mobility that tend to distinguish those who aspire to management positions (Mael, Waldman, & Mulqueen, 2001). Moreover, the ultimate scope of managerial responsibility may be limited to the administration of the professional department. The professional may lack sufficient knowledge and experience of the organization's core business to achieve significant policy-making responsibilities beyond that restricted domain.

Hughes (1965) added a fifth source of tension that is compatible with W. Kornhauser's (1962) analysis. He spoke of the professional's relative detachment from the specifics of a particular case in the sense of having much greater interest in understanding all such cases. It is this interest and curiosity that leads to greater comprehension. In contrast, the organization is generally much more focused on specific actionable instances. "Great corporations, too, although they may seek men [sic] who know the science of management, want an executive's curiosity about and love of the universal aspects of human organization tempered with a certain loyalty and commitment to his employer" (Hughes, 1965, p. 6). This tension, and ultimate equilibrium, between the universal and the particular in a profession is an aspect of the relation between scientific theory and practice, as just noted, that characterizes almost all professions. Hughes observed that "many learned societies show strain between the intellectuals and the professionalizers" (p. 7)—which is largely what led to the formation of the APS in reaction to the perceived "guild orientation" of the clinical practitioners who dominate the APA (cf. Hakel, 1988; T. H. Rosen, 1987). I return to this issue in chapter 9, in a consideration of the paradigm of postmodernism in which, for epistemological reasons, little distinction is made between research and practice.

I add a sixth source of tension and potential ethical dilemmas for the professional in organizations, one that is sometimes signified by the question "who is the client?" I refer to the dual ethical responsibilities professionals like I/O psychologists experience with respect to the individual employees of a client or employer organization as distinct from the organization as a whole. The reader may recall the anecdote taken from Norman (1983), presented in chapter 4, regarding the dilemma of taking his daughter or son on the child seat of his bicycle to visit a friend. The anecdote was offered to illustrate a putative weakness of consequentialist ethical theories—the failure to deal with rights, obligations, duties, or in this instance a promise. A similar situation might be as follows.

Suppose you are a senior human resources manager of a substantial company, and an opening two levels below your position has just become available for which you have been asked by your manager to make a promotion recommendation (in consultation with your direct reports) from among the people in your area. This is not a problem for you because, as a good manager, you are well acquainted with the particular talents, strengths, and weaknesses of most of the potential candidates. The only catch is that the position requires a substantial amount of out-of-town travel. You have narrowed down the choice to two promising candidates, one of whom seems "better" than the other. Unfortunately, this more qualified employee volunteers that she couldn't accept the promotion because of family demands that would be interfered with by the travel requirements of the position. Therefore, with some regret, you recommend the other person to your boss, who takes the matter under advisement, and you so inform the candidates and their managers. However, before a decision is made, the better qualified employee comes to you and explains that she has made satisfactory permanent arrangements to deal with the competing family demands and would very much like to be considered for the promotion.

Is this the same ethical problem faced by Norman (1983) with respect to his upcoming bicycle ride (an obligation to honor his promise to his daughter even if his son would appreciate the ride more)? Although you are not their parent, surely you have an ethical responsibility to treat your employees fairly. Should you, therefore, analogous to Norman's conclusion, unquestionably honor your commitment to the second-ranked employee to whom the job has been tentatively promised? If not, why not? Is there not a substantial difference between the two situations? Unlike Norman you have obligations not only to the two candidates but to the organization as well. If the first-ranked candidate has, by virtue of her past performance, earned the promotion and would indeed contribute more to the organization, this must be given considerable deference. It does not mean that, were we conducting a utilitarian analysis of your options, we should ignore the likely adverse consequences on department morale that might accrue upon reversing your recommendation. What you should actually do in the situation might depend on many other particulars not specified. But that's not the point of the illustration. The point is to emphasize that issues of professional ethics are frequently more complicated for us than personal ethics in that there are additional interests represented besides those of the actors and those immediately affected, in particular the organization and those with whom it interacts, the profession, colleagues, and so on.[79]

---

[79] Additional questions can be raised about how appropriately this situation was handled. One could argue that your obligation was to recommend the better candidate and allow her to make her own decision at that time. If necessary, the person next in line could be offered the position subsequently. Also, it was probably not wise to inform the candidates of your recommendation in advance.

The Case of I/O Psychology

W. Kornhauser (1962) emphasized that these strains and conflicting values did not always lead to actual conflict between professional scientists and their employers: Accommodations are made on both sides. He devoted a chapter (albeit a short one) in his book to "adaptations of professions and organizations." The most salient adaptation to the strain between professional autonomy and bureaucratic control entails the creation of new roles for research administration. The organization develops higher level positions for managers and directors of research who control general administrative policies (e.g., personnel selection, compensation decisions, and budget recommendations), whereas technical matters are decided closer to the level of the actual work, by the professionals themselves and lower level research supervisors. This creates two or more career paths for scientists in the organization, although there is not a great deal of overlap between scientific and managerial competencies, so that the administrative path may not be viable or attractive for everyone. As already noted, commitment to a profession is generally intensive and lifelong. Moreover, organizations vary considerably in the extent to which they are willing to make structural accommodations such as this.

In contrast to W. Kornhauser's (1962) main thesis, a more optimistic note was sounded by Wallace (1995) who disputed the assumption of an inherently conflictual relation between professionals and large bureaucratic employing organizations. Wallace observed lawyers "working under conditions in which they have retained control over the objectives of their work and participate in policy making and thus in helping direct their employing organization by making explicit their professional system of norms and values and by maintaining collegial and supportive ties.... [These] professionals in nonprofessional organizations have preserved autonomy and discretion over their work" (p. 247). Not considered by Wallace, however, was the extent to which these findings may be uniquely characteristic of lawyers—who are interpreting the boundaries of legal business practice for their organizations—and not reflective of the job attributes of engineers, scientists, accountants, or I/O psychologists.

But there is a more interesting observation to be made in this regard. It is my opinion (admittedly unencumbered by consideration of empirical data) that I/O psychologists in industry experience less strain and conflict of the types noted by W. Kornhauser and Hughes than do most other professionals similarly employed. I think there are several reasons why that is to be expected. First, as human resource professionals I/O psychologists work for human resource managers who are likely to be sensitive to the potential conflicts and other human resource issues under consideration here. Notwithstanding that many human resource managers have not trained professionally for their current assignments, they are probably more attuned to these matters than is true for managers of other professional groups in engineering, finance, legal, information systems, or scientific research and development departments.

Second, as I/O psychologists, the substance of our education and training includes the very organizational, structural, managerial, and leadership concerns at issue. Therefore, we ought to be better informed and ready to deal with these matters than most other professional and scientific groups. Third, the explicit adoption and salience of the scientist–practitioner model in I/O psychology (Latham, 2001; Lefkowitz, 1990) may account for a reduced sense of antagonism between these cosmopolitan and local professional orientations.

Fourth, I/O psychologists are directly *useful* to organizations—and perceived by their managers to be so (M. R. Feinberg & Lefkowitz, 1962; Ronen, 1980)—because the professional practice that constitutes our work activities are largely defined by the needs of the organization. Much of what we do in organizations concerns the necessary nuts-and-bolts activities of personnel selection and managerial assessment, performance appraisal, training and development, job analysis and competency modeling, and so on (Campion et al., 1986; Rassenfos, & Kraut, 1988). Even professional practice in the "O" side of the field (e.g., in organization analysis, design, and development) is aimed at the pragmatic objective of enhancing organizational effectiveness. This additional dimension of professional practice has historically been a major distinction between I/O psychology and those of our sister social scientists in sociology and anthropology, who also study organizations but who are not employed in organizations to a significant degree. The same may even be said with respect to the students of organizational behavior as taught in business schools. Even more important and commensurate with our career choices and participation in organizations, it is likely that I/O psychologists have a strong organizational orientation and identification, which has been found to attenuate potential professional—organizational conflict (C. N. Greene, 1978; Sorenson & Sorenson, 1974).

But perhaps even more important, it may be that I/O psychology is one of those professions that, according to Lipartito and Miranti (1998), have flourished by virtue of their integration into modern business systems:

> Some historical models equate the rise of professionalization with the middle class's desire to escape corporate control of its labor. Historically, professions offered an enticing middle ground between independent proprietor and corporate employee. Here the conflict between business and profession is explicit. Professionals seek to avoid corporate supervision and to preserve their autonomy in socializing their expertise....

[But] many occupations, in fact, have risen in status precisely because of their function in the modern business system. These include the older professions of law, engineering, and accountancy, and such newer professions as advertising, public relations, and management. (p. 302)

Those professions, as a consequence, may be expected to exhibit fewer and less extreme values conflicts with business organizations than others do. This is commensurate with Bell's (1985) views:

> Where organization and profession share similar values, as with physicians in hospitals or social workers in welfare agencies, conflicts probably affect the direction of organizational policy only marginally. The effects on policy are more important where professional values diverge sharply from organizational purposes.... From the standpoint of professional autonomy, all organizational hierarchies that attempt to routinize work are similarly threatening. But the threat to substantive professional values ... is less radical where organizational purposes and professional values are closely related. (p. 22)

I believe that I/O psychology generally fits the model of professions that Lipartito and Miranti and Bell have in mind. It is also my opinion that, in particular, individual I/O psychologists who have opted to pursue an organizational career commonly share the perspectives and values that characterize organizations and their managerial hierarchies. This is probably less true, for example, of the biologists, chemists, and physicists who work in industry. (Obviously, to the extent that these reflections have any validity at all, they are generalizations that cannot be expected to characterize every individual.) For example, interviews with particularly successful organizational I/O practitioners—those with high earnings— revealed them to have more of a business than scientific orientation, to be socially compatible with successful business people, and to be unconflicted about the acquisition of wealth as a legitimate objective (Greller, 1984). In fact, it was "not uncommon for a high earner to say, 'I used to be an I/O psychologist,' " reflecting "greater identification with the enterprise than with the profession" (p. 56). I/O psychologists, especially those in administrative positions, remain on average the highest paid psychology specialization (APA, 2000).

Succinctly, then, I/O psychologists employed in large organizations probably experience less strain and fewer conflicts than many other types of professionals in organizations because we tend to have personal values that are more congruent with those of the corporation and its managers, and our domain of expertise encompasses important aspects of organizational policies, systems, and procedures. This compatibility is a consequence of the long-standing integration of the field into the modern business world (the psychologist Walter Dill Scott wrote *The Psychology of Advertising* in 1902) and has in no small measure contributed to the success of I/O psychology as an occupation and career choice. However, as suggested in chapter 12, there is a negative aspect of this integration. The embrace of business objectives and corporate values has not been without cost: much of our ethical and humanistic heritage from psychology has been abandoned. Although it is of no moral significance, it is instructive to realize that this situation may not be unique to I/O psychology:

> In addition to the traditional categories of professions, modern corporate life creates new ones. The systems analyst, the marketing specialist, the labor negotiator, the management theorist, and the public relations expert are necessary ingredients in the modern corporate success formula. These new professionals possess most of the traditional characteristics associated with professions: they rely on a theoretical store of knowledge, are graduated from research-oriented institutions, apply their knowledge to practical problems, and subject their work to review and criticism from colleagues.
>
> Many of the new "technocratic" professions, however, lack a key characteristic associated with traditional professions. With the professions of medicine, law, or teaching, we associate a spirit of altruism or service; but the new technocratic professions often lack this characteristic and thus raise special problems of moral responsibility. We associate the goal of healing with the physician, and of knowledge with the professor (no matter how mercenary doctors or professors may be in fact), yet there are no corresponding goals for the marketing specialist, the public relations manager, or the advertising expert. The standards of the new professional do not explicitly include moral standards, in part because his or her profession does not recognize an altruistic element in its overall goals. The old professions have frequently failed to apply the moral standards articulated in statements of their professional goals; but the new professions fail, it seems, because they do not even attempt to articulate moral standards. (Donaldson, 1982, p. 113)

So we should challenge ourselves by posing the following question: Is I/O psychology more akin to the minimally moral new "technocratic professions" referred to by Donaldson (1982) than to the traditional professions in which responsibility and service to society at large is a major value component? The question will be taken up in chapter 12, but before doing so two faults in Donaldson's presentation should be noted. First, the failure to articulate an explicit morality should not be equated with an amoral posture. Most individuals, for example, try to lead an essentially moral existence without necessarily having articulated an ethical code for guidance. Second, his assertion contrasts the moral professions against the newer professions that serve corporate objectives, as if corporations were entirely or essentially amoral enterprises. Thus, a most relevant question becomes, What is the moral status of business—especially large and enormously powerful corporations? What, if any, is their moral justification? That is the underlying theme of chapters 10 and 11. But a preliminary issue to be dealt with concerns the extent and nature of values in the profession and science of psychology, which is considered in chapter 9.

ADDING FURTHER TO THE FRAMEWORK
FOR ETHICAL DECISION MAKING

23. **It can reasonably be inferred that a number of social and ethical obligations accrue to I/O psychologists by virtue of the status of our field as a profession.** Professional status means that, in many respects, society views what we do as important, defers to our expertise in appropriate areas, and gives us considerable latitude with respect to determining the qualifications to enter the profession and regulate its practice. In return, we are expected to behave as professionals—responsibly—and to utilize our expertise for the benefit of the entire society, not simply to benefit only our direct clients. (This does not imply that the two are necessarily incompatible, although at times they may be.)

24. **Some I/O psychologists work in settings in which they may not have regular contact with professional colleagues (e.g., as solo practitioners or in relatively small organizations) and so may feel relatively isolated when faced with an ethical difficulty.** The worst thing to do under those circumstances is to remain isolated. The advice of professional friends and colleagues, mentors, or former professors should be sought. The ethics committee of the APA also welcomes advisory inquiries.

25. **The sociological study of the professions has revealed several areas of potential conflict between professionals employed in large hierarchical organizations and structural or administrative features of those organizations.** I have speculated that there are several reasons why that is less likely to be the case for I/O psychologists than for other professional groups. Chief among those reasons are that I/O psychology historically has been functionally integrated into the administration of business and that I/O psychologists tend to "self-select" from a population that has an organizational orientation marked by values compatible with those of the corporate enterprise. A warning note is sounded, however, insofar as those values may not always be compatible with the broader obligations owed by professionals to the society that supports their professional status. In other words, the way in which these potential conflicts are resolved or averted may give rise to other values conflicts and attendant ethical issues that, as suggested in chapter 12, are not well recognized in our field.

9

Values in Psychology

In 1951 a young African-American social psychologist at the City College of New York, Kenneth B. Clark, was asked by the National Association for the Advancement of Colored People's (NAACP) Legal Defense and Education Fund (LDEF) to chair a committee of social scientists who would write a legal brief in support of the NAACP–LDEF's lawsuit against the Topeka, Kansas, Board of Education. The social science statement they prepared, *The Effects of Segregation and the Consequences of Desegregation*, played an instrumental role in the Supreme Court's unanimous decision on May 17, 1954, favoring the plaintiffs in *Brown v. Board of Education of Topeka* (347 U.S. 483), which (eventually) led to the desegregation of public schools in the United States (Jackson, 1998). The content of the statement consisted of a review of the social science literature which supported the conclusions that (a) there were no differences between the races in ability to learn; (b) legally segregated education caused psychological damage to African-American children; and (c) desegregation could be implemented relatively smoothly, even in the South.

The account of the committee's work is replete with descriptions of how they tried "to maintain the persona of objective scientific expert while writing for the ultimate adversarial forum—a Supreme Court hearing" (Jackson, 1998, p. 150). The final version of the statement begins:

> The problem of the segregation of racial and ethnic groups constitutes one of the major problems facing the American people today. It seems desirable, therefore, to summarize the contributions which contemporary social science can make toward its resolution. *There are, of course, moral and legal issues involved with respect to which the signers of the present statement cannot speak with*

any special authority and which must be taken into account in the solution of the problem. *There are, however, also factual issues involved with respect to which certain conclusions seem to be justified on the basis of the available scientific evidence. It is with these issues only that this paper is concerned.* (cited in Jackson, p. 151, italics added)

The italicized portions of the preceding quotation express the concern of these psychologists over the extent to which their views would be perceived as related as much to their personal and social values as to their appraisal of the objective scientific evidence.

The view that there is a clear division between scientific facts and values is both an assumption regarding the nature of science (its subject matter, aims, conduct, and products) as well as an implicit value statement regarding that nature—that is, that science *ought* to be distinct from values issues. It is a view, however, that is no longer a unanimous one among philosophers of science or among natural and social scientists, including psychologists. The issue is an integral component of a much larger and more complex controversy. For the sake of exposition, I segmented the controversy into three facets, but they are highly interrelated; only with some difficulty have I been able to discuss them separately. The first, as just illustrated, is the issue of the relation between science and values. The second facet consists of whether the inquiry paradigm (Guba & Lincoln, 1994) of logical positivism, which served natural science so well that it was adopted wholeheartedly by psychology, is adequate to the task of achieving meaningful understanding of human beings or should be replaced by the postmodern paradigm.[80] Third is the matter of the relation between research and practice within the profession of psychology.

It is sometimes the case that those who declaim against the inappropriate intrusion of what appear to them to be social values into what ought to be objective and value-free scientific inquiry are simply objecting to the expression of values different from their own. It is sometimes the case that

---

[80]The term *paradigm* was introduced by Thomas Kuhn (1996) in the groundbreaking first edition of his book *The Structure of Scientific Revolutions*. He defined the term somewhat narrowly as a concrete model of the fundamentals of a scientific field, consisting of a set of "rules and standards for scientific practice" (p. 11) that account for the shared consensus and commitment of those in the field. In the third edition, he discussed definitional problems of the earlier editions and referred to those matters as a "disciplinary matrix." I am using paradigm in its somewhat looser and more popularized version in which it is generally defined as a set of basic beliefs that deals with the nature of the world (Guba & Lincoln, 1994). They are basic in the sense that there is no way to establish their ultimate truth; they are accepted on faith, notwithstanding that they may also be supported with rational argument. Inquiry paradigms or scientific paradigms define for the scientific inquirer the nature of the scientific enterprise, including what are the limits of legitimate inquiry. They do so by way of their answers to fundamental ontological, epistemological, and methodological questions. What is the nature of reality and scientific truth, and what is the nature of our "knowing" such? And how should one go about finding out these things? Similarly, Stricker (1997) summarized: "Thus, a paradigm ... encompasses the whole disciplinary matrix that surrounds a theory, including an epistemological framework, a corpus of knowledge, a means of generating and understanding that information, a set of values, and possibly even a worldview" (p. 443).

we fail to recognize or acknowledge the value assumptions implicit in our own research and practice. Among the best-known examples of this dynamic are the disparaging comments made by Henry E. Garrett, chair of the Psychology Department at Columbia University in the 1940s and 1950s, about Kenneth Clark and the other social scientists whose work was relied on by the Supreme Court in *Brown v. Board of Education*. Garrett, in fact, was a strong advocate of segregationist beliefs and helped organize an international group of scholars dedicated to "preventing race mixing, preserving segregation, and promoting the principles of early 20th century eugenics and 'race hygiene' " (Benjamin & Crouse, 2002, p. 45, quoting historian A. Winston).

SCIENCE AND VALUES

The Positivist Paradigm

The science of psychology was modeled after the natural sciences of the 17th to 19th centuries in the tradition of logical positivism and empiricism as the only fruitful way to uncover reality, truth, or the facts. The natural science model is predicated on the objective, unbiased, and dispassionate ("tough-minded") search for *truth*, which is defined in terms of impartial scientific facts. "The essential position of positivism is that humans can, with the help of the tools of science, gain true knowledge of a reality that exists outside of human thought. Implied in the belief that formal procedures of science will produce a progressively accurate picture of reality are the notions that other modes of reasoning are inadequate for generating valid knowledge ... " (Hoshmand & Polkinghorne, 1992, p. 56). Raw data are to be collected in an objective manner so that it is of no consequence which scientist collects them (assuming all are equally competent), and it is assumed that the process of data collection does not appreciably alter the phenomena under study. Moreover, the only determinants of the problems to be studied and the means of studying them are theoretical relevance and methodological rigor, respectively. Thus, science is conceived to be "value-free." This traditional view is argued forcefully on behalf of psychology by Kendler (1993, 1999) who referred to the "unbridgeable chasm between facts and values" (1999, p. 829) and who asserted "science's incapacity to identify what is good or bad" (1999, p. 832). But rarely specified are the ethical implications of strict adherence to this model when applied to the study of human beings—that is, the consequences of treating research participants essentially as a physical scientist treats inanimate objects. For example, the participants have no voice in deciding what is to be investigated, in what manner, or how the results are to be interpreted, disseminated, or used. By excluding values, the classic positivist paradigm—at least as an ideal—also excludes many ethical considerations: "People who write about methodology often forget that it is a matter of strategy, not of morals" (Homans, 1949, p. 330).

A complicating feature of psychology, however, is that it has been comprised, almost from its inception, of two aspects: scientific research and the application of psychological knowledge and techniques for the betterment of humanity. The preamble of the APA's (1992) *Ethical Principles of Psychologists and Code of Conduct* indicates that psychologists' "goal is to broaden knowledge of behavior and where appropriate, to apply it pragmatically to improve the condition of both the individual and society" (p. 1599).[81] The latter objective is exemplified by the fields of clinical and counseling psychology, educational psychology, and I/O psychology, among many other applications as well (Deutsch, 1969; Mays, 2000; G. A. Miller, 1969; Tyler, 1973). "From the beginning, the American expression of psychology has contained a strong utilitarian component. More than our European counterparts, we have asked what uses can be made of knowledge about human function" (D. R. Peterson, 1991, p. 422).

These two facets of psychology correspond to two conflicting views of education—knowledge for its own sake and learning in order to produce good citizens and the good society—that have been traced back to Socrates and the Sophists, respectively (Furedy & Furedy, 1982). William James (1907) labeled these as "tough-minded" versus "tender-minded" outlooks, and Luria (1976), who viewed them as ethical principles, referred to them as "the ethic of knowledge" and the "ethic of innocence" (p. 332). Leona Tyler (1973) observed that disparaging characterizations like "do-gooder" have often been applied to those "who were mainly interested in what psychology could do to help people and improve the human condition" (p. 1021).

Constructive proponents of the traditional view believe that only by adhering to the separation of science and humanistic values can the former actually serve to promote the latter. That is because it is the value-neutral, unbiased, and objectively determined facts that may then be used legitimately and justified publicly as bases for informed social policy (Kendler, 1993). A two-step process is called for: the production of relevant but impartial empirical data and a separate exploration of its implications for society. Otherwise, what passes for scientific knowledge may easily be dismissed as the mere personal, social, or political preferences of the particular scientist–advocates involved. It is in this context that we understand the difficulties faced by Kenneth Clark and the social science committee members who prepared the NAACP–LDEF brief in the early

---

[81]The preamble of the new APA (2002) code that takes effect June 1, 2003 similarly begins "Psychologists are committed to increasing scientific and professional knowledge of behavior and people's understanding of themselves and others and to the use of such knowledge to improve the condition of individuals, organizations, and society" (p. 1062).

1950s. In the subsequent opinion of some psychologists (cf. Gerard, 1983), the failure of de jure school desegregation to have increased the educational success of minority children in the United States to the extent anticipated is due to the inadequacy of our knowledge regarding the complicated issues that constitute the problem and how to solve it. In other words, Gerard suggested that, in their interpretation of the available research evidence and the attendant optimistic predictions for desegregation, the committee members were overly influenced by their personal values and well-meaning intentions.

The traditional positivist argument against the representation of humanistic or social values in the scientific enterprise entails the exclusion of *all* values from the domain of scientific enquiry. But that classical empiricist tradition from the natural sciences, in particular the fact–value dichotomy, has been under siege for more than a generation. Its critics have charged that it represents an oversimplified erroneous view of the nature of scientific knowledge and process; regardless of its worth as a model (i.e., whether it might be a worthy ideal for which to strive), it does not—never has—accurately characterized actual scientific research. Some go so far as to suggest that "the naive positivist position of the sixteenth through the nineteenth centuries is no longer held by anyone even casually acquainted with these problems [i.e., the critiques noted over the past several decades]" (Guba & Lincoln, 1994, p. 116).

The Role of Values in Science

For quite some time now, a persuasive case has been made for the relatively unacknowledged reality that all scientific research is value laden (Feyerabend, 1975; Kuhn, 1977; B. Schwartz, 1990; Szasz, 1970; Toulmin, 1973) to the extent that many scholars believe that "the controversy is no longer about *whether* values influence scientific practice, but rather about *how* values are embedded in and shape scientific practice" (G. S. Howard, 1985, p. 255). This view is commensurate with those of philosophers of science such as Rorty (1979) and Popper (1972). Although Popper's aim is not essentially antipositivist, he pointed out that reality, truth, or "objective knowledge" (the title of his book) does not reside in the physical world of so-called "facts," as is maintained by "the commonsense theory of knowledge" (p. 63) advanced by the positivists and empiricists. Instead, it "consists of the logical content of our theories, conjectures, [and] guesses" (p. 73). And all knowledge, including even the "subjective knowledge" of our conscious experiences such as the "knowledge of self" depends on these theoretical formulations. According to Popper this world of our theories, although a human construction, nevertheless is real, as demonstrated by their effects on the physical world (e.g., the applications of atomic theory, economic theory, reinforcement theory or goal-setting theory). [82]

Science, therefore, does not consist in the accumulation of facts but in the "invention of ever new theories, and the indefatigable examination of their power to throw light on experience" (Popper, 1972, p. 361). This "examination" consists in the definition of a problem situation, the formulation of a tentative theoretical interpretation, a critical investigation that leads to the elimination of mistaken notions, and the reformulation of the problem; and the process of "conjecture and refutation" is repeated. Thus, theories are never proven true or even confirmed in any absolute or even probabilistic sense by research; they can only be disconfirmed. The search for truth is "the critical search for what is false in our various competing theories" (p. 319).

In addition, the observations we make to test our possible explanations—by means of the process of conjecture and refutation—are always *selective*, that is, determined by our definition of the problem and tentative theoretical explanations. Thus, one of the implications of Popper's work is the realization that knowledge or truth does not lie in "objective facts": Empirical data are not independent of the theoretical perspective(s) within which they are generated. As revealed by the physicist F. Capra (cited in G. S. Howard, 1985):

> Human consciousness plays a crucial role in the process of observation, and in atomic physics *determines to a large extent the properties of the observed phenomena.*... The crucial feature of quantum theory is that the observer is not only necessary to observe the properties of the atomic phenomenon, but is necessary even to bring about these properties. *My conscious decision about how to observe, say, an electron will determine the electron's properties to some extent. If I ask a particle question, it will give me a particle answer; if I ask it a wave question, it will give me a wave answer.* (p. 259, italics added)

Moreover, as Bronowski (1960) noted,

> What we have really seen happen is the breakdown of the plain model of a world outside ourselves where we simply look on and observe.... For relativity derives essentially from the philosophic analysis which insists that there is not a fact and an observer but a joining of the two in an observation. This is the fundamental unit of physics: The actual observation. And this is what the principle of uncertainty showed in atomic physics: That *event and observer are not separable.* (pp. 83–84, italics added)

In addition to the interdependence of observer, theories, and data (i.e., "facts"), a related implication of Popper's position is "the underdetermin-

---

[82]See the "Comment" in the *American Psychologist* by Champion (1985) for a succinct review of the relevance of Popper's work to psychology.

ation of theory" (Guba & Lincoln, 1994): "Not only are facts determined by the theory window through which one looks for them, but different theory windows might be equally well supported by the same set of 'facts.' Although it may be possible, given a coherent theory, to derive by deduction what facts ought to exist, it is never possible, given a coherent set of facts, to arrive by induction at a single, ineluctable theory" (p. 107). In other words, contrary to the traditional positivist view, facts do not speak for themselves. There-fore, to summarize, not only do scientists choose problem situations and tentative explanations of them on the basis of personal considerations (interest, curiosity, fashion, likelihood of success, etc.), but the facts observed have no knowable state of privileged existence apart from the process of human observation, which is theory directed, and scientists must also choose among competing alternative theories on bases other than merely the data. This latter decision process is generally conducted (at least in part—hopefully in great measure) on the basis of criteria that reflect scientific values (Spence, 1985).

Scientific Values

These are also referred to as *epistemic values* (G. S. Howard, 1985) and it must be acknowledged that the scientific process is laden with these value judgments. G. S. Howard discussed five widely agreed-upon value criteria by which scientific theories are evaluated and suggested the possible inclusion of at least five more. These include the degree of *predictive accuracy* enabled by the theory; its *internal coherence*; its *external consistency* or the degree to which it fits with better established theories; its *unifying power*, the theory's capability of integrating disparate knowledge; *fertility* or heuristic value in extending our base of knowledge; *simplicity* or parsimony; *testability*; *potential falsifiability*; the *reproducibility of experiments*; and *measurement accuracy*.

Thus, even in the natural sciences subjectivity is extensive. Not only are data (facts) dependent on theory and the observer, and theories underde-termined by data, but the choice of theory is based on subjective evaluations of epistemic values. And there may be considerable differences among scientists in the relative weighting and application of these criteria. It follows, therefore, that the very bases by which we endow scientific knowledge with a privileged status—these epistemic values—rests on subjective value judgments. "The objectivity of sciences must be understood as emanating from a nexus of judgmental presuppositions, and the efficacy of the entire enterprise is a function of the adequacy of those fundamental assumptive stances" (G. S. Howard, 1985, p. 258). In *The Sociology of Science* Merton (1973) articulated four scientific norms that give institutional and public expression to these epistemic values: *universalism*, judging scientific endeavors by impersonal criteria, regardless of the personal attributes of the scientist; *communalism*, the sharing of scientific data; *disinterestedness,* disregarding one's personal opinions and values; and *organized skepticism,* subjecting all scientific findings to the strict scrutiny of replication, peer review, and so on.

The Practice of Scientific Research

Merton's (1973) norms exist not just in the scientific community. Supporting the value-free conceptualization of science has been the stereotypic image of scientists as dispassionate and neutral observers of natural phenomena that have little if any emotional meaning to them. As a corollary, the public image of the impassioned, driven researcher is likely to be associated with that of the "mad scientist" a la Drs. Jekyll and Frankenstein. However, Mahoney (1976) contrasted the prevalent "storybook image of the scientist" with the actuality of "the biased and passionate ... impetuous truth spinner" (p. 6). The stereotype of the neutral observer–scientist has actually been debunked for quite some time. Biologist Platt (1964) pointed out that personal attachment to one's hypotheses affects one's research and leads to interpersonal conflicts among scientists rather than to a search for truth. Bevan (1980), for example, noted "Doing science is like running a race, and one's colleagues in the field can therefore only be viewed as strong competitors" (p. 780). If that characterization sounds too harsh, one need only recall the recent spectacle of peevish insults, charges, and countercharges traded by the two competing teams of genetic researchers racing to be the first to decode the human genome (Wade, 2001a, 2001b), confirming earlier conclusions that egocentric attributes color scientific research (Mahoney, 1976; Mitroff, 1974). Sociologists have also noted that personal norms and values influence the work of physical scientists at virtually all stages of the enterprise (Hagstrom, 1965; Merton, 1973). Mitroff went so far as to assert "There are very sound psychological reasons why [a scientific] inquirer *should* hold onto his convictions even though his colleagues believe the evidence is against him" (p. xi). The point has even been made that it has been those biases, rather than adherence to the empiricist ideal, that have accounted for the greatest scientific advances in the past (Feyerabend, 1963). Kessel (1969) put it this way:

> Persistence in the face of both contradictory facts and the disapproval of those committed to the prevailing paradigm, the intuitive apprehension of a reality as yet undiscovered, the altering of fundamental presuppositions by the creative act—these are all crucial elements in the progress of science, elements for which the classical conception has little, if any, room. (p. 1004)

Psychological research seems even more vulnerable than the natural sciences to the same sorts of personality quirks, belief systems and other subjective biases of the researcher (MacCoun, 1998; Suedfeld & Tetlock,

1991; Unger, 1983). Krasner and Houts (1984), Kimble (1984), and Lipsey (1974) documented that psychologists can be differentiated with respect to whether they identify primarily with the experimental, scientific, and objective, that is, "tough-minded" positivist or "postpositivist" (Guba & Lincoln, 1994) value position or the humanist position that is focused more on social concern and relevance to the solution of social problems.[83]

Nonscientific Values

It seems rather clear that the bulk of respected contemporary scholarly thought in the natural and social sciences and the philosophy of science has eradicated any reasonable belief in the scientific enterprise as intrinsically objective and totally value free. However, many of those who criticize the conflation of values and psychological science have in mind only the putatively inappropriate intrusion of personal, social, political, and moral values (as these *non-epistemic values* are expressed in the promotion of particular goals and social policies), not the epistemic values by which the adequacy of scientific research and theory are evaluated. The pragmatic question is whether such "intrusions" are preventable. For example, in the context of considering research on justice, Tetlock and Mitchell (1993) believed that "it is difficult, perhaps impossible, to avoid political and moral issues.... The difficulty is especially great, in part, because of the passions evoked in the investigators ..." (p. 246). However, the paradigmatic question that should take precedence is whether such intrusions *should* be avoided. Or, expressed another way, are they really intrusive? In any event, it seems reasonably clear that personal values and prejudices have always affected the way in which questions have been posed and data interpreted in social and behavioral science (Gould, 1981). In an underappreciated contribution to I/O psychology, McCall and Bobko (1990) observed "Although objective scientific method is meant to offset human subjectivity, there are many examples of objectivity actually abetting subjectivity. Rather than pretend that such value structures aren't there, they ought to be made more explicit, perhaps as part of the methodology itself" (p. 396). For example, more than 50 years ago Pastore (1949) showed that among scientists who were prominent in the nature–nurture controversy regarding the source of racial differences in tested IQ, advocacy of *either* a hereditarian or an environmentalist position was associated with one's general political attitudes, conservative or liberal, respectively. The scientists' opinions on the specific scientific question were reflective of their general world views.

---

[83]Postpositivism or neopositivism, in contrast with the positivism of prior centuries, is not value free insofar as epistemic values are acknowledged as intrinsic to the scientific enterprise. It retains the reliance on empirical methods as the accepted path to an understanding of external reality, but it concedes that the understanding will not be perfect and will be probabilistic not certain; theories and their hypotheses cannot be verified, only falsified.

Contemporary *neopositivist* or *postpositivist* psychologists might accept that nonepistemic values and other biasing factors are an unfortunate and unwanted fact of scientific life, but they are to be guarded against, uncovered, and gradually weeded out of the scientific enterprise so that only the more legitimate epistemic values are left as determinants of our scientific progress.

MacCoun's (1998) excellent review discusses several prototypes of biased interpretation of scientific evidence, aside from *fraud* (the conscious intentional effort to fabricate, conceal or distort evidence).[84] These include *cold bias*, which is the unintentional and unconscious bias that may result from a variety of strategic and other cognitive factors, and *hot bias*, which is directionally motivated albeit unintentional and maybe even an unconscious reflection of a preferred outcome. For example, research on these sources of bias has produced a great deal of evidence indicating a *biased assimilation* effect—one's supposedly objective evaluation of scientific methodology and results is influenced strongly by one's initial views (e.g., evidence supporting a view contrary to one's own is evaluated more stringently). Which, if any, of these biases might be contributing to the fact that I/O psychologists employed in industry and concerned with complying with equal employment opportunity laws tend to produce higher selection test validities than their colleagues whose primary employment is in academia (C. R. Russell et al., 1994)? And what might be the mediating behaviors by which the putative motivational differences operate? "Does this suggest that, if two hypothetical investigators were asked to examine the same predictor–criterion relationship, they would conduct their research so differently that dissimilar criterion validities will result? Possibly" (C. R. Russell et al., 1994, p. 169).

Social Advocacy

Recall that the second of psychology's professional goals is "to improve the condition of individuals, organizations, and society" (APA, 2002, p. 1062). The process of attempting to accomplish that, as eloquently stated by Abraham Maslow (1969), unabashedly involves social advocacy in the service of those objectives and values that comprise such "improvements":

> It is now quite clear that the actualization of the highest human potentials is possible—on a mass basis—only under "good conditions." Or more directly, good human beings will generally need a good society in which to grow. Contrariwise, I think it should be clear that a normative philosophy of biology would involve the theory of the good society, defined in terms of "that society

---

[84]MacCoun's analysis is not concerned with the related topic of bias in the conduct of research, including such issues as research design, choice of study populations, statistical analyses, and the effects of experimenter sex or expectancies.

is good which fosters the fullest development of human potentials, of the fullest degree of humanness." (p. 726)

MacCoun (1998) included *advocacy*, "the selective use and emphasis of evidence to promote a hypothesis, without outright concealment or fabrication" (p. 268), as one of the prototypes of biased evidence processing in psychology. However, he concluded that "advocacy is normatively defensible provided that it occurs within an explicitly advocacy based organization, or an explicitly adversarial system of disputing. Trouble arises when there is no shared agreement that such adversarial normative system is in effect" (p. 268). He went on to acknowledge that the widespread acceptance of the traditional public norms for scientists (Merton, 1973) "... surely doesn't preclude advocacy activities on the part of scientists, but it does mean that we must be quite explicit about which hat we are wearing when we speak out, and whether we are asserting our facts ... or asserting our values ..." (p. 280).

Some may feel that Maslow's (1969) criterion of "the fullest development of human potentials" (p. 726) is an inadequate definition of the *good society* and that we lack direction on how to implement the humanitarian goal articulated by the APA. For example, "Although discussions about the role of values in psychology have become frequent in recent years, ... there is still confusion about the moral obligations of psychologists" (Prilleltensky, 1997, p. 517). Prilleltensky suggested that the process of clarification will entail psychologists, first, articulating their individual and collective vision of the good life and the good society, and, second, formulating ways of translating these visions into action. He articulated a number of values, assumptions, and questions about professional practices as a moral framework for assessing different psychological approaches or paradigms. He advanced five values that should be promoted by psychology to live up to its moral obligations: (a) care and compassion for the physical and emotional well-being of others; (b) the ability of people to pursue their own goals (self-determination) while considering other people's needs; (c) respect and appreciation for diverse social groups; (d) citizens having meaningful input into decisions that affect their lives (collaboration and participation); and (e) fair and equitable allocation of bargaining powers, resources, and obligations in society (distributive justice).

Similarly, Koocher and Keith-Spiegel (1998) synthesized from a number of sources a set of nine values or "core ethical principles that we believe should guide the behavior of psychologists" (p. 4): (a) nonmaleficence (avoiding doing harm); (b) respecting autonomy; (c) beneficence (benefitting others); (d) being just, fair, and equitable; (e) being loyal and truthful; (f) according others dignity and respect; (g) treating others with caring and compassion; (h) maintaining professional competence and pursuing excellence; and (i) accepting accountability and responsibility for one's actions. Not surprising is the overlap between the two lists and their similarity to the three-dimensional structure of moral values developed in chapters 5 and 6, based on the long history of moral philosophy and the short history of moral psychology: justice issues, welfare or caring, and honesty or integrity. They also incorporate core principles introduced earlier in the Framework for Ethical Decision Making: universalizability of judgments, universality of concern for all people, and enhancement of the quality of life, especially for those most in need. All of these accounts of the moral domain coalesce nicely with the values reflected in the APA's (2002) new ethical code. The five "general principles," which are meant to be aspirational goals "to guide and inspire psychologists toward the very highest ethical ideals of the profession," (p. 1062) are: beneficence and nonmaleficence, fidelity and responsibility, integrity, justice, and respect for people's rights and dignity.

Prilleltensky (1997) emphasized that a moral system must treat the values he suggested as a complementary set, thus potential conflicts among them may force uncomfortable decisions concerning their relative precedence. Those decisions can only be made in light of the details of the particular situation—an act-based rather than rule-based ethical position. Scholars have noted frequently that difficult ethical dilemmas are those that entail having to choose between two or more right alternatives (Kidder, 1995). Many who have given the matter some thought follow the spirit of the Hippocratic Oath ("First, do no harm") and give considerable primacy to the principle of nonmaleficence: avoiding harm or wrongdoing is more important than doing an equivalent amount of good. Thus, with respect to an I/O psychologist's obligations to job applicants (not to the employing organization), inappropriately rejecting a candidate who would have succeeded if hired (a false-negative prediction) is more momentous than inappropriately hiring a candidate who fails (a false positive). [85] The dilemma for the I/O psychologist, however, is that we have obligations to both the individual applicants and to the organization.

It seems likely that fulfilling the first of Prilleltensky's (1997) criteria, articulating principles for the good society, is easier than meeting the second, translating this vision into action. People, including psychologists, are more likely to agree on the content of the first than on the substance of the second. Nevertheless, agreement is possible among diverse groups of psychologists regarding the ways in which psychology can contribute to the formulation of national policy for the betterment of all citizens (APS, 1992, 1993a, 1993b, 1996a, 1996b).

---

[85]This does not deny or ignore the likely negative effects on the failing and disappointed employee who was hired and perhaps discharged.

However, an interesting issue is raised by Redding's (2001) criticism of social advocacy in psychology, as represented by policy positions advanced by the APA. Echoing a characterization made a decade earlier by Suedfeld and Tetlock (1991), he made a convincing case that the vast majority of psychologists have politically liberal rather than conservative world views and that "Science frequently is interpreted in a manner consistent with the values and beliefs of the scientists doing the research ... As studies have shown, sociopolitical biases influence the question asked, the research methods selected, the interpretation of research results, the peer review process, judgments about research quality, and decisions about whether to use research in policy advocacy ..." (p. 206).[86] This would account, therefore, for his finding that a content analysis of 31 *American Psychologist* articles dealing with social issues during the 1990s indicated that 97% of the articles advanced liberal themes or policies, and only one article reflected more conservative views. In other words, Redding did not dispute the salient role played by personal and social values throughout the scientific enterprise, and he did not advance a case (e.g., as did Kendler, 1999) for value-free science; his concern was with *which* values will be expressed, supported, and promoted. I assume he did not object on principle to the role traditionally played by professions in shaping public policy in areas germane to the profession's expertise (Hughes, 1965). His is a plea for political diversity and sociopolitical pluralism in psychology, which, at first blush, appears eminently reasonable and fair. But some important issues go unrecognized in his arguments.

Redding (2001) had coders judge whether an article contained conservative or liberal views. The conservative position, in comparison with the liberal position, consisted of "whether the articles recognized traditional/ status quo versus progressive/change-oriented themes or positions on social issues; ... advanced either anti- or pro-government involvement in, and spending on, welfare and social programs; were elitist/ meritocracy-oriented versus egalitarian/social justice-oriented in their values; or favored capitalist/ self-reliance versus socialist/communitarian values" (p. 206). Now, it seems logical that people who endorse the capitalist, elitest, status quo society and who, in any event, are against spending public monies on social programs are not well-represented in a profession that avowedly is concerned in part with addressing social problems. Endorsement of the status quo and the views associated with it suggests that one would not in all likelihood perceive the consequences of employment discrimination, inferior schooling and other manifestations of racism, as well as sex discrimination, the number of working poor and homeless in the midst of enormous wealth for a few, and so on, as

---

[86]I suspect that the ideological distribution may not be the same among I/O psychologists. However, I am aware of no systematic data regarding the sociopolitical views of I/O psychologists.

necessarily representing problems. After all, those conditions *are* the status quo. Moreover, if all of these conditions (not problems) reflect primarily the intellectual, social, or moral failure of those affected (i.e., their lack of merit and personal failure to make it in the free-enterprise system) and if one has an egocentric view of society (i.e., self-reliance is the preeminent moral stance so that one has scant interest in social justice), then there is little if anything to be concerned about. If one believes that systemic sociopolitical and socioeconomic factors play little or no role in producing these outcomes, then there is little need to be concerned with ameliorative systemic actions—especially those to be undertaken at public expense. While serving as president of the APA, G. A. Miller (1969) was not optimistic about the likely effectiveness of organizations such as APA addressing social problems *qua* organizations. He nevertheless counseled that APA should not tacitly endorse a system "that presides over the inequitable distribution of health, wealth, and wisdom in our society" (p. 1065). Although he saw little formal role for the APA in this regard, this is nevertheless the famous speech in which Miller advocated "giving psychology away" to the public by each psychologist's individual contribution to the advancement of psychology as a means of promoting human welfare.

THE INQUIRY PARADIGM OF POSTMODERNISM[87]

To whatever extent some of us may hold tenaciously to a positivist or post-positivist conception of value-free natural science, it seems less tenable when applied to the social sciences, including psychology:

> The way in which a social scientist selects problems to work on, the factors cited to explain behavior, and the evidence sought to substantiate these explanations all reflect the significance and meaning the social scientist attaches to them. To focus on a particular problem is to evaluate it as more important than others, and importance is based on evaluation in the light of human values....
>
> *A social science that sought to efface the moral dimension from its descriptions and explanations would simply serve the interests of some other moral conception.* It would reflect values foreign to those that animate our conception of ourselves. (A. Rosenberg, 1995, p. 205, italics added)

The view in social science characterized as *postmodern* (or as *social constructionism*), as distinct from positivistic natural science, involves much

---

[87]Postmodernism is the name of but one of several variations of the point of view to be summarized here. My description is a synthesis of some (not all) of them, and I have chosen this label because it seems to be the most widely recognized, although social constructionism comes close. A. Rosenberg (1995) and Guba and Lincoln (1994) discussed the various versions.

more than simply the values choices A. Rosengerg (1995) noted. It extends beyond realizing that the intrinsic interdependence of theory, data, and interpretation means that the scientific objectivity sought is illusory. It is a perspective which emphasizes that human beings as objects of study are very different in very important ways from the objects studied in the natural sciences and that—most important—those human attributes cannot be understood adequately by the traditional objectivist positivist paradigm but require a different mode of scientific inquiry. A. Howard (1985) put it simply: "if humans possess characteristics that are unlike the characteristics of subject matters studied by other sciences, then an appropriate science of human behavior might need to be somewhat different from other extant sciences" (pp. 259–260).[88]

I do not attempt to do more than present a brief description of this broad humanistic approach as it has been applied to psychology; more extensive summaries are available (Gergen, 1985, 1992, 1994, 2001; Guba & Lincoln, 1994; Rosenau, 1992; A. Rosenberg, 1995). The essential idea is that although the aim of social science is the same as that of natural science—to achieve greater understanding of the phenomena under study—the nature of the subject matter dictates that a different sort of understanding is necessary. In the natural sciences, understanding is characterized as explanation that consists in formulating universal laws that are testable and falsifiable (Popper, 1972). The ultimate expression or confirmation of these laws is the successful prediction and control of the phenomena under study.

In contrast, the postmodernist conceptualization of understanding has much in common with that of the humanities (e.g., history or literary criticism) insofar as it consists of achieving meaning, which necessarily is interpretive in character. *Hermeneutics* is the name given to this process of interpretation. To the extent that meaningfulness may be expressed in the form of certain regularities in the character or occurrence of psychological entities or processes, they are more like rules than universal laws or generalizations.[89] The meaning of human action is provided by the motives, beliefs, and intentions that reflect the rules that govern our actions. "Human action is thus a matter of following rules, and the aim of social science is to uncover these rules" (A. Rosenberg, 1995, p. 93). The rules may be precise or vague, obvious or esoteric, or conscious or unconscious, but they are all communal in nature in that they are shared among a relevant community of people to

---

[88]Some scholars in this area, notably Kuhn (1970, 2000) for one, believe that the interpretive paradigm I discuss in this section is no less true for the natural sciences as for the social sciences. As an amusing aside, Kuhn (2000) who, in the first edition of *The Structure of Scientific Revolutions* 40 years ago, introduced the importance of scientific paradigms plaintively observed "I seldom use that term these days, having totally lost control of it … " (p. 221).

[89]Popper (1972) was of the opinion that "Labouring the difference between science and the humanities has long been a fashion, and has become a bore" (p. 185) because the nature of "understanding" is actually the same for each: i.e., "the method of conjecture and refutation."

whom they apply. Some rules (comprised of beliefs, normative expectations, intentions, etc.) may be shared only by some groups within a culture or by the entire culture; in some instances, they may be shared by several cultures. The primary distinction between a rule and a scientific law or generalization is that the rule can be violated without invalidating it. The rule retains its explanatory power, whereas frequent exceptions to a scientific law result in its being rejected as a causal explanation. For example, a rule such as "it is advisable to respond in certain appropriate ways when your boss asks to speak with you" still holds even if one of your colleagues violates it a number of times. The example suggests another aspect of rules that is not applicable to laws or generalizations: Violations may be punished. In that instance the punishment may be very clear and overt. But acting in ways that are not in accord with some implicit rules may result in more subtle punishment, such as attributions of being irrational, hostile, lazy, or dull.

Whereas the extreme postmodernist would hold that virtually all of social science must be a hermeneutic enterprise, Kuhn (2000) had no problem with accepting a mixture of traditional and social constructionist approaches. Similarly, Gergen (2001) pointed out that although postmodern critiques are highly critical of the dominant empirical hypothesis-testing research tradition on both conceptual and ideological grounds, "there is nothing within the postmodern critiques that is lethal to this tradition ... the postmodern critiques are themselves without foundations: they constitute important voices but not final voices" (p. 808).

Some Specific Tenets

Several specific differences between psychology as conceptualized and practiced for most of the first century of its existence in the tradition of positivistic natural science and the postmodernist movement of the past generation or so have been emphasized. A few of the most important ones are discussed next.

The Significance of Human Actions as the Object of Study

Psychology and the other social sciences face issues that do not exist in the natural sciences or even in most of biological science. Largely through the utility of symbolic language human beings plan and monitor their own actions. Contrary to the backward-looking focus of behaviorism or psycho-analytic theory (in which the major determinants of behavior are one's rein-forcement history or family history, respectively), humans anticipate and try to shape their futures (G. Kelly, 1962; B. D. Smith & Vetter, 1982). Unlike the chemist's solutions, the physicist's particles, the astronomer's galaxies, or even the biologist's organ systems, we study "objects" who are the active agents of their own behavior (Manicas & Secord, 1983). There are several implications of this fact, such as the role of *reflexivity* in human action (G. S. Howard, 1985).

Human beings are *reflexive*, that is, we are generally aware of what we are doing and what is happening to us; we make attributions regarding the determinants of our actions. One implication of this is that, as objects of psychological research, people are not unaware of the research procedures that they experience. Contrary to the assumptions of the classical scientific paradigm, the psychological researcher cannot fail to intervene in the activity of the objects studied. As researchers, we try to deal with this fact methodologically, usually with mixed success, by developing unobtrusive measures, by ethically dubious means like failing to fully inform our research participants of the purpose of the research, or even by deceiving them about its purpose. The postmodernist would say that more frequently we simply ignore the issue, as if it did not exist as a serious threat to our conception of "knowledge." But the full extent of the problem goes beyond merely the way in which people's actions are altered because they are being studied. Everyday behavior is affected by public knowledge of the results of other research. For example, it appears that the standardized test performance of women, African Americans, and other minorities is affected adversely by knowledge concerning the prior performance of members of their social group and the stereotypic interpretations it is given (J. Aronson, Quinn, & Spencer, 1998; Shih, Pittinsky, & Ambady, 1999; Spencer, Steele, & Quinn, 1999; Steele, 1997, 1999; Steele & Aronson, 1995).

A Phenomenological and Contextualized Perspective

In the postmodern perspective the reflexive and planful nature of human activity means that it can only be understood or interpreted adequately from the internal perspective of the person. This point of view has a long history in social science, as illustrated by the phenomenological perspective in psychology, the emic (insider) view in anthropology (as distinct from the outsider's etic view), the early laboratory studies in psychophysics that attempted to systematically relate the external and internal worlds, as well as the more recent ascendance of the cognitive revolution that reintroduced the internal perspective to scientific psychology after more than a generation of behaviorist hegemony.

The most important consequence of the phenomenological perspective is the need to contextualize human action which, in turn, implies (a) abandonment of reliance exclusively on the ideal of controlled experimental methodology and quantification of variables and (b) an emphasis on the cultural context in adequately interpreting human behavior. In this view, the classic experimental procedures "that focus on selected subsets of variables necessarily 'strip' from consideration, through appropriate controls or randomization, other variables that exist in the context that might, if allowed to exert their effects, greatly alter findings. Further, such exclusionary designs, while increasing the theoretical rigor of a study, detract from its *relevance*, that is its applicability or generalizability" (Guba & Lincoln, 1994, p. 106). Moreover, the greater understanding to be achieved by the inclusion of a more fully contextualized study of human actors will therefore also require the use of qualitative data to assess the meanings and purposes of people's actions.

Postmodern social scientists take culture quite seriously—as permeating all human action—and not merely as either moderators of more general or universal laws of behavior or simply as a means of testing the cross-cultural generalizability of those laws (Gergen, Gulerce, Lock, & Misra, 1996). Culture represents the "local context" in which behavior must be understood. "Psychologists as a group are unaware of how small and unrepresentative of human variability is the range of behavior that constitutes American culture.... Because psychologists' ethnocentric understanding of 'the environment' is implicitly limited to the United States today, they have a truncated view of environmental influences on behavior that confirms their bias toward biologized explanations" (Fish, 2000, pp. 555–556).[90] An interesting example of this approach is Greenfield's (1997) explanation of the manner in which cultural differences in the social conventions having to do with values and with ways of knowing and communicating may invalidate the apparent findings of cognitive ability tests when applied outside their culture of origin.

The Centrality of Language and Rejection of Representationalism

To a postmodern social scientist the most important rules that govern human action are those having to do with language because language shapes our conception of reality. And it does not do so by merely being a neutral representation of an assumed objective external reality but by creating that reality. This *social constructionist* point of view denies the traditional *representationalist* assumption that there is an inherent relation between our words and the world (Gergen, 1985, 1992), and it is finding voice in the study of organizations (Hancock & Tyler, 2001). For example:

Although in much of the existing work on organizations and management researchers treat language as a tool of description, constructivists would have us consider that the world we live in and experience is a product of language.

---

[90] For example, estimates of the genetic heritability of a trait are given by the ratio of genetically associated sources of variance to total trait variance (i.e., genetic + environmental sources). Because the research participants in heritability studies (e.g., monozygotic twins "reared apart") frequently share common cultural experiences, the environmental sources of variance are restricted and reduce the total variance, hence contributing to exaggerated estimates of heritability. Thus, heritability estimates are population and context dependent, and do not correspond to absolute measures of genetic determination.

Not only does language describe but it also creates the very world in the description. Indeed, some would argue that it is not possible to experience the world independent of language and that it is impossible to have organizations or their management independent of language. Language, then, is both context and content.

If we view language as context, what happens to our understanding of organizations and their management? What if we consider organizations not as mechanical or political, or even organic, but as linguistic? What would culture be if an organization were a discursive system engaging in multiple discourses? How would we construct management if what got managed was linguistic rather than material (e.g., resources) or organic (e.g., people)? How would we talk about motivation and leadership, and other traditional organization and management topics, if organizations were linguistic systems in which there was only language? (J. Ford, 2001, pp. 328–329)

Thus, according to postmodernism, the traditional positivist view of science and the search for objective knowledge (most especially in the social sciences) is just one among many possible linguistic constructions of reality that positivists justify "by relying on methods that embody these same constructions" (Gergen, 1994, p. 413). Whereas, in the opinion of the postmodernist, the positivist denigrates all other views as unscientific or value biased, the postmodernist does not seek to dominate discourse but to encourage multiple ways of understanding. Thus, "there is nothing about postmodern thought that argues against continuing research ... However, what postmodern thought does discourage is the reification of the languages used by the communities of scientists conducting such research. It militates against the dissemination of this language as 'true' beyond the communities that speak in these particular ways" (Gergen, 1994, p. 414).

Socially Constructed, Value-Laden Truths

The description I have provided so far of a social scientific understanding of human behavior (postmodern version) emphasizes the contextualized interpretation of the interpersonal cultural rules that people use implicitly to shape their reality. The rules consist of semantic conceptions shared among a community defined by that sharing, and there may be as many conceptions of a given construct as there are cultural communities in which it exists.[91] Questions regarding the extent to which these conceptions accurately represent external reality or which among several alternative conceptions is correct are moot; they are simply outside the paradigm. The

---

[91]Positivists believe that this problem is evaded by clearly operationalizing a construct and, if appropriate, translating its exemplars and/or method of measurement into a foreign language. In that way, the cross-cultural generality of the construct can be investigated. The postmodernist would argue that the initial operationalization is probably invested with culture-specific content that invalidates the enterprise.

notion of correctness as a representation of objective truth is an illusory positivist issue. Although postmodernism claims to have placed the traditional empiricist standards of validity in doubt (at least as applied in social science), even Gergen (1985) acknowledged "constuctionism offers no alternative truth criteria" (p. 272). Conversely, some constructions may be more informed, inclusive, and/or sophisticated than others. And in the realm of science, they still must satisfy the normative expectations of the community of concerned scholars. Moreover, of special relevance for I/O psychology, the "proof of the pudding" for postmodernists comes in the effective *application* of their interpretations.

Once the philosophical problems inherent in maintaining the dualism between subject and object are recognized (Rorty, 1979), knowledge becomes the social practices constructed by our shared language, not an attribute or veridical representation of an external object. And because cultural meanings reflect social values (as well as political values, postmodernists emphasize), virtually all meaning is value laden, including scientific meanings. Thus, social constructionist analyses have been applied to such broad psychological topics as person, self, child, gender, aggression, mind, emotion, morality, and so on (cf. Gergen, 1985), the meanings of which are seen as imbued with social and political values that are bounded by particular cultural and historical contexts.

Perhaps the most radical aspect of the postmodernist perspective is the application of the social constructionist view to the institutions of society. In the same way that rules govern individual action, sets of rules combine to form social roles in society (e.g., manager or professor), and the roles combine with others to form organizations and institutions (A. Rosenberg, 1995). And just as uncovering the rules that guide the individual's behavior explains the meaning and significance of his or her actions, explicating the rules and roles that constitute institutions can explain their social and cultural meaning.[92] Therefore, the institutions of society are understood as social constructions, not as inevitable "givens." That is a radical notion because it suggests that, as constructions, institutions can be altered. A. Rosenberg put it well:

> To say that social institutions are "constructed" means roughly that they do not exist independent of people's actions, beliefs, and desires—their reasons for acting. On one interpretation, this claim may not be controversial, for all will grant that without people there is no society thus no social roles to be filled by people. The claim becomes controversial when we add in the idea

---

[92] And an anthropologist would tell us that institutional meanings might not be known consciously by the individual participants in a cultural institution. Explanations may have to be discovered at the societal level. Thus, societies have hidden or deep meanings. The two prominent examples of social science theories that constitute explanations of the hidden meanings of society and its institutions are Freudian psychoanalysis and Marxism (A. Rosenberg, 1995).

that people can do otherwise than what they in fact have done hitherto. They can violate the rules that constrain their actions, and they can construct new rules. That makes social institutions we may have thought were natural and unavoidable look artificial and revisable. (pp. 101–102)

In this sense, postmodernism can be seen as constituting a radical challenge to much of the status quo human enterprise, from literary criticism to social and behavioral science, to the very institutional structure of society itself. That it has met with stiff resistance from many quarters is not surprising. For example, a recent attempt to promote the postmodern perspective in psychology (Gergen, 2001) drew nine published commentaries, some rather vociferous, that characterize it as "untested speculation" (Kruger, 2002, p. 456), "historically frozen" (Krueger, 2002, p. 461), "of little value for the advancement of psychology as a science" (Hofmann, 2002, p. 462), "the dead end of philosophy" (Locke, 1992, p. 458), and "inevitably foster[ing] nihilism" (H. Friedman, 2002, p. 463).

PROFESSIONAL ROLES: RESEARCH AND PRACTICE IN PSYCHOLOGY

As noted earlier, a long-avowed goal of the profession of psychology is betterment of the human condition (APA, 1992, 2002). That this has been an accepted aspect of the role definition of the past generation of psychologists is reflected in surveys of psychology faculty and students who overwhelmingly viewed the relevance of psychology to social problems and the real world as the most important issue facing the field (Lipsey, 1974). It has also been presented as a moral obligation: "... psychologists, as well as members of other scientific disciplines, have a collective obligation to develop knowledge that at least in the long run will contribute to the solutions of the critical problems of the society that literally and figuratively supports their research and themselves" (Spence, 1985, p. 1286). It is not uncommon, however, for leaders in the field to decry the extent to which we have failed to live up to those obligations and expectations: "As the twentieth century wore on, psychological knowledge increased enormously, and psychologists assumed respected and influential positions. But somehow the hopes for continuous improvement in the condition of mankind through psychology declined. It became almost naive to assume that what was discovered through research could have much effect on man's nature or institutions" (Tyler, 1973, p. 1021). Similar negative evaluations of the amount and/or effectiveness of our applications and professional practice have been voiced for 30 years, especially in comparison with the progress and wonders achieved in the physical sciences (Fishman, 1999; G. A. Miller, 1969). For example, after decades of social psychological study of intergroup relations we still arc plagued with racial hostility and conflict; after studying learning and the educational process for the better part of a century we still have mostly disastrous public educational systems and high rates of adult illiteracy; despite the generally acknowledged utility of I/O psychology's contributions to organizations, after many years of both basic and applied research, a considerable gap still remains between organizational research findings and management practices (Rynes et al., 2001); and the predictions that indicate the utility of our personnel selection procedures do not even account hypothetically for more than about one third of the variance in job performance criteria (Schmidt & Hunter, 1998).

The Postmodern Challenge to the Distinction Between Science and Practice

The typical reactions to psychology's alleged failures one is likely to hear from psychologists are: (a) "Yes, that's true, but we are a young field and will produce much useful knowledge in the future"; or a variant of that, (b) "Yes, while that may be true, it's due to the fact that social problems and human behavior are much more complicated and difficult to understand and change than phenomena in the physical world"; or (c) "That's not entirely correct: We have produced a lot of potentially useful knowledge but for a variety of reasons have not been effective in getting it translated into policy applications or used by practitioners." A case can probably be made for each of these three explanations. But convincing arguments refuting each of them are also readily available. Be that as it may, the point I make here is that a very different explanation has been offered by the postmodernist social constructionist school of thought.

In his relatively underappreciated work, Popper (1972) set the groundwork for this view by making the point that the theoretical aim of explanation and the practical aim of technical application "are, in a way, two different aspects of one and the same activity" (p. 348). Indeed, "Perhaps where human beings are concerned, that which is most practical is of most theoretical interest" (G. S. Howard, 1985, p. 263). In recent years, more and more of psychology, regardless of specialty area, has shown "our commitment to real-world phenomena" (Conner, 2001, p. 9) and the "commensurability" of science and practice in psychology has been reasserted forcefully (G. Stricker, 1997).[93] Moreover, there even have been recent signs of a developing rapprochement between natural and social science approaches to the study of human functioning (Damasio et al., 2001).

These trends may, in part, represent reactions to the postmodernist charge that it is the unnecessary and artificial positivist distinction between

---

[93]A cautionary note is sounded by D. R. Peterson (1991) who argued that, because of emphases on traditional scientific research, typical doctoral training in psychology does not equip psychologists for sophisticated professional practice. That is a complaint not unheard of among I/O psychology practitioners as well.

pure science and basic research on the one hand and applied research and professional practice on the other that is responsible for the relatively limited accomplishments of social science in the real world. In that unidirectional ideal model, adopted from the physical sciences, we discover basic knowledge that consists of the general principles uncovered by our controlled laboratory experimentation, which are then transformed into technologies to be applied to real-world problems and clients; professional practice is always assigned a secondary role as the application of knowledge (Hoshmand & Polkinghorne, 1992; D. R. Peterson, 1991). The separation of the two realms is an intrinsic component of the positivist conception of the former as entirely free of the values issues with which the latter is imbued. One unfortunate fallout from this paradigm, however, is that psychologists in many academic specialty areas have tended to bury themselves in the data from laboratory situations and have lost track of the broader questions that may even have stimulated the research (Spence, 1985; Tversky, cited in Conner, 2001). The fundamental impediment is that the basic theoretical principles uncovered in artificially decontextualized, controlled experiments, in which one or only few variables are investigated and the reflexivity of research participants is not accounted for, yields the most limited of truths, biased by the particular theoretical (and other unacknowledged) values of the researcher. No wonder the application of this knowledge to the messy real world has been disappointing and that some I/O psychologists are concerned with reducing the gap between organizational research and practice by encouraging more field research in organizations (Rynes & McNatt, 2001). In a similar vein, J. P. Campbell (1990) chided that we rarely "inquire as to whether the 'role of theory' has anything to do with the problem(s) of concern" (p. 67).

In contrast with the traditional approach adopted from the physical sciences, postmodern psychological researchers begin with a client (individual, group, organization, community, or country) with a problem that needs solving. The problem assessment in terms of the client's objectives, the research, and/or interventions as well as their evaluation all take place in situ (D. R. Peterson, 1991). "In this interpretation of science, the test of knowledge is not whether it corresponds exactly to reality, as it is impossible to ascertain whether there is such a direct correspondence. Instead, *the test for knowledge is whether it serves to guide human action to attain goals*. In other words, the test is pragmatic ... not logical" (Hoshmand & Polkinghorne, 1992, p. 58, italics added).

It is interesting to reflect on the extent to which I/O psychology, despite its generally neopositivist orientation, may have much in common with the postmodern view. Postmodern perspectives have been less in evidence in academic psychology than in the other social sciences—probably because of psychology's strong identification with the natural sciences (Gergen, 2001).

And—with a few exceptions (e.g., Weick, 1995)—they have been even less in evidence in I/O psychology. But our field has from its inception taken real-world organizational problems as both the intellectual and emotional stimulation for systematic inquiry (Boehm, 1980; J. P. Campbell, Daft, & Hulin, 1982) and has emphasized the reciprocity between research (basic or applied) and professional practice (C. L. Cooper & Locke, 2000; Hakel, Sorcher, Beer, & Moses, 1982; Latham, 2000, 2001; Lawler, Mohrman, Mohrman, Ledford, & Cummings, 1985). Nevertheless, the extent to which knowledge created in one of these two realms infuses the other is still perceived as extremely problematic (Rynes et al., 2001). Conversely, the postmodernist critique that such knowledge transfer is invariably and inappropriately assumed to be unidirectional (research informs practice) is probably less true of I/O psychology than for other areas of application.

Fishman (1999) contrasted the postmodern technological model of what he called "pragmatic psychology" with the traditional model. His intent is compatible with Nogami's (1982) concerns for the difference between often-ineffective applied research and what she called "applicable research." Although Fishman's problem-driven, uncontrolled research model emphasizes a variety of methodologies not well represented in I/O psychology, including qualitative methods and case studies (see Coghlan & Brannick, 2000; Gummeson, 1999, for recent exceptions), his description of postmodern pragmatism sounds a great deal like a model of organizationally driven research in the practice of I/O psychology:

> While natural science emphasizes academic freedom of the individual researcher, technology is guided by goals and objectives that are established by the society. While natural science ideally takes place in the laboratory, technology is conducted "in the field," within the actual situation in which a problem presents itself. While basic research focuses on testing hypotheses derived from academic theories, technology focuses on directly altering conditions in the real world. While natural science focuses upon the parameters in its laboratory experiments, technology develops systematic pictures of psychological and social phenomena in the outside world, using standardized measures and large-scale norms.... Finally, while the goal of natural science is theory development and "truth," the goal of technology is to guide practical action by suggesting effective solutions to presenting problems within the constraints of a particular body of knowledge, a given set of skills, and available resources. (p. xxii)

Fishman suggested that his approach represents a middle way between the positivist who attacks the case study as too context specific from which to generalize and the social constructionist who attacks the positivist for trying to achieve generalization by ignoring individual contexts and over simplifying complex phenomena. He did so by advocating the accumulation of multiple cases organized into computer-accessible databases that would eventually permit some generalizations without loss of important contextual factors. This appears to be responsive to Hulin's (2001) observation "... we will never learn about the few underlying general constructs that account for many manifest behaviors and attitudes if we study problems and behaviors one at a time" (p. 230). Similarly, Rynes et al. (2001) presented a taxonomy of means by which tacit and explicit forms of organizational knowledge may be transferred between academics and practitioners, including use of protocol analyses, ethnographies, and action research—all emanating from the practitioner domain.

Potential Value Conflicts and Ethical Dilemmas: Considering Consequences

I anticipate that most I/O psychologists will concur with the orientation of Fishman's pragmatic psychology that real-world (organizational) settings should be recognized as both necessary sites for achieving psychology's goal of bettering the human condition through professional practice, as well as methodologically appropriate sites for conducting meaningful research on fundamental psychological phenomena. But because Fishman's focus is on community psychology, educational reform, and psychotherapy—all exclusively concerned with providing human services—he failed to consider an attendant problem that is extremely relevant for I/O psychologists. It has to do with the values, goals, and objectives of the clients served. His position is that the pragmatic paradigm "supports our democratic ideals by requiring collaboration with program stakeholders in program goal setting" and that "goal and other value questions are to be resolved by open, democratic dialogue among relevant stakeholders" (p. 290). Or, as D. R. Peterson (1991) succinctly stated, "The practitioner does not choose the issue to examine, the client does" (p. 426).

When the meta-objectives of the institutions to be served (e.g., schools and mental health clinics) are entirely commensurate with the humanitarian objectives that comprise the applied portion of psychology's value system, no additional ethical issues are raised. However, when those served are business organizations governed largely (albeit sometimes not exclusively) by a value system of profit making for just one stakeholder group, actions on their behalf may sometimes conflict with our objective "to improve the condition of individuals, organizations, and society" (APA, 2002, p. 1062). This important matter will be explored further later. For now it is sufficient to simply make the point that, to whatever extent one might attempt to advance the case for a value-free conception of scientific psychology and basic psychological research, it clearly does not characterize applied research, much less the practice of applied psychology in business organizations. Those institutions have their own particular value systems and objectives that largely define the role and objectives of the applied psychologist in service to that client. For example, personnel selection and its major components such as test validation are not value-free because they represent solutions to organizational problems that reflect the values and objectives of the organization. In so doing, they determine the very definition of the problem and the range of acceptable solutions, generally without reference to the benefits or harms received by other stakeholders and institutions.

The postmodernist emphasis on applied research inevitably invites consideration of "the sociocultural ramifications of both the research and the manner in which it is framed" (Gergen, 1994). In other words, unlike the niceties of strictly controlled laboratory research procedures, one cannot investigate and manipulate real-world situations unmindful of the effects of such orchestrations. This is a reprise of an issue discussed in chapter 3 regarding ethical responsibility for the foreseeable consequences of one's professional actions, even if those consequences are not the intended purpose of the intervention. Referring to the humanitarian pursuits he called "the ethic of innocence," Luria (1976) admonished that: "Morality does not exist in a vacuum. Human pursuits should always be judged in terms of what their consequences are for other human beings" (p. 333). And finally, Gergen (1985) explained:

> To the extent that psychological theory (and related practices) enter into the life of the culture, sustaining certain patterns of conduct and destroying others, such work must be evaluated in terms of good and ill. The practitioner can no longer justify any socially reprehensible conclusion on the grounds of being a "victim of the facts"; he or she must confront the pragmatic implication of such conclusions within society more generally. (p. 273)

There is both a macrolevel and microlevel challenge implicit in Gergen's statement. The first suggests that one cannot ethically be engaged in furthering the fortunes of powerful institutions in our society while turning a blind eye toward their possible adverse social actions. Similarly, as scientist–practitioners, if we take that hyphenation seriously we cannot ethically hide behind a narrow technological or scientific definition of competent professional practice without considering all of the consequences of that practice. The first challenge comprises much of the substance of chapters 10 and 11, and the second is taken up in chapter 12.

ADDING FURTHER TO THE FRAMEWORK
FOR ETHICAL DECISION MAKING

26.   The role played by values in the scientific enterprise is a topic marked by considerable controversy. The question of what role they ought to play is even more controversial. The question is important, as values entail choices to be made in the conduct of human affairs; hence, the possibility arises of values conflicts and ethical dilemmas. The consensus of current scholarly opinion appears to be (a) even in the physical sciences, arguably the hallmark of the positivist empiricist value-free tradition, epistemic values are intrinsic to scientific inquiry, and personal values of scientists unavoidably play a part in their work; (b) the social and behavioral sciences are even more susceptible to such influences because human beings, who exist in social relationships, are the objects of study by other interested human beings; and (c) social norms, beliefs, and values are clearly suffused throughout applied social science research and professional practice because the clients served provide the goals and objectives that largely define the nature of that research and practice. *Therefore, it would be self-deluding of I/O psychologists to deny that social and political values are inherent in much of our work on behalf of corporations and other organizations. It seems preferable for each of us as individuals as well as for the profession to articulate the extrinsic values that in part shape our work.*

27.   Whether one accepts all of the epistemological, ontological, and methodological critiques by postmodernists, the social-constructionist viewpoint seems to be a potentially fruitful approach to understanding the nature of much of what we study as organizational scientists. Moreover, it should be acknowledged that mainstream psychology has gradually been adopting on its own much of the postmodernist platform without necessarily accepting the overall paradigm. For example: (a) in planning and executing research moral issues (i.e., research ethics—see chaps. 13 and 14) are considered along with the scientific questions (APA, 2002); (b) the use of multivariate statistical techniques, including causal modeling, as well as the continued use of field experiments, quasi-experimental designs, and action research (Coghlan & Brannick, 2000), along with systematic questioning of the generalizability of laboratory research findings (E. A. Locke, 1986), all represent modes of achieving greater contextualization of meaning; (c) growth in the acceptability of qualitative procedures and methods of analysis (case studies, ethnography, discourse analysis, etc.; Gummeson, 1999) as well as the use of insider perspectives (Oyserman & Swim, 2001) reflect more interpretive phenomenological approaches; (d) the cognitive revolution in psychological theory and research begun in the 1960s has given greater recognition to the intentionality and reflexivity of people as objects of study, which was begun as long ago as the Hawthorne studies (Roethlisberger & Dixon, 1939); (e) this was given prominence by Orne's (1962) illumination of the distinction between experimentation in the natural and behavioral sciences, with research participants in the latter subject to the demand characteristics of the experimental situation; and (f) I/O psychologists in particular, like postmodern social scientists, have for at least a generation viewed professional practice both as an inspiration and source of knowledge, as well as a venue for its application. Nevertheless, it is probably still true that "industrial and organizational psychologists tend to use only a limited number of the many available research strategies and tactics" (Sackett & Larson, 1990, p. 419) and that "Ideally, the field would find a better balance between the quantitative and qualitative and show a greater tolerance for and appreciation of all approaches" (McCall & Bobko, 1990, p. 412).

28.   I/O psychologists should recognize that the avowed goal of psychology to use knowledge "to improve the condition of individuals, organizations, and society" (APA, 2002, p. 1062) potentially may conflict with the goals and objectives of organizations for which we work. One could argue, conversely, that the enormous economic and social benefits contributed by business organizations to society indicate that such conflicts are imaginary. It seems to me, however, that the latter position can be maintained only by disregarding the essentially capitalist nature of the corporate enterprise that frequently leads to excesses of concern for shareholder profits, as well as the frequently self-serving features of managerial actions, to the detriment of other employees, stakeholders, and segments of society. The perspective advanced here is that our moral obligation as psychologists is to work toward attenuating those excesses.

10

Business Values:
I. The Classical
Free-Enterprise Model

The normative bill of particulars brought against American corporate business is lengthy, shocking, and saddening. From many quarters and over long stretches of time, a clamorous chorus has sounded out a damning indictment of specific business practices and, in some cases, a condemnation of the institution itself. Greed, selfishness, ego-centeredness, disregard of the needs and well-being of others, a narrow or nonexistent social vision, an ethnocentric managerial creed imposed on nonindustrial cultures, a reckless use of dangerous technologies, an undermining of countervailing institutions such as trade unions, a virtual political takeover of some pluralist government agencies, and a system of self-reward that few either inside or outside business have cared to defend as fair or moral—all of these attributes have been credited to the business account.

—William C. Frederick

Frederick's forthright assessment is rather poignant because he is a supporter and proponent of business, not one of its critics. The bill of particulars he enumerated does not even mention the serious accusations brought by those who see contemporary business organizations as all-powerful corrupters of political democracy and masters of an unjust international order (e.g., Korten, 1995, 1999; Luttwak, 1999; Mokhiber & Weissman, 1999; Soros, 2000). But one would have to be in serious psychological denial to fail to appreciate the enormous positive contributions made by modern business institutions. The widespread material well-being afforded by the resources, products, and services provided are just the beginning. Also to be acknowledged are the economic benefits of employment—viewed from both an individual and societal perspective, the social and psychological gratification experienced by employees performing meaningful work activities (when jobs are structured in that fashion) as well as the emotional security and sense of self-worth attendant upon one's long-term enactment of a career, the philanthropic and community activities supported by businesses, and the potential accumulation of widespread personal wealth made possible through the mechanism of public corporate ownership. What, then, is to be made of the disparity between these two representations of corporate America? How can we best understand the simultaneous existence of this corporate rendering of the Jekyll and Hyde metaphor? What are its moral implications? And most important for our purposes, what is the appropriate ethical stance for I/O psychology, which sustains, supports, and contributes to corporate goals and objectives, and so might be characterized as playing an instrumental role in both scenarios?

Agle and Caldwell (1999), DeGeorge (1987), and Danley (1994) noted that the study of business values and ethics necessitates recognizing several levels of analysis, notwithstanding that the overwhelming bulk of research and theory—including most of the contents of this book—is at the individual level and to a lesser degree the organizational level, and they focus on the relations between the two. A major weakness in the study of business ethics (no less true in the case of I/O psychology) is the "focus primarily upon individual cases while ignoring the larger institutional frameworks.... This obscures the extent to which our intuitions about individualistic ethical judgments are shaped by our views about broader issues of economics, social theory, law, and political philosophy" (Danley, 1994, p. 20). This chapter and the next one are responsive to that criticism.

A relevant illustration of the independence of levels of social analysis was mentioned briefly in commentary on Table 7.1 concerning the institutional business value of "competition." It should be appreciated that competition, as an instrumental (not terminal) business value, is a cherished attribute of the classical free-market economic system (A. Smith, 1776/1976), that is, of the institution of business but not of individual business organizations. Competition is generally forced on companies as a necessary fact of life because there are other companies in the same business. Business activity is aimed at winning not competing—even to the point of eliminating the competition. That's why the enactment of antitrust legislation was necessary. Although competition is romanticized as part of the American ethos and business creed, businesses invariably opt whenever possible for anticompetitive strategies. Thus, we see the monopolies, oligopolies, and trusts of yesteryear and the mergers and acquisitions of recent years.[94]

Adam Smith, the father of modern economics, predicted these patterns 225 years ago, and salient empirical evidence goes back at least as far as to J. P. Morgan who reorganized the entire railroad industry after the panic of 1873 caused by the failure of one railroad and the bank that financed it. He reorganized the industry by consolidating the railroads in a monopolistic process that became known as *Morganizing*. The lesson was learned well by the "robber barons" who followed, such as John D. Rockefeller who monopolized the oil industry. The adverse effects of these anticompetitive practices resulted in the Sherman and Clayton Antitrust Acts and creation of the Federal Trade Commission, all by 1914. These laws were strengthened by the Antitrust Improvements Act of 1976 in response to the growing numbers of mergers and acquisitions. The most dramatic implementation of these laws in recent years was the federal government's suit against Microsoft in 1999. The Microsoft litigation, however, marked something of a shift in the nature of antitrust concerns, reflecting the new technology-based economy. The government's case, on behalf of the public, was not primarily the classic issue of a monopolist's price gouging. In fact, the price of personal computers (PCs) has declined dramatically even as their power and quality have continued to improve; moreover, the cost of the Windows operating system represents a very small portion of the cost of a PC. The issue was one of Microsoft's using its dominance to make threats and exclusionary contracts that forced computer manufacturers and internet service providers to shut out potential rivals such as Netscape. The issue was one of stifling competition by unfairly (and at least in part illegally, as it turns out) enforcing its own Windows technology as essentially the gatekeeping standard for the industry. The concern was innovation, not price, but the company's goal was nevertheless the traditional one of eliminating the competition.

An ironic example of the fact that competition is not a value of individual organizations comes from a domain in which competition is ostensibly the aim of the entire industry—sports entertainment, in which competition among teams is the entertainment service being sold. Therefore, one might surmise that professional baseball teams, for example, would do all they could to enhance the quality of competition among them to increase the overall excitement, suspense, and sales. That could readily be accomplished by greater sharing of the revenues from lucrative television and radio

---

[94]Of course, this does not deny that there are some individuals with greater propensities for risk taking than their more risk-averse counterparts. And they may even seek risk-taking opportunities. This may be a necessary attribute for entrepreneurial success, and these folks may even be willing and eager to incur substantial economic danger for the promise of great reward and may find competition personally thrilling. But risk is still something to be minimized as much as possible in accord with planned goal attainment.

contracts and gate receipts, which currently benefit disproportionately the teams in big markets (e.g., New York City, Atlanta, and Cleveland), and by limiting the total personnel budget for players to the same amount for all teams. That would serve to more nearly equate the level of talent on each ball club and presumably make games more competitive, as well as more interesting by placing a greater premium on innovative field management, player evaluation, and effective team building. (Cooperation, e.g., revenue sharing, is enabled by virtue of major league baseball's having long ago been granted an exemption from antitrust laws.) The owners of the teams with enormous revenues, such as George Steinbrenner of my hometown Yankees, will of course have none of it. (Although, in all fairness, the players' union—fearful of a resultant cap on salaries—also is against large-scale revenue sharing.) As a consequence, the difference in total revenues between the highest and lowest clubs increased from $74 million to $129 million between 1995 and 1999. The comparable increase in payroll differentials was from $45 million to $77 million. That is hardly a level playing field. Those imbalances have resulted in a situation in which (a) every World Series winner from 1995 through 1999 was a team in the first quartile of total payroll; (b) with only one exception during those years, even the World Series runner-up was also in the first quartile; and (c) no team in the third or fourth quartile won any of the 158 playoff games during those years (Levin, Mitchell, Volcker, & Will, 2000). In addition, for the 30 teams, the correlations between total team revenue and number of regular season games won from 1995 to 1999 was .54, .57, .66, .58, and .54, respectively, and between total player payroll and number of regular season games won during the same seasons was .57, .63, .67, .76, and .68.[95] Team performance is sufficiently predictable from the available resources as to make it hardly worth playing the games!

Perhaps these examples of persistent anticompetitive actions and the dismaying bill of particulars brought by Frederick (1995) against American corporations are attributable to a common source. I suggest that the exercise of power, especially as manifested by the single-minded pursuit of short-term profits and increased stock price, is an extremely salient value of business institutions that is determinative. In particular, I argue later that this expression of power, although related to the business values of productivity and efficiency—or what Frederick (1995) called *economizing*—is relatively independent and autonomous. The adverse consequences of the power motive, especially in the service of profit maximization, may be seen directly in the well-documented excesses of exploitative, unethical, and illegal corporate actions. What I find more interesting, however, is the way it may be seen indirectly in attempts to extend the power/profit-motive value to societal

---

[95]Calculated from data in Tables 17, 19, 21, 23, and 25 of Levin et al. (2000).

institutions outside the business domain with the effect of undermining the inherent values that characterize those domains and jeopardizing the fulfillment of their objectives. But I'm getting a little ahead of myself.

THE CLASSICAL LIBERAL MODEL
OF FREE-ENTERPRISE CAPITALISM

For the past generation or so philosophers have proceeded on the belief that moral philosophy and political philosophy are inseparable and that they must include a consideration of the role of government in society, including its economic aspects (i.e., political economy). The general normative focus is on the moral justification of an economic system (e.g., free-market capitalism), and the more specific normative focus is on what should be the appropriate role of individual organizations (mostly corporations) in society.[96]

The classical free-enterprise model of economic activity, based primarily on the economics of Adam Smith (1776/1976) and the political philosophy of John Locke (1689/1988), dominated Western thinking, especially in North America, from the industrial revolution through the 1920s. Following the depression of the 1930s and World War II in the 1940s, an alternative modified conception of free enterprise—emphasizing social responsibility, multiple stakeholders, and the role of the manager as a professional—held sway for about a generation, only to be supplanted for about 20 years by a resurgence of the classical model during the reign of President Reagan's "cowboy economy" (Cavanagh, 1984). It is probably fair to say that, spurred in large measure by what is seen by many as the excesses and inequities associated with the globalization of the capitalist system as well as by public and governmental reactions to the recent spate of corporate scandals, we are now in a period in which the two models may again be in contention—or, as Danley (1994) argued, both may have become inadequate. For example, Danley noted "As markets transcend national boundaries, individual nation states have little ability to deal alone with transnational corporations or international markets. At the world level, there are no mechanisms for coping with market externalities or market failures, or for providing for the needs of the 'losers.' There are virtually no international safety nets ... "(p. 286).[97] The most influential

---

[96]The balance of this chapter and the next owe much to the work of Cavanagh (1984), Danley (1994), Donaldson (1982), Frederick (1995), and Post et al., (1996). Those references should be consulted for a fuller treatment of these issues, which are only summarized briefly here.

[97]*Market externalities* (more commonly, *negative externalities*), also referred to as *neighborhood effects* or *market failures*, are social costs of economic activities that are not paid for by those who purchase the goods and services produced, and they are not borne by the producer. For example, the degradation, property damage and depreciation, medical costs, and so on caused by industrial pollution and the costs of environmental cleanup are not factored into the sales prices of the output of which they are the byproducts. They are often paid for by individual citizens who are adversely affected or by us all through our taxes, which finance remedial projects and programs.

contemporary spokesperson for the unattenuated free-enterprise model has undoubtedly been the economist Milton Friedman.

Milton Friedman

M. Friedman's (1970, 1982) articulate and vehement defense of the classical free-market, antiregulatory model of corporate action was first presented in the early 1960s as a defense against the growing influence of the social responsibility model, and it continues to serve as an inspiration for similar contemporary exhortations (Rappaport, 1990). To appreciate Friedman's position it is important to get past his sometimes overly combative tone: For example, Friedman (1970) stated "Businessmen who talk [about the social responsibilities of business in a free-enterprise system] are unwilling puppets of the intellectual forces that have been undermining the basis of a free society these past decades" (p. 33). His vehemence reflects his passionate belief that the economic freedom of the corporation to exclusively pursue the maximization of profits is an essential component of political freedom. In his view limiting the former necessitates restricting the latter.[98]

If one deconstructs and condenses Friedman's general position, it can be outlined by four main points:

1.   The freedom of corporations to pursue single mindedly the maximization of profits is an expression of inalienable *rights* in a free society; in particular, rights of association of shareholders to freely come together for that purpose and their property rights to use their corporation in that fashion. Friedman acknowledged that those rights are not unlimited: companies, through the actions of their managers, may be expected to obey the law and to adhere to the basic ethical customs of the society such as refraining from fraud. It is not clear whether Friedman meant, by basic ethical customs, anything beyond simply obeying the law.[99]

2.   A free-market economy in which everyone has the right to buy and sell freely is necessary in order to maintain political freedoms such as freedom of speech. Thus, the influence of government should be kept to the bare minimum, based on the principle of protecting the public from harm. There is some grudging justification for antitrust regulations, a

---

[98]M. Friedman restricted his focus to corporations, which are publicly owned. The right of an individual proprietor or owners of a closely held corporation to spend their money any way they wish—even on unjustifiable things like supporting local literacy programs or training unskilled former welfare recipients for a productive life of employment—is not denied. But from a normative standpoint he was clear in his belief that they *ought* not reduce their profits by doing so, and those who fail to disdain such practices are actually "approaching fraud" (M. Friedman, 1970, p. 124).

[99]Defenders of the "anything goes" school of thought frequently exaggerate Friedman's position by omitting his acknowledgment of the necessity to adhere to basic ethical tenets. In all fairness, however, Friedman was not clear on which ethical practices are necessary beyond those enshrined in law.

criminal justice system—including enforcement of the law of contracts and of property rights, regulation of the money supply, some limited "safety net" provision for citizens who cannot be responsible for themselves (i.e., children and the mentally impaired), and some minimal regulation of so-called "neighborhood effects" if they are sufficiently serious, and not much else. This represents Friedman's notion of the "ideal state" in support of a "perfect free market." He recognized, however, that in the real world we have neither.

3.   Since what businesses do best is conduct their business, the most effective way they can contribute to society is by efficiently producing the goods and services they provide. In other words, as indicated by the title of Friedman's classic (1970) statement, "the social responsibility of business is to increase its profits." The assumption is that by responding to the pressures of free competition, businesses become more and more efficient and productive, so that society as a whole benefits.

4.   Corporate executives and managers are agents for the owners and thus have no right to spend the corporation's profits in any ways not in the financial interests of those owners, such as making "expenditures on reducing pollution beyond the amount that is in the best interest of the corporation or that is required by law ... " (M. Friedman, 1970, p. 33). Managers who do so are behaving unethically by violating their social contract with shareholders. Moreover, those managers are in effect inappropriately performing the governmental functions of imposing taxes and determining how they will be disbursed—powers they have neither been elected to possess nor trained to implement.

Friedman's contemporary model is based, in some respects explicitly and in others implicitly, on natural rights theory, social contract theory, utilitarianism, and Adam Smith's (1776/1976) economic theory regarding the production of wealth, which is based on enlightened ethical egoism as the primary explanation of economic activity.

Adam Smith

Adam Smith's (1723–1790) revolutionary recasting of the nature of economics was done in the context of 18th century classical liberalism based on John Locke's conceptions of inalienable rights not to be abridged by government, Jeremy Bentham's hedonistic utilitarianism, and Thomas Hobbes' and Jean Jacques Rousseau's notions of social contract . Smith's brilliance was in literally redefining the nature of wealth as constituting the goods and services produced by a society and elucidating its origins as due to the use of capital under conditions of organizational specialization or the division of labor. Wealth is produced by the efficient utilization of capital and labor, is sought by all as a reflection of merely following one's own self-interest, and it results in the aggregation of maximum benefits for the entire society. In other words, under ideal free-market conditions the egoistic pursuit of one's own concerns will result in maximizing overall utility. The presumed inevitability of this result from the interplay of free markets suggested to Smith the operation of an "invisible hand." But for the system to work, the market must truly be free—that is, protected from the monopolistic tendencies of business people themselves and from the inefficiencies introduced by government intervention, notwithstanding the inherent contradiction that the latter is the only effective means of accomplishing the former.

A. Smith is sometimes interpreted unfairly as having proposed an amoral model of economic activity. But he was more sophisticated than that. He was quite clear on the necessity for trust, honest dealings, and a sense of fairness as an underpinning for the effective operation of the market. He would be appalled at the current wave of insider trading, hiding costs, and inflating revenues to mislead shareholders, as well as personal enrichment of top executives at the expense of shareholders, employees, and consumers. In addition to the moral virtues of honesty, fairness, and trust, he emphasized the significance of beneficence as more important than self-interest at the personal level. In addition, he presaged Hegel, Marx, and 20th century psychologists, such as Abraham Maslow, Charles R. Walker, and Frederick Herzberg, in anticipating the stultifying social and psychological effects on workers of extreme job specialization and routinization. He was sympathetic to that condition and advocated increased educational opportunities for laborers—even though it entailed government activity in the world of commerce. Perhaps most important, Smith's justification of the profit motive was essentially a moral one (utilitarian) in that the competition for profits spurs greater efficiencies and productivity, thus raising the overall economic status of the entire society. He believed—presaging Rawlsian conceptions of justice and/or "trickle-down theory" by 200 years—that, although capitalism might produce disparities in wealth, the poor are better off in its sway than they would otherwise be. Notwithstanding the prominence of the profit motive and individual self-interest in his theory, there is relatively little in A. Smith's writings that invites M. Friedman's vociferous condemnation of "social responsibilities" for business or what Donaldson (1982) called an attitude of "moral disinterest."

Critique of the Classical Free-Enterprise Model

Broadly speaking, the classical model embodies two fundamental issues of political and social economy. The first has to do with the relation between business and government, with a focus on government regulation of the economy and of business organizations versus a laissez-faire approach and free markets. The second focuses on the relation between business and the rest of society, especially with regard to whether businesses have any social responsibilities that might attenuate a strategy of exclusive profit maximization. It might seem that only the second issue is relevant to our focus on the moral implications of business values; however, the two issues are intertwined (in the belief, e.g., that businesses should have the unrestricted and unregulated freedom to pursue profit maximization and should otherwise display moral disinterest). Nevertheless, the two concerns are not coterminous, and each is supported by different rationales, so that critiques of the model tend to focus on one or the other dimension.

With regard to the first issue, most Americans probably are of the opinion that government regulation does not contribute to business productivity, so the question becomes what is the minimum necessary degree of regulation for which we are willing to accept some inefficiencies.[100] The answer, of course, largely reflects one's position regarding values conflicts between the goals of economic productivity and those of social justice, fairness, social responsibility, and protection of the public. Adam Smith himself structured the issue as a matter of degree of regulation rather than an "either–or" choice between free and regulated markets, when he acknowledged the need to protect against the inevitable collusive tendencies of business owners. Voicing a more constructive and empirical point of view, the free-enterprise stalwart Thomas L. Friedman (2002) wrote that what distinguishes our version of capitalism from others in the world, and why it is so envied, is "our system's ability to consistently expose, punish, regulate and ultimately reform" the "greedy excesses" of capitalism by means of "an uncorrupted bureaucracy to manage the regulatory agencies, licensing offices, property laws and commercial courts" (p. 13).

Scholars have suggested that there are four primary flaws in the classical model. I present them next.

The Weaknesses of Natural Rights Theory

A. Smith and M. Friedman's free-enterprise model rests a great deal on Locke's classical liberal (i.e., libertarian) political theory of a minimalist state not harming or interfering with our inalienable rights. As noted earlier, the basic philosophic problems with natural rights theory are the lack of any clear, nontheological basis for such rights, whatever they may be, and the justifiability of Locke's short list of rights versus someone else's longer list. In

---

[100]Even that may be conceding too much too readily to the extreme free marketers. Businesses that dominate their markets (e.g., local utilities) have been known to operate inefficiently and restrict productivity to keep consumer demand and prices high. Conversely, not all government regulation is inefficient or results in a net cost to society.

addition, defining the moral dimension of the state as merely refraining from doing harm seems deficient in its disregard for the moral principles of beneficence and fairness. For example, Danley (1994) portrayed minimalist natural rights theorists as "fanatical in denying the moral relevance of anything except not harming another. This view excludes, not only consideration of social good, but any other goods as well" (p. 51). It eliminates from consideration a great deal of what many think of as the essence of morality: positive duties, obligations, and responsibilities that we accrue as intrinsic to human relationships. Locke's minimalist state is justified by an implicit social contract entered into by people to form that sort of society from the imaginary anarchic "state of nature." To which Danley responded, in effect, "so what?" Such hypothetical agreements among hypothetical people are certainly no basis on which to ignore or deny moral legitimacy to real individuals who may have acted altruistically to create a more beneficent state.

The Limits of Property Rights

The particular right that provides one of the most basic underpinnings of the free-enterprise, profit-maximization model is the notion of *private property rights*. For example, shareholders own the corporation and no one, especially not the government, has the right to require them to do anything that detracts from their attempts to maximize their financial returns—as long as the actions of the company stay within the bounds of law and acceptable moral behavior. The justification of property rights under capitalism is generally traced to John Locke's (1988/1689) philosophy of natural rights that, as noted, provides a somewhat shaky foundation. Be that as it may, it is noteworthy that Locke did not view property rights as anywhere near absolute or unrelated to moral issues. According to Locke, one acquires previously unappropriated property such as land by dint of one's labor, by working it—but under the following two conditions: (a) one is modest in one's appropriations, not acquiring an excess that will spoil; and (b) with the proviso that there is enough comparable property left over for others. Even in Locke's day, the second condition was considered unrealistic (England was getting crowded), and he responded to such criticisms by noting the availability of much land in the New World.[101] More recently, Nozick (1974) updated Locke's second qualification to the more manageable condition that the acquisition and use of the property should not worsen the position of others (or, if so, compensation should be made).

---

[101]Defenders of the classic free-enterprise model might criticize this conception of limited property rights as "unrealistic." But realism as a criterion would not seem to be a fruitful approach given the generally acknowledged assessment that an entirely free-market system does not exist and probably never did.

Obviously, therefore, Locke and Nozick's "right" to use one's property is not independent of a consideration of the consequences of such use on others. And, as Donaldson (1982) pointed out, there is considerable debate among philosophers and political scientists as to when a person's position is worsened in a given instance and whether, therefore, an exclusive profit-maximization strategy can always be justified by the property rights argument. (For example, think of the negative externality of environmental pollution.) Contemporary scholarship reinforces the notion that, because property rights cannot properly be separated from other human rights, the right of ownership is not unrestricted (Munzer, 1992; Pejovich, 1990). As a practical matter, our laws are generally based on the assumption that rights are accompanied by obligations—at least to the extent of placing some limits on the rights. Corporations are not free, for instance, to maximize profits by disregarding federal wage-and-hour regulations. Admittedly, however, the question of just what *nonlegal* obligations the corporation might have remains to be answered, as does whether any of those entail a proactive beneficence over and above merely refraining from doing harm.

Managers Are Not (Merely) Representatives of Shareholder Interests

M. Friedman (1970, 1982) believed that for corporate managers to engage in activities other than profit maximization on behalf of stockholders' interests, such as meeting alleged social responsibilities regarding environmental protection, is "fundamentally subversive" (p. 125)—that it is tantamount to an "explicitly collectivist doctrine" (p. 125). That is because money spent on those social objectives would otherwise go to shareholders as profits, to employees as increased wages, or to consumers in the form of reduced prices. By directing the money elsewhere, the executive "is in effect imposing taxes, on the one hand, and deciding how the tax proceeds shall be spent, on the other" (M. Friedman, 1970, pp. 33, 122). But that seems to be an overstatement. Taxes are mandatory, not volitional; one cannot voluntarily choose to ignore them without expecting legal consequences. Shareholders, however, invest in corporations voluntarily and are free to withdraw their holdings at any time they disagree with the way in which the company is being managed; they may even attempt to replace those managers.

Beyond that, however, Friedman (1970) viewed such socially responsible actions as personal transgressions because "a corporate executive is an employee of the owners of the business [who] has direct responsibility to his employers. That responsibility is to conduct the business in accordance with their desires, which generally will be to make as much money as possible ... in his capacity as a corporate executive, the manager is the agent of the individuals who own the corporation ..." (p. 33). But that argument was empirically and normatively refuted almost as soon as it was made (Stone, 1975). The nature of this alleged "responsibility" to shareholders is rather tenuous. As an empirical matter, management rarely if ever explicitly promises to try to increase profits, much less to maximize them. To make any assertions to shareholders regarding future earnings could be construed as fraud or deceit if they are not realized. Similarly, if managers are defined as agents at all, they are by law agents of the corporation, which has an independent legal identity, not agents of stockholders. Perhaps more important, from a normative perspective, even if promises had been made and/or agency established, it does not follow ethically that there are no justifiable exceptions to be made. Other moral duties and obligations (e.g., avoiding doing gratuitous harm to innocent persons) can override a duty to keep one's promise so that not every choice need result in furthering the financial interests of owners. Therefore, to the extent that managers are in fact strongly motivated to pursue profits, we must look elsewhere than legal mandates and moral imperatives for the justification. (Extrinsic influences like competitive pressures and organizational norms as well as intrinsic sources like the exercise of personal power and self-aggrandizement are not unlikely sources.)

Moreover, this argument errs in assuming that the interests of shareholders are exclusively financial. On what basis can M. Friedman assume that? I own stock in corporations, yet I am in favor of those companies acting in socially responsible ways even if it means foregoing some profits. Many of us are shareholders, but we are also citizens and members of the community. And the same is true of business executives. In fact, a decade ago it was estimated by the Council on Economic Priorities that approximately $600 billion of investments are socially screened, including those made by more than 500 institutional investors (Pava & Krausz, 1996). In addition, corporations themselves value other business goals than short-term profits and share value, for example, enhancing liquidity or market share, furthering technological advances, and expanding or diversifying the business via growth or acquisition.

Limitations of the Fundamental Utilitarian Justification

The primary ethical foundation of the classic laissez-faire free-market model probably rests on the empirical accuracy of utility maximization under those conditions. If any other system produces equal or greater net utility for society, the alleged moral superiority of free markets is undercut. As Danley (1994) pointed out, even M. Friedman's argument that market freedom is indispensable to political freedom ultimately rests on the same justification. No intrinsic defense of political freedom was offered by Friedman; it is valued because freedom "produces the greatest net goodness" (Danley, 1994, p. 88) for all affected parties.

Almost everyone except the most doctrinaire free marketer recognizes, however, that there are no large-scale economic systems constituted of perfect free markets; there may never have been. It is an ideal that could not exist for many reasons. For example, a perfect free market requires the following conditions. (a) Consumers have perfect and complete knowledge of all relevant product and pricing information so that they can immediately change their buying behavior when an entrepreneur offers a better and/or cheaper product. In fact, the three men awarded the 2001 Nobel Memorial Prize in Economic Science—Joseph E. Stiglitz, George A. Akerlof, and A. Michael Spence—won it for their work in explicating the necessary strong role of government in a market system as a consequence of the reality of "imperfect information." (b) All economic behaviors such as consumer purchase decisions and employer personnel decisions are entirely rational (e.g., there would be no such things as consumer brand loyalty, industrial purchases influenced by personal friendships among manufacturers's sales representatives and company purchasing agents, advertising and marketing that create irrational wants such as cyclical changes in clothing fashion, or any racial or sex-based discrimination in hiring and promotion). (c) Sufficient capital is readily available to all those with an acceptable business plan. (d) Sellers always follow competitive pricing policies rather than, say, take advantage of a price rise by a competitor to raise one's own prices. (e) Employees and their families are entirely mobile to follow the vicissitudes of employment opportunities. (f) Citizens decline to empower their government with any interventionist or regulatory powers over the markets—even on behalf of their own health and safety or for emergencies. For example, the $15 billion in grants and loan guarantees by the federal government to the airlines following the September 11, 2001, World Trade Center catastrophe would be prohibited, as well as many other equally nonexistent and/or implausible attributes.

Even Milton Friedman acknowledged that a perfect free market does not exist. Therefore, whether econometric computer simulations can demonstrate hypothetical net utility maximization under ideal free-market conditions is a meaningless exercise. In fact, without a completely free market (i.e., with insufficient competition) it is unlikely that unrestrained individual profit maximization will necessarily produce the best result for society overall (Samuelson, 1993). The empirical question then becomes, under existing world conditions of mixed welfare and market economies that bear varying degrees of resemblance to the classical free market or socialist ideals, can it be demonstrated that a system that more closely resembles the free-market ideal produces a greater net good than those that resemble it less?[102] There are several difficulties that have to be overcome successfully to make such a demonstration.

---

[102]Danley (1994) introduced an additional intriguing complication for Friedman. If the ideal condition has never existed, how do we know that it can be maintained even if we were able to successfully change our mixed economy to the free-market ideal, as Friedman advocated? Moreover, who is to bear the costs of such a monumental systemic shift? And will the overall gains outweigh those costs?

First, actual empirical cross-national economic comparisons are tricky. Although it seems clear that the western mostly free-market economies have produced greater aggregate wealth than the rest of the world, concluding from such case comparisons that there is a direct cause–effect relation between those two sets of variables is uncertain—much less being able to estimate the magnitude of effect. To what extent might the success be attributable in part to western-style political democracy as well as to the market system? Dalton (1974) suggested that cultural factors play a key role in economic development irrespective of the system, and the view that historical, political, and cultural factors such as values are crucial determinants of economic systems and success has become more prevalent (L. E. Harrison & Huntington, 2000). For example, why has Poland done so much better than Russia since the end of the cold war? What accounts for the greater success of capitalist Japan than capitalist Philippines? Is the fact that England and the United States both had relatively high levels of education and technology before the rise of capitalism important? With regard to differences between the U.S. and Western Europe regarding the acceptability of government involvement ("interference"?) in the capitalist free-market system, what role is played by mere historical accident? Europe had relatively strong central governments before the promulgation of Adam Smith's minimalist state; the United States did not. The effects of that historical tradition are apparent even in current times, as with the antitrust authorities of the European Commission blocking the proposed merger of General Electric and Honeywell in the summer of 2001, after it had been approved by the U.S. Justice Department.

Second, relying exclusively on a consequentialist definition of morality means that one must be comfortable with the consequentialist rebuttals to the criticism that utilitarianism omits vital aspects of morality having to do with fulfilling one's duties, meeting one's obligations, and acting in accord with the moral virtues. As noted in chapter 4, the rebuttal entails the adoption of preference utilitarianism, in which such aims can be incorporated in the utilitarian algorithm as representing one's preferences (or welfare utilitarianism, which focuses on one's welfare or what is in one's best interests). In other words, those moral goods—one's preferences or interests—may be included in the definition of utility or what is valued. But if that is the case, then why are the preferences of many for a more just and equal distribution of economic rewards throughout society, as well as other nonmonetary social concerns, not incorporated into the calculation of net utility?

Third, even if one is content to remain exclusively in the consequentialist camp, one is unlikely to surmount on such a large scale the "ethimetric" difficulties of act utilitarianism (see chap. 4), that is, measuring quantitatively the relevant attributes of all consequences of all economic activity under competing systems so that comparisons of net utility could be made. Similarly, many will find the aggregate utility justification ethically flawed in those instances in which the greatest overall good is to be accomplished by committing what would otherwise be viewed as harmful or immoral acts, such as cheating or product misrepresentation (not unknown occurrences under the pressures of profit maximization). The consequentialist response to both criticisms entails using the more generalizable consequentialist theory, rule utilitarianism, as is done by most economists.[103]

Therefore, the moral justification of the capitalist free-market system is distilled to rule-based preference utilitarianism. But that still leaves two key issues to be considered. The first, discussed in chapter 7, concerns the inattention to distributional inequities within the exclusive focus on aggregate or net utility. The other point, just alluded to, concerns the metatheoretical issue of how utility or well-being is defined in the process of putatively demonstrating the utilitarian superiority of the free-market system.

Disregarding for the time being the theoretical issue of defining utility, Table 10.1 presents the hypothetical economic results of four alternative policies. The results pertain to three hypothetical individuals or to the average consequences for three equal-sized groups of people such as those comprising different SES. It assumes that the same definition of utility provides a relevant criterion for each policy alternative and that all persons (or groups of persons) are equally morally deserving of the outcomes.

Because utility theory defines morality entirely in terms of aggregate effects, it provides no basis for choosing between Policy I and Policy II, both with aggregate utilities of 31, despite the fact that two thirds of the population is considerably better off under Policy II—at a cost to the remaining third which seems quite bearable (they are still well above the

TABLE 10.1

Anticipated Outcomes of Four Alternative Economic Policies in Which a Minimum Outcome of 11 Is Necessary to Maintain an Adequate Level of Well-Being.

	Policy I	Policy II	Policy III	Policy IV
Citizen(s) A	30	18	10	14
Citizen(s) B	4	6	10	8
Citizen(s) C	-3	7	10	8
Aggregate Utility	31	31	30	30

Note. From *The Role of the Modern Corporation in a Free Society* by J. R. Danley, 1994, Notre Dame, IN: Notre Dame Press. Copyright © 1994 by Notre Dame Press. Adapted with permission.

---

[103]The reader will recall that rule utilitarianism substitutes culturally based guidelines concerning the generally beneficial or harmful consequences of classes of actions, rather than a specific analysis of the consequences of the act in each particular instance.

point needed to maintain an adequate level of well-being—i.e., minimally acceptable levels of shelter, sustenance, medical care, etc.).

Similarly, there is no basis to choose between Policies III and IV, both with aggregate utilities of 30. Yet Policy III has the advantages of equal outcomes for all, at an amount near the established level of "need," whereas under Policy IV only one group exceeds that level. Moreover, under an exclusive net utility definition of morality we must choose Policies I or II over Policies III or IV despite the fact that two thirds of the population is considerably worse off under the former than the latter. It is this disregard for differential allocation effects in general and for the distributive criteria of "need" or "equality" in particular that lead many to question the utilitarian justification of the free market.

Note that the foregoing concerns do not depend on the *reasons* for the distributional disparities, which also will impact people's moral reasoning. For example, one's views might change if the distributional advantages of Citizen Group A in Table 10.1 are primarily the result of hard work and individual initiative as opposed to inherited wealth. However, it may be that the overall distributional effects for the entire population are in fact determined in large measure by Group A, because they already have greater access to the educational, economic, and social resources of the society, greater inherited wealth, and superior political power such that they exert considerable influence over the politicians charged with actually making these policy decisions. If so, then one must consider the inadequacy of the utilitarian justification from the perspective of social justice. For the pragmatist, the question boils down to the joint consideration of (a) whether the insufficiencies suffered by Groups B and C are more than offset by their putatively better position under the free-market system than under any other system (a Rawlsian concern) and, if so, (b) the extent to which such relative deprivation is the inevitable consequence of the policies needed to achieve the overall result or represent avoidable injustices. Those considerations provide a segue into the final issue to consider.

The most important critique of the utilitarian justification of the free-market system has to do with its limited definition of utility in terms of the aggregate satisfaction of our preferences regarding the acquisition of resources, products, and services. Restricting human goods to that materialistic definition of wealth is simply a myopic vision of human concerns. This, of course, is not an original criticism. Recall from chapter 4 that John Stuart Mill and G. W. F. Hegel each expanded Jeremy Bentham's hedonistic utilitarian "doctrine worthy only of swine" to include a wider representation of human pleasures, including the exercise of personal freedom and autonomy, aesthetic and intellectual gratification, self-realization and self-expression through meaningful employment, as well as social recognition and the assurance of a social identity. In fact, this conceptualization is in keeping with the notion of fulfillment represented by Aristotle's eudaimonia and is experienced, according to Hegel, in the context of a coherent life focus such as might be provided by a commitment to one's work, family, or community. Philosophers frequently refer to these concerns as comprising one's *interests* (cf. Danley, 1994; J. Feinberg, 1984; Perry, 1963), whereas social scientists, including psychologists, generally refer to them as *values*.

The importance of all this has to do with the extent to which the classical free-market definition of utility corresponds to our conceptions of human value and well-being. Even if free markets provide the most efficient source of wealth in terms of the production of goods and services, if such wealth does not adequately capture what we intuitively or explicitly understand to be the components of human welfare, then so what? "It is not unreasonable to believe that even if Friedman's ideal Classical Liberal state would maximize actual preference satisfaction, there may be alternatives which promote greater well being in the broader sense" (Danley, 1994, p. 129). Implicit recognition of this point of view is the growing use of the Human Development Index (HDI) as an alternative to gross national product (GNP) as a means of assessing human welfare at the national level (United Nations Development Programme, 1999). It is based on indicators of longevity, education, and income per capita. Although the United States ranked third among 174 countries in its HDI, among 17 industrialized nations it ranked third in adult illiteracy and *highest* on a composite index of poverty. Among the 45 nations with the highest HDIs, the United States had an infant mortality rate and a rate of expenditure on education (as a percentage of GNP) merely at the arithmetic means of the group.

INDIVIDUAL- AND ORGANIZATION-LEVEL BUSINESS VALUES[104]

One of the most interesting and unusual scholarly considerations of the values that characterize individual business persons and organizations is Frederick's (1995, 1999) controversial theory. It is especially noteworthy because it attempts to explain the frequent misbehavior by businesses in our society as due to fundamental intrinsic values conflicts. I focus on those portions of the theory that seem most useful and appropriate here without embracing the overall model, which has received intense critical commentary (cf. Danley, 2000). For example, one of Frederick's major concerns is to anchor business values in a naturalist biological and physical justification, as a manifestation of basic evolutionary processes for which we

---

[104]Some of the recent research on work values—not related to Frederick's model—is cited in the section on Domain-Relevant Values in chapter 6.

have been culturally reinforced because of their antientropic qualities. This justification is of considerable concern for Frederick because of his presentation of the theory as a normative or prescriptive as well as descriptive model. If we focus on its descriptive usefulness, the naturalist justification becomes less important.

Frederick's model is comprised of four multifaceted values clusters, the first of which, *economizing values*, comprises the values that virtually define in a distinctive manner what is meant by business.[105] The second important set of values that characterizes the business enterprise, *power-aggrandizing values*, are "neither the distinctive property of business firms nor determinative of business's unique function in society" (Frederick, 1995, p. 26). Nevertheless, the first two value clusters are conceived as "master values sets [which] dominate business institutions and business practice" (Frederick, 1999, p. 207). The third and fourth values sets, about which little is said here, *ecologizing* and *technological values*, are contextual in nature, extending both within and beyond the organization's boundaries.

Economizing Values

This value set is comprised of the three original values of business: *economizing, growth,* and *systemic integrity*. Their cumulative meaning is consistent with what I referred to in chapter 7 as the instrumental values of productivity and efficiency. The nature of economizing has to do with all of the intentional actions of individuals, groups, work teams, or organizations that are designed to produce net positive outputs or benefits from a given set of resources, and it may be conceived of as an antientropic energy-transformation process. The forces of growth represent a continuation of the economizing process that is sustained by the repeated reinvestment of resources. Systemic integrity or unit wholeness refers to the integrative processes that characterize any (biological or social–organizational) unit that allows economizing and growth to occur. As I/O psychologists we have long focused on integrating organizational mechanisms—including structural ones like work-flow design, bureaucratic ones like company policies, as well as social–psychological ones such as corporate culture, socialization, loyalty, work- and job-involvement, group cohesiveness, and organizational commitment.

Power-Aggrandizing Values

According to Frederick there are four values that comprise this cluster: *hierarchical (rank- order) organization, managerial decision power, power-system*

---

[105]There is, in addition, a fifth set of "X-factor values" that reflect the idiosyncratic and personal values of the people who populate any given organization and that, therefore, account for much of the interorganizational differences in values among firms.

equilibrium, and *power aggrandizement*. Although they are not unique to the business enterprise, when viewed in tandem with the economizing values they present a familiar characterization of corporate America. Perhaps the most ubiquitous and traditionally accepted aspect of corporate organization is that authority and associated power are arranged hierarchically. Hierarchy is experienced as the legitimate structure within which work gets organized and accomplished, decisions made, social relations are shaped, and social status determined. The perceived legitimacy of status-based power differentials is reflected in the fact that the authority structure is generally maintained as an equilibrium, notwithstanding trends advocating "flatter" rather than "taller" hierarchies in some circumstances. In other words, the first three values components of the power cluster may be viewed as instrumental values in the service of adaptive economizing.

Power Aggrandizement. In contrast, the power-aggrandizement value occupies a special place in Frederick's model because its expression conflicts frequently with the manifestations of both economizing and ecological values. These conflicts yield organizational and societal tensions that may be maladaptive for the organization and destructive for society. Economizing or power-aggrandizing tensions may be seen most dramatically in hostile corporate takeovers, which may be undertaken primarily for the purpose of expanding the power and wealth of the corporate raiders in circumstances in which few economizing gains may be expected, notwithstanding the promulgation of an economizing rationale. The frequent result of these mergers and acquisitions are massive employee lay-offs due to the need to raise cash to service the debt acquired (Cascio, 1993; Rousseau, 1995), not due to the cost or redundancy of labor. But such tensions are probably most frequently observed within the organization in the form of labor–management conflict, middle-management "turf battles," or power struggles among senior managers:

> Whether occurring inside the company, between companies, or between companies and their various external constituencies, these power contests always tend not only to erode the firm's economizing base, diverting it from the economic mission that justifies its societal existence, but also to weaken and damage the life-support activities of many corporate stakeholders. Neither business nor society gains much, if anything, of positive value from these war-like struggles. (Frederick, 1995, p. 11)

But, with respect to the focus of this book, the most important ramification of individual and managerial power is the extent to which it is associated with a great deal of discretionary authority (T. R. Mitchell, Hopper, Daniels, Falvy, & Ferris, 1998) and contributes to the abuse of lower level employees (Vredenburgh & Brender, 1998), as well as to other unethical and even illegal activities (Dunkelberg & Jessup, 2001). Most models of moral behavior assume that among the significant components of ethical decision making is a rational element culminating in a conscious choice or behavioral intention preceding the action (Ajzen, 1988; Ajzen & Fishbein, 1980; cf. Fig. 5.1). The intention that underlies dramatic instances of abusive, unethical, or illegal actions is frequently the pursuit of additional power, recognition, personal enrichment, or corporate profits (Dunkelberg & Jessup, 2001), as illustrated by the managers of the Enron tragedy and other recent examples of executives manipulating financial reports to affect the value of their stock options.

Profit.   One of the points at which my views depart from Frederick's is the secondary and derivative role he ascribed to profit as a value and motive, because he could not attribute it to the natural evolutionary processes by which he normatively justified economizing and power aggrandizing. I agree with his observations that profit is a sign that economizing has occurred and that an individual business can exist without turning a profit; but, conversely, profits can be produced by businesses that seem to contribute little of much meaning to society, thus not fitting the evolutionarily adaptive economizing principle. Therefore, we might agree that both economizing (e.g., productivity and growth) and profit making are potentially separable objectives, as is the case with not-for-profit organizations that strive to be efficient. My own view is that at the level of the intraindividual values structures of business people profit making represents a powerful terminal value that is implemented by economizing values that are instrumental to it, and it is reinforced by socially powerful external sanctions. In fact, a careful reading of Frederick's (1995) book indicates that his position is not very different from my own: "In all cases, profit rests on a base of economizing ..." (p. 53).

Frederick attributed much of the shocking "bill of particulars" against business to power aggrandizement. But, because he did not view profits as one of the essential values of business, he failed to view profit maximizing as a culpable component—as if the only motives for the exercise of power were intrinsic gratifications devoid of the extrinsic and symbolic rewards that also are accrued. In contrast, Donaldson (1982) acknowledged "although the profit motive may ... work to aid society in the sense of sharpening efficiency and motivation, it has often been appealed to as an excuse to fix prices, sell dangerous products, and exploit employees" (p. 167). And, more recently, because CEO compensation has consisted mostly of stock options and financial performance incentives, the form that such malfeasance has taken involves fraudulent financial reporting. "A system that lavishly rewards executives for success tempts those executives, who control much of the information available to outsiders, to fabricate the appearance of success.

Aggressive accounting, fictitious transactions that inflate sales, whatever it takes" (Krugman, 2002, p. 19).[106] This seems to be an extreme example of the more benign "earnings management" that financial analysts have always known corporations practiced to meet predicted earnings figures (Berenson, 2002). Frederick (1995) seemed insufficiently sensitive to the potentially corrupting influences of the synergistic alliance of greed and power aggrandizement in the service of profit maximizing (and vice versa): "An antipathy for business that is rooted in a disdain for or a rejection of profit misses the mark and is closely equivalent to a rejection of the nature-based economizing process that sustains all life" (p. 54). Yet, as alluded to earlier, one of the most interesting and potentially insidious manifestations of American business power and influence is the inappropriate extension of business values—especially profit seeking—to social, educational, religious, and other organizations that are designed to serve the commonweal, not to produce profits.

COMMERCIALIZATION AND PRIVATIZATION

It has been almost four decades since one of my mentors, the late Frederick Herzberg (1966), observed that

> The business organization has given its coloration, methods, skills, objectives and values to all the other institutions that serve Western societies....
>
> Not only have the systems of the businessman [sic] given their complexion to the nonbusiness institution but they have also, in fact, taken over many of its functions, as all dominant institutions eventually do. (pp. 1, 8)

Herzberg did not make the comment in the spirit of condemnation. He was open-minded regarding whether this state of affairs would turn out to be a good or a bad thing. He was concerned with whether business, as the dominant institution, would take a leadership role in enhancing the human condition in the many areas it influences. The question was raised in a very similar manner 30 years later by Post et al. (1996): "Most questions of corporate power concern how business uses its influence, not whether it should have power in the first place. Most people want to know if business power is being used to affirm the broad public-purpose goals, values, and principles considered to be important to the nation as a whole" (p. 276).

---

[106]One is reminded sadly of an aspect of the Viet Nam War, in which the number of enemy dead, reported on the evening news each day, was used as an indication of how well we were doing. (In a guerilla war, the traditional indicator, amount of territory controlled, is unreliable as it changes from day to night.) Military commanders in the field simply inflated the "body counts," as they were known, to present a more favorable picture, just as executives at Enron inflated the company's earnings to profit from the resulting stock increases.

Many critics have responded essentially, "No, they are not!" (Derber, 1998; J. A. Fraser, 2001; Korten, 1995, 1999; Luttwak, 1999; Mokhiber & Weissman, 1999; Rayman, 2001), but that is too large a topic to explore here.

More to the point is the narrower but still very important issue raised by Herzberg concerning the extension and application of business values to nonbusiness institutions and organizations. B. Schwartz (1990) has decried a growing "economic imperialism"—the infusion of an essentially noneconomic activity, organization, or institution with the pursuit of external economic objectives like profit making. The potential danger is that this pursuit pushes the institution in directions it otherwise would not take and that may, in fact, be contrary to its traditional societal function and its specific values, goals, and objectives.

That danger is part of the broader issue of the "commodification" or "commercialization" of society (Hirsch, 1976; B. Schwartz, 1990). For example, in many ways education has ceased to be viewed as the means to creating a well-informed, sophisticated, sensitive, and enlightened citizenry; it is seen as merely a means to job entry and a source of job training, and its cost is therefore an "investment" from which one expects to profit in the future. At the extreme, institutions of higher learning have to be sensitive to market demand to remain in business, and teachers and professors must restrict their curricula to what is immediately useful occupationally or risk the displeasure of students and disapproval of administrators. Many educators are concerned about the adverse consequences on academe (Murray, 2000).

Viewed in this context the *privatization* of goods and services is one facet of the commercialization of society. It may be defined descriptively, and benignly, as "the act of reducing governmental involvement, or increasing private-sector involvement, in an activity or in the ownership of assets" (Savas, 1987, p. 270). Savas presented a concise, albeit one-sided, positive summary of the nature and presumptive advantages of privatization. There are two supporting and interconnected rationales. First, the pragmatic perspective views it instrumentally as a strategic approach to improving the productivity of government functions. The second point of view is more ideological and stems from the minimalist government political philosophy of John Locke and the free-market economics of Adam Smith; it is simply aimed at reducing the role of government. Savas made the interesting point that many critics of the business sector who vigorously oppose the monopolistic tendencies of companies in the private sector are silent about de facto government monopolies in many areas of public service. The reason for that may be that the inefficiency and waste likely to be induced by government monopoly are less onerous than the greedy excesses of monopolistic profiteering. He also presented a useful taxonomy of four types of goods and services and an analysis of how each is affected by five different versions of privatization (e.g., government contracting with or awarding franchises to private organizations or government issuing vouchers to eligible citizens who then choose the supplier). To Savas, "the real issue is monopoly versus competition rather than public versus private, as it is so often posed for rhetorical purposes.... The reason why privatization works so well is ... because privatization offers choice, and choice fosters competition, which leads to more cost-effective performance" (pp. 279, 280). I disagree. Although cost effectiveness ought not be ignored, I think the real issue is whether the infusion of business values such as a press for profits jeopardizes the public good that represents the societal objectives of the institution.

Savas' (1987) analysis itemizes 10 characteristics by which to evaluate the different versions of privatization in comparison with government agency, and they are all presented as positive advantages (e.g., the extent to which each arrangement promotes competition, achieves economies of scale, relates costs to benefits, and limits the number of government employees). But we may achieve economies of scale in schools by increasing the student:teacher ratios or in prisons by meting out egregiously long sentences to minor offenders. Is that really what we want? And although competition may stimulate cost efficiencies, it may also have deleterious effects by pushing people to extremes. How will the educational objectives of a school fare in the face of shareholder or owner pressures for profits? As I argued earlier, competition is not a value espoused by individual businesses or managers. Their aim is not to compete, but to take business away from their competitors—in the extreme, to put the competitor(s) out of business. Is that a relevant value system for schools or health service providers? What happens to those who live in the areas serviced by the schools and medical facilities that have been "bankrupted"? News reports are filled with instances in which many people are offended by the inappropriate extension of business values and principles: for example, production quotas for collecting money from taxpayers by Internal Revenue Service auditors, maltreatment of youthful prisoners in an effort to cut costs at a juvenile prison run by a for-profit corporation, the debacle of "managed" health care by for-profit companies over the past decade, and the threat to independent academic research posed by corporate sponsorship and ownership of the products of the research (Press & Washburn, 2000).

What is missing from most pleas for privatization is a consideration of its relation to each of the separable twin business values of economizing, and power aggrandizement or profit making. Any organization seeking to economize or to make effective use of human resource business practices is to be lauded. Schools may buy supplies more cheaply in bulk, and nearby medical facilities may in some instances be able to share expensive diagnostic equipment. Large bureaucratic organizations may be managed considerably better by experienced and successful business people such as the current and prior Chancellor of New York City's school system, both noneducators. And Archbishop Edward M. Egan, the recently appointed head of the New York Archdiocese, has been known within and outside the Catholic hierarchy for his success in addressing the staffing problems of the church in America with effective recruiting and training of priests. Even the private practitioner (e.g., our clinical psychology colleagues) are advised to follow good business practices (Clay, 2000; Yenney & APA Practice Directorate, 1994), which certainly makes sense. And, in perhaps the largest demonstration of this strategy, the economizing value has been applied wholesale to virtually the entire federal bureaucracy (Gore, 1993).

The danger does not stem from mere economizing; it originates from a press for profits that goads the practitioner, organization, or institution to policies and practices that jeopardize its primary function and supporting values. That is what accounts for the fiasco of Health Maintenance Organizations (HMOs) in the United States in recent years. For example, an investigation of quality-of-care data for over 400 HMOs indicated that investor-owned plans had significantly lower scores on all 14 quality-of-care indicators than did the not-for-profit plans (Himmelstein, Woolhandler, Hellander & Wolfe, 1999). In addition, physicians whose practices are primarily in managed care plans have been found to be considerably less likely to provide charity care and spend fewer hours providing charity care than other physicians (Cunningham, Grossman, St. Peter, & Lesser, 1999). The situation has become so egregious that federal patients' rights legislation is deemed necessary and some of the most independent entrepreneurial types in our society, medical doctors in private practice, are actually starting to band together defensively in unions. HMO incentives, contrary to the primary social function of a health care system and the fundamental values of the medical profession, are based on the *denial* of medical treatment to patients.[107]

Perhaps the most incendiary arena in which the issue of privatization is being contested is that of public education from kindergarten through Grade 12. The fervor with which it is advocated by its proponents belies the observation that the empiricial evidence of success or failure of such conversions appears rather mixed (Steinberg & Henriques, 2002). Using Savas' two rationales for privatization, because the *pragmatic* perspective is not supported clearly by the empirical evidence, one is tempted to conclude that the zeal of its proponents

---

[107]In a dramatic "about face" consequent to the unrelenting criticism of the industry, two HMOs have implemented incentive pay systems for their doctors based on patient satisfaction and other indicators of quality care (Freudenheim, 2001), rather than cost cutting. Wicks (1995) argued that the ethics of medicine and of business are not incompatible, but he did so by setting up and knocking over a "straw-person argument" to the effect that medicine is (not really) all altruistic, and business is (not really) all selfishness and greed, so that an integration is possible. He did not reflect on whether the fundamental values of each may be contradictory; he did not acknowledge the excesses that all too frequently result from the drive for profits and increasing shareholder value.

is based more on *ideological faith* in free markets. The inference is supported by the frequent failure of advocates to articulate the specific ways in which charter schools or voucher systems are expected to cause dramatic improvements in children's education beyond an almost-sloganeering mantra of "choice leads to competition which leads to improvement." For example, rarely articulated are adverse consequences of competition that can be anticipated, such as the diversion of scarce school resources away from the educational enterprise to advertising and promotion as a response to the competitive market. Another indication that the advocacy may be more ideological than pragmatic is when other relevant factors are ignored, such as abysmal pay for teachers; determinants of pupil achievement like class size (Ehrenberg, Brewer, Gamoran, & Willms, 2001); or the fact that major school reform can be undertaken within the public sector, even at the statewide level (V. Phillips, Boysen, & Schuster, 1997).[108]

A case in point is the creation of the Bronx Preparatory Charter School in New York City, as reported recently (Wilgoren, 2001c).[109] These are some of its characteristics: (a) the regular per-pupil state budget and start-up costs have been augmented by almost $1 million from foundations, corporations, and friends; (b) teachers are highly selected from idealistic applicants such as alumni of Teach for America, the national program that places graduates in poor communities, and are imbued with a sense of embarking on a valuable new "mission" (they also spent 7 days on team-building and professional development with an external paid consultant); (c) the school started only with the fifth and sixth grades—seven teachers and 102 students, for an average class size of 14; (d) although charter schools cannot hand pick their students, every student was self-selected in that their families sought admission; and (e) the school year is comprised of 200 days, and classes run from 7:55 a.m. to 5 p.m.—the equivalent of 50% more class time than mandated by the Board of Education!

Several years from now, this school and its students will undergo state assessment and may be found to be successful—especially when compared with other inner-city public schools. It probably does not take a social scientist trained in research design, program evaluation, and the use of appropriate comparison groups to know that attributing its success to privatization per se would be inappropriate. How many failing public schools would be turned around by an infusion of $500,000 per grade, additional teacher training, a reduction of class size to 14, and so forth, while retaining their public accountability?

---

[108]Among 26 member nations of the Organization for Economic Cooperation and Development the United States ranked 22nd in average salary for an experienced teacher as a percentage of average per capita income (Wilgoren, 2001b).

[109]Charter schools receive public funds but are run relatively autonomously, like private schools, with state oversight but no close regulation by the local school district.

Additions to the Framework for Ethical Decision Making are deferred until after the following chapter so as to integrate suggestions from both the classical and revisionist business models.

11

Business Values:
II. The Revisionist Neo-Liberal
Free-Enterprise Model

The cause of business is poorly served when corporate spokespeople concentrate their fire on corporate critics but refuse to speak out against business people and business practices that are illegal or socially irresponsible. By refusing to take a public position against wrong-doing, they invite criticism against all business and convey the image of business as unresponsive to the public interest. Finally, no amount of advocacy advertising is likely to yield results if there is a large gap between the image business is trying to promote and what business is actually doing.

—S. Prakash Sethi

I introduced my discussion of the classical free-enterprise model by noting that it embodied two primary dimensions of political and social economy, one having to do with the role of government vis-à-vis business and the economy, the other concerning the relation between business (especially corporations because of their size) and the rest of society. In the classical model the first dimension is marked by the normative ideals of laissez-faire and free-markets that stem from the classical liberal political tradition; the second is characterized by prescriptions for exclusive profit maximization and moral disinterest. The competing neo-liberal ideology also can be represented clearly by delineating these two issues. But before doing so, a note is in order regarding the set of circumstances that is generally conceded to have prompted the revisionist views: recognition of the growing power of the corporation during the first half of the 20th century, and the resultant managerial revolution.

ANTECEDENTS OF THE REVISIONIST MODEL:
CORPORATE POWER AND THE RISE OF MANAGERIALISM

From the waning decades of the 19th century through the first half of the 20th century a significant concern of economists, social critics, and—interestingly—business leaders was the growing economic and political power and monopolistic anticompetitive tendencies of American corporations, in contrast with the competitive assumptions of the classical model. From this point of view, corporations were envisioned not merely as business enterprises, but as major social institutions whose activities had widespread effects on the commonweal.

This formidable growth of American corporations in the late 19th and early 20th centuries that prompted the enactment of antitrust legislation also prompted the beginning of what was eventually called a *managerial revolution* (Berle & Means, 1932). The growth of corporations in size and the attendant diffusion of stock ownership as more and more capitalization was obtained diminished the role of the original few owners, separated shareholders from the actual running of the firms, and gave prominence to largely autonomous managers. The role of management is thought to have acquired, during this time, both greater power and discretionary latitude in which to exercise it. This was reinforced by the division of labor requiring technical expertise in a range of areas, as well as by the geographic dispersal of the companies. All of this, it was argued, gave rise to the professionalization of management by recognizing the responsibilities that ethically accrue to such discretionary powers. The interested reader should consult A. Kaufman, Zacharias, and Karson (1995) for a history of the struggle between managers and owners in the United States.

Some of the 10 attributes of a profession described earlier (cf. R. T. Hall, 1975) include the confluence of technical expertise, power to control its own standards and means of occupational entry, sense of responsibility, and the acknowledged importance of the societal functions provided—all of which contribute to a profession's responsibility not just to the clients served, but to society at large. In hopes of inculcating this value into the world of business opinion makers like Brandeis (1914/1971), Parsons (1937), and Tawney (1920) promoted and hailed the increased professionalization of managers. By so doing, the aims and values of managers were presumably changed from an exclusive concern for shareholder value to one of enlightened concern for the best interests of society, thus laying the foundation for the corporate social responsibility (CSR) model. This putative transformation in the values, goals and objectives of U.S. corporations and their managers was characterized as "the big change" (Allen, 1952), "the great leap" (Brooks, 1966), or "a new era" (Lilienthal, 1953). "The really great corporate managements have reached a position for the first time in their history in which they must consciously take account of philosophical questions. They must consider the kind of community in which they have faith, and which they will serve, and which they will help to construct and maintain" (Berle, 1954, p. 64).

These antecedent conditions are seen as having given rise to a tapestry of revisionist free-market capitalism, woven of the two complementary strands of neo-Liberal political economy and the normative CSR model.

NEO-LIBERAL POLITICAL AND ECONOMIC THEORY

If the formation of monopolies and oligopolies and generally overweening activities of the "robber barons" during the late 19th and early 20th centuries were not enough to warrant a wholesale challenge to the model of business—government relations characterized as laissez-faire, the onset of the Great Depression in 1929, and the ensuing years of economic and social misery certainly ignited a revisionist explosion known as the New Deal. Among the things that crashed in October 1929 along with the stock market was any residual belief in the self-regulating and self-correcting nature of free markets. Even the massive unemployment of the 1930s was not sufficient to bid down the price of labor, increase hiring, and stimulate production, as predicted by the free-market model. Over time, starting even prior to the Depression, it became accepted that government had to intercede to restrain monopolies *in defense* of the competitive marketplace, to encourage business growth, productivity, and investment by means of fiscal, monetary, and trade policies, to limit the inequities of negative externalities and other market failures, and even (during the depression) to become a major employer. In other words, the view developed that government is needed to promote competition and guide economic activity through the use of incentives and disincentives to business and consumers in the service of legitimate public objectives (e.g., environmental regulations, antidiscrimination laws, or changes in interest rates to encourage investment). This is the antithesis of the classical liberal model, especially M. Friedman's pared-down version of it.

This reflects not only a different explicit economic model—more that of John Maynard Keynes (1935/1964) than Adam Smith—involving constructive government intervention and regulation in service of the public good; it also reflects a different implicit political philosophy regarding the proper relation between the state and its citizens.[110] In the face of enormous and widespread corporate power and the devastation of the Depression, the

---

[110]The extent to which, in the memorable words of then-President Nixon "We are all Keynesians now," is marked by the national unity with which we await each instance of the Federal Reserve Bank's raising and lowering of the prime interest rate in reaction to business cycles. The only challenge to these market interventions one is likely to hear is that "the Fed" does not act quickly or strongly enough.

concept of the minimalist government whose only legitimate aim is Classical Liberalism's prevention of harm seemed inadequate to many. Danley (1994) made the point that classical liberalism (contemporaneous libertarianism or conservatism) has lost sight of the original metamessage of liberalism, which was an underlying commitment to assure people's well-being: "Revisionist Liberals recognize that human well-being requires more than merely leaving individuals alone to compete in the market, and that interference in economic freedom for the sake of improving the conditions of general welfare is a trade-off that is sometimes defensible" (p. 269). Similarly, economist Paul Krugman (2001) admonished "I believe that markets are very good things indeed. But the great economic lesson of the 20th century was that to work, a market system needs a little help from the government: regulation to prevent abuses, active monetary policy to fight recessions" (p. A27). For example, with the failure of Congress to pass an economic stimulus package in the last quarter of 2001, it was anticipated that the recession would worsen. But an uncoordinated and fortuitous rise in government spending (along with that of consumers) was seen by the first quarter of 2002 as responsible for limiting both the severity and length of the recession (Uchitelle, 2002b).

However, given that a pure free market does not exist, and that government involvement in business does frequently detract from efficiency by imposing some regulatory burdens on individual organizations, the question becomes one of whether inefficiencies and added costs are outweighed by the public good. And that question, as the reader will gather by now, cannot be answered by a straightforward empirical assessment because the outcomes reflect individual values preferences. The conflicting objectives are reflected in the contemporary political motto of "compassionate conservatism" which, depending on one's social and political beliefs, represents either a genuine attempt at synthesizing these two sets of objectives or a mere public-relations smokescreen covering an ideological and political agenda of moral disinterest. The shifting tides of political opinion also play a role. Following the recent debacles of financial manipulation, disinformation, employee layoffs, and/or bankruptcies attributable to executives of Enron, Anderson, Merril Lynch, Dynegy, Global Crossing, Tyco International, ImClone Systems, Worldcom, and others, more people seem to appreciate the value of government regulation (T. L. Friedman, 2002; Leonhardt, 2002a; Uchitelle, 2002c).

CORPORATE SOCIAL RESPONSIBILITY (CSR) AND THE MULTIPLE STAKEHOLDER MODEL

The antecedent conditions just described gave rise to the expectation that "to achieve a complete moral picture of a corporations's existence, we must consider not just its capacity to produce wealth, but rather the full range of its effects upon society: its tendencies to pollute or to harm workers, or, alternatively, its tendencies to help employees by providing jobs and other benefits for society" (Donaldson, 1982, p. 38). This perspective became known, in general, as advocating CSR. The assumption was that the managerial revolution had increased the power and discretion of managers to pursue objectives beyond the narrow constraints of profit maximization on behalf of owners. By the third quarter of the 20th century this view had blossomed into a substantial field of scholarship and practice under the rubric of *business and society* (Preston, 1975), dominated by three descriptive and normative models: *social control of business* (SCB), *corporate social performance* (CSP), and *stakeholder theory* (T. M. Jones, 1995). Social Issues in Management (SIM) had already been founded in 1971 as a division of the Academy of Management devoted to "foster[ing] corporate capitalism that is accountable, ethical, and humane" (E. M. Epstein, 1999, p. 253).

The general justification for the normative models is that "the increasing power of corporations must be balanced by a corporate conscience" (Cavanagh, 1984, p. 63), and the perspective is most often fleshed out within the framework of the social contract (cf. Donaldson, 1982; H. B. Jones, 1995; Post et al., 1996). Just as Classical Liberalism extended the model of the social contract from political philosophy to business, as a justification for a laissez-faire relation and the voluntary association of shareholders to further their own financial interests through agreement with management, it is extended still further by the managerialist neo-Liberal model. It is the mechanism by which the very existence of the corporation is justified morally, and the relation between the corporation and all the rest of society is to be understood. It consists of two intertwined normative positions: Business corporations, because of their power, size, and impact on many spheres of public life, have (a) an obligation to help solve social problems and (b) a responsibility to take into account or to balance the interests of the many constituencies who are impacted by its actions and may be said to be parties to implicit social contracts. The social obligations position has led to a focus on the relation between business and society, the ways in which corporations might function as socially responsible citizens, and the means by which their actions in that regard—that is, their CSP—might be assessed (Davenport, 2000; DiNorcia, 1996; Husted, 2000; M. T. Jones, 1999; Pava & Krausz, 1997; Sethi, 1973, 1979; Sethi & Falbe, 1987; Sethi & Swanson, 1981; D. J. Wood, 1991; also see a special issue of *Business & Society*, 2000). Space limitations preclude a consideration of those matters here, but Carroll (1999) presented a concise history of the CSR movement over the past 50 years in the United States. A popular classification scheme for conceptualizing CSP is Carroll's (1991) itemization of the four general obligations of organizations to (a) maximize profits (i.e., meet economic responsibilities), (b) obey the law (legal responsibilities), (c) act within prevailing societal norms (ethical responsibilities), and (d) promote society's welfare in a variety of ways (discretionary responsibilities).

The balance of interests position has led to the development of what has probably been the most prominent model of business ethics over the past 20 years or so, *stakeholder theory*, the study of which has mushroomed following E. Freeman's (1984) seminal work. Descriptively, the basic notion of stakeholder theory is that "an organization's success is dependent on how well it manages the relationships with key groups such as customers, employees, suppliers, communities, financiers, and others that can affect the realization of its purpose" (R. E. Freeman & Phillips, 2002, p. 333). Articulating the corporation's multiple stakeholders serves as a means of focusing attention on those who are affected by the organization's ethically relevant social actions. That is, stakeholders have legitimate interests that may be furthered or harmed by corporate conduct. In fact, that potential to be affected by corporate acts constitutes the most frequently used definition of who qualifies as a stakeholder (Donaldson & Preston, 1995; E. Freeman, 1984).

But stakeholders may also, singly or jointly, have power that influences and constrains the corporation's freedom of action (e.g., social activist groups or competitors). Stakeholders are generally categorized in terms of those who are directly and formally engaged with the business activities of the corporation and are thus referred to as *primary stakeholders* for whom the organization has some direct obligations; they are mostly employees and consumers, but also stockholders, suppliers, and creditors. Indirect obligations may be owed to *secondary stakeholders* with whom the organization maintains indirect relations (not necessarily intentionally), such as its competitors, the local communities in which it is located—including foreign countries, municipal, state, federal, and foreign governments—special interest groups, social activist groups, the general public, and the media.[111] Not only is the nature of the "stake" or interests each constituency has in the organization different, but it stems from different bases (Donaldson & Preston, 1995). For example, the stake of long-term productive employees is based on their effort, commitment, and loyalty to the enterprise; that of customers is based on the explicit and implied promises made to them regarding the effectiveness and safety of the product or service purchased. Not surprising, different stakeholder groups (and even those occupying different roles within a particular stakeholder group) may have different *corporate social orientations*, defined in terms of the extent to which the economic, ethical, legal, and discretionary responsibilities of the organization are emphasized (W. J. Smith, Wokutch, Harrington, &

---

[111]Some business scholars characterize competitors as among the organization's primary stakeholders (e.g., Post et al., 1996). Others place competitors, along with the media, in a separate category of influencers—those who may exert some influence on the firm but have no particular stake in its success (Donaldson & Preston, 1995). Conversely, there may be some stakeholders (e.g., job applicants) who wield no influence.

Dennis, 2001). In its normative version, the stakeholder model has been used as a framework in which to criticize the adverse long-term effects on employees and other stakeholder groups of the preeminence of short-term "shareholder value" as the guiding principle of corporations through the 1980s and 1990s (Kennedy, 2000).

Under normal circumstances the broad outlines of the corporation's business and ethical obligations with respect to its primary stakeholders tend to be relatively stable and well articulated, although not necessarily in all their particulars. For example, with regard to consumers the enduring obligations are to produce the best quality product or provide the best quality service consistent with an optimum pricing strategy and to do it within the bounds of the law and generally accepted ethical standards. In contrast, the "revolutionary" character of the doctrine of CSR is the assertion of moral and social obligations to secondary stakeholders with whom the organization maintains only indirect and/or unintentional relations (most notably, the general public). There is the expectation of new implied social contracts with segments of society beyond the dual obligations of providing affordable quality products or services for consumers and meaningful jobs and fair treatment for employees. In other words, the stakeholder model explicitly includes as part of legitimate corporate obligations the "externalities" that would be ignored within the profit- maximization model. Thus, a full consideration of ethical issues by those who work or conduct research within an organizational environment ought to incorporate the much broader issues of social justice considered in chapter 7.[112] This broad scope is revealed by a statement of the principles of stakeholder management, presented in Figure 11.1.

Implicit in the social responsibility multiple stakeholder model is the recognition that the interests of the many stakeholder groups vary in content and scope and are even frequently in conflict with one another. Hess (2001) presented a concise list of the issues of concern to seven major stakeholder groups. In addition, the various groups differ widely in the degree and kind of social power they can bring to bear in the attempt to achieve their objectives. There may be very broadly focused and powerful stakeholders such as the federal government, as represented by its various specific and cross-industry regulatory bodies, employment, and antitrust laws and taxing authority, and so on; there may be loose coalitions of stakeholders who come together around a specific issue, such as reducing global warming by restricting industrial emissions; and there are stakeholders, such as the media, who may be characterized as simply having an open agenda of potential concerns. Given the management objective of taking account of, or "balancing," the

---

[112]Although stakeholder theory is generally considered to be a liberal point of view (in contemporary nomenclature), R. E. Freeman and Phillips (2002) made a case for construing it as a libertarian perspective.

TABLE 11.1
The Clarkson Principles of Stakeholder Management

Principle	PRINCIPLES OF STAKEHOLDER MANAGEMENT
1	Managers should **acknowledge** and actively **monitor** the concerns of all legitimate stakeholders, and should take their interests appropriately into account in decision-making and operations.
2	Managers should **listen** to and openly **communicate** with stakeholders about their respective concerns and contributions, and about the risks that they assume because of their involvement with the corporation.
3	Managers should **adopt** processes and modes of behavior that are sensitive to the concerns and capabilities of each stakeholder constituency.
4	Managers should **recognize the interdependence** of efforts and rewards among stakeholders, and should attempt to achieve a fair distribution of the benefits and burdens of corporate activity amongst them, taking into account their respective risks and vulnerabilities.
5	Managers should **work cooperatively** with other entities, both public and private, to insure that risks and harms arising from corporate activities are minimized and, where they cannot be avoided, appropriately compensated.
6	Managers should **avoid altogether** activities that might jeopardize inalienable human rights (e.g., the right to life) or give rise to risks which, if clearly understood, would be patently unacceptable to relevant stakeholders.
7	Managers should **acknowledge the potential conflicts** between (a) their own role as corporate stakeholders, and (b) their legal and moral responsibilities for the interests of stakeholders, and should address such conflicts through open communication, appropriate reporting and incentive systems and, where necessary, third party review.

Note. From *Principles of Stakeholder Management: The Clarkson Principles* (p. 4), by the Clarkson Centre for Business Ethics, Joseph L. Rotman School of Management, University of Toronto, 1999, Toronto: Author. Copyright © 1999 by University of Toronto. Reprinted with permission. Emphases in the original.

various stakeholder interests despite their multiplicity, diversity and even incompatibility, along with the fact that salient social issues change over time, a great premium is placed on skillful managerial maneuvering—especially when one considers that managers are themselves vitally concerned stakeholders with their own special interests. A continuum of strategies of corporate social responsiveness has been described, from inaction and resistance to reactive, proactive, and interactive strategies (Post et al., 1996). Interactive strategies entail merging and/or balancing corporate and public goals through ongoing dialogue with all relevant stakeholders, and they are frequently referred to as a *strategic stakeholder approach to management*.[113]

[113]The definition of stakeholder is generally confined to human beings, although a case has been made for considering the natural environment (i.e., "nonhuman nature") as a stakeholder (Starik, 1995). This is reminiscent of the perspective that includes nonhuman animals within the domain of moral philosophy (P. Singer, 1993). Both topics are beyond the scope of this text.

CRITIQUE OF THE REVISIONIST
SOCIAL RESPONSIBILITY MODEL

Regarding the Antecedent Conditions

There seems to be little dispute regarding the phenomenal growth in the power and productivity of corporations beginning in the last decades of the 19th century. What may be questioned, however, is the presumed concomitant increase in the social conscience of management. One can argue, based on the sort of data summarized in Frederick's (1995) "bill of particulars" against business, that this putative values shift was not widely institutionalized and that any increase in managerial discretion was used by many executives in the service of self-aggrandizement and other expressions of power, such as multiple business acquisitions. In fact, during the 1920s—the beginning years of managerialism— managers were primarily concerned with reasserting control over workers, following the end of World War I (cf. Chap. 12). Danley (1994) found little empirical evidence of an enhanced corporate conscience, such as increased philanthropy, that would indicate that the actions of corporate managers became more socially responsible. Thus, he gave little credence to "the big change" (Allen, 1952) as a descriptive thesis of changes in the values, goals, and objectives of American corporations and their managers. Conversely, Donaldson and Preston (1995) reviewed several studies indicating that a substantial number of firms and a great many individual managers reported adhering to the notion that their role is to satisfy a wider set of stakeholders than only shareholders. Nevertheless, I believe that a convincing case remains to be made for the widespread manifestation of a social responsibility motive in corporate action, as distinct from its prevalence in the literature of business and society scholarship. The mere proliferation of corporate codes of conduct does not do it—certainly not when juxtaposed against the scandals of 2002.

Regarding the Political and Economic Theory

There is virtually no disagreement over the descriptive accuracy of the neo-Liberal model of the economy and the role government plays in it. There are no pure free markets, and that is generally accepted as right and necessary. Perhaps the people who best recognize this are the executives who, on the one hand, must contend with a degree of government oversight and regulation of their businesses, but who, on the other hand, have recognized the political dimension of economic policy and have used it so effectively through expansive political campaign contributions, effective lobbying, and otherwise achieving considerable influence over the regulatory agencies.[114] As Danley (1994) put it,

> By the 1970s, the scholarly debate was not whether [regulatory] agencies primarily reflected the interests and needs of the large corporations in industries which were purportedly to be regulated for the public interest. The debate hinged on whether the regulatory agencies originally acted in the public interest and were then captured, or whether in their very inception they represent the influence of corporations seeking to control markets through the facade of the government. (p. 232)

Considerable contentiousness remains, however, with regard to prescriptive or normative advocacy. For example, political battles are fought repeatedly over whether there should be more regulation or deregulation, higher or lower tariffs, quotas or other trade barriers, and whether (or to what extent) private free-market conditions should be extended to other domains as diverse as the delivery of health care and primary education services, the custodial care of prisoners, or the "safety net" provided workers by the federal Social Security fund.

Yet from the standpoint of our consideration of the competing ideals of corporate profit maximization versus social responsibility, the economic arguments are probably moot. Even if one advocates in most respects a more- rather than less-regulated mixed-economy, it holds no necessary imperative for businesses to do anything other than profit maximize within those constraints, as they define social responsibility as simply following the law. The moral issue is not one of economic and political policy per se; it is a question of whether there are sufficient or at least acceptable ethical arguments to be made in support of the CSR approach.

Regarding CSR and Stakeholder Theory

Donaldson and Preston (1995) argued that "the underlying epistemological issue in the stakeholder literature is the problem of justification: Why should the stakeholder theory be accepted or preferred over alternative conceptions?" (p. 73). They observed that there are three versions of stakeholder theory—the descriptive/empirical, instrumental, and normative—each corresponding to a different usage and requiring different types of evidence and appraisals (i.e., they require different sorts of justifications).

In comparison with the instrumental and normative aspects of CSR and stakeholder theory, the descriptive version is relatively uncontroversial. The descriptive/empirical justifications have to do with whether and to what extent the stakeholder model is an accurate description of managerial

---

[114]See A. Kaufman et al. (1995) for a balanced analysis of the financial impact of corporate political action committees.

values, beliefs, and behaviors, as well as corporate actions. To what extent do managers actually employ stakeholder thinking in their strategic decisions? (The most basic descriptive questions, e.g., "Do corporations have multiple stakeholders?," are merely definitional.) Nevertheless, as already noted, Donaldson and Preston (1995) were positive in their assessment of the extent to which managers are sensitive to stakeholder issues, whereas Danley (1994) was skeptical. The first authors illustrate the salience of the stakeholder model descriptively with an example that is familiar to most I/O psychologists—Title VII (of the 1964 Civil Rights Act) employment discrimination litigation. That is, the force of law affirms the legitimate stakeholder status of even those whose relation to the corporation is limited to the position of job applicant. In other words, stakeholder status may be defined more by one's legitimate interest in the organization than by the company's interest in the person(s). At the descriptive level, stakeholder theory has even been cast in a developmental model, suggesting that stakeholders are differentially important to the organization as a function of the organization's life cycle stage (Jawahar & McLaughlin, 2001). Danley cautioned, however, that even if CSR is descriptively correct its proponents frequently conflate that empirical accuracy with a moral justification—a violation of Hume's Law concerning the inability to infer "ought" from "is."

The instrumental version of the theory has to do with the extent to which there are empirically demonstrable connections between stakeholder management (and/or CSR-driven actions in general) and the achievement of traditional corporate objectives and accomplishments. Those would be instrumental justifications having to do with predictive accuracy, and proponents have argued that promoting ethical behavior in the corporation contributes to productivity (Dunfee, 1987). The rationale is as follows:

> There are many reasons to believe that adoption of a "stakeholder" approach to management will contribute to the long-term survival and success of a firm. Positive and mutually supportive stakeholder relationships encourage trust, and stimulate collaborative efforts that lead to "relational wealth," i.e., organizational assets arising from familiarity and teamwork.... In addition, more and more executives are recognizing that a reputation for ethical and socially responsible behavior can be the basis for a "competitive edge" in both market and public policy relationships. (Clarkson Centre for Business Ethics, 1999, p. 2)

However, until relatively recently, a review of the literature could conclude that "the simple hypothesis that corporations whose managers adopt stakeholder principles and practices will perform better financially than those that do not ... has never been tested directly, and its testing involves some formidable challenges (Donaldson & Preston, 1995, p. 77). However, this is an area of considerable research productivity and if we are willing to expand the definition of the independent variable to include a variety of measures of CSR in general rather than stakeholder indicators in particular, then the results appear much more positive.

For example, in a review of 21 prior studies accompanied by their own comparison of 53 socially responsible firms with a sample of other companies matched by size and industry, Pava and Krausz (1996) concluded that "firms which have been perceived as having met social-responsibility criteria have generally been shown to have financial performance at least on a par, if not better, than other firms" (p. 348). The measures of financial performance used included stock prices, return on equity, various measures of financial accounting returns, and so on. Additional later studies not included in their review also report positive relations between CSP and financial performance indices, such as sales and profitability (McMillan, 1996; Stanwick & Stanwick, 1998). Similarly, Roman, Hayibor, and Agle (1999) reviewed 52 studies in which 33 suggest a positive relation between CSR and corporate financial performance (CFP) and only 5 report a negative CSR–CFP relation. Moreover, Gunthorpe (1997) and Rao and Hamilton (1996) both showed that public announcements of unethical behavior had adverse effects on companies's stock prices, indicating that such behavior (at least getting caught at it) is certainly not contributory to shareholder value. And firms actually convicted of some illegality suffered adverse public reactions reflected in significantly lower return on assets and return on sales over the following 5 years (Baucus & Baucus, 1997). Reports documenting the positive relation between CSR and CFP continue to appear (e.g., W. G. Simpson & Kohers, 2002). But in contrast to these optimistic findings, a sour note is introduced by Mayer-Sommer and Roshwalb (1996), who observed that among U.S. military defense contractors two measures of espoused ethical values were positively correlated with the number and cost of convictions for violations of civil and criminal law and reimbursement obligations arising from violations of environmental statutes. Heinze, Sibary, and Sikula (1999) contributed a voice of moderation in this domain with their observation that the strength of the relation between CSR and profits varies considerably from industry to industry. This remains a growing area of empirical investigation, as illustrated by the *Academy of Management Journal*'s (1999) "Special Research Forum on Stakeholders, Social Responsibility, and Performance."

Most of these studies fail to analyze the extent to which the generally positive associations between CSR–CSP and CFP were reflections that (a) social responsiveness pays off economically, (b) financially successful firms are more likely to engage in socially responsible actions, or (c) successful management is likely to include both effective economic performance and social responsiveness. A recent exception is R. Jones and Murrell's (2001) study that indicated that public recognition for exemplary social performance (by being named to *Working Mother* magazine's list of "Most Family-Friendly Companies") led to statistically significant abnormally positive returns to shareholders. However, another exception revealed that a firm's prior financial performance "is generally a better predictor of corporate social responsibility than subsequent performance. Thus associations found between concurrent social responsibility and performance may partially be artifacts of previous high financial performance" (J. B. McGuire, Sundgren, & Schneeweis, 1988, p. 869). Indeed, in an important study of 469 firms using time-lagged correlations over 3 years, Waddock and Graves (1997) confirmed that the relation between CSP and financial performance (return on assets, return on equity, and return on sales) was bidirectional, supporting the existence of a "virtuous circle." Perhaps the key point to take away from these findings is that at the level of management practice there may be no inherent conflict between the aims of corporate profit maximization (at least long-term) and social responsiveness. Conversely, from an ethical perspective one can question the relevance of the instrumental arguments and justification. If the primary grounds for supporting CSR is long-term profit maximization, its moral status as a normatively justified policy arguably is undercut, and CSR could be viewed as just another profit-oriented strategy, albeit of a strategically beneficent sort.

Business scholars and interested philosophers are generally in agreement that the most important issue regarding a potential supporting rationale for CSR in general or stakeholder theory in particular concerns its normative or moral justification. That point of view is obviously in keeping with the aims of this book, but it is one about which there is some contention. Danley (1994) argued forcefully that proponents of the CSR–managerialist position offer little in the way of normative justification beyond mere assertions of its "correctness." (However, note that Danley also found little adequate moral justification for the classic profit-maximization model.) Fieser (1996) argued that businesses have no obligation to be moral beyond merely what the law requires because (a) putative moral obligations beyond explicit legal requirements are optional, and it is simply unreasonable to expect business people to assume such volitional obligations; and (b) in any event, there is no uniformly agreed-upon useful set of moral principles or duties in our society by which to structure obligations beyond those that are incorporated in law.

Both arguments appear fallacious. The first implies either that business people are outside what philosophers call the *moral community* of persons in society or that managerial role requirements are both amoral and trump all other determinants of moral action. In both cases, managers—in the conduct of their jobs, which is presumably independent of their personal behavior—are thereby to be exempted from the rules of morality that we generally accept as intrinsic to the human condition. But at the individual level morality is indeed optional, and there is no basis for such a blanket exemption. The second point simply ignores more than 3,000 years of moral thought that provides guidance as we make our way past life's ethical challenges, and it is logically flawed. As should be clear to the reader at this point, moral philosophy and moral psychological theories are indeed pluralistic and, to some extent, conflicting. But the fact that a single universally endorsed set of moral standards does not exist does not mean that *no* applicable supralegal standards are applicable. To conclude so betrays a fundamental misunderstanding of the values-based nature of moral reasoning and action. The fact that we may not always agree in our ethical judgments does not mean that we should abandon making them and struggling to justify them by "right reasoning."

The CSR–Stakeholder model is sometimes justified normatively by virtue of the failure of the classical profit-maximization model to withstand critique (Donaldson & Preston, 1995). That is, of course, an inadequate strategy: Even if one held free-market profit maximization to be morally bankrupt, it would not imply the ethical superiority of any particular alternative. But, in fact, the CSR–Stakeholder model is essentially consistent with a number of meta-ethical positions and normative ethical theories that can serve as affirmative moral justifications even though the fit is not flawless. In general, it appears to reflect and be consistent with all three of the broad facets representing the domain of moral values and behavior that I proposed: justice or fairness, virtue (i.e., honesty and integrity), and caring—both in terms of nonmaleficence as well as beneficence (Burton & Dunn, 1966; Wicks, Gilbert, & Freeman, 1994). The notions of universalism, the social contract, and Kant's deontology seem especially apropos.

The meta-ethical principle of universalism is a central defining tenet of most normative ethical theories. It refers to the premise that no person's or group's interests have a priori moral precedence over those of any other person's or group's. Given that stakeholders are defined by their interests in the organization, the application of this moral principle seems relatively straightforward. Note, however, the qualifier *a priori* in the statement of the universalist principle. It suggests that the precept does not require that everyone be treated equally, but that there be a justifiable reason for doing so that does not depend on a view of some folks (or, in the case of egoist positions, oneself) as inherently more morally worthy than others. Thus, there may be acceptable justifications for giving precedence to the concerns of some stakeholders over others when they conflict (e.g., legal obligations to primary stakeholders may consistently be given priority over supralegal obligations to secondary stakeholders; some stakeholders may be more important than others based on current needs of the organization).

As noted earlier, the "Achilles heel" of the universalist principle is the empirical reality of our emotional attachments—that is, our partiality. We simply care more for the interests of our family, friends, and colleagues (usually in that order) than we do for those of strangers. And most people also feel a greater affinity with those of similar social background and national identity than with foreigners. Moreover, most people probably experience their concerns for those close to them as moral obligations and duties so that potential conflicts of this sort may readily be construed as moral dilemmas.

Stakeholder theory is most frequently justified within the conceptual framework of the social contract (Post et al., 1996), which is extended to include many secondary stakeholder groups beyond the primary groups of employees and customers. Social contract theory would seem to be ideally suited to provide a normative justification for the stakeholder model, irrespective of whether one is more comfortable with the Hobbesian or Rawlsian versions. The essence of the social contract for Hobbes involves the reciprocal relinquishing of some personal rights to achieve the greater goods of security and social harmony. The implied "contract" consists of the mutual expectations of the corporation and its stakeholders regarding their respective rights and obligations, which presumably works to their mutual advantage. The assertion of one's rights entails the need to recognize the rights of others.

But the Hobbesian version of contract theory has two major normative weaknesses as a potential moral justification for the stakeholder view. One stems from its extremely egoistic assumptions regarding human nature, which lead to the necessity of positing a "sovereign" to oversee and enforce society's "contracts." Therefore, Hobbesian theory provides no hypothetical justification for stakeholder rights beyond those that are codified and enforceable by law. Thus, his philosophy does not afford much moral justification beyond simply the obligation to be law abiding as per the classical model. The second normative weakness has to do with Hobbes' inattention to the power differentials between "contractors," irrespective of their origins; one's "bargaining power" is accepted as part of the status quo. Hobbesian social contracts are not necessarily what most would consider as fair ones; they may reflect vast differences in the bargaining power of the parties. One might acknowledge that this has the virtue of veridicality under capitalist free enterprise, but it fails as a prescriptive moral model of "voluntary contracting" with the corporation (Hessen, 1979; Kelley, 1983).

These flaws are overcome by the Rawlsian versions of social contracting that emphasize the importance of fairness or justice and fairness as reciprocity (Rawls, 1958, 1971). Rawls' normative contracts are made either (a) under the hypothetical "veil of ignorance" that assures impartiality among those who are self-interested, that is, it precludes bargaining based on one's competitive advantage, or (b) under the assumption of "the justice motive" rather than self-interest, meaning that the standard of impartiality or fairness is internalized by those contracting. Especially under the latter circumstances, Rawls envisioned justice evolving from agreements made voluntarily by autonomous and mutually respected parties who are willing to be convinced of the fairness of a position irrespective of their self-interests. Thus, the stakeholder model is rooted in the Rawlsian conception of justice. And Rawls' views, in turn, are based in part on Kantian assumptions.

Stakeholder theory has been justified normatively as providing the basis for "Kantian capitalism" (K. Gibson, 2000). The elements of Kant's morality include the following: (a) of paramount importance is one's moral motivation (good intentions); (b) the importance of motives reflects our standing as autonomous and rational beings; (c) that rationality and those good intentions lead us inevitably to recognize our moral duty despite inclinations to the contrary; (d) the ultimate moral law is the generalized duty to act only on those maxims (principled motives) that are universalizable as a basis for everyone's behavior; and (e) human beings have absolute value (one's value is not contingent on any instrumentalities), and so people are always to be treated with respect and dignity as ends in themselves. Here is Kant's formulation (quoting from chap. 3):

> dictates that we never lose sight of the view of all human beings as having absolute worth in and of themselves and thus should be treated with dignity and respect.... It suggests that we be concerned for other people's objectives as well as our own. It means recognizing that the pursuit of our own goals is limited by their potential infringement on the rights of others; we should not manipulate or use others merely for our own purposes, regardless how worthwhile those purposes may be. It implies respect for the liberty and autonomy of others to pursue their own ends freely.

In a nutshell, the Kantian justification of CSR–Stakeholder theory is that the legitimate interests of corporate stakeholders are to be respected and given credence just as if they were one's own, to the extent, of course, that they do not infringe on the legitimate interests of others. Stakeholders are not to be viewed simply in terms of their utility for accomplishing business objectives. The qualifier regarding lack of infringement emphasizes the "strategic balancing" of multiple stakeholder interests inherent in the stakeholder approach. The question naturally arises, however, concerning the foundation on which the legitimacy of interests rests. What is the basis for such a claim? As mentioned earlier, it usually rests on the capacity to be benefitted or harmed by corporate actions, which raises two issues. First, the determination of "benefit" and especially "harm" may be more ambiguous than ordinarily acknowledged, especially as pertains to the general public as stakeholder. Second, it illustrates the interconnectedness of the normative (moral) and the instrumental justifications of social or business policy.

The major difficulty for the justification of the social responsibility model in general and stakeholder theory in particular is at the operational level (Ullman, 1985). "Evaluation of these theses, whether interpreted descriptively or prescriptively, is extremely difficult given the vagueness of the notion of social responsibility or professionalism" (Danley, 1994, p. 170). To which "social responsibilities" should (any particular) organization attend? What manner of contribution is called for? What levels of involvement are sufficient? What are the standards by which CSP should be measured and evaluated? How are the interests of various stakeholder groups to be determined and assessed? How is the relative importance of those goals and objectives to be determined to achieve a balance among them? Despite more than a quarter-century's attention to the problem of measuring corporate social performance by means of social audits (cf. Bauer & Fee, 1972; Hess, 2001; Kok, van der Wiele, McKenna, & Brown, 2001; Sethi, 1973) most of the empirical research in this area, such as many of the studies reviewed earlier in connection with the instrumental justification of the model, rely on gross reputational indices such as *Fortune* magazine's annual survey of corporate reputations. One attempt to operationalize stakeholder concerns by the Council on Economic Priorities (CEP), a public service research organization, has yielded an organizational appraisal system that uses company questionnaires, publications such as *The Wall Street Journal* and *Business Weekly*, information from government regulatory agencies, and product data from *Consumer Reports* as data sources. Their appraisal system is comprised of 11 dimensions (e.g., environmental, women's, family benefits/worklife and minority issues, charitable giving, and social disclosure) with a total of 50 criteria.[115]

Even if one is sanguine about the moral justification for CSR, an overriding practical issue remains regarding the implementation of such corporate actions. Why should executives want to make those sorts of decisions, and why would they? This is, of course, a variant of the same question that we have considered at the individual level—"why be moral?"—that is, the degree of correspondence between ethical reasoning (knowing what is right) and moral action (doing good). That is why so much attention is paid to the empirical relation between CSR and CFP: It is assumed that if it pays, it will be done. Martin (2002) recently helped illuminate the issues by pointing out the ways in which some manifestations of CSR are not only compatible with but actually enhance shareholder value. Some are mandated by law (e.g., health benefits extended to employees' dependants), and some are volitional but are customary and normatively expected (e.g., corporate philanthropy). Corporations tend to get little credit for those, which Martin referred to as the *civil foundation* of socially responsible corpo-

---

[115]The CEP grading criteria are available on the web at http://www.cepnyc.org/quicktakes.htm

rate practices. One of the most interesting aspects of Martin's analysis is his conceptualization of the *frontier* of socially responsible practices, in which the motivation for the practices is intrinsic and their value to shareholders is either negative or their potential contribution to shareholder value is not apparent at the present time. The trick is to find ways to encourage corporations to take socially responsible actions of the latter sort. It may come from consumer agitation, the encouragement of peers who have already tried and succeeded, publicity received by those successes, lobbying by nongovernmental organizations, or from governmental mandate (e.g., mandatory air bags in cars).

THE TRANSNATIONAL TRUMP CARD[116]

Although there is insufficient space to delve into the issue at any length, before concluding the discussion of the past two chapters, it is important to note that the political and economic framework of the arguments described may have changed substantially and permanently. The discussion was framed by a consideration of alternative normative models of the relation between (national) governments and the corporations that reside within their borders, as well as between the corporations and the remainder of those (national) societies. The mushrooming of the size and scope of the multinational or transnational corporations, such that the sales of many of them exceed the domestic economies of many first-world nations, may render moot much of what the terms of the debate have been for most of the past 100 years. Post et al. (1996) understated the issue euphemistically: "The expansion of global business has created a number of problems. Because global business activity creates new relationships and new forms of activity, existing rules and institutions of government are sometimes inadequate in responding" (p. 183).[117]

Others apparently find the situation more worrisome and have expressed it more bluntly. For example: "The issues today concern not whether a strong national government should regulate the economy and the corporation, but whether the nation-state as we know it is any longer economically and politically viable.... In the global arena, there is no longer necessarily a congruence of interest between the major core corporations and the interests of the nation" (Danley, 1994, pp. 272, 283); or "Incipient global political institutions are too weak to regulate global corporate power, while national governments no longer have sufficient reach to regulate large multinationals" (Cassel, 2001, p. 261); and "much of the activity of multina-

---

[116]Although the terms *transnational* and *multinational* sometimes have somewhat differing connotations, I follow what appears to be the most frequent usage by using them synonymously.

[117]This is not to deny that operating in many countries and cultures with different laws, customs, and regulations places multiple burdens and difficulties on the company as well.

tionals [is] beyond the effective reach of any one country's legal system" (Cragg, 2000, p. 209). Post et al. agreed that the transnational operations of these corporations may exceed the regulatory powers of any single nation so that they become, in effect, "stateless corporations" that owe loyalty to no one nation, regardless of whether they may retain an image of being an American company or a Japanese company. The problem is exacerbated by the consolidation of enormous power in the hands of fewer and fewer such corporations.[118]

The Liberal conception of the corporation, both classical and revisionist versions, included its being a major vehicle for achieving widespread well-being. Although the two theories of political economy differ somewhat in the definition of *well-being,* a system evolved that provided a substantial degree of protection for employees and other stakeholders. Whether the meta-objective and a remnant of employee protection will be retained, despite the pressure of global competition and the push for ever-higher profits, is still being worked out. In a widely read *Harvard Business Review* article Ohmae (1995) heralded the erosion of nation–states and the inevitable rise of region–states—natural and frequently cross-national economic zones shaped by the global economy. He pointed out that political leaders are increasingly finding themselves at the mercy of people and institutions making economic choices over which they have no control, and that they have become dysfunctional in the global economy because of their traditional focus on national or local political issues rather than on the global logic of today's economic activity. Not once, however, did he consider such issues as environmental and consumer protections, wage standards, worker health and safety, monopolistic coercion, and so on that remain in the provenance of national governments. Socially responsible customs and regulations in these fundamental areas are what Martin (2002) referred to as the civil foundation of responsible corporate practices. One of the major problems introduced by globalization is the great variation among countries in the depth of their civil foundations. Ironically, the primary international organizations that have evolved to manage the global economy, such as the World Trade Organization, World Bank, and International Monetary Fund, appear similarly unconcerned with such issues and have defined their roles essentially as facilitators of the classical free market writ-large, with few if any moral interests beyond economic development.

---

[118]In his review of the analytic and empirical social science literatures concerning whether globalization per se has seriously undermined the authority of nation–states, however, Guillen (2001) concluded that the balance of the evidence supports the conclusion that it has not. To the extent that globalization has been associated with the decline of the welfare state and the rise in wage disparities, they appear to be the consequences of the actions of conservative governments such as "attacks on the strength of interest groups, especially labor" (p. 250).

ADDING FURTHER TO THE FRAMEWORK
FOR ETHICAL DECISION MAKING

29.   Ethical deliberations in the world of business cannot reasonably ignore the foundational moral justification of the business enterprise itself, which means appreciating the extent to which moral philosophy is enmeshed with issues of political philosophy and political economy. One's macrolevel values, beliefs, and assumptions regarding the appropriate role of business in society provide a salient context for one's microlevel ethical deliberations.

30.   Contrary to popular belief, scholars have for more than 200 years viewed business from a societal perspective as a moral enterprise—among other things. Even Adam Smith's classic laissez-faire free-market model is embedded in the moral philosophy of the enlightenment (e.g., natural rights theory), and he assumed that a precondition for effective economic transactions was virtuous interpersonal dealings. More fundamentally, however, the justification for free markets and the self-interested pursuit of profits has always been and continues to be the belief that everyone will benefit therefrom.

31.   Notwithstanding those good intentions and its effectiveness in producing wealth, many contemporary business scholars and social theorists from many academic disciplines view the classical free-enterprise economic model as morally deficient and its relatively unrestrained implementation as the cause of a considerable degree of economic injustice. It is viewed as deficient because of its limited conception of what is good, its failure to deal adequately with the extreme and morally questionable inequities it creates, and the antisocial, unethical, and illegal consequences that an excessive pursuit of power and profits frequently produces.

32.   The general perspective of CSR and the multiple stakeholder theory in particular present an alternative conception of the proper role of the corporation in society—judged by an ethical evaluation of all of its effects on society, not simply its effectiveness in producing shareholder value. It is thought by a majority of contemporary business scholars to be a more adequately justified moral position. However, the multiplicity of stakeholders and their differing—often conflicting—interests can serve to increase considerably the difficulty of ethical deliberations by corporate decision makers. This difficulty is exacerbated by our natural partiality and sense of obligation toward those closest to us.

33.   If the recent trends of economic globalization continue (and I have encountered no knowledgeable source who believes they will not) expanded individual moral sensitivity and ethical leadership from the top of the organization will become more and more important as determinants of ethical action, commensurate with the likely continued diminution of external governmental and other regulatory controls on corporate behavior. Recent events do not leave one optimistic in that regard.

12

The Values and Ethics
of Industrial–Organizational
Psychology

The commitment of professionals to the values central to their professions is
what leads society to grant them—individually and collectively—the
authority and resources to pursue those values in the service of others.... it is
the profession's core values that both anchor and trigger the virtues and
duties expected of its members.... The very essence, then, of being a professional, and not just acting as one, is understanding and committing to the
spirit as well as to the letter of the profession's values and ethical
prescriptions.

—Gellerman, Frankel, and Ladenson

This chapter offers for consideration a critique and an expanded vision of
I/O psychology that attempts to go beyond the limited letter of our espoused
values to include a better representation of its spirit as well. Not all of the
ideas put forth are new ones; some reflect criticisms of the field and of
applied social science that have been made earlier by professional colleagues
and predecessors, as well as by external critics. And instances of some of the
advocated changes can already be seen in the research and practice of some
among us. But the appeal here is to elevate those trends to the level of
institutional attributes that will more nearly typify the field of I/O
psychology rather than represent the contributions of a relative few.

This expanded view is comprised of four interrelated facets. Writing
about them separately inevitably entails some redundancy; I tried to keep
that to a minimum. The four aspects of this proposed vision are (a) adoption

of a broader model of values or value system than currently characterizes the field; (b) a greater interest in and concern for the individual employee, along with our predominant concern for organizational needs, goals, and perspectives; (c) an expanded criterion of effectiveness beyond the narrow standard of technical competence to a consideration of the broader societal consequences of our work; and (d) the inclusion of an avowedly normative (i.e., moral) perspective to the field, along with the scientific (i.e., descriptive and predictive) and instrumental (i.e., focus on productivity and organizational effectiveness). The last of these facets is the broadest and to some degree is inclusive of the other three.

THE VALUES MODEL OF I/O PSYCHOLOGY

In the middle of the last century industrial psychology—as it was then known, prior to our hyphenated or slashed social identity—was subjected to considerable criticism both from within the field and from concerned outsiders. Perhaps the harshest and best-informed outsider was the social historian Loren Baritz (1960) who, in *The Servants of Power*, wrote:

> Throughout their professional history, industrial social scientists, without prodding from anyone, have accepted the norms of America's managers. If this attitude had not tended to influence their work, it would deserve merely passing mention. But this commitment to management's goals, as opposed to the goals of other groups and classes in American society, did color their research and recommendations. These men [sic] have been committed to aims other than those of their professional but nonindustrial colleagues. Though the generalization has weaknesses, it seems that making a contribution to knowledge has been the essential purpose of only a few industrial social scientists. Reducing the pressure of unionism while increasing the productivity of the labor force and thereby lowering costs have been among their most cherished goals, because these have been the goals which management has set for them. (pp. 197–198)

Baritz's criticism is two-pronged, comprised of one charge that essentially characterizes the field as unscientific (relatively unconcerned with making a contribution to knowledge) and the other lamenting our putative embrace of the goals, values, and norms of business, including an antilabor orientation, as opposed to other normative perspectives that could have been adopted. I explore each in turn.

I/O Psychology as Unscientific

At the time, Baritz's criticisms of the atheoretical and "unscientific" nature of the field were pretty much on the mark. Such critiques were not unknown among members of the profession itself:

Industrial psychology as management technique is well known and highly successful…. In the main this has meant work on immediate, more or less technical problems….

Meanwhile, industrial psychology as *social science* remains a puny infant—if not, indeed, still in embryo. The problem is serious. (Kornhauser, 1947, p. 224)

But by the time of Baritz's critique industrial psychology, along with the field of psychology in general, was already in the throes of major changes. The so-called "cognitive revolution" in academic psychology in the 1960s, which supplanted the hegemony that behaviorism had enjoyed for more than a generation, was beginning to make inroads into industrial psychology—most notably, at first, in conceptions of managerial decision-making and evaluative processes, such as performance appraisals. More important, the recently evolved field of organizational psychology started to blossom, as indicated by such markers as the first editions of Edgar Schein's (1980) *Organizational Psychology* in 1965, and Katz and Kahn's (1978) *The Social Psychology of Organizations* in 1966. These were, first and foremost, *theoretical* advances that emphasized the system characteristics of organizations and were as much or more concerned with explaining the behavior of groups, subsystems, and the entire organization as of individuals. As Schein (1980) expressed it, "The traditional industrial psychologist either would not have considered questions such as these or could not have dealt with them scientifically because the necessary theoretical and research tools were lacking" (p. 7).

These trends culminated in the development of the field of *organizational behavior* or *organizational theory*, defined as "the study of the structure and functioning of organizations and the behavior of groups and individuals within them" (Pugh, 1966, p. 235; 1969, p. 345). It is a multidisciplinary field, and it was intended from the outset to be distinct from "traditional industrial psychology" by virtue of being "a theoretical research oriented activity" aimed at "understand[ing] the behaviour of men [sic] in organizations, regarding organizational activity as an object of study in its own right, rather than as a setting in which to apply accepted psychological knowledge" (Pugh, 1969, p. 345).

The gravitational pull of the new multidisciplinary and integrative field, coupled with the popularity of organizational psychology, were such that they had a profound effect on the nature of industrial psychology itself. By 1970 it had expanded into industrial *and* organizational psychology, with a substantial theoretical and scientific component even in traditional service areas like job analysis, personnel selection, training, and performance evaluation. Even a casual perusal (if such is possible) of the 3,000+ pages of the *Handbook of Industrial and Organizational Psychology* (Dunnette & Hough, 1990, 1991, 1992; Triandis, Dunnette, & Hough, 1994) reveals that a theoretical and scientific research orientation predominates in virtually every chapter. The very first section of the four-volume set, comprised of five chapters of more than 300 pages, consists entirely of theory and a consideration of metatheoretical issues. And I think it is a fair assessment to characterize even our empirical journals as reflecting research that is, for the most part, if not actually theory driven, at least concerned with theoretical implications. In fact, many of our practitioner colleagues are wont to complain from time to time about the overly theoretical—meaning not readily applicable—nature of our writings and research. Ironically and unfortunately (as well as incorrectly), the prevailing view of the field by colleagues in other psychology specialties remains predominantly "applied industrial psychology—[an] exile from the university—[which] aims to secure optimal performances from employees" (Gardner, 2002, p. B8). And even from within the field, Dunnette (1984) relatively recently felt moved to observe that too many I/O psychologists are technicians rather than scientists or scientist–practitioners. But it seems clear that I/O psychology can no longer reasonably be characterized as unscientific in the sense of being atheoretical. The changes in the field that have been wrought over the past 40 years in that regard have been profound: "… the world's understanding of such subjects as aptitudes, interests, motivation, fatigue, stress, group dynamics, leadership, ethnic and gender differences, and decision making, among others, would be impoverished were it not for the work of industrial and organizational psychologists" (Katzell, 1994, p. 72).

But what about Baritz's other criticism regarding our goals and values (a criticism also embedded in Gardner's much more recent characterization of the field)?

I/O Psychology and the Worker

Baritz's second critique was viewed as exaggerated by some I/O psychologists (Ferguson, 1962–1965; Meltzer & Stagner, 1980; Stagner, 1981a). For example, as early as 1920 Walter Dill Scott's consulting company was strongly advocating labor–management cooperation in the interests of industrial peace, so that the schism that developed between industrial psychology and unions was not inevitable. But it seems clear that most industrial psychologists were sanguine about the purely technocratic character of the field and simply pleased that "industry is now accepting and paying for industrial psychology" (Tiffin, 1956, p. 372).

I/O Psychology and Labor Unions

Although Stagner (1981b) believed that Baritz had distorted the activities of industrial psychologists, he acknowledged that "the tendency of industrial psychologists to ignore labor unions has been remarkable" (p. 321), and he even felt compelled to concede that there was "some justification" that "psychologists have been persuaded to use their selection skills to exclude from employment applicants with prounion sympathies" (1981a, p. 504). This has recently been documented extensively (Zickar, 2001). Reviews of the history of the relation between psychology in general and I/O psychology in particular with working people in general and organized labor in particular reveal considerable disinterest, distrust, and antipathy on both sides (Baritz, 1960; Gordon & Burt, 1981; Huszczo, Wiggins, & Currie, 1984; Shostak, 1964; Zickar, 2001). Gordon and Burt summarized these reactions as reflecting two major sources: (a) the association of I/O psychologists with those who have maintained an adversarial relation to unions, along with the conduct of research and human resources practices, such as attitude surveys and personality testing, which have been used for "union busting" (Hamner & Smith, 1978; Schriesheim, 1978; Zickar, 2001); and (b) the eagerness of I/O psychologists to satisfy the strong management demand for psychological research and services. To these, H. Rosen and Stagner (1980) added (c) the typical secrecy and distrust of outsiders characteristic of many unions as a consequence of years of playing a reactive and adversarial role and (d) the ignorance of most I/O psychologists about unions and the absence of any consideration of them in our training.

But there have been more fundamental determinants of the schism and antipathy between organized labor and I/O psychology, underlying all of the factors reviewed by Gordon and Burt and by Rosen and Stagner. And those are the prevailing zeitgeist of the first third of the 20th century and the extent to which the values and attitudes of industrial psychologists reflected the upper middle-class and managerial perspective of the time (and, to a considerable degree, continue to do so). As noted by Clayton Alderfer (personal communication, July 2002), I/O psychologists are generally not educated to be self-reflective about their social identity or group memberships. Similarly, Walter Nord (1982) was perhaps the first I/O psychologist to point out that our field tends to be rather ahistorical in orientation and, as a result,

> Our ahistorical proclivities have contributed to important distortions in our view of the evolution of organizational forms and the influence of historical processes on the development of I/O psychology....
>
> The evolution of organizational forms, especially those aspects related to the management of people, is also heavily influenced by social, economic, moral, ideological, and political processes....
>
> Consider, for example, the period in U.S. history between 1880–1920— a critical era of great social turmoil, which influenced the development of American work organizations and their environments ... and witnessed the beginnings of modern management theory and applied social science....

Although our I/O psychology field took root in this era, we have given little attention to the social context of these formative years.... In fact, historians who have extensively examined this period differ from I/O psychologists in their picture of the evolution of organizations. In particular, the doctrine of efficiency and the development of social and political institutions, which contributed to the development and viability of modern corporations, were much less the result of technical considerations and more a response to historical conditions than I/O psychologists assumed. (p. 943)

He went on to review historical analyses that have emphasized the critical role of worker exploitation and the attendant violent strikes of the 1890s in contributing to the social unrest that marked this time. And he observed that "although predictions such as the inevitable death of bureaucracy, the satisfaction of lower level needs, self-actualization at work, and increased participation in management by lower level participants may ultimately come true, for most people life along these dimensions has barely improved ... things for many people have gotten considerably worse" (Nord, 1982, p. 942). O'Connor (1999) presented a similar but much more elaborated social analysis of the years following World War I up through the incredibly influential activities of Elton Mayo in helping establish the Harvard Business School and the Human Relations School during the 1920s and 1930s and in the conduct of the famous Hawthorne studies. In 1919 the western world was recovering from World War I, fearful of socialist and/or communist influences and was enduring the great influenza epidemic, inflation, and intense industrial conflict. In Boston, the entire police force went on strike which led to 3 days of looting. Employers were pushing to have rescinded working conditions that had been improved for workers during the war and were buttressing their aims with what amounted to private armies; labor leaders were responding adamantly; and managers were beginning to assert their "professional expertise" in the control of the corporate enterprise, including control over workers. That is the social prism through which the introduction of Frederick Taylor's (1911) mechanistic and reductionist approach to job design, working conditions, employee motivation, and financial compensation was viewed by labor. Unfortunately, Taylorism remains to this day a primary representation of I/O psychology to much of the public—including the working public and their representatives. Although there are signs that I/O psychology is becoming somewhat more self-conscious of its historical roots than it has generally been (Katzell & Austin, 1992; Koppes, 2002), the review served to confirm that "most I–O psychologists were (and continue to be) managerially oriented ... even the studies of worker attitudes were generally motivated more by the interests of management than by concern for employees" (Katzell & Austin, p. 810).

It is impossible to overestimate the role played by Elton Mayo in crystallizing the particular elitest and managerial perspective that came to represent the application of social science in industry and provided the core of a professional identity that I/O psychology has not outgrown or overcome entirely in 75 years. Although Mayo joined the Hawthorne Studies in 1928, after they had been in process for several years, he had already been a recognized social theorist for almost a decade. An abstract of his social, psychological, and political views that he took with him into Western Electric's Hawthorne plant are as follows (O'Connor, 1999):[119]

- A major flaw in democracy is that it has an "individualistic bias" that allows it to take advantage of the emotions and the irrationality of voters. "Reasoning … is deliberately discouraged under the conditions of democratic government" (p. 125).
- Democracy is a "decivilising force" (p. 125) because it exaggerates the irrational in people and is therefore antisocial.
- Correspondingly, democratic influences in industry are to be deplored because they would "place the final power in the hands of the least skilled workers.… The effect would be to determine problems requiring the highest skill by placing the decisions in the hands of those who were unable even to understand the problem" (pp. 125–126).
- The motives of the great majority of people "are largely determined by feeling and irrationality" (p. 126). This is what he meant by "the human factor," which is ignored by the reasoning and logic of economics.
- "Industrial unrest is not caused by mere dissatisfaction with wages and working conditions, but by the fact that a conscious dissatisfaction serves to 'light up,' as it were, the hidden fires of mental uncontrol. Passionate emotions run wildly through the industrial group; tales of capitalistic conspiracy are eagerly accepted, and dispassionate logic is contemptuously spurned" (p. 126).
- The agitator "is usually a genuine neurotic" who "reads his own mental disintegration … into the social world about him; and to him, in consequence, society is the scene of conspiracies and exploitations by reason of which he and his comrades suffer" (p. 126). Labor unrest, therefore, is a symptom of mental disorganization.
- "To any working psychologist, it is at once evident that the general theories of Socialism, Guild Socialism, Anarchism and the like are very largely the phantasy construction of the neurotic … " (p. 127).
- "The worker, dimly aware of his loss of authority and prestige [as a consequence of the industrial revolution and scientific advance], has

---

[119]The material in quotation marks is from various of Mayo's writings, cited by O'Connor (1999). The page references are to the O'Connor article, which contains the original sources.

been encouraged to expect that this loss would be more than compensated by his political enfranchisement.... The general effect has been the exacerbation of class feeling." Thus, democracy is responsible for having "divided society into two hostile camps—an achievement which is the first step downwards to social disintegration" (p. 127).

- "The worker has as little notion of the real ill he suffers as an individual afflicted with melancholia or nervous breakdown" (p. 128). The real ill is a disintegration of personality stemming from a lack of ability to adapt to the conditions of industrial life. Therefore, labor unrest should be studied by psychologists.

In the context of Mayo's preexisting beliefs, which also generally characterized those of managers and the upper class, it is not surprising that the major conclusions and generalizations of the Hawthorne studies (Roethlisberger & Dixon, 1939) were that (a) interpersonal relations and emotional nonrational factors play a dominant role in the behavior and motivation of workers; (b) psychological techniques could be effective means of curing the dissatisfied workers' distorted perceptions of employment conditions, thus aiding his or her adjustment to the demands of working life and increasing his or her efficiency; (c) similarly, effective and enlightened management could satisfy the social and emotional needs of workers, ending the irrational manifestations of hostility in the workplace and obviate the need for workers to organize; and (d) in the absence of worker maladjustment and irrational fantasies, and under skillful and sophisticated management, the workplace could function as it should, conflict free, as a big happy family. Bramel and Friend (1981) presented an analysis of original findings from the study suggesting that these conclusions were reached by virtue of interpretive errors. They found that for very rational reasons "worker resistance to management was commonplace at Hawthorne (despite absence of a union), yet tended to be covered up in the popular writing of Mayo and Roethlisberger" (p. 874). They pointed out that the elitest biases of interpretation have been perpetuated in general psychology textbooks, social psychology and I/O psychology books, and research methodology texts because professional psychologists simply share the same values as Mayo and the other Hawthorne researchers and are therefore comfortable with the implicit social views.

Similarly, Gillespie (1988) illustrated "the political character of scientific experimentation" by means of comparing the "standard account" of the Hawthorne experiments with a close account of the archival records:

The extension of the laboratory into the factory and the resulting experimentation constituted an essentially political process, for the science and politics of work are inseparable. Industrial managers and researchers believed that scientific experimentation on the organization of work and industrial relations would provide a body of objective knowledge that could be applied impartially in the work place, thereby reducing conflict between labor and capital. However, ... the experimenters accepted in large measure the workplace relations of industrial capitalism and repeatedly rejected the viewpoint of workers. In so doing, they unconsciously reified management ideology so that it became scientific knowledge. The scientific findings of the Hawthorne experiments thus reflected the political values of the experimenters and the employers and provided techniques and a scientific ideology for an intensification of production and supervision (pp. 115–116)

Ironically, the human relations movement spawned by these studies reflected a sociopolitical position but posited an apolitical view of workplace problems as due to emotional maladjustment rather than genuine conflicts of interest (O'Connor, 1999). Whereas it is possible to conclude that we have come a long way in our conception of work adjustment (cf. Dawis & Lofquist, 1984; Korman, 1994; Lowman, 1993a), the foregoing portrayal of the tenuous and/or antagonistic relation between I/O psychology and organized labor does not seem to have changed much over the years. There were early attempts sponsored jointly by the Industrial Relations Research Association, the Industrial and Business Division of the American Psychological Association, and the Society for the Psychological Study of Social Issues to forge an active role for psychology in improving labor–management relations (Kornhauser, 1949). During the 1980s, further attempts were made to stimulate our involvement with unions (Huszczo et al., 1984; Meltzer & Stagner, 1980; Rosen & Stagner, 1980; Stagner, 1981a, 1981b). The fact that these efforts have had little apparent effect reinforces the inference that substantial social, cultural, and political forces are at work, including the expression of basic values. The *Handbook of Industrial and Organizational Psychology*, for example, contains no chapter on unions among the 57 chapters comprising the four volumes. The topic is not even covered in chapters devoted to group influences and conflict and negotiation processes in organizations.

However, the most significant professional and ethical questions arise for us when our mere disinterest in organized labor and worker representation is elevated to an active collaboration in the attempt to defeat legal worker attempts to organize or otherwise engage in antiunion actions. At the least, such partisan activities have the potential to limit greatly our usefulness to the organization and all its members. In addition, it places us in the problematic position of working against people's right to attempt to enhance their own well-being within acceptable ethical constraints.[120] Such actions arguably are not legitimate functions for any psychologist.

---

[120]A position one frequently hears in this regard is that many unions are corrupt, are wasteful, do not care about the organization or other (nonunion) employees, and so on, so should be resisted by those whose sympathies lie with the success of the entire enterprise. This seems to imply that management is never self-serving, corrupt, or inefficient. If true, these might be reasons to oppose a particular union (or management) on a particular occasion. However, they may more frequently represent rationalizations or post hoc value justifications (see Chap. 6) of an a priori ideological bias.

The Humanist Tradition and the Scientist–Practitioner Model in Psychology

Approximately 55 years ago an eminent industrial psychologist, Arthur Kornhauser (1947) raised a cry for "industrial psychology as social science." He challenged us with the question *"Do we work on the problems of the private businessman, or on the problems of society?"* (p. 224). One could quarrel with the juxtaposition of those as necessarily antagonistic enterprises—given the fundamental moral (utilitarian) justification for business activity. Nevertheless, in comparison with most short-term applied research aimed at solving immediate bottom-line problems,

> The emphasis of what we are calling industrial psychology as social science is on the broad, long-run, socially significant problems.... For example: what are the strains and the long-run effects which specialized machine processes and assembly lines impose on factory workers? What do unemployment and job insecurity mean in the personal development of working people and their children.... What are the possibilities and the limitations of democratic social participation within industrial units whose structure remains essentially autocratic?... Do men [sic] in top positions of power in industry genuinely believe in democratic participation by working people? What influences, positive and negative, are exerted by labor unions on the personal development and adjustment of working people? (p. 225)

The good news is that some of those issues have, in fact, been the focus of I/O psychology research and practice in the ensuing decades (e.g., Korman, 1994). Ray Katzell (1994; Katzell & Austin, 1992) pointed to a stream of research focusing on nontraditional outcomes (stress, strain, and burnout; health and fitness; the personal consequences of work on people; career development; and the relation between work and leisure, family, and other aspects of life) that are not related directly to the bottom line. The bad news is that, as even Katzell (1994) acknowledged, that stream of work "is still small relative to that comprising economic outcomes" (p. 51).

A meaningful distinction probably can be drawn between the progressive and humanistic research interests of some individual I/O psychologists and the general practice of I/O psychology, as purchased regularly by organizations. In chapter 9, under the rubric of *social advocacy*, the goal of psychology "to improve the condition of individuals, organizations, and society" (APA, 2002, p. 1062) was discussed, especially the difficulty in specifying the particular values that inform professional and moral obligation, along with their implied actions (Prilleltensky, 1997). The important point, however, is to recognize the long-standing nature of this humanist tradition as one of "psychology's two cultures," along with the scientific tradition (Kimble, 1984). Starting in the 1960s, when I/O psychology began to overcome the stigma of merely being a technocratic service profession to business by becoming more theoretically oriented and scientific (Pugh, 1966, 1969), it adopted the scientist–practitioner (S–P) model to articulate and reinforce that change in character. But this did not address the values issue concerning the lack of representation of the humanist tradition from general psychology (Stagner, 1982). The reason for that relates in part to the difference between I/O psychology and clinical psychology, in which field the S–P model was developed. A brief history is helpful.

Following World War II the federal government, mindful of problems that had occurred in the treatment of veterans of the previous war, was concerned with the wide variation in training and practice of clinical psychologists and the coordination among Veteran's Administration hospitals, mental health centers, and university departments of psychology (Baker & Benjamin, 2000; Benjamin, 2001). So in 1949 the U.S. Public Health Service, enlisting the collaboration of the APA, organized and funded a conference to address the standardization of doctoral training in clinical psychology. Seventy-three prominent academicians and practitioners were invited to the University of Colorado at Boulder for a 2-week conference that produced a fairly detailed plan, *Training in Clinical Psychology* (Raimy, 1950). The major result of the Boulder conference was a clear professional consensus that the clinical psychologist should be both a researcher and practitioner (Baker & Benjamin, 2000). Within 5 years, similar conferences were held in order to formalize training in counseling psychology and school psychology; no such structured process preceded the adoption of the S–P model by I/O psychology.

Notwithstanding the relatively explicit written guidelines for the S–P model in clinical psychology, over the course of 50 years there has been considerable disagreement and conflict regarding the nature of the relation that joins the two sets of professional activities, what their relationship ought to be, and their relative importance (Albee, 2000; Belar, 2000; Benjamin, 2001; Hoshmand & Polkinghorne, 1992; G. Stricker, 1997, 2000). In addition, there are both optimistic reports of the extent to which the model is followed in clinical training (O'Sullivan & Quevillon, 1992), as well as pessimistic assessments of the extent to which clinical research has actually influenced clinical practice (Nathan, 2000). It is certainly not surprising, therefore, that in I/O psychology—which has never articulated a formal statement of its conception of the S–P model—similar disagreements and controversies exist regarding the roles played by basic and applied research and professional practice vis-à-vis one another (Dunnette, 1990, 2001; Hulin, 2001; Kanfer, 2001; Latham, 2001; Saari, 2001; Sackett & Larson, 1990).

The important point is that the notion of the scientist-practitioner represents "an incomplete model of values" (Lefkowitz, 1990, p. 48) for I/O psychology, whereas that is not the case for clinical psychology. It is reasonable to equate clinical practice—a helping profession—with the ethical dimension of beneficence and the values of humanism: "Most [clinical] psychologists enter the profession with a desire to promote human welfare and, directly or indirectly, to serve others" (Koocher & Keith-Spiegel, 1998, p. 3). Although it would be unfair and misleading to suggest that I/O psychologists are not also motivated by an ideal of helping people (cf. Church & Burke, 1992), it is probably inaccurate to similarly equate I/O practice with the values of humanism. In the case of I/O psychology the practitioner portion of the S–P model is not driven primarily by the beneficent concerns that are part of the heritage of psychology and part of our professional and ethical obligations. Thus, for I/O psychology the S–P model is incomplete.

It seems readily apparent that the values represented by the practitioner portion of the S–P model in I/O psychology are dominated by the economizing and productivity values of an idealized free-market capitalism. However, that should not be (mis)construed entirely as a criticism. It is obvious that enormous social benefit flows from economic productivity, and the fact that our professional and ethical obligations extend beyond the employees with whom we work directly to the effective functioning of the entire organization is a good thing. But, as has been mentioned by many I/O psychologists, that duality of obligation is also a source of potential ethical conflict (e.g., "who is the client?"). And, as noted in chapter 9, when the meta-objectives of the institution served are commensurate with the humanitarian objectives that comprise one of psychology's two value systems, no ethical issues are raised. However, when those served are business organizations dominated by a value system of continuous short-term profit making for shareholders, actions on their behalf may sometimes conflict with our avowed professional objective "to improve the condition of individuals, organizations, and society" (APA, 2002)—i.e., all three. The likely values conflict requires making explicit and salient our obligation under the professional service ideal to advance the welfare of all stakeholders.

Thus, the expanded vision of I/O psychology put forward here includes extending the S–P model to a scientist–practitioner–humanist model.[121] Neglecting the humanist component and conceiving of the professional and ethical difficulties that we encounter as representing a dialectic of only S–P tensions underestimates their complexity. It also ignores the economic and corporate social values of the current model. This is not meant to suggest, of course, that the practice of I/O psychology has been devoid of the expression

---

[121] At first consideration, it may seem that there is a conceptual disjunction between humanist and scientist or practitioner. Science and professional practice are, after all, domains of activity, or work roles, whereas humanism refers to a values perspective. But the nature of the scientific and practice enterprises are very much defined by their epistemic and pragmatic goals and values, so that the three are commensurable at that level.

of humanistic values. Many I/O psychologists have studied and worked to improve the human condition in areas like worker safety (e.g., Griffin & Kabanoff, 2001), the propriety of using psychological expertise in commercial advertising to children (Kanner & Kasser, 2000), the relation between work and family life (e.g., K. May, 1998), adaptation to shift work (e.g., Hartel, 1998) and other work stressors and dysfunctions (Lowman, 1993a; Spector, 2002), the emotional impact of potential and actual down-sizing (Waldo, 2001), as well as enhancing the reemployment of displaced workers (London, 1996); some of us even contribute professional services pro bono to worthy causes (Klein, 2001; Ryan, 1999). (The itemization is merely illustrative; it is certainly not exhaustive or necessarily representa-tive.) But my concern is that the motives of individual I/O psychologists like these are conditioned only little, if at all, by their being I/O psychologists; neither are they likely to have acquired such values through a process of so-cialization while occupying a corporate internship nor perhaps during their graduate education.

Over the first few decades of its existence, an exception to that institu-tional characterization has been the practice of organization development or human systems development—although anecdotally it seems as if many I/O psychologists and OD specialists question whether they are members of the same profession. Although OD practitioners and I/O psychologists at one time engaged in many of the same work activities (Beer & Walton, 1987; Friedlander & Brown, 1974), there is some evidence that I/O psychol-ogists are less likely to be engaged in such traditional OD interventions as problem-solving sessions, group goal setting, and process consultation (Church & Burke, 1992). In my experience, I/O psychologists are rarely trained in group processes or intergroup relations. A substantial difference between I/O and OD practice appears to be the extent to which values and value conflicts in OD are recognized as intrinsic to the discipline (Alderfer, 1998; Bowen, 1977; Church et al., 1994). Ethical values have been recognized explicitly as a requisite organizing force for the OD profession from the beginning of its emergence as a field (R. Tannenbaum & Davis, 1969). For example: "the future of OD rests in part on its values and the degree to which its practice, theory, and research are congruent with those values" (Friedlander & Brown, 1974, p. 335). And an avowed goal of its leaders has been to develop a consensus around those standards (Gellermann et al., 1990).

Of great concern to OD specialists, and of particular relevance to many of the views I expressed in this book, is the recognition by OD practitioners of a values incongruence between the tenets of their profession and the values of the employing organization or client, which may lead to a resulting values–behavior inconsistency that is personally disturbing (Tichy, 1974). "The OD consultants in Tichy's sample felt that in theory they should be working toward democratic, participative values, yet in practice they found themselves primarily concerned with helping to increase productivity and solve managerial problems" (Bowen, 1977, p. 545).

The following generation of OD practitioners may have resolved this conflict by integrating the dominant business values with those of OD. Recent data from a larger sample of OD practitioners than Tichy surveyed indicates that, although their highest rated value ideals for the field were empowering employees to act, creating openness in communication, and facilitating ownership of process and outcome, the pragmatic values of increasing effectiveness and efficiency, promoting quality of products and services, and enhancing productivity were rated relatively highly, as 7th, 8th, and 10th in importance, from among a list of 31 statements (Church & Burke, 1992). In comparison, a sample of I/O psychologists from SIOP rated the increasing efficiency, enhancing productivity, and promoting quality statements as their very highest ideals. What seems called for, if we are to fulfill society's expectations for a profession, is an increased emphasis on the moral dimension of action, along with (not replacing) the customary economic criteria.

WANTED: A NORMATIVE PERSPECTIVE

As described in the previous section, we have in the last generation essentially obviated the criticism of I/O psychology as an unscientific and atheoretical technology. But a profession is marked not only by its scientific and theoretical underpinnings and the effectiveness of its instrumental practice but by its moral or normative stance regarding human well-being. It seems time for a second "course correction" in this journey, one that more clearly acknowledges the normative component of ethical professional practice—incorporating the humanitarian values that are part of our professional heritage, examines the implicit values by which we have navigated to this point, and explicitly contemplates whether we might not be on the right heading in this regard. The position I advocate is in keeping with the recent pleas by H. Gardner et al. (2001) to understand that meaningful work—what they referred to as "good work"—entails both expertise and making a social contribution (i.e., it is "good" in two senses).

In chapter 8 I offered a tentative analysis that took the form of the classic "good news–bad news" sort. On the positive side, I asserted (without much evidence) that I/O psychologists probably experience fewer and less intense conflicts in corporations than have been described regularly for other professionals in such settings, such as physical scientists. And I further speculated that the reasons had to do with, at least in part, (a) the considerable contribution that our field has made to the effective functioning of such organizations, which is appreciated by those in positions of power; (b) the likelihood that I/O psychologists self-select from among those with strong business orientations and the propensity to develop managerial and organizational identifications (recall the successful practitioner who commented "I used to be an I/O psychologist"); and (c) that I/O psychology is among those professions, like accountancy, advertising, systems analysis, engineering, and others, that have developed and risen in status because of their integration in the modern corporate enterprise.

The other side of that coin, however, is that these are "technocratic professions" that depart in significant ways from the professional model (Donaldson, 1982). Although they are based on a systematic theoretical body of knowledge that requires extensive education, and they enjoy a considerable degree of professional authority and status, they are—in the parlance of a contemporary euphemism—morally challenged. That is, "The standards of the new professional do not explicitly include moral standards, in part because his or her profession does not recognize an altruistic element in its overall goals ... the new professions fail, it seems, because they do not even attempt to articulate moral standards" (Donaldson, 1982, p. 113). Instead, Bell (1985) argued, those professions are characterized more by values of the business organization than by professional norms, values, and ethical standards. This appears to be confirmed by the relatively recent survey of I/O psychologists, already noted, indicating their highest rated ideals for the profession were to increase efficiency, enhance productivity, and promote quality (Church & Burke, 1992). I concluded chapter 8 by posing the question, "Is I/O psychology more akin to the minimally moral new 'technocratic professions' ... than to the traditional professions in which responsibility and service to society at large is a major value component?"

There would have been little doubt about the answer to that question if it were posed when our field began. I/O psychology was established within the prevailing positivistic science of the times, in which even *applied* psychology was considered separate and distinct from ethical, values-related and moral considerations:

> Economic psychotechnics may serve certain ends of commerce and industry, but whether these ends are the best ones is not a care with which the psychologist has to be burdened. For instance, the end may be the selection of the most efficient laborers for particular industries. The psychologist may develop methods in his [sic] laboratory by which this purpose can be fulfilled. But if some mills prefer another goal—for instance, to have not the most efficient, but the cheapest possible laborers—entirely different means for the selection are necessary. The psychologist is, therefore, not entangled in the economic discussions of the day.... He is confined to the statement: If you wish this end, then you must proceed in this way; but it is left to you to express your preference among the ends (Munsterberg, 1913, p. 19)

I believe that such deference continues to characterize much I/O psychology practice almost a century later.

At its inception around the beginning of the last century I/O psychology in the United States was developed within business and industry by virtue of its demonstrable effectiveness in solving organizational problems. That is, its justification was essentially empirical or instrumental in nature. The first well-known industrial psychologists (Hugo Munsterberg, Walter Dill Scott, Walter Van Dyke Bingham, and Louis Leon Thurstone) were able to apply psychological knowledge to produce effective advertising, make accurate assessments of intelligence, and train employees in "scientific salesmanship" or efficient work methods. The facts of our origins appear consistent, whether illuminated positively from within by a member of the profession and participant in those activities (Ferguson, 1962–1965) or outlined in the harsh glare of the scathing critique of our professional integrity as social scientists by Baritz (1960). In Baritz's view, I/O psychology, by emulating the natural science positivist ideal of "value-free" practice, exemplified the moral predicament about which A. Rosenberg (1995) warned many years later: "A social science that sought to efface the moral dimension from its descriptions and explanations would simply serve the interests of some other moral conception" (p. 205). Accordingly, in the opinion of some, I/O psychology came to be "regarded as an appendage of the business community" (Wolf & Ozehosky, 1978, p. 181). Wolf and Ozehosky were mistaken, however, in believing that the field simply needed to become a more objective and "autonomous scientific discipline"; the issue was—and is—one of morality and values, not science. Twenty years later, a leading contemporary organizational psychologist declared "I am concerned that we are allowing the economic and political forces of the times to reduce our capacity for theoretically based self-reflection. *We thus lose the ability to address the ethical dilemmas of this era inside the profession* with data and concepts developed by people who know the work from their own experience" (Alderfer, 1998, p. 74, italics added).

Where Are Our Ethics and Values?

It can be assumed that Baritz's (1960) harsh perspective as a social critic and cultural historian (quoted at the beginning of this chapter) does not correspond with the professional self-image held by most contemporary I/O psychologists, which is probably reflected better in Campion's (1996) expression of professional pride. But how might one attempt to answer the question today? What are the professional values beyond simply the vaguely articulated S–P model that guide I/O psychology and underlie our ethical ideals? What are those ethical standards that presumably reflect the moral nature of our professional activities, and where might one find them? The concerned I/O psychologist might acknowledge the relevance of such questions but dismiss them as moot—after all, we have an ethical code (APA, 2002) and a casebook (Lowman, 1998) for guidance. But the APA ethical code is a generic document meant to apply to all domains of psychology and varieties of psychological practice; moreover, in the opinion of many of us, it is weighted too heavily by issues associated with the provision of health services. Its overly general nature is suggested by the felt need for supplementary explication of the code (Bersoff, 1995; Canter et al., 1994). And our casebook, like many such collections, is an inductive compilation of critical incidents (albeit helpfully referenced to principles from the APA code) that "are meant to stimulate awareness of ethical issues, *not to make policy or to define ethical behavior*" (Lowman, 1998, p. xii, italics added). In comparison, numerous texts exist that define the principles of ethical behavior for other professions—especially managers (e.g., Castro, 1996; Donaldson, 1982, 1989; Maclagan, 1998; Petrick & Quinn, 1997; Schminke, 1998; White, 1993)—and/or that grapple with the normative role of business in society and how the relation is affected by and determines much social policy (e.g., Post et al., 1996; Sethi & Falbe, 1987; Sethi & Swanson, 1981; cf. Chaps. 10 and 11). Why are there no coherent explications of our values and ethics?

In surveys of the SIOP membership concerning their level of interest in several dozen content areas ethics fares no better than the middle of the pack (Schneider & Smith, 1999; Waclawski & Church, 2000). Although integrity and ethics emerge as competencies for I/O psychologists in a job analysis, they are viewed by only 2% and 7% of the sample as among the most difficult or most critical ones, respectively (Blakeney et al., 2002). Neither the values of the field nor the ethics of its practitioners appears to ever have been a major topic in I/O psychology (Katzell & Austin, 1992). And in the "Call for Proposals" for the annual SIOP conferences up through 2002, ethics was not even listed among the more than 40 content categories for submissions. (Upon request, it has been added for the 2003 conference.)

Based on those indicators, if one were to hypothesize that the values and ethics on which our field rests lack salience or are inadequately articulated, what additional evidence might one bring to bear? One way to address the issue is by means of a content analysis of I/O psychology textbooks. Surely, if our moral underpinnings are a significant facet of the profession they will be expressed clearly and prominently in the texts by which we represent ourselves to the world and begin to socialize new entrants to the field. Accordingly, I searched the subject indexes of a convenience sample of 29 I/O psychology textbooks.[122] The topic of *ethics* is listed in just six of the books—mostly as a passing mention of the exis-

---

[122]This was truly a convenience sample comprised of all of those books I own and those in my college library. I excluded special topics books (e.g., motivation and personnel staffing) as probably providing an unfair test of the hypothesis and books of readings because they generally have poor indexes or none at all. If multiple editions of a text were available, I used only the latest one. The sample consisted of 4 texts from the 1960s, 3 from the 1970s, 14 from the 1980s, and 9 from the 1990s.

tence of the APA code and occasionally as a paragraph or so acknowledging a particular issue such as deception in research or the obligation for responsible use of tests in assessment. The term *morals* or *morality* (generally used as a synonym for *ethics*) is not mentioned at all. Mentioned in 11 of the texts, *values* fares better but, in all but two instances, refers to external objects of study (e.g., work values as a component of organization culture or bureaucratic values). In only two instances are values discussed, even briefly, in the context of professional values that inform and shape the research, theory, and practice of I/O psychology. Those two have to do with the value system that putatively underlies the work of OD practitioners—and in one of those instances, it is held up as a difficulty to be overcome:

> Humanistic values represent a problem for the field of organizational psychology because these features can conflict with the objectivity required of a science and because they can dilute a strong concern for performance effectiveness and productivity. This matter is particularly relevant to our discussion of organization development, because its practitioners have often been influenced by strong humanistic values. (Miner, 1992, p. 293)

It is not my intent to single out Miner's sentiments for criticism. In fact, as implied in the previous section and in chapter 9, his position is probably representative of a great many I/O psychologists who adhere to a traditional logical positivist or neopositivist epistemology in which values, other than scientific or epistemic values, are assumed to be outside the domain of all science (notwithstanding the values inherent in "a strong concern for performance effectiveness and productivity"). In fact, there are no chapters concerned with professional ethics or values in the entire *Handbook of Industrial and Organizational Psychology*.

What does it mean to advocate that I/O psychology should incorporate more of a normative or moral perspective? That is, what would such an I/O psychology be like? In what ways might it differ from the current nature of the field? The answers will be informed by an incorporation into our self-image of (a) what we have already discussed as the three foundations of individual ethics and morality (a concern for the principles of fairness and justice, the promotion of welfare and well being, and personal integrity); (b) the professional model that elevates those foundations to the occupational level, emphasizing responsibility to the society at large, not merely to one's direct clients or employer (especially if the client or employer itself disavows any particular ethical or social responsibilities); and (c) the tradition of human betterment that is an integral part of the values of psychology in general (APA, 2002). A prominent example is offered by the changing circumstances of work over the past two decades or so.

The Demise of Loyalty, Job Security, and Careers as We Knew Them

As most Americans are aware millions of employees have been summarily dismissed from their jobs over the past 20 years or so following the merger, acquisition, downsizing, or restructuring of their organizations. There has been no dearth of descriptive and analytic accounts by social scientists and business scholars reporting on the changed nature of jobs, organizations, terms of employment, careers, and the "psychological contracts" between employees and employers that have characterized this period (e.g., Gowing, Kraft, & Quick, 1998; Hall & Associates, 1996; Howard, 1995; Kalleberg, 2000; London, 1995; Rousseau, 1995; Rousseau & Schalk, 2000; V. Smith, 1997). And concerned psychologists have focused on how employees can be motivated to maintain and even enhance their productivity in these changed circumstances (APS, 1993a). What has not been heard much is an avowedly moral voice questioning whether downsizing is just, or when and in what ways it might be justified (Van Buren, 2000), or reflecting on the ethical nature of our professional involvement in the process (Alderfer, 1998). For example, consider the following observations:

- The initial round of organizational downsizing in the early 1980s was largely in response to business pressures, but subsequent occasions have mostly been instances of executives simply imitating their competitors and peers (Rousseau, 1995).
- Similarly, companies are not downsizing because they are losing money. Fully 81% of companies that downsized were profitable in that year (Cascio, 1995).
- Downsizing is not a reaction to the cost of labor per se; it is most frequently an attempt to raise cash needed to service enormous debt burdens acquired through mergers and acquisitions (Cascio, 1993; Rousseau, 1995). It was justified in the 1980s as a response to difficult economic times and international competition, but it was continued through the boom times of the 1990s as well.[123]
- Among 311 companies that downsized employees by more than 3% in any year during the 1980s, the amount of downsizing was not related to their predownsizing financial performance, and level of downsizing did not affect postdownsizing financial performance or long-term stock price (Cascio, 1998; Cascio, Young, & Morris, 1997). Cascio (2002) later reported: "no significant, consistent evidence that employment downsizing led to improved financial performance" (p.

---

[123]Pfeffer (1998) argued that reducing (labor) costs is never the primary objective in any event. Costs are reduced in the belief, more frequently the hope, that it will lead to greater efficiency, productivity, and profits. But it generally doesn't happen. Moreover, labor costs are usually not the major cost component in manufacturing; they are, however, frequently the easiest to reduce.

81) was found for 6,418 instances of changes in employment for S & P 500 companies from 1982 through 2000. The evidence suggests that it does not even effectively reduce costs (Pfeffer, 1998). Similarly, in comparison with the effects of voluntary turnover and individual dismissals, reduction-in-force turnover (downsizing) has been found to have a significantly greater negative impact on the productive efficiency of work units (McElroy, Morrow, & Rude, 2001).

- The chief executives who are responsible for the decisions to downsize generally benefit greatly from it financially through increases in the value of stock options that become more valuable as a result of immediate increases in stock prices (Van Buren, 2000).
- Laid off workers who return to the job market are downwardly mobile and generally take huge pay cuts—frequently working at part-time, short-term, or temporary jobs (Cascio, 1995; Kalleberg, 2000). These jobs, reinforced by outsourcing many technical functions and relocating jobs to cheaper labor markets, tend to produce a bottom-tier workforce of employees who receive no health insurance, pensions, or other fringe benefits (S. Greenhouse, 1998; Kalleberg, 2000; Uchitelle, 2001).
- The spectacular growth of part-time and temporary jobs (reflected in the explosion of temporary help agencies) since the 1970s has been unilaterally employer driven, resulting in the growth of involuntary part-time workers (i.e., those who would prefer full-time work; Kalleberg, 2000). Data suggest that the argument that employees do not really want long-term attachments to their organizations any more "is largely untrue—even if believing these myths comforts the managers who daily test the bounds of employee loyalty and commitment" (Pfeffer, 1998, p. 167).

For the most part, I/O psychology has accepted the economic rationales (or rationalizations) that have justified the changed social contract between employers and employees. As was pointed out previously, we generally defer uncritically to corporate values and objectives as well as to the policies and actions they inspire. In this instance, it entails accepting that "downsizing and other forms of organizational change involving layoffs ... will continue as production and overhead costs remain noncompetitive ... and thus render job insecurity a lasting characteristic of working life" (Sverke & Hellgren, 2002, p. 36). Perhaps, we have been too ready to institutionalize and reify the notion that "downsizing is effective" (McKinley, Zhao & Rust, 2000, p. 227) despite the cautionary message that it is detrimental to organizational learning (S. R. Fisher & White, 2000). Our concerns have been restricted largely to determining the conditions conducive to employees perceiving that the procedures by which it is determined who gets dismissed appear "fair" (Brockner et al., 1994; Skarlicki, Ellard, & Kelln, 1998). For example, we know that downsizing is more likely to be perceived as fair if it is justified by external reasons, such as a substantial loss of market share to a more efficient competitor (Rousseau, 1995), and it is seen as less fair by people who believe that organizations play a social as well as an economic role in society (Watson, Shepard, & Stephens, 1999) and as less ethical by both casualties and survivors of the process than by those higher up who were involved in formulating, implementing, and/or communicating the downsizing decisions (Hopkins & Hopkins, 1999).

In contrast, an explicitly ethical stance has been taken by those business scholars who have voiced a need for a resurgence of "employee relations ethics" (Sikula & Sikula, 2001) in the face of what has been described as "abusive organizations" (Powell, 1998). It is, perhaps, not coincidental that the study of trust in organizations has become a popular topic (Kramer, 1999). However, it has been left largely to social critics to question the moral legitimacy of the corporate world of worker stress, insecurity, overwork, wage stagnation, and alienation that has been created largely in the service of enhancing shareholder value (Fraser, 2001; Kennedy, 2000; Mokhiber & Weissman, 1999). For example, the trend of replacing full-time with part-time workers has been viewed as reflecting the following:

> ... seismic changes in corporate political authority, rather than competitive adjustment in labor-market strategy. The public needs to understand that corporations are changing the nature of jobs to reduce the power of unions and workers, not simply to compete better; in fact, temporary and contract jobs may hurt productivity and competition in the long run. Ultimately, what's at stake here are the basic rights of workers, not whether they can be retrained or assured of benefits. Contingent labor is a political rather than an economic strategy, and requires a political solution: corporate accountability to workers. (Derber, 1998, p. 199)

Relatively few of us within the field have apparently thought to question the moral standing of this changed social contract, despite the fact that the changes have been imposed unilaterally by one extremely powerful party on the other(s). A more typical response to the growing problem of job insecurity is the (nevertheless laudable) attempt "to understand how the negative consequences of job insecurity for employee well-being and work attitudes can be buffered by various moderating variables" (Sverke & Hellgren, 2002, p. 36). But is downsizing to achieve a 15% increase in stock price or as a desperate attempt to redress a foolish and costly corporate acquisition morally equivalent to downsizing in response to serious competition, cost pressures, and financial losses? How much credence should be given to the economic threat when chief executives of "right sizing" organizations simultaneously maintain annual compensation at the seven-, eight-, or even nine-digit levels? For example, earnings at the brokerage firm Merrill Lynch fell by 37% in 2001 (not counting costs related to September 11), so it cut 21% of its staff—15,000 people (Reuters, 2002). The top executives "shared the pain" by having their cash bonuses limited to just $1 million. (The shortfalls from their usual much larger bonuses were made up with more stock.) Some organizations, however, have resorted to downsizing only as a last resort and in conjunction with "responsible restructuring" (Cascio, 2002).

The moral justification of the current changed employment circumstances thrust upon many workers is ambiguous and may be argued pro or con as a function of whether any given instance of organizational retrenchment is primarily a response to intense or unpredictable competitive environments, inexorable technological advances, and more productive organizational design, as compared with an attempt to satisfy the expectations of Wall Street analysts for relentless stock price increases, the aim of exerting greater control over employees, or the result of inadvisable power-aggrandizing company acquisitions.

Also affecting one's moral reasoning should be whether the organization has tried alternative cost-cutting measures prior to the wholesale elimination of jobs. Cascio (1998, 2002) found that, although downsizing did not lead to expected financial gains, restructuring to more effectively use employee talents without making cutbacks was effective, as are high-performance human resource practices (Guzzo, Jette, & Katzell, 1985; Huselid, 1995; Pfeffer, 1994, 1998). Similarly, Tsui, Pearce, Porter, and Tripoli (1997), in a sample of almost 1,000 employees in 85 different jobs in 10 companies, found that "employees seem to respond favorably in terms of both performance and attitudes when employers are willing to commit to fairly long-term relationships with them" (p. 1117). But the share of workers in long-term jobs (at least 10 years tenure) dropped from 41% in 1979 to 35% in 1996; the median time that a 35 to 44-year-old male worker has held his job fell from 7.6 years in 1963 to 6.1 years in 1996 (Mishel et al., 1999). And if personnel cuts are unavoidable, also relevant is the care, respect, and dignity with which employees are treated. For example, to save jobs in anticipation of possible layoffs, some employees at AT&T were selected to become part of an internal unit of full-time employees who have temporary assignments within the company, precluding the need to subsequently hire externally (Smither, 1995).

It is not surprising, therefore, that some I/O psychologists have not only undertaken, from a scientific perspective, to understand the nature of "the new organizational reality" but, from instrumental and caring perspectives, have also recognized that "the stress associated with job loss, relocation, and adjustment to the new, fast-paced environment will require attention to ways to help individuals, groups, and organizations maintain their health and well-being as they work their way through this period of transition on the way to the future" (Gowing et al., 1998, p. xvii). However, the most prevalent of those ways of helping has been attempting to have employees adjust to the reality that their companies no longer accept any responsibility for their career development, beyond providing the opportunity to work hard and succeed along with one's (remaining) coworkers. Therefore, they should not look to their companies to define their career; "they must shoulder the burden of ensuring their own employment security" (London, 1995, p. xv). As D. T. Hall (1996) observed, "what seems to be more important now is the internal career, the person's perceptions and self- constructions of career phenomena" (p. 1).

This is in keeping with the prevailing wisdom as trumpeted by management gurus such as Tom Peters: "corporate loyalty is rubbish.... If I can provide you with exciting new challenges, and if you respond accordingly, well, then I hope we do indeed grow old together—one project at a time" (cited in Wooldridge, 2000, p. 83). "The 'psychological contract' between the employer and the organization has shrunk to what Jack Welch, CEO of General Electric, has called a one-day contract, in which all that counts is the current value that each party contributes to the relationship" (D. T. Hall, 1996, p. 5). Welch is also reputed to have uttered "Loyalty? If I want loyalty I'll buy a dog." Such views have contributed to the creation of what the social historian Richard Sennett (1998) referred to as "ironic man," an archetype in contrast to "the organization man," in which job stability is seen as a negative sign of dependence, weakness, or failure.

Yet managers still expect employees to perform as if they were loyal and committed to the organization. And I/O psychologists support the program with a considerable amount of effort aimed at selecting employees who are conscientious, discovering the means of enhancing their organizational citizenship behaviors and organizational commitment, and helping them adjust to the situation. I believe that we have been too accepting of the inevitability of one particular form of an employer-determined, employee–organization relation. Tsui et al (1997) referred to it as *unbalanced underinvestment*, in which "the employee is expected to undertake broad and open-ended obligations, while the employer reciprocates with short-term and specified monetary rewards, with no commitment to a long-term relationship or investment in the employee's training or career" (p. 1093). In fact, however, they found that employees working in such relationships manifested about the worst levels of performance, citizenship behaviors, attitudes, attendance, perceived fairness of organizational policies, and trust in coworkers compared with other forms of relations.[124]

---

[124]The one form of employee–organization relation that was consistently worse was the *quasi spot contract* relation, which resembles a pure economic exchange: "The employer offers short-term, purely economic inducements in exchange for well-specified contributions by the employee" (Tsui et al., 1997, p. 1091), such as the relations between a brokerage firm and a stockbroker.

Although it is abundantly clear that those I/O psychologists focused on helping people adapt to the changed industrial circumstances are genuine in their concern for employees, there is nevertheless something disquieting about a position that propounds that "The key is to *discourage long-term career planning* and instead to facilitate managers and employees in self-assessment, empowering them to take advantage of opportunities for psychological success as they arise" (D. T. Hall & Richter, 1990, p. 7, italics added). The positions taken by career development specialists seem to afford no moral importance to the fact that (a) employees are generally put in this situation involuntarily by unilateral actions on the part of sometimes-abusive employers whose senior executives may be enriching themselves personally, (b) the economic justifications for the changed social contract are in many instances spurious, (c) the financial benefits to the organization are frequently ephemeral, and (d) not all employees are prepared emotionally to sustain a corporate high-wire act.

Alderfer (1998) made the astute observation that organizational psychology practitioners have not reflected self-consciously on the changed nature of ethical practice since the economic and political changes begun more than 20 years ago ushered in the era of downsizing. "Prior to that time, our profession had primarily been called upon to assist in projects explicitly aimed toward such goals as human development and intergroup cooperation.... After the political and economic changes of 1980, however ... a primary goal of ethically motivated practitioners became reducing harm rather than promoting development" (p. 73).

Security and stability comprise a primary "career anchor" for a substantial number of people (Schein, 1996). Perhaps that is why a formal career self-management training program actually resulted in producing antagonistic effects: less career self-management behavior in trainees than in the untrained control groups (Kossek, Roberts, Fisher, & Demarr, 1998). The moral issue of whether "rightsizing" corporations ought to behave in this fashion does not appear to arise in the literature on the "new career." Similarly, these writings are replete with references to meaningful jobs with challenging work assignments and learning opportunities, along with rewarding collegial relations, that are meant to replace "the old sense of security achieved through educational and career attainments and long-term organizational memberships" (D. T. Hall, 1996, p. 4). But I/O psychologists have been promoting and working to implement enriching, challenging, and rewarding jobs for at least 50 years (cf. C. R. Walker, 1952). It smacks of something very much like rationalization to view these as a newly developed quid pro quo for abandoning hope of achieving a measure of emotional and job security and being treated by the organization as a human being rather than as a temporary and fungible cost. London (1996) sounded a more optimistic note as he considered some of these issues:

Training and development are important to organizational growth. Employee development can be directed to business expansion and, in the process, increase career opportunities within the organization. Organizational restructuring and outplacement can be carried out in ways that create new ventures and job opportunities. Displaced workers can be retrained in needed skills and knowledge and simultaneously learn to demonstrate value and create job opportunities for themselves. Organizations should also consider ways to retain, motivate, and develop older workers rather than displace them. (p. 77)

Unacknowledged Value Positions

Explicitly incorporating a moral perspective into the field means accepting that the positivistic assumption of the separation of facts and values is at best an unrealizable ideal, may have always been an illusion and, in the opinion of many scholars, would be inadvisable in any event (see chap. 9). Social values and moral positions are implicit in much social science research, more so in social science *applied* research, and even more so in the professional *practice* of applied social science—including I/O psychology, in which the organizations served establish the goals and objectives to be accomplished. A. Rosenberg (1995) pointed out that whereas the natural sciences aim, for the most part, at technological progress, the social sciences aim at improving the human condition—which entails making moral choices that the natural sciences are not generally called on to make (e.g., what is and is not an improvement). That is the condition that largely accounts for the importance of his admonition, which bears repeating: "A social science that sought to efface the moral dimension from its descriptions and explanations would simply serve the interests of some other moral conception. It would reflect values foreign to those that animate our conception of ourselves" (p. 205). This, since its inception, is what I/O psychology in great measure has done. For example, in considering the issue of employees who are wrongfully discharged from their jobs, I/O psychologists are likely to counsel organizations against such "troublesome practices" because they may lead to costly litigation against the company, not because they are disrespectful of employee rights, unethical, or simply wrong (cf. Dunford & Devine, 1998).

But also note that there have always been voices of moral dissent from within the field. Responding in the very first volume of the *Journal of Applied Psychology* to Munsterberg's deferential views in *Psychology and Industrial Efficiency* (see the quote from Munsterberg, 1913, p. 19, cited earlier), the industrial psychologist A. A. Roback (1917) wrote:

Can we really divide the world into applied psychologists, legislators, attorneys, social reformers, engineers, etc.? Is it not true that legislators are frequently attorneys, and may not applied psychologists be social reformers as well as scientists?

Why, then, shall we deny the applied psychologist the right of bringing his [sic] observations, not merely his technical knowledge, to bear on the general situation?

Surely the applied psychologist must have a broader outlook on life. He ought to be able to distinguish between what is *desired* and what is *desirable*, between the professional and the moral issues.

The engineer is not beset by the question as to whether it is moral for him to undertake the task [of building a bridge].... his task is to determine merely whether a given project is *practicable*. It is different with the applied psychologist who has also to consider the *ethical implications of this task*.

No connivance on the part of a consulting psychologist can be justified on the ground that applied psychology is an *instrumental science* and is, therefore, not concerned with ends. If we choose to accept this professional view, we shall be involved in no end of difficulties. As no purpose is ultimate, or absolute, there will be a tendency to rule out all ends and to ignore every consideration but what is expedient. (pp. 233, 234, 236, 241)

In a nutshell, incorporating a normative perspective into the field will frequently mean taking an advocacy position concerning the rectitude of professional activities or corporate aims and actions based on moral values and criteria (e.g., is it the right thing to do?) as distinct from traditional scientific criteria (e.g., is it valid?) or instrumental criteria (e.g., is it cost effective?). Obviously, there is considerable room for disagreement about what is the appropriate moral position on many issues, and the moral, scientific, and instrumental perspectives may often conflict. But it is far better to articulate and clarify the moral values and ethical reasoning implicit in our professional practice than to abdicate any responsibility for them or to act as if there are none.

The opinions of I/O psychologists who, in their research or professional practice, claim to take no moral position on issues such as downsizing or affirmative action, for example—expounding a putatively objective–scientific, instrumental, or values neutral stance—generally reflect a normative view representing the organization's economic goals and values. In the words of A. A. Roback (1917), perhaps the first iconoclastic I/O psychologist, almost a century ago, they consistently defer to expediency. Holding views entirely in accord with one's colleagues and social network, as well as with the dominant culture of one's profession and employer, tends to render them phenomenologically neutral, invisible, or nonexistent. Our values often become apparent to us only when they clash with contrasting ones.[125] Although the promotion of many organizational goals and values is

---

[125]This phenomenon has been seen by many I/O practitioners in recent years among White male managers who decried the inappropriate introduction of cultural issues into the organization with the employment of large numbers of women, African Americans, and Latinos. Prior to that, according to these managers, there putatively was no culture in the organization!

usually a defensible position, it is certainly not objective, neutral, nor value free. Moreover, to the extent that the actions in question conflict with more widely accepted moral principles or with our professional goal of human betterment it is ethically dubious, as A. Rosenberg (1995) warned.

But what about questionable corporate actions of which we have had no part in the planning or implementation? Are we to assume some ethical responsibility? After all, I/O psychologists—according to our own complaints—are rarely involved in the significant policy decisions having to do with a corporation's core business (as opposed to its human resource practices). Even when true, however, that seems a morally equivocal position. One can adopt public advocacy positions regarding the adverse social consequences wrought by dubious corporate actions. Our responsibilities can be indirect in that sense. That perspective is in keeping with a developing view of organizations "as private governments, [which] provide members with numerous opportunities for political action to seek greater autonomy, to dissent from organizational polices, to oppose organizational authority, to depose existing leaders, and to transform the political structures within which they work" (Perrucci, Anderson, Schendel, & Trachtman, 1980, p. 162). At times the moral choice will entail advocating positions on issues that conflict with the perceived economic well-being and stated positions of our employers or clients, and thus our own economic self-interest. There is the ethical dilemma. Some may repress or choose to ignore it. Some may rationalize their behavior. My intention is to increase the salience of a moral perspective on such matters and to provide the tools for one's own ethical analysis.

WHAT EVER HAPPENED TO CONCERN FOR THE INDIVIDUAL EMPLOYEE?

Earlier in this chapter I noted the positive transformation of industrial psychology that took place in the 1960s by virtue of the theoretical advances that marked the development of organizational psychology and organizational theory—fields as much or more concerned with explaining the behavior of groups, subsystems, and entire organizations as of individuals. Notwithstanding its theoretical focus, this transformation dovetailed with the dominant economizing values of the corporation emphasizing the macrolevel objectives of productivity and profitability. Werhane (1999) observed that even "the language of employment" reflects a model of economic objects or collectives, not individual human beings. "Employees are talked about as 'human resources,' much like natural resources or manufacturing resources.... We often tend [to] think of employees as a statistical phenomenon and we measure them that way. So when we downsize, we downsize groups of employees, not individuals" (p. 242). In reviewing the history of the field, Katzell and Austin (1992) confirmed the predominant emphasis since the mid-1980s on productivity enhancement as the primary focus of our techniques and interventions.

What seems to have been largely sloughed off during I/O psychology's metamorphosis was our traditional individualist perspective and concern for individually defined personal goals and objectives. Interests and activities that once characterized I/O psychology but are now part of other professional domains and/or are encapsulated subspecialties in which most I/O psychologists claim little or no expertise include individual employee counseling, vocational guidance and development, human factors engineering, employee assistance programs, and occupational health and safety. For example, Highhouse (1999) related the history of personnel counseling and its preeminence in I/O psychology during the 1940s and 1950s and its subsequent demise, and Savickas (2001) noted "The focus on individuals differentiates vocational psychology from the fields of I/O psychology, organizational behavior, and occupational sociology. Of course, vocational psychologists work in organizations, yet when they do they concentrate on individual workers and their careers rather than on the organization and its leadership" (p. 168)[126]

The organizational perspective of our work as social scientists further reinforces professional practice in which we are invariably working as representatives of the organization implementing company-sponsored human resource policies, practices, and procedures. Consequently, to the extent that some of those human resource activities may be experienced by employees as violative of their rights and/or as otherwise invasive or unfair—including instances in which their concern extends to the initiation of formal complaints or lawsuits against the organization—we may automatically be cast in the role of justifying those activities and defending the organization. Thus, regardless of the individual I/O psychologist's personal values or predilections, there is a social–structural determinant that predisposes the profession to one side of most employee–management disputes.

For example, among a sample of 100 I/O psychology experts in personnel selection testing, of whom 70% had been involved in employment discrimination litigation, almost 2/3 of those had worked primarily as an expert on

---

[126]Conversely, although the value of this individualist perspective was extolled, do not lose sight of the avowedly political objectives of personnel counseling during its origins in Elton Mayo's work in the Hawthorne studies: It was developed as a method of "counteract[ing] the increasing tendency for a worker's complaint to be elevated to the status of a union grievance" (Highhouse, 1999, p. 324). Moreover, some contemporary vocational psychologists also decry the absence of a "study of vocations in a broader understanding of social issues, with a focus on how interventions can help empower clients and change inequitable systems" (Blustein, 2001, p. 174). That broader understanding would have to include the organizational point of view that is so well represented in I/O psychology (J. E. A. Russell, 2001). Both perspectives are important.

behalf of defendant–employers. Only 9% had worked primarily on behalf of plaintiffs (Lefkowitz & Gebbia, 1997). It is not difficult to think of other instances in which I/O psychologists maintain a partisan if not adversarial stance on behalf of employer interests or perspectives. In an article entitled "Invasion of Privacy: A Rising Concern for Personnel Psychologists," written by an I/O psychologist (D. W. Arnold, 1990) to alert colleagues to a growing problem, the major thrust of the "concern" referred to is not the putative invasion of workers's privacy by their employers. What is presumed to be the major source of distress for I/O psychologists are legislative initiatives *in support* of employee privacy. What is further decried is that highly publicized employee complaints "create an awareness among job applicants, making subsequent efforts to resist and seek redress for similar [intrusive] inquiries by potential employers more likely" (Arnold, 1990, p. 38).

Similarly, in an article also aimed at serving an educative function for I/O psychologists concerned with employee firing and the common law doctrine of employment at-will (Dunford & Devine, 1998), the employee's recovery of damages as a result of winning a suit for wrongful discharge is lamented as one of the "negative outcomes" of discharge-related lawsuits (p. 904). Another negative outcome of such litigation lamented by the authors is "lowered morale on the part of [the remaining] workers." From a perspective that values the interests of employees, questions naturally arise: Why isn't the recovery of damages by a worker who has been wrongfully discharged a positive outcome? Why is the resulting litigation viewed as the cause of lowered morale rather than the wrongful discharge itself? From a normative frame of reference, wrongful discharge and other similarly motivated actions should be denounced and discouraged not only for instrumental reasons—that they are costly to the organization or the resulting low morale will affect productivity adversely—but because they fail to abide by ethical principles of fairness and justice and are violative of an employee's rights to be treated with dignity and respect; that is, they are simply wrong. The point is not that these authors are necessarily or atypically antagonistic to workers. Their views represent what is probably a majority opinion among I/O psychologists, conditioned by our work on behalf of and identification with the organization and its managerial values system. And this perspective is not new to the field. For example, even during the Great Depression of the 1930s I/O psychology paid virtually no attention to the unemployed (Katzell & Austin, 1992).

Such strong identification can lead to a certain degree of tunnel vision. For the past 20 years or so two of the most frequently investigated research topics in I/O psychology have been organizational commitment (OC) and organizational citizenship behavior (OCB), focusing on the determinants of employees's psychological attachment or loyalty to the organization and their volitional, prosocial, extra-role contributions to organizational functioning, respectively. During this same period of time the dominant fact of corporate life in America has been relentless down sizing, and the replacement of permanent employees with part-time or temporary workers, generally with minimal if any benefits like health insurance. Now, from an instrumental managerial perspective there may be no inherent conflict among these apparently contradictory concerns: It's only the *surviving* employees's OC and OCBs that are of concern to the organization. But how might one judge the moral sensitivity (Rest, 1994) of a profession whose major preoccupations include enhancing worker loyalty to employers who are simultaneously in the process of consigning the notions of career, job security, and fringe benefits to the dustbin of quaint historic relics?[127]

Personnel selection is, of course, also conceptualized and conducted from the organization's perspective. The process could look somewhat different if the perspective of individual employees or, in this case, applicants were afforded more consideration. Simplifying a bit, selection is comprised of two major components, a valid means of assessing job candidates and a set of decision rules by which those assessments are turned into hiring decisions (sometimes called the *referral system*). Arguably, there is no inherent contradiction between the individual and organizational perspectives with regard to the first of those. Organizations have an obvious economizing interest in selecting the most capable employees so as to minimize training time and/or maximize employee longevity, productivity, and profitability. That can be accomplished by using highly valid selection measures or predictors that are used to estimate future job performance. It may safely be assumed that capable and qualified applicants are similarly interested in having their talents recognized and being hired. And it is neither unreasonable nor unfair to accept that candidates truly unqualified for a job ought not be hired and so spared the disappointment and frustration of failing at it and being dismissed. A hypothetically perfectly valid predictor or set of predictors would identify correctly all applicants as either successful or unsuccessful on the job if they were hired: That is, they would be assessed as acceptable and hired or unacceptable and not hired, respectively.[128]

---

[127]A recent example is the unilateral decision of the Allstate Insurance Company to convert its entire sales force of more than 15,000 from regular employees with pensions and health care benefits to independent contractors (Treaster, 2001). Moreover, to keep their reorganized jobs the sales agents had to sign a waiver, or release, that they would not sue Allstate. Unfortunately, a spokesperson for the company was correct when she stated "Releases are used routinely in the American workplace in connection with business reorganizations and have been consistently upheld in court (p. C4)."

[128]As any personnel psychologist will recognize, that is an oversimplification. Predictions or estimates are made of the candidates's scores on a particular criterion measure or set of criteria. Even for a perfectly valid predictor (unknown in actual practice) the extent to which those predictions of criterion performance presage success on the job depends on the relevance and comprehensiveness of the criterion as an indicator of overall job performance and on the location of the (sometimes arbitrary) dividing line between successful and unsuccessful performance on the distribution of criterion scores.

But unfortunately, even the best selection measures (e.g., tests of general mental ability or specific job skills, scored biographical information, and structured employment interviews) are nowhere near perfectly valid. Singly or in combination, they can account for no more than 25% to 40% of the variation in level of job performance among employees (Schmidt & Hunter, 1998). And the job candidate's predicted performance score is merely a point estimate; it is made within a range of error and at a specified level of probability. "Most researchers know both things, but in their statistical zeal, they tend to forget them" (Guion, 1998, p. 337). It is this imperfect level of prediction, along with the nature of the statistical regression procedure by which validity is demonstrated, that causes a divergence of interests between the organization and (some) individual applicants. It occurs with respect to the referral system—that is, the hiring decisions that are based on estimated job performance (or on actual predictor performance). To say that prediction is imperfect is to acknowledge that some applicants are misclassified by our predictor measures. Some are misidentified as acceptable, hired, but subsequently fail to perform successfully on the job (false hires or false positives); others are misidentified as unacceptable, hence not hired, but would have succeeded on the job had they been hired (false rejects or false negatives).

The problem relates to the fact that these two groups are not proportionally equivalent: there are invariably many more false rejects than false hires.[129] The organization's economizing interests are in minimizing still further the number of false positives, which it can do by raising the minimum qualifying standards of performance on the predictor measure(s) (i.e., decreasing the selection ratio) so that fewer applicants are hired, but proportionally more of them are identified correctly as true positives. In fact, with a highly valid predictor it may be possible to hire so few applicants (only the very highest scorers on the predictors) that all of them are successful. But as one might expect the smaller selection ratio serves to increase still further the size of the false rejects group—the candidates who would have succeeded but have been denied employment due in part to the fallibility of our selection technology. At present, no consideration is afforded by organizations to the interests of these candidates, and no substantial acknowledgment is made by I/O psychologists of what may certainly be viewed as an ethical issue in which we are intimately involved.

To the extent that I/O psychologists, as true professionals, should be concerned about the welfare of both the organization and of those incorrectly

---

[129]The relative proportion of false rejects to false hires when introducing a valid predictor is, in part, a function of the proportion of employees who are deemed to be acceptable or successful on the job. The greater the proportion who perform acceptably, the greater will be the proportion of false rejects to false hires. It seems reasonable to assume that for most jobs the proportion of acceptable or successful workers far exceeds those who are unacceptable. (It is hard to conceive of a functioning organization in which most employees are performing unacceptably.) Thus, in most situations, false rejects substantially exceed false hires.

rejected for employment, we may think of this as an ethical dilemma.[130] But acknowledging a dilemma is frequently easier than resolving it. Unfortunately, our options are limited by the inability to differentiate beforehand (i.e., at the applicant stage) between false rejects and true rejects. Most I/O psychologists would probably respond (correctly) to the effect that we are already engaged in the enterprise of attempting to solve this problem in the best way possible for all concerned: striving to maximize the validity of our selection procedures, thus reducing the proportion of misclassifications of both types. But that is an ethically deficient response given the current state of our technology and the low level of improvement in prediction efficiency likely in the foreseeable future.

In acknowledgment of this problem organizations and I/O psychologists have been admonished to allow failing candidates additional opportunities to qualify, such as by retesting, using alternative assessments, or by providing an opportunity for probationary job training (AERA, APA, & NCME, 1985; Equal Employment Opportunity Commission et al., 1978; London & Bray, 1980).[131] It is my impression that these practices are rather rarely instituted. I suggest that organizations also should be encouraged whenever possible to increase somewhat their selection ratios (by relaxing the predictor cut-off scores), thereby hiring more of those who would otherwise be false rejects. This is especially feasible in large-scale or continuous hiring situations in which those people will not displace applicants with higher predictor scores. Although the average level of job performance of the resulting group of hires will be lower than would be the case if a more restrictive cut-off score were used, it is likely to be well within tolerable limits in many situations—especially for lower-level jobs in which the economic utility of valid predictors is more modest than for higher level jobs. After all, we also know that the standard score difference in test performance between low- and high-scoring applicants is generally larger than the difference to be expected between them in subsequent job performance (Hartigan & Wigdor, 1989; Wagner, 1997). As long as the cut-off score remains at the upper levels of the score distribution of a valid predictor the number of previous false rejects now hired and successful will exceed the number of additional false positives.

Of course the dilemma is caused in part by an a priori and unqualified acceptance of the economizing business value system that brooks no diminution of the effort to maximize productivity and profitability for

---

[130]It is a dilemma that is potentially exacerbated whenever so-called "integrity tests" are used for preemployment screening and those who are falsely rejected are characterized as having failed an assessment of their honesty (United States Congress, Office of Technology Assessment, 1990).

[131]However, the latest version of the Standards for Educational and Psychological Testing (AERA, APA, NCME, 1999) considers an applicant's opportunity for retesting to be merely a "privilege" (Standard 11.12).

the individual firm. Within that value system the only permissible standard for personnel selection is the applicants's potential contribution to productivity (at least to the extent that such productivity is well reflected in the particular criterion measure). But the expression of other goals and objectives is at least conceivable, leading to the consideration of other selection values. That is so only if we broaden our perspective to include (a) the welfare of all individuals as well as organizations; (b) other valued outcomes in addition to productivity; and/or (c) maximizing utility for the entire society, not simply for each organization considered independently and competitively. For example, instead of hiring only the highest test scorers, some consideration could be given to selecting (a) those most in need; (b) those who are least likely to obtain other employment, thus putting their families at risk and becoming a drain on public resources; or (c) those most likely to contribute to organizational objectives other than productivity, such as enhancing its public image. Increasing ethnic, racial, or sexual diversity in particular segments of the organization or for the organization as a whole should also be considered. Employment could be reconceptualized in large measure as a *placement* issue for the society as a whole or for a geographic region, in which our objective is to productively employ everyone seeking work, rather than entirely as a *selection* issue for each individual organization in competition with one another. There are not enough "superior" people to go around in any event: By definition, only 5% of any population is above the 95th percentile! Moreover, as Wagner (1997) noted, it is paradoxically true that the greater the number of organizations that use ability tests for selection, the lower will be the overall utility for the society as a whole, approaching the average of the population, thus putting more of a premium on training and on differential job placement. The point is not that the values reflected in these alternative objectives are necessarily "better" than the economizing values, but that they all, including profitability, represent potential values choices that could be considered, discussed, analyzed, and possibly integrated. As noted previously, in considering the problem of imperfect prediction "the personal and societal costs must be considered in addition to the monetary costs, and it is the psychologist's duty to bring these costs to the employer's attention" (London & Bray, 1980, p. 898). Because the field lacks a very salient normative point of view, we tend to be reactive at best rather than proactive in these sorts of matters. For example, I/O psychology's concern for the fairness of our employee assessment methods derived not from a moral or even scholarly perspective of our own, but from sociopolitical ones—as a reaction to the civil rights movement and resulting legislation and jurisprudence (Katzell & Austin, 1992).

Employee Rights

Affording some primacy to the interests of individual workers necessitates consideration of the issue of *employee rights*. Which, if any, of their interests rise to the level of a *right*? What is the rationale or justification for such? And what do we mean by a right anyway? These straightforward questions have revealed themselves to be deceptively complicated philosophical and ethical issues to those who have grappled for answers (cf. Donaldson, 1982; Dworkin, 1977; C. P. Edwards, 1993; Rowan, 2000). And the notion of rights has been neglected in mainstream organizational theory (Keeley, 1983) so that "In the American panoply of rights, workplace rights are the least defined, the least understood, and the least sanctified by social consensus" (C. P. Edwards, 1993, p. 2). Werhane (1999; Werhane & Radin, 1996) suggested that this is due in part to the fact that the American free-enterprise system has distorted the classical political–economic theory of John Locke by segmenting the political or civil realm from the economic. It is a distortion of John Locke's views because his conception of liberty and the pursuit of self-interest was expressly constrained by not violating "the laws of justice." As Werhane (1999) explained,

> Economic phenomena, including employment, are not subject to the same moral constraints as political rights. So, for example, we give those who engage in allegedly obscene or libelous actions the right to due process before being considered guilty; yet people … [who have] been working for the same company for 20 years are laid off or fired without any appeal or redress.
>
> This model of employees as primarily economic phenomena is in contradistinction to the political idea that each employee, as a citizen, is a person with inherent rights. (Pp. 242, 243)

What Is a Right?

The obvious place to begin is with an understanding of what is generally conveyed by the status of something being a right. A right may be defined as a legitimate claim or an entitlement that individuals have by virtue of their social identity, and that protects them in a particular way from the generally prevailing system of social or political governance (Donaldson, 1982; C. P. Edwards, 1993). There are four elements to the definition. First, rights constitute *claims* or *entitlements*. A claim implies a claim *to* something and *against* someone; thus, someone's right ordinarily implies a correlative *duty* on others to respect the claim. Your right to free speech obliges me to permit your expression of opinions with which I disagree. In contrast, an entitlement is a right to do or have something such that it is not necessarily against anyone—that is, no correlative duties can be assigned to particular others. Your

right to associate only with those whom you choose obligates no one to comply with it.

Second, these claims and entitlements are accepted as valid or
legitimate. The basis of their legitimacy may be *moral*, based on cultural
norms or on ethical reasoning that constitutes philosophical rationales of
the sort considered in this book, or it may be *legal*.

Third, one possesses a right merely by virtue of a particular social identity
or group membership for whom the right is intended. The right to vote in the
United States is afforded all adult citizens who have not been convicted of a
felony; the right not to be discriminated against in employment matters due
to a physical impairment is granted by the Americans With Disabilities Act
to all qualified persons with a disability; the right to have the specified terms
of one's employment recognized by one's employer accrues merely by virtue
of being employed. But even that simple situation has become rather
complicated in the past 20 years, with the enormous growth in part-time and
temporary workers who find their employment through temp agencies
(Kalleberg, 2000). Labor laws were written when the nature of employment
(i.e., who worked for whom) was much more clear than it is for such workers,
so that in many instances it has become problematic whether such people
are employees of the agency or of the company at which they may be
working for quite some time (Reich, 2001).

Fourth, rights protect us against the prevailing system of social or political
governance, meaning that "rights are exercised in opposition to or as
limitations upon the ordinary exercise of legitimate power" (C. P. Edwards,
1993, p. 27). In other words, rights are "trumps" that take precedence over
the goals and objectives of the state or other governing bodies (Dworkin,
1977). The most obvious example, of course, is the Bill of Rights of the
American constitution, which limits the powers of the federal government.
Similarly, if certain conditions are met a person with a disability may have
the right to a job even if it requires the employer to make some reasonable
accommodations to enable the person to perform the job, overriding the
employer's right to freely choose whom to hire. The last example suggests
one of the most dynamic aspects of the consideration of rights, and that is
when rights collide. The restaurant owner's right to free association does
not extend to discriminating against serving African Americans. The
employer's right to pay employees as little as possible to maximize profits
stops at the level of the statutory minimum wage.

Manifesto Rights.   Perhaps the most fascinating and certainly the most
controversial topic in the philosophical and political exploration of rights is
the notion of *manifesto rights*, which are especially pertinent to a
consideration of putative employee rights. As indicated in Table 12.1,
manifesto rights are a type of background rights (Dworkin, 1977) that

pertain to rights regarding the broad actions of a society in the abstract. They are often controversial because some are not traditional rights with a cultural or legal precedent; they tend to be politically progressive, if not downright radical, in the sense that they call attention to human interests that have largely been neglected by the existing political system(s); and they present the pragmatic difficulties associated with entitlements rather than claims—that is, it is unclear who has the obligation to provide or enforce the right. Frequently proposed manifesto rights include the right to a job, to decent housing and a decent standard of living for one's family, and to adequate medical care.

The Basis of Employee Rights

In contrast with background or manifesto rights, worker rights are a type of *institutional right*, which stems from a particular institutional source and that justifies decisions by the institution, in this instance the business organization. Based on the general definition of rights, *workers' rights* may be defined as "legitimated claims or privileges (goods) that an employee possesses as a result of being an employee and that the employee may exercise as protection from the established workplace governance" (C. P. Edwards, 1993, p. 28). Edwards also differentiated them from quid pro quo or earned benefits such as wages, fringe benefits, or contractual obligations. One of the reasons workers' rights are of particular interest stems from the general definition of a right as pertaining to those with a specified social identity. Some aspects of social identity are permanent or virtually so (e.g., sex, ethnicity, and citizenship), so that the rights associated with membership in those groups are likewise permanent. This is not so for workers who may be fired (or quit their jobs). Because workers may be fired, thus losing the status that affords them their employee rights, the enforcement of those rights may be problematic and dependent on pragmatic considerations such as the employer's available applicant pool and whether the worker is a union member, as well as the employer's moral stance and commitment to employee rights as reflected in its human resource policies and actions. The question regarding what is the basis for employee rights can be interpreted pragmatically, in which case the answer is that they are established through mechanisms of law (*statutory rights*) such as the 1964 Civil Rights Act, through collective bargaining agreements (*collective contract rights*), or through what C. P. Edwards called *enterprise rights*. Enterprise rights are those that are given unilaterally by employers to their workers explicitly or implicitly.[132] They might include such things as the right to a formal grievance system for complaints, the right to know how one's per-

---

[132]C. P. Edwards (1993) restricted enterprise rights (unnecessarily, I believe) to only those that are granted explicitly.

TABLE 12.1
A Categorization of Rights

Class of Rights	Definition of Types	Justification
Background Rights	**Basic rights, fundamental rights, human rights,** or **moral rights** justify political decisions by the society as a whole in the abstract. They are frequently thought to underlie more specific Institutional Rights. Examples: the right to personal liberty and to not be enslaved or tortured and the right to national self-determination. Included are **manifesto rights** which may be of ambiguous legal and moral status. Examples: the rights of all people to a job, a decent standard of living, and to medical care.	Varies with the underlying philosophical and/or political theory on which the right(s) are based. For example, natural law theory (Locke), hypothetical social contracts (Hobbes; Rawls), or respect for the dignity of persons (i.e., their freedom, well-being, and equal just treatment; Kant).
Institutional Rights	**Legal** and/or **moral rights** that are created by or derived from a specific social institution and justify decisions made by the institution. Examples: **(a) political Rights,** such as freedom of speech or the right to have a contract enforced. **(b) traditional rights,** such as the right to own property or to vote. **(c) civil rights** pertaining to equal treatment under the law. **(d) moral rights,** such as the right not to be deceived, lied to, or cheated; or to have a promise kept. **(e) employer rights,** generally defined as freedom of contract rights. **(f) workers' rights.** Noncontractual entitlements such as the right to a safe workplace or to try to form a union, as opposed to quid pro quo benefits like wages, which are earned. They may be **legal,** such as rights to the statutory minimum wage and to refuse overtime work without being punished; or **moral,** such as the right to not be subject to abusive language by a supervisor. They may also include **enterprise rights** which are granted or promised by employers explicitly or implicitly, such as due process in disciplinary actions (may be of ambiguous, often disputed, legal status).	Legal rights may be based on a constitution, legislation, or other governmental regulations. They may also be based on contract rights that are enforced by law, both individual and collective, such as union–management agreements. Moral rights (which in some instances may also be legal rights) may be based on the rules and policies of informal organizations like social clubs or of formal organizations like corporations. They may also derive from implicit cultural norms and expectations or explicit codes of conduct.

Note. Based in part on Donaldson (1982), C. P. Edwards (1993), and Rowan (2000).

formance will be evaluated, or the right to a "just-cause" standard for be-ing fired. Those that are explicitly codified in organizational policies are more likely to be legally enforceable. Those only implied by customary practices, hence constituting "implicit contracts" or "implied promises," are more tenuous. Despite the fact that enterprise rights are unevenly available from organization to organization, less reliably administered and enforced than collectively bargained or statutory rights, and—most im-portant—may be changed or eliminated at the employer's discretion, Ed-wards nevertheless believed that they have become rather important.[133] That is because of the declining domain of unionized workers and the spotty effectiveness of government regulations in guaranteeing the worker protections they were intended to provide.

The basis for employee rights also can be interpreted more fundamentally as a question regarding the political, economic, or philosophical (i.e., ethical) justification for them. Only the briefest of summaries is possible here. The need to justify employee rights (as a special category of claims and entitlements over and above those of any citizen) may be seen as stemming from the classical free-market economic tradition embedded in the political philosophy of John Locke, the economics of Adam Smith, and notions of the social contract described by Rousseau and Hobbes. That is, if one were to accept that all that is necessary to establish an effective and moral economy is the right of everyone to enter freely into contractual agreements like employment which employees and employers are equally free to terminate at any time, then no additional or special rights for employees are justifiable. Most especially precluded would be those rights (i.e., market intrusions) associated with collective bargaining or government regulation. And, indeed, employment at-will has long been the assumed default option governing employment the United States. But from that perspective, all of the criticisms of the classical free-market model (see chap. 10) may be invoked as justifications for this special category of rights—e.g., its distributional injustices, the disparity in information availability and bargaining power between employer and individual employee, as well as the difficulty and expense of contract enforcement for the employee. These all serve to "establish a market context in which it cannot be presumed that the market will produce the optimal level and mix of workers' rights" (Edwards, 1993, p. 47).

Also relevant are the three facets of moral values that constitute the domain of moral action, which guides the moral community to which we all belong: fairness and justice, welfare or caring, and personal virtue. Indeed, the meta-ethical principle of universalism, Rawlsian social contract theory,

---

[133]Some state courts have begun to interpret the enterprise rights propounded in employee handbooks as implied contracts between the employer and employees, hence legally enforceable.

and "Kantian capitalism" (K. Gibson, 2000) serve as underlying justifications for the corporate social responsibility/multiple stakeholder model of business. These basic ethical precepts also provide the most direct grounds for employee rights. For example, in a Kantian vein, Rowan (2000) assayed that all persons possess needs and goals, or more broadly, interests, which is of great moral relevance because it implies that they ought to have the autonomy and means to formulate a "minimally acceptable life plan" (p. 356), and the freedom to choose among reasonable options.[134] Indeed, the availability of options is what constitutes freedom; the destitute person devoid of almost all life choices is free in only the most limited sense. Thus, the rights to freedom, autonomy, and well-being (the satisfaction of one's interests) are justified. If one accepts that the principles of justice, fairness, and equality or universalism are inherent in the notions of freedom and well-being (my freedom is not inherently more important than yours), then we have come around to an essentially Kantian respect for persons. That is, people, simply because they are human, have a right to be treated fairly in a way that respects their freedom and well-being. Obviously, this pertains to the rights of employees at work as they are among this category. From these fundamental or generic rights flow such particulars as the commonly promoted rights to adequate and fair pay, a safe workplace, due process, and privacy, as well as the rights to refuse unethical directives or to behave responsibly by complaining about dangerous products or unethical practices without fear of reprisal.

Of course this simple enunciation and justification of rights fails to represent the complexity of their implementation. First, a simple assertion of a right to freedom of speech tells us little about its possible limitations. Second, rights may conflict. Your colleague's right to privacy or right to smoke may conflict with your right to a safe or healthful workplace. The ethical resolution of such conflicts generally gives precedence to the avoidance of disrespect, harm, or wrongdoing over the enhancement of dignity, well-being, or liberty. Third, what about employer rights? What is the relationship, for example, between the organization's right to hire and (especially) fire employees, and their rights to respectful and fair treatment?

Employment At-Will (EAW)

As noted earlier, millions of Americans have experienced involuntary permanent loss of a job (or several) over the past 20 years. The reason that has been possible is that the bulk of employees in the United States work

---

[134]Rowan (2000) apparently felt it unnecessary to specify that one's life plan itself (i.e., the gratification of one's needs, goals, and interests), to be justifiable, should comport with the normative principles of the moral community of persons. Obviously, it should. In addition, if it did not, this line of argument could fail by virtue of positing an almost infinite number of rights, corresponding to every need or objective one might have.

under the condition of EAW, meaning that, barring some limitations noted shortly, people "must be left, without interference to buy and sell where they please, and to discharge or retain employees at will for good cause or for no cause, or even for bad cause without thereby being guilty of an unlawful act *per se*. It is a right which an employee may exercise in the same way, to the same extent, for the same cause or want of cause as the employer" (text of a famous 1884 judicial decision, cited by C. P. Edwards, 1993, p.14; also cf. Dunford & Devine, 1998, C. P. Edwards, 1993, and Werhane & Radin, 1996, for concise reviews of EAW).[135]

EAW is a common law doctrine inherited from England where—like most of the rest of the world's industrialized nations—it is no longer the dominant basis for employment as it is in the United States. Business ethicists have frequently decried EAW as incompatible with the development of mutual trust, loyalty, and respect that ought to characterize the workplace (Werhane, 1999). Some organizational scholars have made the case that it is similarly incompatible with the sorts of modern "high performance" and employee-centered human resource practices that build employee commitment and contribute to effective organizational functioning (Dessler, 1999; Huselid, 1995; Pfeffer, 1994, 1998; Pfeffer & Veiga, 1999). In contrast, I/O psychologists have largely ignored the topic or have supported the prevailing corporate perspective by suggesting ways of "protecting at-will organizations from liability associated with discharging employees" (Dunford & Devine, 1998, p. 928).

For the first several decades of the 20th century EAW was virtually the only governing principle of employment relations, and it led to legal interpretations in which employees had virtually no rights. The courts uniformly reasoned that whatever rights might be claimed by an employee against an employer (in the absence of a legal individual contract) could simply and legally be refuted by firing the worker; thus, they were moot. During the middle of the century there was a substantial increase in federal statutory protections for workers in general (e.g., the Fair Labor Standards Act or the Employee Retirement Income Security Act), accompanying regulatory bodies (e.g., the Occupational Safety and Health Administration), as well as civil rights legislation targeted at specific groups of employees (e.g., The Civil Rights Act of 1964, the Equal Pay Act, and the Americans With Disabilities Act). Many states also passed similar laws, and "given the small number of relevant federal laws and their highly specific nature, state law tends to be much more important in discharge-related lawsuits" (Dunford

---

[135]This discussion of EAW pertains to private sector employees only. In the public sector, employees of federal, state, or local governments have many more guaranteed rights. That is because of the political philosophy reflected in the fact that the U.S. constitution was written to protect individual citizens from the state, which includes its role as an employer. It does not pertain to relations among private people (even "quasipeople" like corporations).

& Devine, 1998, p. 907).[136] Almost as important during those years was the growth of labor unions, which were given explicit legal recognition, so that a major source of worker rights and protections emanated from collective-bargaining agreements that would be enforced by the courts. Concomitant with the decline in labor unions and the protections they provided, state courts have partially filled that void by becoming somewhat more "pro-employee" in enforcing what might reasonably be interpreted as implied contracts between employer and employee (e.g., on the basis of statements made in the organization's employee handbook). For reasons of public policy the courts have also afforded workers protection against being fired for behaving ethically and responsibly, such as by alerting the appropriate parties to wrongdoing by the organization (whistle-blowing).

One of the most important limitations on EAW are the institutional enterprise rights of due-process or just cause for dismissal. Werhane and Radin (1996) distinguished between *procedural due process*, as "the right to a hearing, trial, grievance procedure, or appeal" in which the grounds for dismissal can be ascertained and challenged by an employee, and *substantive due process*, which is "the demand for rationality and fairness: for good reasons for decisions" (p. 420). Organizations may be characterized as either at will (a majority in the United States) or those in which some form of just-cause policy for dismissal has been granted to employees as an enterprise right. Unfortunately, as noted in chapter 3, there has been a trend for employers to institute due-process procedures contingent on employees signing away their rights to redress in the courts.

The major organizational justification for EAW is the traditional economizing one of promoting efficiency and productivity. Aside from specific legislative limitations, in a nonunionized, at-will company any employees deemed unproductive, uncooperative, or no longer needed can be terminated expeditiously without the time-consuming and potentially costly procedures of due process. The justification has seemed even more pertinent in recent years as companies have striven to become more "lean and mean" in response to global competition. Long-term commitments to employees have become virtually obsolete, and short-term flexibility in controlling labor costs are more important. "The result is more jobs with lower wages, reduced benefits, more part-time work and temporary workers, more subcontracting, and intensified work schedules" (C. P. Edwards, 1993, p. 15). However, the empirical evidence regarding the extent to which these EAW-based practices have proven to increase productivity is rather mixed (Pfeffer, 1994, 1998; Pfeffer & Veiga, 1999; Tsui et al., 1997; Werhane, 1999), and it is by no means clear that at-will companies are more produc-

---

[136]In an Appendix C. P. Edwards (1993) noted 41 states in which a state court has recognized an implied contract and 6 states in which the existence of an implied contract has been specifically rejected.

tive than just-cause companies or that employees who feel respected, trusted, and protected from capricious personnel actions are not in fact more committed, productive, innovative, and efficient than those who feel vulnerable (Dessler, 1999). Employees are at risk because labor costs are simply easier to reduce than others like capital costs.

From a moral perspective, however, unlike other costs, labor is inseparable from the individual human beings who provide it. The abstract economic objective of "reducing labor costs" can be accomplished only by the dismissal of employees—who are, in this context, conceived of entirely in terms of money saved, not as individual human beings. Although it may be tempting to conclude that this is an unfortunate but nevertheless necessary aspect of a successful free-enterprise economic system, another view—based in fact on the writings of Adam Smith—is possible (Werhane, 1999). As noted earlier, A. Smith conditioned his views of laissez faire free enterprise within the context of principles of fairness and justice. He was primarily focused on a system of political economy—fusing both political and economic concerns—not simply on economic utility for the firm. "Early on, then, Smith linked politics and economics, rights and utility.... Smith's proviso is that system will be successful only when each operates under the constraints of respect for human rights, justice, and fair play, and early on he recognized that poor treatment of employees is both unfair as well as economically questionable on utilitarian grounds" (Werhane, 1999, pp. 243–244).

TECHNICAL COMPETENCE AND SOCIETAL CONSEQUENCES

The ethicality of behavior (i.e., moral action) cannot be judged appropriately without some consideration of the consequences of our actions. This is reflected in the moral dimension of care or well-being and harm-avoidance, and it is true not only within the framework of formal utilitarian theories. "Morality does not exist in a vacuum. Human pursuits should always be judged in terms of what their consequences are for other human beings" (Luria, 1976, p. 333). Many ethicists, like Rest (1986b), have virtually defined what is meant by an ethical situation or dilemma as one in which the consequences of a person's action affects the interests, welfare, or expectations of others. The issue is particularly pertinent for I/O psychology because the business institutions in which and for whom we practice set the agenda for that practice in accord with their own values and objectives; those, in turn, define the organizational problems that we address and largely determine the range of potential applications (hence, consequences) of our work. As noted earlier, a version of this perspective has been promoted recently by Gardner et al. (2001), who suggested that satisfaction in "good work" entails developing one's expertise as well as helping society.

Perhaps the first, maybe the best, but surely the most explicit application of this point of view within the domain of traditional I/O psychology practice is the late Samuel Messick's (1980, 1995) incorporation of *consequences* into a "unified validity framework" for the evaluation of psychological tests. The essence of his approach is that the appropriateness, meaningfulness, and usefulness of tests are inseparable matters. In his scheme, consequences are prominent with regard to "the appraisal of both potential and actual social consequences of the applied testing" (S. Messick, 1995, p. 748). That is, over and above the validity evidence that supports the construct interpretation of the measure, as well as its usefulness, incremental validity, or utility in this situation, one should not ignore the social consequences of its use. And those may fruitfully be contemplated by comparing them with the anticipated consequences of not using the measure or of using alternative assessment procedures. "What matters is not only whether the social consequences of test interpretation and use are positive or negative, but how the consequences came about and what determined them" (p. 748).

Personnel psychologists have not been quick to embrace S. Messick's perspective because it challenges the prevailing positivistic separation in I/O psychology of supposedly objective, value-neutral science (as represented in the demonstration of test *validity*) from value-laden considerations of social consequences (e.g., as reflected in a concern for test fairness or the adverse impact of some tests on minorities). But, as explained earlier, the justification of the fact–value distinction—at least with respect to applied professional practice—is extremely tenuous, and values are implicated at every stage of practice, from problem definition to the interpretation and application of findings. From an ethical perspective it matters less whether moral considerations reflected in concern for the societal consequences of test use are included in an expanded "unified conception of validity" or are conceived as a separate but equally important matter. From a strategic perspective, S. Messick might have invited a warmer reception from the field had he kept the issues separate. But his unified conception is in keeping with much of contemporary social science and with the true nature of professional practice.[137]

I have been involved for the past few years in an employment discrimination matter which provides an illustration of the perspective that Messick

---

[137]As personnel psychologists are aware, expanding and reconceptualizing the nature of validity is not without precedent. Not so many years ago, construct, content, and criterion-related validities were thought of as separate and distinct definitions of validity; now they are viewed as complementary strategies associated with alternative types of inferences to be made from test scores within a single comprehensive conceptualization of construct validity. Similarly, content validity was a strategy that, until relatively recently, was seen as appropriate and necessary only for the validation of measures based on the assessment of overt behaviors, such as job duties and tasks. The profession now generally accepts that if certain conditions are met content validation procedures may also be used appropriately for the validation of covert constructs like job knowledge or abilities.

advocated. Another I/O psychologist and I were retained by attorneys for the African-American plaintiffs in a Title VII lawsuit, to be members of a joint technical panel to oversee the development of valid selection and promotion tests for a state agency in the United States. Joining us on the panel were two I/O psychologists retained by the state to represent their interests. Several years prior, the state defendants had acknowledged pursuing a variety of discriminatory practices for quite some time, by entering into a consent decree with the plaintiffs. The decree specified a number of activities to be undertaken by the state in order to remedy the past discrimination, most of which the state had not done and for which it had been found to be in contempt of court. The expert panel was formed to help expedite the mandated procedures.

In exploring the feasibility of implementing some of the newly developed examinations we learned from plaintiffs's attorneys that some of the more egregious instances of discrimination practiced by the agency had been the exclusive appointment of Whites only to special duties and other "out-of-classification assignments," including provisional noncompetitive promotions to higher level jobs. Because of the recalcitrance of the state in complying with the consent decree there had been no promotional registers for these jobs for many years, so that these provisional appointments were de facto long-term permanent ones. Now, the tasks associated with the special duty assignments and the duties of the higher level jobs into which these White employees had been placed constitute the very job content that the work simulation promotion exams had been designed to reflect. Those employees alone had, in effect, been provided by the agency with the opportunity to practice for the promotional examinations for many months and even years. Obviously, they would have an enormous unfair advantage over the African-Americans (and some other Whites) who had not received such favorable assignments. Use of the tests under these circumstances would lock in years of discriminatory practices for the foreseeable future, as there would be relatively little attrition and promotion in the organization for some time after this wave of promotions filled the accumulated job vacancies. In fact, this problem had been recognized in the consent decree, which had provided for special hands-on "affirmative action training" to take place, in which African Americans would have the opportunity to perform and practice on the "feeder tasks" so as to be prepared to take the promotional examinations on a (more-or-less) equal footing with the Whites who had received the favorable assignments. The agency had never instituted the training.

All four experts, including—most notably—those retained by the state defendants, agreed that the tests could not appropriately be administered in these circumstances. In fact, it is this sort of analysis, taking into account the full ramifications of the situation, that ought to differentiate the contributions to be made by an I/O psychologist beyond those typically afforded by a psychometrician or statistician. It was not enough that a technically competent job had been done in developing content valid examinations; it was clear that a fundamental assumption underlying test interpretation was not being met in these circumstances. Differences in ability test performance between examinees could not reasonably be interpreted as reflecting differences in ability rather than differences in opportunities and de facto test preparation provided by the employer itself. All four experts agreed that the entire context of the situation and the likely *consequences* of test usage could not ethically be ignored. It was then that the state defendants fired their experts.

Perhaps emboldened by new judicial appointments to the appeals court, which had resulted in reversals of some of the trial judge's recent rulings in favor of the plaintiffs, the state retained two different I/O psychologists as its experts, and the court-recognized intervenors in the lawsuit (representing White employees of the agency seeking to prevent reverse discrimination) also for the first time hired their own I/O psychologist expert. Just about all cooperation with me and the other plaintiffs's expert ceased. What had been a constructive and productive collaborative attempt to facilitate the state agency's employment needs, while trying to remedy past employment discrimination and prevent its recurrence, became a contentious adversarial situation akin to that which characterizes such cases at the time of trial.

In subsequent depositions and hearings regarding the implementation of the tests for permanent appointments the I/O psychologist representing the class of intervenors argued simply that the tests were professionally developed and apparently content valid, so they should be used. He did not address the ethical issue regarding the consequences of test usage in this situation. The two new I/O psychologist experts for the state went further. The premises of their argument were (a) ability tests consistently show adverse impact against African-Americans (i.e., mean differences in White–African-American subgroup performance), and (b) there is no compelling evidence in the I/O psychology literature that training would obviate these differences. Therefore, they concluded, in the absence of proof by plaintiffs that the training contemplated would in fact obviate such differences—which plaintiffs had not provided—the tests should be administered. That reasoning is morally equivalent to requiring a victim who is being beaten by a thug on the street to demonstrate that rehabilitation of the attacker will be successful and his own medical treatment will be effective before allowing the police to subdue and arrest the assailant. The anticipated consequences that compel the ethical refusal to recommend testing in this situation are not merely that Whites are likely to do better on the exams than African-Americans, but that they have been unfairly advantaged by the organization to do so. The African-American employees in this agency have clearly been wronged, and in all likelihood harmed, by the organization's actions. The ethical principles of fairness or procedural justice do not require an assumption that the contemplated training will eliminate all subgroup differences.[138] The metaphor of "leveling the playing field" does not imply guaranteeing the outcome of the game, merely that it be determined in an unbiased manner. Once again, in S. Messick's (1995) words, "What matters is not only whether the social consequences of test interpretation and use are positive or negative, but how the consequences came about and what determined them" (p. 748).

ADDING FURTHER TO THE FRAMEWORK
FOR ETHICAL DECISION MAKING

34.   **Virtually from its inception, I/O psychology was reproached by social critics outside the field and by I/O psychologists ourselves as a mere technocratic profession serving the objectives of corporations. One facet of those criticisms—that the field is unscientific, atheoretical, and fails to contribute to the advancement of knowledge in psychology—has not been true for more than a generation. The other facet is more problematic. Many contemporary instances can be cited that support the view that we have not outgrown the organizational–managerial values biases which accounted for our early accomplishments and continued success in serving organizations, even when those organizations stand in opposition to employee rights and well-being.** I have argued that this bias largely goes unrecognized by I/O psychologists because our values are congruent with those of the economic system and corporations within which we function. As a consequence, we misperceive and mischaracterize our activities as entirely scientific, objective, or value free, and sometimes view those who explicitly propound other values positions (e.g., that corporations have broad social responsibilities) as themselves biased, naive, unscientific, or otherwise misguided. The perspective taken throughout this book is that values positions permeate virtually all scientific and moral enterprises, and that our ethical standing will be well served by attempts to articulate and examine the implicit values assumptions that guide our moral reasoning.

---

[138]Ironically, future selection activities in this case shed some indirect light on just this issue. Because of some procedural difficulties in the administration of an employment test for this agency at one of the test sites, the scores of examinees who took the test at that site could not be counted; those folks, unfortunately, had to be retested. Because they might be advantaged by a practice/learning effect, we recommended that all candidates have the option of taking the exam again, with only the higher of their two scores to be counted. As it turned out, among those who were tested twice, African-Americans benefitted disproportionally: They improved their scores substantially more than did Whites (although not eradicating the mean group difference). Extrapolating from the observed learning effect following a simulation exam to the potential learning effect of a hands-on training program is not a very large inferential leap.

35.   Although it is obvious to anyone who cares to look that I/O psychology contains many generous and caring individuals whose professional goals include human betterment, there is room for improving the extent to which the profession qua profession reflects that sensitivity. The expanded vision of the field projected in this chapter attempts to do that. It aspires to do so by advocating (a) adoption of a broader model of values or value system than currently characterizes the field, for example, by adding a humanist dimension to the S–P model; (b) a greater interest in and concern for the well-being of the individual employee that is on a par with our predominant concern for organizational needs, goals, and perspectives; (c) an expanded criterion by which we gauge the effectiveness of our own work beyond the narrow standard of technical competence to a consideration of its broader societal consequences as well; and overall (d) the incorporation of an avowedly normative (i.e., moral) perspective to the field, along with the *scientific* (i.e., descriptive and predictive) and instrumental (i.e., focus on productivity and organizational effectiveness) perspectives that predominate. Although it may not be what he had in mind, this proposal seems compatible with, even if not directly responsive to, J. P. Campbell's (1990) criticism of the field as lacking an "agreed-upon set of substantive goals against which to evaluate the performance of the discipline" (p. 68).

The position taken here is commensurate with Wiley's (1998) examination of the facets of the role of human resource managers in organizations. She emphasized that their professional loyalties and ethical commitments as well as an altruistic norm of service "may place them in direct conflict with their organization's business goals" (p. 147). Nevertheless, a national survey of human resource professionals revealed that they maintained a position of ethical leadership and guidance in their organizations, in which senior managers often sought their advice about ethical issues. A set of potential roles to be played by human resource professionals in their organizations was derived from qualitative survey responses and is presented here as Table 12.2.

36.   The difficulties in implementing the moral agenda proposed in this chapter can hardly be overestimated. But those who attempt to do so will find allies in the management scholars, business ethicists, and progressive business leaders who are already engaged in the process, as well as those earlier-cited I/O psychology colleagues who take seriously psychology's ethical mandate to apply our knowledge of behavior pragmatically to improve the condition of the individual and society as well as the organization.

TABLE 12.2
Potential Roles Available to the I/O Psychologist and Other Human Resource Managers With Respect to Ethical Problems

Roles	Description
Advisory	Advising organizational members on ethical standards and policies
Monitoring	Monitoring actions/behaviors for compliance with laws, policies,and ethical standards
Educator	Instructing or distributing information regarding ethical principles and organizational policies
Advocate	Acting on behalf of individual employees or other organizational stakeholders, and protecting employees from managerial reprisals
Investigative	Investigating apparent or alleged unethical situations or complaints
Questioning	Questioning or challenging the ethical aspects of managers' decisions
Organizational	Explaining or justifying the organization's actions when confronted by agents external to the organization
Model	Modeling ethical practices to contribute to an organizational norm and climate of ethical behavior

Note. Based on Wiley, 1998. *The Journal of Business Ethics, 17,* p. 157. With kind permission from the author and Kluwer Academic Publishers.

III

The Ethical Context
of Research

13

Research Ethics:
I. Informed Consent
and Confidentiality

Trust lies at the heart of virtually every decision that must be made by the researcher, and all human participants in the research process depend on the trust of others at all levels. Research subjects trust the researcher to treat them with dignity and respect, to protect their well-being , and to safeguard them from potential dangers or risks of harm. Researchers trust their subjects to maintain honesty in their responding, to respect the seriousness of the research enterprise, and to maintain their promises not to reveal certain aspects of a study to future participants. Society lends its trust to researchers to pursue worthwhile research questions which stand to benefit humanity, to protect participants from research abuses, and to maintain honesty and objectivity throughout the research process.

—Alan J. Kimmel

In biomedical fields of professional practice and research with human participants utilizing procedures like randomized drug trials or experimental surgery techniques, the core ethical issue is generally the consequentialist one of possible serious harm to the participants from the procedures administered, in relation to their potential benefits. Although that is sometimes also the case for research and practice in clinical psychology or for research with vulnerable groups such as children, the elderly, or the impaired, the safety of research participants is not often the most salient issue for the social and behavioral sciences in general, and it is probably even less frequently the case in I/O psychology. However, as Mann (1994) noted, "psychology subjects may have their self-esteem manipulated, their mood changed, or their abilities questioned" (p. 140). This chapter and the next one cannot hope to explore the entire topic of research ethics, about which many books have been written. In addition to the APA's (1992, 2002) ethical code, excellent, readable treatments are available from Greenberg and Folger (1988), Kimmel (1988, 1996), Rosenthal and Rosnow (1991), Sales and Folkman (2000) and Sieber (1992).

THE SOCIAL NATURE OF THE RESEARCH ENTERPRISE

Notwithstanding some high-profile examples of questionable research procedures involving the deception of research participants, the overriding issue that ought to influence our ethical deliberations is the simple realization that our research is not usually aimed at benefitting directly the people who participate in it as subjects. This is the case whether they are college students in a subject pool or company employees. This does not mean that we should deny that the results of some organizational research have consequences for employee–participants or that employees may benefit from the research indirectly through systemic organizational improvements prompted by the findings. But the research is most frequently driven by organizational objectives or problems defined by those relatively high in the organization's authority structure, and the benefits of the research, if any, may not be experienced by the current participating employees—as with the validation sample in personnel selection research, for example.

In addition, much I/O psychology research is conducted with employee participants and college students in which the aim is to achieve generalizable knowledge of constructs and the relations among them (e.g., organizational commitment, procedural justice, and rater bias), with no expectation that the investigations will necessarily yield immediately useful applications in the organization(s) providing the research sites, much less direct benefits to the research participants themselves. In fact, the participants may be a convenience sample whose members and organization(s) have no special relevance to the topic or aims of the research. Figure 13.1 describes categories of research performed by I/O psychologists based on who are the intended primary beneficiaries of the research. The question of "who benefits?" has implications for the professional and ethical issues covered in this chapter and the next, including informed consent, the obligation to participate in the study, confidentiality of data, and deception. This sort of analysis is similar to one made in clinical psychology or biomedical research, in which a distinction is drawn between therapeutic and nontherapeutic research. Participants in the former, but not the latter, may expect to derive some benefit from having participated.

There are three things to note about the categories of I/O research described in Fig. 13.1. First, of course, is that they are oversimplifications of the complexity of research forms actually carried out. For example, the basic theoretical issues under investigation in Category I type research—for example, investigating the construct validity of alternative types of individual assessments or the nature of cognitive information-retrieval processes—may actually have been inspired by applied organizational questions concerning the utility of assessment centers and the accuracy of performance appraisals, respectively. Secondly, the categorization is more a set of prototypes than a realistic taxonomy within which all empirical studies can be neatly classified. For example, it is very common for I/O psychologists to "piggyback" assessment instruments pertinent to their own Category I or II research interests on to those administered by the organization as part of its own Category III-type enterprise.

Third, and most important, is that Fig. 13.1 serves to emphasize the fact that the extent to which our research is intended to benefit those on whom we depend to carry it out varies considerably. The five prototypic categories form a continuum from Type I, in which there is no intent to provide any benefits for the participants and in which they are unlikely to perceive any advantage for themselves by participating, to Category V, in which the research is focused on serving the interests of the participants.[139] For research categories of Types I, II, III, and sometimes IV, there is no direct value evident to the prospective research subject in participating in the proposed study. Thus, the issue of obtaining subject participation, and the various inducements to participate that may be made, assume considerable ethical importance.

Most research with human participants in the social and behavioral sciences (e.g., in sociology and anthropology, social and experimental psychology, marketing and consumer behavior, or political science) is of Type I or II, and to a lesser extent, III—meaning that the researcher's interest in conducting the study is theoretically motivated or problem driven, and it ordinarily does not include benefitting the prospective participants. They are merely representatives by which general scientific principles may be explored or solutions to applied problems sought. Of course, that doesn't preclude the research having ultimate value for humankind; but, as Shipley

---

[139]Hypothetically, the continuum could be extended beyond Category I, in which participants are not benefitted, to include a type of research in which they actually experience some potential harm. For example, the research design may incorporate an experimental manipulation that is stressful, or the confidentiality of subject responses is not protected adequately in circumstances in which public knowledge of them could be threatening. But in those instances, the harm is either a byproduct of the research or a consequence of insensitivity and poor methodology, respectively, so I have not included it. Nevertheless, if the adverse consequences can be foreseen—even if not intended in the sense of constituting the purpose of the research—there is an ethical issue to address. (Cf. chap. 3 regarding the issue of intentionality in deontological theories.)

I. BASIC PSYCHOLOGICAL RESEARCH IN WHICH NEITHER THE STUDY PARTICIPANTS NOR THE SETTING ARE OF PARTICULAR RELEVANCE TO THE TOPIC.

Many I/O psychologists are interested in studying the same fundamental psychological processes of perception, cognition, attitude formation, emotional responsiveness and other interpersonal influences, individual differences, and so forth, that characterize the substance of academic psychology. The application of the knowledge gained may be of only secondary interest. Depending on the nature of the researcher's employment, organizational employees or college students can provide a readily available *convenience sample* of research participants for such investigations. In general, they are no more (and perhaps no less) appropriate subjects for such investigations than anyone else, and there is no a priori reason to expect them to have any particular interest in the research problem or in participating in the investigation.

II. APPLIED PSYCHOLOGICAL RESEARCH NOT NECESSARILY INTENDED TO BENEFIT DIRECTLY A PARTICULAR ORGANIZATION OR THE STUDY PARTICIPANTS

I/O psychologists generally conduct applied research that is aimed at achieving an understanding of the effective functioning of individual employees, supervisor—subordinate dyads, work teams, management committees and larger units, or the organization as a whole. This work may have the potential to advance the field because it is concerned with organizationally relevant theoretical or applied issues, and/or is conducted with appropriate samples of persons in realistic work settings. For example, much of what we think we know about sex bias in organizations stems from laboratory simulations with college students. But, even in the case of field research with employees, the study may not be responsive to any specific concerns of those in the organization which serves as the research site and may not be of any direct benefit or even interest to the participants.

III. INSTITUTIONAL OR ORGANIZATIONAL RESEARCH BENEFITTING PRIMARILY THE ORGANIZATION

This refers to research aimed at improving the functioning of the specific organization in which it is carried out—for example, by developing new procedures such as an employment selection testing program or by investigating the causes of an organizational problem such as a high rate of voluntary turnover. The hallmark of this category of research is that, despite the applied setting, the study is not generally intended to benefit the employees (or college students, or other organization members) who participate in it and it is unlikely to provide any direct benefits to them. Typical examples include employees serving as knowledgeable sources of information (so-called subject-matter experts, or SMEs) for a job analysis or as examinees in a test validation study the results of which will be applied by the organization to the problem of selecting new job applicants.

IV. INSTITUTIONAL OR ORGANIZATIONAL RESEARCH LIKELY TO ALSO BENEFIT THE STUDY PARTICIPANTS

This is research which also (as with category III) is aimed at improving the functioning of the specific organization in which it is carried out, but in which the results of the study can be expected to also benefit the particular participants as well as other organization members. For example, in evaluating the effectiveness of programs such as alternative training techniques, compensation policies or other interventions, the most effective training procedures or pay plan may be implemented throughout the organization, including even those who served as controls or in an experimental comparison group during the research. (This assumes that what is considered the best option for the organization is the same as for the employees.)

V. THERAPEUTIC RESEARCH INTENDED TO BENEFIT THOSE WHO PARTICIPATE IN THE STUDY (AND FREQUENTLY, BY EXTENSION, THE ORGANIZATION AS WELL)

Sometimes, a problem may be identified in a particular subunit of the organization, or for the organization as a whole, that prompts an investigation and implementation of ways of ameliorating the problem or improving the work life of a target group of employees. It may be difficult sometimes to distinguish between those actions which are more properly thought of as *interventions* (i.e., the implementation of changes in policies, programs or practices) and the research components of the same undertaking. Projects of this sort include quality of work life improvements such as flextime options or various employee assistance programs; task redesign in accord with the principles and aims of job enrichment or team-building; or the analysis and resolution of inter-departmental conflict.

FIG. 13.1.   A categorization of research in I/O psychology based on its intended beneficiaries.

(1977) observed, for the most part the social scientist "does not study the individual but the species" (p. 95). That is why methodological issues like representative sampling, external validity, and the generalizability of research findings are important. But it is also why ethical issues concerning voluntary participation in research, absence of coercion to participate, informed consent, and the well-being of research participants are also so profound.

In that context, the applied research represented by Categories IV and V (including some, but not all, institutional research) is of special interest because it holds the promise of benefitting directly those who have participated in it. Assuming there is some overlap between the interests of the organization and those of its individual members, this is one way in which applied organizational research can be characterized as more ethical than that of our colleagues engaged in a putatively more basic or scientific enterprise. Commensurate with that characterization, an advantage enjoyed by the organizational researcher in I/O psychology engaged in institutional research (Categories III & IV), as well as Type V research, is that employees—and even applicants for employment by the organization—may be assumed to have a conditional obligation to cooperate with such research. That is a reasonable interpretation of the implied social contract between employees–applicants and employer, assuming that the research serves a justifiable organizational purpose, is not threatening or harmful to the people, and does not make egregious demands on them.[140] In my experience, most employees accept this obligation, especially when the purpose of the study is explained adequately.

Conversely, a corollary of that advantage, or right, we enjoy as a consequence of employees' obligations in this regard is the duty to see that their obligation is not abused or experienced as coercive. There is, obviously, an inherent conflict between the principle that all research participation should be explicitly voluntary and the existence of a relatively open-ended implicit obligation of workers to participate in legitimate organizational research. Notwithstanding the implied obligation, adherence to the moral principle of respect for persons requires that we treat research participation as genuinely voluntary and volitional to avoid even the semblance of coercion. This is another area in which our ethical prescriptions may put us at odds with organizational policies, and that may need to be made clear to key decision makers so we can "resolve the conflict in a way that permits adherence to the Ethics Code" (APA, 2002, Ethical Standard 1.03).

An additional abuse of the employees' obligation would be to assume that it extends to their cooperation with our personal research agenda comprised of Category I or II research. Although we may enjoy access to employees who are potential research participants (as a convenience sample), they are not obliged to participate in the conduct of investigations that primarily reflect our individual interests when those are not reflective of the legitimate and reasonable concerns of the organization to which they are obligated. And that is so even if top management has agreed to allow the project to be implemented in their organization. Having made that point, it is also necessary to acknowledge that it is sometimes difficult to differentiate the extent to which a project represents the exploration of our own personal, professional, or scientific interests, versus legitimate organizational concerns.

Therefore, keep in mind that most participants in social science research, including I/O psychology, are generally not in it for self-serving reasons. We owe their participation to other situational and/or motivational factors,

---

[140]The *Standards for Educational and Psychological Testing* (AERA, APA, & NCME, 1985) indicates that IC for testing may be assumed as implied in the case of application for employment or educational admissions (cf. Standard 16.1).

such as their curiosity about the research, their willingness to cooperate in the interests of science or to enhance the effectiveness of the organization, or to comply with the wishes of an authority figure such as the researcher (manager, consultant, or professor). In addition, they may be persuaded that participation will have some educative value, or they may be prevailed upon by a monetary inducement or a requirement for a college course. Psychologists become aware of this issue very early in their professional careers when, as undergraduate psychology majors, they prowl the campus and the neighborhood searching for friends, acquaintances—anyone!— who will agree to participate as a "subject" for them in the experimental psychology laboratory course. Although the point may be learned early, it sometimes seems to be forgotten or its ethical implications unappreciated by some researchers who take subject participation for granted. Consequently, the trust that Kimmel (1996) spoke of in this chapter's epigram needs to be a major component of the social contract between ourselves and our research participants. In addition, as practitioners, we need to keep in mind that trust also plays a key role in our relationships with the users of our applied research. For example, the confidence of company managers in market researchers was predicted best by the perceived integrity of the researchers (e.g., being seen as having high personal standards) more than by their perceived expertise (Moorman, Deshpande, & Zaltman, 1993).

The exceptional importance of trust to the research enterprise is attributable to the power inequities between its participants or subjects on one hand and both the researcher and sponsor of the research on the other. Some time ago, Orne (1962) focused on the psychological experiment as a social relationship in which "the roles of subject and experimenter are well understood and carry with them well-defined mutual role expectations" (p. 777). Greenberg and Folger (1988) explored further the nature of various roles taken by experimental participants. The participant's or respondent's role is influenced greatly by what Orne called the *demand characteristics* of the experimental situation, including—once the person agreed to participate—a willingness to comply with a very wide range of actions upon request. This high degree of compliance is related to most people's general belief in the value of science, a willingness to accept the legitimacy of the research procedures and authority of the researcher, a desire to abide by the compact made when they agreed to participate, and a well-meaning intention to be a good subject. Orne went on to emphasize the importance of recognizing the potential effects on research participants of the contextual demand characteristics of the experimental situation as distinct from the effects of the experimental variables. Participants respond to the totality of the situation, which includes both sets of cues and stimuli, and responses to the situational context may be responsible for artifactual research findings.

Kelman (1972) presented a more elaborated social systems analysis of the power deficiency of the research subject relative to the researcher and sponsor, and viewed many of the problematic ethical issues in research as reflecting the potentially illegitimate exercise of this power. There are three aspects of the prospective research subject's relative disadvantage or vulnerability:

1. *The person's position in society, in general.* The consequences of this structural determinant may be seen in the preponderance of social science research with children, the old, poor, infirm, addicted, hospitalized or otherwise incarcerated, as well as college sophomores and military personnel. Although one might reasonably make the case that some of these groups are over-represented among research participants because they provide the locus of social problems needing solution, most social science research is not of Type IV or V, so it is likely that their greater mere availability plays a significant factor.

2. *The person's position within the organization or institution in which the research is carried out.* Thus, more research is conducted with recruits and enlisted personnel than with officers in the military, more with nonexempt employees and low- and middle-level managers than with high-level executives in corporations, more with prison inmates than with correction officers, and more with college freshman and sophomore members of an introductory psychology subject pool than with seniors. Undoubtedly, the availability factor is also at work here, but just as certain is the role played by those in organizational positions of authority in defining the research problems and providing the resources for its implementation. Moreover, the apparent availability of many of these potential participants may be due to their feeling that they have little prerogative to decline to participate when requested, even indirectly, by those higher up. As noted earlier, the employee's obligation to cooperate with legitimate and reasonable organizational research should not be transformed into a coercive experience.

3. *The person's position within the research situation itself.* As Kelman (1972) noted, "The investigator usually defines and takes charge of the situation on his [sic] own terms and in line with his own values and norms, and the subject has only limited opportunity to question the procedures" (p. 991). This is especially true when the research is carried out in the researcher's facilities (e.g., a college laboratory or a testing room in the human resource division of a corporation), when the researcher is a high-status individual who is in another role relationship with the potential participant (e.g., college professor or high-level manager), and when the subject is uninformed about the nature of the research. Around the same time that the salience of demand characteristics and role relationships in psychological experiments were pointed out by Orne (1962), they

provided the very mechanism by which the limits of obedience to authority were investigated (Milgram, 1963, 1974).

Due to concern about the asymmetric power relations in scientific research with human participants, great attention has been paid during the past 50 years to the ethics of behavioral and social science research.[141] This has consisted of assuring voluntary participation and informed consent to participate; eliminating coercive influences; minimizing the deception of participants; and providing debriefing, feedback, and dehoaxing, as well as securing privacy and confidentiality for participants.[142] Surveys of published empirical research in psychology have indicated that research reports rarely describe obtaining informed consent or having provided debriefing or feedback to participants, and—at least up through the early 1980s—the use of deception was still a problem (Adair, Dushenko, & Lindsay, 1985; Korn & Bram, 1988; Walsh-Bowers, 1995). As an inferential indicator of the relative lack of respect held by researchers for their respondents, Walsh-Bowers noted the frequency with which the term *subjects* was used as opposed to *respondents*, *participants*, or simple descriptors like *men, women, employees*, or even *patients*. Coding more than 3,000 studies from eight major journals, at 6-decade intervals from 1939 to 1989, he found that the usage of *subjects* rose from 60% in 1939 to 91% in 1969, and then it declined to 79% and 76% in 1979 and 1989, respectively. Unfortunately, a preeminent journal in I/O psychology, the *Journal of Applied Psychology*, bucked the later trend with an increase from 73% to 90% in the use of the more derogating term from 1969 to 1989, respectively.

INFORMED CONSENT[143]

Formal Standards

With the partial exceptions of research designs that rely on the collection and analysis of archival or anonymous data or on naturalistic observations of

---

[141] Also playing a prominent role in the focus on ethical matters, including the establishment of federal regulations for the protection of research participants, was the public's revulsion on learning about several dubious and in some cases unconscionable studies in both medical and social research, such as the Tuskegee study of the long-term effects of syphilis (cf. Kimmel, 1988, 1996, for brief reviews).

[142] Most of these issues are equally important in the professional nonresearch activities of I/O psychologists, as well as in research, with the notable exception of deception (and the need for consequent explanations, called *dehoaxing*), which has no acceptable role in professional practice.

[143] Throughout the remainder of this chapter and the next, reference will be made from time to time to applicable ethical guidelines promulgated by the Office for Protection From Research Risks, as appropriate. These primarily consist of the regulations for the *Protection of Human Subjects*, National Institutes of Health, Department of Health and Human Services (1991), the current "Ethical Principles of Psychologists and Code of Conduct" of the American Psychological Association (APA, 2002), as well as the (APA, 2001b) *Publication Manual of the APA* (cf. Appendix C of the manual: Ethical Standards for the Reporting and Publishing of Scientific Information). The OPRR federal regulations may be obtained on the web at http://www.nih.gov/grants/oprr/humansubjects/45cfr46.htm. The reader is advised to consult those sources directly for specific requirements.

persons in public places, empirical psychological research generally requires the assent and cooperation of people to participate or serve as subjects for us. In fact, it has been suggested that we ought to think of our potential participants as another granting agency to which we must apply for necessary resources to implement our proposed research (Rosenthal, 1994).

Psychologists are increasingly concerned with obtaining the informed consent (IC) of those with whom we work. An indication of this involvement, and of its widespread generality, may be inferred from changes made in the APA's revised "Ethical Principles of Psychologists and Code of Conduct" from the 1992 version.[144] Whereas the former document describes the conditions and requirements for obtaining IC entirely within the context of research (Ethical Standards 6.11, 6.12, 6.13, and 6.14), the new code introduces the topic within a newly created set of general standards concerned with many facets of human relations (Standard 3.10), as well as specific standards concerning IC in research (Standards 8.02, 8.03, 8.05, and 8.06), IC in assessments (Standard 9.03), and IC to psychotherapy (Standard 10.01). In other words, a distinction that once was made between the more formal and rigorous IC requirements to be met for research versus those for professional practice (see the *Belmont Report*; National Commission for the Protection of Human Subjects of Biomedical and Behavioral Research, Department of Health, Education, and Welfare, 1979) seems to have disappeared. This is, of course, in keeping with the nature of applied research and practice in I/O psychology, in which a project may include elements of both research and practice. Moreover, in all fairness, even the Belmont Report recognized this complex reality and concluded that if a multifaceted project contained an element of research, that project should undergo review for the protection of human subjects.

The principal purpose of obtaining IC from prospective participants in our research or practice is to ensure that they have the opportunity to protect their own interests and exercise autonomy over their own welfare (Greenberg & Folger, 1988). In general, IC may be defined as the collection of procedures by which people choose to participate in a project, such as a research study or organizational intervention, after being apprized of all matters that might reasonably be expected to influence that decision. Figure 13.2 presents a brief summary of the generally acknowledged requirements for obtaining and documenting IC from research participants. It is a condensation of material from the APA (2002) ethical code and the applicable federal regulations governing research with human participants

---

[144]At the time the draft revisions were published for comment by members of the APA (February, 2001a) it was planned that a further revised draft would be prepared and submitted to the APA Council of Representatives for approval in 2002. The revised code (APA, 2002) was published in December of that year and is effective beginning June 1, 2003.

GENERAL GUIDELINES FOR INFORMED CONSENT (IC)

1. Although the specific content of the psychologist's communication with prospective research participants or clients may be expected to vary with the situation, it should ordinarily include a description or explanation of the following:

(a) the overall purpose of the project, its benefits and any drawbacks, and the person's role in it, including the required duration of participation. It should also contain a description of whom to contact if any questions or concerns arise about the research;

(b) any adverse features, from the possible inconvenience of a significant time commitment to potential risks or threats to comfort, safety or self-esteem, which might reasonably affect the person's decision to participate. (But refer to discussion in chapter 14 re *Deception*, for possible exceptions.)

(c) other aspects of the project that might affect the decision to participate, such as the inability to guarantee anonymity and plans for maintaining the confidentiality of data;

(d) the voluntary nature of participation, and that the person is free to decline to participate or to withdraw from the project (i.e., to revoke his/her decision to participate) at any time, with no adverse consequences. Special care should be taken in this regard, with respect to potential student participants. Or, if there are potential consequences (as there might be for an employee of an organization sponsoring the work), they should be discussed;

(e) when research participation is a course requirement for students, alternative equitable activities should be made available and explained;

(f) if the decision is made to proceed with a study the design of which requires deception or withholding information, or if IC requirements have been waived by an Institutional Review Board (IRB) (see # 7, below) prospective participants should be told, if practicable, that additional information about the study will be provided at a *debriefing* following their participation in the study (or after conclusion of the entire study);

(g) if a beneficial intervention is to be provided to some persons or groups and not others, the basis for assignment is explained, as well as the plans, if any, for extending the intervention to those not originally covered. If the design of the study dictates withholding this information from participants at the beginning of the project, it is made clear by debriefing participants afterwards.

2. The psychologist should avoid exaggerating the potential benefits of the project, or *hyperclaiming* (Rosenthal, 1994), in order to induce participation.

3. The above content should be communicated in language that is clear, unambiguous and readily understandable to the particular persons addressed.

4. Nothing should be communicated that indicates or suggests that persons waive their legal rights or release the researcher, practitioner or sponsor from liability for negligence.

(continued on next page)

(continued from previous page)

5. When feasible, opportunity should be provided for persons to ask and have answered any reasonable questions pertaining to the project, making sure the person understands what has been communicated.

6. Ordinarily, written documentation of IC–a signed consent form containing the above information–should be obtained from each participant, who should be provided with a copy, and the original stored securely.

7. For the following sorts of research or projects, obtaining and documenting IC **may** not be necessary:

(a) studies done under the auspices of state or local governments, designed to study or evaluate public benefit programs;

(b) studies which involve no more than *minimal risk* to participants; the waiver of IC would not adversely affect their rights and welfare; and the research could not be implemented without the waiver;

(c) studies of normal educational practices or programs in educational settings, or routine assessments of organizational practices or effectiveness in other organizations, when participants can not be identified and when disclosure of the data would not place their employability at risk;

(d) studies involving tests, surveys, interviews or observation of public behavior, unless the data are recorded in a manner that permits identification of the participants or if disclosure of data could be damaging to them;

(e) studies involving archival data that are either publicly available or recorded by the researcher in such a way that participants can not be identified;

(f) studies which could not be done unless a waiver of the IC requirements were granted;

(g) when the signed consent form is the only record linking the participant and the research, and a breach of confidentiality would be potentially harmful.

8. If the researcher is associated with an organization which is subject to the federal regulations governing research with human participants, and hence has an Institutional Review Board (IRB), or the activities are otherwise subject to IRB review (e.g., the results are intended for general dissemination by means of professional publication), it is the IRB and not the researcher which decides on whether the proposed research meets the exceptions noted in No. 7, above, as well as other matters (e.g., whether the research qualifies for expedited review).

FIG. 13.2. Guidelines for informed consent. Based in part on material from the APA (2002) and the federal OPRR (1991).

promulgated by the OPRR (1991) and administered locally by institutional review boards (IRBs), as well as generally accepted ethical procedures.

These requirements (as well as those pertaining to privacy, confidentiality, deception, debriefing, etc.) are best understood as reflecting several dimensions of the domain of moral principles noted in earlier chapters: treating people with dignity and respect for their autonomy (so they are free to decide whether to participate in the research and whether to continue their participation); treating them with concern for their well-being and avoiding the infliction of harm (so that if deception or withholding information can be justified by a rigorous review, adequate debriefing will be provided); abiding by principles of justice and fairness (so that people are not coerced into participation by virtue of their lesser social status or other factors); and displaying honesty, integrity, and trustworthiness (so that promises made regarding the confidentiality of replies and the potential benefits, discomforts, or risks of participation are fulfilled). Note that, for the most part, these research requirements are based on deontological principles concerning beneficence and justice and the respect of participant autonomy, dignity, and rights, as well as the researcher's corresponding duties, rather than on consequentialist cost–benefit analyses. A major exception concerns the consequentialist approach to deception which dominates ethical guidelines (cf. chap. 14).

Some Contested Issues Regarding IC

Many problems have been raised concerning the implementation of IC procedures; the literature on the topic is vast, so I have avoided consideration of IC for medical treatments and biomedical research, psychotherapy, and other forms of clinical practice, and for so-called "vulnerable populations" like children. I have also excluded some research done in the 1970s that focused on whether IC might have counterproductive (i.e., negative) effects on participants, especially in therapeutic research (see C. P. Smith, 1983). Also not reviewed are a few potentially relevant sources that might interest the reader, such as whether and how IC is to be obtained when a researcher uses information provided independently by people on the Internet, as in chat rooms or e-mail (American Association for the Advancement of Science, 1999; Childress & Asamen, 1998; Hewson, Laurent, & Vogel, 1996), as well as special concerns regarding student participant pools (Britton, 1979; Chastain & Landrum, 1999; Dalziel, 1996; Scott-Jones, 2000).

Do People Really Understand IC Explanations?

This question has been posed by those who have raised the reasonable point that consent can not be truly informed if the prospective participants have not understood the IC communication completely and accurately. That is why formal requirements specify that the IC content be articulated in clear, unambiguous language understandable by the particular audience (see Fig. 13.2). Stanley, Sieber, and Melton (1987) reviewed the research in this area and noted that the methodological quality of studies investigating the comprehension and retention of IC information was not high. Nevertheless, they concluded that "despite these flaws, these studies show a general trend: comprehension of consent information is relatively poor" (p. 736). Similar findings were reported later by Mann (1994) who found that a longer consent form (attempting to describe a procedure fully) was understood less well than a shorter form that omitted some relevant details. These findings are especially important in light of another conclusion reached by Stanley et al. (1987): Higher levels of comprehension were associated with higher rates of agreement to participate. Another troubling note is introduced by findings indicating that although a sample of undergraduate experimental participants generally described the IC experiences positively, many of them viewed the experiments in which they had participated as too invasive (suggesting that the IC communication was inaccurate and/or incomplete), and only 20% of them viewed the IC process as a decision point at which they could decline to participate (Brody, Gluck, & Aragon, 1997). Congruent with those findings, over 60% of Mann's (1994) undergraduate participants who signed a consent form were under the (mistaken) impression that they had lost their right to sue the researcher, even for negligence.

It seems obvious that considerable attention needs to be paid to the quality of oral and written IC communications. Samples of written consent forms are available for the researcher's use. For instance, the *Principal Investigator's Manual* of my university contains several examples, as does Kimmel (1996). The OPRR "Tips on Informed Consent" advises: "Think of the document primarily as a teaching tool not as a legal instrument."[145] D. L. Smith, Cutting, and Riggs (1995) listed a number of factors that might be expected to affect a person's ability to fully understand the information contained in an IC document: (a) relevant demographic factors like age, SES, and cultural dialects; (b) physical or cognitive attributes, including memory, literacy, and competency, especially if they cause nervousness and distraction; (c) visual or hearing impairments; (d) defensive emotional reactions, such as denial or regression; (e) attributes of the document, such as reading level, use of technical language, and typeface; (f) nature and extent of knowledge and beliefs about research; (g) quality and nature of the manner in which the material is presented; and (h) perceived (or actual) coercion and other situational

---

[145]The "Tips on Informed Consent" is available at: http://www.nih.gov/grants/oprr/humansubjects/guidance/ictips/htm

influences. They recommended writing IC documents at no more than seventh- or eighth-grade reading level (even for highly educated participants) and presenting a thorough oral explanation whenever feasible. In contrast, the scant empirical data that exist suggest that written IC forms used by psychotherapists typically have difficult levels of readability (Handelsman, 1985). The communication of IC information should not be treated in a cursory manner but as an important and integral component of research or practice. As Herbert Kelman observed in the Foreward to Kimmel's (1996) text: "It is still too often the case that ethical considerations are treated as afterthoughts or as obstacles to be gotten out of the way so that the researcher's 'real' work can proceed. In short, the ethical dimension has not been fully internalized by the research community" (p. xv).

Does Obtaining IC Threaten the Validity of Research Findings?

A number of psychologists have raised various methodological objections to the process of obtaining IC; for example, it threatens the representativeness of research samples, hence the generalizability of findings, and that it alters the behavior of participants during the course of the study, hence threatening the internal validity of the research.

The Representativeness Problem. Rosenthal and Rosnow (1975, 1991; Rosnow, 1993, 1997)were the ones primarily responsible for raising the issue of the unrepresentativeness of all-volunteer research samples and the attendant potential problems concerning the generalizability of research results. Kimmel (1996) and C. P. Smith (1983) presented succinct reviews of the issue—that is, the extent to which compliance with the ethical prescription for voluntary participation via IC conflicts with scientific values for performing methodologically good studies. In other words, the more self-selected the sample of participants (by virtue of being all volunteers), the less likely it is to represent a random sample from the population of interest. The problem is especially acute with respect to therapeutic research in medicine and clinical psychology (Blanck, Bellak, Rosnow, Rotheram-Borus, & Schooler, 1992; Tobias, 1997), in which the potential for causing harm due to the erroneous interpretation of artifactual findings is great. But the problem extends even to survey research, in which requiring written IC may reduce the response rate to the survey or to specific items (Lueptow, Mueller, Hammes, & Master, 1977; E. Singer, 1978; Sobal, 1984).

Rosenthal and Rosnow (1991) reported that volunteer research participants, in comparison with nonvolunteers, tend to be more educated, bright, sociable, desirous of approval yet unconventional and nonconforming, arousal seeking, and of higher SES as well as more likely to be women than men. Therefore, rigorously implemented IC procedures, to the extent that prospective participants feel free to act on them (and the findings regarding diminished survey response rates suggest that to some extent they do), effectively render all research as based on volunteers with the just-noted biasing tendencies. For I/O psychologists, this can potentially jeopardize the generalizability of test validation research (e.g., studies utilizing validation samples of volunteers from among current employees) and virtually all studies concerned with understanding work motivation or team processes, as well as other areas of interest.

Given the potential threat to sample representativeness, it is not surprising that some procedural alternatives to obtaining IC have been suggested (cf. C. P. Smith, 1983, for a summary) and that a great deal of attention has been paid to the issue of recruiting research participants, as well as to the dangers of coercion, deception, and withholding relevant information from recruits. Various inducements to participate have been utilized, from the clearly unethical (e.g., deliberately not informing prospective participants about aversive aspects of the research protocol), to generally accepted and widely used procedures (e.g., offering small monetary payment or gifts, extra course credit for students, and putting forward appealing descriptions of the research and its value). A potential ethical issue concerns the point at which the latter largely acceptable techniques might become unethical and unacceptable. How much money or how expensive a gift is appropriate to offer without it being coercive to those most in need? How much extra course credit is acceptable—one third of a grade (e.g., from B to B+) or more? When does an ingenuously enthusiastic and positive description of the research become over selling or hyper claiming (Rosenthal, 1994)? "The psychology of recruiting participants for a research protocol is not dissimilar from other social marketing situations. There is a gray line between applying pressure to participate and being a competent recruiter and researcher. The gray area creates the opportunity for many ethical dilemmas" (Blanck et al., 1992, p. 963).

As applied psychologists we should recognize that these issues pertain to excesses in marketing a project not only to prospective participants but to the organizational decision makers and colleagues whose permission and cooperation is needed to implement it—for example, promising or overestimating the likelihood of positive results in advance or minimizing the intrusiveness of research procedures to the operations of the organization. Obviously, hyperclaiming of this sort has potentially adverse consequences for the future of the psychologist's relation with the organization and the reputation of the profession.

The Problem of Artifactual Findings.   There is some evidence indicating that more fully informed experimental subjects actually behave differently from less informed subjects in the subsequent experiments in which they are participating (Adair et al., 1985; Greenberg & Folger, 1988).

However, these findings are based on a limited domain of behavior such as verbal operant conditioning and the negative aftereffects of noise or crowding. There appears to be little information available regarding how widespread the effect may be, that is, which behavioral domains might be more or less susceptible. Although the causal explanations are not always clear, in some instances the observed differences among experimental groups seem to be related to whether the participants were provided with substantive information concerning the study, and in others the effect was produced merely by the consent procedure itself without conveying even the nature of the impending experiment. And in some instances the result seems to be attributable solely to the specific instruction that one is free to withdraw at any time. The latter findings suggest that the effect is not domain specific. However, on the basis of relatively limited research, IC procedures do not appear to have serious effects in written or interview survey research (E. Singer, 1978; Sobal, 1984) aside from some negative effect on response rates. Response rates to organizational surveys are probably more a function of employees' job satisfaction and opinions regarding how the organization handles the survey data (Rogelberg, Luong, Sederberg, & Cristol, 2000).

It is not unusual, however, for researchers—including those in I/O psychology—to inform participants about impending procedures (experiment, survey, or controlled intervention) in a way that suggests that they believe such biasing effects are likely. That is, information regarding the purpose of the research and some procedures are deliberately withheld (and sometimes misinformation is supplied) presumably because making them known to the participants would affect their behavior, hence biasing the results. Misrepresenting the purpose of the research or supplying a false cover story is the most frequent kind of deception employed in social psychology research (Gross & Fleming, 1982), and a recent informal survey of three I/O psychology journals indicates that the same is true there (Nicolopoulos, 2002). For example, a generation ago, when the positive consequences of job enrichment (increased job satisfaction, autonomy, and performance) had been only recently demonstrated, a question arose as to whether the positive effects might be due to employee participation in planning the work changes rather than, or in combination with, the changes themselves. Accordingly, interventions in which employees worked with managers in planning the job redesign were compared with those in which the changes were introduced "top-down" without employee participation. It was deemed very important that the employees in each group not be aware of the specific research question and procedures, and so they were not mentioned. Similarly, a survey or simulation study might be described innocuously to prospective respondents as "intended to investigate the ways in which people react to or evaluate various aspects of their jobs and organizations." It might even be described more specifically as "focused on understanding the nature of employee evaluations." It is unlikely, however, to be described accurately as concerned with "investigating whether supervisors evaluate more favorably the performance of workers who are similar to them in sex, age, or ethnicity."

The reason for these omissions is the belief that "telling subjects the purpose of the study and the procedures to be followed removes their naivete and spontaneity" (Adair et al., 1985, p. 59). In the latter instance, for example, we might anticipate that mentioning our interest in "similarity bias" in ratings could heighten the salience of the demographic attributes of the employees (real or simulated) who are to be rated and alter the participant–raters' evaluations. However, that concern is based on the implicit assumption that a naive state of relative ignorance regarding the situation one is in (perhaps with some attendant concern or anxiety regarding the research procedures) is the relevant or natural state of the human being to be understood. This is an assumption that may not always be correct and should not be accepted uncritically. Humans are exceedingly curious and continually seek meaning in their lives, even imparting meaning to situations in which it is not apparent; total ignorance about the situation one is in is not a customary state of affairs and is, in fact, a source of anxiety for many. In contrast to the passive or inanimate nature of the objects studied by physical scientists, people are *agentic* and *reflexive* (G. S. Howard, 1985; Manicas & Secord, 1983; B. D. Smith & Vetter, 1982). That is, we are aware of our surroundings, we generally experience ourselves as the instruments of our own behavior, and we anticipate the future and attempt to shape it. Withholding information from human research participants does not render them malleable experimental tabula rasas. In at least some instances it may simply contribute to the artificiality of a situation that is arguably unlike the real-life circumstances to which results are generalized. More problematic, it could induce a process of hypothesis guessing by participants, leading to artifactual reactions that further threaten the interpretability of the research. Granted, there are research questions that could not readily be investigated without keeping the participants ignorant of the purpose and/or procedures of the study. Accordingly, rather than keeping participants *un*informed, researchers sometimes *mis*inform them about key features of the study, thus raising other ethical concerns (see chap. 14 regarding deception).

Are IC Requirements Unreasonable?

Especially given that IC communications may not be well understood by research participants and that they have the potential to introduce artifactual elements into research findings, it has been argued that some requirements are unnecessary or enforced too stringently, even in medicine (Goldworth, 1996). For example, it would be inherently contradictory and foolish to require signed IC forms from respondents to an innocuous and anonymous questionnaire survey. Adair et al. (1985) and Diener and Crandall (1978) reminded us that the procedure was originally developed with biomedical research in mind; the effects of social and behavioral research generally do not have the same harm potential. In a by now famous sardonic remark, M. B. Smith (1976) observed about behavioral science research: "surely temporary boredom is the most common harm" (p. 450). Thus obtaining IC may unnecessarily complicate risk-free research (P. D. Reynolds, 1979). It has also been argued that obtaining formal written IC in an actually stressful experiment may serve to reduce the perceived freedom of participants to withdraw once it has begun, and requiring IC in general may seem to shift the responsibility for ethically questionable practices to the participant (Adair et al., 1985). However, it seems reasonably clear that the researcher is never excused from the responsibility of following ethical practices. Moreover, note that many of these concerns arose early in the history of federal regulation of research with human participants when the rules were less flexible than the current versions. The current OPRR (1991) regulations permit IC requirements to be waived and allow for "expedited review" of harmless research.

Conversely, a reasonable case can be made that the requirements are actually more onerous and less flexible than they seem to be. As Ilgen and Bell (2001b) stated, "in practice, institutional review boards (IRBs) often are reluctant to approve exemptions [to informed consent]. Heavy workloads faced by IRBs create a press toward standard operating procedures that, by their very nature, are resistant to exceptions" (p. 1177). Those authors also warn that such lack of flexibility with regard to obviously innocuous, minimal risk organizational research of the sort I have characterized as Type III, IV, or V (see Fig. 13.1) may serve to encourage disregard for ethical review in general. They may already be correct. A review of the empirical research reported in three I/O psychology journals for 1999, 2000, and 2001 found virtually no mention of formal IC procedures and very few indications of what respondents were actually told prior to the study (Nicolopoulos, 2002). This was confirmed in a survey reported by Ilgen and Bell (2001a), who found that 44% of the authors of field studies published in the *Journal of Applied Psychology* and *Personnel Psychology* acknowledged not having submitted their studies for IRB approval. Ilgen and Bell (2001b) also pointed out a "Catch-22" in the system in that some professional journals require research submitted for publication to have included IC procedures—irrespective of the possibility of having received an IRB exemption.

In addition, although the regulations requiring IRB approval emphasize coverage of "research conducted or supported by any Federal Department or Agency" (§46.103), it also requires that "Each institution engaged in research which is covered by this policy and which is conducted or supported by a Federal Department or Agency shall provide written assurance satisfactory to the Department or Agency head that it will comply with the requirements set forth in this policy" (OPRR, 1991, §46.103). In other words, any research conducted under the auspices of the organization that receives federal support will be expected to comply even if that particular study is not supported. In practice, therefore, the university-based I/O psychology researcher conducting an organizational study that is likely to not require written IC of participants (cf. Fig. 13.2, No. 7 b, c, d, and e) nevertheless must submit a description of the proposed study to his or her university's IRB for such determination. (However, the study probably would qualify for expedited review.)

If that same I/O psychologist is employed not in a university but as an independent consultant or practitioner in a business organization, it might seem that the same study would not receive IRB review: There would be none that had jurisdiction. But as a psychologist and member of the APA, subject to its ethical code, the researcher nevertheless "must consider ... applicable laws and psychology board regulations" (APA, 2002, p. 1062). Moreover, as pointed out by Ilgen and Bell (2001) regarding potentially publishable research, some journals now require documentation of IC procedures for all submissions. If the I/O psychologist does not have a university affiliation (or a collaborator with such) free-standing IRBs exist from which approval may be sought— for a fee, of course.[146]

Anecdotal reports abound of the unreasonableness of IRBs. For example, IRBs sometimes go beyond the ethical aspects of a study to comment on the technical quality of the proposed research design or procedures, and this is frequently viewed as beyond their legitimate mandate. But surely an argument can be made that, given the substantial individual and institutional resources involved in most research endeavors (including participant involvement), doing a poor study that might not justify the internal validity of its findings is a waste and an ethical matter. Nevertheless, whether most IRBs are comprised of members with the collective expertise to render such valid judgments in the many fields of research in which they are called on to review is a legitimate issue. Some psychologists have been concerned about the extent to which many of their colleagues view the application of research ethics as merely "an affront to the integrity of sound research" (Blanck et al.,

---

[146]Such free-standing IRBs may be located with the help of the professional research ethics association, Applied Research Ethics National Association, or through Public Responsibility in Medicine and Research. They can be contacted at http://www.primr.org/arena.html and http://www.primr.org/index.html

1992, p. 959) or who may "feel burdened by an expanding body of ethical rules and regulations" (Rosnow, 1997, p. 345) that reflect a changing social contract between science and society. They have offered constructive suggestions by which ethical guidelines may be seen as a stimulus to conducting more effective research such as by increasing our understanding of the meaning of our data and by including more representative samples. I think we would also do well to realize that our right to do research, which some of us feel is infringed upon inappropriately by IRBs, is more in the nature of an entitlement than a claim (cf. Chap. 12). That is, although we certainly have such a right, invested in our profession by society because of the potentially valuable contributions we can make, there is no correlative duty imposed on any specific others to comply with that right. We need to make our case each time, in the context of the evolving social contract between science and society about which Rosnow (1997) was so concerned.

A review of published research reports in I/O psychology suggests that OPRR requirements are not in fact salient issues in the field. In 1999, 2000, and 2001 there were a total of 46 studies published in the *Academy of Management Journal, Journal of Applied Psychology*, and *Personnel Psychology* that employed intentional deception (Nicolopoulos, 2002).[147] All of the studies were authored or coauthored by people with academic affiliations, yet none of the reports stated that the study had been submitted for review and received IRB approval. A large majority did not mention having obtained IC, and among those that did almost all failed to describe what information had been provided to prospective participants.

PRIVACY, ANONYMITY, AND CONFIDENTIALITY

As noted earlier, there are several moral bases that justify research respondents' claims to privacy and confidentiality (Bok, 1989; Davison, 1995; C. C. Peterson & Siddle, 1995). In addition to those noted previously, once a provision of confidentiality has been made as part of the IC agreement, we incur an obligation to keep the promise. In addition, we may add the utilitarian reason that it helps establish the relationship of trust between researcher–practitioner and participant without which quality research and effective practice are not likely to result.

Privacy and Anonymity

Part of the ethical justification for providing IC (along with respect for autonomy) is allowing people to maintain their privacy. *Privacy* is generally

---

[147] There were 555 articles published in the three journals over the 3 years, 475 (86%) of which were empirical studies (i.e., excluding qualitative and quantitative literature reviews, theoretical articles, reanalyses of previously reported data, computer simulations, etc.). Thus, only 9.7% of the empirical investigations employed deception.

defined as the right to determine how much information about oneself will be revealed to others, in what form it will be provided, and under what circumstances (Kimmel, 1988; Sieber, 1992). It is enshrined in the United States as a constitutional "right to be let alone" (Melton, 1988). Kimmel (1988) noted that privacy may entail *solitude* (voluntary isolation), or it may be desired even in social situations such as with intimacy among small groups or pairs of persons, and *anonymity* (freedom from identification in public settings).

There are four facets of any situation, including a research study, that influence the extent to which a person may consider their privacy violated (Webb, Campbell, Schwartz, Sechrest, & Grove, 1981). The first of these is most relevant to observational research and concerns how public the location is in which the person's behavior is being studied. For example, one might anticipate managers to be more uneasy about an observational study assessing how time spent in their offices is distributed among various activities than a study observing traffic flow patterns in the executive cafeteria. The second facet is the extent to which the person(s) studied are public figures whose personal and legal expectations concerning privacy may be lower than for others. The third dimension has to do with the anonymity of the research data, or whether the person can be linked directly with the information obtained from or about him or her. For most research situations maintenance of anonymity is the best guarantee of privacy.

The last facet noted by Webb et al. (1981) is the nature of the information being collected. Thus, a questionnaire survey focusing on personal opinions and attitudes toward one's superior is likely to be more invasive than one focusing on preferences regarding alternative shift work schedules; a questionnaire seeking to assess personal needs for an employee assistance program providing substance abuse treatment is likely to be experienced as still more invasive. Accordingly, workers experienced less invasion of privacy as a result of electronic performance monitoring when the monitoring was limited to only relevant on-task activities (Alge, 2001). I add a fifth dimension to Webb et al.'s list—the identity of the investigator and/or observer. Although I do not know how the effects of this influence might be manifested, I would anticipate that such attributes as the prestige and status of the researchers and the extent and quality of their personal relationships with participants probably interact with other facets such as the nature of the information collected and degree of confidentiality or anonymity provided in affecting such outcomes as response rates and the amount, quality, and truthfulness of information provided.

Whenever the circumstances of research or practice permit, all information should be obtained and stored in a fashion that maintains the anonymity of respondents. It should be the "default option" for all social and behavioral science research. Some projects require the explicit linking of participants with the information they have provided: For example, longitudinal investigations such as test validation studies in which predictor and criterion scores must be matched, or a study of personnel turnover in which antecedent data must be paired with later separation status. Under those circumstances, the confidentiality of the data are obviously limited. *Confidentiality* refers to the right of people to have the information they provide kept private and to the agreements we make with them concerning what may be done with the data (Folkman, 2000; Sieber, 1992). In the validation and turnover studies just noted, the requirements necessitating the limits on confidentiality are known in advance and should be discussed with participants as part of the IC process. The personal identifiers that link the data sets with the individual employees should be maintained only as long as necessary to provide the linkage, and then they should be destroyed. If the researcher contemplates a follow-up study necessitating the maintenance of personal identifiers, this must be revealed as part of the original IC process.

Another frequently encountered situation in which anonymity may be breached and confidentiality limited involves the mailed or otherwise indirect distribution of a questionnaire survey in which it may be helpful or even necessary to know who has responded and who has not—even if the motive is simply to issue follow-up reminders. Some rather elaborate and ingenious techniques have been developed to preserve the confidentiality or anonymity of respondents in these sorts of situations (Boruch, 1971; Boruch & Cecil, 1982; D. T. Campbell, Boruch, Schwartz, & Steinberg, 1977).

Confidentiality

For the most part, confidentiality is a less salient issue for I/O psychologists (though no less applicable) than it is for clinical, social, or personality psychologist researchers who may conduct investigations in which people's intimate, perhaps embarrassing and humiliating, or even illegal activities may be exposed. Psychotherapists may also be privy to such information, as well as to suicidal or other self-destructive intentions on the part of disturbed clients. And confidentiality may similarly be critical for other applied psychologists who conduct research with vulnerable populations. Researchers and practitioners in these areas have to be concerned with the possibility of their data or records being subpoenaed by a court (APA, Committee on Legal Issues, 1996; Melton, 1988). The research and practice of I/O psychologists tend to be restricted to less personal, work-related concerns with "normal" adult populations. Nevertheless, the confidentiality of data may be threatened by organization members who fail to appreciate the ethical requirements under which behavioral research is conducted and the adverse consequences of violating the trust placed in us by participants. Senior managers, citing the obligation of employees to cooperate with institutional research, have been known to adopt the position that "We paid for (or sponsored the collection of) the data, therefore it's ours—all of it, including the identities of the respondents."

This broaches what is, for many applied psychologists, the familiar question "Who is the client?" For example, it is a prominent issue for clinical psychologists who provide health care services to individuals in organizations, such as in police departments or the military (Staal & King, 2000; Zelig, 1988). It is an issue wherever psychologists are employed by an organization (whether full time or as a consultant) to work with individuals or groups within it. Professional guidelines speak directly to the issue: "The primary responsibility of the psychologist in a professional role is to the client. The psychologist must resolve conflicts of interest between the employer agency and the client on the basis of this responsibility" (APA, 1987, p. 728). That directive is readily interpretable by clinical psychologists in a therapeutic context. Clinicians are trained as health-service providers and, quite naturally, are responsible primarily to their clients—notwithstanding that the setting in which the service is provided is not a private practice but an institution. It is understandable that responsibility to the employing organization is secondary, even if one of the primary purposes might be to ensure that their clients are capable of fulfilling their work role responsibilities (e.g., as police officers or soldiers).

The situation for an I/O psychologist is rather different. The focus of our training is on organizational processes, and we are not trained to provide a therapeutic service for individuals or groups (with some exceptions, e.g., organization development specialists trained in psychodynamic process consultation). It is understandable, therefore, if some I/O psychologists experience this ethical guideline as more complicated and difficult to comply with in reality than it seems to be on the surface.[148] For example, referring to the just-cited APA (1987) quotation, it clearly assumes that there is a distinction between "the employer agency" and "the client." However, many I/O psychologists, most obviously those in consultancy roles, believe that the employer is the client. It is instructive to note how those of our colleagues whose professional activities bear some similarity to clinical or counseling practice (i.e., executive coaching) approach this issue.[149] Witherspoon and White (1996) distinguished between the

---

[148]Perhaps a more appropriate comparison for I/O psychologists would be the clinician employed in a career job at a hospital, treating patients only temporarily during their hospital stay. That psychologist might strongly identify with and be concerned for the well-being and effective functioning of the hospital as an institution. Nevertheless, the primary education, training, and professional socialization of the clinician will have stressed responsibility to the individual patient.

[149]"Executive coaching involves a skilled outside consultant assigned to an executive on a regular basis for one or more specific functions—improve the executive's managerial skills, correct serious performance problems or facilitate long-term development—often to prepare him or her for a future leadership role or top corporate position" (Witherspoon & White, 1996, p. 125). An informal survey found that the typical executive trainee was "either a high potential employee or a successful employee who had one or two weaknesses. It appears that organizations are using executive coaches primarily to develop effective employees, rather than as a means of improving employees who are having serious problems" (M. Harris, 1999, p. 39).

executive or *client* who is the primary person receiving coaching, and the *customer* or client system, which is the organization that contracts and pays for the coaching service. Although they made this distinction, and they went on to note discussions with the parties in advance regarding whose interests the coach is serving, unfortunately they did not indicate whose interests those are or what their priorities are in the event of conflicts between the two. As indicated in chapter 12, in my opinion I/O psychology has historically erred on the side of manifesting greater concern for the organization, frequently to the detriment of individual employees. Whether this emphasis has extended to the professional role of executive coaching is not clear.

The Boundaries of Confidentiality

I have been asked the following questions more than occasionally by graduate students in I/O psychology: "In dealing with employees as a practitioner in an organization, when should I treat information as confidential?" The answer is simple and straightforward and influenced by professional role requirements. As Human Resources professionals we take on advocacy, questioning, and modeling roles in the organization with respect to ethical behavior, reflecting its beneficent and justice components (see Fig. 12.2).[150] Therefore, unless circumstances exist to the contrary and are made clear to the respondent, every nonroutine communication initiated with an employee for the purpose of obtaining information is confidential (and sometimes the routine communications are as well). That includes replies to written questionnaires, individual interviews, team meetings or focus groups, telephone conversations, and so on, whether in connection with a research study or with a company financed intervention project.

There are four types of circumstances in which partial or complete confidentiality might not obtain. The first is when the employee requests it—for example, to "deliver a message" to someone else in the organization. However, one would be prudent to try to find out what that is all about before complying, as it might impact adversely the views of other respondents and one's reputation in the organization. Ordinarily, the request should simply be refused as inconsistent with our ethical obligations. The second circumstance is when the project requires participants to be identified. For example, it is often wise because of potential litigation to document which employees participated in a test validation study; or a summary of survey findings for each work group may need to be supplied to all group members and their managers. On those occasions the planned limitations on confidentiality must be made clear before the employee agrees to participate. The next possibility pertains to the situation in which we become aware through confidential communi-

---

[150]Keep in mind that many lay-people are not well informed about the areas of specialization within psychology and to them all psychologists possess therapeutic skills and attendant responsibilities for confidentiality.

cations (e.g., gratuitous fill-in comments on a questionnaire survey) that someone apparently is seriously disturbed or otherwise seems to be in need of psychological help. The only way to address the problem directly (e.g., by encouraging the person to seek professional help) may be to violate confidentiality. Before doing so, however, one would want to be very sure of the seriousness and immediacy of the person's disturbance, which might be extremely difficult to ascertain.

Last, we may be told of someone's past or intended wrongdoing or that one employee means to harm another. These are very difficult situations in which our assurances of confidentiality conflict with other ethical principles. With regard to the first example, we are generally in no position to differentiate such unconfirmed information from mere gossip and so should proceed very cautiously. The informant should be encouraged to act directly if possible. With respect to the second illustration, our ethical principles require us to prevent harm, whenever feasible, and it may be that in attempting to do so the identity of the information source cannot effectively be concealed. In fact, psychotherapists are held to have a legal duty to warn a likely victim of violence that overrides their duty to maintain the confidentiality of the client–therapist relationship (Bennett, Bryant, VandenBos, & Greenwood, 1990; *Tarasoff v. Board of Regents of the University of California*, 1976). However, it is notoriously difficult even for trained clinicians under favorable conditions to predict a person's dangerousness, and it is doubtful whether a psychologist who is not a therapist is under the same legal obligation. "A serious violation of confidentiality could occur if the researcher inappropriately warns a third party of a potential threat" (Folkman, 2000, p. 52). The I/O psychologist should consult with colleagues and appropriate others before proceeding in such an instance. An experienced organizational consultant points out that because we cannot accurately predict the consequences of violating a commitment to confidentiality, it is a serious mistake to ever do so (Clayton Alderfer, personal communication, July 2002).

Moral dilemmas frequently involve conflicting ethical principles—for example, an obligation to do good or prevent harm versus the duty to abide by promises of confidentiality. Whichever choice one makes, it should be based on a well-reasoned rationale uninfluenced by self-serving motives or conveniently ignoring the issue. (Thus, talking it over with a knowledgeable and trusted colleague is generally a good idea.) Because whichever option one chooses, including doing nothing, entails a breach of one of the operative ethical strictures, one should be as satisfied as possible that the reasons for the breach are good ones.

Methodological Implications of Confidentiality

Just as there is some concern and limited supportive evidence that IC procedures may affect research findings by reducing response rates, introducing sample bias, or influencing the responses of experimental subjects, confidentiality also appears to carry methodological implications. In this instance, however, the threats to research quality appear to be associated with the *absence* of confidentiality. Blanck et al. (1992) reviewed a number of studies suggesting that confidentiality promotes more honest disclosures. However, the effects may be limited to procedures that focus on personally sensitive material. A meta-analysis of experimental studies failed to support the general hypothesis that assurance of confidentiality improves survey response, but it did indicate a significant but modest positive effect when the information asked about was sensitive (E. Singer, Von Thurn, & Miller, 1995). Conversely, those authors also noted the existence of several studies that indicated that elaborate assurances of confidentiality had counterproductive effects, perhaps as a result of arousing respondents' anxiety, perceptions of threat, or suspiciousness. Those effects may be limited to relatively innocuous research for which the assurances might seem incongruous, but "we need to know more about the circumstances under which assurances of confidentiality really reassure respondents and about how best to frame such assurances" (E. Singer et al., 1995, p. 74).

A comparison of personal interviews conducted at home with self-administered questionnaires regarding women's health issues yielded increased judgments of the truthfulness of responses for the latter only when others in the home might have been able to listen in on the interview (Rasinski, Willis, Baldwin, Yeh, & Lee, 1999), thus confirming the relevance of confidentiality when sensitive information is requested. When the setting was private, there was no difference in judged truthfulness of the interview and questionnaire. The authors speculated "When the respondent agrees to an interview, rather than accepting an obligation to tell the truth on all questions, he or she may interpret the obligation as that of reporting truthfully to questions that pose no threat" (p. 482). Correspondingly, anonymity did not improve the rate of response to a nonsensitive mailed survey over a confidential but not anonymous condition (Groves, Price, Olsson, & King, 1997).

ADDING FURTHER TO THE FRAMEWORK
FOR ETHICAL DECISION MAKING

37. Adopting a social perspective on the nature of research in I/O psychology emphasizes that most research is conducted to gratify the scientific or professional interests of the researcher and/or to address an organizational problem—as with institutional research. In both cases the employee–participant cannot necessarily expect to benefit directly from the enterprise and so cannot be expected to have any a priori reason to participate. In addition, the nature of our professional right to do re-

search generally is in the form of an entitlement with no corresponding responsibility imposed on anyone to comply with it. These conditions are reflected in the ethical prescription that research participation must always be voluntary and not coerced. Nevertheless, it is widely accepted that the implied social contract invoked by employment obligates employees to cooperate with legitimate and reasonable institutional research (but not with our personal research agenda for which they are simply a convenience sample). Should a conflict arise between these two contradictory expectations, it ought to be resolved by subordinating the employees's implied contractual obligation to their right to exercise autonomy over their own welfare by refusing to participate.

38.   Deontological principles dominate the ethical strictures governing research participation: treating people with dignity and respect for their autonomy (so they are free to decide whether to participate in the research and whether to continue their participation); having concern for their well-being and avoiding the infliction of harm (so that if deception or withholding information can be justified by a rigorous review, adequate debriefing will be provided); abiding by principles of justice and fairness (so that people are not coerced into participation by virtue of their lesser social status or other factors); and displaying honesty, integrity, and trustworthiness (so that promises made regarding the confidentiality of replies and the potential benefits, discomforts, or risks of participation are fulfilled).

39.   Psychologists are responsible for knowing and adhering to the professional, ethical, and legal requirements for research with human participants, such as using IC and confidentiality, irrespective of the work setting and nature of the research (e.g., both basic theoretical research and applied institutional research).

14

Research Ethics:
II. The Use of Deception

Psychologists always lie!
　　　—A research participant, to Social Psychologist Herbert Kelman

Before discussing the role of deception in behavioral science research it might be helpful to acknowledge that social and behavioral scientists have produced a considerable body of literature studying the nature of deception itself.[151] My focus here is on intentional deceit by researchers as an instrumental technique enabling the conduct of research that presumably could or would not be carried out otherwise. In this context I use the following simple definition: deception consists of intentionally misleading research participants about any aspect of a study.[152] The process frequently entails the creation of what Seeman (1969) euphemistically called "fictional environments" within which a study is carried out.

---

[151]Deception has been investigated as a cognitive process (R. W. Mitchell, 1996) and as a common way of managing interpersonal relationships (Aune, Metts, & Hubbard, 1998; Kagle, 1998; Candida Peterson, 1996; Rowatt, Cunningham, & Druen, 1998; Sagarin, Rhoads, & Cialdini, 1998). Particular attention has also been paid to people's ability to detect deception in others (Bond & Atoum, 2000; DePaulo, Charlton, Cooper, Lindsay, & Muhlenbruck, 1997; Heinrich & Borkenau, 1998), and in that vein it has been viewed through the lens of evolutionary theory as an adaptive advantage (M. T. McGuire & Troisi, 1990). Business ethics scholars have focused on the role of deception versus trust in negotiation (Dees & Cramton, 1995; Strudler, 1995), and I/O psychologists have focused on its maladaptive and criminal manifestations in organizations (Murphy, 1993).

[152]Baumrind (1985) distinguished between intentional and "nonintentional deception" (e.g., failing to disclose everything about a research study). Because the latter is invariably innocuous in nature or not entirely the researcher's fault (e.g., misunderstandings by participants), nothing seems to be gained by introducing what is essentially an oxymoron.

DECEPTION IN I/O PSYCHOLOGY RESEARCH

Because of the nature of the field, the use of deception was never as prevalent in I/O psychology as it has been in social psychology. In fact, with a few exceptions from other social science disciplines, "it is social psychologists who have used deception in research, and have raised these techniques to an art form. In no other area of psychology is deception used so extensively, and when it is used in other areas it almost always is a form of social psychology" (Korn, 1997, p. 10). Accordingly, whereas many reviews have tracked the incidence of deception in social psychology (discussed shortly), and the history of its use in that field has been chronicled (B. Harris, 1988; Herrera, 1997; Korn, 1997), I am aware of no comparable concern having been expressed about I/O psychology research.

The variables and research problems of interest to the I/O psychologist less frequently require deception, and a lower proportion of I/O research consists of laboratory experimentation, which is the methodology in which it is most practiced. For example, a social psychologist might be interested in studying the nature and limits of people's honesty. Because it is generally not possible to know where, when, and how people might behave dishonestly in the normal course of their lives (and because it is a low-incidence event), social psychologists are likely to investigate the problem experimentally, such as by means of "entrapment studies" which "are conducted to investigate moral character by providing opportunities for subjects to engage in dishonest behavior or perform otherwise reprehensible acts" (Kimmel, 1996, p. 151). Conversely, I/O psychologists are more likely to be interested in the extent to which measures of employee conscientiousness or honesty (so-called "integrity tests") are effective real-life predictors of various facets of job performance or other organizational outcomes (Sackett & Wanek, 1996).

Although serious deception does not seem to be prevalent in I/O psychology or organizational behavior research, it is not unknown. For example, equity theory (D. M. Messick & Cook, 1983) is a model of work motivation which posits that individuals compare their perception of the ratio of "outcomes" (i.e., rewards) they receive to the "inputs" they provide (e.g., valuable attributes like one's skills, abilities, and educational qualifications, as well as the effort one expends toward job performance), to the perceived outcome–input ratio(s) of significant "comparison other(s)." The model predicts that if the two ratios are perceived as comparable, a psychologically ̄uitable situation exists; otherwise, the individual will experience a sense ̄equity and will be motivated to behave in ways designed to achieve ̄ such as by adjusting one's "inputs" (e.g., decreasing the amount of ̄ended on the job). Among the great deal of research performed by ̄ogists testing hypotheses based on this model were laboratory studies in which the experimental manipulation consisted of attempting to alter the participants' personal ratio by diminishing their self-perceived inputs to an anticipated (but often bogus) job assignment. This was frequently done by providing fallacious feedback to the participants, indicating that they had performed poorly on a preliminary task or test, showing that they were not well suited for the impending work assignment but would be "employed" nonetheless. Participants were misinformed about their own talents, thus potentially threatening their self-esteem, and in some cases they were not even informed in advance that they were participating in an experiment.[153]

A more recent example is provided in Fig. 14.1, which reproduces verbatim a very upsetting letter received recently by the spouse of one of my students, who manages a rather expensive, trendy (and excellent) restaurant in New York City. His was 1 of 240 well-known restaurants that received this identical letter addressed personally, in each instance, to the owner. It came from an assistant professor of organizational behavior (OB) at the prestigious Business School of an Ivy League University in New York City who was attempting to study what has become a popular concern among businesses in recent years, customer service orientation (Hogan, Hogan, & Busch, 1984).

Aside from the concern one might expect a restaurateur to have for a customer who was sickened by food at his or her restaurant, one must appreciate the highly competitive and precarious existence of restaurants in New York and the heightened threat introduced by the mention of the Better Business Bureau and the Department of Health, to understand the potential emotional impact of this letter. And just for good measure, the personal letter was written on the prestigious university's letterhead and was signed by the faculty member (using his real name)—giving himself a pseudopromotion to professor. By the time about one fourth of the restaurants had responded, the hoax became undone, much to the embarrassment of the university (Kifner, 2001). The researcher wrote a letter of apology to each recipient—this time, on plain nonletterhead paper—acknowledging that "The study was of my own doing and not that of the business school or the university. None of the data collected for the study will be used for publication, and I will not conduct similar studies in the future." A day later, the dean of the business school also wrote to each restaurateur, indicating "While the professor initiated this research project on his own, he failed to think through the toll this study would take on its recipients ... As a result of this incident I have immediately asked the governing academic committee, the Executive Committee, to put

---

[153]In fact, the threat to self-esteem was an experimental confound. That is, it was not the manipulation, which was merely to have the prospective employees perceive that they were fewer inputs.

Ivy League Business School
Ivy League University
Graduate School of Business
New York City Address

[Addressed to Individual
Restaurant Owners]

Dear _____ ,

I am writing this letter to you because I am outraged about a recent experience I had at your restaurant. Not long ago, my wife and I celebrated our first anniversary. To commemorate the event we made plans to dine at [your restaurant]. It was a very special occasion for both of us, and we had been looking forward to the evening for some time.

The evening became soured when the symptoms began to appear about four hours after eating. Extended nausea, vomiting, diarrhea, and abdominal cramps all pointed to one thing: food poisoning. It makes me furious just thinking that our special romantic evening became reduced to my wife watching me curl up in a fetal position on the tiled floor of our bathroom in between rounds of throwing up. I am particularly angry because if I had decided to share my meal with my wife, I would have had to see her suffer the same fate as I did that night.

I begrudgingly accept that occasionally these things happen and that even though you take extreme caution to prevent any cases of food poisoning, the inevitable few will break through. Nevertheless, I am still very angry because it was I who fell ill and only I had to endure that pain.

Had all this happened on any other night of the year I probably would not have bothered to complain, but seeing as how this was a special occasion, I felt incensed and therefore believed it was necessary to write you this letter. We had looked forward to experiencing so many good things at your restaurant, but now, all I am experiencing is extreme irritation. Given that it was our anniversary, we will always bitterly remember this occasion despite how much we wish to forget its aftermath.

In short, I am furious about this entire ordeal. Although it is not my intention to file any report with the Better Business Bureau or the Department of Health, I want you, Mr. [Restaurant Owner], to understand what I went through in anticipation that you will respond accordingly.

I await your response.
Sincerely,
Professor [————————————], PhD
Ivy League University

14.1. An example of deception by concealing the existence of the research study.

place procedures and guidelines for empirical research projects so that this will never happen again." However, something is not quite right here. The researcher's explanation and the first sentence quoted from the dean's letter imply that the professor was either ignorant of the need for IRB approval of research projects or deliberately circumvented the IRB review procedures. Neither implication seems very likely. In any event, those inferences are negated by the second sentence cited from the dean's letter, indicating that the university supposedly did not at that time have "procedures and guidelines for empirical research projects" (as are promulgated and implemented by an IRB). For a major research university, this cannot be the case.

There were 46 (of 475 empirical) articles published in the *Journal of Applied Psychology, Personnel Psychology*, or the *Academy of Management Journal* during 1999, 2000, and 2001 that appeared to use some form of deception (Nicolopoulos, 2002). Most instances seemed relatively innocuous—for example, merely concealing the true purpose of the study to avoid influencing the data, as with studies of rater bias, eyewitness identification, and the investigation of group processes in which the demographic heterogeneity of the group is not revealed as a variable of interest. But there are a sprinkling of studies such as the one that entailed use of a misleading cover story regarding the purpose of the research, a confederate, a bogus role-assignment procedure, and false feedback to the participants. The report of this study makes no mention of any debriefing having been provided at its conclusion. Presumably, the editors and reviewers of the journal also did not think it was necessary.

ATTRIBUTES OF DECEPTION TECHNIQUES

Types of Deception

A number of scholars have described the various deceptive methods that have been used in social and behavioral research, most notably Sieber (1982a; Sieber, Iannuzzo, & Rodriguez, 1995), Kimmel (1996), and Korn (1997). It remains a matter of some concern—affecting the ethical conclusions reached (Lawson, 2001). Figure 14.2 displays a simple categorization scheme by which the varieties of deception can be classified, based on the nature of the researcher's role in the deception and the potential level of risk to participants. *Passive deception* means the failure to reveal everything that could be revealed about the study, that is, deception by concealment or omission. In contrast, *active deception* consists in affirmatively misleading research participants or candidates about some feature(s) of the research. The assessment of the potential level of risk or harm that participants might experience is generally a subjective judgment that may be easy to make at the extremes but more difficult to do for studies that fall in the middle of the continuum. Physical harms are generally seen as more severe than psychological or emotional harms (Collins, 1989). In addition, the severity may vary with such additional factors as the identity of the participants or the research setting. The dichotomization into minimal risk and substantial risk potential is clearly an oversimplification. On the other hand, it is probably prudent to consider any situation that is not clearly of minimal risk to be of substantial risk.

The varieties of deception that have been practiced can be summarized conveniently in three categories or content areas, which are represented within the four cells depicted in Fig. 14.2. These include deception regarding (a) the very existence of the study, (b) the actual purpose of the study or research problem being investigated, and (c) various aspects of the study's methodology or procedures. For example, the Ivy League OB assistant professor actively deceived the restaurant owners both about the existence of the research project and, by extension, its purpose, by using a bogus cover story. In contrast, naturalistic or contrived observational studies in which researchers observe people in public venues, such as with

ROLE OF THE RESEARCHER

		PASSIVE (Concealing)	ACTIVE (Misleading)
	MINIMAL	(1a) The existence of the study.	(1b) The existence of the study.
		(2a) The true purpose or problem being investigated.	(2b) The true purpose or problem being investigated.
POTENTIAL		(3a) Aspects of the study's procedures.	(3b) Aspects of the study's procedures.
LEVEL OF	SUBSTANTIAL	(1c) The existence of the study.	(1d) The existence of the study.
RISK/HARM		(2c) The true purpose or problem being investigated.	(2d) The true purpose or problem being investigated.
		(3c) Aspects of the study's procedures.	(3d) Aspects of the study's procedures.

FIG. 14.2.   A simple taxonomy of 12 categories of research deception based on the nature of the researchers's role in the deception, the anticipated level of risk incurred by participants, and three content areas.

the entrapment studies noted earlier, simply conceal the existence of an ongoing study. The example I offered earlier of innocuously describing survey or simulation research regarding possible rater bias as concerned with understanding the nature of employee evaluations passively omits mention of the true problem being investigated, in the belief that explaining the purpose of the study would distort the ratings data collected. And I concede that to be a relatively harmless or minimal risk deception.

The last area, in which participants are deceived about some aspect(s) of the research procedures, subsumes a great variety of deceptive maneuvers such as being given false instructions or false information about stimulus materials (e.g., phony equipment, as in Milgram's, 1963, 1974, obedience study, or fake scenarios in questionnaire studies using putatively genuine descriptions of people or situations), use of a confederate (or, with increasing frequency in recent years, a "virtual confederate" in the form of a computer) to misinform or mislead, providing erroneous feedback and/or manufactured data about the participant or about others, using a surreptitious staged manipulation in field settings, collecting irrelevant "filler" data, and misinforming the person about when the study will begin (i.e., the participant is unaware the study has begun, or the relation between two studies is concealed; Sieber, 1982a; Sieber et al., 1995). The students in the equity theory research whose self-perceived "inputs" into a bogus job situation were deceptively devalued by providing them with phony feedback regarding their abilities is an example from I/O research.

The Severity of Deception

It is sometimes useful to think about the severity or intensity of the deception used or contemplated in a study (Sieber, 1982a, 1982b); this is something that members of an IRB are frequently called on to assess. Thus, some instances of deception may be considered mild or innocuous and some extreme (Greenberg & Folger, 1988; Korn, 1997), with others falling in-between. It is probably true that virtually all behavioral research involves some deception—of the passive sort—insofar as not every aspect of the study, including its theoretical implications, hypotheses under investigation and procedural details, are ever communicated to participants. They do not need to be. This is what Baumrind (1985) called *unintentional deception.* Overall judgments of the severity of deceit are sometimes difficult to make because each may be influenced idiosyncratically by all aspects of the deception that we have been considering as well as by additional matters such as the content domain of the research, the particular constructs investigated, and the quality, extent, and timing of any dehoaxing and desensitization provided to the participants. If one were to perform a policy-capturing study assessing the relative contribution of the various components of the research to the overall judgment of severity of deception, my guess is that the most important factor would be the perceived potential level of risk or harm to the participants, followed by the adequacy of debriefing. I would also expect that the purpose served by the deception—that is, the researcher's intent—would play an important, perhaps moderating, role in influencing severity judgments. Deception entirely for the purpose of masking the nature of the study in the belief that participants must be naive to manifest the phenomena under investigation, is likely to be perceived as less severe (all else being comparable) than deception intended to induce people into participating or continuing to participate. In recent years the latter tactic has, in fact, been considered unethical: "Psychologists never deceive research participants about significant aspects that would affect their willingness to participate, such as physical risks, discomfort, or unpleasant emotional experiences" (APA, 1992, Standard 6.15[b]).

Note, however, that this dictate has been loosened in the recent revision to the ethical code: "Psychologists do not deceive prospective participants about research that is reasonably expected to cause physical pain or severe emotional stress" (APA, 2002, Standard 8.07[b]). Whereas we had been required to avoid creating mere risks, discomfort, or unpleasantness, the new standards require avoiding only physical pain or severe stress. Given the extremely rare occurrence of psychological research that causes physical pain and the almost as infrequent incidence of inflicted severe emotional stress, the code revision widens the scope of potentially acceptable deception.

The Frequency of Deception

As mentioned earlier, social psychologists have attended rather closely to the incidence of deception in their published research (Adair et al., 1985; R. Carlson, 1971; Gross & Fleming, 1982; McNamara & Woods, 1977; Menges, 1973; Nicks, Korn, & Mainieri, 1997; Seeman, 1969; Sieber et al., 1995; L. J. Stricker, 1967; Vitelli, 1988). Although inferences regarding a trend are difficult to sustain because of somewhat differing definitions of deception that were used in each of these reviews, most found an increase in deception during the 1950s, 1960s and early 1970s, to a rate well exceeding half of all published studies, and a decline from the late 1970s through the 1980s to below 50%. Sieber et al (1995) reported the beginnings of an upswing in the 1990s, whereas Nicks et al. (1997), in a more comprehensive survey, found a continuation of the downward trend. Sieber et al. (1995) make the case that the trend (in both directions) is a function of changes in the frequency of studies published on topics that rarely require deception, such as attribution, environmental psychology, sex roles (gender), sex differences, socialization, and personality, rather than due to changes in the relative popularity of deceptive methodology per se. Nicks et al. agreed in part with that interpretation of the decline in deception but also cited the growing influences of the APA ethical code and federal regulation of research with humans, as well as a decreased emphasis on randomized laboratory experiments and corresponding increase in surveys and field studies.

I have found no corresponding surveys of the nature or frequency of deception in I/O psychology, suggesting that it has not been perceived as a problem. That is probably attributable to the joint effects of the nature of the constructs studied, the greater proportion of applied field studies in I/O psychology focusing on pragmatic organizational issues, and a correspondingly lower rate of laboratory experimentation with students. A brief review of three I/O psychology journals (*Journal of Applied Psychology, Personnel Psychology* and *Academy of Management Journal*) for 3 recent years (1999–2001) estimates the rate of deception at approximately 10% (Nicolopoulos, 2002). Because the rate of deception in social psychology has been found to be the highest for studies of compliance, conformity, altruism, aggression, equity, and dissonance (Gross & Fleming, 1982), it is enticing to speculate on what effect might be had on research procedures in I/O psychology, including the use of deception, as we branch out to study new topics such as emotions in organizations (Ashforth & Humphrey, 1995; George & Jones, 1996; Lazarus & Cohen-Charash, 2001; Lefkowitz, 2000) that may require deceptive experimental mood-induction procedures.

EFFECTIVENESS AND EFFECTS OF DECEPTION

Does it Work?

As noted in the previous chapter, there is some evidence to suggest that IC procedures may alter the behavior of research participants—more so in experimental than nonexperimental studies—thus producing artifactual findings. By extension, the primary purpose of deception is to maintain the naivete of participants to ensure the internal validity of the research. As I also noted, however, an argument can be made that, for at least some circumstances and/or areas of research, the imposed artificial state of ignorance that constitutes the temporary world of the naive research subject is itself artifactual. Kruglanski (1975) emphasized the active and interpretive nature of humans even while serving as research subjects and that their search for meaning may entail a suspicious questioning of research experiences. In any event, especially given the ethical challenges to the practice, it makes sense to ask whether deception even works.

Suspiciousness

In the heyday of deception research Kelman (1970) mused "I have increasing doubts about the effectiveness of deception as a method for social research" (p. 70). In that chapter he not only acknowledged ethical misgivings but pragmatic concern about whether the widespread use of deceptive techniques, especially among college students, was producing experimental subjects who would be preoccupied with trying to figure out what the research is really all about and either acting accordingly or resentfully, behaving to the contrary. As cited in the epigram that begins this chapter, he reported one student as observing, "Psychologists always lie" (p. 71). Kelman was worried that "the experimenter can no longer assume that the conditions that he [sic] is trying to create are the ones that actually define the situation for the subject. Thus, the use of deception, while it is designed to give the experimenter control over the subject's perceptions and motivations, may actually produce an unspecifiable mixture of intended and unintended stimuli that make it difficult to know just what the subject is responding to" (p. 71). He speculated that the long-term continued use of deception would be self-defeating as there would be more and more sophisticated and/or cynical subjects. As Seeman (1969) voicing similar doubts put it, "In view of the frequency with which deception is used in research we may soon be reaching a point where we no longer have naive subjects, but only naive experimenters" (p. 1026). Research participants may react to artifactual cues in the experimental situation that suggest to them the existence of a deception. This was illustrated in the aborted restaurant study of consumer service orientation. The hoax was initially suspected and ultimately revealed by several restaurateurs who noted that the letter of complaint failed to mention details that would be expected following such an (actual) episode—for example, the date and time of occurrence and the dish(es) ordered. The fact that no reservation listing or credit card receipt could be found in the professor's name also added to the suspiciousness. The adverse publicity received by this ill-advised study and the potential ramifications to the field of OB are just the sort of consequences about which many critics of deception are concerned (cf. Baumrind, 1985).

Accordingly, there has been for some time a great deal of professional interest regarding the potential suspiciousness of research participants, especially college students. Kimmel (1996) reviewed the resulting empirical research up through the 1970s and concluded "There has not been a great deal of research on the extent of subjects' suspiciousness in the research setting and the existing studies present something of a mixed bag" (p. 96). However, he acknowledged elsewhere that, with regard to applied marketing research, the increase in refusal rates by consumers is in part due to deceptive research practices (Kimmel & Smith, 2001). Greenberg and

Folger (1988) agreed that we are insufficiently informed: "In view of the prevalence of deceptive practices ... surprisingly little is known about the extent to which subjects are aware of the deceptions employed" (p. 162). Kimmel (1996) reported on studies that found (a) a substantial proportion of research participants who had been debriefed about the true purpose of the study, including student members of a subject pool, leaked crucial information to other potential participants—even those who had agreed to secrecy; and, tending to confirm Kelman's (1970) and Seeman's (1969) concern, (b) over time, the degree of suspiciousness among participants and the proportion of studies reporting suspicious participants were related to the number of deceptive studies reported. With regard to the impact of such suspiciousness on research results, he again found the results inconsistent. Some studies found no differences between the data obtained from suspicious and presumably naive subjects, whereas some studies did. In addition, again reminiscent of Kelman's and Seeman's warnings, some studies have found that prior experience in a deceptive experiment increased suspicions and affected performance in subsequent research.

Some concern over this issue has continued through the 1980s and 1990s. For example, Epley and Huff (1998) found that although participants reported little negative reaction to being deceived in an experiment and debriefed about it, after 3 months they were still more suspicious of experiments than was an uninformed group. (The uninformed group was not told about the deception until the 3-month follow-up interview.) They acknowledged, however, not knowing whether the long-term suspicions would result in changed behavior in subsequent experiments. Although student participants may be expected to differ in degree of gullibility regarding the deceptions of experimental confederates (Oliansky, 1991), prospective research participants who have been deceived previously in an experiment are more likely to expect it in the future than those who have not (Krupat & Garonzik, 1994). Complicating the situation greatly is the realization that it may be difficult even to assess accurately the extent to which suspiciousness exists. K. M. Taylor and Shepperd (1996) found that participants may refuse to divulge in the postexperimental inquiry or manipulation check that they were suspicious of the experimental procedures. This may be the most disquieting aspect of the problem, as it implies an absence or loss of trust in the researcher and the research process.

Proposed Alternatives

Stimulated primarily by the moral ambivalence associated with deception as well as by the ambiguities regarding its efficacy, a number of methodological substitutes or alternatives have been suggested and tried. (I hope that the irony of considering truth telling a "substitute strategy" is not overlooked.) This is commensurate with the dictates of the APA (2002) ethical code, which admonishes that "Psychologists do not conduct a study involving deception unless they have determined that the use of deceptive techniques is justified by the study's significant prospective scientific, educational, or applied value *and that effective nondeceptive alternative procedures are not feasible*" (Standard 8.07[a], italics added).

Describing these options in detail is beyond the scope of this book, but they have been described or reviewed by Greenberg and Folger (1988), Kelman (1972), Kimmel (1996), C. P. Smith (1983), and others. By far the most frequently implemented and evaluated alternative is *role playing* in which people are fully informed about all pertinent aspects of the study procedures—including the experimental manipulations—and asked to participate as if they were in the actual situation. Kelman (1972) viewed this as just one of a variety of participatory research procedures designed to restructure the ethical nature of the research enterprise. According to its proponents, studies using role-playing subjects have yielded results comparable to those that have employed deception. A similar procedure is that of *role-taking* in which participants imagine themselves in a presented situation without even enacting the role. This has been used, for example, by a colleague of mine to study interpersonal rejection—students read and projected themselves into a realistic scenario. They did not have to actually be placed in a humiliating situation. The major argument against role-based procedures has been that, at best, the results pertain to people's hypothetical or anticipated behavior (how they think they would behave if they were in the real situation), which is probably subject to social desirability biases, not their likely actual behavior. But this criticism overlooks the corresponding epistemological ambiguities of deception research noted earlier, and perhaps it underestimates the degree to which participant role players may identify with their parts and become emotionally engaged in the circumstances (Haney, Banks, & Zimbardo, 1973; Zimbardo, Haney, Banks, & Jaffe, 1973).

The array of additional options includes using simple self-report measures (e.g., of past dishonest behaviors, rather than using an entrapment study); obtaining limited IC, or forewarning prospective participants that some aspects of the study may not be as they appear to be, but that this will be explained later; and a form of role-playing, structured game-like simulations such as with "mock-jury" research. Two things should be kept in mind: (a) the external or ecological validity of information gleaned from these methods is controversial, and (b), although they may have been proposed as alternatives to deception, some methods can also be used in conjunction with deception procedures, such as when the true purpose of a simulation study is concealed. Most important, however, is the widespread view that among the reasons deception has remained relatively prevalent in social psychology research is that these alternatives have, for the most part, not worked very well (Adair et al., 1985; Christensen, 1988). As a prophyl-axis procedure aimed at reducing the severity of deception, the use of *quasi-controls* has been advocated by Orne (1969) and Suls and Rosnow (1981). This consists of having respondents imagine themselves undergoing the research as described (a form of role taking) and reacting to it before the study is actually conducted with other participants. Alternative research protocols can be explored this way, and the least deceptive one that nevertheless maintains the necessary features of the design can be the one implemented.

Effects on Those Deceived

The moral justifications for the use of deception are consequentialist arguments in which the procedure is condoned if the potential benefits can be seen as outweighing the likely harms. In that context, therefore, the possible adverse effects on research participants of having been deceived has been a salient empirical issue. C. P. Smith (1983) and Kimmel (1996) reviewed a great many studies investigating the matter and have come away with similar conclusions: "the negative effects of deception appear to be minimal" (Kimmel, 1996, p. 104), and "there is little evidence of harm or long-term negative effects, possibly because most research procedures are not more serious or harmful than everyday life events" (C. P. Smith, 1983, p. 316). Moreover, additional studies report similar findings (Epley & Huff, 1998; C. B. Fisher & Fryberg, 1994; S. H. Schwartz & Gottlieb, 1981; C. P. Smith & Berard, 1982; C. P. Smith & Richardson, 1983), although some negative reactions have been reported (Lindsay & Adair, 1990; Oliansky, 1991), and even C. P. Smith acknowledged "In most studies of participants' reactions, however, there are a few subjects who did not have a good experience" (p. 317).

The data from these studies are of two sorts: follow-up inquiries of actual research participants who had been deceived and the reactions of people who were asked to read descriptions of studies in which participants were deceived (i.e., role taking). The general absence of negative reactions to deception (e.g., when former participants believe in the importance of the research and accept the necessity for using deceit to investigate the problem) are especially noteworthy because the same respondents generally make it clear that they did (or would) not like being stressed, harmed, or embarrassed. Such adverse experiences, not deception per se, are what they object to. Broder (1998) emphasized the distinction that should be maintained between obnoxious experimental treatments (which should be avoided) and the act of deceiving participants (which may be rather benign in nature and unavoidable in order to carry out the research).

Nonetheless, the fact that most participants appear to be sanguine about having been deceived does not mean, as noted earlier, that they may not be suspicious of researchers and future research participation. Interestingly, the opinions and attitudes toward the research and one's actual or projected participation in it tend to be more favorable among those who actually took part in research and were deceived than among those who merely imagined having participated. The reason(s) for that distinction are not clear. It has been explained optimistically as due to the likelihood that deceived (and rather elaborately debriefed) participants are more likely to have found the experience interesting and of educational value. It has also been attributed more negatively to cognitive dissonance reduction (Baumrind, 1985)—that is, evaluating the experience as interesting and worthwhile as a means of justifying one's feelings of embarrassment or shame at having been duped. This would be commensurate with the finding noted earlier that participants may be unwilling to communicate their suspiciousness about the study to the researcher even after it is concluded. Baumrind (1985) went on to question the construct validity of participants' post-experimental self-reports as measures of possible harm: "After all, if self-reports could be regarded as accurate measures of the impact of experimental conditions, we could dispense entirely with experimental manipulation and behavioral measures, substituting instead vivid descriptions of environmental stimuli to which subjects would be instructed to report how they would act" (p. 168).

THE NORMATIVE ETHICAL ARGUMENTS

The use of deception by researchers is problematic and of great concern to many psychologists, and it continues to generate debate (Broder, 1998; Kimmel, 1998; Korn, 1998; Ortmann & Hertwig, 1997, 1998). It seems to strike a deadly blow at the ethical heart of the research enterprise—the trust that we ask of our participants. It also appears to be antithetical to our humanistic tradition and to the respect for people's dignity and autonomy that is the spirit of IC. So, when deception is used it is generally because of a belief that "the phenomena that the psychologist hopes to observe would be destroyed if he [sic] revealed the true purpose of the experiment to his subjects ... Without deception, it would be impossible—at least within the limits of our current research technology—to obtain the kind of information that many psychological experiments are designed to produce" (Kelman, 1972, p. 996). The use of deception represents a particular resolution of a conflict between values: arguably, a trumping of the concerns of individuals for privacy, self-determination, and respect by the entitlement rights of the researcher, the profession, and society to produce knowledge. However, I am not aware of the existence of any moral arguments asserting that scientists have a right to produce knowledge, much less a duty to do so, that would necessarily override the individual human rights being threatened.

It does seem true that at least some problems could not be investigated without use of deception—and not only those employing obnoxious manipulations. This makes the stakes in the deception debate very high for the field. For example, in studies of incidental learning participants are instructed to respond in some irrelevant way to experimental stimuli not knowing that a memory test of the stimuli will follow. A plausible cover story is necessary to conceal the true nature of the study: Otherwise, the learning would be intentional not incidental. Broder (1998) used this example to make the point that "The ethical question concerning deception in this research therefore cannot be whether deception is necessary within this research (because it is) but rather whether this research is necessary. This must of course be the topic of public discussion in which psychologists will have to defend their claims about the relevance of their research. But this is the case for every empirical science" (p. 806). However, the implicit assumption that a bogus cover story creates the uniform psychological reality necessary to permit valid inferences from the results has not gone unchallenged (Baumrind, 1985).

Views on the general matter of deception can be formulated as representing one or another of the leading types of normative ethical theories discussed in chapters 3 and 4. They consist of deontological theories concerned with right and wrong and the origins of those judgments; and consequentialist (or utilitarian) theories concerned with the harmful and beneficial effects of actions. Each category contains both rule-based and act-based versions. In all instances, my preference is for normative stances that reflect the meta-ethical position of universalism, rather than egoism (i.e., no person's or group's interests, including one's own, is more important than any other's unless specifically justified), and universalizability (whatever form of moral reasoning is adopted, we assume it is applied consistently irrespective of who is making the decision). Rule-deontological positions emphasize invariant principles based on such considerations as one's moral duty and respect for people (Kant), contractarian social justice (Hobbes and Rawls), individual rights (Locke), and/or self-realization through social concern or institutional and political reform (Hegel and Marx). The difficulties encountered in implementing rule-based views (e.g., what to do when two or more "absolute" moral principles conflict) led to development of the act-deontological model that allows for the preeminence of some principles over others or permits of some qualifications of a general rule. For example, the absolute prohibition against killing ("Thou shalt not") is excepted by most but not all people in the case of war, to protect an innocent person's life, to punish a capital offender, and for legal termination of a pregnancy. When the effects of particular actions are used as a basis for making the qualifications or for choosing among alternatives, the deontological approach takes on some of the trappings of consequentialism.

The act-utilitarianism model was developed largely by Bentham to render moral reasoning more objective and measurable (see chap. 4). He believed that ethical choices should and could be determined not by vague abstractions and metaphysical or religious dictates but by whichever action produces the greatest aggregate good for all those affected by it. The model is afflicted with a host of theoretical, pragmatic, and empirical difficulties: How should *good* be defined and by whom?; can all the consequences of an action be known?; and even if known, they may not all be measurable; and even if known and measurable, they may not be comparable on a common metric to assess the net effects of alternative actions, as required. And even if all that is possible, can it be accomplished in time to actually be used for decision making? Utilitarian conclusions also sometimes fly in the face of common and intuitive moral principles like promise keeping, truth telling, or fulfilling duties and obligations; and finally, the criterion of the greatest overall good ignores the potential injustice of maldistributions of the benefits and costs among individuals and groups.

Mills' secondary principles evolved into rule utilitarianism in response to some of these problems. Rule utilitarianism employs ethical principles based on culturally influenced views of their relative utility for society overall. For example, most cultures have learned that telling the truth is, in general, more culturally adaptive than never knowing when one is being lied to; its utility doesn't need to be assessed in every individual ethically relevant situation. Consequently, rule utilitarianism "is seen as more consistent with the logic of moral reasoning and the common understanding of morality as a social code, where individuals have convictions about moral obligations and minimum moral standards. Thus, it is seen as more intuitively plausible and less likely to be at odds with nonconsequentialist reasoning than act-utilitarianism" (Kimmel, 2001, p. 673). But because these rules are treated more as guidelines or default options than as absolute standards, the practical advantage gained in decision making can be offset by a certain degree of indeterminacy in rule-utilitarian analyses. In other words, in contrast to an act-utilitarianism analysis in which one is obliged to act on the most utile option (if it can be determined), several alternative courses of action may be permissible under a rule-utilitarian analysis.

The Modified Act-Utilitarian Argument Permitting Deception

The predominant view in the social and behavioral sciences—at least the view that is officially codified in numerous ethical statements (e.g., APA, 2002)—is essentially an act-utilitarian argument. It is a modification of the traditional utilitarian position in that it provides a justification for permitting deception when certain conditions are met; it generally does not purport to make deception obligatory under any circumstances—even if that alternative could be shown to yield the greatest good in a particular situation. For example, even proponents do not suggest that deception research should be reinstituted as the "standard operating procedure" for psychological research, only that "ethics committees should not institute rejection of powerful deception experiments as their standard operating procedure" (West & Gunn, 1978, p. 36). In that sense, it seems to me that there is an implicit acknowledgment in this position of the morally dubious nature of deception. That interpretation is confirmed by a reading of the APA (2002) ethical code. Standard 8.07 begins "Psychologists do not conduct a study involving deception *unless* ... " (italics added). Standard 8.07 goes on to specify that the permissibility of deception must be justified by the particular study's "significant prospective scientific, educational, or applied value and that effective nondeceptive alternative procedures are not feasible." Permissibility is also contingent on meeting all of the other safeguards against causing harm: review by an IRB, affording as much IC as possible, and extensive debriefing. The tacit acknowledgment that deception is, at best, a "necessarily evil" that must be justified affirmatively in each individual instance is also reflected in the absence of any other form of supporting ethical rationale from rule-utilitarianism or a deontological approach. Formally, there is no reason why deception could not be justified by a *rule-utilitarian* argument—For example, the scientific and societal benefits of research in general and over the long run could be viewed as outweighing the discomforts or harm to participants which might in some instances be unavoidable, so that only egregious cases of deception need be guarded against. But I am not aware of that argument ever having been made, and I would not support it.

Hypothetically, the decision to proceed with deceptive research is based on a subjective assessment that the degree of harm or extent of costs likely to be associated with its implementation is substantially exceeded by the anticipated benefits. However, it is generally taken for granted that virtually all the costs may be visited upon the participants and the benefits mostly accrue to the researcher and to society, so that review procedures for the protection of human participants are likely to focus almost exclusively on the extent of the costs or potential harms (Rosnow, 1997). This is why the empirical debate over the extent to which participants actually have been harmed or offended by being deceived is so spirited. Moreover, it has been pointed out that the review process seldom considers the costs and benefits of *not* doing the research, thus failing to acknowledge sufficiently the potential benefits to society that may be lost by not allowing it to be done (Rosenthal & Rosnow, 1984; Rosnow, 1997).

The Rule-Deontological Prohibition

The simplest, most straightforward arguments against the use of deceptive methods is that they are unequivocally wrong, irrespective of whether participants are actually harmed. They are wrong because they violate our duty to do no harm and to respect the autonomy, dignity, and worth of all people by dealing with them truthfully and not treating them instrumentally like "research material" (Veatch, 1987) and/or because they unjustly assign all of the costs of the research enterprise to one group. Hypothetically, an *act-deontological* argument could be made against deception that allowed exceptions under certain circumstances, such as when the anticipated value of the research is high and the severity of deception low (but notice that a consequentialist perspective has sneaked in to make the argument). Presumably a *rule-deontological* argument could even be made in *favor* of deception if researchers' responsibilities to their profession, society, and the advancement of knowledge were seen as uniformly more important than their obligations to research participants. But I have not come across a serious statement of that position—probably because it is antithetical to the very essence of ethical thought.

The Rule-Utilitarian Objection

Some protagonists in the deception debate identify the "moral philosophizing" objections to it as exclusively deontological in nature (e.g., Christensen, 1988, p. 669). That overlooks the prevalence of rule-utilitarian objections, such as those articulated by Baumrind (1985). She argued persuasively that the use of deception violates three rules that are of enormous adaptive advantage in western society, thus causing substantial harms to research participants, the profession, and society. The first rule is the right of self-determination, which is reflected in the right of research participants to IC. "Thus, subjects have the right to judge for themselves whether being lied to or learning something painful about themselves constitutes psychological harm for them" (p. 167). The second rule consists in the obligation of a fiduciary (the researcher) to protect the welfare of the beneficiary, in this case the research participant. And third is the obligation, especially of a fiduciary like a researcher or professor in relation to students, to be loyal and trustworthy, not undermining the trust offered by the participant–student.

   In making the case regarding harms done to participants by deception Baumrind (1985) challenged much of the evidence that has been garnered ostensibly demonstrating that participants do not feel harmed or even wronged by deception if adequate explanation of the need for the process is provided. The evidence, she pointed out, is generally based on superficial questionnaire or interview responses obtained by people not trained clinically to "uncover true feelings of anger, shame, or altered self-image in participants who believe that what they say should conform with their image of a 'good subject' " (p. 168). She made the argument that the profession is harmed by deception research because social support for behavioral science research is jeopardized when we promote values that conflict with the generally accepted tenets of moral conduct. In fact, the commitment to truth of the researchers themselves may be undermined. Earlier in this chapter evidence was reviewed regarding the increased suspiciousness and lack of trust engendered in research participants as a result of having been deceived. Baumrind warned that such attitudes may generalize to all expert authorities, thus having deleterious effects for society at large. Her forceful attack on deception is also based on a belief "that the scientific and social benefits of deception research cannot be established with sufficient certitude to tip the scale in favor of procedures that wrong subjects" (p. 170).

POSTRESEARCH PROCEDURES: MANIPULATION CHECKS, DEBRIEFING, DEHOAXING, AND DESENSITIZATION

Respect and concern for the well-being of research participants should extend beyond the boundaries of the data-gathering steps to include what I will generically refer to as *postresearch procedures*. The issue is more important than the amount of space that can be devoted to it here. Consequently, the reader is referred to more thorough reviews of the topic (Greenberg & Folger, 1988; B. Harris, 1988; Kimmel, 1996; Tesch, 1977) and to extremely helpful procedural protocols provided by experienced researchers (Holmes, 1976a, 1976b; Mills, 1976). The general term *post-experimental procedures*, or the more inclusive postresearch procedures encompasses several activities that are relevant to nonexperimental procedures like questionnaire surveys or experience-based learning activities, such as games and simulations, as well as to experiments (Lederman, 1992; Stewart, 1992).[154]

Multiple Aims and Objectives

The researcher-initiated exchanges between investigator and participant following the data-collection phase of a study have three types of objectives: (a) methodological—to check on the efficacy of experimental manipulations, measures, and procedures; (b) educational—to inform and educate the participants about the study and the value of behavioral and social science research; and (c) ethical—to reverse any misconceptions due to deception and to ameliorate any adverse consequences as a result of it (Greenberg & Folger, 1988; B. Harris, 1988; Tesch, 1977). Although those distinctions are still useful in elucidating the different functions that may be going on simultaneously in postresearch procedures, in the quarter century

---

[154]I am not entirely happy with the designation of these procedures as occurring postresearch as it might imply a secondary status to them; but I have not thought of a better term.

since Tesch first pointed out the distinctions, it has come to be accepted that the educational responsibilities we owe to research participants are also to be included as part of our ethical obligations (APA, 2002, Standard 8.08).

The Methodological Functions: Procedural Inquiry, Manipulation Checks, and Safeguards Against Leakage

These steps are generally applicable to experimental research only, and in contrast with the other purposes of postresearch procedures, they are for the benefit of the researcher, not the participants. They mostly involve collecting additional information from the participants, whereas the others primarily entail imparting information (Greenberg & Folger, 1988). The information sought is of three types, all contributing to the establishment of the internal validity of the experimental findings. The first thing ordinarily of interest to the experimenter is a manipulation check to assess whether the independent variable was operative as intended—That is, did it produce the effects on the participants or create the conditions desired? Suppose, for example, I conduct an experiment investigating the effect of mood state on cognitive information processing—for example, the encoding, storage, and retrieval of performance data used in making employee appraisal ratings. If my study entails comparing the evaluations made by people who are frustrated or angry with those who are in a pleasant emotional state (as well as an untreated comparison group), I might decide that I have to create experimental conditions that induce those contrasting moods in different participants before obtaining their ratings data. My ability to interpret the results of the study accurately will depend on my confirmation that they did, in fact, feel frustrated or happy, depending on which experimental treatment they received. I will attempt to find that out from them after they conclude the experimental tasks. (This assumes, of course, that we can rely on such verbal reports. But I may have some pertinent observational data regarding their behavior during the experiment as well.)

The second reason for conducting the inquiry is an assessment of the extent to which the behavior of the participants might have been influenced by extraneous demand characteristics of the research (Orne, 1962). Similarly, if there has been some deception involved (as might very well be necessary for my mood-induction study), the researcher will want to have some idea whether the participants were suspicious about it or accepted the "genuineness" of the situation. Unfortunately, as noted earlier, it is not at all clear that the experimental participants will be willing to reveal their suspicions (K. M. Taylor & Shepperd, 1996) or whether such suspiciousness necessarily impacts their behavior during the experiment (Kimmel, 1996). The third methodological aim—frequently salient in the university subject pool environment—consists of the researcher's attempt to impress on the participants the need to not reveal any features of the study to potential participants that would invalidate their participation. However, as is the case regarding the communication of their suspicions, the evidence is equivocal that such pledges to secrecy by participants will be kept (Kimmel, 1996). Although it is tempting to simply derogate the trustworthiness and lack of ethical standards of students who leak such information, it may reflect an antipathy resulting from the negative reactions those students have had with the research enterprise. In any event, it sometimes results in the researcher delaying a full debriefing until after completion of the study, at which time some students may no longer be available and may, therefore, be left with the recollections and effects of a bad experience. But "if scientific or humane values justify delaying or withholding this information [about the study], psychologists take reasonable measures to reduce the risk of harm" (APA, 2002, Standard 8.08[b]).

The Educational Function: Debriefing

The ubiquitous term *debriefing* derives historically from military usage—in particular, the British Royal Air Force during World War II—in which pilots were briefed at the beginning of a mission and interrogated or debriefed at its conclusion (B. Harris, 1988). The term was introduced into the language of experimental psychology by Stanley Milgram (1964), and it was ultimately used generically to refer to one or more of several different procedures with rather different objectives (E. Aronson & Carlsmith, 1968). For example, the term may be used in psychiatry to refer to post-traumatic interventions, such as those offered to victims of the World Trade Center (September 11, 2001) attack, designed to help "promote the emotional processing of traumatic events through the ventilation and normalisation of reactions and preparation for possible future experiences" (Bisson & Deahl, 1994, p. 717).

The overall importance of debriefing (in the global sense) is suggested by some findings that a majority of research participants do not find their participation particularly enjoyable or interesting, and the debriefing was not a positive experience (Brody, Gluck, & Aragon, 2000; Lindsay & Adair, 1990). This is a matter of some concern because, in the opinion of some experienced researchers, "the most important determinant of the subject's feeling about the research experience ... is the debriefing" (C. P. Smith, 1983, p. 323). In fact, student participants in one survey "found the experiences to be boring, irrelevant, and a waste of time. In a few cases ... students ... expressed considerable contempt for the entire psychological research endeavor.... No student ... could say anything intelligible about the experiment's purpose or design" (Coulter, 1986, p. 317). This appears to have nothing to do with deception or noxious experimental manipulations: "Faculty seem to have underestimated the introductory students' dislike of research participation in apparently innocuous studies" (Lindsay & Adair,

1990, p. 292). Brody et al. (2000) also reported a substantial variability in the content, format, and quality of debriefing practices followed by researchers—even within a single university department of psychology. They also noted that the most frequent student complaint was that information provided during the debriefing was insufficient and unclear. "None of the participants spontaneously mentioned educational value as an outcome of their research participation" (p. 23).

Given the frequently mandatory nature of student participation in research, it seems imperative for both educational and ethical reasons that the research experience be academically justifiable (Coulter, 1986). This is commensurate with the ethical guideline to "provide a prompt opportunity for participants to obtain appropriate information about the nature, results, and conclusions of the research" (APA, 2002, Standard 8.08). At first blush, it might seem that this imperative is significantly less salient for applied research in I/O psychology, which is less likely to involve laboratory experimentation with students and more likely to entail survey procedures with more mature employees. However, even surveys are sometimes long, demanding, boring, mildly invasive, or otherwise upsetting; employees may also feel that, as a result of organizational pressures, their participation is as mandatory as that of a student in a university subject pool. They too deserve to understand the purpose and potential value of the research (perhaps to the organization or all employees), and they may even be pleased to learn about the nature of their contribution to it.

The Ethical Functions: Dehoaxing and Desensitization

Standards 8.07(c) and 8.08(a) of the APA (1992) ethical code obligate psychologists to explain to participants as early as is feasible any deception that has occurred and to "correct any misconceptions that participants may have." That process is called *dehoaxing*. Most psychologists accept that appropriate dehoaxing also includes a detailed explanation of why the deception was necessary and a personal apology for having done so (e.g., S. S. Smith & Richardson, 1983). A proposed change in the revised code makes explicit what many researchers have believed for some time, by adding "When psychologists become aware that research procedures have harmed a participant, they take reasonable steps to minimize the harm" (APA, 2002, Standard 8.08[c]). This is what is meant by *desensitization* in this context. The distinction between the two related procedures was first made by D. S. Holmes (1976a, 1976b).

D. S. Holmes (1976a) described the objective of dehoaxing as follows: "the problem is to convince the subjects that the fraudulent information they were given (e.g., that they are seriously maladjusted) was in fact fraudulent and thereby relieve any anxiety engendered by that information" (p.

859). However, the participants may find themselves in a virtual "Catch-22": If they believe the researcher's description of having just deceived them, why should they believe that they are not being deceived again? Perhaps they are being set up for a more complex manipulation involving a deception within a deception (yes, it has been done). Or perhaps they interpret the experimenter's explanation as a benign expression of sympathy, but still untrue, for one who is so "seriously maladjusted."

Despite those difficulties, D. S. Holmes (1976a, 1977) found that dehoaxing could, if done carefully and thoughtfully, effectively eliminate the misinformation participants received attendant upon a research deception. Hollingsworth (1977) was less sanguine about its effectiveness, especially with respect to false feedback about personal qualities, such as one's intelligence or sociability. Some researchers have advocated that experimenters spend as much or more time with participants after the experiment is over as they did during the data collection (Greenberg & Folger, 1988). In response to the possibility that dehoaxing may not be effective— that is, the false beliefs may persist despite debriefing (Holmes, 1976a)— Misra (1992) demonstrated that including "a formal discussion of the belief perseverance phenomenon" as a feature of the dehoaxing enhanced its effectiveness. And Eyde (2000) recommended that participants be reassured that extensive pilot testing had been done to assure that the deception was believable "and that the participant's acceptance of the ruse was not a reflection of the participant's gullibility, but rather of the lab's care and skill in designing the process" (p. 71). Of course, such difficulties would be obviated by a blanket proscription against noxious deceptions.

Among the 46 recent published studies in I/O psychology that used deception, most did not report providing any debriefing or dehoaxing (Nicolopoulos, 2002). Among those that did, most did not provide any information about its content, including whether the deception was revealed and explained. These are some typical descriptions of the debriefing procedures, quoted in their entirety: "Following this, the experimenter debriefed and thanked the participants"; "Finally, participants were debriefed and dismissed"; "Participants completed a posttask questionnaire, were debriefed, thanked, and allowed to leave"; "Finally, all participants were debriefed and paid"; "After completing the questionnaire, participants were debriefed and dismissed." Just two informative descriptions of appropriate procedures were found. For example, "Following the exercises, participants completed a post-experimental questionnaire and were debriefed, thanked, and allowed to leave. The debriefing provided information about the purpose of the study and the roles of the confederates, made apologies for the deception, and provided a phone number for participants who had further questions or concerns."

I cannot recall encountering a research study in I/O psychology in which the nature and severity of the deception and potential harm to participants was so great as to warrant *desensitization* procedures, which D. S. Holmes (1976b) defined as "the process of helping the subjects deal with new information about themselves acquired as a consequence of the behaviors they exhibited during the experiment" (p. 868). The classic example, of course, is the majority of Milgram's (1963, 1964, 1974) research participants who, in their (bogus) role of research assistant, discovered that they were compliant enough to obey the authoritative researcher's instructions to administer (bogus but realistic) severe electric shocks to inefficient learners who were actually research confederates. Many of them showed quite significant signs of distress during the experiment. Among the many serious matters to be considered in performing research of that nature (which probably would never receive IRB approval today) is the necessary prescreening of prospective participants that would be needed to eliminate any possibility of employing even a single psychologically "fragile subject" (Norris, 1978). In writing about such relatively extreme instances of deception, Diana Baumrind (1985)—in a rather deontological vein—notes that "Effective debriefing does not nullify the wrong done participants by deceiving them and may not even repair their damaged self-image or ability to trust adult authorities" (p. 172).

I think that her summary of the general and educational debriefing protocol developed by Mills (1976) is a fitting conclusion to this section:

> The experiment is explained very gradually and every point reviewed until the subject understands. Subjects are given time to reorganize their perceptions of the experiment and their responses to it, from possible humiliation and discomfort to self-acceptance and, it is to be hoped, sympathetic understanding of the researcher's perspective. Subjects are offered a genuine opportunity to withdraw their data after having received a full explanation of the purposes of the experiment. Moreover, by adding to the investigators' emotional and fiscal costs, painstaking and effective debriefing procedures introduce a noncoercive but persuasive deterrent to investigators who are contemplating deception research. (Baumrind, 1985, p. 173)

ADDING FURTHER TO THE FRAMEWORK
FOR ETHICAL DECISION MAKING

40.   Intentionally deceiving research participants remains a contentious issue in social, behavioral, and biomedical research. Despite the categorical objections of some, the ethical consensus, as articulated for example in the APA (2002) ethical code, reflects a reluctant act-utilitarian permissibility. "Psychologists do not conduct a study involving deception unless ... [it] is justified by the study's significant

prospective scientific, educational, or applied value and that effective nondeceptive alternative procedures are not feasible" (Standard 8.07[a]). Moreover, it must be explained to participants "as early as is feasible" (8.07[c]), and the decision to deceive must be approved by an appropriate review committee, such as an IRB.

IV

Conclusion

15

Taking Moral Action

An ethical problem may sometimes stir automatic reactions in us (cf. Haidt's, 2001, intuitionist view). In other words, we may have an "immediate, prereflective response" (Kitchener, 1984, p. 44) to an ethical situation that is based on our moral values and sensitivity, as well as on our introjected prior experiences with similar situations. But however useful these intuitive responses might sometimes be in situations requiring an immediate reaction, even Kitchener acknowledged that they often are not enough. And the immediacy of our reaction is no guarantee of its appropriateness in any event. Some problems may be of the sort that are apprehended and readily resolved by reference to an ethical code, casebook, or other available source. But some dilemmas may be even more complex and difficult, such as when ethical principles conflict (Pryzwansky & Wendt, 1999; Sales & Lavin, 2000). In this last chapter I present a suggested strategy for approaching, analyzing, and resolving ethical issues of the more troublesome kind. It is predicated on the belief that the nearly infinite variety of human interaction virtually guarantees that each of us will at some time be confronted by a problem with moral implications that is not articulated adequately in our professional or organizational codes or casebooks. On such occasions it is helpful to have an overall strategy and some general guidelines to follow as a path to taking moral action.

The strategy offered here consists of three stages. The first stage refers to the anticipatory steps that every professional ought to maintain with the objective of preventing or minimizing the occurrence of ethical problems. The second stage is in the nature of a predecisional audit based on a distillation of the 40 summary items or learning points gleaned from the preceding chapters. The third is a recommended

11-step procedure for making ethical decisions and taking ethical action, to be implemented following one's personal predecisional audit taking. But before embarking on a description of those stages it is necessary to revisit briefly a preliminary question. How might one determine when to invoke these (latter two) sets of procedures? That is, how does one determine that a problem is ethical or moral in nature? What is the domain of moral action?

THE DOMAIN OF MORAL ACTION

As derived from normative ethical theories like the ones reviewed in Part I, as well as from the study of moral psychology and moral and social values, a problem is generally considered to have ethical implications if it involves one or more of several dimensions of human interaction that most ethicists agree reflect fundamental moral or ethical principles and that are enshrined as such in formal codes of conduct (e.g., APA, 1992, 2002; Canadian Psychological Association [CPA], 2000). Wittmer (2001) noted that two additional elements of an ethical situation are that one is faced with a choice and that one's actions are expected to have significant impact on the welfare of others. Thus, he concluded, "an *ethical situation* is taken to be essentially one in which *ethical dimensions are relevant and deserve consideration in making some choice that will have significant impact on others*" (p. 483).

The function served by the ethical dimensions or moral principles is to guide one's deliberations by providing the criteria with which reasoning and action can be assessed and justified from a moral perspective. As noted throughout this book, however, the principles are abstract and general, so the criteria tend to be rather vague. Indeed, that is why ethical codes such as that of the APA and the CPA articulate more specific ethical standards that are reflective of the general principles. In addition, the principles contain no intrinsic attributes that determine their relative importance (although avoiding causing physical harm or pain to another is at or near the top of the list of most moral philosophers). Their generality and indeterminate rank order is a cause of some difficulty when they suggest conflicting resolutions. Even the best ethical analysis, therefore, will sometimes leave the decision maker in a quandary; in fact, the use of ethical principles for guidance might make the decision more complex (Newman & Brown, 1996). Even on those occasions, however, the process may nevertheless help sharpen the issues.

Depending on how narrowly or broadly conceived and multifaceted each of the principles is defined, the domain of moral action has been represented by as few as two dimensions (e.g., Justice and Welfare), or by as many as six or seven. I have categorized them into five subdomains.

Respect for People

The origins of this subdomain are largely deontological—distinctively Kantian—as well as based on theories of human rights like John Locke's and Hegelian notions of self-realization. It directs our attention to actions that reflect the rights of all persons to be treated with respect and dignity and to be allowed to exercise their rights to privacy or confidentiality, freedom, autonomy, and self-expression. We are to view these rights and liberties as universalizable—that is, as much applicable to anyone else as to ourselves— and as bounded by corresponding reciprocal obligations. Your autonomy rights (e.g., to pursue your research objectives) do not necessarily extend to the point where they supercede my right to decide whether I wish to participate in that research.

Fairness and Justice

This dimension is informed primarily by ethical theories based on the social contract and by political, sociological, and psychological concepts of procedural and distributive justice. It is, perhaps, among the more nebulous of the ethical principles and more subject to interindividual variability in interpretation as a function of one's personal and social values (cf. Skitka & Tetlock, 1993). Being just may be conceived characterologically as the essence of virtue. Being treated justly or fairly may be viewed in a Kantian sense as having an appropriate balance of rights and duties. Social justice refers to the properties of a social system, such as an organization or an entire nation, and is generally defined in terms of a fair distribution of the system's benefits and burdens. Normative ideas of what constitutes appropriate distributive criteria—hence which outcomes are seen as right or wrong—tend to be culturally determined by the nature of the economic and political system of a society. For example, the American preference is for equity (merit) over equality and need, even to the point of tolerating extreme and dysfunctional disparities in income and wealth. Models of social justice from political philosophy help us distinguish between outcomes that merely reflect the differential opportunities and degrees of economic and political power between people, and impartial outcomes that can be defended rationally and accepted as fair even by those with vested interests.

Caring: Beneficence

This principle derives from consequentialist moral theory and the empathy-based perspective of an "ethics of care" in moral psychology— especially as reflected in the traditional service ideal of the professions. For example, "providers of I/O psychological services are guided primarily by the principle of promoting human welfare" (APA, Committee on Standards for Providers of Psychological Services, 1981, p. 668). An ethics of care is driven very much by the meta-principle of universalism—that no one's interests, especially one's own, counts for more than those of anyone else's unless reasonably justified. But we can expect the universalist standard to be at odds with the fact that we care more for some persons than others. In addition, those to whom we owe some special obligation, duty, or responsibility may justifiably make a special claim on our concerns. Consequently, in an organizational setting those special cares and concerns that we feel for particular friends and coworkers may conflict at some point with the universalist norms of fairness as impartiality and equal treatment, or as equity and merit, which are meant to be the primary determinants of our professional behavior toward others. "Playing favorites" is generally frowned upon.

In earlier chapters I pointed out that some deontological (e.g., libertarian rights-based) views focus exclusively on the avoidance of doing harm; doing good is not viewed as an ethical obligation. Indeed, for some persons calling someone a do-gooder is a dismissive insult. As noted earlier, the classical libertarian position seems to be an anemic version of morality and an egoistic denial of the adaptive advantages of prosocial and cooperative behavior. Nevertheless, it does seem reasonable to acknowledge some limitations of the construct and the extensiveness of one's obligation to be beneficent. It may be difficult to differentiate between moral acts of benefi-cence and mere socially conventional behavior. There is an ambiguous boundary between being unethical and simply being rude. The principle of beneficence seems most appropriate in relation (a) to those who help further our interests (e.g., employees, students, clients, and research participants) especially when they occupy positions of lesser status and power and (b) to the extent that we may be in a position uniquely capable of providing benefit to them (Beauchamp & Childress, 1994). In other words, the extent to which one may be expected to do good depends in part on one's social status and on the circumstances of one's role relationships (Newman & Brown, 1996).

Caring: Nonmaleficence

Although this principle shares some intellectual lineage with the subdomain of beneficence, it is not merely the opposite side of the same coin, and so I have listed it separately. Refraining from unjustifiably doing harm is the principle about which there is the greatest consensus among moral philoso-phers. It differs from the principle of beneficence primarily in its uncondi-tional and noncontingent nature. Whereas the extensiveness of our moral obligations to do good—especially our emotional commitment to it—may be structured and delimited by the nature of our social identity and role relationships, the obligation to not cause harm is generally thought to apply to all. The principle pertains most appropriately and is felt most keenly with respect to those in vulnerable positions; for I/O psychologists, these people are likely to be employees, students, and research participants. It also extends to a wariness against the possibility that others might misuse our work (e.g., individual assessments, survey findings, or other information obtained confidentially). The importance or primacy of this principle is suggested in the APA (2002) code of ethics: "When conflicts occur among psychologists' obligations or concerns, they attempt to resolve these conflicts in a responsible fashion that avoids or minimizes harm" (Principle A: Beneficence and Nonmaleficence). In other words, nonmaleficence is to be given particular deference in the resolution of ethical dilemmas.

Moral Virtue or Character

The sources of this subdomain are many, including classical Greek philosophy, religious teachings, and a Kantian sense of duty, as well as psychological considerations regarding the relative consistency of moral behavior. Some ethical statements include principles that may be considered aspects of this subdomain—for example, fidelity, integrity in relationships, scientific integrity, and trust (APA, 1992, 2002; CPA, 2000; M. B. Smith, 2000). But rather than singling out specific attributes like those just mentioned and having to justify the exclusion of others, I have opted to emphasize the broader perspective connoted by moral virtue or moral character.[155] I consider virtue and character to be roughly synonymous, referring to relatively stable personality attributes with the same behavioral manifestations. Included in the domain are traditional moral virtues like truthfulness, integrity, and trust, as well as other attributes that have only more recently been construed by moral psychologists: moral sensitivity (Rest, 1994), moral motivation (Stocker, 1976), moral emotions, and self-sanctions (Bandura 1991). Moral virtue differs somewhat from the first four subdomains (respect, justice, beneficence, and nonmaleficence) in that, rather than simply denoting an ethical principle (i.e., a content domain), it focuses on the locus of moral action—the person—and emphasizes the role played by traits of moral character in initiating and shaping the process of ethical reasoning and acting. Moral character refers to both a constellation of ethical traits (e.g., honesty and integrity) and to the motivational source

---

[155]The restriction of virtues to those that are moral in nature excludes such traditional and "selfish virtues" as respectability, chastity, perseverance, prudence, fortitude, and so on that fall outside the domain of ethical considerations as customarily defined by moral philosophers. I also use the term virtue without any religious connotations.

of behavior that reflects all of the ethical principles, including respect for persons, justice, beneficence, and nonmaleficence.

STAGE I: ANTICIPATING PROBLEMS

A practical approach to professional ethics should emphasize prevention (Pryzwansky & Wendt, 1987). To use an analogy from public health medicine, if moral problem solving represents the "treatment" for a dilemma, this stage consists of maintaining good "moral hygiene." Although Canter et al. (1994) presented a seven-step process of ethical decision making, the first six steps are actually preventive in nature and focus on developing and maintaining the knowledge base on which ethical reasoning depends. Those six steps are discussed next.

1.   **Know the ethics code.** Canter et al. (1994) referred specifically to the code of the APA (1992), but one might also include that of the CPA (2000) as well as codes promulgated by other appropriate organizations or groups of professionals, such as the Academy of Management (2002), the International Personnel Management Association (1990), and the Society for Human Resource Management (1990), and by organization and human systems development specialists (Gellermann et al., 1990). In a similar vein, it is also useful to become familiar with the sorts of ethical problems most likely to be encountered by psychologists in general (cf. APA Ethics Committee, 1988, 2000, 2001; Christa Peterson, 1996; Pope & Vetter, 1992), the particular problems associated with one's field (Eyde & Quaintance, 1988; Eyde et al., 1993; London & Bray, 1980; Lowman, 1998), or with specific areas of specialization (e.g., Hollander, 1998; Loch, Conger, & Oz, 1998; Sashkin & Prien, 1996). To the extent that psychologists sometimes blunder into ethical indiscretions due to ignorance (Keith-Spiegel, 1977), familiarizing oneself with these guidelines and maintaining one's awareness of updates and revisions to the codes (e.g., APA, 2001a) may provide a degree of immunization. Indeed, "lack of awareness or misunderstanding of an ethical standard is not itself a defense to a charge of unethical conduct" (APA, 2002, p. 1061).

2.   **Know the applicable state laws and federal regulations.** This includes a substantial array of regulations and statutes, including state laws regulating the licensing of psychologists and dealing with issues of confidentiality, malpractice, and research with human subjects. Especially pertinent for I/O psychologists are statutes and regulations governing employment practices, such as the Civil Rights Acts of 1964 and 1991, the Americans With Disabilities Act, the Age Discrimination in Employ-

ment Act, and the *Uniform Guidelines on Employee Selection Procedures* (EEDC, CSC, DOL, DOJ, 1978).

3. Know the rules and regulations of the Institution where you work. There are two purposes served by this knowledge. The first is rather straightforward, having to do with assuring appropriate and competent professional practice in keeping with the organization's expectations. The second is more problematic and concerns potential issues of person–organization fit. At the broadest level it is not unusual for professionals to experience values conflicts with respect to the goals and objectives of the organizations in which they are employed, and these may sometimes manifest themselves in specific ethical dilemmas. The operative stance to be adopted is articulated clearly in the standards of the APA (2002) code:

> 1.03. Conflicts Between Ethics and Organizational Demands. If the demands of an organization with which psychologists are affiliated or for whom they are working conflict with this Ethics Code, psychologists clarify the nature of the conflict, make known their commitment to the Ethics Code, and to the extent feasible, resolve the conflict in a way that permits adherence to the Ethics Code.

Of course, in light of this standard, the preferred strategy is to anticipate potential conflicts in advance of their occurrence so that mutually acceptable strategies can be agreed on when circumstances are calm. (See Point 7 of this list.)

4. Engage in continuing education in ethics. Canter et al. (1994) enumerated many of the steps that may be taken in this regard: taking courses or workshops in ethics, subscribing to journals that focus on ethical and professional issues, reading books on ethics pertaining to one's particular area of practice (and research), and attending seminars and workshops. I add the practice of initiating exchanges with colleagues about ethical issues and promoting the topic at professional conferences, which would have the beneficial effect of increasing the topic's salience.

5. Identify when there is a potential ethical problem. In a sense, one might say that this is what much of this book is about—an attempt to heighten the reader's awareness of potential ethical issues by highlighting (among other things) the role played by one's personal characteristics, attitudes, and values in the definition and approach to such problems. Canter et al. (1994) focused predominantly on clinical practice and the danger of practicing beyond one's professional expertise. The issue of competence certainly generalizes beyond clinical practice. But of more general importance is appreciating the varied manifestations of the five ethical principles constituting the domain of moral action, which serve to alert us that we may be facing an ethical challenge.

6.   Learn a method for analyzing ethical obligations in often complex situations. Canter et al. (1994) recommended use of a decision-making model of the sort presented below as the third and final stage of the overall strategy for taking moral action. I believe that the second, predecisional stage is also helpful and that the value of any decision-making routine is greatly limited without some rudimentary mastery of moral philosophy. Moreover, I add another guideline to Canter et al.'s list.

7.   Maintain a mind-set of ethical watchfulness. Several of the foregoing recommendations coalesce around the notion of avoiding ethically ambiguous situations or clarifying them before one gets involved. R. G. L. Pryor's (1989) notion of watchfulness seems like a reflection, at least in part, of one's moral sensitivity (Rest, 1994) in the service of minimizing ethical difficulties. Watchfulness is enabled by staying familiar with the relevant knowledge domain (Points 1–4 of this list), especially with respect to potential conflicts among obligations owed to different parties; adopting an ethical perspective with respect to the evaluation of any suggested new procedures, strategies, or policies (Point 5); and exercising caution and taking time for reflection and/or consultation (Point 6). "The watchful psychologist seeks, where appropriate, to draw on the collective wisdom of the profession" (R. G. L. Pryor, 1989, p. 298). For example, some I/O psychologists have thoughtfully enumerated ethical problems that are likely to be encountered by practitioners in the field (Eyde & Quaintance, 1988; London & Bray, 1980; Lowman, 1991, 1998). Similarly, The APA has published a number of helpful and informative documents such as those that "set forth both the expectations employed psychologists may properly anticipate will be met by their employers and the obligations that employers may properly expect psychologists to meet" (APA, Committee on Academic Freedom and Conditions of Employment, 1987, p. 724) and "general guidelines of practice to promote the best interests and welfare of the users of [covered psychological] services" (APA, Board of Professional Affairs & Committee on Professional Standards, 1987, p. 1).

STAGE II: A PREDECISIONAL AUDIT—THE FRAMEWORK FOR ETHICAL DECISION MAKING

Assuming that one encounters a challenging ethical problem despite having taken the foregoing preventive measures, I suggest that the first steps in the solution of the problem might be to review the perspectives embodied in the 40 summary conclusions or learning points derived in the preceding chapters. This stage is still predecisional because the points deal with contextual or background factors—such as orienting information from ethical models, moral psychology, and social and political theory. They are meant to prompt reflections about one's own values and those of the organization(s) and institution(s) within which one functions in the belief that in dealing with potential ethical dilemmas it is best to "clarify and refine our values and ethics before we need to draw on them" (Gellermann et al., 1990, p. 88). Many of the learning points are very general in nature, and so they are relevant to a wide array of ethical difficulties but not *necessarily* pertinent to any particular problem at hand. The predecisional review is meant to sensitize or cue the actor to potentially salient or enlightening matters that could be useful in the decisional stage of ethical reasoning and taking moral action.

Rather than recapitulating the 40 points seriatim, I summarized and integrated them into six groups according to their sources. To enable more convenient reference, I also indicated their original numbering and the chapters in which they were derived.

Learning Points From Ethical Theory (Chaps. 2, 3, and 4)

The nature of ethical principles has historically been framed by a Manichean battle between those who view them as reflections of subjective feelings and beliefs and those who view them as representations of objective moral facts, including those of divine origin. An unsuccessful attempt at a resolution has been to take one's cues regarding the specification of normative ethical principles from the empirical facts of human behavior, like viewing as moral those attributes having a high incidence in the population or high heritability. But the logic is flawed, and the diversity of human behavior is too great: What *is* does not provide a sufficient justification for what *ought* to be (Point 6, Hume's Law). A useful middle-ground is the emphasis on ethical reasoning (Point 1). We can accept normative prescriptions based on a well-reasoned rationale and the solution to a moral dilemma if it is supported by better arguments than the alternative solutions. As psychologists, however, we are well aware of the potential distortions to which rational deliberations are subject, and so we accept the need for exposing those deliberations to others. Similarly, we are also mindful that behavior tends to be influenced by a variety of motives and external influences so that one's moral reasoning and intentions do not invariably lead to the corresponding moral action (Point 4). The study of moral psychology illuminates many of those additional determinants of action.

A rational, analytic approach also provides a middle-ground solution between the idiosyncratic cultural relativist and the cultural universals positions regarding ethical standards (Point 5). The middle way posits a certain number of core values that develop in response to the common problems faced by all societies in having to regulate the behavior of it members; but those values may be expressed in a dazzling variety of culturally linked social customs and practices.

Among the important assumptions or meta-issues underlying moral reasoning are universalizability (Points 2, and 9a) and universalism (Points 3 and 9b). That is, in the first instance, the quality of an ethical solution to a given situation should be the same irrespective of who is in the situation. Therefore, your recommendation to a colleague is probably not an ethical one if, faced with exactly the same moral dilemma, you would not behave in the way recommended. Second, ethical behavior has to mean more than the expression of mere self-interest. Unless reasonably justified (e.g., by duties and obligations one owes to particular others), no person's interests— including one's own—count for more morally than anyone else's. In addition, the essence of ethics and morality is the right treatment of others, generally respecting their dignity, autonomy, and striving for social recognition and self-realization (Points 9c and 9d).

Although some morally enjoined actions such as the proscription against incest might be associated with immediately and intuitively felt emotional reactions (Haidt, 2001), most ethical dilemmas involve competing motives or values conflicts and are more likely to engender rational attempts at solution. Because most of us are reasonably well socialized, our ethical solutions are not necessarily experienced as being forced upon us against our will, as Kantian notions of doing one's duty seem to imply. Conversely, we may feel pangs of conscience and guilt over the most mundane transgressions. Therefore, although our emotional feelings or upset may be useful introspective clues to what is salient for us, they are not reliable indicators of the moral rectitude of our intentions or actions (Point 8).

The structure of moral reasoning generally takes either a deontological or consequentialist form, based in the first instance on principles of right and wrong, duty, obligations, rights, virtues, or fairness and justice and in the second case on the balance of anticipated benefit and harm accruing to all those affected by the contemplated actions. However, both forms of normative theory have been subject to extensive criticism; as a consequence, they have undergone a variety of structural modifications, some of which tend to render them more alike—for example, the development of rule-utilitarianism and act-deontological views (Point 7). For those reasons, and because some problems seem to lend themselves more readily to one form of analysis than the other, it is prudent to be familiar with both views so that we may avail ourselves of the appropriate one. Unfortunately, the two approaches sometimes lead to conflicting conclusions.

Because ethics has to do not only with personal convictions and morality but with the regulation of behavior and power relations between and among people, organizations, and economic and social institutions, it is essentially political in nature, as reflected explicitly in the fields of political philosophy and political economy (Point 10). The implied social contract between employee and employer is an example of such, in which each party has a right to expect dutiful, respectful, and ethical behavior on the part of the other (Point 11).

Learning Points From the Psychological Study of Moral Behavior (Chap. 5)

The fundamental psychological capacities that enable the development of a mature moral perspective (e.g., empathic sensitivity and an appreciation of the consequences of one's actions) seem to appear very early in life in virtually all cultures, suggesting that ethical behavior is among the critically important and indispensable features of human existence. This implies that ethical considerations should be afforded considerable deference in human affairs and not be conceived of as a discretionary afterthought (Point 12). Common paradigms of ethical challenges studied by moral psychologists include contemplating an action that would harm or wrong another, anticipating someone's being harmed by a third party, having conflicting obligations to two or more persons, and facing a situation in which two or more of one's important values are in conflict (Point 13). Notwithstanding the common core of human potentials, these capacities develop into culturally distinctive patterns of ethical concern. For example, in portions of Africa, the Middle East, Southeast Asia, and the Far East, communitarian group-based principles are more salient than the individualistic rights-based conceptions of justice typical in the west (Point 14). And perhaps most important, the study of moral psychology reveals that ethical conduct is certainly no less complex than other varieties of social behavior (Point 15). It is conditioned by developmental and dispositional antecedents with perceptual, cognitive, and motivational components; it reflects schema-based reasoning processes as well as other consistencies of personality and character. Yet there are many influences that dispose toward a lack of individual consistency too: conflicting values and competing objectives, the consequences of prior ethical decisions, contemporaneous social pressures and other contextual influences including organizational norms and expectations (which may themselves be internally inconsistent), and others. Consequently, there is no good reason to anticipate that invariably behaving ethically is to be taken for granted.

Learning Points From the Study of Individual and Social Values (Chaps. 6 and 7)

Values refer to the relative importance with which we view generalized end states (terminal values) or standards of conduct (instrumental values; Point

16). As core aspects of personality, akin to assumptions one takes for granted, they play a directing role in the formation of our specific beliefs, attitudes, and actions concerning how things ought to be. Not all values are ethical or moral; those that are pertain to the domain of moral action as just noted (Point 18). Particulars of our upbringing such as "national background, social class, family roots, education and life experiences" (Hofstede, 2001, p. 523) result in individual differences in values and in what is perceived as just (Point 20). Consequently, social conflicts frequently involve principled differences among individuals or groups who disagree about the relative priority of such generalized means and/or ends. In a related manner, intrapersonal conflicts, including ethical dilemmas, also often involve competing values. The complexity of social and moral attitudes and action is increased still further by virtue of (a) distinctions between one's espoused (normative) values and one's less conscious experiential (normal) "values in use" and (b) the unattractive role sometimes played by principled values statements as mere post-hoc rhetorical devices for rationalizing discriminatory and/or self-serving motives (Points 17 and 19).

Despite the fact that the primary purposes of many societal institutions and individual organizations do not concern moral matters per se, their actions can nevertheless be viewed from an ethical standpoint, that is, with respect to the principles defining the domain of moral action (Point 22). This seems eminently true in the case of modern business corporations because of the extraordinary influence and power they wield over people's lives. This sort of perspective invokes consideration of social justice issues concerning the distribution of benefits and burdens throughout society. United States cultural norms and the capitalist free-market economic system predispose to an equity- or merit-based criterion of distributive justice; with few exceptions, it has been demonstrably effective in maximizing the production and aggregation of material wealth. However, quite a convincing argument can be made for the moral superiority of the distributive justice criteria of equality or need over merit (Point 21). At the least, in keeping with widely accepted ethical principles, justice criteria of need and equality ought to be invoked as a means of attenuating the morally dubious extreme distributional inequities of the so-called free-market system.

Learning Points From the Study of Institutional—Professional, Scientific, and Organizational—Values (Chaps. 8, 9, and 12)

The privileges that accrue to members of a profession entail corresponding obligations to the society that has bestowed that status on the occupation. Chief among these is the expectation that professional expertise will be used "to improve the condition of individuals, organizations, and [the entire] society" (APA, 2002, p. 1062), not just for the paying clients (Points 23 and

28). A number of likely points of friction between the structural and cultural features as well as the objectives of large organizations and the values and expectations of professionals who may be employed in them have been well-documented. These include, in the case of public corporations, the overriding importance of enhancing shareholder value to the relative neglect of other stakeholder groups. Although there are reasons to anticipate that I/O psychologists may experience less of those sorts of frictions than members of some other professions, those reasons themselves are troubling to the extent that they suggest a failure to embrace the professional service ideal (Point 25). Although the decades-old criticism of I/O psychology as "unscientific" has not been justifiable for quite some time, the charge that the field has not outgrown the organizational, managerial, and antilabor biases that helped account for its success still seems pertinent (Point 34).

Many I/O psychologists consider themselves exclusively scientific and objective in their research and practice, by which they frequently mean that those activities are not influenced by any personal or social values —that their work is value free. This logical positivist tradition adopted from the natural sciences has undergone serious challenge by postmodern or *social constructivist* perspectives for more than a generation, even with respect to basic research. The challenge seems more credible with respect to applied research and professional practice. Without necessarily taking sides categorically in this intellectual manifestation of contemporary "culture wars," it seems difficult to imagine how one could accept the value-free assumption when many of the very constructs and problems we investigate, as well as the goals and objectives of our professional practice, are influenced greatly if not defined entirely by the corporate enterprise and its dominant value structure (Points 26 and 27). That our field's professional values are so commensurate with those of the organizational cultures in which we work tends to render them invisible to many of us so that the field is mischaracterized as value free (Point 34). It would seem preferable to articulate all of the values that should and do get reflected in our work, from whatever sources—as well as those which are not represented or are controverted—to more fully appreciate the consequences and implications of what we do.

A more morally sensitive (Rest, 1986b, 1994) I/O psychology would have to incorporate an explicitly normative perspective to accompany the scientific and instrumental perspectives that dominate the field (Point 35). To the questions "Is it valid?" and "Is it cost-effective?" we need to add "Is it right?" This would encompass a broader system of values to include psychology's humanistic tradition, greater concern for the individual employee to balance our organizational outlook, and a recognition of the extent to which the societal consequences of our work are as germane as is its technical competence. This transformational enterprise will be supported by those employee-centered human resource specialists, progressive business leaders, management scholars, other psychologists, and business ethicists who have already begun it (Point 36).

Learning Points From the Study of Business Values (Chaps. 10 and 11)

Business is a moral enterprise. That is, the consequences of business activity are very much within the domain of moral action—involving interpersonal behavior and personal decision making with beneficent and potentially maleficent effects subject to standards of fairness and justice. It's ultimate justification is the utilitarian one of maximizing the aggregate good. Even the fundamental free-market model of economic activity was couched by Adam Smith (1976) in terms of the classical liberal moral philosophy of natural rights theory and the assumption of virtuous dealings (Point 29 and 30). Moreover, with respect to the domain of moral action, the recent sociopolitical, technological, and economic changes known as globalization have placed large business organizations in even more dominating positions relative to government and the other institutions of society (Point 33).

Notwithstanding the general success of the free-market economic model, many contemporary business scholars, social theorists, and others have challenged its adequacy as a moral model and the consequences it fosters. It is viewed as promoting a narrow conceptualization of life's goods, vast and morally indefensible distributional inequities regarding those goods, and egregiously harmful effects based on the excessive pursuit of power and profits (Point 31). An alternative model has been promoted by those critics, involving the notion of corporate social responsibility (CSR) and recognition of multiple stakeholders with legitimate claims on the concerns of the corporation (Point 32). Their objective is to "foster corporate capitalism that is accountable, ethical, and humane" (E. M. Epstein, 1999, p. 253). This alternative version of political economy and philosophy does not appear to be represented much in I/O psychology scholarship and practice; thus, the macrolevel values that provide the salient context for our normative views are dominated by the profit-maximization–shareholder value perspective.

Learning Points From the Ethical Principles of Research With Human Participants (Chapters 13 & 14)

Deontological principles dominate the ethical standards governing research participation: treating people with dignity and respect for their autonomy (so they are free to decide whether to participate in the research and whether to continue their participation); having concern for their well-being and avoiding the infliction of harm (so that if deception or withholding information can be justified by a rigorous review, adequate debriefing will be provided); abiding by principles of justice and fairness (so that people are not coerced into participation by virtue of their lesser social status or other factors); and displaying honesty, integrity, and trustworthiness (so that promises made regarding the confidentiality of replies and the potential benefits, discomforts, or risks of participation are fulfilled; Point 38). In addition, the bulk of our research, whether basic or applied, is aimed at fulfilling our own intellectual and professional goals and/or organizational objectives; it is not often, like so-called therapeutic research, designed to benefit directly the specific students, employees, or others who participate in it. Consequently, they have little, if any, moral or social responsibility to comply with our professional desires (Point 37). In other words, to whatever extent we as professionals have a right to conduct the research for which we have been trained, it is more of an entitlement than a claim. Moreover, it is prudent to proceed on that premise notwithstanding the case that can be made for employees having an obligation to cooperate with legitimate organizational research. And it is our responsibility to know and adhere to the professional and ethical standards and government regulations that codify these principles, irrespective of the setting in which the research is conducted (Point 39).

Despite the categorical objections of some, the ethical consensus in psychology regarding the intentional deception of research participants reflects a reluctant act-utilitarian permissibility. "Psychologists do not conduct a study involving deception unless ... [it] is justified by the study's significant prospective scientific, educational, or applied value and that effective nondeceptive alternative procedures are not feasible" (APA, 2002, Standard 8.07[a]). Moreover, it must be explained to participants "as early as is feasible" (Standard 8.07[c]). In addition, the decision to deceive must be approved by an appropriate review committee, such as an IRB (Point 40).

STAGE III: A MODEL FOR MAKING ETHICAL DECISIONS AND TAKING MORAL ACTION

A number of scholars have attempted to provide helpful decision-making models, checklists, flowcharts, or decision trees as aids in producing satisfactory and satisfying solutions to moral dilemmas (Canadian Psychological Association, 2000; T. L. Cooper, 1998; Gellerman et al., 1990; Gortner, 1991; L. J. Haas & Malouf, 1995; Koocher & Keith-Spiegel, 1998; Lewis, 1991; Nagle, 1987; Newman & Brown, 1996; Sales & Lavin, 2000), and some of these are reviewed by Wittmer (2001) and by Pryzwanski and

Wendt (1999).[156] An optimistic appraisal of these procedures is that they not only are helpful with respect to the deliberations at hand, but that repeated use of them for each ethics-related incident will help "fine-tune and shape appropriate responses"(Koocher & Keith-Spiegel, 1998, p. 12), thus providing cumulative improvements in one's ethical problem-solving skills. In fact, it may not be too far-fetched to suggest that guided and practiced striving to do the right thing contributes to becoming more of the right kind of person (and, according to Aristotle, experiencing the ultimate good– happiness).

Conversely, it may be that "in the case of any approach that analyzes the ethical decision-making process primarily in terms of a determinate, well-defined, and ordered sequence of steps, there is a near total lack of fit between subject matter and method" (Ladenson, cited in Gellermann et al., 1990, p. 90). I confess to a considerable, albeit reluctant, degree of sympathy with Ladenson's opinion; complex social situations with moral aspects often involve a bewildering mix of antecedent conditions, contrasting interpretations and personal beliefs, competing values and motives, divided loyalties, and contradictory principles and institutional demands. After concluding 14 chapters that attempt to shed some light on those complexities, ending with a normative list of invariant decision-making steps—mirroring the lamentable limitations of codes and casebooks—could be overly simplistic and anticlimactic.

But, on balance, I believe there is a positive contribution to be made by such moral mnemonics if they focus our attention on the *process* of decision making and taking moral action, rather than on specific rules or standards. After all, the scant empirical evidence that exists suggests that I/O psychologists "cannot always agree on what behaviors are appropriate, and even when they do agree on what to do, they often disagree on why" (S. I. Tannenbaum, Greene, & Glickman, 1989, p. 234). There is no doubt that most complex ethical dilemmas will be comprised of idiosyncratic details at a level of specificity much beyond what can be anticipated and described in this or any other decision model. But the overall process is generalizable even if the particulars of the problems vary. I agree with S. I. Tannenbaum et al. (1989), who concluded that "the task of ethics training is to convey ethical reasoning processes … the ethics reasoning process enables us to generalize to new and unique situations" (p. 234).

The recommended process consists of 11 nondiscrete (i.e., overlapping) steps, within four broad identifiable phases: problem identification,

---

[156]The following section owes much to their work. The models are normative—prescriptive problem-solving aids—and very different from the empirically grounded descriptive or conceptually derived predictive models such as the one in Fig. 5.1 or as illustrated by Miceli, Van Scotter, Near, and Rehg's (2001) model predicting whistle-blowing behavior in response to perceived wrongdoing.

information gathering, problem analysis and choice, and following through.

Problem Identification

1. Decide Whether the Problem is an Ethical One.

What is the nature of the difficulty? Do you have an intuitive reaction that this is more than just a technical problem to be solved or a matter of mere social convention? An ethical problem will generally invoke one or more principles from "The Domain of Moral Action." It may entail the threatened disrespect of some people (or a person), such as by violating their rights to privacy or autonomy or failing to honor an obligation to them; the potential imposition of unjustified ill effects on some or the distribution of undeserved rewards to others; a temptation to refrain from affording some benefit or care to another that one is readily capable of providing, or to inflict (or fail to prevent) harm, especially on those who possess lower social status, fewer resources, or less power; or a violation of the moral virtues concerning truthfulness, fidelity, trust, and so on, especially to those with whom we have a fiduciary relationship or are particularly vulnerable.

2. Understand the Structure and Complexity of the Problem.

That is, what are the key issues and who is affected? As noted earlier, a great many ethical difficulties can be encompassed in a simple taxonomy consisting of four ethical paradigms (that are not, however, mutually exclusive): considering harming or wronging another, especially when motivated by self-serving reasons, notwithstanding that there may be some external pressure to do so; having foreknowledge of someone's harmful intentions to a third party, as when one is privy to an organization's confidential plan to downsize; having conflicting responsibilities or obligations to two or more people, as occurs frequently among I/O psychologists who are retained by organization decision makers other than the employees with whom they work; and confronting a situation in which two or more important personal values are in conflict—that is, giving expression to one will deny expression of the other(s)—as is the case for the researcher who is disturbed by the realization that his or her research question can only be addressed adequately by means of perpetrating a deception on the experimental participants.

But the essence of the difficulty may have as much to do with the particular persons involved as with the structure of the dilemma. Can you identify all of the parties directly involved and the wider array of stakeholders who are potentially affected? They may include individual employees, students, research participants, trainees, or interns; or the issues may involve peers—colleagues, competitors, or perhaps a superior; at the macrolevel, there may be potential consequences for the client/organization/employer as an entity or for particular employee groups, consumers, or shareholders; a salient issue may be the reputation of our profession as a consequence of your actions or impacts on society at large. Last, but not least of course, are the implications for oneself. Especially challenging are situations in which the pressure to engage in some ethically questionable activity stems from one's employer or client, so that resisting may have potentially adverse personal consequences. To what extent does the particular "cast of characters" make a difference in your experience of the problem? Would it be the same problem, would there even be a problem, if different persons were involved? That is, would your likely actions be the same? If not, you should explore why that is so and whether the inconsistency can be justified comfortably. For example, would the just-noted researcher be less likely to implement deception in a field study with coworkers as research participants than with students? Both the structure of the dilemma (e.g., the number of conflicting elements) and the variety of persons affected contribute to the degree of moral complexity with which one is faced.

Initial Information Gathering

3. Get the Facts.

To what extent does understanding and addressing the problem depend on factual matters potentially subject to confirmation? It makes little sense to begin a thoughtful process of ethical reasoning if it is likely to be based on incorrect premises. How certain can you be that the circumstances of the problem are as you perceive them? It will be helpful to be able to make clear distinctions between factual matters and one's unconfirmed assumptions (e.g., concerning the antecedent conditions giving rise to the difficulty) or between one's personal beliefs and values that may be invoked. Similarly, one needs to think about the degree of certainty associated with one's expectations regarding the anticipated consequences of alternative courses of action (see below). Virtually all ethical decision-making models focus on a consideration of the consequences associated with the various options being pondered. But how certain can you be of the consequences? It would be reassuring to consult any knowledgeable and trusted others who might provide a consensus on which to base one's judgments.

4. Assess the Seriousness of the Problem.

At least as important as the complexity of the problem, in all likelihood more so, is its moral intensity, which is determined by the nature of the potential consequences (D. Collins, 1989; T. M. Jones, 1991). And the most salient consequences are those that are harmful.[157] Most people agree that physical harms (pain, injury, and suffering) are the most serious, followed by economic or financial harm, and "mere" emotional or psychological harm—in that order. In the utilitarian tradition of assessing aggregate outcomes, the overall magnitude of the anticipated harms ought to play a key role in one's deliberations. For example, any given harm is magnified by the number of people affected. A moral problem is also likely to be viewed as more intense because the potential consequences have a greater probability of occurring. Therefore, you should begin to think about whether you have enough reliable information to begin mapping out the consequences of your alternative options and their comparative likelihoods of actually happening.

Two other sets of elements are likely to contribute to the felt intensity of the ethical issue. The first of these are temporal factors, such as whether a decision must be made in haste, affording little time for reflection, and the degree of immediacy with which the consequences follow the action taken. Under conditions of extreme haste we may be forced to rely on our intuitive "gut reactions" with accompanying feelings of uncertainty about having done the best thing. So an important early decision is to determine how quickly you must do something. A situation in which you know that your actions will initiate ill effects immediately will ordinarily make the dilemma more painful, but this is likely to be an inherent feature of the situation that cannot be changed; it is probably not an "action item." The second set of factors has to do with personal dimensions of the situation, such as the degree of connectedness one has to the person(s) affected, whether more than one person is impacted, or the distinction between harming (or benefitting) an individual and an impersonal entity such as a corporation. For example, most people are more likely to return an excess refund of money received from an individual than the same amount received from an insurance company (although some employees may feel as personally responsible to their organization as to a personal friend).

Problem Analysis and Choice

5. *Restate the Problem in Ethical Terms.*

The troubling issues will probably have been encountered or presented to you in pragmatic operational terms (e.g., "Should I or should I not do such-and-such?"). Ethical reasoning is facilitated by articulating the problem in ethical terms, which you ought to be able to do based on your identification

---

[157]In this context I use *harm* as a broadly conceived construct extending beyond the two ethical principles of beneficence and nonmaleficence to include adverse effects associated with disrespectful, unjust, hurtful, or disloyal actions as well. The notion is stretched to encompass deontological "wrongs."

of the problem and initial information gathering. You will have already decided in Step 1 that the problem is ethical in nature, involving one or more of the five broad principles constituting the domain of moral action. It is time to articulate as clearly as possible which ethical principles are involved. Is it that people's rights are being violated or that some are being taken advantage of unfairly? Are you under pressure to violate a promise of confidentiality or to take personnel actions that will be gratuitously hurtful for reasons that you believe are inadequate? In all likelihood, you are conflicted (or else there would not be a problem). What, as precisely as you can identify them, are the causes of the conflict? It may be that circumstances suggest that two or more ethical principles are in opposition and you will not be able to adhere to one without violating the other. For example, the source of the "pressure" to violate confidentiality just mentioned may be coming from a sense of responsibility to prevent wrongdoing or harm. Or perhaps the structure of the situation is that you feel justifiably tempted to behave unvirtuously. Once the problem has been specified in terms that identify clearly the ethical stakes at risk, you are almost ready to undertake more formal and analytic ethical reasoning—which you no doubt have implicitly begun by now, in any event. But there is a preliminary step that may obviate the need for doing so.

6.   Is There a Ready Solution? Concession, Compromise, Codes, and Consensus.

Because you now have a pretty good understanding of the ethical issues, you are in a position to recognize potential solutions that may be readily available without having to initiate more analytic processes. There are four possibilities. First, you may, however reluctantly, concede that you simply cannot justify going ahead with (or refraining from preventing) a contemplated dubious act based on self-serving motives despite how well rationalized they are and despite the frustration caused by your concession. I trust that you would not, for example, deceive your IRB by intentionally withholding relevant information, irrespective of how "unreasonable" the particular committee members seem to be. This is the sort of commonly encountered pseudo dilemma in which one really knows all along what is the right thing to do—and that you will, ultimately, do it; the conflict reflects one's reluctance, frustration, or annoyance at being placed in such circumstances. In these situations, the concession is to oneself—more precisely, acting on a moral principle that outweighs whatever the competing motive(s) may be or acknowledging a "bottom- line" ethical position you are unwilling to violate.

Second, once the ethical issues have been specified clearly, a compromise may more readily be perceived. It might be as straightforward as acknowledging that one of the two or more ethical principles in opposition is significantly more important than the other(s) and should be given deference.

The third possibility harks back to the anticipatory steps outlined earlier as part of Stage I: Know the ethics codes, applicable laws and regulations, professional standards, relevant organizational policies, and other normative statements of professional propriety, such as the SIOP-sponsored case illustrations (Lowman, 1998) and other sources mentioned earlier in this book. It may just be that the issue distressing you—or a close parallel—is not unique and has been thought through and documented previously by colleagues. (Although it is possible that details of the situation you are in render the written guidelines inapplicable and/or insufficient.) In addition, I hope that you have available to you colleagues and friends with whom you can consult on the matter. Despite how vexatious the problem is for you—from your uncomfortable position in the middle of it—it is possible that they will uniformly see the situation as less conflicting. A fourth possibility, therefore, is that a consensus among trusted and knowledgeable colleagues may be all that is needed to resolve the dilemma—provided that it is acceptable to you. (There is no reason to believe that a colleague's judgments are necessarily less fallible than your own or that there may not be genuine differences between you and colleagues in values and ethical reasoning.)

7. *Acknowledge Your Personal Beliefs, Values, and Egoistic Biases as Well as Any External Pressures Relevant to the Issues.*

If no ready solution is apparent, you will need to proceed further with more formal ethical reasoning. But before doing so, it is necessary to explore the extent to which your personal perspective, values, or even biases play a role in those processes. If, as is almost invariably the case, one has a personal stake in the matter at hand, a near-ubiquitous issue will be satisfying oneself that the action taken is not merely a reflection of self-serving motives. In listing the potential options you have and their associated consequences (discussed next), special attention needs to be paid to the ethical justification of those options that further your self-interest. The origin of those forces may include discomforting external pressures from the client, employer, or significant others, such as one's boss.

It is also important to reflect on one's system of values, both the normative or espoused values that may be more readily accessible, as well as one's experiential, less conscious "values in use" that may be expected to impact one's judgment. Our values can be counted on to play a role in how we structure and understand the situation, evaluate the alternatives we construe, and decide on a course of action. Some of the intrapersonal conflict in ethical decision making can be attributed to the lack of clarity characterizing most people's understanding of their diverse value system

(D. Brown & Crace, 1996; DiNorcia & Tigner, 2000). Introspectively achieving greater understanding of one's values and their relative ordering may even, perhaps, prevent reaching a decision that is primarily a post hoc "values justification" rationalization for the expression of egoistic or prejudicial motives.

Building on your understanding of the key issues and who is affected (Step 2), a necessary companion process to making more salient one's own preferences and values is the attempt to appreciate the way in which other participants and affected parties experience the situation based on their concerns and motives. This appreciation is a requisite ingredient of the universalist assumption in moral reasoning, yet the circumstances may not be conducive to your finding out directly from other stakeholders what are their interests—hence, requiring your empathic sensitivities to do so.

8. *Enumerate Options and Their Consequences.*

In light of the foregoing seven steps, you should be in a position to generate a list of potential options or alternative courses of action, along with the consequences that may be anticipated from each. L. J. Haas and Malouf (1995) suggested that this step assume the nature of a "brainstorming" process in which emphasis is placed on producing novel and creative potential solutions that attempt to reconcile competing ethical principles. Similarly, Koocher and Keith-Spiegel (1998) advised that alternatives should be developed without regard to their feasibility, utility, riskiness, cost, appropriateness, or even their ethicality! Their advice is aimed at maximizing the array of options that can be considered—including the option of doing nothing—to enhance the probability of arriving at the best one. They recommended that, in enumerating the consequences anticipated from each option, whenever relevant the "consequences should include economic, psychological, and social costs; short-term, ongoing and long-term effects; the time and effort necessary to effect each decision, including any resource limitations; any other risks, including the violation of individual rights; and any benefits" (p. 14). As already noted, specification of consequences should include consideration of the effects on all identifiable stakeholders (Step 2), and special attention should be paid to the issue of the actual likelihood of occurrence of the anticipated consequences (Step 3). This advice is consistent with the exercise of one's moral imagination (Werhane, 1999), as discussed in chapter 5.

In addition to the self-reflection and insights promoted in Step 7, it is useful at this time also to contemplate the effects of other potentially relevant features of your "personal equation," such as the maturity of your moral character—that is, your degree of moral sensitivity and moral identity—and whether your moral musings tend to be shaped by a particular form of normative thinking. Are you generally dismissive of ethical considerations, frequently viewing them as idealistic and unnecessary intrusions on the real concerns of getting things done? Or are moral principles a key element of your self-identity? Do you tend to think in moralistic (deontological) terms of right and wrong that will preempt any utilitarian analysis? If so, your specification of consequences will focus on the ethical principles reflected in the options. Does your moralistic approach permit of any qualifications or exceptions? Or are you something of an ethical pragmatist, more likely to entertain utilitarian considerations of the ways in which people are benefitted and harmed by a contemplated action, in search of maximizing the good or minimizing the hurt? Similarly, do you tend toward optimism or pessimism as a dispositional attribute? Are you inclined to an unhappy or sarcastic cynicism regarding the motives of others? The matters alluded to by these questions may all affect the nature and range of alternatives you contemplate and your projections of their likely consequences, hence your choice of which one (or ones) to implement. Moreover, according to Nisan (1990, 1991), our ethical choices at any point in time are affected by previous recent ethical choices we have made, as reflected in the motivational influence of our moral balance. In other words, the generation of alternatives and specification of their likely consequences is not an entirely rational and objective enterprise as is frequently implied by decision-making strategies such as this. Some effort and personal insight is required to assure their accuracy in the hopes of arriving at the best solution.

9. Evaluate and Choose.

If you have approached the process in a thoughtful manner up to this point, you will probably be able to arrive at a best choice. It is important to accept that it is unlikely to be a "perfect" choice—that is, one with an absence of negative features and associated misgivings. (If one were available, you probably would not have needed to embark on this process.) Moreover, additional discussion at this time with a knowledgeable and sympathetic colleague, friend, professor, or mentor may prove extremely helpful in achieving an accurate assessment of the alternatives.

In evaluating the positive and negative consequences identified with each option, a number of guiding principles are worth keeping in mind: (a) universalism or equality of interests—Have I given appropriate consideration to the interests of everyone affected, adequately justifying why the interests of some may legitimately be given greater weight than others? (b) Right reasoning—Am I sanguine that the reasons substantiating this choice are better than the arguments that favor the other alternatives? In particular, am I satisfied that my own self-interest has not been the major determinative factor? (c) Universalizability: Would I advise anyone else like me in this same situation to do what I am choosing to do? Alternatively, does it pass the "family test"? That is, would I be pleased to explain to my family what I am about to do? Answers to those sorts of questions will be influenced by personal attributes like your level of moral identity and degree of moral motivation. In addition, if Nisan's (1990, 1991) notion of moral balance has some validity, that sense of identity will not result in an invariant ethical posture, but will reflect a "limited morality" in which we permit ourselves to deviate somewhat from the ideal, in response to other influences. The degree of such deviation, however, is likely to be limited by the motivation to preserve our moral identity.

For I/O psychologists, organizational influences may play an important part in the decision process, constituting one influential source threatening to upset our moral balance. Organizational ethical culture or a firm's moral atmosphere has an impact on the ethical decision making of employees (see Ford & Richardson, 1994 for a review). Of particular interest is Jansen and Von Glinow's (1985) observation that organizational reward systems may influence behavior in ways that contradict the dominant espoused ethical norms of the organization, thus establishing counternorms such as "do whatever it takes to get the job done on time." What, if any, organizational precedents, unacknowledged norms, or other social pressures might militate against your decision and need to be anticipated?

Following Through

10. Implement the Choice.

As discussed in the early chapters of this book and illustrated in Fig. 5.1, the implementation of a moral choice into moral action should not be taken for granted. There are many factors that account for the imperfect correlation between intentions and behavior. In some instances, for example, one is not able simply to take unilateral action, and implementing a course of action may require the cooperation of others and a very different skill set than was necessary to arrive at the choice (L. J. Haas & Malouf, 1995; Newman & Brown, 1996). This is especially liable to be the case for I/O psychology practitioners working in complex social systems like large corporations. It is not unlike the distinction between the knowledge needed to design a factorial experiment and the wider set of knowledge, skills, and abilities required to carry it out effectively in an organizational field setting.

After making a tentative decision, the first step in implementation will generally be to discuss the choice with the key stakeholders likely to be affected by it and to share that information with as many of those concerned as is feasible (Koocher & Keith-Spiegel, 1998). A focus of the discussion might be on whether there are any hitherto unforseen difficulties in implementation that were not incorporated in the specification of consequences on which the decision process was based. These may simply be practical problems concerning timing, resources, and the like, or it may be that others are able to envision that the proposed action is an inadequate solution to the dilemma or perhaps raises new problems.

A key consideration at this point is your assessment of whether there are forces like organizational counternorms keeping you from doing what you have chosen to do. L. J. Haas and Malouf (1995) noted what they referred to as "the 'prudence' aspect of this question" (p. 18), having to do with the fact that an ethical choice sometimes comes at considerable cost to the person implementing the decision. This may be especially true in an organizational context. For example, in comparison with higher level managers, lower level managers and supervisors are less likely to believe that their organizations are managed ethically and are more likely to report having had to compromise their personal principles to conform with organizational expectations (Posner & Schmidt, 1987). It has been suggested, however, that subordinates who are at higher levels of cognitive moral development (a la Kohlberg) will be less affected by their supervisors' influence (Wimbush, 1999). Try to be aware of the social sanctions mediated by organizational reward structures, normative expectations, and other indications of valued policies and practices such as leadership and compliance processes (Ciulla, 1998; R. S. Peterson, 2001) as these influence your taking moral action.

Also pertinent at this point are your internalized self-sanctions (Bandura, 1986, 1991) associated with aspects of your moral identity. The contemplated satisfaction and enhanced self-respect stemming from the confirmation and enactment of one's moral ideals and the converse self-condemnation anticipated from a failure to live up to them are salient influences for most people. Situations in which one is confronted unavoidably with instances of unethical behavior on the part of others (e.g., high-ranking managers) in the organization may be especially threatening. Nielsen (1989) contrasted a number of strategies that can be taken from the standpoint of an individual in opposition to the offending parties (e.g., secretly or quietly blowing the whistle within or outside the organization or anonymously threatening to do so and conscientiously refusing to implement an unethical policy) with collaborative solutions in which people have successfully worked with others to build a more ethical organization. There are difficulties and limitations associated with both sets of strategies.

11. Evaluation and Review.

It is important to take the time to ponder the results of your actions. One technique is to use the five ethical principles to evaluate the results. Has the problem been resolved only to yield a new moral dilemma? Might that have been anticipated? It is probably wise to accept that the resolution of ethical problems may not be entirely emotionally satisfying: "resolution is ordinarily an approximate state" (T. L. Cooper, 1998, p. 27). Nevertheless, to what extent have your actions met the needs of the situation? Did any particular stakeholders get the short end of the stick? If so, why? Did the consequences turn out as expected? If not, to what extent is it attributable to having misread the situation initially (see Steps 2 and 3)? As pointed out in the *Canadian Code of Ethics for Psychologists* (Canadian Psychological Association, 2000), at this point one should accept responsibility for the consequences of one's action, correct any negative consequences, and reengage in the decision-making process if the ethical issue is not resolved.

Perhaps most important, what have you learned from this experience that will be useful for the next dilemma encountered? A potential value of engaging in a process such as this is the increased ease with which it may be called on in the future, as well as the structure it provides in recognizing and understanding what might have gone wrong. As Gellermann et al. (1990) noted, "Reflect on the results of your action; clarify your vision and beliefs; refine your values and ethics; and give feedback to your consciousness as a means of heightening your ethical sensitivity and developing your ability to act ethically in the future" (p. 87). It may be unreasonable to expect an entirely satisfactory resolution of every ethical dilemma, but producing increasingly skilled efforts to do so should be the objective.

References

Abelson, R. (2000, July 6). New philanthropists put donations to work. *The New York Times*, p. C1.

Academy of Management. (2002). Academy of Management code of ethical conduct. *Academy of Management Journal, 45,* 291–294.

Academy of Management Journal. (1999). Special research forum on stakeholders, social responsibility, and performance. *42,* (5).

Adair, J. G., Dushenko, T. W., & Lindsay, R. C. (1985). Ethical regulations and their impact on research practice. *American Psychologist, 40,* 59–72.

Adams, R. M. (1976) Motive utilitarianism. *The Journal of Philosophy, 73,* 467–481.

Agle, B. R., & Caldwell, C. B. (1999). Understanding research on values in business: A level of analysis framework. *Business & Society, 38,* 326–387.

Ajzen, I. (1988). *Attitudes, personality, and behavior.* Chicago: Dorsey.

Ajzen, I., & Fishbein, M. (1980). *Understanding attitudes and predicting social behavior.* Englewood Cliffs, NJ: Prentice-Hall.

Albee, G. W. (2000). The Boulder model's fatal flaw. *American Psychologist, 55,* 247–248.

Alderfer, C. P. (1998). Group psychological consulting to organizations: A perspective on history. *Consulting Psychology Journal, 50,* 67–77.

Alge, B. J. (2001). Effects of computer surveillance on perceptions of privacy and procedural justice. *Journal of Applied Psychology, 86,* 797–804.

Allen, F. (1952). *The big change.* New York: Harper.

Almond, B. (1993). Rights. In P. Singer (Ed.), *A companion to ethics* (pp. 259–272). Cambridge, MA: Blackwell.

American Association for the Advancement of Science. (1999, June 25). Net news. *Science, 284,* p. 2051.

American Educational Research Association, American Psychological Association & National Council on Measurement in Education. (1985). *Standards for educational and psychological testing.* Washington, DC: American Psychological Association.

American Educational Research Association, American Psychological Association & National Council on Measurement in Education. (1999). *Standards for educational and psychological testing.* Washington, DC: American Educational Research Association.

413

American Psychological Association. (1987). Guidelines for conditions of employment of psychologists. *American Psychologist, 42,* 724–729.

American Psychological Association. (1992). Ethical principles of psychologists and code of conduct. *American Psychologist, 47,* 1597–1628.

American Psychological Association. (2000). What does it pay to be a psychologist? *Monitor on Psychology, 31,* 13.

American Psychological Association. (2001a). Ethical principles of psychologists and code of conduct: Draft for comment. *Monitor on Psychology, 32,* 77–89.

American Psychological Association. (2001b). *Publication manual of the American Psychological Association* (5th ed.). Washington, DC: American Psychological Association.

American Psychological Association. (2002). Ethical principles of psychologists and code of conduct. *American Psychologist, 57,* 1060–1073.

American Psychological Association, Board of Professional Affairs & Committee on Professional Standards. (1987). General guidelines for providers of psychological services. *American Psychologist, 42,* 1–12.

American Psychological Association, Committee on Academic Freedom and Conditions of Employment. (1987). Guidelines for conditions of employment of psychologists. *American Psychologist, 42,* 724–729.

American Psychological Association, Committee on Legal Issues. (1996). Strategies for private practitioners coping with subpoenas or compelled testimony for client records or test data. *Professional Psychology: Research and Practice, 27,* 245–251.

American Psychological Association, Committee on Standards for Providers of Psychological Services. (1981). Specialty guidelines for the delivery of services by industrial/organizational psychologists. *American Psychologist, 36,* 664–669.

American Psychological Association, Ethics Committee. (1988). Trends in ethics cases, common pitfalls, and published resources. *American Psychologist, 43,* 564–572.

American Psychological Association, Ethics Committee. (2000). Report of the ethics committee, 1999. *American Psychologist, 55,* 938–945.

American Psychological Association, Ethics Committee. (2001). Report of the ethics committee, 2000. *American Psychologist, 56,* 680–688.

American Psychological Society. (1992, February). Human capital initiative: Report of the national behavioral science research agenda committee [Special issue]. *APS Observer.*

American Psychological Society. (1993a, October). Human capital initiative. Report 1: The changing nature of work [Special issue]. *APS Observer.*

American Psychological Society. (1993, December). Human capital initiative. Report 2: Vitality for life: Psychological research for productive aging [Special issue]. *APS Observer.*

American Psychological Society. (1996a, February). Human capital initiative. Report 3: Reducing mental disorders: A behavioral science research plan for psychopathology [Special issue]. *APS Observer.*

American Psychological Society. (1996b, April). Human capital initiative. Report 4. Doing the right thing: A research plan for healthy living [Special issue]. *APS Observer.*

Anderson, S., Cavanagh, J., Collins, C., Hartman, C., & Yeskel, F. (2000). *Executive excess 2000: Seventh annual CEO compensation survey.* Boston: United for a Fair Economy.

Anscombe, G. E. M. (1958). Modern moral philosophy. *Philosophy, 33,* 1–19.

Argyris, C. (1970). *Intervention theory and method.* Reading, MA: Addison-Wesley.

Argyris, C., & Schon, D. A. (1978). *Organizational learning.* Reading, MA: Addison-Wesley.

Arnold, D. W. (1990). Invasion of privacy: A rising concern for personnel psychologists. *The Industrial-Organizational Psychologist, 28*(2), 37–39.

Aronfreed, J. (1994). Moral development from the standpoint of a general psychological theory. In B. Puka (Ed.), *Moral development: A compendium.* (Vol. 1, pp. 170–185). New York: Garland.

Aronson, E., & Carlsmith, J. M. (1968). Experimentation in social psychology. In G. Lindzey & E. Aronson (Eds.), *Handbook of social psychology*, (rev. ed., Vol. 2, pp. 1–79). Reading, MA: Addison-Wesley.

Aronson, J., Quinn, D. M., & Spencer, S. J. (1998). Stereotype threat and the academic underperformance of women and minorities. In J. K. Swim & C. Stangor (Eds.), *Prejudice: The target's perspective* (pp. 83–103). San Diego: Academic.

Arrington, R. L. (1998). *Western ethics: An historical introduction*. Malden, MA: Blackwell.

Ashforth, B. E., & Humphrey, R. H. (1995). Emotion in the workplace: A reappraisal. *Human Relations, 48*, 97–125.

Aune, R. K., Metts, S., & Hubbard, A. S. E. (1998). Managing the outcomes of discovered deception. *The Journal of Social Psychology, 138*, 677–689.

Austin, J., & Villanova, P. (1992). The criterion problem. *Journal of Applied Psychology, 77*, 836–874.

Badaracco, J. L. (1998, March–April). The discipline of building character. *Harvard Business Review, 76*, pp. 115–124.

Baier, K. (1993). Egoism. In P. Singer (Ed.), *A companion to ethics* (pp. 197–204). Cambridge, MA: Blackwell.

Baker, D. B., & Benjamin, L. T. (2000). The affirmation of the scientist-practitioner: A look back at Boulder. *American Psychologist, 55*, 241–247.

Balkin, D. B., Markman, G. D., & Gomez-Mejia, L. R. (2000). Is CEO pay in high-technology firms related to innovation? *Academy of Management Journal, 43*, 1118–1129.

Ball-Rokeach, S. J., Rokeach, M., & Grube, J. (1984). *The great American values test: Influencing behavior and belief through television*. New York: The Free Press.

Bandura, A. (1986). *Social foundations of thought and action: A social cognitive theory*. Englewood Cliffs, NJ: Prentice-Hall.

Bandura, A. (1991). Social cognitive theory of moral thought and action. In W. M. Kurtines & J. L. Gewirtz (Eds.), *Handbook of moral behavior and development: Vol. 1. Theory* (pp. 45–103). Hillsdale, NJ: Lawrence Erlbaum Associates.

Barber, B. (1965). Some problems in the sociology of the professions. In K. S. Lynn (Ed.). *The professions in America* (pp. 15–34). Boston: Houghton Mifflin.

Bar-Hillel, M., & Yaari, M. (1993). Judgments of distributive justice. In B.A. Mellers & J. Baron (Eds.), *Psychological perspectives on justice: Theory and applications* (pp. 55–84). New York: Cambridge University Press.

Baritz, L. (1960). *The servants of power: A history of social science in American industry*. Westport, CT: Greenwood.

Barkema, H. C., & Gomez-Mejia, L. R. (1998). Managerial compensation and firm performance: A general research framework. *Academy of Management Journal, 41*, 135–145.

Barnett, T., & Vaicys, C. (2000). The moderating effect of individuals' perceptions of ethical work climate on ethical judgments and behavioral intentions. *Journal of Business Ethics, 27*, 351–362.

Baron, J. (1997). Biases in the quantitative measurement of values for public decisions. *Psychological Bulletin, 122*, 72–88.

Barry, B. (1989). *A treatise on social justice: Vol. 1. Theories of justice*. Berkeley, CA: University of California Press.

Barry, B., & Stephens, C. U. (1998). Objections to an objectivist approach to integrity. *Academy of Management Review, 23*, 162–169.

Bartels, L. K., Harrick, E., Martell, K., & Strickland, D. (1998). The relationship between ethical climate and ethical problems within human resource management. *Journal of Business Ethics, 17*, 799–804.

Bass, B. M., & Steidlmeier, P. (1999). Ethics, character, and authentic transformational leadership behavior. *Leadership Quarterly, 10*, 181–217.

Batson, C. D. (1989). Personal values, moral principles, and a three-path model of prosocial motivation. In N. Eisenberg, J. Reykowski, & E. Staub (Eds.), *Social and moral values: Individual and societal perspectives* (pp. 213–228). Hillsdale, NJ: Lawrence Erlbaum Associates.

Baucus, M. S., & Baucus, D. A. (1997). Paying the piper: An empirical examination of longer-term financial consequences of illegal corporate behavior. *Academy of Management Journal, 40,* 129–151.

Bauer, R., & Fee, D. H., Jr. (1972). *The corporate social audit.* New York: Russell Sage Foundation.

Baumeister, R. F., Stillwell, A. M. N., & Heatherton, T. F. (1994). Guilt: An interpersonal approach. *Psychological Bulletin, 115,* 243–267.

Baumrind, D. (1985). Research using intentional deception: Ethical issues revisited. *American Psychologist, 40,* 165–174.

Bazerman, M. H., Messick, D. M., Tenbrunsel, A. E., & Wade-Benzoni, K. A. (Eds.). (1997). *Environment, ethics, and behavior: The psychology of environmental valuation and degradation.* San Francisco: New Lexington.

Beauchamp, T. L., & Childress, J. F. (1994). *Principles of biomedical ethics* (4th ed.). New York: Oxford University Press.

Bebchuk, L. A., Fried, J. M., & Walker, D. I. (2002). *Managerial power and rent extraction in the design of executive compensation.* (NBER Working Paper No. w9068). Cambridge, MA: National Bureau of Economic Research.

Bebeau, M. J. (1994). Influencing the moral dimensions of dental practice. In J. R. Rest & D. Narvaez (Eds.), *Moral development in the professions* (pp. 121–146). Hillsdale, NJ: Lawrence Erlbaum Associates.

Becker, T. E. (1998). Integrity in organizations: Beyond honesty and conscientiousness. *Academy of Management Review, 23,* 154–161.

Beer, M., & Walton, A. E. (1987). Organization change and development. *Annual Review of Psychology, 38,* 339–367.

Belar, C. D. (2000). Scientist Practitioner ≠ Science + Practice. *American Psychologist, 55,* 249–250.

Bell, R. (1985). Professional values and organizational decision making. *Administration & Society, 17,* 21–60.

Belman, D. (1992). Unions, the quality of labor relations, and firm performance. In L. Mishel & P. B. Voos (Eds.), *Unions and economic competitiveness* (pp. 41–107). Armonk, NY: M. E. Sharpe.

Benjamin, L. T., Jr. (2001). American psychology's struggles with its curriculum: Should a thousand flowers bloom? *American Psychologist, 56,* 735–742.

Benjamin, L. T., Jr. (2002). Revisiting psychology's core curriculum. *American Psychologist, 57,* 454–455.

Benjamin, L. T., Jr., & Crouse, E. M. (2002). The American Psychological Association's response to *Brown v. Board of Education:* The case of Kenneth B. Clark. *American Psychologist, 57,* 38–50.

Bennett, B. E., Bryant, B. K., VandenBos, G. R., & Greenwood, A. (1990). *Professional liability and risk management.* Washington, DC: American Psychological Association.

Berenson, A. (2002, June 29). Tweaking numbers to meet goals comes back to haunt executives. *The New York Times,* pp. A1, C3.

Berg, J. (1993). How could ethics depend on religion? In P. Singer (Ed.), *A companion to ethics* (pp. 525–533). Cambridge, MA: Blackwell.

Berle, Jr., A. A. (1954). *The 20th century capitalist revolution.* New York: Harcourt, Brace and World.

Berle, A. A., Jr., & Means, G. C. (1932). *The modern corporation and private property.* New York: Macmillan.

Bernoulli, D. (1954). Exposition of a new theory on the measurement of risk. *Econometrica*, 22, 23–36. (Original work published 1738)

Bernstein, J., Boushey, H., McNichol, E., & Zahradnick, R. (2002). *Pulling apart: A state-by-state analysis of income trends*. Washington, DC: Center on Budget and Economic Priorities & Economic Policy Institute.

Bersoff, D. N. (1995). *Ethical conflicts in psychology*. Washington, DC: American Psychological Association.

Beu, D., & Buckley, M. R. (2001). The hypothesized relationship between accountability and ethical behavior. *Journal of Business Ethics, 34*, 57–73.

Bevan, W. (1980). On getting in bed with a lion. *American Psychologist, 35*, 779–789.

Bisson, J. I., & Deahl, M. P. (1994). Psychological debriefing and prevention of post-traumatic stress: More research is needed. *British Journal of Psychiatry, 165*, 717–720.

Blackburn, R. T., & Fox, T. G. (1983). Physicians' values and their career stage. *Journal of Vocational Behavior, 22*, 159–173.

Blakeney, R., Broenen, R., Dyck, J., Frank, B., Glenn, D., Johnson, D., & Mayo, C. (2002). Implications of the results of a job analyses of I–O psychologists. *The Industrial–Organizational Psychologist, 39*, 29–37.

Blanck, P. D., Bellak, A. S., Rosnow, R. L., Rotheram-Borus, M. J., & Schooler, N. R. (1992). Scientific rewards and conflicts of ethical choices in human subjects research. *American Psychologist, 47*, 959–965.

Blasi, A. (1980). Bridging moral cognition and moral action: A critical review of the literature. *Psychological Bulletin, 88*, 1–45.

Bledstein, B. J. (1976). *The culture of professionalism: The middle class and the development of higher education in America*. New York: Norton.

Bloom, M. (1999). The performance effects of pay dispersion on individuals and organizations. *Academy of Management Journal, 42*, 25–40.

Blum, L. (1987). Particularity and responsiveness. In J. Kagan & S. Lamb (Eds.), *The emergence of morality in young children* (pp. 306–337). Chicago: University of Chicago Press.

Blumenthal, R. G. (2000, September 4). Capitalist plot? The pay gap between workers and chiefs looks like a chasm. *Barron's*, p. 10.

Blustein, D. L. (2001). Extending the reach of vocational psychology: Toward an inclusive and integrative psychology of working. *Journal of Vocational Behavior, 59*, 171–182.

Boehm, V. (1980). Research in the "real world": A conceptual model. *Personnel Psychology, 33*, 495–503.

Bok, S. (1989). *Secrets*. New York: Pantheon.

Bolin, A., & Heatherly, L. (2001). Predictors of employee deviance: The relationship between bad attitudes and bad behavior. *Journal of Business and Psychology, 15*, 405–418.

Bolinger, D. (1982). *Language: The loaded weapon*. London: Longman.

Bolton, B. (1980). Second-order dimensions of the Work Values Inventory (WVI). *Journal of Vocational Behavior, 17*, 33–40.

Bommer, M., Gratto, C., Gravander, J., & Tuttle, M. (1987). A behavioral model of ethical and unethical decision making. *Journal of Business Ethics, 6*, 265–280.

Bond, C. F., Jr., & Atoum, A. O. (2000). International deception. *Personality and Social Psychology Bulletin, 26*, 385–395.

Boruch, R. F. (1971). Maintaining confidentiality of data in educational research: A systemic analysis. *American Psychologist, 26*, 413–430.

Boruch, R. F., & Cecil, J. S. (1982). Statistical strategies for preserving privacy in direct inquiry. In J. E. Sieber (Ed.). *The ethics of social research: Surveys and experiments* (pp. 207–232). New York: Springer-Verlag.

Bowen, D. B. (1977). Value dilemmas in organization development. *Journal of Applied Behavioral Science, 13*, 543–556.

Boyd, D. (1994). The character of moral development. In B. Puka (Ed.), *Moral development: A compendium* (Vol. 6, pp. 449–477). New York: Garland.

Boyle, B. A., Dahlstrom, R. F., & Kellaris, J. J. (1998). Points of reference and individual differences as sources of bias in ethical judgments. *Journal of Business Ethics, 17,* 517–525.

Bradley, F. H. (1935). *Ethical studies* (2nd ed.). Oxford, England: Clarendon.

Braithewaite, V. A., & Law, H. G. (1985). Structure of human values: Testing the adequacy of the Rokeach Value Survey. *Journal of Personality and Social Psychology, 49,* 250–263.

Bramel, D., & Friend, R. (1981). Hawthorne, the myth of the docile worker, and class bias in psychology. *American Psychologist, 36,* 867–878.

Brandeis, L. D. (1971). *Business—A profession.* New York: Kelley. (Original work published 1914)

Bredemeier, B. J. L., & Shields, D. L. L. (1994). Applied ethics and moral reasoning in sport. In J. R. Rest & D. Narvaez (Eds.), *Moral development in the professions* (pp. 173–188). Hillsdale, NJ: Lawrence Erlbaum Associates.

Brief, A., Dukerich, J. M., & Doran, L. I. (1991). Resolving ethical dilemmas in management: Experimental investigations of values, accountability, and choice. *Journal of Applied Social Psychology, 21,* 380–396.

Brien, A. (1998). Professional ethics and the culture of trust. *Journal of Business Ethics, 17,* 391–409.

Britton, B. K. (1979). Ethical and educational aspects of participating as a subject in psychology experiments. *Teaching of Psychology, 6,* 195–198.

Brockner, J., Konovsky, M., Cooper-Schneider, R., Folger, R., Martin, C., & Bies, R. (1994). Interactive effects of procedural justice and outcome negativity on victims and survivors of job loss. *Academy of Management Journal, 37,* 397–409.

Brody, J. L., Gluck, J. P., & Aragon, A. S. (1997). Participants' understanding of the process of psychological research: Informed consent. *Ethics & Behavior, 7,* 285–298.

Brody, J. L., Gluck, J. P., & Aragon, A. S. (2000). Participants' understanding of the process of psychological research: Debriefing. *Ethics & Behavior, 10,* 13–25.

Broder, A. (1998). Deception can be acceptable. *American Psychologist, 53,* 805–806.

Bronner, E. (2001, July 15). Posner v. Dershowitz: A famous judge and a famous lawyer scrutinize the Supreme court's role in the presidential election. *The New York Times Book Review,* 11–12.

Bronowski, J. (1960). *The common sense of science.* Middlesex, England: Penguin.

Brooks, J. N. (1966). *The great leap: The past twenty-five years in America.* New York: Harper & Row.

Brown, D., & Crace, R. K. (1996). Values in life role choices and outcomes: A conceptual model. *Career Development Quarterly, 44,* 211–223.

Buckle, S. (1993). Natural law. In P. Singer (Ed.), *A companion to ethics* (pp. 161–174). Cambridge, MA: Blackwell.

Burton, B. K., & Dunn, C. P. (1996). Feminist ethics as moral grounding for stakeholder theory. *Business Ethics Quarterly, 6,* 133–147.

Business & Society. (2000). Revisiting corporate social performance [Special issue]. *39, 4.*

Cameron, L. D., Brown, P. M., & Chapman, J. G. (1998). Social value orientations and decisions to take proenvironmental action. *Journal of Applied Social Psychology, 28,* 675–697.

Campbell, D. T., Boruch, R. F., Schwartz, R. D., & Steinberg, J. (1977). Confidentiality-preserving modes of access to files and to interfile exchange for useful statistical analysis. *Evaluation Quarterly, 1,* 269–300.

Campbell, J. P. (1990). The role of theory in industrial and organizational psychology. In M. D. Dunnette & L. M. Hough (Eds.), *Handbook of industrial and organizational psychology* (2nd ed., Vol. 1, pp. 39–73). Palo Alto, CA: Consulting Psychologists Press.

Campbell, J. P., Daft, R. L., & Hulin, C. L. (1982). *What to study: Generating and developing research questions.* Beverly Hills: Sage.

Campion, M. A. (1996). Why I'm proud to be an I/O psychologist. *The Industrial–Organizational Psychologist, 34*(1), 27–29.

Campion, M. A., Adams, E. F., Morrison, R. F., Spool, M. D., Tornow, W. W., & Wijting, J. P. (1986). I/O psychology research conducted in nonacademic settings and reasons for nonpublication. *The Industrial-Organizational Psychologist, 24*(1), 40–43.

Canadian Psychological Association. (2000). *Canadian code of ethics for psychologists,* (3rd ed.). Ottawa, Canada: Author.

Canter, M. B., Bennett, B. E., Jones, S. E., & Nagy, T. F. (1994). *Ethics for psychologists: A commentary on the APA ethics code.* Washington, DC: American Psychological Association.

Caprara, G. V., Barbaranelli, C., Pastorelli, C., Bandura, A., & Zimbardo, P.G. (2000). Prosocial foundations of children's academic achievement. *Psychological Science, 11,* 302–306.

Carlson, D. S., & Perrewe, P. L. (1995). Institutionalization of organizational ethics through transformational leadership. *Journal of Business Ethics, 14,* 829–838.

Carlson, R. (1971). Where is the person in personality research? *Psychological Bulletin, 75,* 203–219.

Carroll, A. B. (1987). In search of the moral manager. *Business Horizons, 30*(2), 7–16.

Carroll, A. B. (1991). CSP measurement: A commentary for methods for evaluating an illusive construct. In J. E. Post (Ed.), *Research in corporate social performance and policy* (Vol. 12, pp. 385–401). Greenwich, CT: JAI.

Carroll, A. B. (1999). Corporate social responsibility: Evolution of a definitional construct. *Business & Society, 38,* 268–295.

Carruth, R. (1999). Regional market integration in the transatlantic marketplace. *Business & Society, 38,* 402–414.

Carter, R. T. (1991). Cultural values: A review of empirical research and implications for counseling. *Journal of Counseling & Development, 70,* 164–173.

Carter, R. T., Gushue, G. V., & Weitzman, L. M. (1994). White racial identity development and work values. *Journal of Vocational Behavior, 44,* 185–197.

Cascio, W. F. (1993). Downsizing: What do we know? What have we learned? *Academy of Management Executive, 7,* 95–104.

Cascio, W. F. (1995). Whither industrial and organizational psychology in a changing world of work? *American Psychologist, 50,* 928–939.

Cascio, W. F. (1998). Learning from outcomes: Financial experiences of 311 firms that have downsized. In M. K. Gowing, J. D. Kraft, & J. C. Quick, (Eds.), *The new organizational reality: Downsizing, restructuring, and revitalization* (pp. 55–70). Washington, DC: American Psychological Association.

Cascio, W. F. (2002). Strategies for responsible restructuring. *Academy of Management Executive, 16,* 80–91.

Cascio, W. F., Young, C. E., & Morris, J. R. (1997). Financial consequences of employment-change decisions in major U.S. corporations. *Academy of Management Journal, 40,* 1175–1189.

Cassel, D. (2001). Human rights and business responsibilities in the global marketplace. *Business Ethics Quarterly, 11,* 261–274.

Castro, B. (Ed.). (1996). *Business and society: A reader in the history, sociology, and ethics of business.* New York: Oxford University Press.

Cavanagh, G. F. (1984). *American business values* (2nd ed.). Englewood Cliffs, NJ: Prentice-Hall.

Champion, R. (1985). The importance of Popper's theories to psychology. *American Psychologist, 40,* 1415–1417.

Chandler, R. C. (2001). Deontological dimensions of administrative ethics revisited. In T.L. Cooper (Ed.), *Handbook of administrative ethics* (2nd ed., pp. 179–193). New York: Marcel Dekker.

Chapman, A. D. (1981). Value-orientation analysis: The adaptation of an anthropological model for counseling research. *Personnel and Guidance Journal, 59,* 637–642.

Chastain, G., & Landrum, R. E. (Eds.). (1999). *Protecting human subjects: Departmental subject pools and institutional review boards.* Washington, DC: American Psychological Association.

Chia, A., & Mee, L. S. (2000). The effects of issue characteristics on the recognition of moral issues. *Journal of Business Ethics, 27,* 255–269.

Childress, C. A., & Asamen, J. K. (1998). The emerging relationship of psychology and the internet: Proposed guidelines for conducting internet intervention research. *Ethics & Behavior, 8,* 19–35.

Choi, I., Nisbett, R. E., & Norenzayan, A. (1999). Causal attribution across cultures: Variation and universality. *Psychological Bulletin, 125,* 47–63.

Christensen, L. (1988). Deception in psychological research: When is its use justified? *Personality and Social Psychology Bulletin, 14,* 664–675.

Church, A. H., & Burke, W. W. (1992). Assessing the activities and values of organization development practitioners. *The Industrial–Organizational Psychologist, 30,* 59–66.

Church, A. H., Burke, W. W., & Van Eynde, D. F. (1994). Values, motives, and interventions of organization development practitioners. *Group and Organization Management, 19,* 5–50.

Chusmir, L. H., & Parker, B. (1991). Gender and situational differences in managers' lives: A look at work and home lives. *Journal of Business Research, 23,* 325–335.

Ciulla, J. B. (Ed.). (1998). *Ethics, the heart of leadership.* Westport, CT: Praeger.

Clarkson Centre for Business Ethics, University of Toronto. (1999). *Principles of stakeholder management: The Clarkson principles.* Toronto: Author.

Clarkson Centre for Business Ethics, University of Toronto. (2000). *Research in stakeholder theory, 1997–1998: The Sloan Foundation minigrant project.* Toronto: Author.

Clay, R. A. (2000). Why every private practitioner needs a business plan. *Monitor on Psychology, 31,* 48–49.

Clymer, A. (1999, September 9). Sharp divergence found in views of military and civilians. *The New York Times,* p. A.20.

Coghlan, D., & Brannick, T. (2000). *Doing action research in your own organization.* Thousand Oaks, CA: Sage.

Cohen, R. (2000, October 15). The ethicist: Fair or foul? *The New York Times Magazine,* p. 48.

Cohen, R. (2001, September 23). The ethicist: Blood ties. *The New York Times Magazine,* pp. 30–31.

Cohen, R. (2002, April 8). The politics of ethics. *The Nation, 274,* 21–23.

Colby, A., & Kohlberg, L. (1987). The measurement of moral judgment (Vols. 1 & 2). New York: Cambridge University Press.

Cole, D., Sirgy, M. J., & Bird, M. M. (2000). How do managers make teleological evaluations in ethical dilemmas? Testing part of and extending the Hunt–Vitell model. *Journal of Business Ethics, 26,* 259–269.

Coles, R. (1997). *The moral intelligence of children.* New York: Penguin Group.

Collins, C., Hartman, C., & Sklar, H. (1999). *Divided decade: Economic disparity at the century's turn.* Boston: United for a Fair Economy.

Collins, D. (1989). Organizational harm, legal condemnation and stakeholder retaliation: A typology, research agenda and application. *Journal of Business Ethics, 8,* 1–13.

Colquitt, J. A. (2001). On the dimensionality of organizational justice: A construct validation of a measure. *Journal of Applied Psychology, 86,* 386–400.

Colquitt, J. A., Conlon, D. E., Wesson, M. J., Porter, C. O. L. H., & Ng, K. Y. (2001). Justice at the millennium: A meta-analytic review of 25 years of organizational justice research. *Journal of Applied Psychology, 86,* 425–445.

Colvin, A. J. S., Batt, R., & Katz, H. C. (2001). How high performance human resource practices and workforce unionization affect managerial pay. *Personnel Psychology, 54,* 903–934.

Comte-Sponville, A. (2001). *A small treatise on the great virtues: The uses of philosophy in everyday life.* New York: Metropolitan Books/Henry Holt.

Connor, A. (2001). From brain researcher to social scientist, they all answer to "psychologist." *APS Observer, 14*(1), 1, 8–9, 11.

Cooke, R. A., & Rousseau, D. M. (1988). Behavioral norms and expectations. *Group and Organization Studies, 13,* 245–273.

Cooper, C. L., & Locke, E. A. (Eds.). (2000). *Industrial and organizational psychology: Linking theory with practice.* Oxford, England: Blackwell.

Cooper, T. L. (1998). *The responsible administrator: An approach to ethics for the administrative role* (4th ed.). San Francisco: Jossey-Bass.

Cooper, T. L. (Ed.). (2001). *Handbook of administrative ethics.* New York: Dekker.

Copleston, F. (1994). *A history of philosophy: Vol. V. Modern philosophy: The British philosophers from Hobbes to Hume.* New York: Doubleday.

Coulter, X. (1986). Academic value of research participation by undergraduates. *American Psychologist, 41,* 317.

Cragg, W. (2000). Human rights and business ethics: Fashioning a new social contract. *Journal of Business Ethics, 27,* 205–214.

Cropanzano, R. (1993). *Justice in the workplace: Approaching fairness in human resource management.* Hillsdale, NJ: Lawrence Erlbaum Associates.

Cropanzano, R., Byrne, Z. S., Bobocel, D. R., & Rupp, D. E. (2001). Moral virtues, fairness heuristics, social entities, and other denizens of organizational justice. *Journal of Vocational Behavior, 58,* 164–209.

Cropanzano, R., & Randall, M.L. (1993). Injustice and work behavior: A historical review. In R. Cropanzano (Ed.), Justice in the workplace: Approaching fairness in human resource management (pp. 3–20). Hillsdale, NJ: Lawrence Erlbaum Associates.

Crystal, G. S. (1991). *In search of excess: The overcompensation of American executives.* New York: Norton.

Cunningham, P. J., Grossman, J. M., St. Peter, R. F., & Lesser, C. S. (1999). Managed care and physicians' provision of charity care. *Journal of the American Medical Association, 281,* 1087–1092.

Dalai Lama. (1999). *Ethics for the new millennium.* New York: Riverhead.

Dalton, G. (1974). *Economic systems and society.* Kingsport, TN: Kingsport.

Dalziel, J. R. (1996). Students as research subjects: Ethical and educational issues. *Australian Psychologist, 31,* 119–123.

Damasio, A. R., Harrington, A., Kagan, J., McEwen, B. S., Moss, H., & Shaikh, R. (Eds.). (2001). *Unity of knowledge: The convergence of natural and human science* (Vol. 935). New York: Annals of the New York Academy of Sciences.

Damon, W. (1999). The moral development of children. *Scientific American, 281,* 72–79.

Danley, J. R. (1994). *The role of the modern corporation in a free society.* Notre Dame, IN: University of Notre Dame Press.

Danley, J. R. (2000). Philosophy, science and business ethics: Frederick's new normative synthesis. *Journal of Business Ethics, 26,* 111–122.

D'Aquilla, J., & Bean, D. (2000). Does a tone at the top that fosters ethical decisions impact financial reporting decisions?: An experimental analysis. Seventh International Conference Promoting Business Ethics, September, 21–23. *Proceedings, 1,* 81–89.

Darley, J. M., Messick, D. M., & Tyler, T. R. (2001). *Social influences on ethical behavior in organizations.* Mahwah, NJ: Lawrence Erlbaum Associates.

Davenport, K. (2000). Corporate citizenship: A stakeholder approach for defining corporate social performance and identifying measures for assessing it. *Business & Society, 39,* 210–219.

Davison, G. (1995). The ethics of confidentiality: Introduction. *Australian Psychologist, 30,* 153–157.

Davidson, R. E. (1985). Professional conflicts within organizations. *Sociology and Social Research, 69,* 210–220.

Davis, M. (1994). *Empathy: A social–psychological approach.* Madison, WI: Brown & Benchmark.

Davis, N. A. (1993). Contemporary deontology. In P. Singer (Ed.), *A companion to ethics* (pp. 205–218). Cambridge, MA: Blackwell.

Dawis, R. V. (1991). Vocational interests, values, and preferences. In M. D. Dunnette & L. M. Hough (Eds.), *Handbook of industrial & organizational psychology,* (Vol. 2, pp. 833–871). Palo Alto, CA: Consulting Psychologists Press.

Dawis, R. V., & Lofquist, L. H. (1984). *A psychological theory of work adjustment.* Minneapolis: University of Minnesota Press.

Deal, T. E., & Kennedy, A. A. (1999). *The new corporate cultures: Revitalizing the workplace after downsizing, mergers, and reengineering.* Cambridge, MA: Perseus.

Deci, E. L., & Ryan, R. M. (1991). Intrinsic motivation and self-determination in human performance. In R. M. Steers & L. W. Porter (Eds.), *Motivation and work behavior* (5th ed., pp. 44–58). New York: McGraw-Hill.

Dees, J. G., & Cramton, P. C. (1995). Deception and mutual trust: A reply to Strudler. *Business Ethics Quarterly, 5,* 823–832.

DeForest, M. (1994). Thinking of a plant in Mexico? *Academy of Management Executive, 8,* 33–40.

DeGeorge, R. (1987). The status of business ethics: Past and future. *Journal of Business Ethics, 6,* 201–212.

DeLeon, L. (1994). The professional values of public managers, policy analysts and politicians. *Public Personnel Management, 23,* 135–152.

DePaulo, B. M., Charlton, K., Cooper, H., Lindsay, J. J., & Muhlenbruck, L. (1997). The accuracy–confidence correlation in the detection of deception. *Personality and Social Psychology Review, 1,* 346–357.

Derber, C. (1998). *Corporation nation: How corporations are taking over our lives and what we can do about it.* New York: St. Martin's Griffin.

Dessler, G. (1999). How to earn your employees' commitment. *Academy of Management Executive, 13,* 58–67.

Deutsch, M. (1969). Socially relevant science: Reflections on some studies of interpersonal conflict. *American Psychologist, 24,* 1076–1092.

Deutsch, M. (1975). Equity, equality, and need: What determines which value will be used as the basis of distributive justice? *Journal of Social Issues, 31,* 137–149.

Deutsch, M. (1985). *Distributive justice.* New Haven, CT: Yale University Press.

De Waal, F. (1996). *Good natured: The origins of right and wrong in humans and other animals.* Cambridge, MA: Harvard University Press.

Dewey, J. (1939). *Theory of valuation.* Chicago: University of Chicago Press.

Diener, E., & Crandall, R. (1978). *Ethics in social and behavioral research.* Chicago: University of Chicago Press.

Dillon, S. (2001, February 15). Profits raise pressures on U.S.-owned factories in Mexican border zone. *The New York Times,* p. A16.

DiNorcia, V. (1996). Environmental and social performance. *Journal of Business Ethics, 15,* 773–784.

DiNorcia, V., & Tigner, J. (2000). Mixed motives and ethical decisions in business. *Journal of Business Ethics, 25,* 1–13.

Dobrin, A. (1993). *Being good and doing right: Readings in moral development.* Lanham, MD: University Press of America.

Donaldson, T. (1982). *Corporations and morality.* Englewood Cliffs, NJ: Prentice-Hall.

Donaldson, T. (1989). *The ethics of international business.* New York: Oxford University Press.

Donaldson, T., & Dunfee, T. W. (1994). Toward a unified conception of business ethics: Integrative social contracts theory. *Academy of Management Review, 19,* 252–284.

Donaldson, T., & Preston, L. E. (1995). The stakeholder theory of the corporation: Concepts, evidence, and implications. *Academy of Management Review, 20,* 65–91.

Douglas, P. C., Davidson, R. A., & Schwartz, B. N. (2001). The effect of organizational culture and ethical orientation on accountants' ethical judgments. *Journal of Business Ethics, 34,* 101–121.

Dubinsky, A. J., & Loken, B. (1989). Analyzing ethical decision making in marketing. *Journal of Business Research, 19,* 83–107.

Duckett, L. J., & Ryden, M. B. (1994). Education for ethical nursing practice. In J. R. Rest & D. Narvaez (Eds.), *Moral development in the professions* (pp. 51–70). Hillsdale, NJ: Lawrence Erlbaum Associates.

Duff, A., & Cotgrove, S. (1982). Social values and the choice of careers in industry. *Journal of Occupational Psychology, 55,* 97–107.

Dunfee, T. W. (1987). Work-related ethical attitudes: A key to profitability? In S. P. Sethi & C. M. Falbe (Eds.), *Business and society: Dimensions of conflict and cooperation* (pp. 292–310). Lexington, MA: Lexington.

Dunford, B. B., & Devine, D. J. (1998). Employment at-will and employee discharge: A justice perspective on legal action following termination. *Personnel Psychology, 51,* 903–934.

Dunkelberg, J., & Jessup, D. R. (2001). So then why did you do it? *Journal of Business Ethics, 29,* 51–63.

Dunnette, M. D. (1984, August). *I/O psychology in the 80s: Fads, fashions, and folderol revisited.* Paper presented at the 92nd Annual Conference of the American Psychological Association, Toronto.

Dunnette, M. D. (1990). Blending the science and practice of industrial and organizational psychology: Where are we and where are we going? In M. D. Dunnette & L. M. Hough (Eds.), (1990). *Handbook of industrial and organizational psychology* (2nd ed., Vol. 1, pp. 1–27). Palo Alto, CA: Consulting Psychologists Press.

Dunnette, M. D. (2001). Science and practice in applied psychology: A symbiotic relationship. *Applied Psychology: An International Review, 50,* 222–224.

Dunnette, M. D., & Hough, L. M. (Eds.). (1990). *Handbook of industrial and organizational psychology* (2nd ed., Vol. 1). Palo Alto, CA: Consulting Psychologists Press.

Dunnette, M. D., & Hough, L. M. (Eds.). (1991). *Handbook of industrial and organizational psychology* (2nd ed., Vol. 2). Palo Alto, CA: Consulting Psychologists Press.

Dunnette, M. D., & Hough, L. M. (Eds.). (1992). *Handbook of industrial and organizational psychology* (2nd ed., Vol. 3). Palo Alto, CA: Consulting Psychologists Press.

Durkheim, E. (1953). *Sociology and philosophy.* New York: The Free Press. (Original work published 1898)

Durkheim, E. (1956). *The division of labor in society.* New York: The Free Press. (Original work published 1893)

Dworkin, R. (1977). *Taking rights seriously.* Cambridge, MA: Harvard University Press.

Dyck, B., & Kleysen, R. (2001). Aristotle's virtues and management thought: An empirical exploration of an integrative pedagogy. *Business Ethics Quarterly, 11,* 561–574.

Earley, P. C., & Gibson, C. B. (1998). Taking stock in our progress on individualism–collectivism: 100 years of solidarity and community. *Journal of Management, 24,* 265–304.

Eckensberger, L. H., & Zimba, R. F. (1997). The development of moral judgment. In J. W. Berry, P. R. Dasen, & T. S. Saraswathi (Eds.), *Handbook of cross-cultural psychology* (Vol. 2, pp. 299–338). Boston: Allyn & Bacon.

Edwards, C. P. (1987). Culture and the construction of moral values: A comparative ethnography of moral encounters in two cultural settings. In J. Kagan & S. Lamb (Eds.), *The emergence of morality in young children* (pp. 123–151). Chicago: University of Chicago Press.

Edwards, C. P. (1993). Culture and the construction of moral values: A comparative ethnography of moral encounters in two cultural settings. In A. Dobrin (Ed.), *Being good and doing right: Readings in moral development* (pp. 93–120). Lanham, MD: University Press of America.

Edwards, J. T., Nalbandian, J., & Wedel, K. R. (1981). Individual values and professional education: Implications for practice and education. *Administration & Society, 13*, 123–143.

Edwards, R. (1993). *Rights at work: Employment relations in the post-union era.* Washington, DC: Brookings Institution.

Ehrenberg, R. G., Brewer, D. J., Gamoran, A., & Willms, J. D. (2001). Class size and student achievement. *Psychological Science in the Public Interest, 2*, 1–30.

Eichenwald, K. (2002a, January 13). Audacious climb to success ended in a dizzying plunge. *The New York Times*, p. A1, A26.

Eichenwald, K. (2002b, February 3). Enron panel finds inflated profits and self-dealing. *The New York Times*, p. A1, A27.

Eisenberg, N., & Miller, P. A. (1987). Empathy, sympathy and altruism: empirical and conceptual links. In N. Eisenberg & J. Strayer (Eds.), *Empathy and its development* (pp. 292–316). Cambridge, England: Cambridge University Press.

Eisenberg, N., Reykowski, J., & Staub, E. (1989). Introduction. In N. Eisenberg, J. Reykowski, & E. Staub (Eds.), *Social and moral values: Individual and societal perspectives* (pp. xi– xv). Hillsdale, NJ: Lawrence Erlbaum Associates.

Eiser, J. R. (1987). *The expression of attitude.* New York: Springer-Verlag.

Elizur, D. (1984). Facets of work values: A structural analysis of work outcomes. *Journal of Applied Psychology, 69*, 379–389.

Elizur, D., & Sagie, A. (1999). Facets of personal values: A structural analysis of life and work values. *Applied Psychology: An International Review, 48*, 73–87.

Elliott, P. (1972). *The sociology of the professions.* New York: Herder and Herder.

Ellis, A. (1992). Do I really hold that religiousness is irrational and equivalent to emotional disturbance? *American Psychologist, 47*, 428–429.

Emler, N., & Hogan, R. (1991). Moral psychology and public policy. In W. M. Kurtines & J. L. Gewirtz (Eds.), *Handbook of moral behavior and development: Vol. 3. Application* (pp. 69–93). Hillsdale, NJ: Lawrence Erlbaum Associates.

Engel, G. V. (1970). Professional autonomy and bureaucratic organization. *Administrative Science Quarterly, 15*, 12–21.

England, G. W. (1967). Personal value systems of American managers. *Academy of Management Journal, 10*, 53–68.

England, G. W., & Lee, R. (1974). The relationship between managerial values and managerial success in the United States, Japan, India, and Australia. *Journal of Applied Psychology, 59*, 411–419.

Epley, N., & Huff, C. (1998). Suspicion, affective response, and educational benefit as a result of deception in psychology research. *Personality and Social Psychology Bulletin, 24*, 759–768.

Epstein, E. M. (1999). The continuing quest for accountable, ethical, and humane corporate capitalism: An enduring challenge for social issues in management in the new millennium. *Business & Society, 38*, 253–267.

Epstein, S. (1989). Values from the perspective of cognitive–experiential self-theory. In N. Eisenberg, J. Reykowski, & E. Staub (Eds.), *Social and moral values: Individual and societal perspectives* (pp. 3–22). Hillsdale, NJ: Lawrence Erlbaum Associates.

Equal Employment Opportunity Commission, Civil Service Commission, Department of Labor, and Department of Justice. (1978, August 25). Uniform guidelines on employee selection procedures. *Federal Register, 43*(166), p. 38290–38315.

Erikson, E. H. (1964). The golden rule in the light of new insight. In E. H. Erikson (Ed.), *Insight and responsibility: Lectures on the ethical implications of psychoanalytic insight* (pp. 219–243). New York: Norton.

Ermann, M. D., & Lundman, R. J. (Eds.). (1996). *Corporate and governmental deviance: Problems of organizational behavior in contemporary society* (5th ed.). New York: Oxford University Press.

Etzioni, A. (Ed.). (1969). *The semi-professions and their organization.* New York: The Free Press.

Etzioni, A. (1996). *The new golden rule: Community and morality in a democratic society.* New York: Basic Books.

Executive compensation scoreboard. (2000, April 17). *Business Week*, pp.114–142.

Eyde, L. D. (2000). Other responsibilities to participants. In B. D. Sales & S. Folkman (Eds.), *Ethics in research with human participants* (pp. 61–73). Washington, DC: American Psychological Association.

Eyde, L. D., & Quaintance, M. K. (1988). Ethical issues and cases in the practice of personnel psychology. *Professional Psychology: Research and Practice, 19*, 148–154.

Eyde, L. D., Robertson, G. J., Krug, S. E., Moreland, K. L., Robertson, A. G., Shewan, C. M., Harrison, P. L., Porch, B. E., Hammer, A. L., & Primoff, E. S. (1993). *Responsible test use: Case studies for assessing human behavior.* Washington, DC: American Psychological Association.

Falkenberg, L., & Herremans, I. (1995). Ethical behaviours in organizations: Directed by the formal or informal systems? *Journal of Business Ethics, 14*, 133–143.

Feather, N. T. (1982). Reasons for entering medical school in relation to value priorites and sex of student. *Journal of Occupational Psychology, 55*, 119–128.

Feather, N. T. (1992). Values, valences, expectations and actions. *Journal of Social Issues, 48*, 109–124.

Feinberg, J. (1984). *Harm to others: The moral limits of the criminal law.* New York: Oxford University Press.

Feinberg, M. R., & Lefkowitz, J. (1962). Image of industrial psychology among corporate executives. *American Psychologist, 17*, 109–111.

Ferguson, L. W. (1962–1965). *The heritage of industrial psychology* (14 pamphlets). Hartford, CT: Finlay.

Feyerabend, P. K. (1963). How to be a good empiricist—A plea for tolerance in matters epistemological. In B. Baumrin (Ed.), *Philosophy of science: The Delaware seminar.* (Vol. 2, pp. 3–41). New York: Wiley.

Feyerabend, P. K. (1975). *Against method.* London: Redwood Barn.

Fieser, J. (1996). Do businesses have moral obligations beyond what the law requires? *Journal of Business Ethics, 15*, 457–468.

Finkel, N. J., & Groscup, J. L. (1997). When mistakes happen: Commonsense rules of culpability. *Psychology, Public Policy, and Law, 3*, 65–125.

Finkel, N. J., Watanabe, H., & Crystal, D. S. (2001). Commonsense notions of unfairness in Japan and the United States. *Psychology, Public Policy, and Law, 7*, 345–380.

Fish, J. M. (2000). What anthropology can do for psychology: Facing physics envy, ethnocentrism, and a belief in "race." *American Anthropologist, 102*, 552–563.

Fisher, C. B., & Fryberg, D. (1994). Participant partners: College students wight the costs and benefits of deceptive research. *American Psychologist, 49*, 417–427.

Fisher, S. R., & White, M. A. (2000). Downsizing in a learning organization: Are there hidden costs? *Academy of Management Review, 25*, 244–251.

Fishman, D. B. (1999). *The case for pragmatic psychology*. New York: New York University Press.

Fletcher, J. (1966). *Situation ethics: The new morality*. Philadelphia,: Westminster.

Folger, R. (2001). Fairness as deonance. In S. Gilliland, D. Steiner, & D. Skarlicki (Eds.), *Theoretical and cultural perspectives on organizational justice* (pp. 3–33). Greenwich, CT: Information Age Publishing.

Folger, R., & Lewis, D. (1993). Self-appraisal and fairness in evaluations. In R. Cropanzano (Ed.), *Justice in the workplace: Approaching fairness in human resource management* (pp. 107–131). Hillsdale, NJ: Lawrence Erlbaum Associates.

Folkman, S. (2000). Privacy and confidentiality. In B. D. Sales & S. Folkman (Eds.), *Ethics in research with human participants* (pp. 49–58). Washington, DC: American Psychological Association.

Forbes top CEOs: Corporate America's most powerful people. (2001). *Forbes Magazine* [online serial]. Available: http://www.forbes.com/CEOS

Ford, J. (2001). Call for papers. Academy of Management Review special topic forum. Language and organization. *Academy of Management Review, 26*, 328–330.

Ford, R. C., & Richardson, W. D. (1994). Ethical decision making: A review of the empirical literature. *Journal of Business Ethics, 13*, 205–221.

Forsyth, D. R. (1992). Judging the morality of business practices: the influence of personal moral philosophies. *Journal of Business Ethics, 11*, 461–470.

Fountain, J. W. (2002 January 5). On an icy night, little room at the shelter. *The New York Times*, pp. A1, A9.

Fowler, J. W. (1981). *Stages of faith: The psychology of human development and the quest for meaning*. San Francisco: HarperSanFrancisco.

Fox, H. R., & Spector, P. E. (2002). Occupational health psychology: I–O psychologists meet with interdisciplinary colleagues to discuss this emerging field. *The Industrial–Organizational Psychologist, 39*, 139–142.

Franke, G. R., Crown, D. F., & Spake, D. F. (1995). Gender differences in ethical perceptions of business practices: A social role theory perspective. *Journal of Applied Psychology, 82*, 920–934.

Frankena, W. K. (1973). *Ethics*, (2nd ed.). Englewood Cliffs, NJ: Prentice-Hall.

Fraser, J. A. (2001). *White-collar sweatshop: The deterioration of work and its rewards in corporate America*. New York: Norton.

Frazer, M. J., & Kornhauser, A. (1986). *Ethics and social responsibility in science education*. Oxford: Pergamon.

Frederick, W. C. (1995). *Values, nature, and culture in the American corporation*. New York: Oxford University Press.

Frederick, W. C. (1999). An Appalachian coda: The core values of business. *Business & Society, 38*, 206–211.

Freeman, E. (1984). *Strategic management: A stakeholder approach*. Boston: Pitman.

Freeman, R. B. (1996, September–October). Toward an apartheid economy? *Harvard Business Review, 74*, 114–121.

Freeman, R. E. ,& Phillips, R. A. (2002). Stakeholder theory: A libertarian defense. *Business Ethics Quarterly, 12*, 331–349.

Freidson, E. (1973). Professions and the occupational principle. In E. Freidson (Ed.), *The professions and their prospects* (pp. 19–38). Beverly Hills: Sage.

Freidson, E. (1986). *Professional powers: A study of the institutionalization of formal knowledge*. Chicago: University of Chicago Press.

French, W., & Weis, A. (2000). An ethics of care or an ethics of justice. *Journal of Business Ethics, 27*, 125–136.

Freudenheim, M. (2001, July 11). In a shift, an H.M.O. rewards doctors for quality care. *The New York Times*, pp. C1, C4.

Frey, B. F. (2000). The impact of moral intensity on decision making in a business context. *Journal of Business Ethics, 26*, 181–195.

Friedlander, F., & Brown, L. D. (1974). Organization development. *Annual Review of Psychology, 25*, 313–341.

Friedman, H. (2002). Psychological nescience in a postmodern context. *American Psychologist, 57*, 462–463.

Friedman, M. (1970, September 13). The social responsibility of business is to increase its profits. *The New York Times Magazine*, 32–33, 122, 124, 126.

Friedman, M. (1982). *Capitalism and freedom*, (2nd ed.). Chicago: Chicago University Press.

Friedman, T. L. (2000). *The lexus and the olive tree*. New York: Anchor Books.

Friedman, T. L. (2002, July 28). In oversight we trust. *The New York Times*, Section 4, p. 13.

Fritz, J. M. H., Arnett, R. C., & Conkel, M. (1999). Organizational ethical standards and organizational commitment. *Journal of Business Ethics, 20*, 289–299.

Fritzsche, D. J. (1995). Personal values: Potential keys to ethical decision-making. *Journal of Business Ethics, 14*, 909–922.

Fritzsche, D. J., & Becker, H. (1984). Linking management behavior to ethical philosophy—An empirical investigation. *Academy of Management Journal, 27*, 166–175.

Fudge, R. S., & Schlacter, J. L. (1999). Motivating employees to act ethically: An expectancy theory approach. *Journal of Business Ethics, 18*, 295–304.

Furedy, J. J., & Furedy, C. (1982). Socratic versus sophistic strains in the teaching of undergraduate psychology: Implicit conflicts made explicit. *Teaching of Psychology, 9*, 14–20.

Gambino, R. (1973, November–December). Watergate lingo: A language of non-responsibility. *Freedom at Issue*, 7–9, 15–17.

Gardner, H. (2002, February 22). Good work, well done: A psychological study. *The Chronicle of Higher Education*, Section 2, B7–B9.

Gardner, H., Csikszentmihalyi, M., & Damon, W. (2001). *Good work: When excellence and ethics meet*. New York: Basic Books.

Geertz, C. (1973). *The interpretation of cultures*. New York: Basic Books.

Gellermann, W., Frankel, M. S., & Ladenson, R. F. (1990). *Values and ethics in organization and human systems development: Responding to dilemmas in professional life*. San Francisco: Jossey-Bass.

Gelman, R., & Baillargeon, R. (1983). A review of some Piagetian concepts. In J. H. Flavell & E. M. Markman (Eds.), *Handbook of child psychology. Vol. 3: Cognitive development* (pp. 167–230). New York: Wiley.

George, J. M., & Jones, G. R. (1996). The experience of work and turnover intentions: Interactive effects of value attainment, job satisfaction, and positive mood. *Journal of Applied Psychology, 81*, 318–325.

Gerard, H. B. (1983). School desegregation: The social science role. *American Psychologist, 38*, 869–877.

Gergen, K. J. (1985). The social constructionist movement in modern psychology. *American Psychologist, 40*, 266–275.

Gergen, K. J. (1992). Social construction and moral action. In D. N. Robinson (Ed.), *Social discourse and moral judgment*. (pp. 9–27). San Diego: Academic.

Gergen, K. J. (1994). Exploring the postmodern: Perils or potentials? *American Psychologist, 49*, 412–416.

Gergen, K. J. (2001). Psychological science in a postmodern context. *American Psychologist, 56*, 803–813.

Gergen, K. J. (2002). Psychological science: To conserve or create? *American Psychologist, 57*, 463–464.

Gergen, K. J., Gulerce, A., Lock, A., & Misra, G. (1996). Psychological science in cultural context. *American Psychologist, 51*, 496–503.

Gewirtz, J. L. (1972). Some contextual determinants of stimulus potency. In R. D. Parke (Ed.), *Recent trends in social learning theory* (pp. 7–33). New York: Academic.

Giacobbe-Miller, J. (1995). A test of the group values and control models of procedural justice from the competing perspectives of labor and management. *Personnel Psychology, 48*, 115–142.

Giacobbe-Miller, J. K., Miller, D. J., & Victorov, V. I. (1998). A comparison of Russian and U.S. pay allocation decisions, distributive justice judgments, and productivity under different payment conditions. *Personnel Psychology, 51*, 137–163.

Gibbs, J. C. (1991). Toward an integration of Kohlberg's and Hoffman's moral development theories. *Human Development, 34*, 88–104.

Gibson, K. (2000). The moral basis of stakeholder theory. *Journal of Business Ethics, 26*, 245–257.

Gillespie, R. (1988). The Hawthorne experiments and the politics of experimentation. In J. G. Morawski (Ed.), *The rise of experimentation in American psychology* (pp. 114–137). New Haven, CT: Yale University Press.

Gilliland, S., Steiner, D., & Skarlicki, D. (Eds.). (2001). *Theoretical and cultural perspectives on organizational justice*. Greenwich, CT: Information Age.

Gilligan, C. (1982). *In a different voice: Psychological theory and women's development*. Cambridge, MA: Harvard University Press.

Gilligan, C., & Wiggins, G. (1987). The origins of morality in early childhood relationships. In J. Kagan & S. Lamb (Eds.), *The emergence of morality in young children* (pp. 277–305). Chicago: University of Chicago Press.

Goldworth, A. (1996). Informed consent revisited. *Cambridge Quarterly of Healthcare Ethics, 5*, 214–220.

Gomez-Mejia, L. R., & Balkin, B. B. (1992). *Compensation, organizational strategy and firm performance*. Cincinnati, OH: Southwestern.

Goode, E. (1999, June 1). For good health, it helps to be rich and important. *The New York Times*, pp. A1, A9.

Goode, W. J. (1960). Encroachment, charlatanism, and the emerging profession: Psychology, sociology, and medicine. *American Sociological Review, 25*, 902–914.

Goode, W. J. (1969). The theoretical limits of professionalization. In A. Etzioni (Ed.), *The semi-professions and their organization* (pp. 266–313). New York: The Free Press.

Gooden, R. E. (1993). Utility and the good. In P. Singer (Ed.), *A companion to ethics*, pp. 241–248. Cambridge, MA: Blackwell.

Goodstein, L. D. (1983). Managers, values, and organization development. *Group and Organization Studies, 8*, 203–220.

Gordon, M. E., & Burt, R. E. (1981). A history of industrial psychology's relationship with American unions: Lessons from the past and directions for the future. *International Review of Applied Psychology, 30*, 137–156.

Gore, A. (1993). *From red tape to reality: Creating a government that works better and costs less* (Report of the National Performance Review). Washington, DC: U.S. Government Printing Office, No. 040-000-00592-7.

Gortner, H. F. (1991). *Ethics for public managers*. New York: Greenwood.

Gortner, H. F. (2001). Values and ethics. In T. L. Cooper (Ed.), *Handbook of administrative ethics* (2nd ed., pp. 509–528). New York: Marcel Dekker.

Gorusch, R. L., & Ortberg, J. (1983). Moral obligation and attitudes: Their relation to behavioral intentions. *Journal of Personality and Social Psychology, 44*, 1025–1028.

Gottschalk, P. (1993). Changes in inequality of family income in seven industrialized countries. *American Economic Review, 83*, 136–142.

Gould, S. J. (1981). *The mismeasure of man*. New York: Norton.

Gowing, M. K., Kraft, J. D., & Quick, J. C. (Eds.). (1998). *The new organizational reality: Downsizing, restructuring, and revitalization.* Washington, DC: American Psychological Association.

Grant, J. D., & Wagar, T. H. (1992). Willingness to take legal action in wrongful dismissal cases: Perceptual differences between men and women. *Perceptual and Motor Skills, 74,* 1073–1074.

Gray, J. (2000). *Two faces of liberalism.* New York: The New Press.

Greenberg, J., & Folger, R. (1988). *Controversial issues in social research methods.* New York: Springer-Verlag.

Greene, C. N. (1978). Identification modes of professionals: Relationship with formalization, role strain, and alienation. *Academy of Management Journal, 21,* 486–492.

Greene, J. D., Sommerville, R. B., Nystrom, L. E., Darley, J. M., & Cohen, J. D. (2001, September 14). An fMRI investigation of emotional engagement in moral judgment. *Science, 293,* 2105–2108.

Greenfield, P. M. (1997). You can't take it with you: Why ability assessments don't cross cultures. *American Psychologist, 52,* 1115–1124.

Greenhouse, L. (2001, March 22). Court says employers can require arbitration of disputes. *The New York Times,* pp. C1, C6.

Greenhouse, S. (1998, March 30). Equal work, less-equal perks: Microsoft leads the way in filling jobs with "permatemps." *The New York Times,* pp. D1, D6.

Greenhouse, S. (2002, June 25). Suits say Wal-Mart forces workers to toil off the clock. *The New York Times,* pp. A1, A18.

Greller, M. M. (1984). High earnings for I/O psychologists. *The Industrial–Organizational Psychologist, 21,* 55–58.

Griffin, M. A., & Kabanoff, B. (2001). Global vision: The psychology of safety. *The Industrial–Organizational Psychologist, 38,* 123–127.

Grimshaw, J. (1993). The idea of a female ethic. In P. Singer (Ed.), *A companion to ethics* (pp. 491–499). Cambridge, MA: Blackwell.

Gross, A. E., & Fleming, I. (1982). Twenty years of deception in social psychology. *Personality and Social Psychology Bulletin, 8,* 402–408.

Groves, B. W., Price, J. H., Olsson, R. H., & King, K. A. (1997). Response rates to anonymous versus confidential surveys. *Perceptual and Motor Skills, 85,* 665–666.

Guba, E. G., & Lincoln, Y. S. (1994). Competing paradigms in qualitative research. In N. K. Denzin & Y. S. Lincoln (Eds.), *Handbook of qualitative research* (pp. 105–117). Thousand Oaks, CA: Sage.

Guillen, M. F. (2001). Is globalization civilizing, destructive or feeble? A critique of five key debates in the social science literature. *Annual Review of Sociology, 27,* 235–260.

Guimond, S. (1995). Encounter and metamorphosis: The impact of military socialization on professional values. *Applied Psychology: An International Review, 44,* 251–275.

Guion, R. M. (1998). *Assessment, measurement, and prediction for personnel decisions.* Mahwah, NJ: Lawrence Erlbaum Associates.

Gummeson, E. (1999). *Qualitative methods in management research.* Thousand Oaks, CA: Sage.

Gunthorpe, D. L. (1997). Business ethics: A quantitative analysis of the impact of unethical behavior by publicly traded corporations. *Journal of Business Ethics, 16,* 537–543.

Guzzo, R. A., Jette, R. D., & Katzell, R. A. (1985). The effects of psychologically based intervention programs on worker productivity: A meta-analysis. *Personnel Psychology, 38,* 275–291.

Haas, L. J., & Maouf, J. L. (1995). *Keeping up the good work: A practitioner's guide to mental health ethics* (2nd ed.). Sarasota, FL: Professional Resource Press.

Haas, R. D. (1997). Business ethics. *Executive Excellence, 14*(6), 17.

Haber, S. (1991). *The quest for authority and honor in the American professions, 1750–1900.* Chicago: University of Chicago Press.

Habermas, J. (1990). *Moral consciousness and communicative action.* Cambridge, MA: MIT Press.

Hackman, J. R., & Oldham, G. R. (1980). *Work redesign.* Reading, MA: Addison-Wesley.

Hagstrom, W. O. (1965). *The scientific community.* New York: Basic Books.

Haidt, J. (2001). The emotional dog and its rational tail: A social intuitionist approach to moral judgment. *Psychological Review, 108,* 814–834.

Hakel, M. D. (1988). Introducing the American Psychological Society. *The Industrial- Organizational Psychologist, 26,* 22–24.

Hakel, M. D., Sorcher, M., Beer, M., & Moses, J. L. (1982). *Making it happen: Designing research with implementation in mind.* Beverly Hills: Sage.

Hall, D. T. (1996). Introduction: Long live the career—a relational approach. In D. T. Hall, & Associates (Eds.), *The career is dead—long live the career: A relational approach to careers* (pp. 1–12). San Francisco: Jossey-Bass.

Hall, D. T., & Associates. (Eds.). (1996). *The career is dead—long live the career: A relational approach to careers.* San Francisco: Jossey-Bass.

Hall, D. T., & Richter, J. (1990). Career gridlock: Baby boomers hit the wall. *Academy of Management Executive, 4,* 7–22.

Hall, R. T. (1975). *Occupations and the social structure* (2nd ed.). Englewood Cliffs, NJ: Prentice-Hall.

Hamner, W. C., & Smith, F. J. (1978). Work attitudes as predictors of unionization activity. *Journal of Applied Psychology, 63,* 415–421.

Hancock, P., & Tyler, M. (2001). *Work, postmodernism and organization.* Thousand Oaks, CA: Sage.

Handelsman, M. M. (1985, April). *Use, readability, and content of written informed consent for treatment.* Paper presented at the annual convention of the Rocky Mountain Psychological Association, Tucson, AZ.

Haney, C., Banks, W. C., & Zimbardo, P. G. (1973). Interpersonal dynamics in a simulated prison. *International Journal of Criminology and Penology, 1,* 69–97.

Hare, R. M. (1981). *Moral thinking.* Oxford, England: Oxford University Press.

Hare, R. M. (1993). Universal prescriptivism. In P. Singer (Ed.), *A companion to ethics* (pp. 451–463). Cambridge, MA: Blackwell.

Harrington, S. J. (1997). A test of a person–issue contingent model of ethical decision making in organizations. *Journal of Business Ethics, 16,* 363–375.

Harris, B. (1988). Key words: A history of debriefing in social psychology. In J. G. Morawski (Ed.), *The rise of experimentation in American psychology* (pp. 188–212). New Haven, CT: Yale University Press.

Harris, M. (1999). Practice network: Look, it's an I/O psychologist.... No, it's a trainer.... No, it's an executive coach! *The Industrial–Organizational Psychologist, 36,* 38–42.

Harris, R. J. (1993). Two insights occasioned by attempts to pin down the equity formula. In B. A. Mellers & J. Baron (Eds.), *Psychological perspectives on justice: Theory and applications* (pp. 32–54). New York: Cambridge University Press.

Harrison, J. S., & Fiet, J. O. (1999). New CEOs pursue their own self-interests by sacrificing stakeholder value. *Journal of Business Ethics, 19,* 301–308.

Harrison, L. E., & Huntington, S. P. (2000). *Culture matters: How values shape human progress.* New York: Basic Books.

Hart, D., Atkins, R., & Ford, D. (1998). Urban America as a context for the development of moral identity in adolescence. *Journal of Social Issues, 54,* 513–530.

Hart, D. K. (2001). Administration and the ethics of virtue: In all things, choose first for good character and then for technical expertise. In T. L. Cooper (Ed.), *Handbook of administrative ethics* (pp. 131–150). New York: Marcel Dekker.

Hartel, C. E. J. (1998). Vantage 2000: The consequences and distinctiveness of shiftwork. *The Industrial–Organizational Psychologist, 35,* 76–79.

Hartigan, J. A., & Wigdor, A. K. (1989). *Fairness in employment testing.* Washington, DC: National Academy Press.

Hartshorne, H., & May, M. A. (1928). *Studies in the nature of character.* New York: Macmillan.

Hatch, E. (1983). *Culture and morality: The relativity of values in anthropology.* New York: Columbia University Press.

Hazer, J. T. ,& Alvares, K. M. (1981). Police work values during organizational entry and assimilation. *Journal of Applied Psychology, 66,* 12–18.

Heinrich, C. U., & Borkenau, P. (1998). Deception and deception detection: The role of cross–modal inconsistency. *Journal of Personality, 66,* 687–712.

Heinze, D., Sibary, S., & Sikula, Sr., A. (1999). Relations among corporate social responsibility, financial soundness, and investment value in 22 manufacturing industry groups. *Ethics & Behavior, 9,* 331–347.

Herrera, C. D. (1997). A historical interpretation of deceptive experiments in American psychology. *History of the Human Sciences, 10,* 23–36.

Herzberg, F. (1966). *Work and the nature of man.* Cleveland, OH: World.

Herzberg, F., Mausner, B., & Snyderman, B. (1959). *The motivation to work.* New York: Wiley.

Hess, D. (2001). Regulating corporate social performance: A new look at social accounting, auditing, and reporting. *Business Ethics Quarterly, 11,* 307–330.

Hessen, R. (1979). *In defense of the corporation.* Stanford, CA: Hoover Institution.

Hewson, C. M., Laurent, D., & Vogel, C. M. (1996). Proper methodologies for psychological and sociological studies conducted via the internet. *Behavior Research Methods, Instruments & Computers, 28,* 186–191.

Highhouse, S. (1999). The brief history of personnel counseling in industrial–organizational psychology. *Journal of Vocational Behavior, 55,* 318–336.

Himmelstein, D. U., Woolhandler, S., Hellander, I., & Wolfe, S. M. (1999). Quality of care in investor-owned vs not-for-profit HMOs. *Journal of the American Medical Association, 282,* 159–163.

Hinings, C. R., Thibault, L., Slack, T., & Kikulis, L. M. (1996). Values and organizational structure. *Human Relations, 49,* 885–916.

Hirsch, F. (1976). *Social limits to growth.* Cambridge, MA: Harvard University Press.

Hoffman, M. L. (1977). Moral internalization: Current theory and research. In L. Berkowitz (Ed.), *Advances in experimental social psychology* (Vol. 10, pp. 86–133). New York: Academic.

Hoffman, M. L. (1983). Affective and cognitive processes in moral internalization. In E. T. Higgins, D. N. Rubie & W. W. Hartup (Eds.), *Social cognition and social development: A sociocultural perspective* (pp. 236–274). Cambridge, MA: Cambridge University Press.

Hoffman, M. L. (1988). Moral development. In M. H . Bornstein & M. E. Lamb (Eds.), *Developmental psychology: An advanced textbook* (pp. 497–548). Hillsdale, NJ: Lawrence Erlbaum Associates.

Hoffman, M. L. (1991). Commentary. *Human Development, 34,* 105–110.

Hofmann, S. G. (2002). More science, not less. *American Psychologist, 57,* 462.

Hofstede, G. (1980). *Culture's consequences: International differences in work-related values.* Beverly Hills: Sage.

Hofstede, G. (2001). *Culture's consequences: Comparing values, behaviors, institutions, and organizations across nations.* Thousand Oaks, CA: Sage.

Hofstede, G., Neuijen, B., Ohayv, D. D., & Sanders, G. (1990). Measuring organizational cultures: A qualitative and quantitative study across twenty cases. *Administrative Science Quarterly, 35,* 286–316.

Hofstede, G., & Spangenberg, J. (1987). Measuring individualism and collectivism at occupational and organizational levels. In C. Kagitcibasi (Ed.), *Growth and progress in cross-cultural psychology* (pp. 113–122). Lisse, Netherlands: Swets & Zeitlinger.

Hogan, J., Hogan, R., & Busch, C. M. (1984). How to measure service orientation. *Journal of Applied Psychology, 69,* 167–173.

Hollander, E. P. (1998). Ethical challenges in the leader–follower relationship. In J. B. Ciulla (Ed.), *Ethics, the heart of leadership* (pp. 49–61). Westport, CT: Praeger.

Hollingsworth, R. (1977). Effectiveness of debriefing. *American Psychologist, 32,* 780–782.

Holmes, D. S. (1976a). Debriefing after psychological experiments: I. Effectiveness of post-deception dehoaxing. *American Psychologist, 31,* 858–867.

Holmes, D. S. (1976b). Debriefing after psychological experiments: II. Effectiveness of post-deception desensitizing. *American Psychologist, 31,* 868–875.

Holmes, D. S. (1977). Valins's postdeception dehoaxing revisited. *American Psychologist, 32,* 385.

Holmes, S. A. (1996, November 18). Quality of life is up for many blacks, data say. *The New York Times,* pp. A1, B10.

Homans, G. C. (1949). The strategy of industrial sociology. *American Journal of Sociology, 54,* 330–337.

Hood, J. M. (1996). *The heroic enterprise: Business and the common good.* New York: The Free Press.

Hopkins, W. E., & Hopkins, S. A. (1999). The ethics of downsizing: Perceptions of rights and responsibilities. *Journal of Business Ethics, 18,* 145–156.

Horney, K. (1950). *Neurosis and human growth.* New York: Norton.

Hoshmand, L. T., & Polkinghorne, D. E. (1992). Redefining the science-practice relationship and professional training. *American Psychologist, 47,* 55–66.

Hosmer, L. T., & Masten, S. E. (1995). Ethics vs. economics: The issue of free trade with Mexico. *Journal of Business Ethics, 14,* 287–298.

Howard, A. (1995). *The changing nature of work.* San Francisco: Jossey-Bass.

Howard, G. S. (1985). The role of values in the science of psychology. *American Psychologist, 40,* 255–265.

Hughes, E. C. (1965). Professions. In K. S. Lynn (Ed.), *The professions in America* (pp. 1–14). Boston: Houghton Mifflin.

Hulin, C. (2001). Applied psychology and science: Differences between research and practice. *Applied Psychology: An International Review, 50,* 225–234.

Hultman, K. (1976). Values as defenses. *Personnel and Guidance Journal, 54,* 269–271.

Hume, D. (1978). *A treatise of human nature.* Oxford, U.K.: Oxford University Press.

Hunt, S. D., & Vitell, S. (1986). A general theory of marketing ethics. *Journal of Macromarketing, 6,* 5–16.

Huselid, M. A. (1995). The impact of human resource management practices on turnover, productivity, and corporate financial performance. *Academy of Management Journal, 38,* 635–672.

Husted, B. W. (2000). A contingency theory of corporate social performance. *Business & Society, 39,* 24–48.

Huszczo, G. E., Wiggins, J. G., & Currie, J. S. (1984). The relationship between psychology and organized labor: Past, present, and future. *American Psychologist, 39,* 432–440.

Ilgen, D. R. (1999). Teams embedded in organizations. *American Psychologist, 54,* 129–139.

Ilgen, D. R., & Bell, B. S. (2001a). Conducting industrial and organizational psychological research: Institutional review of research in work organizations. *Ethics & Behavior, 11,* 395–412.

Ilgen, D. R., & Bell, B. S. (2001b). Informed consent and dual purpose research. *American Psychologist, 56,* 1177.

International Personnel Management Association. (1990). *IPMA code of ethics.* Alexandria, VA: Author.

Jackson, J. P., Jr. (1998). Creating a consensus: Psychologists, the Supreme Court, and school desegregation, 1952–1955. *Journal of Social Issues, 54,* 143–177.

Jaffee, S., & Hyde, J. S. (2000). Gender differences in moral orientation: A meta-analysis. *Psychological Bulletin, 126,* 703–726.

James, K. (1993). The social context of organizational justice: Cultural, intergroup, and structural effects on justice behaviors and perceptions. In R. Cropanzano (Ed.), *Justice in the workplace: Approaching fairness in human resource management* (pp. 21–50). Hillsdale, NJ: Lawrence Erlbaum Associates.

James, W. (1907). *Pragmatism: A new name for some old ways of thinking.* New York: Longmans.

Janis, I. (1982). *Victims of groupthink* (2nd ed.). Boston: Houghton Mifflin.

Jansen, E., & Von Glinow, M. A. (1985). Ethical ambivalence and organizational reward systems. *Academy of Management Review, 10,* 814–822.

Jawahar, I. M., & McLaughlin, G. L. (2001). Toward a descriptive stakeholder theory: An organizational life cycle approach. *Academy of Management Review, 26,* 397–414.

Jehl, D. (2001, March 25). Regulations czar prefers new path. *The New York Times,* pp. A1, A28.

Jenkins, G. D., Jr., Mitra, A., Gupta, N., & Shaw, J. D. (1998). Are financial incentives related to performance? A meta-analytic review of empirical research. *Journal of Applied Psychology, 83,* 777–787.

Johnston, D. C. (1999, September 5). Gap between rich and poor found substantially wider. *The New York Times,* p. A16.

Johnston, D. C. (2001, February 14). Dozens of rich Americans join in fight to retain the estate tax. *The New York Times,* pp. A1, A26.

Jones, G. E., & Kavanagh, M. J. (1996). An experimental examination of the effects of individual and situational factors on unethical behavioral intentions in the workplace. *Journal of Business Ethics, 15,* 511–523.

Jones, H. B., Jr. (1995). The ethical leader: An ascetic construct. *Journal of Business Ethics, 14,* 867–874.

Jones, M. T. (1999). The institutional determinants of social responsibility. *Journal of Business Ethics, 20,* 163–179.

Jones, R., & Murrell, A. J. (2001). Signaling positive corporate social performance. *Business & Society, 40,* 59–78.

Jones, S. E. (2001). Ethics code draft published for comment. *Monitor on Psychology, 32*(2), 76–89.

Jones, T. M. (1991). Ethical decision-making by individuals in organizations: An issue-contingent model. *Academy of Management Review, 16,* 366–395.

Jones, T. M. (1995). Instrumental stakeholder theory: Synthesis of ethics and economics. *Academy of Management Review, 20,* 404–437.

Jordan, A. E., & Meara, N. M. (1990). Ethics and the professional practice of psychologists: The role of virtues and principles. *Professional Psychology: Research and Practice, 21,* 107–114.

Kagan, J. (1987). Introduction. In J. Kagan & S. Lamb (Eds.), *The emergence of morality in young children* (pp. ix–xx). Chicago: University of Chicago Press.

Kagle, J. D. (1998). Are we lying to ourselves about deception? *Social Service Review, 72,* 234–250.

Kahneman, D., Slovik, P., & Tversky, A. (1982). *Judgment under uncertainty: Heuristics and biases.* New York: Cambridge University Press.

Kalleberg, A. L. (2000). Nonstandard employment relations: Part-time, temporary and contract work. *Annual Review of Sociology, 26,* 341–365.

Kanfer, R. (2001). I/O psychology: Working at the basic-applied psychology interface. *Applied Psychology: An International Review, 50,* 235–240.

Kanner, A. D., & Kasser, T. (2000). Stuffing our kids: Should psychologists help advertisers manipulate children?, *The Industrial–Organizational Psychologist, 38,* 183–187.

Karp, D. G. (1996). Values and their effect on pro-environmental behavior. *Environment and Behavior, 28,* 111–133.

Katz, D. (1960). The functional approach to the study of attitudes. *Public Opinion Quarterly, 24,* 163–204.

Katz, D., & Kahn, R. (1978). *The social psychology of organizations* (2nd ed.). New York: Wiley.

Katzell, R. A. (1994). Contemporary meta-trends in industrial and organizational psychology. In H. C. Triandis, M. D. Dunnette, & L. M. Hough (Eds.), *Handbook of industrial and organizational psychology* (2nd ed., Vol. 4, pp. 1–89). Palo Alto, CA: Consulting Psychologists Press.

Katzell, R. A., & Austin, J. T. (1992). From then to now: The development of industrial- organizational psychology in the United States. *Journal of Applied Psychology, 77,* 803–835.

Kaufman, A., Zacharias, L., & Karson, M. (1995). *Managers vs. owners: The struggle for corporate control in American democracy.* New York: Oxford University Press.

Kaufman, L., & Gonzalez, D. (2001, April 24). Labor standards clash with global reality. *The New York Times,* pp. A1, A10.

Kecharananta, N., & Baker, H. G. (1999). Capturing entrepreneurial values. *Journal of Applied Social Psychology, 29,* 820–833.

Keeley, M. (1983). Values in organizational theory and management education. *Academy of Management Review, 8,* 376–386.

Kegan, R. (1993). The evolution of moral meaning-making. In A. Dobrin (Ed.), *Being good and doing right: Readings in moral development.* (pp. 15–35). New York: Latham.

Keister, L. A. (2000). *Trends in wealth inequality.* Cambridge, England: Cambridge University Press.

Keith-Spiegel, P. (1977). Violation of ethical principles due to ignorance or poor professional judgment versus willful disregard. *Professional Psychology: Research and Practice, 8,* 288–296.

Keith-Spiegel, P., & Koocher, G. P. (1985). *Ethics in psychology: Professional standards and cases.* New York: Random House.

Keith-Spiegel, P., & Whitley, Jr., B. E. (2001). Academic dishonesty [Special issue]. *Ethics & Behavior, 11*(3).

Kelly, Jr., E. W. (1995). Counselor values: A national survey. *Journal of Counseling and Development, 73,* 648–653.

Kelly, G. (1962). *The psychology of personal constructs.* New York: Norton.

Kelley, M. (1983). Values in organizational theory and management education. *Academy of Management Review, 8,* 376–386.

Kelman, H. C. (1970). Deception in social research. In N. K. Denzin (Ed.), *The values of social science* (pp. 65–86). Chicago: Aldine.

Kelman, H. C. (1972). The rights of the subject in social research: An analysis in terms of relative power and legitimacy. *American Psychologist, 27,* 989–1016.

Kendler, H. H. (1993). Psychology and the ethics of social policy. *American Psychologist, 48,* 1046–1053.

Kendler, H. H. (1999). The role of value in the world of psychology. *American Psychologist, 54,* 828–835.

Kennedy, A. A. (2000). *The end of shareholder value: Corporations at the crossroads.* Cambridge, MA: Perseus.

Kenrick, D. T., & Funder, D. C. (1988). Profiting from controversy: Lessons from the person-situation debate. *American Psychologist, 43,* 23–34.

Kessel, F. (1969). The philosophy of science as proclaimed and science as practiced: "Identity" or "dualism"? *American Psychologist, 24,* 999–1005.

Keynes, J. M. (1964). *The general theory of employment , interest, and money.* New York: Harcourt Brace Jovanovich. (Original work published 1935)

Kidder, R. M. (1995). *How good people make tough choices.* New York: Morrow.

Kifner, J. (2001, September 8). Scholar sets off gastronomic false alarm. *The New York Times*, pp. A1, B2.

Kimball, B. A. (1992). The "true professional ideal" in America. Cambridge, MA: Blackwell.

Kimble, G. A. (1984). Psychology's two cultures. *American Psychologist, 39*, 833–839.

Kimmel, A. J. (1988). *Ethics and values in applied social research*. Newbury Park, CA: Sage.

Kimmel, A. J. (1996). *Ethical issues in behavioral research: A survey*. Cambridge, MA: Blackwell.

Kimmel, A. J. (1998). In defense of deception. *American Psychologist, 53*, 803–805.

Kimmel, A. J. (2001). Ethical trends in marketing and psychological research. *Ethics & Behavior, 11*, 131–149.

Kimmel, A. J., & Smith, N. C. (2001). Deception in marketing research: Ethical, methodological, and disciplinary implications. *Psychology and Marketing, 18*, 663–689.

Kinnane, J. F., & Bannon, M. M. (1964). Perceived parental influence and work-value orientation. *Personnel and Guidance Journal, 43*, 273–279.

Kinnier, R. T. (1995). A reconceptualization of values clarification: values conflict resolution. *Journal of Counseling and Development, 74*, 18–24.

Kitchener, K. S. (1984). Intuition, critical evaluation and ethical principles: The foundation for ethical decisions in counseling psychology. *The Counseling Psychologist, 12*, 43–55.

Klein, E. (2001). Pro bono: What, why, and how? *The Industrial–Organizational Psychologist, 38*, 112–113.

Kleining, J. (1996). *The ethics of policing*. New York: Cambridge University Press.

Kluckhohn, C. (1951). Values and value orientations in the theory of action: An exploration in definition and classification. In T. Parsons & E. Shils (Eds.), *Toward a general theory of action* (pp. 388–433). Cambridge, MA: Harvard University Press.

Kluckhohn, F. R., & Strodtbeck, F. L. (1961). *Variations in value orientations*. Evanston, IL.: Row, Peterson.

Knapp, S. (1999). Utilitarianism and the ethics of professional psychologists. *Ethics & Behavior, 9*, 383–392.

Kohlberg, L. (1973). Continuities in childhood and adult moral development revisited. In P. B. Baltes & K. Schaie (Eds.), *Life-span developmental psychology: Personality and socialization* (pp. 179–204). New York: Academic.

Kohlberg, L. (1981). *Essays on moral development: Vol. 1. The philosophy of moral development: Moral stages and the idea of justice*. San Francisco: Harper and Row.

Kohlberg, L. (1984). *Essays on moral development: Vol. 2. The psychology of moral development*, San Francisco: Harper & Row.

Kohlberg, L., Levine, C., & Hewer, A. (1983). Moral stages: A current formulation and a response to critics. In J. A. Meacham (Ed.), *Contributions to human development*, (Vol. 10, p. 174). New York: Karger.

Kohlberg, L., & Ryncarz, R. A. (1990). Beyond justice reasoning: Moral development and consideration of a seventh stage. In C. N. Alexander & E. J. Langer (Eds.), *Higher stages of human development: Perspectives on adult growth* (pp. 191–207). New York: Oxford University Press.

Kok, P., van der Wiele, T., McKenna, R., & Brown, A. (2001). A corporate social responsibility audit within a quality management framework. *Journal of Business Ethics, 31*, 285–297.

Kolata, G. (2001, March 25). Researchers find big risk of defect in cloning animals. *The New York Times*, pp. A1, A14.

Koocher, G., & Keith-Spiegel, P. (1998). *Ethics in psychology: Professional standards and cases* (2nd ed.). New York: Oxford University Press.

Koppes, L. L. (2002). Using the jigsaw classroom to teach the history of I/O psychology and related topics. *The Industrial–Organizational Psychologist, 39*, 109–112.

Korman, A. K. (Ed.). (1994). *Human dilemmas in work organizations: Strategies for resolution*. New York: Guilford.

Korn, J. H. (1997). *Illusions of reality: A history of deception in social psychology.* Albany, NY: State University of New York Press.

Korn, J. H. (1998). The reality of deception. *American Psychologist, 53,* 805.

Korn, J. H., & Bram, D. R. (1988). What is missing in the method section of APA journal articles? *American Psychologist, 43,* 1091–1092.

Kornhauser, A. (1947). Industrial psychology as management technique and as social science. *American Psychologist, 2,* 224–229.

Kornhauser, A. (1949). *Psychology of labor-management relations.* Champaign, IL: Industrial Relations Research Association.

Kornhauser, W. (1962). *Scientists in industry.* Berkeley, CA: University of California Press.

Korten, D. C. (1995). *When corporations rule the world.* West Hartford, CT: Kumarian.

Korten, D. C. (1999). *The post-corporate world: Life after capitalism.* San Francisco: Berrett-Koehler.

Kossek, E. E., Roberts, K., Fisher, S., & Demarr, B. (1998). Career self-management: A quasi-experimental assessment of the effects of a training intervention. *Personnel Psychology, 51,* 935–962.

Kracher, B., & Wells, D. L. (1998). Employee selection and the ethic of care. In M. Schminke (Ed.), *Managerial ethics* (pp. 81–97). Mahwah, NJ: Lawrence Erlbaum Associates.

Kramer, R. M. (1999). Trust and distrust in organizations: Emerging perspectives, enduring questions. *Annual Review of Psychology, 30,* 569–598.

Krasner, L., & Houts, A. C. (1984). A study of the "value" systems of behavioral scientists. *American Psychologist, 39,* 840–849.

Krebs, D. L., Vermeulen, S. C. A., Carpendale, J. I., & Denton, K. (1991). Structural and situational influences on moral judgment: The interaction between stage and dilemma. In W. M. Kurtines & J. L. Gewirtz (Eds.),, *Handbook of moral behavior and development: Vol. 2. Research* (pp. 139–169). Hillsdale, NJ: Lawrence Erlbaum Associates.

Kristiansen, C. M., & Zanna, M. P. (1988). Justifying attitudes by appealing to values: A functional perspective. *British Journal of Social Psychology, 27,* 247–256.

Kristiansen, C. M., & Zanna, M. P. (1994). The rhetorical use of values to justify social and intergroup attitudes. *Journal of Social Issues, 50,* 47–65.

Kronzon, S., & Darley, J. (1999). Is this tactic ethical? Biased judgments of ethics in negotiation. *Basic and Applied Social Psychology, 21,* 49–60.

Krueger, J. I. (2002). Postmodern parlor games. *American Psychologist, 57,* 461–462.

Kruger, D. J. (2002). The deconstruction of constructivism. *American Psychologist, 57,* 456–457.

Kruglanski, A. W. (1975). The human subject in the psychology experiment: Fact and artifact. In L. Berkowitz (Ed.), *Advances in experimental social psychology* (Vol. 8, pp. 101–147). New York: Academic.

Krugman, P. (1994). *The age of diminished expectations.* Cambridge, MA: MIT Press.

Krugman, P. (2001, December 11). Laissez not fair. *The New York Times,* p. A27.

Krugman, P. (2002, June 4). Greed is bad. *The New York Times,* p. A19.

Krupat, E., & Garonzik, R. (1994). Subjects' expectations and the search for alternatives to deception in social psychology. *British Journal of Social Psychology, 33,* 211–222.

Kuhn, T. (1970). The structure of scientific revolutions (2nd ed.). *International encyclopedia of unified science: Foundations for the unity of science, Vol. 2.* Chicago: University of Chicago Press.

Kuhn, T. (1977). *The essential tension.* Chicago: University of Chicago Press.

Kuhn, T. (1996). *The structure of scientific revolutions* (3rd ed.). Chicago: University of Chicago Press.

Kuhn, T. (2000). *The road since structure.* Chicago: University of Chicago Press.

Kurzynski, M. J. (1998). The virtue of forgiveness as a human resource management strategy. *Journal of Business Ethics, 17,* 77–85.

Kymlicka, W. (1993). The social contract tradition. In P. Singer (Ed.), *A companion to ethics* (pp. 186–196). Cambridge, MA: Blackwell.

Landy, F. J., Barnes, J. L., & Murphy, K. R. (1978). Correlates of perceived fairness and accuracy of performance evaluation. *Journal of Applied Psychology, 63,* 751–754.

Latham, G. (2000). The reciprocal effects of science on practice: Insights from the practice and science of goal setting. *Canadian Psychology, 42,* 1–11.

Latham, G. (2001). The reciprocal transfer of learning from journals to practice. *Applied Psychology: An International Review, 50,* 201–211.

Lavelle, L. (2000, October 16). CEO pay: The more things change …. *Business Week,* Issue 3703, 106–108.

Lawler, E. E., III, Mohrman, A. M., Jr., Mohrman, S. A., Ledford, G. E., Jr., & Cummings, T. G. (Eds.). (1985). *Doing research that is useful for theory and practice.* San Francisco: Jossey-Bass.

Lawrence, P. R., & Lorsch, J. W. (1969). *Organization and environment: Managing differentiation and integration.* Homewood, IL: Irwin.

Lawson, E. (2001). Informational and relational meanings of deception: Implications for deception methods in research. *Ethics & Behavior, 11,* 115–130.

Lazarus, R. S., & Cohen-Charash, Y. (2001). Discrete emotions in organizational life. In R. L. Payne & G. L. Cooper (Eds.), *Emotions at work: Theory, research and applications for management* (pp. 45–81). Chichester, England: Wiley.

Lear, R. W. (2000). Compensation obscenity. *Chief Executive, 14,* p. 14.

Lederman, L. C. (1992). Debriefing: Toward a systematic assessment of theory and practice. *Simulation & Gaming, 23,* 145–160.

Lee, J. (2001, February 21). Discarded dreams of dot-com rejects. *The New York Times,* p. C1.

Lefkowitz, J. (1990). The scientist–practitioner model is not enough. *The Industrial–Organizational Psychologist, 28*(1), 47–52.

Lefkowitz, J. (2000). The role of interpersonal affective regard in supervisory performance ratings: A literature review and proposed causal model. *Journal of Occupational and Organizational Psychology, 73,* 67–85.

Lefkowitz, J., & Gebbia, M. (1997). The "shelf-life" of a test validation study: A survey of expert opinion. *Journal of Business and Psychology, 11,* 381–397.

Lefkowitz, J., Gebbia, M. I., Balsam, T., & Dunn, L. (1999). Dimensions of biodata items and their relationships to item validity. *Journal of Occupational and Organizational Psychology 72,* 331–350.

Leonhardt, D. (2001a, April 1). Executive pay: A special report. *The New York Times,* Sec. 3, pp. 1, 8.

Leonhardt, D. (2001b, April 1). Leaving shareholders in the dust. *The New York Times,* Sec. 3, pp. 1, 9.

Leonhardt, D. (2002a, February 10). How will Washington read the signals?: The race is on for tougher regulation of business. *The New York Times,* pp. C1, C13.

Leonhardt, D. (2002b, April 7). Did pay incentives cut both ways? *The New York Times,* Section 3, pp. 1, 6, 7.

Lerman, D. L., & Mikesell, J. J. (1988). Rural and urban poverty: An income/net worth approach. *Policy Studies Review, 7,* 765–781.

Lerner, M. J. (Ed.). (1975). The justice motive in social behavior [Special issue]. *Journal of Social Issues, 31*(3).

Levin, R. C., Mitchell, G. J., Volcker, P. A., & Will, G. F. (2000 July). *The report of the independent members of the commissioner's blue ribbon panel on baseball economics.* Major League Baseball.

Levine, J. M., & Moreland, R. L. (1990). Progress in small group research. *Annual Review of Psychology, 41,* 585–634.

Lewis, C. W. (1991). *The ethics challenge in public service: A problem-solving guide.* San Francisco: Jossey-Bass.

Lickona, T. (1994). Research on Piaget's theory of moral development. In B. Puka (Ed.), *Fundamental research in moral development* (Vol. 2, pp. 321–342). New York: Garland.

Lilienthal, D. (1953). *Big business: A new era.* New York: Harper.

Lindsay, R. C. L., & Adair, J. G. (1990). Do ethically recommended research procedures influence the perceived ethicality of social psychological research? *Canadian Journal of Behavioural Science, 22,* 282–294.

Lipartito, K. J., & Miranti, P. J. (1998). Professions and organizations in twentieth century America. *Social Science Quarterly, 79,* 301–320.

Lipsey, M. W. (1974). Research and relevance: A survey of graduate students and faculty in psychology. *American Psychologist, 29,* 541–553.

Litz, R. A. (1998). Self-deception and corporate social responsibility: A microlevel conception. *Research in Corporate Social Performance and Policy, 15,* 125–143.

Loch, K. D., Conger, S., & Oz, E. (1998). Ownership, privacy and monitoring in the workplace: A debate on technology and ethics. *Journal of Business Ethics, 17,* 653–663.

Locke, E. A. (Ed.). (1986). Generalizing from laboratory to field settings: Research findings from industrial–organizational psychology, organizational behavior, and human resource management. Lexington, MA: Lexington.

Locke, E. A. (1988). The virtue of selfishness. *American Psychologist, 43,* 481.

Locke, E. A. (2002). The dead end of postmodernism. *American Psychologist, 57,* 458.

Locke, E. A., & Becker, T. (1998). Rebuttal to a subjectivist critique of an objectivist approach to integrity in organizations. *Academy of Management Review, 23,* 170–175.

Locke, E. A., & Woiceshyn, J. (1995). Why businessmen should be honest: The argument from rational egoism. *Journal of Organizational Behavior, 16,* 405–414.

Locke, J. (1988). Two treatises of government. In P. Laslett (Ed.), *Two treatises of government* (pp. 141–428). New York: Cambridge University Press. (Original work published 1689)

Loe, T. W., Ferrell, L., & Mansfield, P. (2000). A review of empirical studies assessing ethical decision making in business. *Journal of Business Ethics, 25,* 185–204.

London, M. (Ed.). (1995). *Employees, careers, and job creation: Developing growth-oriented human resource strategies and programs.* San Francisco: Jossey-Bass.

London, M. (1996). Redeployment and continuous learning in the 21st century: Hard lessons and positive examples from the downsizing era. *Academy of Management Executive, 10,* 67–78.

London, M., & Bray, D. W. (1980). Ethical issues in testing and evaluation for personnel decisions. *American Psychologist, 35,* 890–901.

Lounsbury, M. (2002). Institutional transformation and status mobility: The professionalization of the field of finance. *Academy of Management Journal, 45,* 255–266.

Lowman, R. L. (1991). Ethical human resources practice in organizational settings. In D. Bray and Associates. (Eds.), *Working with organizations and their people: A guide to human resources practice* (pp. 194–218). New York: Guilford.

Lowman, R. L. (1993a). Counseling and psychotherapy of work dysfunctions. Washington, DC: American Psychological Association.

Lowman, R. L. (1993b). An ethics code for I/O psychology: For what purpose and at what cost? *The Industrial–Organiztional Psychologist, 31*(1), 90–92.

Lowman, R. L. (Ed.). (1998). *The ethical practice of psychology in organizations.* Washington, DC: American Psychological Association.

Lublin, J. S. (1999, April 8). Lowering the bar. *The Wall Street Journal,* p. R1.

Lueptow, L., Mueller, S. A., Hammes, R. R., & Masters, L. S. (1977). The impact of informed consent regulations on response rate and response bias. *Sociological Methods and Research, 6,* 183–204.

Luria, S. E. (1976). Biological aspects of ethical principles. *Journal of Medicine and Philosophy, 1,* 332–336.

Luttwak, E. (1999). *Turbo-capitalism: Winners and losers in the global economy.* New York City: HarperCollins.

Lynn, K. S. (Ed.). (1965). *The professions in America.* Boston: Houghton Mifflin.

MacCoun, R. J. (1998). Biases in the interpretation and use of research results. *Annual Review of Psychology, 49,* 259–287.

Maclagan, P. (1998). *Management and morality.* London: Sage.

Mael, F. A. (1991). A conceptual rationale for the domain and attributes of biodata items. *Personnel Psychology, 44,* 763–792.

Mael, F. A., Waldman, D. A., & Mulqueen, C. (2001). From scientific work to organizational leadership: Predictors of management aspiration among technical personnel. *Journal of Vocational Behavior, 59,* 132–148.

Mahoney, M. J. (1976). *Scientist as subject: The psychological imperative.* Cambridge, MA: Ballinger.

Maio, G. R., Roese, N. H., Seligman, C., & Katz, A. (1996). Rankings, ratings, and the measurement of values: Evidence for the superior validity of ratings. *Basic and Applied Social Psychology, 18,* 171–181.

Manicas, P. T., & Secord, P. E. (1983). Implications for psychology of the new philosophy of science. *American Psychologist, 38,* 399–413.

Mann, T. (1994). Informed consent for psychological research: Do subjects comprehend consent forms and understand their legal rights? *Psychological Science, 5,* 140–143.

Mappes, T. A., & Zembaty, J. S. (1997). (Eds.), *Social ethics: Morality and social policy,* (5th ed.). New York: McGraw-Hill.

Marshall, B., & Dewe, P. (1997). An investigation of the components of moral intensity. *Journal of Business Ethics, 16,* 521–530.

Martin, R. L. (2002, March). The virtue matrix: Calculating the return on corporate responsibility. *Harvard Business Review, 80*(3), 69–75.

Martinez, S. M., & Dorfman, P. W. (1998). The Mexican entrepreneur: An ethnographic study of the Mexican empresario. *International Studies of Management and Organization, 28,* 91–124.

Maslow, A. H. (1969). Toward a humanistic biology. *American Psychologist, 24,* 724–735.

Maslow, A. H. (1998). *Toward a psychology of being* (3rd ed.). New York: Wiley.

Mason, E. S., & Mudrack, P. E. (1997). Are individuals who agree that corporate social responsibility is a "fundamentally subversive doctrine" inherently unethical? *Applied Psychology: An International Review, 16,* 135–152.

Mattick, P. (2000, March 26). You've got an attitude. Review of "On the Emotions" by Richard Wollheim. *The New York Times,* Book Review Section, Vol. 149, p. 28.

May, D. R., & Pauli, K. P. (2002). The role of moral intensity in ethical decision making. *Business & Society, 41,* 84–117.

May, K. (1998). Work in the 21st Century: The role of I/O in work–life programs. *The Industrial–Organizational Psychologist, 36,* 79–82.

Mayer-Sommer, A. P., & Roshwald, A. (1996). An examination of the relationship between ethical behavior, espoused ethical values, and financial performance in the U.S. defense industry: 1988–1992. *Journal of Business Ethics, 15,* 1249–1274.

Mays, V. M. (2000). A social justice agenda. *American Psychologist, 55,* 326–327.

McAndrew, F. T. (2002). New evolutionary perspectives on altruism: Multilevel-selection and costly-signaling theories. *Current Directions in Psychological Science, 11,* 79–82.

McCabe, D. M. (1997). Alternative dispute resolution and employee voice in nonunion employment: An ethical analysis of organizational due process procedures and mechanisms—The case of the United States. *Journal of Business Ethics, 16,* 349–356.

McCall, Jr., M. W., & Bobko, P. (1990). Research methods in the service of discovery. In M. D. Dunnette & L. M. Hough (Eds.), *Handbook of industrial and organizational psychology* (2nd ed., Vol. 1, pp. 381–418). Palo Alto, CA: Consulting Psychologists Press.

McCullough, M. E., Kilpatrick, S. D., Emmons, R. A., & Larson, D. B. (2001). Is gratitude a moral affect? *Psychological Bulletin, 127*, 249–266.

McDonald, G., & Pak, P. C. (1996). It's all fair in love, war, and business: Cognitive philosophies in ethical decision making. *Journal of Business Ethics, 15*, 973–996.

McDonough, W. J. (1996, September–October). The challenge to U.S. business. *Harvard Business Review, 74*(5), 125.

McElroy, J. C., Morrow, P. C., & Rude, S. N. (2001). Turnover and organizational performance: A comparative analysis of the effects of voluntary, involuntary, and reduction-in-force turnover. *Journal of Applied Psychology, 86*, 1294–1299.

McGuire, J. B., Sundgren, A., & Schneeweis, T. (1988). Corporate social responsibility and firm financial performance. *Academy of Management Journal, 31*, 854–872.

McGuire, M. T., & Troisi, A. (1990). Deception. *International Journal of Contemporary Sociology, 27*, 75–87.

McKillip, J., & Owens, J. (2000). Voluntary professional certifications: Requirements and validation activities. *The Industrial–Organizational Psychologist, 38*, 50–57.

McKinley, W., Zhao, J., & Rust, K. G. (2000). A sociocognitive interpretation of organizational downsizing. *Academy of Management Review, 25*, 227–243.

McMillan, G. S. (1996). Corporate social investments: Do they pay? *Journal of Business Ethics, 15*, 309–314.

McNamara, J. R., & Woods, K. M. (1977). Ethical considerations in psychological research: A comparative review. *Behavior Therapy, 8*, 703–708.

Meara, N. M. (2001). Just and virtuous leaders and organizations. *Journal of Vocational Behavior, 58*, 227–234.

Meglino, B. M., & Ravlin, E. C. (1998). Individual values in organizations: Concepts, controversies, and research. *Journal of Management, 24*, 351–389.

Mellers, B. A. (2000). Choice and the relative pleasure of consequences. *Psychological Bulletin, 126*, 910–924.

Mellers, B. A., & McGraw, A. P. (2001). Anticipated emotions as guides to choice. *Current Directions in Psychological Science, 10*, 210–214.

Mellers, B. A ., Schwartz, A., Ho, K., & Ritov, I. (1997). Decision affect theory: Emotional reactions to the outcomes of risky options. *Psychological Science, 8*, 423–429.

Melton, G. B. (1988). When scientists are adversaries, do participants lose? *Law and Human Behavior, 12*, 191–198.

Meltzer, H., & Stagner, R. (1980). Industrial organizational psychology: 1980 overview. Epilogue. *Professional Psychology, 11*, 543–546.

Menges, R. J. (1973). Openness and honesty versus coercion and deception in psychological research. *American Psychologist, 28*, 1030–1034.

Merton, R. K. (1973). *The sociology of science: Theoretical and empirical investigations.* Chicago: University of Chicago Press.

Messick, D. M., & Cook, K. S. (Eds.). (1983). *Equity theory: Psychological and sociological perspectives.* New York: Praeger.

Messick, D. M. (1993). Equality as a decision heuristic. In B.A. Mellers & J. Baron (Eds.), *Psychological perspectives on justice: Theory and applications* (pp. 11–31). New York: Cambridge University Press.

Messick, S. (1980). Test validity and the ethics of assessment. *American Psychologist, 35*, 1012–1027.

Messick, S. (1995). Validity of psychological assessment: Validation of inferences from persons' responses and performances as scientific inquiry into score meaning. *American Psychologist, 50*, 741–749.

Miceli, M. P., Van Scotter, J. R., Near, J. P., & Rehg, M. T. (2001). Responses to perceived organizational wrongdoing: Do perceiver characteristics matter? In J. M. Darley, D. M.

Messick, & T. R. Tyler (Eds.), *Social influences on ethical behavior in organizations* (pp. 119–135). Mahwah, NJ: Lawrence Erlbaum Associates.

Milgram, S. (1963). Behavioral study of obedience. *Journal of Abnormal and Social Psychology, 67,* 371–378.

Milgram, S. (1964). Issues in the study of obedience: A reply to Baumrind. *American Psychologist, 19,* 849.

Milgram, S. (1974). *Obedience to authority.* New York: Harper & Row.

Miller, D. T. (1999). The norm of self-interest. *The American Psychologist, 54,* 1053–1060.

Miller, G. A. (1969). Psychology as a means of promoting human welfare. *American Psychologist, 24,* 1063–1075.

Mills, J. (1976). A procedure for explaining experiments involving deception. *Personality and Social Psychology Bulletin, 2,* 3–13.

Miner, J. B. (1992). *Industrial–organizational psychology.* New York: McGraw-Hill.

Minton, C., Kagan, J., & Levine, J. (1971). Maternal control and obedience in the two-year-old. *Child Development, 42,* 1873–1894.

Mischel, W., Shoda, Y., & Mendoza-Denton, R. (2002). Situation–behavior profiles as a locus of consistency in personality. *Current Directions in Psychological Science, 11,* 50–54.

Mishell, L., Bernstein, J., & Schmitt, J. (1999). *The state of working America, 1998–1999.* Ithaca, NY: Cornell University Press.

Mishell, L., Bernstein, J., & Schmitt, J. (2001). *The state of working America, 2000–2001.* Ithaca, NY: Cornell University Press.

Misra, S. (1992). Is conventional debriefing adequate? An ethical issue in consumer research. *Journal of the Academy of Marketing Science, 20,* 269–273.

Mitchell, R. W. (1996). The psychology of human deception. *Social Research, 63,* 819–861.

Mitchell, T. R., Hopper, H., Daniels, D., Falvy, J. G., & Ferris, G. R. (1998). Power, accountability, and inappropriate actions. *Applied Psychology: An International Review, 47,* 497–517.

Mitchell, T. R., & Scott, W. G. (1990). America's problems and needed reforms: Confronting the ethic of personal advantage. *Academy of Management Executive, 4,* 23–35.

Mitroff, I. I. (1974). *The subjective side of science: A philosophical inquiry into the psychology of the Apollo moon scientists.* New York: Elsevier.

Mitroff, I. I., & Denton, E. A. (1999). *A spiritual audit of corporate America: A hard look at spirituality, religion, and values in the workplace.* San Francisco: Jossey-Bass.

Mobley, W. H., Griffeth, R. W., Hand, H. H., & Meglino, B. M. (1979). Review and conceptual analysis of the employee turnover process. *Psychological Bulletin, 86,* 493–522.

Mokhiber, R., & Weissman, R. (1999). *Corporate predators: The hunt for mega-profits and the attack on democracy.* Monroe, ME: Common Courage.

Moore, G. E. (1903). *Principia ethica.* Cambridge, England: Cambridge University Press.

Moorman, C., Deshpande, R., & Zaltman, G. (1993). Factors affecting trust in market research relationships. *Journal of Marketing, 57,* 81–102.

Moorman, R. H., & Blakely, G. L. (1995). Individualism–collectivism as an individual difference predictor of organizational citizenship behavior. *Journal of Organizational Behavior, 16,* 127–142.

Morris, D. (2001). Business ethics assessment criteria: Business v. philosophy—survey results. *Business Ethics Quarterly, 11,* 623–650.

Morris, S. A., & McDonald, R. A. (1995). The role of moral intensity in moral judgments: An empirical investigation. *Journal of Business Ethics, 14,* 715–726.

Mueller, D. J., & Wornhoff, S. A. (1990). Distinguishing personal and social values. *Educational and Psychological Measurement, 50,* 691–699.

Mueller, J. (1996, September–October). Don't round up the usual suspects. *Harvard Business Review, 74*(5), 126.

Munsterberg, H. (1913). *Psychology and industrial efficiency.* Boston: Houghton-Mifflin.

Munzer, S. R. (1992). *A theory of property.* New York: Cambridge University Press.

Murphy, K. R. (1993). *Honesty in the workplace.* Pacific Grove, CA: Brooks/Cole.

Murray, B. (1999, March). More graduates seeking socially responsible jobs: Students are pledging to pursue work that improves the world. *Monitor on Psychology, 30,* 1, 34.

Murray, B. (2000, February). Can academic values mesh with fiscal responsibility? *Monitor on Psychology,* 46–47.

Musser, S. J., & Orke, E. A. (1992). Ethical value systems: A typology. *Journal of Applied Behavioral Science, 28,* 348–362.

Myers, S. L. (2001, January 20). Defense chief cites collective blame on Cole. *The New York Times,* pp. A1, A4.

Nagle, R. J. (1987). Ethics training in school psychology. *Professional School Psychology, 2,* 163–171.

Nagy, T. F. (2000). *Ethics in plain english: An illustrative casebook for psychologists.* Washington, DC: American Psychological Association.

Nathan, P. E. (2000). The Boulder model: A dream deferred—Or lost? *American Psychologist, 55,* 250–252.

National Commission for the Protection of Human Subjects of Biomedical and Behavioral Research, Department of Health, Education, and Welfare. (1979), *Belmont report: Ethical principles and guidelines for the protection of human subjects of research.* FR Doc. 79-12065. GPO 887–809. Washington, DC: U.S. Government Printing Office.

National Conference of Catholic Bishops. (1986). *Economic justice for all: Catholic social teaching and the U.S. economy.* Washington, DC: United States Catholic Conference.

Near, J. P., & Miceli, M. P. (1995). Effective whistle-blowing. *Academy of Management Review, 20,* 679–708.

Newman, D. L., & Brown, R. D. (1996). *Applied ethics for program evaluation.* Thousand Oaks, CA: Sage.

New York Academy of Sciences. (1999). *Socioeconomic status and health in industrial nations: Social, psychological and biological pathways.* New York, NY: New York Academy of Sciences, Vol. 896.

Nichols, D., & Subramaniam, C. (2001). Executive compensation: Excessive or equitable. *Journal of Business Ethics, 29,* 339–351.

Nicks, S. D., Korn, J. H., & Mainieri, T. (1997). The rise and fall of deception in social psychology and personality research, 1921 to 1994. *Ethics & Behavior, 7,* 69–77.

Nicolopoulos, V. (2002). [Deception survey of three I/O psychology journals]. Unpublished raw data.

Nielsen, R. P. (1989). Changing unethical organizational behavior. *The Academy of Management Executive, 3,* 123–130.

Nieves, E. (2000, February 20). Many in Silicon Valley cannot afford housing, even at $50,000 a year. *The New York Times,* p. A20.

Nisan, M. (1990). Moral balance: A model of how people arrive at moral decisions. In T. Wren (Ed.), *The moral domain* (pp. 283–314). Cambridge, MA: MIT Press.

Nisan, M. (1991). The moral balance model: Theory and research extending our understanding of moral choice and deviation. In W. M. Kurtines & J. L. Gewirtz (Eds.), *Handbook of moral behavior and development: Vol. 3. Application* (pp. 213–249). Hillsdale, NJ: Lawrence Erlbaum Associates.

Nisbett, R. E., Peng, K., Choi, I., & Norenzayan, A. (2001). Culture and systems of thought: Holistic vs. analytic cognition. *Psychological Review, 108,* 291–310.

Noddings, N. (1986). *Caring: A feminine approach to ethics and moral education.* Berkeley: University of California Press.

Nogami, G. Y. (1982). Good-fast-cheap: Pick any two: Dilemmas about the value of applicable research. *Journal of Applied Social Psychology, 12,* 343–348.

Nord, W. R. (1982). Continuity and change in industrial/organizational psychology: Learning from previous mistakes. *Professional Psychology, 13*, 942–953.

Norman, R. (1983). *The moral philosophers: An introduction to ethics.* Oxford, England: Clarendon.

Norris, N. P. (1978). Fragile subjects. *American Psychologist, 33*, 962–963.

Notturno, M. A. (2000). *Science and the open society: The future of Karl Popper's philosophy.* Budapest, Hungary: Central European University Press.

Nozick, R. (1974). *Anarchy, state, and utopia.* New York: Basic Books.

Nozick, R. (1993). *The nature of rationality.* Princeton, NJ: Princeton University Press.

Nucci, L., & Turiel, E. (1978) Social interactions and the development of social concepts in preschool children. *Child Development, 49*, 400–407.

Nucci, L. & Weber, E. K. (1991). The domain approach to values education. In W. M. Kurtines & J. L. Gewirtz (Eds.), *Handbook of moral behavior and development: Vol. 3. Application* (pp. 251–266). Hillsdale, NJ: Lawrence Erlbaum Associates.

Oakley, E. F., III, & Lynch, P. (2000). Promise-keeping: A low priority in a hierarchy of workplace values. *Journal of Business Ethics, 27*, 377–392.

O'Connor, E. S. (1999). The politics of management thought: A case study of the Harvard Business School and the Human Relations School. *Academy of Management Review, 24*, 117–131.

Office for Protection From Research Risks, National Institutes of Health, Department of Health and Human Services. (1991 June 18). Protection of human subjects. Title 45, *Code of Federal Regulations*, Part 46. [GPO 1992 0-307-551].

Ohmae, K. (1995, January–February). Putting global logic first. *Harvard Business Review, 73*(3) 154–160.

Oliansky, A. (1991). A confederate's perspective on deception. *Ethics & Behavior, 1*, 253–258.

Oliver, B. L. (1999). Comparing corporate managers' personal values over three decades, 1967-1995. *Journal of Business Ethics, 20*, 147–161.

Oliver, M. L., & Shapiro, T. M. (1995). *Black wealth/white wealth.* New York: Routledge.

O'Neill, O. (1993). Kantian ethics. In P. Singer (Ed.), *A companion to ethics* (pp. 175–185). Cambridge, MA: Blackwell.

Oppel, R. A., Jr. (2002, July 7). Senate panel says Enron's board could have stopped high-risk practices. *The New York Times*, p. A17.

Organ, D. W., & Greene, C. N. (1981). The effects of formalization on professional involvement: A compensatory process approach. *Administrative Science Quarterly, 26*, 237–252.

Organ, D. W., & Ryan, K. (1995). A meta-analytic review of attitudinal and dispositional predictors of organizational citizenship behavior. *Personnel Psychology, 48*, 775–802.

Orne, M. T. (1962). On the social psychology of the psychological experiment: With particular reference to demand characteristics and their implications. *American Psychologist, 17*, 776–783.

Orne, M. T. (1969). Demand characteristics and the concept of quasi-controls. In R. Rosenthal & R. L. Rosnow (Eds.), *Artifact in behavioral research* (pp. 143–179). New York: Academic.

Ortmann, A., & Hertwig, R. (1997). Is deception acceptable? *American Psychologist, 52*, 746–747.

Ortmann, A., & Hertwig, R. (1998). The question remains: Is deception acceptable? *American Psychologist, 53*, 806–807.

O'Sullivan, J. J., & Quevillon, R. P. (1992). 40 Years later: Is the Boulder model still alive? *American Psychologist, 47*, 67–70.

Oyserman, D., Coon, H. M., & Kemmelmeier, M. (2002). Rethinking individualism and collectivism: Evaluation of theoretical assumptions and meta-analyses. *Psychological Bulletin, 128*, 3–72.

Oyserman, D., & Swim, J. K. (2001). Stigma: An insider's view. *Journal of Social Issues, 57*, 1–14.

Ozanian, M. D. (2000, May 15). Upward bias. *Forbes Magazine* [On-line serial]. Available: http://www.forbes.com/forbes/2000/0515/6511210a.html

Paine, F. T., Deutsch, D. R., & Smith, R. A. (1967). Relationship between family background and work values. *Journal of Applied Psychology, 51*, 320–323.

Paolillo, J. G. P., & Vitell, S. J. (2002). An empirical investigation of the influence of selected personal, organizational and moral intensity factors on ethical decision making. *Journal of Business Ethics, 35*, 65–74.

Parker, M. (Ed.). (1998). *Ethics and organizations*. London: Sage.

Parsons, T. (1937). Remarks on education and the professions. *International Journal of Ethics, 47*, 365–369.

Parsons, T. (1954). *Essays in sociological theory*. New York: The Free Press.

Pastore, N. (1949). *The nature–nurture controversy*. New York: King's Cross.

Patterson, D. M. (2001). Causal effects of regulatory, organizational and personal factors on ethical sensitivity. *Journal of Business Ethics, 30*, 123–159.

Pava, M. L., & Krausz, J. (1996). The association between corporate social responsibility and financial performance: The paradox of social cost. *Journal of Business Ethics, 15*, 321–357.

Pava, M. L., & Krausz, J. (1997). Criteria for evaluating the legitimacy of corporate social responsibility. *Journal of Business Ethics, 16*, 337–347.

Pearl Meyer, & Partners. (2000, August 23). *91% of CEO pay rides on performance*. [Press release]. New York: Author.

Pejovich, S. (1990). *The economics of property rights: Towards a theory of comparative systems*. Dordrecht, The Netherlands: Kluwer Academic.

Pence, G. (1993). Virtue theory. In P. Singer (Ed.), *A companion to ethics* (pp. 249–258). Cambridge, MA: Blackwell.

Perrucci, R., Anderson, R. M., Schendel, D. S., & Trachtman, L. E. (1980). Whistle-blowing: Professionals' resistance to organizational authority. *Social Problems, 28*, 149–164.

Perry, R. B. (1963). The definition of value in terms of interest. In P. W. Taylor (Ed.), *The moral judgment: Readings in contemporary meta-ethics* (pp. 72–94). Englewood Cliffs, NJ: Prentice-Hall.

Peterson, Candida (1996). Deception in intimate relationships. *International Journal of Psychology, 31*, 279–288.

Peterson, Christa (1996). Common problem areas and their causes resulting in disciplinary actions. In L. J. Bass, S. T. DeMers, J. R. P. Ogloff, C. Peterson, J. L. Pettifor, R. P. Reaves, T. Retfalvi, N. P. Simon, C. Sinclair, & R. M. Tipton (Eds.), *Professional conduct and discipline in psychology* (pp. 71–89). Washington, DC: American Psychological Association.

Peterson, C. C., & Siddle, D. A. T. (1995). Confidentiality issues in psychological research. *Australian Psychologist, 30*, 187–190.

Peterson, D. R. (1991). Connection and disconnection of research and practice in the education of professional psychologists. *American Psychologist, 46*, 422–429.

Peterson, R. S. (2001). Toward a more deontological approach to the ethical use of social influence. In J. M. Darley, D. M. Messick, & T. R. Tyler (Eds.), *Social influences on ethical behavior in organizations* (pp. 21–36). Mahwah, NJ: Lawrence Erlbaum Associates.

Petrick, J. A., & Quinn, J. F. (1997). *Management ethics: Integrity at work*. Thousand Oaks, CA: Sage.

Pettit, P. (1993). Consequentialism. In P. Singer (Ed.), *A companion to ethics* (pp. 230–240). Cambridge, MA: Blackwell.

Pfeffer, J. (1994). *Competitive advantage through people: Unleashing the power of the workforce*. Boston: Harvard Business School Press.

Pfeffer, J. (1998). *The human equation: Building profits by putting people first*. Boston: Harvard Business School Press.

Pfeffer, J., & Veiga, J. F. (1999). Putting people first for organizational success. *The Academy of Management Executive, 13*, 37–48.

Phillips, K. P. (1990). *The politics of rich and poor: Wealth and the American electorate in the Reagan aftermath.* New York: Harper Perennial.

Phillips, V., Boysen, T. C., & Schuster, S. A. (1997). Psychology's role in statewide education reform: Kentucky as an example. *American Psychologist, 52,* 250–255.

Piaget, J. (1965). *The moral judgment of the child.* New York: Free Press. (Original work published 1932)

Pigden, C. R. (1993). Naturalism. In P. Singer (Ed.), *A companion to ethics* (pp. 421–431). Cambridge, MA: Blackwell.

Platt, J. R. (1964, October 16). Strong inference. *Science, 146,* 347–353.

Podsakoff, P. M., & MacKenzie, S. B. (2000, April). *The impact of organizational citizenship behavior on organizational performance: A review of the empirical literature.* Paper presented at the annual meeting of the Society for Industrial and Organizational Psychology, New Orleans.

Pope, K. S., & Vetter, V. A. (1992). Ethical dilemmas encountered by members of the American Psychological Association: A national survey. *American Psychologist, 47,* 397–411.

Popper, K. R. (1972). *Objective knowledge: An evolutionary approach.* Oxford, England: Clarendon.

Posner, B. Z., Randolph, W. A., & Schmidt, W. H. (1987). Managerial values across functions: A source of organizational problems. *Group and Organization Studies, 12,* 373–385.

Posner, B. Z., & Schmidt, W. H. (1987). Ethics in American companies: A managerial perspective. *Journal of Business Ethics, 6,* 383–391.

Posner, B. Z., & Schmidt, W. H. (1996). The values of business and federal government executives: More different than alike. *Public Personnel Management, 25,* 277–289.

Post, J. E ., Frederick, W. C., Lawrence, A. T., & Weber, J. (1996). *Business and society: Corporate strategy, public policy, ethics* (8th ed.). New York: McGraw-Hill.

Powell, G. N. (1998). The abusive organization. *Academy of Management Executive, 12,* 95–96.

Pratto, F., & Shih, M. (2000). Social dominance orientation and group context in implicit group prejudice. *Psychological Science, 11,* 515–518.

Pratto, F., Sidanius, J., Stallworth, L. M., & Malle, B. F. (1994). Social dominance orientation: A personality variable predicting social and political attitudes. *Journal of Personality and Social Psychology, 67,* 741–763.

Pratto, F., Stallworth, L. M., Sidanius, J., & Siers, B. (1997). The gender gap in occupational role attainment: A social dominance approach. *Journal of Personality and Social Psychology, 72,* 37–53.

Press, E., & Washburn, J. (2000, March). The kept university. *The Atlantic Monthly,* 39–54.

Preston, L. E. (1975). Corporation and society: The search for a paradigm. *Journal of Economic Literature, 13,* 434–453.

Prilleltensky, I. (1997). Values, assumptions, and practices: Assessing the moral implications of psychological discourse and action. *American Psychologist, 52,* 517–535.

Pryor, R. (1979). In search of a concept: Work values. *The Vocational Guidance Quarterly, 27,* 250–258.

Pryor, R. (1982). Values, preferences, needs, work ethics, and orientations to work: Toward a conceptual and empirical integration. *Journal of Vocational Behavior, 20,* 40–52.

Pryor, R. G. L. (1989). Conflicting responsibilities: A case study of an ethical dilemma for psychologists working in organizations. *Australian Psychologist, 24,* 293–305.

Pryzwansky, W. B., & Wendt, R. N. (1987). *Psychology as a profession: Foundations of practice.* New York: Pergamon.

Pryzwansky, W. B., & Wendt, R. N. (1999). *Professional and ethical issues in psychology: Foundations of practice.* New York: Norton.

Pugh, D. S. (1966). Modern organizational theory: A psychological and sociological study. *Psychological Bulletin, 66,* 235–251.

Pugh, D. S. (1969). Organizational behaviour: An approach from psychology. *Human Relations, 22,* 345–354.

Puka, B. (1991). Toward the redevelopment of Kohlberg's theory: Preserving essential structure, removing controversial content. In W. M. Kurtines & J. L. Gewirtz (Eds.), *Handbook of moral behavior and development: Vol. 1. Theory* (pp. 373–393). Hillsdale, NJ: Lawrence Erlbaum Associates.

Rachels, J. (1993a). *The elements of moral philosophy* (2nd ed.). New York: McGraw-Hill.

Rachels, J. (1993b). Subjectivism. In P. Singer (Ed.), *A companion to ethics* (pp. 432–441). Cambridge, MA: Blackwell.

Raelin, J. A. (1984). An examination of deviant/adaptive behavior in the organizational careers of professionals. *Academy of Management Review, 9*, 413–427.

Raelin, J. A. (1989). An anatomy of autonomy: Managing professionals. *Academy of Management Executive, 3*, 216–228.

Raelin, J. A. (1994). Three scales of professional deviance within organizations. *Journal of Organizational Behavior, 15*, 483–501.

Raimy, V. (Ed.). (1950). *Training in clinical psychology.* New York: Prentice-Hall.

Ralston, D. A., Gustafson, D. J., Elsass, P. M., Cheung, F., & Terpstra, R. H. (1992). Eastern values: A comparison of managers in the United States, Hong Kong, and the People's Republic of China. *Journal of Applied Psychology, 77*, 664–671.

Rand, A. (1964). *The virtue of selfishness.* New York: Signet.

Rao, S. M., & Hamilton, J. B., III. (1996). The effect of published reports of unethical conduct on stock prices. *Journal of Business Ethics, 15*, 1321–1330.

Rappaport, A. (1990, February 4). Let's let business be business. *The New York Times*, p. F13.

Rasinski, K. A., Willis, G. B., Baldwin, A. K., Yeh, W., & Lee, L. (1999). Methods of data collection, perceptions of risks and losses, and motivation to give truthful answers to sensitive survey questions. *Applied Cognitive Psychology, 13*, 465–484.

Rassenfos, S. E., & Kraut, A. I. (1988). Survey of personnel research departments. *The Industrial–Organizational Psychologist, 25*(4), 31–37.

Ravlin, E. C., & Meglino, B. M. (1987). Effect of values on perception and decision-making: A study of alternative work values measures. *Journal of Applied Psychology, 72*, 666–673.

Rawls, J. (1958). Justice as fairness. *Philosophical Review, 67*, 164–194.

Rawls, J. (1971). *A theory of justice.* Cambridge, MA: Harvard University Press.

Rayman, P. M. (2001). *Beyond the bottom line: The search for dignity at work.* New York: Palgrave.

Reber, A. S. (1993). *Implicit learning and tacit knowledge: An essay on the cognitive unconscious.* New York: Oxford University Press.

Redding, R. E. (2001). Sociopolitical diversity in psychology: The case for pluralism. *American Psychologist, 56*, 205–215.

Reese, H. W., & Fremouw, W. J. (1984). Normal and normative ethics in behavioral sciences. *American Psychologist, 39*, 863–876.

Reich, R. B. (1996, September–October). Seven modest steps toward more equality. *Harvard Business Review, 74*(5), 122.

Reich, R. B. (2001, January 9). Working, but not "employed." *The New York Times*, p. A19.

Reis, H. T., Collins, W. A., & Berscheid, E. (2000). The relationship context of human behavior and development. *Psychological Bulletin, 126*, 844–872.

Rest, J. R. (1984). The major components of morality. In W. Kurtines & J. Gewirtz (Eds.). *Morality, moral behavior, and moral development* (pp. 24–40). New York: Wiley.

Rest, J. R. (1986a). *Manual for the defining issues test.* Minneapolis: Center for the Study of Ethical Development, University of Minnesota.

Rest, J. R. (1986b). *Moral development: Advances in research and theory.* New York: Praeger.

Rest, J. R. (1994). Background: Theory and research. In J. R. Rest & D. Narvaez (Eds.), *Moral development in the professions* (pp. 1–26). Hillsdale, NJ: Lawrence Erlbaum Associates.

Rest, J. R., & Narvaez, D. (Eds.). (1994). *Moral development in the professions.* Hillsdale, NJ: Lawrence Erlbaum Associates.

Reuters. (2002, February 28). Merrill trims executive bonuses. *The New York Times*, p. C7.

Reynolds, P. D. (1979). *Ethical dilemmas and social science research*. San Francisco: Jossey-Bass.

Reynolds, T. J., & Jolly, J. P. (1980). Measuring personal values: An evaluation of alternative methods. *Journal of Marketing Research, 17*, 531–536.

Richtel, M. (2001, May 5). What, us worry? Layoff: A spring break for some in the dot-com generation. *The New York Times*, pp. C1, C4.

Rilling, J. K., Gutman, D. A., Zeh, T. R., Pagnoni, G., Berns, G. S., & Kilts, C. D. (2002). A neural basis for social cooperation. *Neuron, 35*, 395–405.

Rips, L. J. (2001). Two kinds of reasoning. *Psychological Science, 12*, 129–134.

Roback, A. A. (1917). The moral issues involved in applied psychology. *Journal of Applied Psychology, 1*, 232–243.

Robert, C., & Wasti, S. A. (2000, April). *Individualism/collectivism and the exploration of person–organization fit*. Poster session presented at the annual conference of the Society for Industrial and Organizational Psychology, New Orleans.

Roe, R. A., & Ester, P. (1999). Values and work: Empirical findings and theoretical perspective. *Applied Psychology: An International Review, 48*, 1–21.

Roethlisberger, F., & Dickson, W. J. (1939). *Management and the worker*. Cambridge, MA: Harvard University Press.

Rogelberg, S. G., Luong, A., Sederberg, M. E., & Cristol, D. S. (2000). Employee attitude surveys: Examining the attitudes of noncompliant employees. *Journal of Applied Psychology, 85*, 284–293.

Rokeach, M. (1973). *The nature of human values*. New York: Macmillan.

Rokeach, M., & Ball-Rokeach, S. J. (1989). Stability and change in American value priorities, 1968–1981. *American Psychologist, 44*, 775–784.

Roman, R. M., Hayibor, S., & Agle, B. R. (1999). The relationship between social and financial performance: Repainting a portrait. *Business & Society, 38*, 109–125.

Ronen, S. (1980). The image of I/O psychology: A cross-national perspective by personnel executives. *Professional Psychology, 11*, 399–406.

Rorty, R. (1979). *Philosophy and the mirror of nature*. Princeton, NJ: Princeton University Press.

Ros, M., Schwartz, S. H., & Surkiss, S. (1999). Basic individual values, work values, and the meaning of work. *Applied Psychology: An International Review, 48*, 49–71.

Rosen, H., & Stagner, R. (1980). Industrial/organizational psychology and unions: A viable relationship? *Professional Psychology, 11*, 477–483.

Rosen, T. H. (1987). Reorganizing to meet the needs of scientific psychology. *The Industrial–Organizational Psychologist, 24*(4), 62–63.

Rosenau, P. (1992). *Postmodernism and the social sciences*. Princeton, NJ: Princeton University Press.

Rosenberg, A. (1995). *Philosophy of social science* (2nd ed.). Boulder, CO: Westview.

Rosenberg, M. (1957). *Occupations and values*. Glencoe, IL: Free Press.

Rosenthal, R. (1994). Science and ethics in conducting, analyzing and reporting psychological research. *Psychological Science, 5*, 127–134.

Rosenthal, R., & Rosnow, R. L. (1975). *The volunteer subject*. New York: Wiley.

Rosenthal, R., & Rosnow, R. L. (1984). Applying Hamlet's question to the ethical conduct of research: A conceptual addendum. *American Psychologist, 39*, 561–563.

Rosenthal, R., & Rosnow, R. L. (1991). *Essentials of behavioral research: Methods and data analysis* (2nd ed.). New York: McGraw-Hill.

Rosnow, R. L. (1993). The volunteer problem revisited. In P. D. Blanck (Ed.), *Interpersonal Expectations: Theory, research, applications* (pp. 418–436). New York: Cambridge University Press.

Rosnow, R. L. (1997). Hedgehogs, foxes, and the evolving social contract in psychological science: Ethical challenges and methodological opportunities. *Psychological Methods, 2*, 345–356.

Rousseau, D. M. (1985). Issues of level in organizational research. In L. L. Cummings & B. M. Staw (Eds.), *Research in organizational behavior* (Vol. 7, pp. 1–38). Greenwich, CT: JAI.

Rousseau, D. M. (1990). Assessing organizational culture: The case for multiple methods. In B. Schneider, (Ed.), *Organizational climate and culture* (pp. 153–192). San Francisco: Jossey-Bass.

Rousseau, D. M. (1995). *Psychological contracts in organizations: Understanding written and unwritten agreements.* Thousand Oaks, CA: Sage.

Rousseau, D. M., & Schalk, R. (Eds.). (2000). *Psychological contracts in employment: Cross-national perspectives.* Thousand Oaks, CA: Sage.

Rowan, J. R. (2000). The moral foundation of employee rights. *Journal of Business Ethics, 24*, 355–361.

Rowatt, W. C., Cunningham, M. R., & Druen, P. B. (1998). Deception to get a date. *Personality and Social Psychology Bulletin, 24*, 1228–1242.

Ruse, M. (1993). The significance of evolution. In P. Singer (Ed.), *A companion to ethics* (pp. 500–510). Cambridge, MA.: Blackwell.

Russell, C. R., Settoon, R. P., McGrath, R. N., Blanton, A. E., Kidwell, R. E., Lohrke, F. T., Scifres, E. L., & Danforth, G. W. (1994). Investigator characteristics as moderators of personnel selection research: A meta-analysis. *Journal of Applied Psychology, 79*, 163–170.

Russell, J. E. A. (2001). Vocational psychology: An analysis and directions for the future. *Journal of Vocational Behavior, 59*, 226–234.

Ryan, A. M. (1999). SIOP's pro bono initiative. *The Industrial–Organizational Psychologist, 36*, 135–138.

Rynes, S. L., Bartunek, J. M., & Daft, R. L. (2001). Across the great divide: Knowledge creation and transfer between practitioners and academics. *Academy of Management Journal, 44*, 340–355.

Rynes, S. L., & McNatt, D. B. (2001). Bringing the organization into organizational research: An examination of academic research inside organizations. *Journal of Business and Psychology, 16*, 3–19.

Saari, L. M. (2001). Wider forms of the reciprocal model. *Applied Psychology: An International Review, 50*, 241–244.

Sackett, P. R. (1986). Results of society survey on scientist-practitioner issues. *The Industrial–Organizational Psychologist, 24*(1), 37–39.

Sackett, P. R., Callahan, C., DeMeuse, K., Ford, J. K., & Kozlowski, S. (1986). Changes over time in research involvement by academic and nonacademic psychologists. *The Industrial–Organizational Psychologist, 24*(1), 44–49.

Sackett, P. R., & Larson, J. R., Jr. (1990). Research strategies and tactics in industrial and organizational psychology. In M. D. Dunnette & L. M. Hough (Eds.), *Handbook of industrial and organizational psychology* (2nd ed., Vol. 1, pp. 419–489). Palo Alto, CA: Consulting Psychologists Press.

Sackett, P. R., & Wanek, J. E. (1996). New developments in the use of measures of honesty, integrity, conscientiousness, dependability, trustworthiness, and reliability for personnel selection. *Personnel Psychology, 49*, 787–829.

Sagarin, B. J., Rhoads, K. V. L., & Cialdini, R. B. (1998). Deceiver's distrust: Denigration as a consequence of undiscovered deception. *Personality and Social Psychology Bulletin, 24*, 1167–1176.

Sagie, A., Elizur, D., & Koslowsky, M. (1996). Work values: A theoretical overview and a model of their effects. *Journal of Organizational Behavior, 17*, 503–514.

Sagiv, L., & Schwartz, S. H. (1995). Value priorities and readiness for out-group social contact. *Journal of Personality and Social Psychology, 69*, 437–448.

Sales, B. D., & Folkman, S. (Eds.). (2000). *Ethics in research with human participants.* Washington, DC: American Psychological Association.

Sales, B. D., & Lavin, M. (2000). Identifying conflicts of interest and resolving ethical dilemmas. In B. D. Sales & S. Folkman (Eds.), *Ethics in research with human participants* (pp. 109–128). Washington, DC: American Psychological Association.

Sampson, E. E. (1977). Psychology and the American ideal. *Journal of Personality and Social Psychology, 35,* 762–782.

Samuelson, P. A. (1993). Altruism as a problem involving group versus individual selection in economics and biology. *American Economic Review, 83,* 143–148.

Sargent, J., & Matthews, L. (1999). Exploitation or choice? Exploring the relative attractiveness of employment in the Maquiladoras. *Journal of Business Ethics, 18,* 213–227.

Sashkin, M., & Prien, E. P. (1996). Ethical concerns and organizational surveys. In A. I. Kraut (Ed.). *Organizational surveys: Tools for assessment and change* (pp. 381–403). San Francisco: Jossey-Bass.

Savage, L. J. (1954). *The foundations of statistics.* New York: Wiley.

Savas, E. S. (1987). Privatization. In S. P. Sethi & C. M. Falbe (Eds.), *Business and society: Dimensions of conflict and cooperation* (pp. 270–281). Lexington, MA: Lexington.

Savickas, M. L. (2001). Envisioning the future of vocational psychology. *Journal of Vocational Behavior, 59,* 167–170.

Schein, E. H. (1980). *Organizational psychology.* Englewood Cliffs, NJ: Prentice-Hall. (Original work published 1965)

Schein, E. H. (1990). Organizational culture. *American Psychologist, 45,* 109–119.

Schein, E. H. (1996). Career anchors revisited: Implications for career development in the 21st century. *Academy of Management Executive, 10,* 80–88.

Schmidt, F. L., & Hunter, J. E. (1998). The validity and utility of selection methods in personnel psychology: Practical and theoretical implications of 85 years of research findings. *Psychological Bulletin, 124,* 262–274.

Schminke, M. (1998). The magic punchbowl: A nonrational model of ethical management. In M. Schminke (Ed.), *Managerial ethics: Moral management of people and process* pp. 197–214). Mahwah, NJ: Lawrence Erlbaum Associates.

Schminke, M., Ambrose, M. L., & Noel, T. W. (1997). The effect of ethical frameworks on perceptions of organizational justice. *Academy of Management Journal, 40,* 1190–1207.

Schminke, M., & Wells, D. (1999). Group processes and performance and their effects on individuals' ethical frameworks. *Journal of Business Ethics, 18,* 367–381.

Schneewind, J. B. (1993). Modern moral philosophy. In P. Singer (Ed.), *A companion to ethics* (pp. 147–160). Cambridge, MA: Blackwell.

Schneider, J., & Smith, K. (1999). SIOP 1999 member survey results. *The Industrial-Organizational Psychologist, 37*(2), 24–29.

Schokkaert, E., & Sweeney, J. (1999). Social exclusion and ethical responsibility: Solidarity with the least skilled. *Journal of Business Ethics, 21,* 251–267.

Schriesheim, C. A. (1978). Job satisfaction, attitudes toward unions, and voting in a union representation election. *Journal of Applied Psychology, 63,* 548–552.

Schwab, K. (2000). Neighbors on the same planet [Interview]. *Newsweek, 135*(5), 82.

Schwartz, B. (1990). The creation and destruction of value. *American Psychologist, 45,* 7–15.

Schwartz, S. H. (1992). Universals in the content and structure of values: Theoretical advances and empirical tests in 20 countries. *Advances in Experimental Social Psychology, 25,* 1–65.

Schwartz, S. H. (1994). Are there universal aspects in the structure and contents of human values? *Journal of Social Issues, 50,* 19–45.

Schwartz, S. H. (1999). A theory of cultural values and some implications for work. *Applied Psychology: An International Review, 48,* 23–47.

Schwartz, S. H., & Bilsky, W. (1987). Toward a psychological structure of human values. *Journal of Personality and Social Psychology, 53,* 550–562.

Schwartz, S. H., & Bilsky, W. (1990). Toward a theory of the universal content and structure of values: Extension and cross-cultural replications. *Journal of Personality and Social Psychology, 58,* 878–891.

Schwartz, S. H., & Gottlieb, A. (1981). Participants' postexperimental reactions and the ethics of bystander research. *Journal of Experimental Social Psychology, 17,* 396–407.

Scott-Jones, D. (2000). Recruitment of research participants. In B. D. Sales & S. Folkman (Eds.), *Ethics in research with human participants* (pp. 27–34). Washington, DC: American Psychological Association.

Seberhagen, L. W. (1993a). An ethics code for I/O psychology: Good behavior at low cost. *The Industrial–Organizational Psychologist, 31*(2), 69–71.

Seberhagen, L. W. (1993b). An ethics code for statisticians—What next? *The Industrial–Organizational Psychologist, 30*(3), 71–74.

Seckel, A. (Ed.). (1987). *Bertrand Russell on ethics, sex, and marriage.* Amherst, NY: Prometheus.

Seeman, J. (1969). Deception in psychological research. *American Psychologist, 24,* 1025–1028.

Sennett, R. (1998). *The corrosion of character: The personal consequences of work in the new capitalism.* New York: Norton.

Sethi, S. P. (1973). Corporate social audit: An emerging trend in measuring corporate social performance. In D. Votaw & S. P. Sethi (Eds.), *The corporate dilemma* (pp. 214–231). Englewood Cliffs, NJ: Prentice-Hall.

Sethi, S. P. (1979). A conceptual framework for environmental analysis of social issues and evaluation of business response patterns. *Academy of Management Review, 4,* 63–74.

Sethi, S. P. (1987). Corporate political activism. In S. P. Sethi & C. M. Falbe (Eds.), *Business and society: Dimensions of conflict and cooperation* (pp. 529–545). Lexington, MA: Lexington.

Sethi, S. P. (1999). Codes of conduct for global business: Prospects and challenges of implementation. In The Clarkson Centre for Business Ethics, *Principles of stakeholder management* (pp. 9–20). University of Toronto: Author.

Sethi, S. P., & Falbe, C. M. (Eds.). (1987). *Business and society: Dimensions of conflict and cooperation.* Lexington, MA: Lexington.

Sethi, S. P., & Swanson, C. L. (Eds.). (1981). *Private enterprise and public purpose: An understanding of the role of business in a changing social system.* New York: Wiley.

Sherif, M., Harvey, O. J., White, B. J., Hood, W. R., & Sherif, C. W. (1961). *Intergroup conflict and cooperation: The robbers cave experiment.* Norman, OK: Institute of Group Relations.

Shih, M., Pittinsky, T. L., & Ambady, N. (1999). Stereotype susceptibility: Identity salience and shifts in quantitative performance. *Psychological Science, 10,* 80–83.

Shipley, T. (1977). Misinformed consent: An enigma in modern social science research. *Ethics in Science and Medicine, 4,* 93–106.

Shklar, J. N. (1990). *The faces of injustice.* New Haven, CT: Yale University Press.

Shostak, A. (1964). Industrial psychology and the trade unions: A matter of mutual indifference. In G. Fisk (Ed.), *The frontiers of management psychology* (pp. 144–154). New York: Harper.

Shweder, R. A., Mahapatra, M., & Miller, J. G. (1987). Culture and moral development. In J. Kagan & S. Lamb (Eds.), *The emergence of morality in young children* (pp. 1–83). Chicago: University of Chicago Press.

Sidanius, J., Pratto, F., & Bobo, L. (1996). *Journal of Personality and Social Psychology, 70,* 476–490.

Sieber, J. E. (1982a). Deception in social research I: Kinds of deception and the wrongs they may involve. *IRB: A Review of Human Subjects Research, 4,* 1–6.

Sieber, J. E. (1982b). Deception in social research III: The nature and limits of debriefing. *IRB: A Review of Human Subjects Research, 6,* 1–4.

Sieber, J. E. (1992). *Planning ethically responsible research*. Newbury Park, CA: Sage.

Sieber, J. E., Iannuzzo, R., & Rodriguez, B. (1995). Deception methods in psychology: Have they changed in 23 years? *Ethics & Behavior, 5*, 67–85.

Sikula, A. F. (1973, January–February). The values and value systems of governmental executives. *Public Personnel Management, 2*(1), 16–22.

Sikula, A., Sr., & Sikula, J. (2001). Employee relations ethics [Special issue]. *Ethics & Behavior, 1*(1).

Silberbauer, G. (1993). Ethics in small-scale societies. In P. Singer (Ed.), *A companion to ethics* (pp. 14–28). Cambridge, MA: Blackwell.

Simon, H. A. (1985). Human nature in politics: The dialogue of psychology with political science. *American Political Science Review, 79*, 293–303.

Simon, H. A. (1990). A mechanism for social selection and successful altruism. *Science, 250*, 1665–1668.

Simon, H. A. (1993). Altruism and economics. *American Economic Review, 83*, 156–161.

Simpson, E. L. (1994). Moral development research: A case study of scientific cultural bias. In B. Puka (Ed.), *Moral Development: A Compendium* (Vol. 4). New York: Garland.

Simpson, W. G., & Kohers, T. (2002). The link between corporate social and financial performance: Evidence from the banking industry. *Journal of Business Ethics, 35*, 97–109.

Sims, R. L., & Keon, T. L. (1999). Determinants of ethical decision making: The relationship of the perceived organizational environment. *Journal of Business Ethics, 19*, 393–401.

Sims, R. R. (1992). Linking groupthink to unethical behavior in organizations. *Journal of Business Ethics, 11*, 651–662.

Singelis, T. M., Triandis, H. C., Bhawuk, D., & Gelfand, M. J. (1995). Horizontal and vertical dimensions of individualism and collectivism: A theoretical and measurement refinement. *Cross-Cultural Research: The Journal of Comparative Social Science, 29*, 240–275.

Singer, E. (1978). Informed consent: Consequences for response rate and response quality in social surveys. *American Sociological Review, 43*, 144–162.

Singer, E., Von Thurn, D. R., & Miller, E. R. (1995). Confidentiality assurances and response: A quantitative review of the experimental literature. *Public Opinion Quarterly, 59*, 66–77.

Singer, M., Mitchell, S., & Turner, J. (1998). Consideration of moral intensity in ethicality judgements: Its relationship with whistle-blowing and need-for-cognition. *Journal of Business Ethics, 17*, 527–541.

Singer, M. S. (2000). Ethical and fair work behavior: A normative-empirical dialogue concerning ethics and justice. *Journal of Business Ethics, 28*, 187–209.

Singer, P. (Ed.). (1993). *A companion to ethics*. Cambridge, MA: Blackwell.

Singer, P. (1995). *Practical ethics* (2nd ed.). New York: Cambridge University Press.

Skarlicki, D. P., Ellard, J. H., & Kelln, B. R. C. (1998). Third-party perceptions of a layoff: Procedural, derogation, and retributive aspects of justice. *Journal of Applied Psychology, 83*, 119–127.

Skitka, L. J., & Tetlock, P. E. (1993). Of ants and grasshoppers: The political psychology of allocating public assistance. In B. A. Mellers & J. Baron (Eds.), *Psychological perspectives on justice: Theory and applications* (pp. 205–233). New York: Cambridge University Press.

Slovik, P., Fischoff, B., & Lichtenstein, S. (1985). Regulation of risk: A psychological perspective. In R. G. Noll (Ed.), *Regulatory policy and the social sciences* (pp. 239–343). Berkeley: University of California Press.

Smith, A. (1976). An inquiry into the nature and causes of the wealth of nations. In E. Cannan (Ed.), Chicago: University of Chicago Press. (Original work published 1776)

Smith, B. D., & Vetter, H. J. (1982). *Theoretical approaches to personality*. Englewood Cliffs, NJ: Prentice-Hall.

Smith, C. P. (1983). Ethical issues: research on deception, informed consent, and debriefing. In L. Wheeler & P. Shaver (Eds.), *Review of personality and social psychology* (Vol. 4, pp. 297–328). Beverley Hills: Sage.

Smith, C. P., & Berard, S. P. (1982). Why are human subjects less concerned about ethically problematic research than human subjects committees? *Journal of Applied Social Psychology, 12,* 209–221.

Smith, C. P., & Richardson, D. (1983). Amelioration of deception and harm in psychological research: The important role of debriefing. *Journal of Personality and Social Psychology, 44,* 1075–1082.

Smith, D. L., Cutting, J. C., & Riggs, R. O. (1995). Ensuring subjects' understanding of informed consent. *Research Management Review, 7,* 25–33.

Smith, M. (1993). Realism. In P. Singer (Ed.), *A companion to ethics* (pp. 399–410). Cambridge, MA: Blackwell.

Smith, M. B. (1976). Some perspectives on ethical/political issues in social science research. *Personality and Social Psychology Bulletin, 2,* 445–453.

Smith, M. B. (2000). Moral foundations in research with human participants. In B. D. Sales & S. Folkman (Eds.), *Ethics in research with human participants* (pp. 3–10). Washington, DC: American Psychological Association.

Smith, M. B., Bruner, J. S., & White, R. W. (1956). *Opinions and personality.* New York: Wiley.

Smith, S. S., & Richardson, D. (1983). Amelioration of deception and harm in psychological research: The important role of debriefing. *Journal of Personality and Social Psychology, 44,* 1075–1082.

Smith, V. (1997). New forms of work organization. *Annual Review of Sociology, 23,* 315–339.

Smith, W. C. (1963). *The meaning and end of religion.* New York: Macmillan.

Smith, W. J., Wokutch, R. E., Harrington, K. V,. & Dennis, B. S. (2001). An examination of the influence of diversity and stakeholder role on corporate social orientation. *Business & Society, 40,* 266–294.

Smither, J. W. (1995). Creating an internal contingent workforce: Managing the resource link. In M. London (Ed.), *Employees, careers, and job creation: Developing growth-oriented human resource strategies and programs* (pp. 142–164). San Francisco: Jossey-Bass.

Snarey, J. R. (1985). Cross-cultural universality of social–moral development: A critical review of Kohlbergian research. *Psychological Bulletin, 97,* 202–232.

Snarey, J. R. (1986). The relationship of social–moral development with cognitive and ego development: A cross-cultural study. *Behavior Science Research, 20,* 132–146.

Snell, R. S. (1996). Complementing Kohlberg: Mapping the ethical reasoning used by managers for their own dilemma cases. *Human Relations, 49,* 23–49.

Sobal, J. (1984). The content of survey introductions and the provision of informed consent. *Public Opinion Quarterly, 48,* 788–793.

Society for Human Resource Management. (1990). *Code of ethics.* Alexandria, VA: Author.

Society for Industrial and Organizational Psychology. (1987). *Principles for the Validation and Use of Personnel Selection Procedures* (3rd ed.). College Park, MD: Author.

Solomon, R. C. (1992). *Ethics and excellence: Cooperation and integrity in business.* New York: Oxford University Press.

Sonnert, G., & Commons, M. L. (1994). Society and the highest stages of moral development. *Politics and the Individual, 4,* 31–55.

Sorensen, J. E., & Sorensen, T. L. (1974). The conflict of professionals in bureaucratic organizations. *Administrative Science Quarterly, 19,* 98–106.

Soros, G. (1998). *The crisis of global capitalism [open society endangered].* New York: PublicAffairs.

Soros, G. (2000). *Open society [reforming global capitalism].* New York: PublicAffairs.

Spector, P. E. (2002). Employee control and occupational stress. *Current Directions in Psychological Science, 11,* 133–136.

Spence, J. T. (1985). Achievement American style: The rewards and costs of individualism. *American Psychologist, 40,* 1285–1295.

Spencer, S. J., Steele, C. M., & Quinn, D. M. (1999). Stereotype threat and women's math performance. *Journal of Experimental Social Psychology, 35,* 4–28.

Staal, M. A., & King, R. E. (2000). Managing a multiple relationship environment: The ethics of military psychology. *Professional Psychology: Research and Practice, 31,* 698–705.

Stagner, R. (1981a). The future of union psychology. *International Review of Applied Psychology, 30,* 321–328.

Stagner, R. (1981b). Training and experiences of some distinguished industrial psychologists. *American Psychologist, 36,* 497-505.

Stagner, R. (1982). Past and future of industrial/organizational psychology. *Professional Psychology, 13,* 892–903.

Stanley, B., Sieber, J. E., & Melton, G. B. (1987). Empirical studies of ethical issues in research. *American Psychologist, 42,* 735–741.

Stanwick, P. A., & Stanwick, S. D. (1998). The relationship between corporate social performance and organizational size, financial performance, and environmental performance: An empirical examination. *Journal of Business Ethics, 17,* 195–204.

Starik (1995). "Should trees have managerial standing?" Toward stakeholder status for non-human nature. *Journal of Business Ethics, 14,* 207–217.

Staw, B. M., & Epstein, L. D. (2000). What bandwagons bring: Effects of popular management techniques on corporate performance, reputation, and CEO pay. *Administrative Science Quarterly, 45,* 523–556.

Steele, C. M. (1997). A threat in the air: How stereotypes shape intellectual identity and performance. *American Psychologist, 52,* 613–629.

Steele, C. M. (1999, August). Thin ice: "Stereotype threat" and black college students. *The Atlantic Monthly, 284*(2), 44–54.

Steele, C. M., & Aronson, J. (1995). Contending with a stereotype: African-American intellectual test performance and stereotype threat. *Journal of Personality and Social Psychology, 69,* 797–811.

Steinberg, J., & Henriques, D. B. (2002, July 16). Complex calculations on academics: Edison schools and detractors rely on test scores and surveys. *The New York Times,* p. A10.

Steininger, M., Newell, J. D., & Garcia, L. T. (1984). *Ethical issues in psychology.* Homewood, IL: Dorsey.

Stephens, G. K., & Greer, C. R. (1995). Doing business in Mexico: Understanding cultural differences. *Organizational Dynamics, 24,* 39–55.

Stern, P. C., Dietz, T., & Guagnano, G. A. (1998). A brief inventory of values. *Educational and Psychological Measurement, 58,* 984–1001.

Stevenson, C. L. (1944). *Ethics and language.* New Haven, CT: Yale University Press.

Stewart, L. P. (1992). Ethical issues in postexperimental and postexperiential debriefing. *Simulation & Gaming, 23,* 196–211.

Stocker, M. (1976). The schizophrenia of modern ethical theories. *The Journal of Philosophy, 73,* 453–466.

Stokes, G., Mumford, M. D., & Owens, W. A. (1994). *Biodata handbook: Theory, research, and use of biographical information in selection and performance prediction.* Palo Alto, CA: CPP Books.

Stone, C. D. (1975). *Where the law ends: The social control of corporate behavior.* New York: Harper Colophon.

Stricker, G. (1997). Are science and practice commensurable? *American Psychologist, 52,* 442–448.

Stricker, G. (2000). The scientist–practitioner model: Ghandi was right again. *American Psychologist, 55,* 253–254.

Stricker, L. J. (1967). The true deceiver. *Psychological Bulletin, 68,* 13–20.

Strudler, A. (1995). On the ethics of deception in negotiation. *Business Ethics Quarterly, 5,* 805–822.

Strum, S. (1987). *Almost human: A journey into the world of baboons.* New York: Random House.

Suedfeld, P., & Tetlock, P. E. (Eds.). (1991). *Psychology and social advocacy.* Washington, DC: Hemisphere.

Sullivan, E. V. (1994). A study of Kohlberg's structural theory of moral development: A critique of liberal social science ideology. In B. Puka (Ed.), *Moral development: A compendium* (Vol. 4, pp. 46–70). New York: Garland.

Sullivan, J. L., & Transue, J. E. (1999). The psychological underpinnings of democracy: A selective review of research on political tolerance, interpersonal trust, and social capital. *Annual Review of Psychology, 50,* 625–650.

Suls, J. M., & Rosnow, R. L. (1981). The delicate balance between ethics and artifacts in behavioral research. In A. J. Kimmel (Ed.), *Ethics of human subject research* (pp. 49–54). San Francisco: Jossey-Bass.

Sverke, M., & Hellgren, J. (2002). The nature of job insecurity: Understanding employment uncertainty on the brink of a new millennium. *Applied Psychology: An International Review, 51,* 23–42.

Swanson, D. L. (1999). Toward an integrative theory of business and society: A research strategy for corporate social performance. *Academy of Management Review, 24,* 506–521.

Sweeney, J. (1996, September–October). Give workers a voice. *Harvard Business Review, 75*(5), 124.

Szasz, T. S. (1970). *Ideology and insanity.* New York: Doubleday.

Tannenbaum, R., & Davis, S. A. (1969). Values, man, and organizations. *Industrial Management Review, 10,* 67–86.

Tannenbaum, S. I., Greene, V. J., & Glickman, A. S. (1989). The ethical reasoning process in an organizational consulting situation. *Professional Psychology: Research and Practice, 20,* 229–235.

Tarasoff v. Board of Regents of the University of California, 17 Cal. 3d 425, Cal. Rptr. 14, 551 P.2d 334 (1976).

Tawney, R. H. (1920). *The acquisitive society.* New York: Harcourt, Brace & Howe.

Taylor, F. W. (1911). *The principles of scientific management.* New York: Harper.

Taylor, K. M., & Shepperd, J. A. (1996). Probing suspicion among participants in deception research: Comment. *American Psychologist, 51,* 886–887.

Tesch, F. E. (1977). Debriefing research participants: Though this be method there is madness to it. *Journal of Personality and Social Psychology, 35,* 217–224.

Tetlock, P. E. (1992). The impact of accountability on judgment and choice: Toward a social contingency model. In M.P. Zanna (Ed.), *Advances in Experimental Social Psychology,* (Vol. 25, pp. 331–377). New York: Academic.

Tetlock, P. E., & Mitchell, G. (1993). Liberal and conservative approaches to justice: Conflicting psychological portraits. In B. A. Mellers & J. Baron (Eds.), *Psychological perspectives on justice: Theory and applications* (pp. 234–255). New York: Cambridge University Press.

Thoma, S. (1994). Moral judgments and moral action. In J. R. Rest & D. Narvaez (Eds.), *Moral development in the professions* (pp. 199–212). Hillsdale, NJ: Lawrence Erlbaum Associates.

Thoma, S., Rest, J. R., & Barnett, R. (1986). Moral judgment, behavior, decision making, and attitudes. In J. R. Rest (Ed.), *Moral development: Advances in theory and research* (pp. 133–175). New York: Praeger.

Thomas, L. (1993). Morality and psychological development. In P. Singer (Ed.), *A companion to ethics* (pp. 464–475). Cambridge, MA: Blackwell.

Thompson, G. (2001a, February 11). Chasing Mexico's dream into squalor. *The New York Times,* pp. A1, A6.

Thompson, G. (2001b, December 26). Fallout of U.S. recession drifts south into Mexico. *The New York Times*, pp. C1, C2.

Thorne, L., & Saunders, S. B. (2002). The socio–cultural embeddedness of individuals' ethical reasoning in organizations (cross-cultural ethics). *Journal of Business Ethics, 35*, 1–14.

Thornhill, R., & Palmer, C. T. (2000). Why men rape. *The Sciences, 40*(1), 30–36.

Tichy, N. M. (1974). Agents of planned social change: Congruence of values, cognition, and actions. *Administrative Science Quarterly, 19*, 164–182.

Tiffin, J. (1956). How psychologists serve industry. *Personnel Journal, 36*, 372–376.

Tjeltveit, A. C. (1999). *Ethics and values in psychotherapy.* London: Routledge.

Tobias, J. S. (1997). BMJ's present policy. *British Medical Journal, 314*, 1111–1114.

Toulman, S. (1973). *Human understanding.* Chicago: University of Chicago Press.

Treaster, J. B. (2001, December 28). U.S. sues Allstate, whose agents cite age discrimination. *The New York Times* pp. A1, C4.

Trevino, L. K. (1986). Ethical decision making in organizations: A person–situation interactionist model. *Academy of Management Review, 11*, 601–617.

Triandis, H. C. (1995). *Individualism and collectivism.* Boulder, CO: Westview Press.

Triandis, H. C., Dunnette, M. D., & Hough, L. M. (Eds). (1994). *Handbook of industrial and organizational psychology* (2nd ed., Vol. 4). Palo Alto, CA: Consulting Psychologists Press.

Tsui, A. S., Pearce, J. L., Porter, L. W., & Tripoli, A. M. (1997). Alternative approaches to the employee-organization relationship: Does investment in employees pay off? *Academy of Management Journal, 40*, 1089–1121.

Tuck, R. (1979). *Natural rights theories: Their origin and development.* Cambridge, England: Cambridge University Press.

Turiel, E. (1983). *The development of social knowledge: Morality and convention.* Cambridge, England: Cambridge University Press.

Turiel, E., Killen, M., & Helwig, C. (1987). Morality: It's structure, functions and vagaries. In J. Kagan & S. Lamb (Eds.), *The emergence of morality in young children* (pp. 155–243). Chicago: University of Chicago Press.

Turiel, E., Smetana, J. G., & Killen, M. (1991). Social contexts in social cognitive development. In W. M. Kurtines & J. L. Gewirtz (Eds.), *Handbook of moral behavior and development: Vol. 2. Research* (pp. 307–332). Hillsdale, NJ: Lawrence Erlbaum Associates.

Tyler, L. (1973). Design for a hopeful psychology. *American Psychologist, 28*, 1021–1029.

Uchitelle, L. (2001, August 5). Now, the pink slip is all in a day's work. *The New York Times*, pp. A1, A11.

Uchitelle, L. (2002a, January 20). The rich are different. They know when to leave. *The New York Times*, Section 4, pp. 1, 5.

Uchitelle, L. (2002b, March 23). Sharp rise in federal spending may have helped ease recession. *The New York Times*, pp. A1, C4.

Uchitelle, L. (2002c, July 28). Broken system? Tweak it, they say. *The New York Times*, Section 3, pp. 1, 12.

Ullman, A. (1985). Data in search of a theory: A critical examination of the relationships among social performance, social disclosure, and economic performance. *Academy of Management Review, 10*, 540–577.

Unger, R. K. (1983). Through the looking glass: No wonderland yet! (The reciprocal relationship between methodology and models of reality.) *Psychology of Women Quarterly, 8*, 9–32.

United Nations (1948). Universal declaration of human rights. General Assembly resolution 217A (III), Dec. 10.

United Nations Development Programme. (1999). *Human development report 1999.* New York: Oxford University Press.

United Nations Development Programme. (2000). *Poverty report 2000: Overcoming human poverty.* New York : Author.

United States Congress (1977/1998). Foreign Corrupt Practices Act. 15 U.S.C., Secs. 78dd-1, et seq.

United States Congress, Office of Technology Assessment. (1990). *The use of integrity tests for pre-employment screening.* Washington, DC: U.S. Government Printing Office. [OTA-SET-442].

Van Buren, H. J., III. (2000). The windingness of social and psychological contracts: Toward a theory of social responsibility in downsizing. *Journal of Business Ethics, 25,* 205–219.

Van Natta, D., Jr., & Berenson, A. (2002, January 15). Enron's chairman received warning about accounting: Letter sent by executive. *The New York Times,* pp. A1, C8.

Vardi, Y. (2001). The effects of organizational and ethical climates on misconduct at work. *Journal of Business Ethics, 29,* 325–337.

Veatch, R. M. (1987). *The patient as partner.* Bloomington: Indiana University Press.

Victor, B., & Cullen, J. B. (1988). The organizational bases of ethical work climates. *Administrative Science Quarterly, 33,* 95–119.

Viswesvaran, C., & Ones, D. (2002). Examining the construct of organizational justice: A meta-analytic evaluation of relations with work attitudes and behaviors. *Journal of Business Ethics, 38,* 193–203.

Vitelli, R. (1988). The crisis issue assessed: An empirical analysis. *Basic and Applied Social Psychology, 9,* 301–309.

Vredenburgh, D., & Brender, Y. (1998). The hierarchical abuse of power in work organizations. *Journal of Business Ethics, 17,* 1337–1347.

Waclawski, J., & Church, A. H. (2000). The 2000 SIOP Member survey results are in! *The Industrial–Organizational Psychologist, 38*(1), 59–68.

Waddock, S. A., & Graves, S. B. (1997). Quality of management and quality of stakeholder relations: Are they synonymous? *Business & Society, 36,* 250–280.

Wade, N. (2001a, May 3). Genome feud heats up as academic team accuses commercial rival of faulty work. *The New York Times,* p. A15.

Wade, N. (2001b, May 18). Link between human genes and bacteria is hotly debated by rival scientific camps. *The New York Times,* p. A17.

Wagner, R. K. (1997). Intelligence, training, and employment. *American Psychologist, 52,* 1059–1069.

Waldo, D. (2001). Lessons for employers in a slowing economy. *The Industrial- Organizational Psychologist, 39*(1), 50–51.

Waldron, J. (Ed.). (1984). *Theories of rights.* Oxford, England: Oxford University Press.

Walker, C. R. (1952). *The man on the assembly line.* Cambridge, MA: Harvard University Press.

Walker, J. E., Tausky, C., & Oliver, D. (1982). Men and women at work: Similarities and differences in work values within occupational groupings. *Journal of Vocational Behavior, 21,* 17–36.

Walker, L. (1984). Sex differences in the development of moral reasoning: A critical review. *Child Development, 55,* 183–201.

Wallace, J. E. (1995). Organizational and professional commitment in professional and non-professional organizations. *Administrative Science Quarterly, 40,* 228–255.

Walsh, M. W. (2000, November 3). Court considers if employer can force pledge not to sue. *The New York Times,* p. A1.

Walsh-Bowers, R. (1995). The reporting and ethics of the research relationship in areas of interpersonal psychology, 1939–1989. *Theory & Psychology, 5,* 233–250.

Walters, B., Hardin, T., & Schick, J. (1995). Top executive compensation: Equity or excess? Implications for regaining American Competitiveness. *Journal of Business Ethics, 14,* 227–234.

Watson, G. W., Shepard, J. M., & Stephens, C. U. (1999). Fairness and ideology: An empirical test of social contracts theory. *Business & Society, 38,* 83–108.

Wayne, L. (1999, November 14). Flat tax goes from 'snake oil' to G.O.P. tonic. *The New York Times*, pp. A1, A30.

Wayne, L. (2002, January 13). Before debacle, Enron insiders cashed in $1.1 billion in shares: Lawsuit contends other investors were misled. *The New York Times*, p. A1, A27.

Weaver, G. R., Trevino, L. K., & Cochran, P. L. (1999). Corporate ethics programs as control systems: Influences of executive commitment and environmental factors. *Academy of Management Journal, 42*, 41–57.

Webb, E. J., Campbell, D. T., Schwartz, R. D., Sechrest, L., & Grove, J. B. (1981). *Non-reactive measures in the social sciences* (2nd ed.). Boston: Houghton-Mifflin.

Weber, J. (1993). Exploring the relationship between personal values and moral reasoning. *Human Relations, 46*, 435–463.

Weber, J. (1996). Influences upon managerial moral decision-making: Nature of the harm and magnitude of consequences. *Human Relations, 49*, 1–22.

Wegner, D. M., & Wheatley, T. (1999). Apparent mental causation: Sources of the experience of will. *American Psychologist, 54*, 480–492.

Weick, K. E. (1995). *Sensemaking in organizations*. Thousand Oaks, CA: Sage.

Weinberg, C. R. (2000, September). CEO compensation: How much is enough? *Chief Executive Magazine,* Issue 159, 48–63.

Werhane, P. H. (1999). *Moral imagination and management decision-making.* New York: Oxford University Press.

Werhane, P. H. (1999). Justice and trust. *Journal of Business Ethics, 21, 237–249.*

Werhane, P. H., & Radin, T. J. (1996). Employment practices in the contemporary American workplace. In W. W. Gasparski & L. V. Ryan (Eds.), *Human action in business: Praxiological and ethical dimensions* (pp. 417–433). New Brunswick, NJ: Transaction.

West, S. G., & Gunn, S. P. (1978). Some issues of ethics and social psychology. *American Psychologist, 33*, 30–38.

Weston, J. S. (1996, September–October). Invest in human capital. *Harvard Business Review, 74*(5), 123.

White, T. I. (1993). *Business ethics: A philosophical reader.* Upper Saddle River, NJ: Prentice Hall.

Wicks, A. C. (1995). Albert Schweitzer or Ivan Boesky? Why we should reject the dichotomy between medicine and business. *Journal of Business Ethics, 14*, 339–351.

Wicks, A. C., Gilbert, D. R., Jr., & Freeman, R. E. (1994). A feminist reinterpretation of the stakeholder concept. *Business Ethics Quarterly, 4*, 475–497.

Wiley, C. (1998). Reexamining perceived ethics issues and ethics roles among employment managers. *Journal of Business Ethics, 17*, 147–161.

Wilgoren, J. (2001a, March 22). Helping hands at Spring break. *The New York Times*, p. A24.

Wilgoren, J. (2001b, June 13). Education study finds U.S. falling short: Teachers are found not benefitting in era of economic expansion. *The New York Times*, p. B1.

Wilgoren, J. (2001c, August 23). New curriculum in the Bronx is built on an ideal. *The New York Times*, pp. B1, B10.

Wilkins, D. B. (1996). Redefining the "professional" in professional ethics: An interdisciplinary approach to teaching professionalism. *Law and Contemporary Problems, 58*, 241–258.

Williams, O. F. (2000). *Global codes of conduct: An idea whose time has come.* Notre Dame, IN: University of Notre Dame Press.

Wilson, E. O. (2000). *Sociobiology: The new synthesis, twenty-fifth anniversary edition.* Boston: Harvard University Press. (Original work published 1975)

Wilson, W. J. (1996). *When work disappears: The world of the new urban poor.* New York: Knopf.

Wimbush, J. C. (1999). The effect of cognitive moral development and supervisory influence on subordinates' ethical behavior. *Journal of Business Ethics, 18*, 383–395.

Wimbush, J. C., Shepard, J. M., & Markham, S. E. (1997a). An empirical examination of the multi-dimensionality of ethical climate in organizations. *Journal of Business Ethics, 16*, 67–77.

Wimbush, J. C., Shepard, J. M., & Markham, S. E. (1997b). An empirical examination of the relationship between ethical climate and ethical behavior from multiple levels of analysis. *Journal of Business Ethics, 16*, 1705–1716.

Witherspoon, R., & White, R. P. (1996). Executive coaching: A continuum of roles. *Consulting Psychology Journal: Practice and Research, 48*, 124–133.

Wittmer, D. P. (2001). Ethical decision-making. In T. L. Cooper (Ed.), *Handbook of administrative ethics* (2nd ed., pp. 481–507). New York: Marcel Dekker.

Wojciszke, B. (1989). The system of personal values and behavior. In N. Eisenberg, J. Reykowski, & E. Staub (Eds.), *Social and moral values: Individual and societal perspectives* (pp. 229–252). Hillsdale, NJ: Lawrence Erlbaum Associates.

Wolf, R. N., & Ozehosky, R. J. (1978). Industrial psychology: In need of a learned lawyer? *Professional Psychology, 9*(2), 178–182.

Wolff, E. N. (1995). *Top heavy: A study of the increasing inequality of wealth in America.* New York: Twentieth Century Fund Press; Distributed by Brookings Institute, Washington, D.C.

Wong, D. (1993). Relativism. In P. Singer (Ed.), *A companion to ethics* (pp. 442–450). Cambridge, MA: Blackwell.

Wood, A. (1993). Marx against morality. In P. Singer (Ed.), *A companion to ethics* (pp. 511–524). Cambridge, MA: Blackwell.

Wood, D. J. (1991). Corporate social performance revisited. *Academy of Management Review, 16*, 691–718.

Wooldridge, A. (2000, March 5). Come back, company man! *The New York Times Magazine,* Vol. 149, pp. 82–83.

Wooler, S. (1985). Let the decision maker decide!: A case against assuming common occupational value structures. *Journal of Occupational Psychology, 58*, 217–227.

Workman, M. (2001). Collectivism, individualism, and cohesion in a team-based occupation. *Journal of Vocational Behavior, 58*, 82–97.

Wyld, D. C., & Jones, C. A. (1997). The importance of context: The ethical work climate construct and models of ethical decision making—An agenda for research. *Journal of Business Ethics, 16*, 465–472.

Yenney, S. L., & American Psychological Association Practice Directorate. (1994). *Business strategies of a caring profession: A practitioner's guidebook.* Washinton, DC: American Psychological Association.

Zajonc, R. B. (1980). Feeling and thinking: Preferences need no inferences. *American Psychologist, 35*, 151–175.

Zelig, M. (1988). Ethical dilemmas in police psychology. *Professional Psychology: Research and Practice, 19*, 336–338.

Zickar, M. J. (2001). Using personality inventories to identify thugs and agitators: Applied psychology's contribution to the war against labor. *Journal of Vocational Behavior, 59*, 149–164.

Zimbardo, P. G., Haney, C., Banks, W., & Jaffe, D. (1973, April 8). The mind is a formidable jailer: A Pirandellian prison. *The New York Times Magazine,* pp. 38–60.

Zipkin, A. (2000, October 18). Getting religion on corporate ethics: A scourge of scandals leaves its mark. *The New York Times,* p. C1, C10.

Author Index

Kimble, G. A., 215, 290, 434
Kimmel, A. J., 332, 337, 339n141, 344, 345,
        352, 360, 363, 368, 369, 370, 371,
        372, 374, 377, 378, 379, 434
King, K. A., 357, 429
King, R. E., 354, 452
Kinnane, J. F., 136, 434
Kinnier, R. T., 151, 434
Kitchener, K. S., 387, 435
Klein, E., 293, 435
Kleining, J., 435
Kleysen, R., 148, 423
Kluckhohn, C., 138, 435
Kluckhohn, F. R., 435
Knapp, S., 9, 67, 74, 435
Kohers, T., 272, 450
Kohlberg, L., 6, 94, 95, 99, 100n36, 101, 105,
        107, 147, 420, 435
Kok, P., 277, 435
Kolata, G., 7n1, 435
Konovsky, M., 301, 418
Koocher, G., 217, 292, 401, 402, 408, 410, 435
Koocher, G. P., 434
Koppes, L. L., 286, 435
Korman, A. K., 289, 290, 435
Korn, J. H., 339, 360, 363, 365, 366, 372,
        435, 442
Kornhauser, A., 283, 289, 290, 426, 435
Kornhauser, W., 196, 199, 200, 202, 435
Korten, D. C., 235, 256, 435
Koslowsky, M., 146, 448
Kossek, E. E., 304, 435
Kozlowski, S., 190, 199, 448
Kracher, B., 85, 436
Kraft, J. D., 299, 303, 428
Kramer, R. M., 301, 436
Krasner, L., 215, 436
Krausz, J., 246, 265, 272, 443
Kraut, A. I., 203, 446
Krebs, D. L., 102, 113n44, 436
Kristiansen, C. M., 150, 436
Kronzon, S., 123, 436
Krueger, J. I., 227, 436
Krug, S. E., 392, 425
Kruger, D. J., 227, 436
Kruglanski, A. W., 367, 436
Krugman, P., 171, 176, 255, 264, 436
Krupat, E., 369, 436
Kuhn, T., 208n80, 211, 221n88, 222, 436
Kurzynski, M. J., 122, 436
Kymlicka, W., 22n7, 55, 436

L

Ladenson, R. F., 293, 392, 395, 401, 402, 412,
        427

Landrum, R. E., 343, 419
Landy, F. J., 160, 436
Larson, D. B., 122, 439
Larson, J. R., Jr., 234, 291, 448
Latham, G., 203, 230, 291, 436
Laurent, D., 343, 431
Lavelle, L., 170, 436
Lavin, M., 387, 401, 448
Law, H. G., 146, 418
Lawler, E. E., III, 230, 436
Lawrence, A. T., 177n67, 239n96, 255, 265,
        266n111, 268, 275, 278, 297, 445
Lawrence, P. R., 124, 154, 436
Lawson, E., 363, 436
Lazarus, R. S., 367, 437
Lear, R. W., 169, 437
Lederman, L. C., 377, 437
Ledford, G. E., Jr., 230, 436
Lee, J., 180n71, 437
Lee, L., 357, 446
Lee, R., 157n53, 424
Lefkowitz, J., 165, 203, 291, 309, 367, 425, 437
Leonhardt, D., 171, 264, 437
Lerman, D. L., 174n63, 437
Lerner, M. J., 437
Lesser, C. S., 258, 421
Levin, R. C., 238, 238n95, 437
Levine, C., 95, 435
Levine, J., 90, 440
Levine, J. M., 87, 437
Lewis, C. W., 401, 437
Lewis, D., 160, 425
Lichtenstein, S., 68, 451
Lickona, T., 91n33, 92, 93, 101, 437
Lilienthal, D., 262, 437
Lincoln, Y. S., 208, 208n80, 211, 213, 215,
        220n87, 221, 224, 429
Lindsay, J. J., 359n151, 422
Lindsay, R. C., 339, 346, 348, 349, 366, 371,
        413
Lindsay, R. C. L., 371, 379, 437
Lipartito, K. J., 196, 203, 437
Lipsey, M. W., 215, 227, 437
Litz, R. A., 150, 437
Loch, K. D., 392, 437
Lock, A., 224, 427
Locke, E. A., 22, 22n7, 227, 230, 233, 421,
        437, 438
Locke, J., 22, 25, 239, 244, 438
Loe, T. W., 83n32, 124n46, 125n47, 128, 438
Lofquist, L. H., 289, 422
Lohrke, F. T., 216, 447
Loken, B., 83n32, 423
London, M., 293, 299, 303, 304, 312, 313,
        392, 394, 438
Lorsch, J. W., 124, 154, 436

Subject Index